NEW YORK STATE
EDUCATION DEPARTMENT REPORTS

JUDICIAL DECISIONS OF THE COMMISSIONER OF EDUCATION

CURRENT REPORTS

OFFICIAL EDITION

The State Education Department

Office of Counsel

Albany

Cite this Volume

as

44 Ed Dept Rep _____

QUESTIONS ABOUT THIS PUBLICATION?

For CUSTOMER SERVICE ASSISTANCE concerning replacement pages, shipments, billing, reprint permission, or other matters,

please call Customer Service Department at 800-833-9844
email customer.support@lexisnexis.com
or visit our interactive customer service website at *www.lexisnexis.com/printcdsc*

For EDITORIAL **content questions** concerning this publication,

please call 800-446-3410 ext. 7447
or email: *LLP.CLP@lexisnexis.com*

For **information on other LEXISNEXIS MATTHEW BENDER publications,**

please call us at 800-223-1940
or visit our online bookstore at *www.lexisnexis.com/bookstore*

ISBN: 0-8205-8070-8

Education Law § 101 provides that the Deputy Commissioner of Education "in the absence or disability of the commissioner or when a vacancy exists in the office of commissioner, shall exercise and perform the functions, powers and duties conferred or imposed on the commissioner by this chapter."

LexisNexis®

Matthew Bender & Company, Inc.
Editorial Offices
P.O. Box 7587
Charlottesville, VA 22906-7587
800-446-3410
www.lexisnexis.com

Product Number 3190010

(Pub. 31890)

THE STATE EDUCATION DEPARTMENT

RICHARD P. MILLS
Commissioner of Education

KATHY A. AHEARN
Counsel and
Deputy Commissioner
for Legal Affairs
Chief of Staff

ERIN M. O'GRADY-PARENT
Deputy Counsel

RICHARD J. TRAUTWEIN
JOAN S. GAVRILIK
MARY ELLEN CLERKIN
Assistant Counsels

OFFICE OF COUNSEL

MARY ELLEN LORINI
RICHARD L. NABOZNY
CHARLES E. O'BRIEN
KATHLEEN E. SURGALLA
ERIC JAY BRAUN
SUSAN A. NACCARATO
PATRICIA L. BOOCHEVER
NANCY H. HALLECK
AMY D. SCHALLOP
KATHERINE J. GAFFNEY
DAVID P. FORD
WILLIAM J. LYNCH
VICTORIA HUNTER HAY
KATHLEEN MARINELLI
LOUISE M. DeCANDIA

TABLE OF CONTENTS

USER'S GUIDE

USER'S GUIDE

HOW TO USE

Subscribers will receive a soft cover bound book three times a year containing the official text of all judicial decisions of New York's Commissioner of Education issued during the given period. At year's end, subscribers will be issued a hard cover bound edition containing all of the decisions for the current volume. Each quarterly issue of the *Reports* contains the latest decisions rendered by the Commissioner. Subject indices are included in the back of the book to aid in case research. These quarterly bound reports should be retained until the end of the current volume's year, at which time a hard cover bound edition of all decisions rendered for the current year will be issued. Each volume year, which runs from July to June, the decisions reported in the *Reports* are compiled, together with cumulative indices, into a single bound volume for the year.

The following is a description of each section found in the *New York State Education Department Reports*.

CONTENTS

Commissioner's Decisions

This section contains the full text of decisions of New York's Commissioner of Education. Each decision is formatted to include decision number, parties involved, decision date, appearances of counsel and the full opinion text.

Table of Decisions

This table is an alphabetical listing of the parties involved in the reported decisions. Alongside each entry is the case decision number as assigned by the Commissioner of Education.

Subject Index

The subject index is arranged alphabetically by major topical area and then further into subcategories within a topical area. The Subject Index contains a small summary of the legal principles derived from the reported decisions. The researcher, after locating the major area and subcategories of interest, should note the decision number and refer to the full text of the opinion in the Commissioner's Decisions section to locate "on-point" decisions. PLEASE NOTE: In no listing for the major topical area and/or subcategories of interest is found, it signifies that no decisions have been rendered on those topics during the time period covered by the volume.

Statutory Reference Table

The Statutory Reference Table lists New York rules, regulations and consolidated laws as well as federal regulations and statues cited in the Commissioner's Decisions. The principal headings, which are in boldface type, indicate the regulation or law applicable to the sections listed below each heading. The cited sections are listed in numeric order with references to the decisions numbers in which they are cited.

Table of Judicial Review

This section lists, in numeric order, those of the Commissioner's Decisions which have been appealed. Each listing includes the name of the case, the venue, and the status of the appeal.

HOW TO RESEARCH

Research should be initiated in the latest soft cover bound edition of the *New York State Education Department Reports* in order to locate the most current decisions first. Consult previous volumes of the *New York State Education Department Reports* for earlier reported cases.

To Research by Subject:

STEP ONE: Think of a major category descriptor that applies to the subject matter you wish to research. Turn to the alphabetically arranged Subject Index and locate that descriptor. Narrow your search by locating one or more of the subcategories that describe your topic. Examine the case summaries and review the full text of the decision in the Commissioner's Decisions section.

Example: If you are researching a question concerning the dismissal of a probationary teacher, you would look in the Subject index under the major category "TEACHERS," and under the subcategories "Probationary Appointment—Dismissal."

STEP TWO: You may have to examine terms which are synonymous with your topic if you cannot find a listing for your precise terminology. Note the decision number and turn to the Commissioner's Decisions section to review the full text to determine if the case is "on-point" for you.

PLEASE NOTE: If you are unable to locate any decision listings under your topic and synonyms for your topic, it signifies that no decisions have been rendered on that topic during the time frame covered by the volume.

STEP THREE: Consult the Table of Judicial Review to determine whether the selected decisions are under appeal and are still "good law."

To Locate a Specific Decision:

If the researcher knows the names of one or more of the parties involved in a particular case, he or she can find the decision number of that case by turning to the Table of Decisions, where the cases are listed alphabetically by party name.

JUDICIAL DECISIONS

OF THE

COMMISSIONER OF EDUCATION

Decision No. 15,075

Appeal of IZABEL SKUGOR, on behalf of RAFAELA JERONIMO ROWEDER, from action of the Board of Education of the Sewanhaka Central High School District regarding residency.

(July 2, 2004)

APPEARANCES OF COUNSEL

Douglas E. Libby, Esq., attorney for respondent, *Bernadette Gallagher-Gaffney, Esq.*, of counsel

DECISION OF THE COMMISSIONER

MILLS, Commissioner.—Petitioner appeals the determination of the Board of Education of the Sewanhaka Central High School District ("respondent") that her niece, Rafaela Jeronimo Roweder, is not a district resident. The appeal must be dismissed.

By registration form dated March 24, 2003, petitioner, a resident of respondent's district, sought admission of Rafaela to the district's schools beginning in September 2003. Rafaela is the daughter of petitioner's sister who lives in Brazil. At the time petitioner applied for Rafaela's admission, Rafaela was not yet living with her.

On the sworn registration form, petitioner indicated that Rafaela "wants to come here and live with me to improve her English before she starts college." Petitioner also stated that this arrangement would be temporary and that Rafaela's parents would provide one-half of Rafaela's financial support. In a sworn affidavit, which was part of the registration materials, petitioner reiterated that Rafaela wanted "to have an opportunity to come to this country and learn the English language with proficiency," and that the proposed living arrangement would last for one year. Also, in a sworn affidavit, Rafaela's parents confirmed that the arrangement would allow Rafaela to study in another country and would last one year.

By letter dated May 9, 2003, respondent's Administrative Assistant to the Superintendent notified petitioner that Rafaela was not entitled to attend the public schools of the district on the basis of "parental residence out-of-district" and "temporary residence established for attending district schools."

On May 20, 2003, petitioner appealed this determination to the district's administrative review officer. An administrative hearing was held on June 17, 2003. At the hearing petitioner testified that Rafaela would be moving to her home in July or August 2003, that Rafaela would attend respondent's schools in the eleventh grade, and that after one year Rafaela would return to Brazil. Petitioner stated that she agreed to have Rafaela live with her because her sister was experiencing financial problems. Petitioner also stated that another reason for the living arrangement was to allow Rafaela to improve her English before starting college. Petitioner submitted a Brazilian court document, dated June 13, 2003, certifying that petitioner was granted temporary custody of Rafaela and that petitioner "may request, separately and jointly, anything pertaining to such minor, including enrolling her in social and health programs, receive benefits, without affecting the rights and obligations of the permanent custody holder." Petitioner testified that she would provide 100 percent of Rafaela's financial support, but that she would consult with Rafaela's parents on educational and medical issues.

When questioned about why she had not stated in the registration materials that Rafaela was coming to live with her because of her parents' financial difficulties, petitioner stated that she "didn't think there was going to be any question about that," and gave no further explanation. Also, when questioned about why she indicated in the registration materials that Rafaela's parents would contribute one-half of Rafaela's financial support, petitioner stated that she recently visited her sister in Brazil and realized that her sister would not be able to provide any support.

On July 28, 2003, respondent's review officer issued a determination that Rafaela was not a district resident and therefore not entitled to attend respondent's schools. This appeal ensued. On August 29, 2003, petitioner's request for interim relief was denied.

In this appeal, petitioner claims that Rafaela lives with her and requests a determination that Rafaela is a district resident entitled to attend the district's schools without the payment of tuition. Respondent claims that its determination that Rafaela is not a district resident was rational and supported by the record. In addition, respondent claims that the petition should be dismissed because it was not properly verified.

Section 275.5 of the Commissioner's regulations requires that all pleadings in an appeal to the Commissioner must be verified. Respondent claims that petitioner's verification is defective. The petition, which is dated August 20, 2003, states that Rafaela arrived in the United States "today." However, the verification is dated August 19, 2003. Respondent contends, therefore, that petitioner could not have verified the fact of petitioner's arrival on August 20, 2003. I find this error to be *de minimis*. Whether Rafaela arrived on August 19th or 20th is not material to the issues in this appeal, and I do not find that the inconsistency in the dates prejudiced respondent. A liberal interpretation of the rules is appropriate where the petitioner is *pro se* and there is no prejudice to respondent (*Appeal of Metze*, 42 Ed Dept Rep 40, Decision No. 14,768, *Appeal of Smith*, 40 *id.* 172, Decision No. 14,452). Accordingly, I decline to dismiss the petition for lack of proper verification.

The appeal must be dismissed, however, on the merits. Education Law §3202(1) provides in pertinent part:

> A person who is over the age of five and under twenty-one years of age who has not received a high school diploma is entitled to attend the public schools maintained in the district in which such person resides without the payment of tuition.

The purpose of this statute is to limit the obligation of the school district to provide tuition-free education to students whose parents or legal guardians reside within the district (*Appeal of a Student with a Disability*, 43 Ed Dept Rep ___, Decision No. 14,926; *Appeal of Gimenez*, 42 *id.* 176, Decision No. 14,812; *Appeal of Curran*, 42 *id.* 49, Decision No. 14,772). A child's residence is presumed to be that of his or her parents or legal guardians (*Appeal of a Student with a Disability*, *supra*; *Appeal of Gimenez*, *supra*; *Appeal of Curran*, *supra*). This presumption can be rebutted where it is shown that the parents have relinquished total custody and control to someone residing in the district (*Appeal of a Student with a Disability*, *supra*;

Appeal of Maxwell, 42 Ed Dept Rep 134, Decision No. 14,799). While it is not necessary to establish parental custody and control through a formal guardianship proceeding, it is necessary to demonstrate that a particular location is a child's permanent residence, and that the individual exercising control has full authority and responsibility with respect to the child's support and custody (*Appeal of a Student with a Disability, supra*; *Appeal of Hutchinson*, 42 Ed Dept Rep 310, Decision No. 14,865).

In addition, where the sole reason the child is residing with someone other than the parent is to take advantage of the schools of the district, the child has not established residence (*Appeal of a Student with a Disability, supra*; *Appeal of Hutchinson, supra*; *Appeal of Maxwell, supra*).

In this case, petitioner has failed to rebut the presumption that Rafaela's residency is with her parents in Brazil. Petitioner has not established that Rafaela's permanent residence is with her or that petitioner's parents have made a total transfer of custody and control. The Brazilian court certification specifically grants temporary custody to petitioner and provides that the rights and obligations of the permanent custody holder, Rafaela's parents, would not be affected. Furthermore, petitioner states that she will consult with Rafaela's parents on educational and medical matters involving Rafaela.

Petitioner admits that Rafaela will only live with her for one year, and will return to Brazil to live with her parents. Furthermore, petitioner stated in the registration materials that Rafaela's parents would pay one-half of Rafaela's expenses. Petitioner only raised the issue of financial hardship after respondent denied Rafaela's admission to its schools. Petitioner admits that a reason for Rafaela coming to live with her was to improve her English prior to going to college. As stated above, Rafaela may not establish residency solely to take advantage of the district's schools to improve her English.

Based on the totality of the record, I find that respondent's determination was neither arbitrary nor capricious and will not overturn it.

THE APPEAL IS DISMISSED.

Decision No. 15,076

Appeal of JUAN LOPEZ, on behalf of his nephew GIANCARLO HERNANDEZ, from action of the Board of Education of the Hicksville Union Free School District regarding residency.

(July 2, 2004)

APPEARANCES OF COUNSEL

Guercio & Guercio, attorneys for respondent, *Gary L. Steffanetta, Esq.*, of counsel

DECISION OF THE COMMISSIONER

MILLS, Commissioner.—Petitioner appeals the determination of the Board of Education of the Hicksville Union Free School District ("respondent") that his nephew, Giancarlo, is not a district resident. The appeal must be dismissed.

In 2001, Giancarlo moved to his uncle's home and attended school in respondent's district. In or about November 2003, the district received information that Giancarlo was not a district resident. Respondent's residency officer sent a letter to Giancarlo's mother, dated November 7, 2003, giving her an opportunity to submit proof of Giancarlo's residency within the district. On November 14, 2003, the officer held a residency hearing at which Giancarlo's mother and aunt were present. The residency officer concluded that Giancarlo was not a district resident and this appeal ensued. Petitioner's request for interim relief was denied on January 9, 2004.

Petitioner contends that he is Giancarlo's guardian and that Giancarlo is entitled to attend respondent's schools tuition-free. Respondent contends that the appeal must be dismissed because, among other things, the notice of petition and petition were never served on respondent.

Section 275.8(a) of the Commissioner's regulations requires that the petition be personally served upon each named respondent. If a school district is named as party respondent, service upon the school district shall be made personally by delivering a copy of the petition to the district clerk, to any trustee or any member of the board of education, to the superintendent of schools, or to a person in the office of the superintendent who has been designated by the board of education to accept service.

Respondent contends that the petition was not personally served in accordance with §275.8. The affidavit of service submitted by petitioner is defective in that, with the exception of the notary's signature, it is blank. Therefore, I must dismiss the appeal for lack of personal service upon respondent (*Appeal of Grant*, 42 Ed Dept Rep 184, Decision No. 14,816; *Appeal of K.R.*, 40 *id.* 189, Decision No. 14,457; *Appeal of Bd. of Educ. of the Sachem Cent. School Dist.*, 31 *id.* 277, Decision No. 12,641).

THE APPEAL IS DISMISSED.

Decision No. 15,077

Appeal of VIVIENNE MENDEZ, on behalf of her daughter YANIQUE HAYNES, from action of the Board of Education of the Uniondale Union Free School District regarding residency.

(July 2, 2004)

APPEARANCES OF COUNSEL

Ingerman Smith L.L.P., attorneys for respondent, *Lawrence W. Reich, Esq.*, of counsel

DECISION OF THE COMMISSIONER

MILLS, Commissioner.—Petitioner challenges the determination of the Board of Education of the Uniondale Union Free School District ("respondent") that her daughter, Yanique Haynes, is not a district resident. The appeal must be sustained.

In September 2002, petitioner enrolled her daughter in respondent's schools as a seventh grade student. On the enrollment application, petitioner listed their residence as Uniondale, within respondent's district. The enrollment application indicated a previous address in Roosevelt, within the Roosevelt Union Free School District.

In September 2003, the district received an anonymous message on its residency "Hot Line" that petitioner and her daughter did not reside in Uniondale. In response, an investigator conducted two surveillances at the Roosevelt address. On October 9, 2003, at approximately 7:07 a.m., the investigator observed a green Toyota parked in the driveway. The investigator learned that the Toyota was registered to petitioner at the Roosevelt address. On October 22,

2003, at approximately 7:56 a.m., the investigator observed petitioner and her daughter exit the Roosevelt residence and drive the Toyota to respondent's middle school, where the student was dropped off. The district also used the computer search engine "Auto Track" to match petitioner's address to the Roosevelt address as of October 2002.

By letter, dated November 10, 2003, respondent's administrative assistant for central registration ("registration assistant") and the interim superintendent advised petitioner that her daughter was not entitled to attend district schools because she resided outside the district. The letter indicated that a meeting could be arranged at which petitioner could provide additional documentation to support her residency claim before a final determination was made.

On November 19, 2003, the registration assistant met with petitioner to consider her evidence of residency. On November 20, 2003, he advised petitioner by telephone of his determination that she did not reside within the district. By letter dated December 10, 2003, he confirmed that determination based upon surveillance reports and documentary evidence indicating that petitioner continued to reside in Roosevelt. The letter advised that petitioner's daughter would be excluded as a non-resident after December 12, 2003. This appeal ensued. Petitioner's request for interim relief was granted on December 15, 2003.

Petitioner contends that her daughter resides with her in respondent's district. To support her claim, petitioner submits a bank statement for a checking account in her name at the Uniondale address. Petitioner also submits 15 receipts recording cash payments in the amount of $600 per month from August 2002 through October 2003 for an apartment rental in Uniondale. Petitioner states that her daughter's grandmother resides at the Roosevelt address and that the student goes there after school.

Respondent contends that it properly determined that petitioner and her daughter are not district residents. Respondent relies on petitioner's automobile registration, driver's license and computer search that all listed the Roosevelt address and its surveillance.

Education Law §3202(1) provides, in pertinent part:

> A person over five and under twenty-one years of age who has not received a high school diploma is entitled to attend the public schools maintained in the district in

which such person resides without the payment of tuition.

The purpose of this statute is to limit the obligation of school districts to provide tuition-free education to students whose parents or legal guardians reside within the district (*Appeal of B.C.*, 43 Ed Dept Rep ___, Decision No. 14,946; *Appeal of D.E.*, 43 *id.* ___, Decision No. 14,908). A child's residence is presumed to be that of his or her parents or legal guardian (*Appeal of B.C.*, *supra*; *Appeal of D.E.*, *supra*). Residency for purposes of Education Law §3202 is established based on two factors: physical presence as an inhabitant within the district, and intent to reside in the district (*Appeal of B.C.*, *supra*; *Appeal of D.E.*, *supra*).

Based on the record before me, I find insufficient evidence to support respondent's determination that petitioner is not a district resident. The surveillance, conducted on only two occasions, yielded inconclusive and unpersuasive results in view of petitioner's statement that her daughter spends time at her grandmother's Roosevelt residence. This limited surveillance of the Roosevelt home does not, therefore, establish that petitioner and her daughter reside there. Moreover, respondent's investigator did not conduct a surveillance at the Uniondale address, despite petitioner's claim that she resides there. The documents listing petitioner's residence as Roosevelt are also not conclusive proof that she still resides there, particularly in light of the rent receipts and banking records addressed to her Uniondale address.

On the record before me, I find that respondent's determination that Yanique is not a district resident is based upon insufficient evidence and is therefore arbitrary and capricious.

THE APPEAL IS SUSTAINED.

IT IS ORDERED that respondent permit Yanique Haynes to attend school in the Uniondale Union Free School District without the payment of tuition.

Decision No. 15,078

Appeal of ROBIN L. CRAIG, on behalf of ASHLEY and SHADONNA PENDLETON, from action of the Board of Education of the South Colonie Central School District regarding residency.

(July 15, 2004)

APPEARANCES OF COUNSEL

Tabner, Ryan and Keniry, LLP, attorneys for respondent, *William F. Ryan, Jr., Esq*., of counsel

DECISION OF THE COMMISSIONER

MILLS, Commissioner.—Petitioner challenges the determination of the Board of Education of the South Colonie Central School District ("respondent") that her daughters, Ashley and ShaDonna, are not district residents. The appeal must be sustained.

Petitioner enrolled her daughters in respondent's schools in September 2003. Previously they attended the schools of a neighboring district. By letter dated October 27, 2003, respondent's superintendent notified petitioner that a residency hearing would be held on October 31, 2003. At that hearing, petitioner stated that she and her daughters had recently moved to a Launfal Street residence ("Launfal") within the district, and she submitted a temporary driver's license. Several days later, petitioner submitted a letter from the owner of the Launfal residence stating that petitioner resided there. Thereafter, petitioner's daughters continued to attend respondent's schools.

After receiving information that petitioner resided at a Lark Street residence ("Lark") in the neighboring district, the district on February 11, 2004, conducted a second residency hearing. At that hearing, petitioner maintained that she resides at the Launfal residence, within the district. She explained that she is separated from her husband who resides at the Lark address with his niece and the niece's children.

At the February hearing, the district presented evidence it had acquired with the assistance of a private investigator purportedly showing that petitioner still resides at the Lark address. By letter dated February 12, 2004, the superintendent notified petitioner that her daughters would no longer be entitled to attend respondent's schools because they were not district residents. This appeal ensued. Petitioner's request for interim relief was granted on February 27, 2004.

Petitioner claims that her daughters live with her at Launfal and requests a determination that they are district residents entitled to attend the district's schools without the payment of tuition.

Respondent claims that its residency determination was rational and supported by the record. In addition, respondent requests attorney's fees and costs.

Education Law §3202(1) provides, in pertinent part:

> A person over five and under twenty-one years of age who has not received a high school diploma is entitled to attend the public schools maintained in the district in which such person resides without the payment of tuition.

The purpose of this statute is to limit the obligation of school districts to provide tuition-free education to students whose parents or legal guardians reside within the district (*Longwood Cent. School Dist. v. Springs Union Free School Dist.*, 1 NY3d 385; *Appeal of B.C.*, 43 Ed Dept Rep __, Decision No. 14,946; *Appeal of B.O. and D.O.*, 42 *id.* 42, Decision No. 14,769; *Appeal of Metze*, 42 *id.* 40, Decision No. 14,768). Residence for purposes of Education Law §3202 is established based upon two factors: physical presence as an inhabitant within the district and intent to reside in the district (*Longwood Cent. School Dist. v. Springs Union Free School Dist.*, *supra*; *Appeal of B.C.*, *supra*; *Appeal of B.O. and D.O.*, *supra*; *Appeal of Metze*, *supra*). Moreover, for purposes of Education Law §3202(1), a person can have only one legal residence (*Appeal of B.C.*, *supra*).

Petitioner states that she and her husband separated in August 2003 and that, while her husband is not her daughters' biological or adoptive father, he acts as their father in all other respects, and her daughters spend weekends with him. She also states that she and her husband own the Lark house, but that she moved out because she could not afford the house on her own. Petitioner further asserts that her father lives across the street from the Lark house and that she often helps him there. Petitioner also contends that her husband's niece frequently uses petitioner's car. Petitioner has submitted photocopies of mail she received at the Launfal residence, including bank and credit card statements. She also submitted unsworn statements from her husband, her father, her husband's niece and a neighbor.

Respondent relies on three computer search reports and observations by its private investigator. Respondent also points to the lack of separation or custody documents.

The first computer report, by Locate Plus, shows eight separate addresses for petitioner, including the marital residence and her father's residence. The dates overlap and cover a period from 1985 until July 1, 2003. Even if the report covered only the relevant period of time, it is impossible to ascertain from this list any single address where petitioner lived at a date certain. The report also lists a telephone search, but petitioner's name does not appear on the list. Similarly, her name does not appear on the list of vehicle registrations included in the report.

The second computer search, the Comprehensive Report, identifies the owner and nine other past and current residents of the Launfal address, again with overlapping dates, from October 1992 to January 2004. Petitioner's name does not appear on the list.

The third computer search, another Comprehensive Report, details numerous addresses purportedly occupied by petitioner dating from 1984. Again, there are overlapping dates so that it appears that petitioner has had an Alabama address, as well as the Lark address, as recently as December 2003.

Respondent also relied on the private investigator's testimony regarding his surveillance. Respondent states that on January 20, 2004, the investigator observed a gray minivan enter the Launfal driveway. Three females exited the house and were driven in the minivan to the school bus stop. On January 21, 2004, the investigator observed two females leave the Lark residence at 6:15 a.m. and drive away in the minivan with a third female. After arriving at the Launfal residence, three females exited that house and drove in the same minivan to the school bus stop. The investigator also testified that he made several evening observations at the Launfal residence and did not observe the minivan at that address.

Although petitioner's evidence is not overwhelming, I find respondent's evidence even less compelling and insufficient to support its determination that petitioner is not a district resident. The computer searches provide an abundance of conflicting information while failing to confirm where petitioner resides.

The investigator's observations are also unconvincing. There is no indication that the investigator positively identified petitioner or her daughters on the two observation dates. This is especially important given petitioner's explanation that she loans her vehicle, which appears to be registered to her husband, to her husband's niece.

Respondent does not provide information on the number and length of evening observations purportedly made by the investigator. It is, therefore, impossible to evaluate the significance, if any, of his failure to observe the vehicle at the Launfal residence on those occasions.

Petitioner's explanation of her personal circumstances also reasonably accounts for respondent's evidence. Petitioner asserts that she lives with a friend at the Launfal residence while trying to improve her financial situation. She does not pay rent, but instead helps with childcare and groceries. Petitioner explains that she does not have a separation agreement because of the cost of an attorney and feels it is unnecessary. There is apparently no custody agreement because there is no legal relationship between her husband and her daughters. Petitioner's name is still connected to the Lark address because she still owns it with her husband. Her daughters visit there frequently and petitioner is often at her father's house nearby. And petitioner's husband's niece and her children may well have been the individuals the investigator observed leaving the Lark residence, using petitioner's vehicle.

In sum, I find that respondent had an insufficient factual basis to determine that petitioner resides outside the district, and I therefore set aside that determination (*See, Appeal of Trapani*, 40 Ed Dept Rep 653, Decision No. 14,576; *Appeal of Staton*, 40 *id.* 134, Decision No. 14,440). Respondent may revisit the issue of petitioner's residency in the future if it obtains additional information indicating that petitioner and her children are not district residents.

THE APPEAL IS SUSTAINED.

IT IS ORDERED that respondent allow Ashley and ShaDonna Pendleton to attend school in the South Colonie School District without the payment of tuition.

Decision No. 15,079

Appeal of a STUDENT SUSPECTED OF HAVING A DISABILITY, by her parent, from action of the Board of Education of the Mamaroneck Union Free School District regarding special education.

(July 15, 2004)

APPEARANCES OF COUNSEL

Shaw & Perelson, LLP, attorneys for respondent, *Lisa S. Rusk* and *David S. Shaw, Esqs.*, of counsel

DECISION OF THE COMMISSIONER

MILLS, Commissioner.—Petitioner appeals the determination by the Board of Education of the Mamaroneck Union Free School District ("respondent") that his daughter is not eligible for special education services. The appeal must be dismissed.

In June 2003, petitioner referred his daughter to respondent's Committee on Special Education ("CSE") for evaluation. In August 2003, the CSE met and determined the student was not eligible for special education.

Petitioner disputed the CSE's determination and ultimately requested and received a hearing before an impartial hearing officer ("IHO"). In March 2004, petitioner commenced this appeal. In April 2004, the IHO issued a decision in the impartial hearing.

Petitioner contends that respondent failed to pay for an independent evaluation or initiate an impartial hearing. Petitioner also contends that respondent failed to perform required evaluations prior to convening the CSE and disregarded evaluations supporting a classification of learning disability for his daughter. Petitioner argues that unnecessary delays by respondent denied his daughter services.

Petitioner seeks an order that respondent classify his daughter as learning disabled and grant her testing accommodations. In the alternative, petitioner seeks an order that respondent pay for independent evaluations and provide testing accommodations.

Respondent contends that the appeal should be dismissed for lack of jurisdiction. Respondent also maintains that the appeal is moot and that petitioner failed to join the IHO as a necessary party.

Federal and state law establish procedural safeguards to ensure the opportunity for parental participation in, and the appeal of, decisions relating to eligibility for special education services to children with disabilities. The Individuals with Disabilities Education Act ("IDEA") and Education Law §4404 provide parents with the right to an impartial hearing regarding a complaint on any matter relating to the identification, evaluation, or educational placement of a child, or the provision of a free appropriate public education to such child (20 USC §1415).

Petitioner's claims relate entirely to respondent's alleged procedural violations of the IDEA and its alleged failure to find his daughter eligible for special education services. Because these are special education issues governed by the IDEA and the relief sought includes a directive to the CSE to classify petitioner's daughter as learning disabled, provide her with testing accommodations, pay for independent evaluations, and other determinations of his daughter's rights to special education services and procedures, they are properly the subject of an impartial hearing brought pursuant to Education Law §4404(1) and §200.5(c) of the Commissioner's regulations. A hearing officer must, in the first instance, determine these issues.

The record reflects that petitioner received an impartial hearing and decision from the IHO. A person who is dissatisfied with the decision of an IHO may appeal such decision to the State Review Officer ("SRO") pursuant to Education Law §4404(2). Consequently, this appeal must be dismissed for lack of jurisdiction (Education Law §4404(1) and (2); 8 NYCRR §200.5(c); *Appeal of a Student with a Disability*, 40 Ed Dept Rep 170, Decision No. 14,451; *Appeal of a Student with a Disability*, 39 *id.* 354, Decision No. 14,257; *Appeal of a Student with a Disability*, 39 *id.* 1, Decision No. 14,154).

In light of this disposition, I need not address the parties' remaining claims.

THE APPEAL IS DISMISSED.

Decision No. 15,080

Appeal of ALISHA TUCKER, on behalf of her daughter JAVAYA CARLTON, from action of the Board of Education of the Greenburgh Central School District regarding residency.

(July 15, 2004)

APPEARANCES OF COUNSEL

Keane & Beane, P.C., attorneys for respondent, *Mark D. Pellis, Esq.*, of counsel

DECISION OF THE COMMISSIONER

MILLS, Commissioner.—Petitioner appeals the determination of the Board of Education of the Greenburgh Central School District ("respondent") that her daughter, Javaya, is not a district resident. The appeal must be dismissed.

Sometime in or around January 2004, petitioner told Javaya's kindergarten teacher that she lived outside respondent's district. By letter dated February 2, 2004, respondent's superintendent offered petitioner an opportunity to submit information concerning Javaya's residency. Receiving no response, the superintendent notified petitioner by letter dated February 9, 2004, that Javaya would be excluded from district schools because petitioner was not a district resident.

On February 10, 2004, petitioner told the superintendent's secretary that she was employed as a school bus monitor by the private bus company that transports children to respondent's schools, and therefore, believed her daughter was entitled to attend respondent's schools. When advised that her employment with the bus company did not entitle her daughter to attend respondent's schools, petitioner stated that her daughter stayed with an aunt in the district Sundays through Fridays. When she learned that a transfer of custody and control to her aunt was necessary, petitioner stated that she was moving in with her aunt on February 13, 2004.

On or about February 13, 2004, petitioner submitted a landlord affidavit, a letter from her aunt and a water bill. On February 25, 2004, petitioner met with the district's director of pupil personnel services. She asserted that her employment previously entitled her to send her daughter to school in the district, but stated that she now resided with her aunt in the district, and submitted various documents including an interim license and a temporary auto insurance identification card with her aunt's address. Following a review of the information submitted, the superintendent notified petitioner of her final determination that petitioner was not a district resident. This appeal ensued. Petitioner's request for interim relief was denied on March 12, 2004.

Petitioner asserts that she currently resides with her aunt within respondent's district. She further states that her daughter attended respondent's schools by living weekdays with her uncle during the 2002-2003 school year, and with her aunt during the 2003-2004 school year.

Respondent contends that its residency determination should be upheld because petitioner admits that she lived outside the district until February 2004 and submitted unreliable documents to establish residency after that date.

Education Law §3202(1) provides in pertinent part:

> A person over five and under twenty-one years of age who has not received a high school diploma is entitled to attend the public schools maintained in the district in which such person resides without the payment of tuition.

The purpose of this statute is to limit the obligation of school districts to provide tuition-free education to students whose parents or legal guardians reside within the district (*Appeal of B.O. and D.O.*, 42 Ed Dept Rep 42, Decision No. 14,769; *Appeal of L.W.*, 41 *id.* 372, Decision No. 14,717; *Appeal of Pierre*, 40 *id.* 538, Decision No. 14,551). Residence is established by one's physical presence as an inhabitant within the district combined with an intent to remain (*Longwood Cent. School Dist. v. Springs Union Free School Dist.*, 1 NY3d 385; *Appeal of B.O. and D.O.*, *supra*; *Appeal of Metze*, 42 Ed Dept Rep 40, Decision No. 14,768).

In an appeal to the Commissioner of Education pursuant to Education Law §310, petitioner has the burden of establishing the facts upon which she seeks relief (8 NYCRR §275.10; *Appeal of Brown*, 42 Ed Dept Rep 17, Decision No. 14,760). Furthermore, residency determinations will not be set aside unless they are arbitrary, capricious or unreasonable (*Appeal of Gurka*, 43 Ed Dept Rep ___, Decision No. 15,072; *Appeal of Brown*, *supra*).

Petitioner has failed to meet the burden of proving that respondent's determination was arbitrary, capricious or unreasonable because she makes inconsistent statements and produces inconsistent documents concerning her residency. Although petitioner states that she lived outside the district from August 2002 until February 2004, she annexed two documents in which she represented to the district that she resided there in 2003—a kindergarten registration form dated March 7, 2003, and a landlord affidavit indicating that she rented an apartment from her aunt within the district commencing September 1, 2003. The documentation provided by petitioner is similarly inconsistent and questionable. The water bill contains no name, and the interim license and temporary auto insurance identification were issued after respondent challenged her residency.

Moreover, the landlord's affidavit is inconsistent with petitioner's statements and with a landlord affidavit previously submitted.

Petitioner has also failed to establish a transfer of custody and control of Javaya to her aunt or uncle. The fact that Javaya may have spent some time with them is not determinative.

Based on the record before me, I find that petitioner has not sustained her burden of establishing that respondent's determination is arbitrary, capricious, or unreasonable.

THE APPEAL IS DISMISSED.

Decision No. 15,081

Appeal of YOLANDA GIOVANNIELLO, on behalf of her daughter BREANNA, from action of the Board of Education of the Cold Spring Harbor Central School District regarding attendance zones.

(July 15, 2004)

APPEARANCES OF COUNSEL

Ehrlich, Frazer & Feldman, attorneys for respondent, *Jerome H. Ehrlich, Esq.*, of counsel

DECISION OF THE COMMISSIONER

MILLS, Commissioner.—Petitioner appeals the determination of the Board of Education of the Cold Spring Harbor Central School District ("respondent") that her daughter, Breanna, may not attend school outside of the attendance zone in which she resides. The appeal must be dismissed.

Respondent's district has two elementary schools: West Side Elementary School ("West Side") and Lloyd Harbor Elementary School ("Lloyd Harbor"). Respondent has established attendance zones for both schools.

Under respondent's general policy, the location of a child's residence determines which elementary school the child attends. Thus, a child who resides within the West Side attendance zone must attend West Side and a child who resides within the Lloyd Harbor attendance zone must attend Lloyd Harbor. There are two exceptions to this policy: (1) a classified student may attend a school outside of the student's attendance zone upon direction of the Committee on Special Education; and (2) a sixth-grade student is permitted to complete that grade at the student's former elementary school when the student's family moves into a different attendance zone, as long as the student resided in the original attendance zone on October 1 of the school year in question.

At the beginning of the 2003-2004 school year, two of petitioner's three daughters, Breanna, a fourth grader, and Jackie, a sixth grader, attended West Side. The family then resided at Crosby Place in Cold Spring Harbor, which is within West Side's attendance zone. On or about September 22, 2003, petitioner notified the West Side principal that her family would be moving from Cold Spring Harbor to Lloyd Harbor, in Lloyd Harbor's attendance zone, and requested that both Breanna and Jackie be permitted to continue attending West Side. The principal advised petitioner to address her request to the superintendent.

Petitioner submitted her request to the superintendent, who advised petitioner that Jackie could complete sixth grade at West Side, provided that she resided within West Side's attendance zone on October 1, 2003, and that petitioner provide Jackie's transportation. However, the superintendent denied petitioner's request for Breanna to continue at West Side based on respondent's attendance zone policy.

According to the petition, on or about October 20, 2003, petitioner and her family moved to Abbington Drive in Lloyd Harbor, within the Lloyd Harbor attendance zone. This appeal ensued. Petitioner's request for interim relief was denied on November 19, 2003.

Petitioner argues that Breanna and her family will suffer "innumerable hardships" if Breanna is required to transfer to Lloyd Harbor. She claims that Breanna has difficulty adjusting to change and questions the effect the change may have on her academic performance. Finally, petitioner claims that Breanna should be allowed to continue attending West Side because it has fewer fourth grade students per class than Lloyd Harbor.

Respondent maintains that petitioner has failed to establish that she is entitled to the requested relief. Respondent argues that pupil placement is a matter of educational policy, within the discretion of the district. Respondent claims its attendance zone policy is rational and that its decision regarding petitioner's daughter is consistent with this policy. In addition, respondent claims that its policy balances the student population between the two elementary schools. Additionally, respondent maintains that the differences in class size at West Side and Lloyd Harbor are not pedagogically significant.

Pursuant to Education Law §1709(3) and (33), a board of education has the authority and responsibility to manage and administer the affairs of the school district, including the assignment of pupils to schools therein (*Matter of Older, et al. v Board of Ed.*, 27 NY2d 333; *Appeal of P.S.*, 39 Ed Dept Rep 806, Decision No. 14,387; *Appeal of Ibrahim*, 39 *id.* 155, Decision No. 14,200). In the assignment of pupils to schools, a board of education has broad discretion (*Matter of Addabbo v. Donovan*, 22 AD2d 383; *aff'd* 16 NY2d 619, *cert den* 382 US 905; *Appeal of the Lancaster Parent Alliance*, 38 Ed Dept Rep 356, Decision No. 14,053). Accordingly, a board's decision regarding school assignments will only be overturned when found to be arbitrary, capricious or contrary to sound educational policy (*Matter of Older, supra*). Moreover, petitioner bears the burden of demonstrating that respondent's action is arbitrary, capricious or contrary to sound educational policy (*Appeal of Johnson*, 37 Ed Dept Rep 465, Decision No. 13,906; *Appeal of Sherwood, et al.*, 33 *id.* 410, Decision No. 13,096; *Appeal of McNerney, et al.*, 28 *id.* 250, Decision No. 12,097). I find that petitioner has failed to meet that burden.

Respondent's policy requires students to attend the elementary school in the attendance zone in which they reside, with two limited exceptions that are not applicable to Breanna. There is no dispute that Breanna resides in the Lloyd Harbor attendance zone. Thus, petitioner has no legal basis to insist that Breanna remain at West Side.

The fact that Breanna may have some difficulty adjusting to a new school, while regrettable, is not a basis for overturning respondent's decision (*Appeal of Sponcy*, 33 Ed Dept Rep 126, Decision No. 12,998; *Appeal of Cullen*, 32 *id.* 179, Decision No. 12,798). While I am sympathetic to petitioner's wishes to have Breanna attend the same school as her sister, there is no legal basis to grant the relief petitioner seeks (*Appeal of Kershaw*, 37 Ed Dept Rep 186, Decision No. 13,837; *Appeal of Barbara D. and James D.*, 34 *id.* 118, Decision No. 13,252).

I conclude that respondent's decision in this matter is not arbitrary, capricious or contrary to sound educational policy and therefore, I will not disturb it.

THE APPEAL IS DISMISSED.

Decision No. 15,082

Appeal of EULAH NELSON, on behalf of her grandson CHRISTIAN ROBINSON, from action of the Board of Education of the Pittsford Central School District regarding residency.

(July 15, 2004)

APPEARANCES OF COUNSEL

Harris Beach LLP, attorneys for respondent, *Laura M. Purcell, Esq.*, of counsel

DECISION OF THE COMMISSIONER

MILLS, Commissioner.—Petitioner challenges the determination of the Board of Education of the Pittsford Central School District ("respondent") that her grandson, Christian, is not a district resident. The appeal must be dismissed.

Since September 1998, Christian has attended respondent's schools. Respondent permitted Christian to enroll based upon his mother's representation that she resided with her parents (Christian's grandparents) on Mile Post Lane within the district.

In June 2003, the principal of Jefferson Road Elementary School notified respondent's director of pupil services that Christian had made comments indicating that he did not reside within the district. The director of pupil services contacted respondent's director of transportation to learn whether Christian was riding the bus to and from the Mile Post Lane residence.

The director of transportation spoke with Christian's bus driver, who informed him that the Mile Post Lane residence was Christian's grandparents' house and that Christian's mother lived elsewhere. The bus driver further stated that Christian did not take the bus in the morning because his mother drove him to school, and that each afternoon, Christian's mother picked him up in her car after he was dropped off at the bus stop near the Mile Post Lane residence.

At the beginning of the 2003-2004 school year, Christian's bus driver reported to the assistant to the transportation director ("assistant") that Christian did not ride the bus in the mornings and that in the afternoons his mother picked him up from the bus stop in a white Honda. The assistant determined that the white Honda was registered to Christian's mother at a French Road residence in Rochester, within the Brighton Central School District.

The director of pupil services contacted a private investigator, who surveilled both the Mile Post Lane and French Road residences from September 22 to September 26, 2003, and again from October 20 to October 24, 2003. On seven mornings, he observed Christian being driven to school from his mother's French Road residence or the bus stop near the Mile Post Lane residence. On seven afternoons, the investigator observed Christian being dropped off by the school bus, near the Mile Post Lane residence, and either picked up by his mother or transported to church activities by his grandparents. On eight evenings, he observed Christian being driven to his mother's French Road residence after church activities.

By letter dated December 2, 2003, the director of pupil services advised Christian's mother that, based upon the district's investigation, the district had determined that Christian was not a district resident and was not entitled to attend respondent's schools after December 19, 2003. By letter dated December 8, 2003, petitioner stated that guardianship had been given to her and her husband. This appeal ensued. Petitioner's request for interim relief was denied on December 29, 2003.

Petitioner contends that Christian is a district resident because his mother transferred guardianship and surrendered parental control to petitioner and her husband. Petitioner admits that Christian's mother remarried and moved out of the district in October 2002. Petitioner claims, however, that Christian has continued to reside with her and her husband because it is in Christian's best interest to remain in a stable environment.

Respondent contends that petitioner has failed to demonstrate that Christian is a district resident because the transfer of Christian's custody and control to petitioner and her husband was neither total nor permanent.

In an appeal to the Commissioner pursuant to Education Law §310, a petitioner has the burden of demonstrating a clear right to the relief requested and the burden of establishing the facts upon which they seek relief (8 NYCRR §275.10; *Appeal of Green*, 40 Ed Dept Rep 278, Decision No. 14,479; *Appeal of a Student with a Disability*, 40 *id*. 121, Decision No. 14,436).

Education Law §3202(1) provides in pertinent part:

> A person over five and under twenty-one years of age who has not received a high school diploma is entitled to attend the public schools maintained in the district in which such person resides without the payment of tuition.

The purpose of this statute is to limit the obligation of school districts to provide tuition-free education to students whose parents or legal guardians reside within the district (*Appeal of Humphrey*, 43 Ed Dept Rep___, Decision No. 14,940; *Appeal of Thomas*, 41 *id.* 84, Decision No. 14,622; *Appeal of Oliver*, 41 *id.* 30, Decision No. 14,603). A child's residence is presumed to be that of his or her parents or legal guardian (*Appeal of Humphrey, supra*; *Appeal of Thomas, supra*; *Appeal of Santana*, 40 Ed Dept Rep 57, Decision No. 14,420). This presumption may be rebutted upon a determination that there has been a total, and presumably permanent, transfer of custody and control to someone residing in the district (*Appeal of Maxwell*, 42 Ed Dept Rep 134, Decision No. 14,799; *Appeal of Donohue*, 41 *id.* 26, Decision No. 14,601; *Appeal of Juarez*, 39 *id.* 184, Decision No. 14,208). A residency determination will not be set aside unless it is arbitrary and capricious (*Appeal of A.F.*, 41 Ed Dept Rep 115, Decision No. 14,633; *Appeal of Karmin*, 41 *id.* 72, Decision No. 14,618).

Upon the record before me, petitioner has failed to rebut the presumption that Christian resides with his mother. Respondent's surveillance supports its determination that Christian lives with his mother outside of the district. Petitioner has not submitted any evidence to challenge the surveillance findings.

Furthermore, petitioner has failed to prove that there was total and permanent transfer of custody and control to petitioner and her husband. The petition states that both petitioner and Christian's mother support Christian and provide him with food, shelter and clothing. The petition also asserts that both petitioner and Christian's mother exercise control over his activities and behaviors. In addition, the petition claims that Christian communicates with his mother daily and spends every weekend with her. The record further shows that only Christian's mother has interacted with district personnel regarding educational and related matters.

Moreover, petitioner failed to provide evidence of a transfer of guardianship. According to respondent, petitioner did not notify the district of the purported transfer until after it determined that

Christian was not a district resident. Where the sole reason the child claims to reside with someone other than the parent is to take advantage of the schools of the district, the child has not established residence (*Appeal of a Student with a Disability*, *supra*; *Appeal of West*, 36 Ed Dept Rep 76, Decision No. 13,662).

Based on these facts, I find that petitioner has failed to provide sufficient evidence to rebut the presumption that Christian resides with his mother outside the district. Accordingly, respondent's determination is neither arbitrary nor capricious and will not be set aside.

THE APPEAL IS DISMISSED.

Decision No. 15,083

Appeal of D.K. and R.S., Jr., on behalf of A.K., from action of the Board of Education of the Maplewood-Colonie Common School District regarding residency.

(July 15, 2004)

APPEARANCES OF COUNSEL

William M. Hoblock, Esq., attorney for respondent

DECISION OF THE COMMISSIONER

MILLS, Commissioner.—Petitioners challenge the determination of the Board of Education of the Maplewood-Colonie Common School District ("respondent") that A.K. is not a district resident entitled to attend its schools tuition-free. The appeal must be dismissed.

Petitioner D.K. is A.K.'s mother and petitioner R.S., Jr., is A.K.'s brother. On March 24, 2004, Albany County Family Court awarded petitioners joint legal custody of A.K. Pursuant to the court order, R.S., Jr. has primary physical custody over A.K. and her parents have "[p]arenting [t]ime with [A.K.] at times and places mutually agreed to by the parties." A.K. is 14 years old and lives with her brother in Maplewood, within respondent's district. D.K. resides in the City of Watervliet, outside respondent's district.

Respondent's district has one school for kindergarten through eighth grade. Apart from educating resident students on a tuition-free basis, respondent also accepts certain nonresident students selected by lottery on a tuition basis.

Upon completing eighth grade, resident students of the district have the option of attending high school, tuition-free, in either the City of Watervliet at Watervliet High School or at Shaker High School in the North Colonie Central School District pursuant to instruction contracts with each district. In either case, the resident student's tuition is paid for by the district. Nonresident students who have attended the district do not have the same option.

During sixth, seventh and most of eighth grade, A.K. resided outside the district with her parents in Watervliet and attended respondent's district on a tuition basis.

In April 2003, A.K. and her mother moved into the district to live with R.S., Jr. in Maplewood. Upon completing eighth grade, A.K. chose to attend Shaker High School in North Colonie Central School District, at respondent's expense. D.K. moved back to her Watervliet home, and respondent asked her to provide documentation of A.K.'s residency. By letter dated March 26, 2004, D.K. was informed that A.K. was not entitled to attend Shaker High School tuition-free and was advised to register A.K. at Watervliet High School. Petitioners commenced this appeal on April 9, 2004. Their request for interim relief was granted on April 20, 2004.

Petitioners claim that A.K. is a resident of respondent's district because she lives with her brother in Maplewood. They contend that Albany County Family Court awarded physical custody of A.K. to her brother on March 24, 2004, because it was in her best interest to finish out the school year at Shaker High School.

Respondent contends that A.K. is not a district resident because she lives with her parents on weekends in Watervliet and the only reason joint custody was arranged with R.S., Jr. was to take advantage of the schools of the district.

Education Law §3202(1) provides in pertinent part:

> A person over five and under twenty-one years of age who has not received a high school diploma is entitled to attend the public schools maintained in the district in which such person resides without the payment of tuition.

The purpose of this statute is to limit the obligation of school districts to provide tuition-free education to students whose parents or legal guardians reside within the district (*Appeal of Humphrey*, 43 Ed Dept Rep ___, Decision No. 14,940; *Appeal of Thomas*, 41 *id.* 84, Decision No. 14,622; *Appeal of Oliver*, 41 *id.* 30, Decision No. 14,603). A child's residence is presumed to be that of his or her parents or legal guardian (*Appeal of Humphrey*, *supra*; *Appeal of Thomas*, *supra*; *Appeal of Santana*, 40 Ed Dept Rep 57, Decision No. 14,420). This presumption may be rebutted upon a determination that there has been a total, and presumably permanent, transfer of custody and control to someone residing in the district (*Appeal of Maxwell*, 42 Ed Dept Rep 134, Decision No. 14,799; *Appeal of Donohue*, 41 *id.* 26, Decision No. 14,601; *Appeal of Juarez*, 39 *id.* 184, Decision No. 14,208). A residency determination will not be set aside unless it is arbitrary and capricious (*Appeal of A.F.*, 41 Ed Dept Rep 115, Decision No. 14,633; *Appeal of Karmin*, 41 *id.* 72, Decision No. 14,618).

Where the sole reason the child is residing with someone other than the parent is to take advantage of the schools of the district, the child has not established residence (*Appeal of Gratton*, 43 Ed Dept Rep ___, Decision No. 14,922; *Appeal of Pierre*, 40 *id.* 538, Decision No. 14,551; *Appeal of Mendoza*, 39 *id.* 74, Decision No. 14,178). Applications by parents to transfer custody or legal guardianship of their children merely to achieve residence status for the children to take advantage of the local schools should not be granted (*Matter of Proios*, 111 Misc. 2d 252; *Appeal of Cron*, 38 Ed Dept Rep 149, Decision No. 14,005). Even if custody orders or letters of guardianship are issued by a court, the presumption of a child's residence with the guardian or custodian can be rebutted if it can be shown that the guardianship or transfer of custody was established merely for the purpose of circumventing a district's nonresident policy (*Appeal of Cron*, *supra*; *Appeal of Gilbert*, 37 Ed Dept Rep 43, Decision No. 13,798; *Appeal of Pinto*, 30 *id.* 374, Decision No. 12,499).

The record before me indicates that the parents have not relinquished custody of A.K. They continue to share custody of their daughter and have simply added R.S., Jr. as joint custodian. The joint custody order was arranged so that A.K. would spend school days with her brother and would return to her parents' residence for a "visit" on weekends. The Family Court petition clearly suggests that the sole reason for the addition of R.S., Jr. as joint custodian was to establish a residence in Maplewood so that A.K. could finish the school year at Shaker High School. Petitioners only commenced the Family Court proceeding after respondent determined that A.K. was a non-resident. The record thus amply supports respondent's conclusion that the reason for obtaining the joint custody order was to achieve residence status in order to take advantage of the educational programs provided by respondent's school district.

Under these circumstances, I find that petitioners have not rebutted the presumption that A.K.'s residence remains with her parents, in the City School District of the City of Watervliet. Accordingly, I find no basis to disturb respondent's determination that A.K. is not a district resident.

THE APPEAL IS DISMISSED.

Decision No. 15,084

Appeal of CHAZY LEGACY ASSOCIATION from action of the Board of Education of the Chazy Union Free School District regarding the appointment of a director of physical education.

(July 15, 2004)

APPEARANCES OF COUNSEL

Harris Beach LLP, attorneys for respondent, *Dennis Curtin, Esq.*, of counsel

DECISION OF THE COMMISSIONER

MILLS, Commissioner.—Petitioner appeals the failure of the Board of Education of the Chazy Union Free School District ("respondent") to appoint a director of physical education. The appeal must be dismissed.

Petitioner alleges that respondent failed to appoint a director of physical education, as required by the Commissioner's regulations. Petitioner seeks an order directing respondent to appoint an individual to that position.

Respondent admits that, at the time the appeal was initiated, it did not employ a director of physical education. On May 11, 2004, however, respondent appointed a director of physical education for the 2004-2005 school year. Respondent asserts that the appeal is moot.

The Commissioner will only decide matters in actual controversy and will not render a decision on a state of facts which no longer exists or which subsequent events have laid to rest (*Appeal of Schuler*, 43 Ed Dept Rep ___, Decision No. 15,058; *Appeal of Baldauf*, 43 *id.* ___, Decision No. 15,049; *Appeal of Kushner*, 43 *id.* ___, Decision No. 15,040). The 2003-2004 school year has ended. Respondent has employed a director of physical education for the 2004-2005 school year in compliance with §135.4(c)(4)(iii) of the Commissioner's regulations. As petitioner seeks no further relief, the appeal is moot.

THE APPEAL IS DISMISSED.

Decision No. 15,085

Appeal of MAXINE SLOLEY-RAYMOND, on behalf of her sister LETISHA MCDERMOTT, from action of the Board of Education of the Elmsford Union Free School District regarding residency.

(July 15, 2004)

APPEARANCES OF COUNSEL

Keane & Beane, P.C., attorneys for respondent, *Mark D. Pellis* and *Stephanie M. Roebuck, Esqs.*, of counsel

DECISION OF THE COMMISSIONER

MILLS, Commissioner.—Petitioner appeals the determination of the Board of Education of the Elmsford Union Free School District ("respondent") that her sister, Letisha, is not a district resident. The appeal must be dismissed.

Letisha began attending the district's schools in September 2002. In January 2004, respondent learned that Letisha might reside in another district and retained a private investigator. Based on surveillance conducted on seven dates, the investigator concluded that Letisha resided with her parents in the Bronx.

By letter dated March 5, 2004, respondent's superintendent informed Letisha's parents that because they had not responded to her request for information on Letisha's residence, Letisha would be excluded from the district's schools effective March 12, 2004. This appeal ensued. Petitioner's request for interim relief was granted on March 29, 2004.

Petitioner alleges that Letisha resides with her in the district. She contends that Letisha lives with her because their mother is experiencing financial hardships, and intends to reside with her until she enters college in four years.

Respondent asserts that petitioner has not rebutted the surveillance evidence indicating that Letisha resides with her parents in the Bronx. It further contends that Letisha's parents have not relinquished total custody and control to petitioner because Letisha's parents, and not petitioner, have been involved in all discussions with school authorities concerning Letisha's educational progress. Respondent also claims that petitioner has failed to offer any evidence supporting her allegation that Letisha's parents are experiencing financial difficulties.

Education Law §3202(1) provides in pertinent part:

> A person over five and under twenty-one years of age who has not received a high school diploma is entitled to attend the public schools maintained in the district in which such person resides without the payment of tuition.

The purpose of this statute is to limit the obligation of the school district to provide tuition-free education to students whose parents or legal guardians reside within the district (*Appeal of a Student with a Disability*, 43 Ed Dept Rep ___, Decision No. 14,926; *Appeal of O.W.*, 43 *id.* ___, Decision No. 14,949). A child's residence is presumed to be that of his or her parents or legal guardians (*Appeal of a Student with a Disability, supra*; *Appeal of O.W., supra*). This presumption can be rebutted where it is shown that the parents have relinquished total custody and control to someone residing in the district (*Appeal of a Student with a Disability, supra*; *Appeal of O.W., supra*). While it is not necessary to establish parental custody and control through a formal guardianship proceeding, it is necessary to demonstrate that a particular location is a child's permanent residence, and that the individual exercising control has full authority and responsibility with respect to the child's support and custody (*Appeal of a Student with a Disability, supra*; *Appeal of O.W., supra*). Moreover, where the sole reason the child is residing with someone other than the parent is to take advantage of the schools of the district, the child has not established residence (*Appeal of a Student with a Disability, supra*; *Appeal of O.W., supra*).

A residency determination will not be set aside unless it is arbitrary and capricious (*Appeal of Newby*, 42 Ed Dept Rep 107, Decision No. 14,790; *Appeal of Leontakianakos*, 42 *id.* 10, Decision No. 14,757). In an appeal to the Commissioner of Education, the petitioner has the burden of demonstrating a clear legal right to the relief requested and the burden of establishing the facts upon which she seeks relief (8 NYCRR §275.10; *Appeal of B.H. and B.H.*, 43 Ed Dept Rep __, Decision No. 14,919; *Appeal of J.T.*, 43 *id.* __, Decision No. 14,917).

Petitioner's evidence of residency is essentially limited to the conclusory statements of petitioner and Letisha's mother that Letisha resides with petitioner in the district due to financial circumstances. She has not submitted any evidence to rebut the investigator's report.

Furthermore, petitioner has not established that Letisha's parents have relinquished custody and control. In fact, petitioner admits that Letisha's parents have not surrendered parental control. She also has not refuted that Letisha's parents alone have been involved in all discussions with school authorities concerning Letisha's educational progress. Accordingly, respondent's determination was not arbitrary or capricious.

THE APPEAL IS DISMISSED.

Decision No. 15,086

Appeal of THOMAS EJBISZ, on behalf of his daughter SARAH, from action of the Board of Education of the Cheektowaga-Sloan Union Free School District regarding residency.

(July 15, 2004)

APPEARANCES OF COUNSEL

Jaeckle Fleischmann & Mugel, LLP, attorneys for respondent, *Matthew C. Van Vessem, Esq.*, of counsel

DECISION OF THE COMMISSIONER

MILLS, Commissioner.—Petitioner appeals the determination of the Board of Education of the Cheektowaga-Sloan Union Free School District ("respondent") that his daughter Sarah is not a district resident. The appeal must be dismissed.

On February 2, 2004, petitioner's family, including Sarah, moved out of respondent's district. By letter dated March 2, 2004, respondent's superintendent notified petitioner that Sarah could not continue to attend respondent's schools because she was not a resident. This appeal ensued. Petitioner's request for interim relief was granted on April 20, 2004.

Petitioner concedes that Sarah no longer resides in the district and does not intend to return. Respondent contends that this concession requires that the appeal be dismissed.

Education Law §3202(1) provides, in pertinent part:

> A person over five and under twenty-one years of age who has not received a high school diploma is entitled to attend the public schools maintained in the district in which such person resides without the payment of tuition.

The purpose of this statute is to limit the obligation of school districts to provide tuition-free education to students whose parents or legal guardians reside within the district (*Appeal of Marshall*, 43 Ed Dept Rep __, Decision No. 14,911; *Appeal of B.O. and D.O.*, 42 *id.* 42, Decision No. 14,769; *Appeal of Metze*, 42 *id.* 40, Decision No. 14,768). A student's residence is presumed to b that of his or her parent or legal guardian (*Appeal of Steele*, 43 Ed Dept Rep ___, Decision No. 15,068; *Appeal of DiFalco*, 43 *id.* ___, Decision NO. 14,903). Residence for purposes of Education Law §3202 is established based upon two factors: physical presence as an inhabitant within the district and an intent to reside in the district (*See*, *Longwood CSD v. Springs UFSD*, 1 NY3d 385; *Appeal of Marshall*, *supra*; *Appeal of B.O. and D.O.*, *supra*).

Neither Sarah nor her parents are physically present, nor do they intend to reside in respondent's district. Accordingly, Sarah is not district resident and has no right to attend district schools tuition-free.

THE APPEAL IS DISMISSED.

Decision No. 15,087

Appeal of ALEISHA L. GARVIN, on behalf of her daughter JAZMYNE GARVIN ARCHER, from action of the Board of Education of the Uniondale Union Free School District regarding transportation.

(July 16, 2004)

APPEARANCES OF COUNSEL

Ingerman Smith, L.L.P., attorneys for respondent, *Lawrence W. Reich, Esq.*, of counsel

DECISION OF THE COMMISSIONER

MILLS.—Petitioner appeals the denial by the Board of Education of the Uniondale Union Free School District ("respondent") of her request for her daughter's transportation to a nonpublic school. The appeal must be dismissed.

Petitioner and her daughter, Jazmyne, reside within respondent's district. Jazmyne attends the Portledge School, a nonpublic school in Locust Valley. For the past nine years, including the 2003-2004 school year, respondent transported Jazmyne to the Portledge School. By letter dated August 8, 2003, the district clerk notified petitioner that the Portledge School was "beyond the 15 mile limit for transportation" and denied petitioner's transportation request for the 2003-2004 school year. Thereafter, by letter dated August 12, 2003, the district clerk granted petitioner's 2003-2004 transportation request without explanation.

By letter dated December 2003, the assistant superintendent for business affairs notified parents of students attending certain nonpublic schools, including the Portledge School, that the schools were beyond the district's 15 mile transportation limitation. Petitioner received that notice. The letter stated that "[a]lthough transportation has been provided to the above schools in the past, beginning with the 2004-2005 school year we will no longer do so." This appeal ensued. Petitioner's request for interim relief was denied on February 23, 2004.

On May 18, 2004, the assistant superintendent for business affairs notified petitioner:

> Another mileage check was conducted to determine the distance from your residence to the Portledge School in Locust Valley, New York. As a result, it has been established that the school is less than 15 miles away and your child, Jazmyne Archer, will be eligible for transportation for the 2004-05 school year.

The Commissioner will only decide matters in actual controversy and will not render a decision on a state of facts which no longer exists or which subsequent events have laid to rest (*Appeal of Schuler*, 43 Ed Dept Rep ___, Decision No. 15,058; *Appeal of Baldauf*,

43 *id.* ___, Decision No. 15,049). Respondent concedes that petitioner resides within 15 miles of the Portledge School and that Jazmyne is eligible for transportation for the 2004-2005 school year. Since respondent has agreed to provide the requested transportation and petitioner seeks no further relief, the appeal is moot.

THE APPEAL IS DISMISSED.

Decision No. 15,088

Appeal of KANISA HOLDER, on behalf of her son CYRUS, from action of the Board of Education of the Uniondale Union Free School District regarding residency.

(July 16, 2004)

APPEARANCES OF COUNSEL

Law Firm of Anthony D. Denaro, P.C., attorneys for petitioner, *Lawrence S. Lefkowitz, Esq.*, of counsel

Ingerman Smith, LLP, attorneys for respondent, *Lawrence W. Reich, Esq.*, of counsel

DECISION OF THE COMMISSIONER

MILLS, Commissioner.—Petitioner appeals the determination of the Board of Education of the Uniondale Union Free School District ("respondent") that her son, Cyrus, is not a district resident. The appeal must be dismissed.

Petitioner enrolled Cyrus in first grade in respondent's schools in the fall of 2003. At that time, she indicated that she resided in the district. In January 2004, the district's administration commenced an investigation of petitioner's residency. By letter dated February 13, 2004, the interim superintendent notified petitioner of his finding that she was not a district resident and that, as of March 5, 2004, Cyrus was ineligible to attend school in the district. The letter further notified petitioner of her right to present evidence regarding her residency.

On March 1, 2004, petitioner attended a residency conference. By letter dated March 2, 2004, respondent's designee informed petitioner of his decision that Cyrus was not a district resident. He further determined that petitioner's primary residence is outside the district in Roosevelt. This appeal ensued. On April 9, 2004, petitioner's request for interim relief was granted.

Petitioner contends that respondent's determination is not supported by the evidence in the record and that she was not afforded appropriate due process. Respondent asserts that it complied with the procedural requirements of §100.2(y) of the Commissioner's regulations and that the record supports its determination that petitioner and her son are not district residents.

Education Law §3202(1) provides in pertinent part:

> A person over five and under twenty-one years of age who has not received a high school diploma is entitled to attend the public schools maintained in the district in which such person resides without the payment of tuition.

The purpose of this statute is to limit the obligation of school districts to provide tuition-free education to students whose parents or legal guardians reside within the district (*Appeal of General*, 43 Ed Dept Rep ___, Decision No. 14,948; *Appeal of Burnett*, 42 *id.* 208, Decision No. 14,825; *Appeal of J.M.*, 42 *id.* 80, Decision No. 14,783). Residency for purposes of Education Law §3202 is established based upon two factors: physical presence and an intent to reside in the district (see, *Longwood C.S.D. v. Springs U.F.S.D.*, 1 NY3d 385; *Appeal of General, supra*; *Appeal of Burnett, supra*). A child's residence is presumed to be that of his or her parents or legal guardians (*Appeal of Short*, 43 Ed Dept Rep ___, Decision No. 14,945; *Appeal of Washington*, 42 *id.* 197, Decision No. 14,820).

A residency determination will not be overturned unless it is arbitrary and capricious (*Appeal of General, supra*; *Appeal of Short, supra*). In an appeal to the Commissioner, petitioner has the burden of demonstrating a clear legal right to the relief requested and the burden of establishing the facts upon which she seeks relief (8 NYCRR §275.10; *Appeal of General, supra*; *Appeal of Short, supra*).

In his March 2, 2004, letter, respondent's designee indicated that his determination was based on telephone records, a surveillance report, Cyrus's statement that he had moved to Roosevelt, petitioner's statement that she sleeps at the Roosevelt address, and the statement of a tenant at the Uniondale address indicating that petitioner did not reside there.

Petitioner asserts that her family owns property in Uniondale, Hempstead and Roosevelt, that she spends time at each of the properties, but that she and Cyrus reside at her father's house in respondent's district. Petitioner asserts that she spends time at her grandparents' house in Roosevelt because she is attempting to open a daycare center at that address. She maintains that she sometimes sleeps at that address because she occasionally babysits late in the evening or early in the morning. She submits two letters from individuals for whom she provides child care at her grandparents' house in Roosevelt.

Petitioner also submits a statement from the tenant at the Uniondale address. The tenant states that she hears petitioner "coming and going but I really do not pay this any attention because it is none of my business. However, [petitioner] does reside at this address and have [sic] been for quite some time." Petitioner also submits tax receipts indicating that her father owns the Uniondale property. Finally, petitioner submits correspondence addressed to her at the Uniondale address.

In addition to the evidence referred to in the March 2, 2004, letter, respondent submits copies of petitioner's employment earning statements and vehicle registration data listing the Roosevelt address and utility bills sent to petitioner at a Hempstead address for service provided to her at the Roosevelt address.

Based on the record before me, I find that respondent's determination is neither arbitrary nor capricious. Petitioner has not presented sufficient evidence to establish that she and her son actually reside in respondent's district. The correspondence, tax receipts and tenant's statement are unpersuasive in view of the contrary evidence submitted by respondent. In addition, petitioner submits a letter dated March 10, 2004, from her then current employer stating that on March 1 petitioner worked from 8:30 a.m. to 2:30 p.m. This information belies petitioner's claim that she was present at the Roosevelt address during the relevant period because she provides childcare services from that location. I also note that petitioner's application to operate a daycare center was not filed with the New York State Office of Children and Family Services until March 4, 2004—two days after respondent's residency determination. Accordingly, I find that petitioner has not met her burden of proof and respondent's determination is supported by the record.

Petitioner's assertion that she was not afforded due process is also without merit. Section 100.2(y) of the Commissioner's regulations requires that, prior to making a determination of residency "the board or its designee shall afford the child's parent . . . the opportunity to submit information concerning the child's right to attend school in the district." When petitioner's residency was questioned, petitioner received written notice of the opportunity to provide information and documentation to respondent's designee, thus satisfying the requirements of §100.2(y).

While the appeal must be dismissed, I note that petitioner retains the right to reapply to the district for admission of her son at any time should circumstances change (*Appeal of Normandin*, 43 Ed Dept Rep __, Decision No. 14,950; *Appeal of a Student with a Disability*, 43 *id.* __, Decision No. 14,926).

THE APPEAL IS DISMISSED.

Decision No. 15,089

Appeal of CHRIS C. CORDISCO, on behalf of his daughter VICTORIA, from action of the Board of Education of the Rhinebeck Central School District regarding the distribution of textbooks.

(July 21, 2004)

APPEARANCES OF COUNSEL

Shaw & Perelson, LLP, attorneys for respondent, *Margo L. May, Esq.*, of counsel

DECISION OF THE COMMISSIONER

MILLS, Commissioner.—Petitioner challenges the policy of the Board of Education of the Rhinebeck Central School District ("respondent") in relation to the loan of textbooks to his daughter, Victoria. The appeal must be dismissed.

Petitioner and Victoria reside in respondent's school district. Victoria attends St. Joseph School, a nonpublic elementary school located in Millbrook, New York. On petitioner's behalf, St. Joseph School requested from the district a loan of textbooks for Victoria for the 2003-2004 school year. The district failed to order all of the requested textbooks. This appeal ensued. Petitioner requests that I direct respondent to order the requested books for all district students attending St. Joseph School and find that respondent's textbook loan policy is in violation of Education Law §701.

After the commencement of this appeal, on November 13, 2003, the district ordered all remaining requested textbooks for district students attending St. Joseph School, including petitioner's daughter. Further, respondent is considering a policy and regulation establishing formal procedures regarding textbook loans to nonpublic school students.

This appeal must be dismissed as moot. The Commissioner will only decide matters in actual controversy and will not render a decision on a state of facts which no longer exists or which subsequent events have laid to rest (*Appeal of Kushner*, 43 Ed Dept Rep _____, Decision No. 15,040; *Appeal of Reynolds*, 42 *id.* 231, Decision No. 14,834; *Appeal of N.S.*, 42 *id.* 190, Decision No. 14,817). Because the district ordered all of the requested textbooks for district students attending St. Joseph School, including petitioner's daughter, the appeal is moot.

THE APPEAL IS DISMISSED.

Decision No. 15,090

Appeal of CAROL M. HAUK, on behalf of ALYSA BRENHOCH, from action of the Board of Education of the Rush-Henrietta Central School District regarding residency.

(July 23, 2004)

APPEARANCES OF COUNSEL

DesMarteau & Beale, attorneys for respondent, *George DesMarteau, Esq.*, of counsel

DECISION OF THE COMMISSIONER

MILLS, Commissioner.—Petitioner appeals the determination of the Board of Education of the Rush-Henrietta Central School District ("respondent") that her step-granddaughter, Alysa, is not a district resident. The appeal must be dismissed.

Petitioner resides within respondent's district. Alysa and her mother moved in with petitioner in August 2003, and Alysa began attending respondent's elementary school in September. In November 2003, Alysa's mother moved into an apartment outside of the district. By letter dated December 5, 2003, respondent's Director of Student Management and School Safety asked petitioner and Alysa's mother to complete Custodial and Parental Affidavits. Based upon the information contained in the affidavits, respondent determined that Alysa was not a district resident. This appeal ensued. Petitioner's request for interim relief was denied on January 29, 2004.

Petitioner claims that she provides all of Alysa's food, shelter and clothing, and exercises control over Alysa's activities and behavior. She also maintains that Alysa's mother is emotionally and financially unable to care for her at this time. Petitioner alleges she has applied to be Alysa's guardian.

Respondent asserts that Alysa's living arrangement with petitioner is temporary and would terminate if Alysa's mother were to relocate to respondent's district. Respondent also claims that petitioner has provided no documentary evidence to support her allegations. Finally, respondent maintains that the petition fails to comply with the notice provisions of §275.11 of the Commissioner's regulations.

The appeal must be dismissed because petitioner failed to serve a notice of petition on respondent. It is the notice of petition that alerts a party to the fact that he or she is required to appear in the appeal, and to answer the objections contained in the petition (8 NYCRR §275.11; *Appeal of Khalid*, 40 Ed Dept Rep 621, Decision No. 14,570; *Appeal of Heller*, 38 *id.* 335, Decision No. 14,048; *Application of the Bd. of Educ. of the Ardsley Union Free School Dist.*, 38 *id.* 221, Decision No. 14,019). A petition that does not contain the language required by §275.11 is fatally defective, and does not secure jurisdiction over the intended respondent (*Appeal of Khalid*, *supra*).

Aside from the fatally defective notice of petition, the appeal must also be dismissed on the merits. Education Law §3202(1) provides in pertinent part:

> A person over five and under twenty-one years of age who has not received a high school diploma is entitled to attend the public schools maintained in the district in which such person resides without the payment of tuition.

The purpose of this statute is to limit the obligation of school districts to provide tuition-free education to students whose parents or legal guardians reside within the district (*Appeal of Humphrey*, 43

Ed Dept Rep ____, Decision No. 14,940; *Appeal of Thomas*, 41 *id*. 84, Decision No. 14,622; *Appeal of Oliver*, 41 *id*. 30, Decision No. 14,603). A child's residence is presumed to be that of his or her parents or legal guardian (*Appeal of Humphrey*, *supra*; *Appeal of Thomas*, *supra*; *Appeal of Santana*, 40 Ed Dept Rep 57, Decision No. 14,420). This presumption may be rebutted upon a determination that there has been a total, and presumably permanent, transfer of custody and control to someone residing in the district (*Appeal of Scott*, 43 Ed Dept Rep ___, Decision No. 15,024; *Appeal of Maxwell*, 42 *id*. 134, Decision No. 14,799; *Appeal of Donohue*, 41 *id*. 26, Decision No. 14,601). Moreover, where the sole reason the child is residing with someone other than the parent is to take advantage of the schools of the district, the child has not established residence (*Appeal of Gratton*, 43 Ed Dept Rep ___, Decision No. 14,922; *Appeal of Pierre*, 40 *id*. 538, Decision No. 14,551; *Appeal of Mendoza*, 39 *id*. 74, Decision No. 14,178). A residency determination will not be set aside unless it is arbitrary and capricious (*Appeal of A.F.*, 41 Ed Dept Rep 115, Decision No. 14,633; *Appeal of Karmin*, 41 *id*. 72, Decision No. 14,618).

Petitioner has failed to establish that Alysa's mother has permanently transferred custody to her. In the residency affidavits submitted to respondent, Alysa's mother states that Alysa's living arrangement with petitioner is "semi-permanent/indefinite," depending upon whether or not she can move back into the district. Petitioner also alleges she has applied for guardianship of Alysa, but no documents in the record support this claim. Under these circumstances, I find that petitioner has failed to rebut the presumption that Alysa's residence is that of her mother and has failed to demonstrate that respondent's determination was arbitrary, capricious or unreasonable (*see*, *Appeal of Scott*, *supra*; *Appeal of Gratton*, *supra*). Accordingly, I find no basis to disturb respondent's determination that Alysa is not a district resident.

While the appeal must be dismissed for the above reason, I note that petitioner and Alysa retain the right to reapply for admission at any time and present any new information for respondent's consideration (*Appeal of Vinci*, 40 Ed Dept Rep 505, Decision No. 14,539; *Appeal of D.F.*, 39 *id*. 106, Decision No. 14,187; *Appeal of Swezey*, 39 *id*. 81, Decision No. 14,180).

THE APPEAL IS DISMISSED.

Decision No. 15,091

Appeal of C.R. and C.R., on behalf of M.R., from action of the Board of Education of the City School District of the City of North Tonawanda regarding exclusion from school due to lack of immunization.

(July 26, 2004)

APPEARANCES OF COUNSEL

Norton / Radin / Hoover / Freedman, attorneys for respondent, *Andrew J. Freedman, Esq*., of counsel

DECISION OF THE COMMISSIONER

MILLS, Commissioner.—Petitioners appeal the determination of the Board of Education of the City School District of the City of North Tonawanda ("respondent") that their daughter, M.R., is not entitled to an exemption from the immunization requirements under Public Health Law ("PHL") §2164. The appeal must be sustained.

In April 2003, petitioners registered M.R. for kindergarten at respondent's Meadow Elementary School. By letter dated March 25, 2003, an attorney requested an exemption from the immunization requirement under PHL §2164(9) on petitioners' behalf. Section 2164(9) provides:

This section shall not apply to children whose parent, parents, or guardian hold genuine and sincere religious beliefs which are contrary to the practices herein required, and no certificate shall be required as a prerequisite to such children being admitted or received into school or attending school.

On May 19, 2003, respondent afforded petitioners an opportunity to meet with the district's coordinator of student health and the district's attorney regarding their exemption request for M.R. Petitioners' then-attorney, who had made the written request, participated via telephone.

By letter dated May 30, 2003, the coordinator of student health summarily denied petitioners' request for an exemption. The letter stated, in pertinent part, "[W]hile it is apparent that you are personally against immunizations, you could not articulate the religious basis for this request .... While your opposition to immunizations seems sincere, I have determined on behalf of the District that it is not religious in nature as required by the statute."

This appeal ensued. Petitioners' request for interim relief was denied on August 27, 2003.

The issue in this appeal is whether petitioners' opposition to immunization stems from sincerely held religious beliefs. The exemption from immunization does not extend to persons whose views are founded upon medical or purely moral considerations, scientific or secular theories, or philosophical and personal beliefs (*Farina v. Bd. of Educ. of the City of New York*, 116 F Supp 2d 503). However, it is not necessary for persons to be members of a recognized religious organization whose teachings oppose inoculation (*Sherr v. Northport-East Northport Union Free School Dist.*, 672 F Supp 81). The courts have found that "[b]ecause the statutory exception of PHL §2164(9) is for persons whose opposition to immunizations stems from genuine and sincere 'religious' beliefs, . . . the Court must first determine whether [petitioners'] purported beliefs are religious, and only if they are, determine whether those beliefs are genuinely and sincerely held" (*Farina v. Bd. of Educ. of the City of New York, supra* at 507; *see also Galinsky v. Bd. of Educ. of City of New York*, 213 F 3d 626; *Turner v. Bd. of Educ. of the Liverpool Central School Dist.*, 186 F Supp 2d 187).

Whether a religious belief is sincerely held can be a difficult factual determination that must be made, in the first instance, by school district officials (*Appeal of Quigley*, 41 Ed Dept Rep 399, Decision No. 14,724; *Appeal of Bork*, 39 *id.* 549, Decision No. 14,307; *Appeal of Murphy*, 34 *id.* 648, Decision No. 13,439). In making this determination, school officials must make a good faith effort to assess the credibility of petitioners' statements and sincerity and may consider petitioners' demeanor and forthrightness (*Appeal of Quigley, supra; Appeal of Murphy, supra; see Farina v. Bd. of Educ. of the City of New York, supra; Matter of Christine M.*, 157 Misc.2d 4). While school officials are not required to simply accept a statement of religious belief without some examination, they similarly should not simply reject a statement without further examination (*Appeal of Murphy, supra*).

In an appeal to the Commissioner, petitioners bear the burden of establishing the facts upon which they seek relief and demonstrating a clear legal right to the relief requested (8 NYCRR §275.10; *Appeal of Goldin*, 43 Ed Dept Rep ___, Decision No. 15,009; *Appeal of L.S.*, 41 *id.* 270, Decision No. 14,683). For the reasons set forth below, I find that petitioners have met this burden.

Respondent gave petitioners a full opportunity to explain their beliefs during the May 19 meeting held between petitioners, their attorney, respondent's student health coordinator and respondent's attorney. A transcript of that meeting reveals that Mrs. R. stated the following beliefs:

> God created us in his image . . . with His immune system and His body . . . that if we were to give our children immunizations, that we would be showing a lack of faith in God: showing Him that we didn't believe in what He gave us. And that would be . . . against our practices.
>
> . . .
>
> If God gave us something to work with, like the immune system, we cant [sic] go against what he did . . . what he gave us. . . . [A]s far as our immune system and the health of our bodies we feel very strongly that we cannot defile what God has given us.
>
> . . .
>
> We don't vaccinate. Whether this [vaccine] would be good or bad, they're all equal to us. It's just not done.
>
> . . .
>
> If the child was ill we would treat the child. But if the child was healthy we are not going to put something into them that's not necessary.

Mrs. R. stated that she came to this realization at a particular point in time during a sermon on faith when the pastor, referring to Proverb 3:5-6,[1] asked, "[In] what ways are you not showing your faith to God?" She realized that she was not trusting Him with her children. Afterward, petitioners talked and prayed about it. Petitioners stated that since that time, M.R. has not been immunized and their two-year-old child has never received any immunizations. Both petitioners agreed that they would treat a sick child.

In their petition, petitioners explain that they are Wesleyans, attend services weekly at the Eastern Hills Wesleyan Church and show their Christian beliefs daily by the way they live their lives. As

---

[1] "Trust in the Lord with all your heart and lean not on your own understanding; in all your ways acknowledge Him, and He will make your paths straight."

examples, they state that they pray as a family at certain times each day, tithe, pray for guidance in daily living, study from the bible and "do devotionals . . . witness to others . . . and try to live in the image of Christ." They state that their beliefs about immunizations do not stem directly from Wesleyan teachings, but rather from their own interpretation of scripture and where that leads them in their relationship with God. "Neither are our beliefs frowned upon by our church, but accepted as personal interpretation as allowed in our church doctrine." They believe that "according to the Bible disease is unclean and that its injection into the body is defilement. . . . [I]mmunizations are unclean because they contain disease. . . . [B]ecause they are unclean they are unholy."

Respondent cites *Farina v. Bd. of Educ.*, (*supra*), for the proposition that "merely stating that God provides an immune system is not enough to demonstrate that Plaintiff's belief is a genuine and sincere religious belief." However, this record is in direct contrast to that in *Farina*. There the court determined that the Farinas' objections to immunizations were not religious in nature but personal and represented a belief that inoculations would be damaging to the physical health of their children. The court found Mrs. Farina's testimony evasive and inconsistent, and concluded that the testimony and documentation upon which the Farinas relied appeared to be not of their own deeply held convictions, but borrowed from outside sources to obtain the exemption. The court described Mrs. Farina's testimony as "boilerplate religious sentiments" and rejected her testimony because it doubted the sincerity of her professed beliefs, not the religious nature of the beliefs.

Here, respondent found petitioners' beliefs to be sincerely held, but questioned their religious nature. However, as respondent points out, the beliefs expressed by petitioners concerning the immune system are very similar to those professed by Mrs. Farina, which the court acknowledged were "religious." At the May 19 meeting, petitioners articulated that they believe that immunization shows a lack of faith in God and specified the precise origin of their belief. Petitioners do not reject medical intervention in all circumstances, but differentiate between defilement of a healthy body, which is contrary to their beliefs, and treatment of a sick one. Their testimony appeared consistent and straightforward. There is no evidence that petitioners' position is based on philosophical, scientific, medical or personal preference.

I conclude that the weight of the evidence supports petitioners' contentions. I also find that respondent fails to adequately explain its rejection of otherwise convincing testimony. I cannot, therefore, defer to respondent's assessment of petitioners' credibility, to the extent such an assessment was made (*see e.g.*, *Appeal of Grihin*, 38 Ed Dept Rep 399, Decision No. 14, 064).

Accordingly, based on the record before me, I find respondent's determination to be arbitrary, capricious and unreasonable.

THE APPEAL IS SUSTAINED.

Decision No. 15,092

Appeal of KEVIN P. and ADELAIDA O'BRIEN on behalf of CRYSTAL F. DELL'ERA from action of the Chester Union Free School District regarding residency.

(July 26, 2004)

APPEARANCES OF COUNSEL

Shaw & Perelson, LLP, attorneys for respondent, *David S. Shaw* and *Jillian E. Cass, Esqs.*, of counsel

DECISION OF THE COMMISSIONER

MILLS, Commissioner.—Petitioners appeal the determination of the Board of Education of the Chester Union Free School District ("respondent") that Crystal Dell'Era is not a district resident. The appeal must be dismissed as untimely.

An appeal to the Commissioner must be commenced within 30 days from the making of the decision or the performance of the act complained of, unless excused by the Commissioner for good cause shown (8 NYCRR §275.16; *Appeal of Recore*, 42 Ed Dept Rep 283, Decision No. 14,856; *Appeal of Phillips*, 40 *id*. 241, Decision No. 14,471). Petitioners were informed of respondent's determination on March 18, 2004. Petitioners served the petition on June 3, 2004, beyond the thirty-day period. Petitioners offer insufficient reason for the delay. Therefore, the appeal must be dismissed.

While the appeal must be dismissed, I note that petitioners retain the right to reapply to the district for admission on Crystal's behalf at any time and to present any new information for respondent's consideration (*Appeal of Santoianni*, 40 Ed Dept Rep 237, Decision No. 14,470; *Appeal of D.F.*, 39 *id*. 106, Decision No. 14,187; *Appeal of Swezey*, 39 *id*. 81, Decision No. 14,180).

THE APPEAL IS DISMISSED.

Decision No. 15,093

Appeal of I.B. on behalf of her children, S.R., E.B. and C.B., from action of the Bayport-Bluepoint Union Free School District regarding residency.

(July 30, 2004)

APPEARANCES OF COUNSEL

Cooper, Sapir & Cohen, P.C., attorneys for respondent, *David M. Cohen, Esq.*, of counsel

DECISION OF THE COMMISSIONER

MILLS, Commissioner.—Petitioner appeals the determination of the Board of Education of the Bayport-Bluepoint Union Free School District ("respondent") that her children are not district residents. The appeal must be dismissed.

Petitioner's children have attended respondent's schools since August 2000. In November 2003, petitioner advised the Sylvan Avenue elementary school principal that she was going to be evicted from her apartment and wanted to use a post office box as her new address. The principal told petitioner that a post office box was not acceptable. In December, petitioner told the principal's secretary that she was still living at the apartment, but wanted to use a post office box number for her address.

In January 2004, the principal's secretary contacted the apartment complex and was told that petitioner had moved out in November 2003. The secretary then contacted petitioner, who informed her that she was living at a Stephen Court address in Bayport. However, the secretary knew petitioner did not reside there because a friend of hers lived at that address. The principal met with petitioner who admitted that she did not reside at the Stephen Court address, but refused to tell the principal where she lived.

By letter dated January 14, 2004, respondent's attendance officer requested that petitioner provide him with documentation supporting residency by January 22, 2004. On February 5, 2004, petitioner submitted a new registration form to the district indicating she and her children were residing at a different Stephen Court address with a friend. The friend provided an affidavit stating petitioner and her children resided with her.

Thereafter, the district's investigator visited the alleged Stephen Court residence on three occasions. On February 14, 2004, the owner told him that petitioner was not home. On February 16, the owner told the investigator that petitioner and her children did not stay there every night, and that their belongings were not there. On March 14, 2004, the owner told the investigator that petitioner and her children had not stayed there for the past month. Based on this investigation, the attendance officer again contacted petitioner who still maintained that she resided at the Stephen Court address.

By letter dated March 17, 2004, the attendance officer notified petitioner that absent proof of residency her children would be excluded from school after March 26, 2004. According to respondent, when petitioner picked up her son at the middle school on March 26, 2004, she told the principal that she tried to enroll her children in the South County School District, because she lived in East Patchogue.

This appeal ensued. Petitioner's request for interim relief was granted on April 8, 2004.

Petitioner claims that she and her children reside at Stephen Court in respondent's school district. Respondent requests that I reject petitioner's reply because it is untimely, raises new issues, and is not properly verified. As to the merits, respondent contends that its determination was not arbitrary or capricious.

I will first address respondent's procedural contentions regarding the reply. A reply "shall be served within 10 days after service of the answer to which it responds.... If the answer has been served by mail..., the date of mailing and the four days subsequent thereto shall be excluded in computing the 10-day period." (8 NYCRR §275.14(a)) Respondent served its answer on April 20, 2004, and petitioner's reply was served on June 3, 2004, well beyond the allowable time frame. Accordingly, petitioner's reply is untimely and I will not consider it.

Education Law §3202(1) provides, in pertinent part:

> A person over five and under twenty-one years of age who has not received a high school diploma is entitled to attend the public schools maintained in the district in

> which such person resides without the payment of tuition.

The purpose of this statute is to limit the obligation of school districts to provide tuition-free education to students whose parents or legal guardians reside within the district (*Appeal of McSween*, 42 Ed Dept Rep 59, Decision No. 14,775; *Appeal of Thomas*, 41 *id.* 84, Decision No. 14,622; *Appeal of Oliver*, 41 *id.* 30, Decision No. 14,603).

A student's residence is presumed to be that of his or her parents or legal guardians (*Appeal of Donohue*, 41 Ed Dept Rep 26, Decision No. 14,601; *Appeal of Weaver*, 39 *id.* 588, Decision No. 14,320; *Appeal of Williams*, 39 *id.* 73, Decision No. 14,177). Residence is established by one's physical presence as an inhabitant within the district combined with an intent to remain (*Longwood Cent. School Dist. v. Springs Union Free School Dist.*, 1 NY3d 385; *Appeal of B.O. and D.O.*, 42 Ed Dept Rep 42, Decision No. 14,769; *Appeal of Metze*, 42 *id.* 40, Decision No. 14,768). In an appeal to the Commissioner of Education pursuant to Education Law §310, petitioner has the burden of establishing the facts upon which she seeks relief (8 NYCRR §275.10; *Appeal of Brown*, 42 Ed Dept Rep 17, Decision No. 14,760). A residency determination will not be set aside unless it is arbitrary, capricious or unreasonable (*Appeal of Gurka*, 43 Ed Dept Rep ___, Decision No. 15,072; *Appeal of Brown*, *supra*).

Petitioner states she and her children reside at a Stephen Court address with a friend and provides an affidavit from her friend to that effect. However, the friend's affidavit was executed prior to the district's residency investigation. That investigation revealed petitioner and her children were not living at the friend's residence, and petitioner was unable to produce any other evidence of residence in the district.

I find that petitioner has failed to provide sufficient evidence or explanation to refute respondent's findings. Thus, on the evidence before me, I cannot conclude that respondent acted arbitrarily or capriciously in determining that petitioner and her children are not district residents. Accordingly, respondent's determination will not be set aside.

While the appeal must be dismissed, petitioner retains the right to reapply to the district for admission on her children's behalf at any time and to present new information for respondent's consideration (*Appeal of Perez*, 42 Ed Dept Rep 71, Decision No. 14,779; *Appeal of Santoianni*, 40 *id.* 237, Decision No. 14,470).

THE APPEAL IS DISMISSED.

Decision No. 15,094

Appeal of D.K., on behalf of his son C.K., from action of the Board of Education of the Starpoint Central School District regarding exclusion from school due to the lack of immunization.

(August 10, 2004)

APPEARANCES OF COUNSEL

Norton / Radin / Hoover / Freedman, attorneys for respondent, *Andrew J. Freedman, Esq.*, of counsel

DECISION OF THE COMMISSIONER

MILLS, Commissioner.—Petitioner appeals the determination of the Board of Education of the Starpoint Central School District ("respondent") that his son is not entitled to an exemption from the immunization requirement under Public Health Law ("PHL") §2164. The appeal must be dismissed.

Petitioner resides outside of respondent's district. His son, C.K., resides with C.K.'s mother in respondent's district. In April 2003, petitioner contacted the district about enrolling C.K. in September 2003. He requested that his son be allowed to attend school without the immunizations required by PHL §2164. PHL §2164(9) provides:

> This section shall not apply to children whose parent, parents, or guardian hold genuine and sincere religious beliefs which are contrary to the practices herein required, and no certificate shall be required as a prerequisite to such children being admitted or received into school or attending school.

On August 6, 2003, respondent's elementary school principal and attorney met with petitioner to ascertain the basis for his request. After hearing petitioner's arguments for a religious exemption and reviewing the information he provided in support of his request, the principal denied an exemption by letter dated August 11, 2003, because she determined that petitioner's opposition to immunization was "not religious in nature as required by the statute." Petitioner's request for interim relief was denied on September 8, 2003.

Petitioner contends that his objections to immunizations are based on sincerely held religious beliefs and seeks an order reversing respondent's decision to exclude his son from school.

Respondent maintains that the petition should be dismissed because petitioner is not a district resident and he failed to join C.K.'s mother as a necessary party. Respondent further argues that petitioner's objections to immunizations are not based on sincerely held religious beliefs, but rather on personal, philosophical and medical beliefs and, therefore, he failed to meet his burden of proof.

Respondent objects to petitioner's reply on the grounds that it was not timely submitted or properly served. The record reflects that my Office of Counsel granted petitioner's request for an extension of time to file his reply until October 7, 2003, and that petitioner served his reply on that date. Accordingly, I find that the reply was timely served (*Appeal of Campbell*, 40 Ed Dept Rep 417, Decision No. 14,515; *Appeal of Shaver*, 38 *id.* 570, Decision No. 14,096). In addition, §275.8(b) of the Commissioner's regulations requires a party to serve all pleadings and papers subsequent to the petition on the adverse party's counsel. Although petitioner's service of his reply papers on the district clerk was improper, I will excuse petitioner's mistake as he is not represented by counsel and respondent was not prejudiced thereby (*Appeal of Mennella*, 39 Ed Dept Rep 306, Decision No. 14,245).

I reject respondent's assertion that petitioner is not a proper party to this proceeding and that C.K.'s mother is a necessary party. PHL §2164(7)(b) states, "A parent, a guardian or any other person in parental relationship to a child denied school entrance or attendance may appeal by petition to the commissioner of education in accordance with the provisions of section three hundred ten of the education law." Petitioner shares legal custody of C.K. and provided a statement in support of his position from C.K.'s mother. Therefore, I decline to dismiss the appeal on this basis.

The issue in this appeal is whether petitioner's opposition to immunization stems from sincerely held religious beliefs. The exemption from immunization does not extend to persons whose views are founded upon medical or purely moral considerations, scientific or secular theories, or philosophical and personal beliefs (*Farina v. Bd. of Ed. of the City of New York*, 116 F Supp 2d 503). However, it is not necessary for persons to be members of a recognized religious organization whose teachings oppose inoculation

(*Sherr v. Northport-East Northport Union Free School Dist.*, 672 F Supp 81). Whether a religious belief is sincerely held can be a difficult factual determination that must be made, in the first instance, by school district officials (*Appeal of Quigley*, 41 Ed Dept Rep 399, Decision No. 14,724; *Appeal of Bork*, 39 *id.* 549, Decision No. 14,307; *Appeal of Murphy*, 34 *id.* 648, Decision No. 13,439). In making this determination, school officials must make a good faith effort to assess the credibility of petitioner's statements and sincerity and may consider petitioner's demeanor and forthrightness (*Appeal of Quigley*, *supra*). While school officials are not required to simply accept a statement of religious belief without some explanation, they similarly should not simply reject a statement without further examination (*Appeal of Murphy*, *supra*).

In an appeal to the Commissioner, petitioner has the burden of demonstrating a clear legal right to the relief requested and the burden of establishing the facts upon which he seeks relief (8 NYCRR §275.10; *Appeal of Garmaeva*, 43 Ed Dept Rep ___, Decision No. 14,988; *Appeal of Goldin*, 43 *id.* ___, Decision No. 14,904). In this appeal, the principal and respondent's attorney gave petitioner an opportunity to explain his position. Petitioner states that he is a practicing Unitarian and that he is trained in Reiki. He meditates and prays on a daily basis and has listened to audiotapes produced by an organization entitled the Aladdin Fellowship for 27 years. He states that he has "the sincere belief that disease is not a natural state of our bodies, and that perfect health is an expression of being in harmony with our divine nature. . . . Part of this process involves releasing disease from our bodies, rather than suppressing it."

After affording petitioner an opportunity to explain his beliefs, and after assessing his credibility, respondent's administrators found that petitioner failed to articulate the religious basis or origin of his beliefs. Instead, they concluded that petitioner's opposition to immunization is rooted in personal theories, philosophy, a fear of medical science and preference for holistic medicine.

Although petitioner's opposition to immunizations may be sincere, it did not appear to school officials that his opposition is religious in nature as required by the statute. Based on the record before me, I cannot find that respondent's determination was arbitrary or capricious.

THE APPEAL IS DISMISSED.

Decision No. 15,095

Appeal of JOSE and NORMA CHORRO, on behalf of MARCELLA PAOLA CUELLAR CORTEZ, from action of the Board of Education of the Sewanhaka Central High School District regarding residency.

(August 13, 2004)

APPEARANCES OF COUNSEL

Douglas E. Libby, Esq., attorney for respondent

DECISION OF THE COMMISSIONER

MILLS, Commissioner.—Petitioners challenge the determination of the Board of Education of the Sewanhaka Central High School District ("respondent") that Marcella Paola Cuellar Cortez ("Marcella") is not a district resident. The appeal must be dismissed.

Marcella came to stay with petitioners to take an English course in November and December of 2003 while on break from her school in El Salvador. Marcella's mother, who is petitioner Jose Chorro's cousin, and sister reside in El Salvador, and Marcella's father is deceased.

In February 2004, petitioners applied for Marcella's admission to respondent's schools. By letter dated February 5, 2004, a district administrator denied Marcella admission. Petitioners appealed the determination to an administrative review officer. By letter dated March 5, 2004, the review officer denied Marcella's admission because her mother was not a district resident. This appeal ensued, and petitioners' request for interim relief was denied on May 20, 2004.

Petitioners contend that Marcella resides with them and will continue to reside with them until she finishes college. They assert that Marcella wishes to complete her high school and college education in the United States. Petitioners request a determination that Marcella is a district resident and entitled to attend respondent's schools without payment of tuition.

Respondent contends that Marcella is not a district resident because there has been no transfer of custody and control to petitioners.

Education Law §3202(1) provides in pertinent part:

> A person who is over the age of five and under twenty-one years of age who has not received a high school diploma is entitled to attend the public schools maintained in the district in which such person resides without the payment of tuition.

The purpose of this statute is to limit the obligation of school districts to provide tuition-free education to students whose parents or legal guardians reside within the district (*Appeal of a Student with a Disability*, 43 Ed Dept Rep ___, Decision No. 14,926; *Appeal of Gimenez*, 42 *id.* 176, Decision No. 14,812; *Appeal of Curran*, 42 *id.* 49, Decision No. 14,772). A child's residence is presumed to be that of his or her parents or legal guardians (*Appeal of a Student with a Disability*, *supra*; *Appeal of Hutchinson*, 42 Ed Dept Rep 310, Decision No. 14,865). This presumption can be rebutted where it is shown that the parents have relinquished total custody and control to someone residing in the district (*Appeal of a Student with a Disability*, *supra*; *Appeal of Maxwell*, 42 Ed Dept Rep 134, Decision No. 14,799).

While it is not necessary to establish parental custody and control through a formal guardianship proceeding, it is necessary to demonstrate that a particular location is a child's permanent residence, and that the individual exercising control has full authority and responsibility with respect to the child's support and custody (*Appeal of a Student with a Disability*, *supra*; *Appeal of Hutchinson*, *supra*). In addition, where the sole reason the child is residing with someone other than the parent is to take advantage of the schools of the district, the child has not established residence (*Appeal of a Student with Disability*, *supra*; *Appeal of Hutchinson*, *supra*; *Appeal of Maxwell*, *supra*).

In this case, petitioners have failed to rebut the presumption that Marcella's residency is with her mother in El Salvador. Petitioners did not submit any evidence in support of their contentions. Respondent submitted the documents petitioners supplied to them during the administrative review of the residency determination, which included Marcella's birth certificate, her father's death certificate and a "Power of Attorney" executed by Marcella's mother. The "Power of Attorney" gives petitioners the authority to act on Marcella's mother's behalf in "all legal, medical and educational matters," but that document alone is not sufficient to transfer permanent custody and control of Marcella.

Respondent also submitted the transcript of the review hearing during which petitioners admitted that they would consult with Marcella's mother on issues related to her education and health. Petitioners also admitted that Marcella's mother provides some financial support. Finally, petitioners admitted that Marcella is living with them in order to attend school. Petitioners, therefore, have not established that Marcella's mother has transferred custody and control.

Under these circumstances, I find that petitioners have not rebutted the presumption that Marcella's residence remains with her mother. Accordingly, I find no basis to disturb respondent's determination that Marcella is not a district resident.

THE APPEAL IS DISMISSED.

Decision No. 15,096

Appeal of G.P., on behalf of her son U.P., from action of the Board of Education of the Sag Harbor Union Free School District regarding residency.

(August 13, 2004)

APPEARANCES OF COUNSEL

Bracken, Margolin & Gouvis, LLP, attorneys for petitioner, *Linda U. Margolin, Esq.*, of counsel

Guercio & Guercio, attorneys for respondent, *Christine LaPlace, Esq.*, of counsel

DECISION OF THE COMMISSIONER

MILLS, Commissioner.—Petitioner appeals the determination of the Board of Education of the Sag Harbor Union Free School District ("respondent") that her son, U.P., is not a district resident. The appeal must be sustained.

Petitioner registered her son with respondent's district in September 2001. Based on her representation that she and her husband were building a home on Harry's Lane in the district, respondent permitted U.P. to attend kindergarten during the 2001-2002 school year.

In September 2002, the district apparently questioned whether the family had moved into the Harry's Lane residence. By letter dated September 8, 2002, petitioner's husband advised the district that the house was in the "final stages" of construction and that he estimated that the family would move in within three months. Although respondent's superintendent subsequently advised petitioner and her husband that respondent would not permit U.P. to attend the district's schools under these circumstances, respondent continued to allow U.P. to attend school tuition free during the 2002-2003 school year.

At some point during the 2003-2004 school year, respondent hired an investigator, who conducted surveillance on multiple days between March 11 and April 20, 2004, at the Harry's Lane address as well as the Bel-Aire Cove Motel ("the motel") in Hampton Bays, which petitioner's husband owns and manages, and where respondent apparently suspected petitioner's family of living. The investigator advised the district that the Harry's Lane residence was still under construction and that petitioner and her family did not live there.

By letter dated April 14, 2004, the superintendent invited petitioner and her husband to attend an April 16, 2004, "meeting" pursuant to §100.2(y) of the Commissioner's regulations where she would determine whether U.P. was a district resident. Petitioner's husband appeared at the meeting and requested a postponement until April 20, 2004, to allow him to retain counsel. Although the request was granted, neither petitioner nor her husband appeared at the April 20, 2004, proceeding, which was conducted in their absence.

By decision dated April 21, 2004, and hand-delivered to petitioner and her husband, the superintendent determined that U.P. is not a district resident based on the investigative evidence that the Harry's Lane house was still under construction and "uninhabitable" and that during the period of surveillance, petitioner's family was not seen at the house on "weekends or evening hours." The superintendent further informed U.P.'s parents that the child would be excluded from the district's schools after April 23, 2004. This appeal ensued. Petitioner's request for interim relief was granted on May 7, 2004.

In support of her residency claim, petitioner explains that her husband has personally performed most of the construction work on the Harry's Lane house and that from December 2002 through the end of the summer of 2003, he was unable to work on the house as much as anticipated because of petitioner's diagnosis and treatment for a serious illness. Petitioner maintains, however, that the family moved into the house at the beginning of the 2003-2004 school year so that U.P. could continue to attend respondent's schools, notwithstanding that the town had not yet issued a certificate of occupancy. Petitioner claims that although the kitchen was unfinished at that time, the house had water, heat, electricity and working bathrooms. She explains that the family essentially uses only the second floor of the house, temporarily placing a kitchen table and chairs, microwave and refrigerator in one of the bedrooms and using a bathroom sink to wash dishes. Petitioner also submits photographs to document these arrangements.

Petitioner further maintains that although the family generally sleeps in the Harry's Lane home, her husband picks up U.P. after school and brings him to the motel, where petitioner often meets them after finishing work at 7:00 p.m. Depending on her husband's work schedule, the family sometimes does not return to Harry's Lane until 10:00 p.m. Further, because her husband generally works through the night on Fridays and Saturdays, petitioner and her son visit him at the motel on weekends.

Respondent contends that it properly determined that petitioner's son is not a district resident based on the investigator's surveillance evidence and petitioner's failure to submit any evidence to support her residency claim. Respondent also contends that I should not consider any evidence submitted by petitioner that was not presented to respondent at the residency hearing.

Preliminarily, I will address respondent's procedural claims. The purpose of a reply is to respond to new material or affirmative defenses set forth in an answer (8 NYCRR §§275.3 and 275.14). A reply is not meant to buttress allegations in the petition or to belatedly add assertions that should have been in the petition (*Appeal of General*, 43 Ed Dept Rep __, Decision No. 14,948). I will accept petitioner's reply papers because I find that, in large measure, the allegations and exhibits are responsive to new material or affirmative defenses raised by respondent in its answer. I will also accept, pursuant to §276.5 of the Commissioner's regulations, the affidavit submitted by respondent with a letter dated July 6, 2004, responding to information contained in petitioner's reply papers.

Respondent also objects to the documentary evidence submitted by petitioner to support her residency claim on the grounds that it was not presented at the residency hearing. Petitioner explains that the April 14, 2004, letter informing her and her husband of the April 16, 2004, "meeting" advised them that any information they wished to submit "must be received no later than April 15, 2004" and that she and her husband were not able to gather the necessary documentation in this short timeframe. Further, based on the superintendent's letter, petitioner's husband did not realize, until he arrived at the appointed time, that the superintendent intended to conduct a hearing, which prompted petitioner's husband's request for an adjournment to retain counsel. Petitioner further explains that the superintendent would only postpone the hearing to the following Tuesday, April 20, 2004, that she and her husband were unable to find a lawyer by then, were "scared" to attend the hearing without counsel, and did not ask for a further extension because "the superintendent had already said this was the last date she would give us." Under these circumstances, and in light of the fact that respondent has had an opportunity to respond to petitioner's submission, I will accept petitioner's evidence (*see*, *Appeal of Short*, 43 Ed Dept Rep ___, Decision No. 14,945).

Education Law §3202(1) provides, in pertinent part:

> A person over five and under twenty-one years of age who has not received a high school diploma is entitled to attend the public schools maintained in the district in which such person resides without the payment of tuition.

The purpose of this statute is to limit the obligation of school districts to provide tuition-free education to students whose parents or legal guardians reside within the district (*Appeal of Marshall*, 43 Ed Dept Rep __, Decision No. 14,911; *Appeal of B.O. and D.O.*, 42 *id.* 42, Decision No. 14,769). Residence for purposes of Education Law §3202 is established by one's physical presence as an inhabitant within the district combined with an intent to remain in the district (*Longwood Cent. School Dist. v. Springs Union Free School Dist.*, 1 NY3d 385; *Appeal of Marshall*, *supra*; *Appeal of B.O. and D.O.*, *supra*). For purposes of Education Law §3202(1), a person can have only one legal residence (*Appeal of Marshall*, *supra*). Mere ownership of property in a school district does not confer residency status (*Appeal of Rosen* 43 Ed Dept Rep __, Decision 14,929; *Appeal of Felenczak*, 39 *id.* 125, Decision No. 14,191; *Appeal of Duhaney*, 38 *id.* 94, Decision No. 13,991).

There does not appear to be any dispute that petitioner and her husband own property on Harry's Lane and are constructing a house there that they intend to occupy as their primary residence. There is some dispute as to whether the house is substantially complete, as petitioner contends, or "uninhabitable," as respondent contends. However, pending home construction, in and of itself, does not establish residency (*Appeal of Sobel*, 43 Ed Dept Rep ___, Decision No. 14,931; *See, Appeal of Embler and Schwerbel*, 40 Ed Dept Rep 17, Decision No. 14,406; *Appeal of Duhaney, supra*). Petitioner must establish that her family actually resides in the house.

Respondent's investigator conducted surveillance at the Harry's Lane address on approximately 19 days between March 11 and April 20, 2004. On most of these occasions, the investigator arrived at the home early in the morning, generally between 5:15 a.m. and 6:30 a.m. On 14 of those occasions, the investigator observed at least one vehicle parked in the driveway. On seven occasions, he observed either a truck registered to petitioner's husband or a sport utility vehicle ("SUV") registered to petitioner's mother-in-law. On the remaining seven occasions, both of these vehicles were present. Although respondent's investigator states that he never observed petitioner or her son at the Harry's Lane address, it appears that on the days there was at least one car parked at the house in the early morning, he did not remain at the residence for any length of time to see whether anyone might leave for work or school.

Further, although the investigator also reported seeing a car registered to petitioner parked at the motel on a number of occasions during the surveillance period, petitioner explains that she does not use this car during the winter months because it performs poorly in the snow, and instead, uses her mother-in-law's SUV, and that she continued to use the SUV in March and April 2004.

Although respondent's investigator apparently testified at the hearing that the house "appeared to be uninhabitable," his surveillance photographs suggest otherwise. Although the photographs reflect that the property has no lawn or landscaping, the exterior of the house appears to be substantially, if not entirely, finished. Further, while a photograph of a portion of the first floor interior, apparently taken through a window, reveals what appears to be a stack of lumber on the floor, the interior appears substantially complete. Moreover, the investigator did not photograph the second floor, where petitioner claims the family is living.

Based on all the facts and circumstances, I find that petitioner has sustained her burden of establishing residency. Contrary to respondent's assertion, I do not find respondent's surveillance evidence persuasive proof that petitioner and her family do not reside at the Harry's Lane residence. To the contrary, the proof is largely consistent with petitioner's claim that the family stays on the second floor of the home, but often does not arrive home until 10:00 p.m. The evidence establishes that the investigator observed either one or two of the vehicles used by petitioner and her husband parked in the driveway on most mornings when he conducted surveillance. Further, it is not surprising that the investigator did not observe activity at the house because, for the most part, his observations were made very early in the morning when petitioner and her family would likely still be sleeping. The investigator's more limited surveillance at other times during the weekdays or on the weekend, revealing no activity at the house, are consistent with petitioner's assertions that she and her husband both work during the day, that she often spends time in the evening with her husband and son at the motel that he manages, and that the family spends time over the weekend either at the motel or visiting relatives.

In sum, I find insufficient evidence in the record to support respondent's determination that petitioner is not a district resident. Even if I were to disregard the additional evidence submitted by petitioner, I would reach the same conclusion.

THE APPEAL IS SUSTAINED.

Decision No. 15,097

Appeal of TANISHA WELCH, on behalf of her daughter MEDINA, from action of the Board of Education of the Baldwin Union Free School District regarding residency.

(August 13, 2004)

APPEARANCES OF COUNSEL

Ingerman Smith LLP, attorneys for respondent, *Susan M. Gibson, Esq.*, of counsel

DECISION OF THE COMMISSIONER

MILLS, Commissioner.—Petitioner appeals the determination of the Board of Education of the Baldwin Union Free School District ("respondent") that her daughter Medina is not a district resident. The appeal must be dismissed.

Petitioner alleges that she and her daughter were forced to move from their residence in the district to a location outside the district because the person they were residing with moved out of state. Petitioner alleges that she has been trying to find another residence within the district but has been unable to do so. Petitioner states that she hopes to find a residence in the district by September and asks that Medina be permitted to complete the 2003-2004 school year in respondent's district.

Respondent contends that its residency determination is neither arbitrary, capricious nor unreasonable and that the appeal should be dismissed as moot.

The appeal must be dismissed as moot. The Commissioner will only consider matters in actual controversy and will not render a decision on a state of facts which no longer exists or which subsequent events have laid to rest (*Appeal of Swanson*, 39 Ed Dept Rep 312, Decision No. 14,247; *Appeal of Foshee*, 38 *id*. 346, Decision No. 14,051). For relief, petitioner asks that her daughter be permitted to attend respondent's schools for the balance of the 2003-2004 school year. On June 8, 2004, an interim order was granted directing respondent to admit Medina to the schools of the district pending an ultimate determination of this appeal. Because the 2003-2004 school year has ended and petitioner has obtained the relief she seeks, the matter is moot and the appeal must be dismissed (*Appeal of D'Angelo*, 39 Ed Dept Rep 849, Decision No. 14,399; *Appeal of Lascala*, 38 *id*. 16, Decision No. 13,974).

THE APPEAL IS DISMISSED.

Decision No. 15,098

Appeal of DONALD CROSS, on behalf of his daughter NATALIE, from action of the Board of Education of the Burnt Hills-Ballston Lake Central School District and Superintendent William E. Hostetter regarding residency.

(August 13, 2004)

APPEARANCES OF COUNSEL

The Nicholas D. Morsillo Law Firm, attorney for petitioner, *Nicholas D. Morsillo, Esq*., of counsel

Robert E. Van Vranken, Esq., attorney for respondents

DECISION OF THE COMMISSIONER

MILLS, Commissioner.—Petitioner appeals the determination of the Board of Education of the Burnt Hills-Ballston Lake Central School District and Superintendent William E. Hostetter ("respondents") that his daughter, Natalie, is not a district resident. The appeal must be dismissed.

On September 3, 2003, petitioner's wife registered Natalie for school, listing Rustic Bridge Road, within the district, as Natalie's address. Shortly thereafter, two district employees who resided on the same road informed the superintendent that neither the student nor her parents resided there. The employees reported that they observed petitioner or his wife transport Natalie on a regular basis to the bus stop at that address.

By letter dated September 30, 2003, the superintendent notified petitioner and his wife that he had information that Natalie was not a district resident. Specifically, he suggested that Natalie was residing on Kruger Road in Pattersonville, outside the district, and was being transported each day to board the bus at Rustic Bridge Road. The superintendent therefore requested information regarding Natalie's residency. Petitioner claims he never received this letter. The superintendent did not receive a response.

By letter dated October 22, 2003, the superintendent again requested residency information, stating that Natalie would be removed from school if the parents failed to respond by October 31, 2003. Petitioner telephoned the superintendent on October 29 and informed him that he was repairing and renovating the Rustic Bridge Road property and intended to move there by January 1, 2004. The superintendent requested, but never received, written confirmation of this intention.

By letter dated January 9, 2004, the superintendent informed petitioner and his wife that he had no evidence that they had relocated to the Rustic Bridge Road address, and that Natalie would be removed from school by January 23, 2004, if they did not confirm their residency within the district. By letter dated January 30, 2004, the superintendent informed petitioner and his wife that they were not district residents and Natalie's last day of enrollment would be February 6, 2004.

By letter dated February 2, 2004, petitioner's counsel requested a residency hearing and asserted that, as of August 1, 2003, petitioner had transferred guardianship of Natalie to her grandfather (petitioner's father), who resided at the Rustic Bridge Road address. A meeting was held before the assistant superintendent, acting as the board of education's designee, on February 12, 2004. It was agreed that subsequent to the meeting, petitioner and his father could submit modified guardianship affidavits with additional information regarding the purported transfer of Natalie's custody to her grandfather. Two documents were submitted to the superintendent on February 18, 2004. By letter dated February 18, 2004, the superintendent informed petitioner of his determination that Natalie was not a district resident and would be excluded from the district's schools effective March 5, 2004. This appeal ensued. Petitioner's request for interim relief was denied on March 16, 2004.

Petitioner asserts that he owns the property on Rustic Bridge Road and pays school taxes to the district. He also asserts that as of August 1, 2003, he transferred guardianship of Natalie to her grandfather, who also resides at the Rustic Bridge Road address, and that Natalie permanently resides there with her grandfather.

Respondents argue that petitioner never moved into the Rustic Bridge Road home and admittedly resided outside the district. Respondents also argue that petitioner has failed to rebut the presumption that Natalie resides with her parents, because there has been no transfer of custody or control to Natalie's grandfather.

Education Law §3202(1) provides in pertinent part:

> A person over five and under twenty-one years of age who has not received a high school diploma is entitled to attend the public schools maintained in the district in which such person resides without the payment of tuition.

The purpose of this statute is to limit the obligation of school districts to provide tuition-free education to students whose parents or legal guardians reside within the district (*Appeal of Thomas*, 43 Ed Dept Rep __, Decision No. 14,963; *Appeal of Normandin*, 43 *id.* __, Decision No. 14,950; *Appeal of General*, 43 *id.* __, Decision No. 14,948). Residency for purposes of Education Law §3202 is established by one's physical presence combined with an intent to reside in the district (*Longwood Cent. School Dist. v. Springs Union Free School Dist.*, 1 NY3d 385; *Appeal of Thomas, supra*; *Appeal of General, supra*).

A child's residence is presumed to be that of his or her parents or legal guardians (*Appeal of D.H.C.*, 43 Ed Dept Rep ___, Decision No. 15,053; *Appeal of Donohue*, 41 *id.* 26, Decision No. 14,601). This presumption may be rebutted upon a determination that there has been a total, and presumably permanent, transfer of custody and control to someone residing in the district (*Appeal of D.H.C.*, *supra*; *Appeal of Donohue*, *supra*; *Appeal of Burdi*, 39 Ed Dept Rep 176, Decision No. 14,206). Moreover, where the sole reason the child is residing with someone other than the parent is to attend the schools of the district, the child has not established residence (*Appeal of Maxwell*, 42 Ed Dept Rep 134, Decision No. 14,799; *Appeal of Pierre*, 40 *id.* 538, Decision No. 14,551; *Appeal of Cron*, 38 *id.* 149, Decision No. 14,005).

A person can only have one legal residence (*Catlin v. Sobol*, 155 AD2d 24, rev'd on other grnds, 77 NY2d 552 (1991); *Appeal of O'Herron*, 41 Ed Dept Rep 1, Decision No. 14,591; *Appeal of LaQuerre*, 40 *id.* 565, Decision No. 14,558; *Appeal of Embler*, 40 *id.* 17, Decision No. 14,406). If a person owns or rents property both within and outside the school district, only one property can be considered one's legal residence (*Appeal of Reynolds*, 41 Ed Dept Rep 32, Decision No. 14,604; *Appeal of Scaffa*, 40 *id.* 177, Decision No. 14,453). The mere fact that one rents or owns a house or property in the district, or even pays taxes in the district, does not necessarily confer residence status (*Appeal of O'Herron*, *supra*; *Appeal of Smith*, 40 Ed Dept Rep 126, Decision No. 14,438).

A residency determination will not be overturned unless it is arbitrary and capricious (*Appeal of General*, *supra*; *Appeal of Newby*, 42 Ed Dept Rep 107, Decision No. 14,790). In an appeal to the Commissioner, petitioner has the burden of demonstrating a clear legal right to the relief requested and the burden of establishing the facts upon which he seeks relief (8 NYCRR §275.10; *Appeal of General*, *supra*; *Appeal of T.K.*, 43 Ed Dept Rep __, Decision No. 14,935).

In this case, the petition states that petitioner resides on Kruger Road in Pattersonville, outside the district. The fact that petitioner owns and pays school taxes on the Rustic Bridge Road property, without more, does not make him a district resident nor does it entitle his daughter to attend district schools.

Petitioner alternatively argued for the first time in February 2004 that on August 1, 2003, he transferred guardianship of Natalie to his father, who resides at the Rustic Bridge Road address. *Appeal of Samuel*, 39 *id.* 94, Decision No. 14,183. Although this guardianship agreement is dated August 1, 2003, the date cannot be verified because it is not notarized. The agreement also bears petitioner's wife's signature, dated February 12, 2004.

Other than the statement in the guardianship agreement, there is no evidence that petitioner transferred total and permanent custody and control of Natalie to his father. In fact, the evidence belies that conclusion. Petitioner's wife, rather than Natalie's grandfather, registered Natalie for school on September 3, 2003 (*see Appeal of G.B.*, 41 Ed Dept Rep 137, Decision No. 14,639). In addition, two private investigators witnessed petitioner and his wife regularly departing Kruger Road in Pattersonville and transporting Natalie to the bus stop at Rustic Bridge Road.

The petition states that petitioner established Natalie's residence in anticipation of the family moving to Rustic Bridge Road, thus avoiding a mid-year change in schools. In fact, the agreement specifies that guardianship is being transferred because the parties desire that Natalie attend the district schools. The Commissioner has repeatedly held that residency is not established where custody is transferred so that the student may attend the local schools (*Appeal of A.F.*, 41 Ed Dept Rep 115, Decision No. 14,633; *Appeal of Vinci*, 40 *id.* 505, Decision No. 14,539; *Appeal of Samuel*, 39 *id.* 94, Decision No. 14,183).

I therefore find respondents' determination to be neither arbitrary nor capricious. In light of this determination, I need not address the parties' remaining arguments. If, at some future date, petitioner and his family do, indeed, relocate to the Rustic Bridge Road address within respondents' district, petitioner may at that time reapply for Natalie's admission (*see Appeal of Sobel*, 43 Ed Dept Rep __, Decision No. 14,931).

THE APPEAL IS DISMISSED.

Decision No. 15,099

Appeal of MABEL CRUMP, on behalf of FAITH ANN ADAMS, from action of the Board of Education of the City School District of the City of New Rochelle regarding residency.

(August 13, 2004)

APPEARANCES OF COUNSEL

Kehl, Katzive & Sigmond. LLP, attorneys for respondent, *Terri E. Simon, Esq.*, of counsel

DECISION OF THE COMMISSIONER

MILLS, Commissioner.—Petitioner, a district resident, appeals the determination of the Board of Education of the City School District of the City of New Rochelle ("respondent") that her granddaughter, Faith Ann Adams, is not district resident. The appeal must be dismissed.

In the spring of 2003, district officials became aware that Faith, then a sophomore at respondent's high school, might be living with her mother outside the district on Hancock Avenue in Mount Vernon. Respondent's director of pupil services ("director") asked the attendance officer ("officer") to investigate Faith's residency. On the school mornings of May 19 through 22, 2003, between 7:00 and 7:50 a.m., the officer parked in his car near petitioner's residence but did not observe Faith exit the house. On the school mornings of May 28 and 29, and June 2 and 3, 2003, between 7:05 and 7:17 a.m., the officer parked next door to the Hancock Avenue address and observed Faith exit the side door and board the #42 bus to New Rochelle. On June 3, the officer followed the #42 bus to an intersection where he saw Faith transfer to the #45 bus that proceeds to the district's high school. Despite this evidence, respondent apparently took no action regarding Faith's residency at the end of the 2002-2003 school year.

The record indicates that the officer conducted additional surveillance at the beginning of the 2003-2004 school year. On the school mornings of September 8 and 9, at approximately 7:15 a.m., he observed Faith leave her mother's house on Hancock Avenue and board bus #42 and transfer to bus #45. On the school days of September 16 and 17, at approximately 3:35 p.m., the officer observed Faith talking to friends on Hancock Avenue in Mount Vernon. On September 26, 2003, at 7:00 a.m., the officer observed Faith, her mother and two young children leave the Hancock Avenue address and enter a white Ford Explorer. The mother discharged the younger children at an elementary school in Mount Vernon, and then left Faith at the district's high school. On school days of October 20 through 24, from 7:10 to 8:15 a.m., the officer parked near petitioner's residence, but did not observe Faith exit the residence on any of those days. Finally, on the school days of February 10 through 12, 2004, between 7:40 and 7:55 a.m., the officer observed a maroon Taurus pick up Faith and two younger children at the Hancock Avenue address. He followed the vehicle as it discharged the two children at elementary school in Mount Vernon and Faith at the district's high school.

Based on this investigation, the director notified petitioner by letter dated March 15, 2004, that she had information that Faith did not reside with petitioner. The director invited petitioner to submit documentation by March 26, 2004, substantiating Faith's residency, after which she intended to make a final decision. The letter, a copy of which was sent to Faith's mother, also referred to a May 3, 2001, Order of Custody/Visitation from the Westchester Family Court, that granted joint custody of Faith to petitioner and Faith's mother, with physical custody awarded to petitioner.

Petitioner failed to respond to the director's March 15 letter, although Faith's mother attempted to reach the director twice by telephone. By letter dated March 31, 2004, the director informed petitioner (with a copy to Faith's mother) of her determination that Faith did not reside with petitioner and was therefore ineligible to attend the schools of the district after April 16, 2004. The director also noted that petitioner referred school staff members to Faith's mother when staff asked to speak or meet with petitioner.

On April 14, 2004, petitioner met with the director. Petitioner offered no documentation to verify that Faith resided with her, but merely stated that Faith lived with her, although she sometimes stayed overnight in Mount Vernon when she worked late or babysat for her siblings. When questioned why she referred staff to Faith's mother, petitioner replied that Faith's mother "can understand better" and "I want her to be involved." After the director refused to change her decision, this appeal ensued. Petitioner's request for an interim order was granted on April 27, 2004.

Petitioner claims she is Faith's legal guardian and that Faith resides with her in the district. Respondent contends that its surveillance substantiates that Faith resides in Mount Vernon with her mother and is thus not entitled to attend respondent's schools.

Education Law §3202(1) provides in pertinent part:

> A person over five and under twenty-one years of age who has not received a high school diploma is entitled to attend the public schools maintained in the district in

which such person resides without the payment of tuition.

The purpose of this statute is to limit the obligation of school districts to provide tuition-free education to students whose parents or legal guardians reside within the district (*Appeal of a Sloley-Raymond*, 44 Ed Dept Rep ___, Decision No. 15,085; *Appeal of O.W.*, 43 *id.* ___, Decision No. 14,949). A child's residence is presumed to be that of his or her parents or legal guardians (*Appeal of a Sloley-Raymond*, *supra*; *Appeal of O.W.*, *supra*). This presumption can be rebutted where it is shown that the parents have relinquished total custody and control to someone residing in the district (*Appeal of a Solely-Raymond*, *supra*; *Appeal of O.W.*, *supra*). While it is not necessary to establish parental custody and control through a formal guardianship proceeding, it is necessary to demonstrate that a particular location is a child's permanent residence, and that the individual exercising control has full authority and responsibility with respect to the child's support and custody (*Appeal of a Sloley-Raymond*, *supra*; *Appeal of O.W.*, *supra*). Moreover, where the sole reason the child is residing with someone other than the parent is to take advantage of the schools of the district, the child has not established residence (*Appeal of a Sloley-Raymond*, *supra*; *Appeal of O.W.*, *supra*).

A residency determination will not be set aside unless it is arbitrary and capricious (*Appeal of Newby*, 42 Ed Dept Rep 107, Decision No. 14,790; *Appeal of Leontakianakos*, 42 *id.* 10, Decision No. 14,757). In an appeal to the Commissioner of Education, the petitioner has the burden of demonstrating a clear legal right to the relief requested and the burden of establishing the facts upon which she seeks relief (8 NYCRR §275.10; *Appeal of B.H. and B.H.*, 43 Ed Dept Rep __, Decision No. 14,919; *Appeal of J.T.*, 43 *id.* __, Decision No. 14,917).

In this case, petitioner submitted no documentation or evidence of Faith's residency other than her conclusory statement that Faith resides with her in the district. This is insufficient to rebut the presumption that Faith resides with her mother outside the district. Although a court order purportedly grants physical custody of Faith to petitioner, the order is three years old and is contradicted by much of the other evidence. Personal observations of the officer over 19 days of surveillance show that Faith does not actually reside with petitioner. Petitioner submitted no evidence to rebut the investigator's report. Nor did petitioner provide any legitimate explanation to refute respondent's surveillance other than asserting that Faith sometimes stayed with her mother when she worked late or babysat.

Moreover, petitioner has not established that Faith's mother has relinquished custody and control to petitioner. Faith's mother is clearly involved in Faith's education, as evidenced by the fact that she telephoned the director in response to the director's March 15 letter. Accordingly, respondent's determination was not arbitrary or capricious, and will not be set aside.

THE APPEAL IS DISMISSED.

Decision No. 15,100

Appeal of TANIA SMITH, on behalf of her daughters, JAMIA and TAYLA, from action of the Board of Education of the Uniondale Union Free School District regarding residency.

(August 23, 2004)

APPEARANCES OF COUNSEL

Ingerman Smith, L.L.P., attorneys for respondent, *Lawrence W. Reich, Esq.*, of counsel

DECISION OF THE COMMISSIONER

MILLS, Commissioner.—Petitioner appeals the determination of the Board of Education of the Uniondale Union Free School District ("respondent") that her daughters, Jamia and Tayla, are not district residents. The appeal must be sustained.

Petitioner, her husband, children and parents lived together on Leslie Lane, within respondent's district. In 2003, petitioner and her husband separated, and he moved to Orchard Street in Hempstead, outside the district. In March 2004, respondent began to suspect the children did not reside in the district when Tayla told a teacher that she lived on Orchard Street in Hempstead. Based on this information, respondent began a residency investigation.

Respondent's investigation revealed that petitioner and her husband both have mail delivered to the Orchard Street address. Respondent's investigator conducted surveillance on four occasions during a two-week period between March 30 and April 13, 2004. Another surveillance was conducted on June 25, 2004, after the commencement of this appeal.

By letter dated April 16, 2004, respondent's Administrative Assistant for Central Registration notified petitioner that her children were no longer eligible to attend respondent's schools because she did not reside within the district and would be excluded as of April 30, 2004. A registration review conference was held on May 5, 2004, at which petitioner was allowed to present evidence of residency. By letter dated May 18, 2004, the Administrative Assistant notified petitioner of his conclusion that she and her children were not residents of the district. This appeal ensued. Petitioner's request for interim relief was denied on July 7, 2004.

Petitioner claims that she and her children are district residents. To support her claim, petitioner submits a driver's license (issued in 1999 and renewed in May 2004), a payroll statement for February 2004, a 2003 W-2 form, and a 2003 tax return. She claims her children spend two to three nights a week with their father, and live with her the rest of the time at Leslie Lane.

Respondent alleges that its surveillance proves that petitioner lives at Orchard Street with her husband. It also maintains that, because the post office delivers mail to petitioner at the Orchard Street address, she does not reside at Leslie Lane. Additionally, respondent contends that because petitioner claimed only one child as a dependent on her income taxes for 2003, the other child must be living at Orchard Street. Finally, respondent notes that, while petitioner alleges she is separated from her husband, she has not produced a separation agreement.

Education Law §3202(1) provides, in pertinent part:

> A person over five and under twenty-one years of age who has not received a high school diploma is entitled to attend the public schools maintained in the district in which such person resides without the payment of tuition.

The purpose of this statute is to limit the obligation of school districts to provide tuition-free education to students whose parents or legal guardians reside within the district (*Appeal of Jones*, 42 Ed Dept Rep 129, Decision No. 14,797; *Appeal of L.W.*, 41 *id.* 372, Decision No. 14,717; *Appeal of Pierre*, 40 *id.* 538, Decision No. 14,551). Residence for purposes of §3202 is established by one's physical presence as an inhabitant within the district combined with an intent to reside in the district (*Longwood Cent. School Dist. v. Springs Union Free School Dist.*, 1 NY3d 385; *Appeal of Silvestro*, 40 Ed Dept Rep 259, Decision

No. 14,476; *Appeal of Lavelanet*, 39 *id.* 56, Decision No. 14,171). A child's residence is presumed to be that of his or her parents or legal guardians (*Appeal of James*, 41 Ed Dept Rep 487, Decision No. 14,752; *Appeal of Santana*, 40 *id.* 57, Decision No. 14,420; *Appeal of Lavelanet, supra*). Where a child's parents live apart, the child can have only one legal residence (*Appeal of Lavelanet, supra*; *Appeal of Plesko*, 37 Ed Dept Rep 238, Decision No. 13,850).

Respondent's investigator conducted surveillance at Orchard Street on four days between March 30 and April 13, 2004. During the first surveillance he saw "a woman" leave the Orchard Street residence at 8:10 a.m., get into a car registered to petitioner and drive away. The second surveillance commenced at 7:50 a.m. on March 31, 2004. The investigator observed a woman drive two children to school at 8:11 a.m. in a car registered to petitioner. The investigator was then informed by teachers at the school that the two girls were Jamia and Tayla. The third observation began at 6:58 a.m. on April 2, 2004, and revealed a man driving petitioner's children to school in a car registered to petitioner. The fourth surveillance occurred on April 13, 2004, at 7:54 a.m. Once again the investigator observed a man driving the children to school in a car registered to petitioner.

These actions are not inconsistent with petitioner's explanation that the children spend two to three nights per week with their father. Petitioner also admits she has spent some nights at Orchard Street due to reconciliation attempts with her husband. On no occasion did the investigator observe the Leslie Lane address, the address at which petitioner maintains she has continuously resided.

The lack of a legal separation agreement is not conclusive evidence that petitioner lives with her husband. Neither is the tax return showing petitioner claimed only one of her children as a dependant for 2003. In fact, that return lists petitioner's address as Leslie Lane. Finally, respondent's allegation—that the post office delivers mail with petitioner's name on it to Orchard Street—is not determinative. Moreover, this allegation is contradicted by petitioner's driver's license, earnings statement, W-2 and tax return.

In sum, I do not find respondent's surveillance evidence persuasive proof that petitioner has taken up residence at Orchard Street. I further find that respondent's other evidence is inconclusive. Accordingly, I am constrained to find, on the record before me, that respondent's determination, that petitioner's children are not district residents, is based on insufficient evidence and is arbitrary and capricious.

THE APPEAL IS SUSTAINED.

Decision No. 15,101

Appeal of WILDA ST. VILLIEN, on behalf of her daughter TAMAR DENACE, from action of the Board of Education of the Valley Stream Central High School District regarding residency.

Appeal of WILDA ST. VILLIEN, on behalf of her son DARREN DESRAMEAUX, from action of the Board of Education of the Valley Stream Central High School District regarding residency.

(August 23, 2004)

APPEARANCES OF COUNSEL

Guercio & Guercio, attorneys for respondent, *John P. Sheahan, Esq.*, of counsel

DECISION OF THE COMMISSIONER

MILLS, Commissioner.—In separate appeals, petitioner challenges the determination of the Board of Education of the Valley Stream Central High School District ("respondent") that her daughter, Tamar, and her son, Darren, are not district residents. Because the appeals raise similar issues of law and fact, they are consolidated for decision. The appeals must be dismissed.

Petitioner enrolled Tamar and Darren in respondent's schools in the fall of 2003. At that time she indicated that they all resided with petitioner's cousin in the district. Sometime thereafter, the district's administration began an investigation of petitioner's residency, and on March 22, 2004, petitioner attended a residency conference.

By letter dated March 23, 2004, respondent's superintendent notified petitioner of his finding that Tamar and Darren were not district residents and that, as of April 2, 2004, they were ineligible to attend school in the district. On May 12, 2004, petitioner's requests for interim relief were granted.

Petitioner contends that she and her children live in the district. Respondent contends that the petitions are untimely. Respondent further contends that petitioner and her children reside in Queens.

The appeals must be dismissed as untimely. An appeal to the Commissioner must be instituted within 30 days from the making of the decision or the performance of the act complained of, unless excused by the Commissioner for good cause shown (8 NYCRR §275.16). The superintendent's March 23, 2004, letter notified petitioner that her children would be excluded from respondent's schools, yet petitioner did not commence the appeals until April 27, 2004. Petitioner has not offered any reason for the delay. Consequently, the appeals must be dismissed as untimely (*Appeal of Eveillard*, 42 Ed Dept Rep 78, Decision No. 14,782; *Appeal of Perez*, 42 *id*. 71, Decision No. 14,779).

Even if the appeals were not dismissed as untimely, they would be dismissed on the merits. Education Law §3202(1) provides in pertinent part:

> A person over five and under twenty-one years of age who has not received a high school diploma is entitled to attend the public schools maintained in the district in which such person resides without the payment of tuition.

The purpose of this statute is to limit the obligation of school districts to provide tuition-free education to students whose parents or legal guardians reside within the district (*Appeal of Holder*, 44 Ed Dept Rep ___, Decision No. 15,088; *Appeal of General*, 43 *id*. ___, Decision No. 14,948; *Appeal of Burnett*, 42 *id*. 208, Decision No. 14,825). Residency for purposes of Education Law §3202 is established based upon two factors: physical presence and an intent to reside in the district (*Longwood Central School Dist. v. Springs Union Free School Dist.*, 1 NY3d 385; *Appeal of Holder, supra*; *Appeal of General, supra*). A child's residence is presumed to be that of his or her parents or legal guardians (*Appeal of Short*, 43 Ed Dept Rep ___, Decision No. 14,945; *Appeal of Washington*, 42 *id*. 197, Decision No. 14,820).

A residency determination will not be overturned unless it is arbitrary and capricious (*Appeal of Holder, supra*; *Appeal of General, supra*). In an appeal to the Commissioner, petitioner has the burden of demonstrating a clear legal right to the relief requested and the burden of establishing the facts upon which she seeks relief (8 NYCRR §275.10; *Appeal of General, supra*; *Appeal of Short, supra*).

In his March 23, 2004, letter, respondent's superintendent indicated that the determination was based on district surveillance and a number of documents that listed petitioner's address in Queens, including, a real estate record, Department of Motor Vehicle records and telephone book listing.

Petitioner admits that she used to live in Queens but claims that she and her children moved in with petitioner's cousin in respondent's district in July 2002. She contends that her estranged husband continues to reside in the home she owns in Queens. The only documentary evidence that petitioner submits in support of her claim of residency is her driver's permit and an expired automobile insurance card listing her cousin's address.

In contrast, respondent has submitted evidence that suggests that petitioner does not reside in the district. Between November 2003 and February 2004, respondent's investigator conducted surveillance on six occasions, during the early morning hours before school, at the alleged in-district residence. Neither petitioner nor Tamar was observed leaving the in-district residence, and yet Tamar was in school on time on those days. Petitioner's only explanation for the observations made by respondent's investigator is that he made a mistake or was confused. Petitioner fails to submit any evidence from her cousin supporting her claim that she and her children reside with her.

Petitioner's evidence is insufficient to support her claim of residency and therefore I find that petitioner has failed to meet her burden of proof (See *Appeal of K.M.*, 42 Ed Dept Rep 104, Decision No. 14,788). Accordingly, based on the record before me, I do not find that respondent's determination was arbitrary or capricious.

While the appeals must be dismissed, I note that petitioner has the right to reapply to the district for admission of her children at any time should circumstances change (*Appeal of Holder, supra*; *Appeal of Normandin*, 43 Ed Dept Rep ___, Decision No. 14,950; *Appeal of a Student with a Disability*, 43 *id.* ___, Decision No. 14,926).

THE APPEALS ARE DISMISSED.

Decision No. 15,102

Appeal of MICHAEL J. CROWLEY, on behalf of his children MICHAEL and KRISTIN, from action of the Board of Education of the Bronxville Union Free School District regarding residency.

(August 23, 2004)

APPEARANCES OF COUNSEL

Bertine, Hufnagel, Headley, Zeltner, Drummond & Dohn, LLP, attorneys for respondent, *John J. Hughes, Esq.*, of counsel

DECISION OF THE COMMISSIONER

MILLS, Commissioner.—Petitioner challenges the determination of the Board of Education of the Bronxville Union Free School District ("respondent"), rendered January 25, 2002, which found that his children were not residents of the district during the first semester of the 2001-2002 school year. The appeal must be dismissed.

The residency determination at issue in this appeal was the subject of a previous appeal brought by the children's mother, Barbara J. Crowley, which was dismissed on February 5, 2004, (*Appeal of Crowley*, 43 Ed Dept Rep ____, Decision No. 15,025). No judicial review of that determination has been sought. The facts are stated in the previous decision, and will not be repeated here.

Petitioner claims that respondent's residency determination, based upon a hearing conducted January 23, 2002, was not provided to him in writing within two business days, as required by Commissioner's regulation §100.2(y). He further claims that he first saw the residency decision in March 2002 (this is disputed by respondent), when he received it as an attachment to a letter dated March 25, 2002, from respondent's counsel, demanding payment for tuition for the first semester of the 2001-2002 school year. Petitioner claims that this procedure violated his rights, because he did not receive a copy of the residency determination until more than 30 days after the determination was made, and therefore received it after his time to appeal to the Commissioner had already expired.

Respondent contends that the appeal should be dismissed as untimely and under the doctrines of laches, collateral estoppel and *res judicata*. Respondent also objects to the submission of certain documents. As to the merits, respondent maintains that it complied with the regulation and its decision is not arbitrary or capricious.

Petitioner's basic premise is that respondent did not comply with the requirements of §100.2(y). I find that respondent did comply. The board's determination letter dated January 25, 2002, which was timely sent to Barbara J. Crowley and admittedly received by her, misquotes the Commissioner's regulation. The January 25, 2002, letter, purporting to quote the regulation, states that "such board or its designee shall, within two business days, provide written notice of its determination to the child's parents, to the person in parental relation to the child, or to the child, as appropriate." In fact, the regulation states that "such board or its designee shall, within two business days provide written notice of its determination to the child's *parent* . . . ." (emphasis added). There is no question that such notice was timely sent to, and received by, Barbara J. Crowley, the parent who attended the hearing on January 23, 2002, and with whom both children lived. Accordingly, I find that the procedure used by respondent complied with the regulation.

Even if a second notification were required, petitioner received the January 25, 2002, determination in March 2002. Although an appeal commenced by him then would have been untimely, under Commissioner's regulation §275.16, the Commissioner has the authority to excuse late commencement of an appeal "for good cause shown." If service on petitioner had been required, and was made two months late, as he claims (this is disputed by respondent), a late appeal commenced within 30 days of his receipt of the determination might well have been excused because of the impossibility of commencing it earlier. Here, however, petitioner did not commence an appeal in March 2002, but instead waited until March 3, 2004, to commence this appeal. Petitioner offers no excuse whatsoever for his inaction for nearly two years after receiving a copy of respondent's determination. While petitioner argues that his purported right to receive his own copy of the determination was violated in 2002, he apparently believes that such a violation allows him an unlimited time within which to commence an appeal. There is no factual or logical reason for such a position. Because he has offered no reason for waiting two years to commence this appeal, I find there is no basis upon which to exercise my discretion.

I note that neither the prior appeal by Barbara J. Crowley (commenced August 12, 2003), nor this appeal was commenced until after respondent sued Mr. and Mrs. Crowley and obtained a money judgment in Supreme Court, Westchester County, in June 2003 for tuition for the time period during which Barbara J. Crowley and the children were found not to be district residents. It is evident that the purpose of this appeal is to undermine the underlying basis for the judgment of Supreme Court, Westchester County. Any attack on that judgment must be made through the court system, not through an appeal to the Commissioner of Education.

In light of this disposition, I need not address any other issues raised in this appeal.

THE APPEAL IS DISMISSED.

Decision No. 15,103

Appeal of NADINE COLLINS, on behalf of ANTHONY and DANTE McLAUGHLIN, from action of the Board of Education of the Baldwin Union Free School District regarding residency.

(August 23, 2004)

APPEARANCES OF COUNSEL

Wanda L. Selinger, Esq., attorney for petitioner

Ingerman Smith, LLP, attorneys for respondent, *Susan M. Gibson, Esq.*, of counsel

DECISION OF THE COMMISSIONER

MILLS, Commissioner.—Petitioner appeals the determination of the Board of Education of the Baldwin Union Free School District ("respondent") that her children, Anthony and Dante, are not district residents. The appeal must be dismissed.

Petitioner registered Anthony and Dante with respondent in September 2002 and represented at that time that she resided on Milburn Avenue in Baldwin, within respondent's district.

In March 2004, the principal of the Meadow Elementary School reported to respondent's Registrar and Residency Investigator ("investigator") that Anthony was usually late for school, was picked up everyday after school, and that she had learned that petitioner's family had moved to Hempstead. Based on this information, the investigator conducted surveillance on the mornings of March 17 through 19, 2004, and March 22 through 24, 2004, at a home owned by petitioner on Elizabeth Avenue in Hempstead. On all six dates, the investigator observed the children leaving the Hempstead home, and being driven to the Meadow School. In addition, the investigator subsequently visited the Milburn Avenue address and found the home boarded up and posted with a February 18, 2004, notice warning that the building was unsafe.

By letter dated March 23, 2004, respondent's Director of Pupil Services advised petitioner that the district had reason to believe that her family did not reside in the district and invited petitioner to attend a March 29, 2004, meeting where she would have the opportunity to present evidence to support her residency claim. At the meeting, petitioner essentially admitted that she had vacated the Milburn Avenue residence a year earlier and was living at the Hempstead address, but claimed that she intended to return to her home in the district once construction on the house resumed.

By letter dated April 14, 2004, respondent's Director of Pupil Services advised petitioner that the district had determined that the family did not reside in the district based on, among other things, petitioner's admission that she did not reside at the Milburn Avenue home during the past year. The letter advised petitioner that her children would be excluded from school effective April 21, 2004. This appeal ensued. Petitioner's request for interim relief was granted on May 24, 2004.

Petitioner maintains that she was forced to vacate the Baldwin home in May 2003 because the house was uninhabitable due to demolition and construction. She claims that, in the interim, she has stayed either at the Baldwin residence of her youngest child's grandmother or her Elizabeth Avenue home in Hempstead, which she uses for her child daycare business.

Petitioner claims that she intends to renovate the Baldwin home and move back in, but admits that, in October 2003, construction stopped due to a dispute with her contractor and financing issues. Petitioner asserts that construction has now resumed, and submits an affidavit from a plumber she has hired. Petitioner explains that she sold the Baldwin home in June 2002 to her children's father "to pay off [the] mortgage and obtain the funds needed to remodel the house," but asserts that legal ownership is not dispositive.

Respondent maintains that it properly determined that petitioner is not a district resident because she is living in Hempstead and has no intention of returning to the Milburn Avenue home. In support of its position, respondent submits, among other things, surveillance reports showing the children leaving the Hempstead home on multiple occasions and being transported to school, as well as evidence that the Milburn Avenue home is in foreclosure and has been declared unsafe because of a crack in the foundation.

Education Law §3202(1) provides, in pertinent part:

> A person over five and under twenty-one years of age who has not received a high school diploma is entitled to

> attend the public schools maintained in the district in which such person resides without the payment of tuition.

The purpose of this statute is to limit the obligation of school districts to provide tuition-free education to students whose parents or legal guardians reside within the district (*Appeal of Marshall*, 43 Ed Dept Rep __, Decision No. 14,911; *Appeal of B.O. and D.O.*, 42 *id.* 42, Decision No. 14,769; *Appeal of Metze*, 42 *id.* 40, Decision No. 14,768). Residence for purposes of Education Law §3202 is established by one's physical presence as an inhabitant within the district and an intent to reside in the district (*Longwood Cent. School Dist. v. Springs Union Free School Dist.*, 1 NY3d 385; *Appeal of Marshall*, *supra*; *Appeal of B.O. and D.O.*, *supra*). A residence is not lost, moreover, until it is abandoned and another is established through action and intent (*Appeal of Scaffa*, 40 Ed Dept Rep 177, Decision No. 14,453; *Appeal of Britton*, 33 *id.* 198, Decision No. 13,022; *Appeal of Kurtz*, 32 *id.* 112, Decision No. 12,776).

A person's temporary absence from the school district of residence does not necessarily constitute either the establishment of a residence in the district where one is temporarily located, or the abandonment of one's permanent residence (*Appeal of Weisberg*, 39 Ed Dept Rep 737, Decision No. 14,365, judgment granted dismissing petition to review, *Weisberg v. Mills, et al.*, Sup. Ct., Albany Co., Special Term (Malone, J.), November 27, 2000, n.o.r.; *Appeal of Schwartzburt*, 37 *id.* 139, Decision No. 13,825; *Appeal of Kenneth R.*, 30 *id.* 297, Decision No. 12,471). To determine one's intent as to whether a living arrangement is indeed temporary, the Commissioner must consider evidence regarding the family's continuing ties to the community and their efforts to return (*Appeal of Weisberg*, *supra*; *Appeal of Schwartzburt*, *supra*; *Appeal of Gannon*, 37 Ed Dept Rep 135, Decision No. 13,823). Respondent's determination concerning residency will not be set aside unless the determination is arbitrary and capricious (*Appeal of Weisberg*, *supra*).

Petitioner admits that she does not presently reside at the Milburn Avenue residence because it is uninhabitable. Further, although petitioner claims that she sometimes stays with her youngest child's grandmother in Baldwin, she neither claims nor supplies proof that she resides at that location. In contrast, respondent's surveillance supports the conclusion that petitioner and her sons currently reside in Hempstead. Thus, petitioner's residency claim distills to whether

her absence from the district is temporary, as she contends, or permanent, as respondent contends.

Although petitioner claims that she intends to return to the district, she has failed to supply sufficient evidence demonstrating progress toward achieving that objective. The record reflects that petitioner vacated the Milburn Avenue house well over a year ago, and although the house is uninhabitable, in need of substantial renovations, and has been declared unsafe by the Town of Hempstead because of a crack in the foundation, the only work done on it thus far is the installation of "a waste line and vents" by a plumber. Further, although petitioner submits an estimate from a contractor for certain work on the home, petitioner has failed to establish that she has actually hired a contractor. Nor does petitioner explain how she intends to rectify the structural problem currently rendering the house unsafe. The record further reflects that petitioner no longer owns the home, and the property is in foreclosure.

A school district cannot be expected to allow students to continue to attend its schools indefinitely based on an expressed intent to return to the district (*Appeal of Weisberg, supra*). Petitioner's claimed intent to return to the district is insufficient to establish residency, absent either substantial progress repairing and renovating the Milburn Avenue house or, at the very least, a concrete and realistic plan to do so. Under these circumstances, I cannot conclude that respondent's determination is arbitrary or capricious (*see, Appeal of Weisberg, supra*; *Appeal of Gannon, supra*).

THE APPEAL IS DISMISSED.

Decision No. 15,104

Appeal of W.D. and P.Z-D., on behalf of their son L.D., from action of the Board of Education of the Quogue Union Free School District regarding residency.

(August 26, 2004)

APPEARANCES OF COUNSEL

Kevin A. Seaman, Esq., attorney for petitioners

Guercio & Guercio, attorneys for respondent, *Matthew R. Fleming, Esq.*, of counsel

DECISION OF THE COMMISSIONER

Petitioners appeal the determination of the Board of Education of the Quogue Union Free School District ("respondent") that their son, L.D., is not a district resident. The appeal must be sustained in part.

In August 2003, petitioners registered L.D. as a student in the district's pre-K program based on an address on Quogue Street within the district. In early September 2003, respondent's superintendent received information that petitioners were actually residing at Oneck Lane in Westhampton Beach, outside the district. After he observed petitioners and their vehicles at Oneck Lane, the superintendent hired a private investigator. By letter dated November 4, 2003, the superintendent notified petitioners of his intention to hold a residency hearing.

At the hearing on November 21, 2003, petitioners testified that at the time they registered L.D., W.D. was employed at the Inn at Quogue, within the district, and had been offered a cottage there to reside in with his family after Labor Day. After they moved in, W.D. lost his job and the family had to move. Petitioners then leased a dwelling on Quaquanantuck Lane in the district, from October 1, 2003, through June 15, 2004, and on September 23, 2003, paid in advance the full lease amount of $7,000. Petitioners moved into an unheated cottage on the property until December 1, when they moved into the main house.

P.Z-D. testified that she also owns a residence on Oneck Lane in Westhampton Beach, outside the district, where she had resided for 29 years and where her elderly mother continues to reside. P.Z-D. further testified that prior to December 1, the family occasionally stayed overnight at the Oneck Lane house for several reasons including that P.Z-D. was undergoing chemotherapy treatment and needed her mother's assistance with childcare. P.Z-D. explained that her mother is elderly and needs assistance, that the cottage was not available during weekends in October, and that the cottage was not winterized.

By letter dated December 15, 2003, a hearing officer designated by respondent informed petitioners of his determination that L.D. was not a district resident and would be excluded from the pre-K program as of January 5, 2004. This appeal ensued. Petitioners' request for interim relief was granted on January 15, 2004.

Petitioners assert that they are district residents. They contend that the surveillance report is deficient and that the hearing officer arbitrarily rejected legitimate explanations for their presence at Oneck Lane. They also complain that neither the superintendent nor respondent reviewed the hearing officer's findings. They request annulment of the hearing officer's decision.

Respondent asserts that the hearing officer was properly appointed and had authority to make the residency determination. Respondent contends that the evidence supports the hearing officer's rational determination that petitioners are not district residents.

Education Law §3202(1) provides in pertinent part:

> A person over five and under twenty-one years of age who has not received a high school diploma is entitled to attend the public schools maintained in the district in which such person resides without the payment of tuition.

The purpose of this statute is to limit the obligation of school districts to provide tuition-free education to students whose parents or legal guardians reside within the district (*Appeal of Thomas*, 43 Ed Dept Rep __, Decision No. 14,963; *Appeal of Normandin*, 43 *id.* __, Decision No. 14,950; *Appeal of General*, 43 *id.* __, Decision No. 14,948). Residency for purposes of Education Law §3202 is established based upon two factors: physical presence and intent to reside in the district (*Longwood Cent. School Dist. v. Springs Union Free School Dist.*, 1 NY3d 385; *Appeal of Thomas*, *supra*; *Appeal of General*, *supra*). A child's residence is presumed to be that of his or her parents or legal guardians (*Appeal of General*, *supra*; *Appeal of Sobel*, 43 Ed Dept Rep ___, Decision No. 14,931).

A person can only have one legal residence (*Catlin v. Sobol*, 155 AD2d 24, rev'd on other grnds, 77 NY2d 552 (1991); *Appeal of O'Herron*, 41 Ed Dept Rep 1, Decision No. 14,591; *Appeal of LaQuerre*, 40 *id.* 565, Decision No. 14,558; *Appeal of Embler*, 40 *id.* 17, Decision No. 14,406). If a person owns or rents property both within and outside the school district, only one property can be considered one's legal residence (*Appeal of Reynolds*, 41 Ed Dept Rep 32, Decision No. 14,604; *Appeal of Scaffa*, 40 *id.* 177, Decision No. 14,453). The mere fact that one rents or owns a house or property in the district, or even pays taxes in the district, does not necessarily confer residence status (*Appeal of O'Herron*, *supra*; *Appeal of Smith*, 40 Ed Dept Rep 126, Decision No. 14,438).

A residency determination will not be overturned unless it is arbitrary and capricious (*Appeal of General*, *supra*; *Appeal of Newby*, 42 Ed Dept Rep 107, Decision No. 14,790). The hearing officer's December 15, 2003, cover letter to petitioners, containing his determination, states that "[a] determination was made on December 11, 2003, that your son is not a resident of the Quogue Union Free School District" and that he is not entitled to attend district schools effective January 5, 2004. This in fact is contrary to the actual determination wherein the hearing officer states: "I conclude that prior to August of 2003, the parents were domiciled at . . . Oneck Lane in the Westhampton Beach Union Free School District" and that "their domicile up to the date of the hearing remained . . . Oneck Lane . . . ." However, the hearing officer also states that "[t]hereafter, *the parents attempted and did establish a residence within the Quogue Union Free School District* solely for the purpose of having their son, [L.D.], enroll in that District's Pre-K program . . . ." (Emphasis added)

The hearing officer's language suggests that although petitioners established residency within the district, L.D. is not entitled to attend district schools because the reason they relocated was for school purposes. Families may, and often do, relocate and establish residency based on their preference of school districts, particularly as their children reach school age. This is not to be confused with situations in which parents rent or purchase property in a district for the sole purpose of having their children attend district schools without intending to become district residents (*see*, *Appeal of Perez*, 42 Ed Dept Rep 71, Decision No. 14,779). Nor should it be confused with situations in which parents transfer custody and control of their child to a third party merely for the purpose of establishing the child's residency, apart from the parents, in order for the child to take advantage of district schools (*see*, *Appeal of Cuesta*, 42 Ed Dept Rep 6, Decision No. 14,755).

In this case, since the hearing officer found petitioners to be district residents and since there is no indication that L.D. lives apart from his parents, the determination that L.D. is not a district resident and not entitled to attend district schools is arbitrary, capricious and unreasonable and must be set aside.

As to whether petitioners were residents prior to the December 11, 2003, determination, the hearing officer's determination that petitioners thereafter established a residence within the Quogue Union Free School District renders the issue moot. The Commissioner of Education will only consider matters in actual controversy and will not render a decision on a state of facts which no longer exists or which subsequent events have laid to rest (*Appeal of Steinbrecher*, 43 Ed Dept Rep ___, Decision No. 15,008; *Appeal of T.B. and N.B.*, 42 *id.* 142, Decision No. 14,803; *Appeal of Tobias*, 41 *id.* 51, Decision No. 14,612).

THE APPEAL IS SUSTAINED TO THE EXTENT INDICATED.

Decision No. 15,105

Appeal of EMMA INNOCENT, on behalf of her daughter DAPHNE, from action of the Board of Education of the Islip Union Free School District regarding residency.

(August 26, 2004)

APPEARANCES OF COUNSEL

Ingerman Smith, L.L.P., attorneys for respondent, *Susan M. Gibson, Esq.*, of counsel

DECISION OF THE COMMISSIONER

Petitioner appeals the determination of the Board of Education of the Islip Union Free School District ("respondent") that her daughter, Daphne, is not district resident. The appeal must be dismissed.

In February 2004, the district's senior administrative aide ("aide") received a report that Daphne was being dropped off within the district and walking to school. Accordingly, the district's residency investigator initiated a surveillance of petitioner's alleged Moffitt Boulevard address. The investigator reported that when he visited that address on February 26, at 6:45 a.m., an adult male answered and stated that no one named Daphne lived there.

When the investigator interviewed Daphne at school on March 9, she insisted that she lived on Moffitt Boulevard. Daphne told the investigator that she had stayed at her father's house the previous night and also stays with her boyfriend, but refused to provide either address. The investigator then called petitioner who admitted she did not reside in the district but stated she was trying to obtain a residence there. Petitioner also admitted that Daphne stays with her father in Wheatley Heights, outside the district, and requested that future correspondence be directed there.

In a letter dated March 10, 2004, respondent's superintendent advised petitioner that Daphne was not a district resident and offered her the opportunity to provide evidence of Daphne's residency.

On March 25, 2004, petitioner met with the aide and admitted she lived outside the district in Brooklyn, but stated that Daphne was living with friends in the district. On March 26, 2004, petitioner submitted an affidavit in which she swore that she resided in Brentwood (not Brooklyn), that Daphne had been living with petitioner's sister in the district until the sister sold her house, and that Daphne was now living with a friend in the district. Petitioner also swore that she was looking for an apartment and planned to move into the district within a month to 45 days, and that she would provide for Daphne's necessities. Petitioner's friend, Ms. Steizinger, submitted a custodian's affidavit dated March 26, stating that Daphne would reside with her on Willow Street in the district for about a month until petitioner found an apartment. By letter dated May 29, 2004, the superintendent agreed to permit Daphne to complete the 2003-2004 school year at the district's schools based on the statements in the two affidavits.

Subsequent to the superintendent's March 29, 2004, letter, the aide received an anonymous tip that petitioner and Daphne were residing in Massapequa, outside the district. Consequently, the district continued its investigation at the Brentwood address listed in petitioner's affidavit and the Willow Street address listed in Ms. Steizinger's affidavit. The investigator reported that when he visited the Brentwood address at 6:30 a.m. on March 30, the adult female who answered the door told him that no one by the name of "Innocent" resided there. He also reported that when he visited the Willow Street address on March 31 looking for Daphne, the adult female who answered the door told him that no child lived there. Five more visits to that address yielded negative results. On April 20, 2004, the investigator observed the Massapequa address from 6:10 a.m., until he confirmed Daphne was in school at 7:50 a.m., but did not see her exit the residence.

By letter dated April 22, 2004, the superintendent informed petitioner that based on information provided by the investigator, he had reason to believe that Daphne was not residing on Willow Street, within the district. Therefore, Daphne would be excluded from the district's schools effective April 30, 2004. This appeal ensued. Petitioner's request for interim relief was granted on May 27, 2004.

Petitioner asserts that she and Daphne reside with Ms. Steizinger on Willow Street in the district, and that Daphne intends to live there for one year until she graduates from high school in 2005. Respondent asserts that the petition fails to state a claim upon which relief may be granted and that neither petitioner nor Daphne reside in the district.

Education Law §3202(1) provides in pertinent part:

> A person over five and under twenty-one years of age who has not received a high school diploma is entitled to attend the public schools maintained in the district in which such person resides without the payment of tuition.

The purpose of this statute is to limit the obligation of school districts to provide tuition-free education to students whose parents or legal guardians reside within the district (*Appeal of Sloley-Raymond*, 44 Ed Dept Rep ___, Decision No. 15,085; *Appeal of O.W.*, 43 *id.* ___, Decision No. 14,949). A child's residence is presumed to be that of her parents or legal guardians (*Appeal of Sloley-Raymond, supra*; *Appeal of O.W., supra*). This presumption can be rebutted where it is shown that the parents have relinquished total custody and control to someone residing in the district (*Appeal of Slolely-Raymond, supra*; *Appeal of O.W., supra*). Moreover, where the sole reason the child is residing with someone other than the parent is to take advantage of the schools of the district, the child has not established residence (*Appeal of Sloley-Raymond, supra*; *Appeal of O.W., supra*).

A residency determination will not be set aside unless it is arbitrary and capricious (*Appeal of Newby*, 42 Ed Dept Rep 107, Decision No. 14,790; *Appeal of Leontakianakos*, 42 *id.* 10, Decision No. 14,757). In an appeal to the Commissioner of Education, the petitioner has the burden of demonstrating a clear legal right to the relief requested and the burden of establishing the facts upon which she seeks relief (8 NYCRR §275.10; *Appeal of B.H. and B.H.*, 43 Ed Dept Rep __, Decision No. 14,919; *Appeal of J.T.*, 43 *id.* __, Decision No. 14,917).

In this case, petitioner has given inconsistent and conflicting addresses and information, and has failed to rebut any of the district's surveillance reports. Surveillance indicates that petitioner and Daphne do not live in the district, either on Moffitt Boulevard, the address on record with the district, or on Willow Street, the address she alleges in the petition. In fact, petitioner admitted three times that she lived outside the district.

In addition, there is no evidence that petitioner transferred custody or control of Daphne to Ms. Steizinger. In sum, petitioner has submitted no documentation or evidence to rebut the presumption that Daphne resides with her, somewhere outside the district. Accordingly, respondent's determination was not arbitrary or capricious, and will not be set aside.

THE APPEAL IS DISMISSED.

Decision No. 15,106

Appeal of ANTHONY ANTONIADIS, on behalf of his daughter JODIE, from action of the Board of Education of the Amherst Central School District regarding transportation.

(August 31, 2004)

APPEARANCES OF COUNSEL

Linda L. Kaumeyer, Esq., attorney for respondent

DECISION OF THE COMMISSIONER

MILLS, Commissioner.—Petitioner appeals the denial by the Board of Education of the Amherst Central School District ("respondent") of his request for his daughter's transportation to a nonpublic school. The appeal must be dismissed.

Petitioner and his daughter, Jodie, reside within respondent's district. During the 2003-2004 school year, Jodie attended seventh grade at Christ the King School ("Christ the King"), a nonpublic school located within the district. Petitioner resides one-half mile from the school.

Respondent's transportation policy provides that students in grades six through eight who reside "one mile or more from school will be transported to and from school." In addition, in 1998, pursuant to Education Law §3635-b, respondent established a "child safety zone" near petitioner's home because it determined that certain intersections were hazardous. Respondent provides transportation to Christ the King students who reside within the boundaries of the child safety zone, notwithstanding the distance of their homes from the nonpublic school. Petitioner resides outside the designated child safety zone.

In establishing the child safety zone, respondent determined, pursuant to New York State Department of Transportation regulations, that a hazardous condition existed at an intersection located within the district (Kensington Avenue and Bentham/Avalon/Ridgewood Drives). Respondent determined the students whose most direct walking route to or from school required them to cross that intersection and prescribed the child safety zone to include the residences of those students. Based on this determination, respondent established a child safety zone bounded by the southeast side of Kensington Avenue, Avalon and Ridgewood Drives, Bennington Drive and Lamarck Drive. Students residing within that zone received transportation because their most direct walking route to the school they attended (Christ the King) required them to cross at the identified hazardous intersection. Respondent did not include within its established child safety zone the street on which Jodie resides because she was not required to cross the identified hazardous intersection at Kensington/Bentham/Avalon/ Ridgewood when walking to school.

Although not requested to do so at the time, respondent also analyzed other intersections within the district, including the intersection of Kensington Avenue and Walton Drive, and determined that no hazardous condition existed there.

In March 2003, petitioner requested afternoon transportation for Jodie from Christ the King to home. The request was denied because petitioner's residence is less than one mile from school. By letter dated August 28, 2003, to the district's school safety coordinator, petitioner again requested transportation for Jodie stating that her "most direct route home . . . is within the established child safety zone."

By letter dated September 8, 2003, the school safety coordinator denied petitioner's written transportation request and his verbal request to extend the child safety zone to include petitioner's residence. She stated that Jodie was ineligible for transportation because petitioner's residence was not located within the designated child safety zone. With respect to petitioner's request to extend the child safety zone to include his residence, the school safety coordinator proposed alternative walking routes that would avoid any hazardous intersections. She further notified petitioner of the procedures for formally petitioning respondent to establish a new or revised child safety zone.

At respondent's September 16, 2003, board meeting, petitioner appealed the safety coordinator's decision denying Jodie transportation and reiterated his request that respondent extend the child safety zone to include his residence. By letter dated September 22, 2003, respondent denied petitioner's requests. On that same day, petitioner apparently wrote to the president of the board setting forth additional issues, although neither party has submitted a copy of that letter. By letter dated September 23, 2003, respondent's attorney notified petitioner that the president of the board wished to present petitioner's letter to respondent at its October 7, 2003, meeting. The September 23 letter stated, "in order to afford you the opportunity to have the Board address the issues in your recent letter, the District will suspend the commencement of your time to appeal until Friday, October 10, 2003, to accommodate your request."

On October 7, 2003, petitioner appeared before respondent during executive session, but respondent did not alter its decision to deny petitioner's requests. This appeal ensued. On November 19, 2003, petitioner's request for interim relief was denied.

Petitioner contends that, although Jodie does not reside within the child safety zone, she is nevertheless entitled to transportation because her most direct walking route home from school requires her to walk through the designated child safety zone. In the alternative, petitioner asserts that respondent should extend the current child safety zone to include his residence. Finally, petitioner contends that the alternative walking route respondent proposed for Jodie measures 1.2 miles, thus entitling her to transportation under respondent's transportation policy.

Respondent asserts that Jodie is not entitled to transportation because her residence is outside the designated child safety zone, that petitioner's request to extend the current zone or create a new zone is untimely and unwarranted, and that the alternative walking route proposed for Jodie does not exceed one mile.

I must first address a procedural matter. Petitioner has submitted written argument in reply to respondent's memorandum of law. Respondent has not objected to this submission. Pursuant to §§276.4 and 276.5 of the Commissioner's regulations, I will accept petitioner's reply memorandum for consideration.

Petitioner first argues that Jodie is entitled to transportation because her most direct route from home to school requires her to walk through a child safety zone. Education Law §3635-b(2) provides in pertinent part:

> A board of education ... is authorized to adopt a resolution providing for pupil transportation in child safety zones, subject to voter approval, where applicable, of a proposition to expend money for such transportation. ... Such transportation may be provided without regard to like circumstances based solely upon the fact that the pupil resides within [the mileage limitation] from the school such pupil legally attends.... Such transportation may be provided upon the determination by the board that a hazardous zone exists which in the opinion of the board would be reasonably alleviated by the establishment of a child safety zone. For purposes of this section, child safety zone means *a designated area* of a school district, including at least one personal residence, *within which children who reside at a lesser distance* from the school they legally attend than the minimum transportation limit of the district *will be provided transportation* on the basis that their most direct walking route to school will traverse a hazardous zone (emphasis added).

The statutory language is clear in defining "child safety zone" as a designated area of a school district *within which* children *who reside* at a lesser distance than the minimum transportation limits will be provided transportation (emphasis supplied). Therefore, a student must reside within the geographic boundary of the designated child safety zone to be entitled to transportation under Education Law §3635-b (See also, *Appeal of Trader*, 43 Ed Dept Rep ___, Decision No. 14,967). Because petitioner resides outside the child safety zone, Jodie is not entitled to transportation pursuant to §3635-b.

Petitioner also challenges respondent's refusal to grant his alternative request that the child safety zone be extended to include his residence or that a new child safety zone be created that includes his residence. Petitioner based his request on the assertion that Jodie must cross either the intersection one block west of her residence at Kensington Avenue/Walton Drive as respondent suggests, or at Kensington Avenue/Lamarck, Drive located on one boundary of the current child safety zone.

Respondent correctly maintains that petitioner's September 2003 request to extend the current child safety zone or create a new zone was untimely. Education Law §3635-b(4) requires that requests seeking designation of a child safety zone be made by petition signed by 25 qualified voters of the district or five percent of the number of voters who voted in the previous annual election of board members, whichever is greater. It further provides that such petitions "shall not be submitted later than the first day of March preceding the school year for which transportation is being requested." Petitioner failed to submit a petition with the requisite number of signatures, and his request for designation of an expanded or new child safety zone for the 2003-2004 school year was not submitted by March 1, 2003, as required (*Appeal of Chapman*, 40 Ed Dept Rep 558, Decision No. 14,556). Respondent assertion that petitioner's request was untimely is, therefore, correct.

Despite petitioner's late request, respondent reviewed petitioner's claim that the intersections at Kensington Avenue/Lamarck Drive and Kensington Avenue/Walton Drive are hazardous. Based on the 1998 analysis by an independent transportation consultant, respondent concluded that no other intersections within the district constituted hazards. Respondent specifically analyzed the intersection at Kensington Avenue/Walton Drive, which is part of its proposed alternate walking route for Jodie. Respondent concluded that the intersection did not meet the New York State Department of Transportation criteria to be considered hazardous.

In this appeal, petitioner sets forth a number of conclusory allegations regarding the safety of that intersection. In an appeal to the Commissioner of Education, the petitioner has the burden of demonstrating a clear legal right to the relief requested (8 NYCRR §275.10) and the burden of establishing the facts upon which he seeks relief (*Appeal of a Student with a Disability*, 43 Ed Dept Rep ___, Decision No. 15,073; *Appeal and Application of Davis*, 43 *id.* ___, Decision No. 15,007). Except for a letter from the Amherst Police Department providing general information regarding accident statistics along Kensington Avenue "between Main and Saratoga," petitioner submits no proof of his allegations regarding the conditions at the specific intersection of Kensington Avenue/Walton Drive, the alternative route proposed by respondent. Thus, petitioner fails to demonstrate that respondent's determination regarding the safety of the intersection is unreasonable.

Petitioner also asserts that the alternative walking route respondent suggests for Jodie is not the most direct route and, further, that the alternative route measures 1.2 miles, entitling her to transportation under respondent's general transportation policy.

Section 191.4 of the Department of Transportation regulations provides, in pertinent part:

> The route used between home and school must avoid hazardous locations when a more reasonable route is available. . . . [B]efore a [child safety zone] can be established, alternative solutions must be investigated. Sometimes, a hazard can be mitigated by changing the route which the student walks to one that is slightly shorter or longer.

Respondent asserts that its proposed route is a reasonable alternative in that the intersection Jodie would be required to cross (Kensington Avenue/Walton Drive) is not hazardous. Respondent denies that the alternate route exceeds one mile. Other than his conclusory allegation, petitioner offers no proof of his assertion that the proposed alternative route exceeds one mile. Therefore, I need not address petitioner's claim for transportation on that basis.

THE APPEAL IS DISMISSED.

Decision No. 15,107

Appeal of L.T., on behalf of R.T., from action of the Board of Education of the East Islip Union Free School District regarding student discipline.

(August 31, 2004)

APPEARANCES OF COUNSEL

Ingerman Smith, L.L.P., attorneys for respondent, *Deborah Richardson de Cuevas, Esq.*, of counsel

DECISION OF THE COMMISSIONER

MILLS, Commissioner.—Petitioner appeals the suspension of her son, R.T., by the Board of Education of the East Islip Union Free School District ("respondent"). The appeal is sustained.

In September 2003, R.T. commenced his junior year at respondent's East Islip High School. On October 30, 2003, R.T. was suspended for five days for being under the influence of alcohol on school premises, insubordination, threatening a teacher, leaving school grounds without permission and using foul language. On November 7, 2003, a hearing officer conducted a superintendent's hearing pursuant to Education Law §3214 on these charges:

> <u>Charge #1</u>
>
> That on October 30, 2003, [R.T.] was under the influence of alcohol while on the premises of East Islip Union Free School District.
>
> <u>Charge #2</u>
>
> That on October 30, 2003, [R.T.], after having been directed to remain in the nurse's office of the East Islip High School, left the nurse's office and the premises of the East Islip High School.
>
> <u>Charge #3</u>
>
> That on October 30, 2003, [R.T.], while on the premises of the East Islip High School, threatened another by stating, "That b—— is dead."
>
> <u>Charge #4</u>
>
> That on October 30, 2003, [R.T.], while leaving the premises of the East Islip High School without authorization, stated to staff members, "F—- you guys."

The hearing officer found R.T. guilty of all four charges and, upon review of his anecdotal record, recommended that R.T. be permanently suspended from the district's schools. The hearing officer also determined that, because of his age, R.T. was not entitled to alternative instruction. The superintendent of schools adopted the hearing officer's recommendations.

By letter dated November 20, 2003, petitioner appealed the superintendent's decision and also requested alternative instruction for R.T. By letter dated December 3, 2003, the superintendent notified petitioner of her right to submit written information for respondent's consideration on appeal. Thereafter, R.T. was provided alternative instruction.

Petitioner submitted two letters to respondent, dated January 2 and January 6, 2004. In her letters, she stated that she was not represented by counsel at the superintendent's hearing and that she never received a written decision from the superintendent. She challenged the determination of R.T.'s guilt and the penalty imposed.

By letter dated January 8, 2004, respondent notified petitioner that, at its meeting of January 6, 2004, it upheld the superintendent's decision. This appeal ensued. On April 13, 2004, petitioner's request for interim relief was denied.

Petitioner asserts that she was not adequately prepared for the November 7, 2003, superintendent's hearing. She also asserts that respondent had pre-determined her appeal prior to its January 6, 2004, meeting. Finally, petitioner seeks an order returning R.T. to school. Respondent maintains that its determination was, in all respects, proper and that the penalty is appropriate.

As a threshold matter, respondent seeks permission to submit a late answer and additional affidavit pursuant to §276.5 of the Commissioner's regulations. Most of respondent's defenses and exhibits were previously submitted in a timely manner in opposition to petitioner's stay request. Upon review of respondent's application, and noting no objection by petitioner, I have accepted respondent's answer and additional affidavit for consideration.

In an appeal to the Commissioner of Education, the petitioner has the burden of demonstrating a clear legal right to the relief requested and the burden of establishing the facts upon which she seeks relief (8 NYCRR §275.10; *Appeal of Crump*, 44 Ed Dept Rep ___, Decision No. 15,099; *Appeal of B.H. and B.H.*, 43 *id.* ___, Decision No. 14,919). Section 3214(3)(c)(1) provides, in pertinent part:

> No pupil may be suspended for a period in excess of five school days unless such pupil and the person in parental relation to such pupil shall have had an opportunity for a fair hearing, upon reasonable notice, at which such pupil shall have the right of representation by counsel, with the right to question witnesses against such pupil and to present witnesses and other evidence on his behalf.

Although petitioner contends that she was not prepared for the November 7, 2003, disciplinary hearing, she does not assert that she was not provided notice of R.T.'s right to representation by counsel or to present and cross-examine witnesses. Nor does she allege that she had insufficient time to obtain counsel prior to the hearing. At the hearing, the hearing officer reviewed R.T.'s rights under Education Law §3214(3)(c)(1) and specifically asked petitioner and R.T. if they had any questions. Neither petitioner nor R.T. requested an adjournment to obtain counsel or otherwise indicated that they did not understand their rights under Education Law §3214.

Petitioner claims that at its January 6, 2004, meeting, respondent acted too hastily in upholding the superintendent's decision and, therefore, she believes respondent had made its decision prior to hearing her appeal. Petitioner's claim consists solely of conclusory allegations. She presents no evidence that respondent acted with bias or otherwise improperly prejudged the merits of her appeal.

Finally, petitioner seeks R.T.'s reinstatement. A decision to suspend a student from school pursuant to Education Law §3214 must be based on competent and substantial evidence that the student participated in the objectionable conduct *Bd. of Educ. of Monticello Cent. School Dist. v. Commissioner of Educ.*, 91 NY2d 133; *Bd. of Educ. of City of New York v. Mills, et al.*, 293 AD2d 37). Petitioner admits that on October 30, 2003, R.T. was under the influence of alcohol. At the November 7, 2003, superintendent's hearing, the high school principal provided direct testimony that he observed R.T. under the influence of alcohol (Charge 1), that R.T. ignored his directive and left the nurse's office without permission (Charge 2), and that he saw R.T. leave school premises without authorization and heard him direct foul language to security staff (Charge 4). The principal also testified that he had received reports from staff that R.T. made a threatening statement against a teacher (Charge 3).

In addition to the principal, respondent also presented a teacher, N.K., who testified that she heard R.T. threaten another teacher [Mrs. P.] (Charge 3). Petitioner challenges the characterization of the statement made by R.T. She claims R.T. did not threaten Mrs. P. but instead referred to her in vulgar terms. Petitioner asserts that Mrs. P. told her that she did not feel threatened by R.T. However, petitioner did not call Mrs. P. as a witness at the hearing. In view of the eyewitness testimony respondent presented at the hearing, I find that the determination of guilt is supported by competent and substantial evidence.

In cases of student discipline, however, the sanction imposed must be proportionate to the severity of the offenses involved (*Appeal of Y.M.*, 43 Ed Dept Rep ___, Decision No. 14,968; *Appeal of M.F. and*

J.F., 43 *id.* ___, Decision No. 14,960). The test to be applied in reviewing a penalty is whether it is so excessive as to warrant substitution of the Commissioner's judgment for that of the board (*Appeal of Y.M., supra*; *Appeal of M.F. and J.F., supra*; *Appeal of J.C. and P.C.*, 41 Ed Dept Rep 395, Decision No. 14,723). A permanent suspension is an extreme penalty that is generally educationally unsound except under extraordinary circumstances such as where the student exhibits "an alarming disregard for the safety of others" and where it is necessary to safeguard the well-being of other students (*Appeal of Y.M., supra*; *Appeal of Coleman*, 41 Ed Dept Rep 101, Decision No. 14,628; *Appeal of McNamara*, 37 Ed Dept Rep 326, Decision No. 13,871). The record in this case is somewhat unclear as to whether R.T.'s suspension was "permanent" or through June 30, 2005, which would have been the end of R.T.'s senior year. The circumstances of this case, however, do not merit either penalty.

R.T. was found guilty of intoxication, insubordination, using foul language and making a verbal threat. While a verbal threat must be taken seriously, R.T. has no history of violent or threatening behavior.

In support of its penalty, respondent points to R.T.'s anecdotal record over a period of approximately one and one-half years and alleges that the current charges, when considered with his past record, warrant R.T.'s expulsion. R.T.'s record reveals 25 incidents of: using foul language, leaving school grounds, failing to follow directions and engaging in disrespectful and/or disruptive behavior. A prior five-day suspension of R.T. for possession of "a weapon" stemmed from his waving around a stage prop theatrical sword. Although I agree that a significant period of suspension is appropriate in view of R.T.'s anecdotal record and the current charges, the extraordinary penalty of expulsion, or even suspension through June 30, 2005, is not warranted. Indeed, none of R.T.'s prior suspensions exceeded five days — thirteen of them were in-school suspensions. Even the incident with the stage prop sword resulted in only a five-day suspension. These prior incidents do not now create a basis, when viewed with the current incident, for either a permanent suspension or suspension through June 30, 2005, that may effectively end R.T.'s chance to graduate from high school. Thus, after carefully reviewing the record before me, I do not find R.T.'s conduct extreme enough to warrant the penalty imposed.

R.T. has already been suspended from school from October 30, 2003, through June 30, 2004—a period of eight months. Such period should sufficiently impress upon R.T. the seriousness of his prior misconduct. I encourage R.T. to profitably use this opportunity to return to school in respondent's district to earn his high school diploma.

THE APPEAL IS SUSTAINED.

IT IS ORDERED that respondent admit R.T. to school in the East Islip Union Free School District; and

IT IS FURTHER ORDERED that respondent remove any reference to a permanent suspension or suspension through June 30, 2005, from R.T.'s disciplinary record and adjust such record in accordance with the terms of this decision.

Decision No. 15,108

Appeal of a STUDENT WITH A DISABILITY, by his parent, from action of the Board of Education of the Grand Island Central School District regarding residency.

(August 31, 2004)

APPEARANCES OF COUNSEL

Bouvier, O'Connor, LLP, attorneys for respondent, *Chris G. Trapp, Esq.*, of counsel

DECISION OF THE COMMISSIONER

MILLS, Commissioner.—Petitioner appeals the determination of the Board of Education of the Grand Island Central School District ("respondent") that her son is not a district resident. The appeal must be dismissed.

Petitioner's son is a 15-year-old student with a disability who attended eighth grade at respondent's middle school during the 2003-2004 school year. Petitioner and her son resided in respondent's district from December 2003 until February 25, 2004, at which time they moved into her mother's residence in the City of Buffalo. At a March 11, 2004, meeting of its Committee on Special Education ("CSE"), respondent learned of petitioner's relocation outside the district. By letter dated March 25, 2004, respondent's Director for Pupil Personnel Services advised petitioner that her son was no longer a resident eligible to enroll in its middle school, and would be excluded from attendance, effective April 2, 2004. This appeal ensued. Petitioner's request for interim relief was granted on April 20, 2004.

Petitioner claims that she left her Grand Island residence because she was the victim of domestic violence at the hands of her partner and housemate. Petitioner contends that her current living arrangement with her mother in Buffalo is temporary until she can rent an apartment in Grand Island. Petitioner also argues in this appeal, apparently for the first time, that she and her son should be considered homeless.

Respondent contends that petitioner resides in Buffalo and has not established residency in Grand Island. Respondent alleges that petitioner voluntarily moved out of Grand Island for her own convenience, but prefers that her son remain in respondent's district because she feels that he will receive a better education there. Respondent disputes that petitioner and her son are homeless, and maintains that Buffalo school records indicate that petitioner and her son resided previously in their current Buffalo residence. Respondent further contends that the appeal should be dismissed for failure to exhaust administrative remedies.

I will first address the procedural issue of exhaustion of remedies. Section 100.2(y) of the Commissioner's regulations specifically states that the board of education or its designee may make residency determinations. Respondent does not deny that its Director for Pupil Personnel Services is its designee for the purpose of making residency determinations. Thus, respondent cannot now claim that petitioner failed to exhaust her administrative remedies where there is no showing that the Director was not authorized to act for respondent (*Appeal of Zavesky*, 40 Ed Dept Rep 517, Decision No. 14,543; *Appeal of Smith*, 40 *id.* 172, Decision No. 14,452; *Appeal of Berliner*, 38 *id.* 181, Decision No. 14,010.

Education Law §3202(1) provides, in pertinent part:

> A person over five and under twenty-one years of age who has not received a high school diploma is entitled to attend the public schools maintained in the district in which such person resides without the payment of tuition.

The purpose of this statute is to limit the obligation of school districts to provide tuition-free education to students whose parents or legal guardians reside within the district (*Appeal of Wingert*, 43 Ed Dept Rep ___, Decision No. 15,059; *Appeal of D.H.C.*, 43 *id.* ___, Decision No. 15,053; *Appeal of Geithner*, 43 id. ___, Decision No. 15,047). A student's residence is presumed to be that of his or her parent or legal guardian (*Appeal of Wingert*, *supra*; *Appeal of D.H.C.*, *supra*; *Appeal of Geithner*, *supra*). In this case, petitioner admits that her son is living with her outside the district. She contends that her absence from the district is temporary and that, under federal and State laws governing homeless children, her son is eligible to attend respondent's schools.

Education Law §3209(1)(a), as amended, effective July 1, 2003, defines a homeless child as:

> (1) a child or youth who lacks a fixed, regular, and adequate night-time residence, including a child or youth who is:
>
> (i) sharing the housing of other persons due to a loss of housing, economic hardship or a similar reason;
>
> (ii) living in motels, hotels, trailer parks or camping grounds due to the lack of alternative adequate accommodations;
>
> (iii) abandoned in hospitals;
>
> (iv) awaiting foster care placement; or
>
> (v) a migratory child. . . who qualifies as homeless under any of the provisions of clauses (i) through (iv) of this subparagraph or subparagraph two of this paragraph; or
>
> (2) a child or youth who has a primary nighttime location that is:
>
> (i) a supervised publicly or privately operated shelter designed to provide temporary living accommodations. . .
>
> (ii)a public or private place not designed for, or ordinarily used as, a regular sleeping accommodation for human beings. . . .

Section 100.2(x) of the Commissioner's regulations, as amended, effective March 6, 2003, also contains this definition. Both the Education Law and Commissioner's regulations conform to the definition of "homeless children and youths" in the federal McKinney-Vento Homeless Assistance Act ("McKinney-Vento" 42 USC §11302). McKinney-Vento and Education Law §3209 permit homeless children to attend the school district in which they were last enrolled if they are temporarily housed in another school district (42 USC §11432(g)(3)(A); Education Law §3209(2)(a)).

Petitioner's son does not fit the definition of homeless child under state or federal law. He has a fixed, regular night-time residence and there is insufficient evidence on record that such residence is inadequate. The petition includes only conclusory statements by petitioner's mother that her residence cannot accommodate three additional people on a permanent basis, and by petitioner that a single bathroom for six people is not adequate. Petitioner has the burden of demonstrating a clear legal right to the relief requested and establishing the facts upon which relief is sought (8 NYCRR §275.10; *Appeal of D.R.*, 43 Ed Dept Rep ___, Decision No. 14,944). Petitioner has not established that she is sharing the housing of other persons due to loss of housing rather than a preference to move back into her family residence.

While it is unfortunate that petitioner felt the need to leave her Grand Island apartment, there is no proof in the record that petitioner lost her Grand Island apartment and is required to live in the kind of shelter or other accommodation described in §3209. Indeed, school records indicate that petitioner and her son previously resided at the same Buffalo address. Consequently, the provisions of Education Law §3209(2) and McKinney-Vento regarding choice of district for homeless children are not applicable in petitioner's circumstances (see, *Appeal of D.R.*, *supra*).

Therefore, respondent's determination that petitioner's son may not attend its schools without payment of tuition was not arbitrary, capricious or unreasonable. I find no basis on which to substitute my judgment for that of respondent.

I have considered the parties remaining contentions and find them without merit.

THE APPEAL IS DISMISSED.

Decision No. 15,109

Appeal of WILLIAM SIGSBY, on behalf of his son JOSHUA, from action of the Board of Education of the East Greenbush Central School District regarding residency.

(August 31, 2004)

APPEARANCES OF COUNSEL

Ferrara, Fiorenza, Larrison, Barrett & Reitz, P.C., attorneys for respondent, *David G. Maestri, Esq.*, of counsel

DECISION OF THE COMMISSIONER

MILLS, Commissioner.—Petitioner challenges the determination of the Board of Education of the East Greenbush Central School District ("respondent") that his son, Joshua, is not a district resident. The appeal must be dismissed.

Petitioner and his wife purchased a home in respondent's district in August 2003. On August 28, 2003, petitioner enrolled his son in respondent's district and informed respondent's registrar that they intended to move into the house that fall after renovations were completed. Petitioner provided the registrar with an address outside the district where he and his family would be living while the house was being renovated. The registrar informed petitioner that Joshua would be permitted to attend the district's schools tuition-free provided that residency was established by December 31, 2003.

In February 2004, respondent's administrators became aware that Joshua still did not reside in the district. By letter dated March 26, 2004, respondent's registrar requested additional information from petitioner. After reviewing petitioner's submissions, including a district residency questionnaire, a utility bill for the house in the district, and an automobile insurance card, respondent's superintendent informed petitioner by letter dated April 29, 2004, that Joshua was not entitled to attend respondent's schools without payment of tuition. That letter also informed petitioner that he could apply school taxes paid on the house in the district to the tuition bill. This appeal ensued.

Petitioner contends that the renovations are taking longer than anticipated because the discovery of black mold necessitated more extensive renovation than had been planned. Petitioner asserts that Joshua is allergic to this type of mold and that they cannot move into the house until it is removed. Petitioner maintains that they intend to move into the house soon. Petitioner also contends that he was unaware that he could become liable for tuition costs. Petitioner requests a determination that Joshua is a resident of the district and entitled to attend its schools without payment of tuition.

Respondent argues that petitioner fails to establish that he and his family are district residents. Respondent asserts that under its policy, if pending legal residence is not established by January 1 of the current school year tuition will be charged. Respondent asserts that when petitioner registered Joshua on August 28, 2003, the registrar informed petitioner that he would be liable for tuition retroactively if residency was not established by December 31, 2003. Respondent also argues that the petition should be dismissed because petitioner did not submit an affidavit of service with the petition.

Section 275.9 of Commissioner's regulations requires that an affidavit of personal service be transmitted to my Office of Counsel within five days after the service of any pleadings or paper. The record indicates that the petition was properly served on respondent on May 28, 2004, but the affidavit of service was not received by my Office of Counsel until June 22, 2004. Respondent, however, expresses no prejudice from petitioner's filing delay. Accordingly, I find such delay to be harmless error (*See Appeal of McSween*, 42 Ed Dept Rep 59, Decision No. 14,775).

Education Law §3202(1) provides in pertinent part:

> A person over five and under twenty-one years of age who has not received a high school diploma is entitled to attend the public schools maintained in the district in which such person resides without the payment of tuition.

The purpose of this statute is to limit the obligation of school districts to provide tuition-free education to students whose parents or legal guardians reside within the district (*Longwood Cent. School Dist. v. Springs Union Free School Dist.*, 1 NY3d 385; *Appeal of B.C.*, 43 Ed Dept Rep __, Decision No. 14,946; *Appeal of B.O. and D.O.*, 42 *id*. 42, Decision No. 14,769). Residence for purposes of Education Law §3202 is established based upon two factors: physical presence as an inhabitant within the district and intent to reside in the district (*Longwood Cent. School Dist. v. Springs Union Free School Dist.*, *supra*; *Appeal of B.C.*, *supra*; *Appeal of B.O. and D.O.*, *supra*; *Appeal of Metze*, *supra*). Moreover, for purposes of Education Law §3202(1), a person can have only one legal residence (*Appeal of B.C.*, *supra*). Mere ownership of property in a school district does not confer residency status (*Appeal of Johnson*, 43 Ed Dept Rep __, Decision No. 14,943; *Appeal of Crosier*, 42 *id*. 232, Decision No. 14,835; *Appeal of O'Herron*, 40 *id*. 204, Decision No. 14,461).

Based on the record before me, I find respondent's determination that petitioner and his family are not district residents to be reasonable. Petitioner admits that he and his family are not living in the house. Petitioner and his family are not physically present in the district and, therefore, are not district residents (*Appeal of Duhaney*, 38 Ed Dept Rep 94, Decision No. 13,991).

In the event that petitioner and his family relocate to respondent's district at some future date, petitioner can reapply for Joshua's admission to respondent's schools at that time.

THE APPEAL IS DISMISSED.

Decision No. 15,110

Appeal of L.H., on behalf of her granddaughter T.H. and step-granddaughter M.S., from action of the Board of Education of the Rush-Henrietta Central School District regarding residency.

(August 31, 2004)

APPEARANCES OF COUNSEL

William C. Dedes, Esq., attorney for petitioner

DesMarteau & Beale, attorneys for respondent, *George DesMarteau, Esq.*, of counsel

DECISION OF THE COMMISSIONER

MILLS, Commissioner.—Petitioner challenges the determination of the Board of Education of the Rush-Henrietta Central School District ("respondent") that her granddaughter, T.H., and step-granddaughter, M.S., are not district residents. The appeal must be dismissed.

T.H. has attended respondent's schools since approximately September 2000, and M.S. since approximately February 2001, based upon their father's/step-father's representation that he (their "father") and their mother resided with his parents (petitioner and her husband) on Sussex Road within respondent's district.

During the 2003-2004 school year, T.H.'s school needed to contact someone to transport her from school. Although her student file listed petitioner as the first person to contact in such a situation, T.H. asked that her mother be contacted instead and provided the school with her mother's telephone number. After learning that this telephone number was for a residence on Appleton Street in Rochester, within the City School District of the City of Rochester, respondent's Director of Student Management & School Safety ("director") conducted a residency investigation.

During the investigation, it was discovered that the girls' father and mother were residing together at the Appleton Street residence in Rochester, outside respondent's district. According to the director's affidavit, the girls' father had moved to Rochester to live with their mother in February 2001, at the same time that M.S. moved into petitioner's home. The director further learned that, on June 22, 2001, the Monroe County Family Court appointed petitioner guardian of both girls. The director claims that, on at least two occasions, the girls' father informed him that T.H. is listed as an insured under his health care policy and that he contributes to the financial support of both girls.

By letter dated March 31, 2004, the director advised the girls' mother that he had determined that T.H. and M.S. were not district residents and would be excluded from respondent's schools after April 7, 2004.

On April 27, 2004, the director held a residency conference with petitioner and the girls' parents. According to the director, during this conference, both parents stated that they are involved in the girls' educational programs and attend parent-teacher conferences. They also acknowledged that the girls were frequently at their Appleton Street residence, including most weekends. They claimed that they made the decision to give custody of M.S. to petitioner because she was experiencing some emotional problems as a result of the death of a family member in her mother's home.

By letter dated May 13, 2004, the director affirmed his March 31, 2004, decision that T.H. and M.S. were not district residents and stated that they would be excluded after May 21, 2004. This appeal ensued. Petitioner's request for interim relief was granted on June 7, 2004.

Petitioner contends that T.H. and M.S. are district residents because their parents have transferred guardianship and surrendered parental control to her. To substantiate her claim, petitioner submitted her Letters of Guardianship, her 2000 school tax bill, T.H.'s Henrietta Public Library Card, M.S.'s discharge summary from Niagara Falls Medical Center and a dental appointment reminder, statements from a pediatric practice, a mailing from the Girl Scouts, a social security check and a birthday party invitation all addressed to T.H. and/or M.S. at petitioner's address on Sussex Road.

Respondent argues that petitioner has failed to demonstrate that T.H. and M.S. are district residents because the transfer of their custody and control to petitioner was neither total nor permanent. Respondent further argues that the primary reason they are living with petitioner is to attend respondent's schools. Respondent contends that M.S.'s discharge summary also supports this conclusion.

Education Law §3202(1) provides in pertinent part:

> A person over five and under twenty-one years of age who has not received a high school diploma is entitled to attend the public schools maintained in the district in which such person resides without the payment of tuition.

The purpose of this statute is to limit the obligation of school districts to provide tuition-free education to students whose parents or legal guardians reside within the district (*Appeal of Humphrey*, 43 Ed Dept Rep __, Decision No. 14,940; *Appeal of Thomas*, 41 *id.* 84, Decision No. 14,622; *Appeal of Oliver*, 41 *id.* 30, Decision No. 14,603). A child's residence is presumed to be that of his or her parents or legal guardian (*Appeal of Humphrey, supra*; *Appeal of Thomas, supra*; *Appeal of Santana*, 40 Ed Dept Rep 57, Decision No. 14,420). This presumption may be rebutted upon a determination that there has been a total, and presumably permanent, transfer of custody and control to someone residing in the district (*Appeal of Maxwell*, 42 Ed Dept Rep 134, Decision No. 14,799; *Appeal of Donohue*, 41 *id.* 26, Decision No. 14,601; *Appeal of Juarez*, 39 *id.* 184, Decision No. 14,208). While it is not necessary to establish parental custody and control through a formal guardianship proceeding (*Appeal of Burdi*, 39 Ed Dept Rep 176, Decision No. 14,206), it is necessary to demonstrate that a particular location is a child's permanent residence, and that the individuals exercising control have full authority and responsibility with respect to the child's support and custody (*Appeal of Burdi, supra*; *Appeal of Garretson*, 31 Ed Dept Rep 542, Decision No. 12,729).

Moreover, where the sole reason a child is residing with someone other than the parent is to take advantage of the schools of the district, the child has not established residence (*Appeal of Donohue, supra*; *Appeal of Cron*, 38 Ed Dept Rep 149, Decision No. 14,005;

Appeal of a Student with a Disability, 37 *id.* 29, Decision No. 13,796). Parents may not transfer custody or legal guardianship of their children merely to achieve residence status for the children to take advantage of the local schools (*Matter of Proios*, 111 Misc 2d 252; *Appeal of a Student with a Disability, supra*; *Appeal of O'Malley*, 35 Ed Dept Rep 550, Decision No. 13,629). Even if custody orders or letters of guardianship are issued by a court, the presumption of a child's residence with the guardian or custodian can be rebutted if it can be shown that the guardianship or transfer of custody was established merely for the purpose of circumventing a district's nonresident policy (*Appeal of Gilbert*, 37 Ed Dept Rep 43, Decision No. 13,798).

I agree that the purported transfer of T.H.'s and M.S.'s custody and control to petitioner is not total or permanent. The record shows that the girls' parents contribute to their financial support, are involved with their educational programs and attend their parent-teacher conferences. In addition, the parents acknowledged to the director that the girls frequently visit their Appleton Street residence and spend most weekends with them. The petition also states that the girls will only live with petitioner until they graduate from high school.

In addition, there is sufficient evidence that the girls are living with petitioner for the purpose of attending respondent's schools. M.S.'s discharge summary states that her parents felt that her main difficulty was with her school situation, that she was picked on by her peers, that she had difficulty with her teachers and peers and that her parents were discussing the possibility of moving out of Rochester so that she could attend a different school. M.S. moved to petitioner's home shortly after her discharge. Nowhere in the discharge summary does it state that she was experiencing emotional problems due to the death of a family member.

Also, when applying for guardianship, petitioner indicated that the girls' mother worked evenings and was unable to care for her children. Later, the mother told the director that she no longer worked evenings and in fact, operates a in-home day care business.

A student may establish residence apart from his or her parents for other bona fide reasons, such as family conflict (*Appeal of Donohue, supra*; *Appeal of Burdi, supra*; *Appeal of Menci*, 35 Ed Dept Rep 61, Decision No. 13,465), or the hardships of single parenting (*Appeal of Burdi, supra*; *Appeal of McMullan*, 29 Ed Dept Rep 310,

Decision No. 12,304). There is no evidence of such a bona fide reason in this case.

A residency determination will not be set aside unless it is arbitrary and capricious (*Appeal of Wingert*, 43 Ed Dept Rep ___, Decision No. 15,059; *Appeal of Vazquez*, 42 *id*. 245, Decision No. 14,841). On the record before me, I cannot find that respondent's residency determination is arbitrary and capricious.

THE APPEAL IS DISMISSED.

Decision No. 15,111

Appeal of D.L., on behalf of her daughter J.Q., from action of the Board of Education of the Bayport-Blue Point Union Free School District regarding exclusion from school due to lack of immunization.

(August 31, 2004)

APPEARANCES OF COUNSEL

Felicia Pasculli, Esq., attorney for petitioner

Cooper, Sapir & Cohen, P.C., attorneys for respondent, *David M. Cohen, Esq*., of counsel

DECISION OF THE COMMISSIONER

MILLS, Commissioner.—Petitioner appeals the determination of the Bayport-Blue Point Union Free School District ("respondent") that her daughter is not entitled to an exemption from the immunization requirements under Public Health Law ("PHL") §2164. The appeal must be dismissed.

In April 2003, J.Q. transferred to respondent's high school from the Center Moriches Union Free School District. In September 2003, respondent received J.Q.'s school records, which indicated that she had received all required immunizations from her birth in 1987 through 1994, but had not received her required Hepatitis B vaccination. When respondent asked petitioner about this, she responded by submitting a letter dated September 24, 2003, requesting an exemption from the vaccination based on "religion and beliefs that nothing be placed into our body that doesn't belong there."

Respondent's attorney and assistant superintendent met with petitioner on October 22, 2003, to interview her concerning the request for an exemption. According to respondent, which petitioner does not deny, during this interview petitioner admitted that J.Q. had received all required immunizations between 1987 and 1994, and had also received a Mantoux test for tuberculosis in August 2002. Petitioner explained that J.Q. had had a number of adverse reactions to various medications until the age of two and a half. She also explained that she had become more deeply involved in her belief in God, and felt nothing should be placed in the body that could be damaging or that could offset the flow of blood. She admits, however, that her daughter eats processed foods even though chemicals in foods may be damaging.

Respondent claims that petitioner also stated that immunizations are experimental and that she and her daughter are concerned with adverse reactions. Petitioner stated that her daughter's health was her primary concern, but she was not seeking a medical exemption from immunization because it is costly and difficult to obtain.

By letter dated November 6, 2003, respondent denied petitioner's request. The letter gave no reason for the denial but stated that respondent would review a request for a medical exemption if proper documentation was provided. This appeal ensued. Petitioner's request for interim relief was denied on December 31, 2003.

Petitioner argues that it is her sincere and genuinely held religious belief that one must prohibit the introduction of any foreign substance into the bloodstream, including immunizations. She maintains that this belief has developed through her practice of the Catholic faith and her study of religion over the past several years. She asserts that many vaccines are derived from cells of aborted fetuses, and allowing her daughter to receive them would be an endorsement of pro-abortion ideals which are contrary to her religious beliefs. Petitioner also claims that her application for a religious exemption for immunization was granted in 2000 by another school district in Suffolk County.

Respondent alleges that petitioner has failed to state a claim upon which relief can be granted. It also contends that petitioner failed to verify her affidavit and that its determination was not arbitrary and capricious. Respondent argues that the true basis of petitioner's opposition to the vaccine is medical, not religious. Respondent also avers that the vaccine for Hepatitis B is not produced with human blood or blood product.

I will first address respondent's assertion concerning petitioner's failure to verify her affidavit. Affidavit is defined as "[a] written or printed declaration or statement of facts, made voluntarily, and confirmed by the oath or affirmation of the party making it, taken before a person having authority to administer such oath or affirmation" (Black's Law Dictionary 58 [6th ed 1990]). While it is true that an unsworn statement is not a valid affidavit, the "affidavit" in this case is annexed to the petition and precedes the verification thereto. In these circumstances, and in the absence of any prejudice to respondent, I will in my discretion, accept petitioner's unsworn statement (*see*, *Appeal of Ravix*, 36 Ed Dept Rep 89, Decision No. 13,667).

The issue in this appeal is whether petitioner's opposition to immunization stems from sincerely held religious beliefs. Whether a religious belief is sincerely held can be a difficult factual determination that must be made, in the first instance, by school district officials (*Appeal of Quigley*, 41 Ed Dept Rep 399, Decision No. 14,724; *Appeal of Bork*, 39 *id.* 549, Decision No. 14,307; *Appeal of Murphy*, 34 *id.* 648, Decision No. 13,439). In making this determination, school officials must make a good faith effort to assess the credibility of petitioner's statements and sincerity and may consider petitioner's demeanor and forthrightness (*Appeal of Quigley*, *supra*). While school officials are not required to simply accept a statement of religious belief without some explanation, they similarly should not simply reject a statement without further examination (*Appeal of Murphy*, *supra*). The exemption from immunization does not extend to persons whose views are founded upon medical or purely moral considerations, scientific or secular theories, or philosophical and personal beliefs (*Farina v. Bd. of Educ. of the City of New York*, 116 F Supp 2d 503). It is not necessary, however, for persons to be members of a recognized religious organization whose teachings oppose inoculation (*Sherr v. Northport-East Northport Union Free School Dist.*, 672 F Supp 81).

In an appeal to the Commissioner, petitioner has the burden of demonstrating a clear legal right to the relief requested and the burden of establishing the facts upon which he seeks relief (8 NYCRR §275.10; *Appeal of Garmaeva*, 43 Ed Dept Rep ___, Decision No. 14,988; *Appeal of Goldin*, 43 *id.* ___, Decision No. 14,904).

Respondent's administrators gave petitioner a full opportunity to explain her position at their meeting on October 22, 2003. At that time, petitioner gave several reasons for her objection to immunization. After affording petitioner an opportunity to explain her beliefs, and after assessing her credibility, respondent's administrators found that petitioner failed to demonstrate that her opposition to immunization stems from sincerely held religious beliefs. Respondent thus concluded that petitioner was more concerned with the effect of the Hepatitis B vaccine on her daughter's physical health than on her spiritual well-being. Based on the record before me, I cannot find that respondent's determination was arbitrary or capricious.

THE APPEAL IS DISMISSED.

Decision No. 15,112

Application to reopen the Appeals of FATHER CONSTANTINE L. SITARAS and SAINT BASIL ACADEMY, on behalf of E.M., S.M., and A.P., et al., from action of the Board of Education of the Garrison Union Free School District regarding residency.

(September 1, 2004)

APPEARANCES OF COUNSEL

Michael K. Lambert, Esq., attorney for petitioners

Donoghue, Thomas, Auslander & Drohan, attorneys for respondent, *Daniel Petigrow, Esq.*, of counsel

DECISION OF THE COMMISSIONER

Respondent Board of Education of the Garrison Union Free School District seeks to reopen *Appeals of Sitaras, et al.* (43 Ed Dept Rep __, Decision No. 15,044) which, in a consolidated decision, sustained in part a challenge by St. Basil Academy ("St. Basil") and its Executive Director, Father Constantine Sitaras ("petitioners") to respondent's determination that 26 students residing at St. Basil are not district residents. The application must be denied.

Section 276.8 of the Commissioner's regulations governs applications to reopen. It provides that such applications are addressed solely to the discretion of the Commissioner and will not be granted in the absence of a showing that the original decision was rendered under a misapprehension of fact or that there is new and material evidence that was not available at the time the decision was made.

In the underlying appeal, I found, among other things, that although petitioners failed to establish that the children at issue were district residents, those children who have a parent or guardian residing in New York State are entitled, pursuant to Education Law §3202(6), to attend school in respondent's district on a tuition basis at the expense of the child's school district of residence or responsible social services district.

Respondent alleges that my determination that Education Law §3202(6) governs is based on a misapprehension of fact. Specifically, respondent contends that St. Basil is not covered by Education Law §3202(6) because it operates a private boarding school. Respondent submits a number of documents to support this contention. Respondent also asserts that because it operates only a kindergarten through grade eight (K-8) school, it cannot "receive" high school age children pursuant to Education Law §3202(6). Finally, respondent contends that it was not given the opportunity, as provided in Education Law §3202(6), to establish that it has valid and sufficient reasons for refusing to receive the St. Basil children for instruction in its schools. Respondent therefore attempts to do so in this application for reopening.

The application must be dismissed. I find no misapprehension of fact in the original decision, nor do I find any new and material evidence that was not available at the time of the original decision. Contrary to respondent's assertions, the record establishes that, although St. Basil is chartered to operate a boarding school, it has not done so since 1997. Moreover, respondent has failed to establish that any of the information it seeks to submit was unavailable at the time I rendered my determination.

A reopening may not be used to augment previously undeveloped factual assertions and arguments or to advance new legal arguments (*Application to reopen Appeal of Osoris*, 38 Ed Dept Rep 273, Decision No. 14,031; *Application to reopen the Appeal of the Bd. of Educ. of the Longwood Cent. School Dist.*, 36 *id.* 245, Decision No. 13,714; *Application to reopen the Appeal of a Student with a Disability*, 33 *id.* 659, Decision No. 13,185). Accordingly, I will not address respondent's claim that it cannot "receive" high school children because it only operates a K-8 school, a fact explicitly acknowledged in my decision. Similarly, I will not address respondent's new legal argument that it has "valid and sufficient reasons" to refuse to receive the St. Basil children in its schools under Education Law §3202(6).

THE APPLICATION IS DENIED.

Decision No. 15,113

Appeal of C.F., on behalf of his granddaughter K.F., from action of the Board of Education of the Sewanhaka Central High School District regarding residency.

(September 7, 2004)

APPEARANCES OF COUNSEL

Douglas E. Libby, Esq., attorney for respondent

DECISION OF THE COMMISSIONER

MILLS, Commissioner.—Petitioner, a district resident, appeals the determination of the Board of Education of the Sewanhaka Central High School District ("respondent") that his granddaughter, K.F., is not a district resident. The appeal must be dismissed.

K.F.'s parents were divorced in October 2003. Her mother, who resides in a neighboring district, was granted legal custody of K.F. and her brother, who resides in Florida with their father. In January 2004, K.F.'s mother asked petitioner to let K.F. live with him because K.F. was skipping school and having discipline problems at home. K.F. moved in with petitioner and she attended elementary school in the district.

In April 2004, petitioner submitted a registration form for K.F. to attend the district's Floral Park Memorial High School for the 2004-2005 school year. By letter dated April 22, 2004, an administrative assistant to respondent's superintendent informed petitioner that K.F. was not entitled to attend the schools of the district on the basis of "Parental Residence Out-of-District and Custody Concerns." By letter dated April 26, 2004, petitioner appealed that decision.

On May 11, 2004, a residency hearing was held at which petitioner and K.F.'s mother testified. Petitioner testified that K.F. lives with him and that the arrangement would last as long as necessary. When asked if he was supporting K.F. financially, he replied "more or less," but estimated that K.F.'s mother provides about 15% financial support. He also stated that he could not claim K.F. on his 2004 income tax because her mother had legal custody. K.F.'s mother testified that she supplied K.F. with whatever she needed when she visited on weekends, that K.F. has medical insurance through her, that she and petitioner would both make decisions regarding K.F.'s schooling, and that petitioner has physical custody of K.F. She further stated that she "didn't want to release custody because I'm not getting rid of my child, and so I'm not renouncing to my custody . . . to the custody that is rightfully mine."

By letter dated June 9, 2004, the hearing officer concluded that the evidence and testimony did not establish that there had been a total and permanent transfer of care, custody and control from K.F.'s mother to petitioner, and therefore the presumption that K.F. resided with her mother outside the district had not been rebutted. This appeal ensued. Petitioner's request for interim relief was denied on July 22, 2004.

Petitioner asserts that K.F. resides with him in the district and he has assumed full responsibility for her upbringing and educational needs. Respondent claims that the appeal is untimely. It also asserts that the hearing officer's decision is rational and supported by the record.

I will first address the procedural issue. An appeal to the Commissioner must be commenced within 30 days from the making of the decision or the performance of the act complained of, unless excused by the Commissioner for good cause shown (8 NYCRR §275.16). Respondent asserts that the appeal must be dismissed as untimely because petitioner did not properly serve the petition until July 13, 2004, 34 days after the hearing officer issued her determination on June 9, 2004. However, there is nothing in the record to indicate when petitioner actually received the determination. Affording the usual five days for mailing, excluding Sundays and holidays (*Appeal of Spensieri*, 40 Ed Dept Rep 51, Decision No. 14,419), the date of receipt would be June 14, 2004, and the appeal is thus timely. I need not discuss, therefore, the delay caused by the initial improper service of the petition on the administrative assistant to respondent's superintendent.

Education Law §3202(1) provides in pertinent part:

> A person over five and under twenty-one years of age who has not received a high school diploma is entitled to attend the public schools maintained in the district in which such person resides without the payment of tuition.

The purpose of this statute is to limit the obligation of school districts to provide tuition-free education and related services to students whose parents or legal guardians reside within the district (*Appeal of Sloley-Raymond*, 44 Ed Dept Rep ___, Decision No. 15,085; *Appeal of J.G.*, 43 *id.* ___, Decision No. 15,045; *Appeal of Y.R.*, 42 *id.* 376, Decision No. 14,886).

A child's residence is presumed to be that of his or her parents (*Appeal of J.G.*, *supra*; *Appeal of T.C.*, 43 Ed Dept Rep ___, Decision No. 14,910; *Appeal of Donohue*, 41 *id.* 26, Decision No. 14,601). That presumption can be rebutted where it is shown that the parents have relinquished total custody and control to someone residing within the district (*Appeal of Maxwell*, 42 Ed Dept Rep 134, Decision No. 14,799; *Appeal of Lapidus*, 40 *id.* 21, Decision No. 14,408). While it is not necessary to establish parental custody and control through a formal guardianship proceeding, it is necessary to demonstrate that a particular location is a child's permanent residence, and that the individual exercising control has full authority and responsibility with respect to the child's support and custody (*Appeal of Maxwell*, *supra*).

Moreover, where the sole reason the child is residing with someone other than the parent is to take advantage of the schools of the district, the child has not established residence (*Appeal of Hutchinson*, 42 Ed Dept Rep 310, Decision No. 14,865; *Appeal of Maxwell*, *supra*; *Appeal of Lapidus*, *supra*). However, a student may establish residence apart from his or her parents for other bona fide reasons, such as family conflict (*Appeal of Maxwell*, *supra*; *Appeal of Lapidus*, *supra*; *Appeal of Juarez*, 39 Ed Dept Rep 184, Decision No. 14,208).

It is undisputed that K.F. lives with petitioner within respondent's district. At the time of the hearing, K.F.'s mother indicated that K.F. stayed with her on weekends, and that she purchased clothes, food and necessities when K.F. visited, which petitioner estimated to be 15% of K.F.'s support. According to the petition, however, K.F.'s relationship with her mother is "deplorable," and the scheduled weekend visits between K.F. and her mother have deteriorated to just a few hours, with no overnights or weekend visits. However, at the hearing, K.F.'s mother stated that she was not relinquishing custody because it was rightfully hers.

While there may be bona fide family issues unrelated to the district's educational program that prompted K.F.'s move, K.F.'s mother has not relinquished custody and control. Therefore, in light of the mother's statement, I am constrained to find that respondent's determination was not arbitrary and capricious and it will not be set aside.

While the appeal must be dismissed, I note that petitioner retains the right to reapply to the district for admission of his granddaughter at any time should circumstances change (*Appeal of Holder*, 44 Ed Dept Rep ___, Decision No. 15,088; *Appeal of Normandin*, 43 *id.* ___, Decision No. 14,950).

THE APPEAL IS DISMISSED.

Decision No. 15,114

Appeal of JOSETTA WALKER, on behalf of her daughter NADIRAH GATHERS, from action of the Board of Education of the Roosevelt Union Free School District regarding transportation.

(September 17, 2004)

APPEARANCES OF COUNSEL

Koehler & Isaacs, LLP, attorneys for petitioner, *Joey Jackson, Esq.*, of counsel

Jaspan Schlesinger Hoffman, LLP, attorneys for respondent, *Lawrence J. Tenenbaum, Esq.*, of counsel

DECISION OF THE COMMISSIONER

AHEARN, Acting Commissioner.—Petitioner appeals the determination of the Board of Education of the Roosevelt Union Free School District ("respondent") denying her daughter, Nadirah, transportation to a nonpublic school. The appeal must be dismissed.

In December 2003, petitioner withdrew her daughter from respondent's elementary school, enrolled her in a nonpublic school, and requested that respondent provide transportation. By letter dated January 13, 2004, respondent's assistant superintendent for business advised petitioner that the district would transport Nadirah for a monthly charge of $449. By letter dated February 13, 2004, petitioner appealed this decision to respondent. By letter dated March 17, 2004, respondent upheld the decision to deny petitioner's request.

Respondent apparently transported Nadirah to the nonpublic school in February, March and April, 2004, notwithstanding petitioner's failure to pay the sum requested, but refused to transport her thereafter. Petitioner commenced her appeal on May 24, 2004. Her request for interim relief was denied on June 18, 2004.

The appeal must be dismissed as untimely. An appeal to the Commissioner of Education must be commenced within 30 days of the making of the decision or the performance of the act complained of, unless excused by the Commissioner for good cause shown (8 NYCRR §275.16; *Appeal of Trader*, 43 Ed Dept Rep ___, Decision No. 14,967; *Appeal of Recore*, 42 *id.* 283, Decision No. 14,856; *Appeal of Phillips*, 40 *id.* 241, Decision No. 14,471). Respondent notified petitioner by letter dated March 17, 2004, that her transportation request was denied. Petitioner did not commence this appeal until May 24, 2004, well beyond the 30-day timeframe, and offers no excuse for the delay.

The appeal must also be dismissed as moot. The Commissioner of Education will only consider matters in actual controversy and will not render a decision on a state of facts that no longer exists or which subsequent events have laid to rest (*Appeal of Cordisco*, 44 Ed Dept Rep ___, Decision No. 15,089; *Appeal of Schrader*, 42 *id.* 47, Decision No. 14,771; *Appeal of E.F.*, 42 *id.* 23, Decision No. 14,762). Since the 2003-2004 school year has ended, petitioner's request for transportation during that school year is moot. The record also reflects that respondent has granted petitioner's timely request for transportation for the 2004-2005 school year. Accordingly, there is no possibility of any further meaningful relief and the appeal must be dismissed.

THE APPEAL IS DISMISSED.

Decision No. 15,115

Appeal of J.J., on behalf of P.S., from action of the Board of Education of the Cobleskill-Richmondville Central School District regarding student discipline.

Appeal of J.J., on behalf of M.S., from action of the Board of Education of the Cobleskill-Richmondville Central School District regarding student discipline.

(September 22, 2004)

APPEARANCES OF COUNSEL

Michael West, Esq., attorney for respondent

DECISION OF THE COMMISSIONER

MILLS, Commissioner.—In separate appeals, petitioner challenges respondent's suspension of her children, P.S. and M.S., for the remainder of the 2003-2004 school year. Because the appeals raise common issues of law and fact, they are consolidated for decision. The appeals must be dismissed.

On September 9, 2003, P.S. and M.S. were involved in an altercation on school premises with another student, J.S., who allegedly uttered racist slurs at them. As a result, P.S. punched J.S. on the side of the face and M.S. threw a book at J.S., which missed him and struck a teacher's aide instead. M.S. and P.S. were suspended on that date, pending a superintendent's hearing.

M.S. and P.S. were charged with being insubordinate, disorderly and violent and endangering the safety, morals, health and welfare of himself/herself and others. A joint hearing was held on September 17 and September 26, 2003. The hearing officer issued his findings of fact and recommendation on October 8, 2003, concluding that M.S. and P.S. each committed the offense charged and recommending that they be suspended for the remainder of the school year.

Respondent's superintendent issued a decision dated October 14, 2003, which modified the hearing officer's recommended penalty to the extent that the students would be allowed to petition the school district to return sooner. Petitioner subsequently appealed to respondent. At its November 10, 2003, meeting, respondent upheld the superintendent's October 14, 2003, decision. Although it appears that petitioner submitted petitions for the readmission of M.S. and P.S. on December 10, 2003, there is no indication in the record that the students were allowed to return to school prior to the end of the school year.

Respondent contends that the appeals must be dismissed as untimely. An appeal to the Commissioner of Education pursuant to Education Law §310 must be initiated within 30 days of the action or decision complained of, unless excused by the Commissioner for good cause shown (8 NYCRR §275.16). Petitioner commenced her appeals on December 9, 2003, within 30 days of respondent's November 10,

2003, determination upholding the superintendent's decision. Therefore, I find both appeals to be timely.

Turning to the merits, I note that petitioner does not dispute her children's involvement in the altercation and admits that P.S. struck J.S. and that M.S. threw a book at J.S., inadvertently striking a teacher's aide. However, petitioner contends that the penalty of suspension for the remainder of the school year is excessive.

In cases of student discipline, the sanction imposed must be proportionate to the severity of the offense involved (*Appeal of A.L., Jr.*, 42 Ed Dept Rep 368, Decision No. 14,883; *Appeal of T.N.*, 42 *id.* 235, Decision No. 14,836). The test to be applied in reviewing a penalty is whether it is so excessive as to warrant substitution of the Commissioner's judgment for that of the board (*Appeal of A.L., Jr., supra*; *Appeal of T.N., supra*; *Appeal of D.C.*, 41 Ed Dept Rep 277, Decision No. 14,684).

Upon the record before me, I find that the students' suspension for the remainder of the school year is not so excessive as to require substitution of my judgment for that of respondent.

The teacher's aide suffered serious physical injury as a result of being struck by the book thrown by M.S., including a cut to the inside lip that required eight stitches, a broken tooth that required a root canal, headaches, dizziness and a possible concussion. The record further indicates that even more than three months after the incident, the employee still had not returned to work. Because of the serious injury that occurred as a result of M.S.'s conduct, the penalty imposed in this case is distinguishable from that imposed in *Appeal of Esther F.*, 39 Ed Dept Rep 357, Decision No. 14,258, and other cases cited by petitioner.

With respect to P.S., the record indicates that in addition to punching J.S. in the face, he also used obscene and threatening language, screamed and yelled, and incited M.S. and other students to participate in the altercation. The hearing officer stated that the hearing testimony indicated that immediately prior to P.S.'s assault on J.S., the latter student was in the process of withdrawing, but that P.S.'s conduct caused the incident to escalate into a violent event.

I also find without merit petitioner's contention that respondent failed to consider that J.S. allegedly used racial slurs to incite M.S. and P.S. to engage in reckless behavior. The hearing officer specifically noted in his findings and recommendation that the behavior and culpability of J.S., by his use of obscene, threatening or inciteful language, was reprehensible, but did not justify the subsequent escalation of the event by M.S. and P.S. into one of physical violence.

THE APPEALS ARE DISMISSED.

Decision No. 15,116

Application to reopen the Appeal of STEPHANIE KUSHNER from action of the Board of Education of the East Williston Union Free School District regarding a school district election.

(September 22, 2004)

APPEARANCES OF COUNSEL

Guercio & Guercio, attorneys for respondent, *Gary L. Steffanetta, Esq*., of counsel

DECISION OF THE COMMISSIONER

MILLS, Commissioner.—Petitioner seeks to reopen *Appeal of Kushner*, 43 Ed Dept Rep ___, Decision No. 15,040, regarding the decision of the Board of Education of the East Williston Union Free School District ("respondent") to reject her challenge to the eligibility of another board candidate. The application must be denied.

Section 276.8 of the Commissioner's regulations governs applications to reopen. It provides that such applications are addressed solely to the discretion of the Commissioner and will not be granted in the absence of a showing that the original decision was rendered under a misapprehension of fact or that there is new and material evidence that was not available at the time the decision was made.

Petitioner argues that the appeal should be reopened because she alleges I did not consider the definition of a "city" or the ramifications of violating a board policy. Respondent contends that the application does not set forth any new and material evidence, and that the decision clearly addresses the material facts and the issue in dispute.

Petitioner has not demonstrated that the decision was rendered under a misapprehension of fact nor has she presented any new or material evidence that was not available at the time the decision was made. Essentially, she has attempted to reargue the original appeal. My decision references petitioner's failure to establish that her opponent held a "city" office and indicates that respondent should review its policy which contained inapplicable language. It is well settled that mere reargument of issues presented in a prior appeal is not a basis for reopening an appeal (*Application of Satler*, 41 Ed Dept Rep 293, Decision No. 14,690; *Application of Tanzer*, 40 *id*. 229, Decision No. 14,467).

THE APPLICATION TO REOPEN IS DENIED.

Decision No. 15,117

Appeal of FELICIA M. RITTERS, on behalf of her daughter ALYSE, from action of the Board of Education of the Hyde Park Central School District and Superintendent David Burpee regarding transportation.

(September 22, 2004)

APPEARANCES OF COUNSEL

Donoghue, Thomas, Auslander & Drohan, attorneys for respondents, *Daniel Petigrow, Esq*., of counsel

DECISION OF THE COMMISSIONER

MILLS, Commissioner.—Petitioner appeals the determination of the Board of Education of the Hyde Park Central School District ("respondent board") and its Superintendent, David Burpee, (collectively referred to as "respondents") to deny her daughter, Alyse, door-to-door transportation from their residence to a nonpublic school. The appeal must be dismissed.

On October 6, 2003, petitioner enrolled Alyse in a nonpublic school and submitted a transportation request to respondent board's Transportation Department. Alyse previously attended the district's Haviland Middle School and was transported from her residence to that school. Petitioner's October 6 transportation request asked that Alyse be transported to and from their residence and also to and from a daycare provider on an "as needed" basis. The transportation director offered to transport Alyse to and from the daycare provider, which is located on an existing route. Petitioner refused this arrangement, and respondent board arranged for Alyse to be picked up at a point approximately one mile from petitioner's residence.

This appeal ensued. Petitioner's request for interim relief was denied on December 11, 2003.

Petitioner contends that respondent board should transport Alyse door-to-door from her residence to the nonpublic school she attends. Petitioner asserts that respondent board previously sent a separate bus to transport Alyse to the district's middle school and that extending the existing nonpublic bus route to her residence would be less costly than the prior arrangement. Petitioner contends that another nonpublic student in similar circumstances is receiving transportation and that the district's administrators are discriminating against her and her daughter in retaliation for past complaints.

Respondents argue that the petition should be dismissed as against the superintendent because he was not personally served with the petition. Respondents assert that it was neither arbitrary nor capricious to deny petitioner's request for door-to-door transportation. Respondents also contend that the transportation supervisor offered to transport Alyse to and from the daycare provider named in petitioner's transportation request, but that petitioner refused to accept that arrangement.

Initially, I will address the procedural issue of service. Section 275.8(a) of the Commissioner's regulations requires that the petition be personally served upon each named respondent. Petitioner's affidavit of service does not indicate that she personally served the superintendent, nor has she submitted any response to this defense. Accordingly, the appeal must be dismissed as against the superintendent for lack of service (*Appeal of Lopez*, 44 Ed Dept Rep ___, Decision No. 15,076; *Appeal of Grant*, 42 *id.* 184, Decision No. 14,816).

Pursuant to Education Law §3635(2), a request for transportation to a nonpublic school must be submitted no later than the first day of April preceding the school year for which transportation is requested. The purpose of this deadline is to enable school districts to budget funds and make necessary arrangements to provide transportation reasonably and economically (*Appeal of Calabrese*, 43 Ed Dept Rep __, Decision No. 14,982; *Appeal of Sarant*, 41 *id.* 70, Decision No. 14,617). However, a district may not reject a late request for transportation if there is a reasonable explanation for the delay (Education Law §3635(2)). It is the responsibility of the board of education to determine whether a parent has offered a reasonable explanation for submitting a late request (*Appeal of J.D.*, 42 Ed Dept Rep 373, Decision No. 14,884; *Appeal of Tarricone*, 38 *id.* 623, Decision No. 14,105; *Appeal of Shevlin*, 38 *id.* 365, Decision No. 14,056). The board's determination will not be set aside unless it constitutes an abuse of discretion (*Appeal of J.D.*, *supra*; *Appeal of Tarricone*, *supra*). A belated decision to enroll a student in a private school is not a reasonable explanation for the late submission of a transportation request (*Appeal of J.D.*, *supra*; *Appeal of Attubato*, 38 Ed Dept Rep 511, Decision No. 14,082; *Appeal of Matero*, 36 *id.* 242, Decision No. 13,713).

Even absent a reasonable explanation for the delay, a late transportation request must be granted if the requested transportation can be provided under existing transportation arrangements at no additional cost to the district (*Appeal of Aguanno*, 41 Ed Dept Rep 326, Decision No. 14,700; *Appeal of R.O.*, 40 *id.* 137, Decision No. 14,441; *Appeal of Mogilski*, 37 *id.* 446, Decision No. 13,901). The Commissioner has consistently sustained denials of untimely applications for transportation where the transportation requested would impose additional costs upon the school district (*Appeal of J.D.*, *supra*; *Appeal of Joanne M.*, 40 Ed Dept Rep 686, Decision No. 14,584; *Appeal of Matero*, *supra*.

The parties agree that to accommodate petitioner's request, the district would have to extend an existing bus route four miles. According to respondent board, this extension would cost an additional $1,096.87 in transportation-related labor and maintenance and would result in additional staff supervision costs. Petitioner has not submitted any evidence to refute respondent board's cost estimates.

After reviewing the record in this appeal, I conclude that respondent board did not abuse its discretion in denying petitioner's late request for door-to-door transportation.

As for petitioner's remaining contentions, petitioner did not submit any evidence to support her conclusory allegations of disparate treatment or discrimination. In an appeal to the Commissioner pursuant to Education Law §310, a petitioner has the burden of demonstrating a clear right to the relief requested and the burden of establishing the facts upon which she seeks relief (8 NYCRR §275.10; *Appeal of Nelson*, 44 Ed Dept Rep __, Decision No. 15,082; *Appeal of Green*, 40 *id.* 278, Decision No. 14,479; *Appeal of a Student with a*

Disability, 40 *id.* 121, Decision No. 14,436). Petitioner has failed to meet her burden of proof and those claims must be dismissed.

THE APPEAL IS DISMISSED.

Decision No. 15,118

Appeal of S.Y. from action of the Board of Cooperative Educational Services for Ulster County relating to a personnel matter.

(September 22, 2004)

APPEARANCES OF COUNSEL

Jerold S. Slate, Esq., attorney for petitioner

Kuntz, Spagnuolo, Scapoli & Schiro, P.C., attorneys for respondent, *Vanessa M. Gronbach, Esq.*, of counsel

DECISION OF THE COMMISSIONER

MILLS, Commissioner.—Petitioner challenges actions of the Board of Cooperative Educational Services for Ulster County ("respondent") regarding a personnel memorandum. The appeal must be dismissed.

Petitioner is a culinary arts instructor employed by respondent. By memorandum dated May 9, 2002, petitioner and two other culinary arts teachers expressed concerns about the return of a suspended student, from the Onteora Central School District ("Onteora"), to respondent's culinary arts program. The memorandum was addressed to respondent's Director of Career Technical Education and Adult Services ("Director") and was faxed to Onteora's superintendent.

By memorandum dated May 10, 2002, respondent's school principal addressed their concerns. Thereafter, petitioner received a formal "memo of correction" dated May 21, 2002, from the Director stating that the instructors violated board policy and protocol by directly contacting the Onteora superintendent instead of going through respondent's administrative channels. This memo was placed in petitioner's personnel file.

More than one year later, by letter dated June 4, 2003, petitioner's attorney requested that the "memo of correction" be removed from petitioner's personnel file. The Director agreed to remove the "memo of correction" and replaced it with a memorandum dated June 25, 2003, that stated:

> In May of 2002, you sent a letter to Dr. Hal Rowe, Superintendent of Onteora Schools. Although you were concerned about the potential threat imposed by the behavior of your student and although your intentions were sincere, your direct communication with the superintendent was inappropriate.
>
> Communication with administration from our component districts must flow from you to your Principal and follow an appropriate chain of command.
>
> I appreciate your following these guidelines in the future.

By letter dated July 1, 2003, petitioner's attorney requested an opportunity to meet with respondent, which was denied. A series of correspondence between respondent's attorney and petitioner's attorney ensued, the last of which was dated August 26, 2003. Petitioner commenced this appeal on December 1, 2003.

Petitioner contends that he did not violate any known policy or protocol by directly contacting the Onteora superintendent and that the June 25, 2003, memorandum violated his rights as a teacher and threatened his ability to communicate issues of public safety. Petitioner requests that the memorandum and any other materials connected to the incident be removed from his file and from the records of any educational institutions that might contain copies.

Respondent argues that the appeal is untimely and that petitioner failed to exhaust administrative remedies pursuant to the terms of the collective bargaining agreement. Respondent further maintains that the June 25, 2003, memorandum was a proper exercise of administrative authority, and that the memorandum was not written to forbid petitioner's speech, but to remind petitioner to comply with school policy. Respondent states that the memorandum will be removed from petitioner's file after one year if no similar activity occurs.

The appeal must be dismissed as moot. The Commissioner will only decide matters in actual controversy and will not render a decision on a state of facts which no longer exists or which subsequent events have laid to rest (*Appeal of D.W.*, 43 Ed Dept Rep ___, Decision No. 14,965; *Appeal of L.B.*, 43 *id.* ___, Decision No. 14,952; *Appeal of N.S.*, 42 *id.* 190, Decision No. 14,817). In response to a request from my Office of Counsel pursuant to §275.6 of the Commissioner's regulations, respondent submitted an affirmation from its attorney dated July 16, 2004, that confirms that the memorandum and letter were removed from petitioner's personnel file on June 25, 2004, and that no other documents pertaining to the incident remain in the file or other administrative files. No additional meaningful relief, therefore, can be granted. Accordingly, the appeal is moot.

In light of this disposition, I need not address the parties' remaining contentions or submissions.

THE APPEAL IS DISMISSED.

Decision No. 15,119

Appeal of DAVID E. MERANDY from action of the Board of Education of the Haldane Central School District regarding an election.

(September 30, 2004)

APPEARANCES OF COUNSEL

Keane & Beane, P.C., attorneys for respondent, *Stephanie M. Roebuck, Esq.*, of counsel

DECISION OF THE COMMISSIONER

MILLS, Commissioner.—Petitioner, an unsuccessful candidate for reelection to the Board of Education of the Haldane Central School District ("respondent"), challenges the results of the May 18, 2004, school board election. The appeal must be dismissed.

On May 18, 2004, respondent conducted an election wherein three candidates ran for two seats on the board. Petitioner received 772 votes and the other two candidates received 863 and 778 votes respectively. This appeal ensued. Petitioner's request for interim relief was denied on June 28, 2004.

Petitioner alleges that operational difficulties with, and the attempted repair of, one of the voting machines may have inadvertently affected the results of the school board election, and he questions the number of absentee ballots received. Petitioner requests that the voting machine be examined by a certified technician, that the votes be recounted, that he be granted access to the absentee ballots, and that a new election be conducted, if appropriate. In addition, petitioner requests permission to submit additional information pursuant to §276.5 of the Commissioner's regulations.

Respondent alleges that the voting machine malfunction and attempted repair did not affect the results of the election, and denies knowledge of a problem with the absentee ballot count. Respondent alleges that the appeal should be dismissed for failure to state a cause of action and failure to name the successful candidates as necessary parties. Respondent also alleges that petitioner requests relief that the Commissioner may not grant in an appeal brought pursuant to Education Law §310.

The petition must be dismissed for failure to join necessary parties. A party whose rights would be adversely affected by a determination of an appeal in favor of petitioner is a necessary party and must be joined as such (*Appeal of Milazzo*, 43 Ed Dept Rep ___, Decision No. 14,999; *Appeal of Stolbach*, 43 *id.* ___, Decision No. 14,977; *Appeal of Gilmore and Jordon-Thompson*, 42 *id.* 334, Decision No. 14,874). The rights of the successful candidates would be affected if the school board election were declared void and a new election ordered. Section 275.8(d) of the Commissioner's regulations provides in pertinent part: "If an appeal involves the validity of a school district meeting or election, . . . a copy of the petition must be served upon the trustee or board of trustees or board of education as the case may be, *and upon each person whose right to hold office is disputed and such person must be joined as a respondent*" (emphasis added). Joinder requires that an individual be clearly named as a respondent in the caption of the petition and served with a copy of the notice of petition and petition to inform the individual that he or she should respond to the petition and enter a defense (*Appeal of Milazzo, supra*; *Appeal of Stolbach, supra*; *Appeal of Gilmore and Jordan-Thompson, supra*). In this case, petitioner has not named or personally served the individual members of respondent board who were successful candidates in this election. Therefore, the appeal must be dismissed for failure to join necessary parties.

In light of this disposition, I need not address petitioner's application to submit additional information or the parties' remaining contentions.

THE APPEAL IS DISMISSED.

Decision No. 15,120

Appeal of A.F., on behalf of his son D.F., from action of the Board of Education of the Syosset Central School District regarding student discipline.

(September 30, 2004)

APPEARANCES OF COUNSEL

Reisman, Peirez & Reisman, L.L.P., attorneys for petitioner, *E. Christopher Murray, Esq.*, of counsel

Farrell Fritz, P.C., attorneys for respondent, *A. Kathleen Tomlinson, Esq.*, of counsel

DECISION OF THE COMMISSIONER

MILLS, Commissioner.—Petitioner appeals actions of the Board of Education of the Syosset Central School District ("respondent") regarding the suspension of his son, D.F. The appeal must be dismissed.

At all relevant times, D.F. was an 11-year-old sixth-grade student at one of respondent's middle schools. As part of an English class assignment, D.F. was required to maintain a journal. After completing the assignment, D.F. continued to maintain his journal. In it, he wrote stories of a violent and sexual nature using the names of other students at the school, allegedly with their permission. On October 3, 2003, he read portions of the journal to his English class without incident. According to respondent, the teacher did not hear anything violent or inappropriate because he was busy taking attendance.

Later that day, when D.F. asked if he could read some journal excerpts during his voluntary lunchtime program, the instructor asked to read them first. The instructor found the contents disturbing and notified the school's administration.

After petitioner and his wife met with several school administrators, D.F. was suspended from October 8 through October 15, 2003. A superintendent's hearing was scheduled for October 14, 2003, and rescheduled for October 21, 2003, at petitioner's request. On October 23, 2003, the hearing officer recommended sustaining the charges and imposing a 30-day suspension. By letter dated October 23, 2003, the superintendent adopted the recommendations of the hearing officer.

On October 28, 2003, petitioner's attorney appealed the suspension to respondent. This appeal ensued. Petitioner's request for interim relief was denied on November 14, 2003. By letter dated November 18, 2003, respondent's president notified petitioner that respondent affirmed the superintendent's determination.

Petitioner requests that I overturn the suspension or greatly reduce it. Among other things, respondent maintains that the suspension of D.F. was proper.

The appeal must be dismissed as moot. The Commissioner will only decide matters in actual controversy and will not render a decision on a state of facts which no longer exists or which subsequent events have laid to rest (*Appeal of D.W.*, 43 Ed Dept Rep ___, Decision No. 14,965; *Appeal of L.B.*, 43 *id.* ___, Decision No. 14,952; *Appeal of N.S.*, 42 *id.* 190, Decision No. 14,817). Petitioner does not request expungement of D.F.'s records. Since D.F. has served the suspension, no further meaningful relief can be granted and the appeal must be dismissed as moot (*Appeal of R.R. and K.R.*, 41 Ed Dept Rep 405, Decision No. 14,726; *Appeal of D.H.*, 41 *id.* 142, Decision No. 14,640; *Appeal of N.B.*, 40 *id.* 515, Decision No. 14,542).

In light of this disposition, I need not address the parties' remaining contentions.

THE APPEAL IS DISMISSED.

Decision No. 15,121

Appeal of SUZANNE COWLEY, on behalf of her daughters DANA and KRISTIN, from action of the Board of Education of the Greece Central School District regarding transportation.

(September 30, 2004)

APPEARANCES OF COUNSEL

Harris Beach LLP, attorneys for respondent, *James A. Spitz* and *Laura M. Purcell, Esqs.*, of counsel

DECISION OF THE COMMISSIONER

MILLS, Commissioner.—Petitioner appeals the decision of the Board of Education of the Greece Central School District ("respondent") denying her request to change the location of her daughters' transportation pick-up point. The appeal must be dismissed.

Prior to the 2003-2004 school year, district students were provided transportation directly from home to school. As a cost-saving measure, respondent eliminated door-to-door transportation for the 2003-2004 school year and adopted a system of centralized bus stops. Petitioner's daughters and 22 other children were assigned a pick-up point at the intersection of Long Pond Road and Larkins Crossing.

In the fall of 2003, petitioner and other parents requested that the bus stop be relocated to an allegedly safer address on Long Pond Road, some 30 feet from the intersection. By letter dated December 1, 2003, respondent's director of transportation ("director") denied the request. This appeal ensued.

Petitioner claims that the bus stop is hazardous and that respondent ignored safety concerns and police statistics regarding the intersection. Petitioner asserts that the bus passes the proposed new bus stop, so there would be no rerouting or additional stops. Petitioner asserts, therefore, that respondent has acted arbitrarily and capriciously in denying her request to relocate the bus stop. Petitioner seeks permanent relocation of the bus stop to the Long Pond Road address and confirmation from the district that her children will not suffer any repercussions as a result of her actions.

Respondent asserts that the appeal must be dismissed as untimely. Respondent further contends that petitioner has failed to prove that the district's decision was arbitrary or capricious or that the bus stop at issue is unsafe. Respondent also asserts that petitioner seeks an inappropriate remedy under Education Law §310.

I must first address two procedural issues. Petitioner's reply contains affidavits from a parent and a daycare provider of children who use the bus stop in question. The purpose of a reply is to respond to new material or affirmative defenses set forth in an answer (8 NYCRR §§275.3 and 275.14). A reply is not meant to buttress allegations in the petition or to belatedly add assertions that should have been in the petition (*Appeal of Crosier*, 42 Ed Dept Rep 232, Decision No. 14,835). The affidavits contain allegations that could have been included in the petition. Therefore, while I have reviewed petitioner's reply, I have not considered those portions containing new allegations or exhibits that are not responsive to new material or affirmative defenses set forth in the answer.

The appeal must also be dismissed as untimely. An appeal to the Commissioner must be commenced within 30 days from the making of the decision or the performance of the act complained of, unless excused by the Commissioner for good cause shown (8 NYCRR §275.16). By letter dated December 1, 2003, respondent notified petitioner of its "final decision" on her request and that it "consider[ed] the matter closed." Petitioner acknowledged receiving the letter on December 3, 2003, which therefore required her to initiate this appeal no later than January 2, 2004. Respondent states that district offices were open for business on that date, yet petitioner failed to serve the petition until January 6, 2004, rendering the appeal untimely.

Even if it were not dismissed on procedural grounds, the appeal would be dismissed on the merits. A board of education may exercise its discretion when designating pick-up points provided that the board uses care in exercising such discretion (*Appeal of Eason*, 43 Ed Dept Rep ___, Decision No. 14,970; *Appeal of Gulla*, 39 *id.* 716, Decision No. 14,358; *Appeal of Rheaume-Wellenc*, 37 *id.* 83, Decision No. 13,811). In establishing pick-up points, a board of education must consider and balance considerations of pupil safety and convenience, routing efficiency and costs (*Appeal of Eason*, *supra*; *Appeal of Gulla*, *supra*; *Appeal of Rheaume-Wellenc*, *supra*; *Appeal of Warner*, 37 Ed Dept Rep 469, Decision No. 13,907).

Education Law §3635 does not require a school district to provide students transportation directly to and from their homes (*Ossant v. Millard*, 72 Misc. 2d 384; *Appeal of O'Connell*, 37 Ed Dept Rep 22, Decision No. 13,794) and boards of education have discretion to require students to walk to pick-up points from which transportation will be provided (*Appeal of Raymond*, 39 Ed Dept Rep 774, Decision No. 14,376; *Appeal of Hobbs*, 38 *id.* 203, Decision No. 14,015; *Appeal of Marsh*, 36 *id.* 134, Decision No. 13,680). It is the responsibility of the parents, not the district, to see that their child safely reaches the pick-up point (*Pratt v. Robinson*, 39 NY2d 554; *Appeal of Rheaume-Wellenc*, *supra*).

According to the director, the change to a centralized system generated over 1,400 parental requests for pick-up point changes. She states that as of February 2004, 828 changes were approved where: all parents of students assigned to a bus stop agreed to a location change; or there were medical needs of a student; or safety factors required a change.

Here, the parents of two children at the bus stop in question would not agree to relocate the stop. The district investigated changing the stop of those two students to achieve unanimity. However, the bus operations expeditor ("expeditor") concluded that was not feasible because it would have required the two students to walk a greater distance and to walk in the streets in the winter.

The director and the expeditor also analyzed the safety of the bus stop using the criteria for child safety zones under Education Law §3635-b. According to the expeditor, the children walk on a sidewalk approximately five feet wide located approximately eight feet from the road, and they do not cross an intersection. Accordingly, he found no basis to recommend a change in pick-up point to the director. He also noted no other hazards to warrant a recommendation to change the stop location. The director's supervisor and the assistant superintendent for finance also visited the site and determined that a change was not warranted.

After examining the evidence presented by the parties, I conclude that respondent acted reasonably and within its discretion in declining to change the pick-up point. The record indicates that respondent thoroughly investigated petitioner's concerns and applied consistent criteria in evaluating petitioner's request. While I am sympathetic to petitioner's concerns about safety, I find no basis to overturn respondent's decision.

In light of this disposition, I need not address petitioner's remaining arguments.

THE APPEAL IS DISMISSED.

Decision No. 15,122

Appeal of A.S. and S.K., on behalf of their son S.S., from action of the Board of Education of the Valley Stream Central High School District regarding student discipline.

(October 7, 2004)

APPEARANCES OF COUNSEL

Guercio & Guercio, attorneys for respondent, *John P. Sheahan, Esq.*, of counsel

DECISION OF THE COMMISSIONER

MILLS, Commissioner.—Petitioners appeal the suspension of their son, S.S., by the Board of Education of the Valley Stream Central High School District ("respondent"). The appeal must be dismissed.

By separate letters dated December 19, 2003, petitioners and S.S. were notified of a hearing scheduled for January 8, 2004, on charges against S.S. for disorderly conduct and endangering the health, safety and welfare of others by possessing a knife on school property on December 18, 2003. At the time of the incident, S.S. was a 17 year-old senior in respondent's high school.

After two adjournments requested by petitioners, a hearing was scheduled for February 9, 2004, before respondent's assistant superintendent as the designated hearing officer. Petitioners, S.S., their attorney, respondent's attorney, and the high school principal appeared on that date. After the hearing officer explained the hearing process and informed petitioners and S.S. of their rights, including their right to appeal the outcome of the hearing, respondent's attorney informed the hearing officer that the parties had agreed to a stipulation, the terms of which were then read into the hearing record. The parties agreed that S.S. would plead no contest to the charges and serve a five-month suspension until the end of the 2003-2004 school year, and that the matter would be resolved without further administrative proceedings by the district or petitioners. S.S. would also be entitled to attend an alternative program and summer school to complete his courses, with a limited number of allowable absences. If S.S. failed to graduate by the end of the summer, he would voluntarily withdraw from school and enroll in an alternative program, such as a GED program. In addition, petitioners agreed to special education testing, to be provided by the district.

The hearing officer recommended the settlement to the superintendent. By letter to S.S. dated February 10, 2004, the superintendent accepted the settlement. In his letter, the superintendent advised S.S. that he could "appeal the decision of the superintendent's hearing to the Board of Education in writing within 30 days."

By letter dated March 8, 2004, petitioners appealed to the superintendent, requesting that he reconsider the terms of the settlement. After meeting with petitioners on March 11, the superintendent denied their appeal on March 12. By letter dated March 18, 2004, petitioners requested that the superintendent provide transportation for S.S. to his classes, change his school hours, or change the location of his classes. The superintendent denied this request on March 24. This appeal ensued. Petitioners' request for interim relief was denied on June 16, 2004.

Petitioners deny that S.S. brought a knife to school and claim that S.S. only admitted he had a knife under pressure from the principal because the principal had him arrested and told him he would go to jail. They admit that S.S. cut classes over a period of two years but assert he was never referred for counseling or academic intervention services. Petitioners claim that respondent is forcing S.S. out of school and into a GED program. They also contend that the alternative education S.S. received is inadequate. They request that their late petition be excused because respondent did not advise them of their right to appeal to the Commissioner. Petitioners seek to have S.S. readmitted as a regular high school student and the charges removed from his record.

Respondent asserts that the appeal must be dismissed because petitioners failed to exhaust their administrative remedies and, in the alternative, waived their rights to further administrative proceedings. It also claims that the petition is untimely and fails to state a claim upon which relief may be granted. Respondent further contends that the settlement is valid and there is no reason to invalidate it. Finally, respondent maintains that it is not obligated to provide S.S. with alternative education because he is over the compulsory education age.

Education Law §3214(3)(c)(1) provides that an appeal to the board of education lies from a superintendent's disciplinary determination. Accordingly, the decision of a superintendent to suspend a student following a hearing must be appealed to the board of education prior to initiating an appeal to the Commissioner of Education (*Appeal of D.C.*, 41 Ed Dept Rep 190, Decision No. 14,661; *Appeal of P.R. and C.R.*, 41 *id.* 48, Decision No. 14,611). Both the hearing officer and the superintendent's letter of February 10 advised petitioners of their right to appeal to the board of education, yet the record is devoid of any evidence that petitioners did so. Accordingly, petitioners' claims must be dismissed for failure to exhaust administrative remedies.

Although the appeal is dismissed on procedural grounds, I am compelled to comment on the stipulation entered into at the beginning of the suspension hearing on February 9. Since no hearing was held, the stipulation essentially amounted to a waiver of petitioners' rights under Education Law §3214. I have previously recognized that, under certain conditions, parents may waive a student's due process rights under §3214 (*Appeal of a Student with a Disability*, 42 Ed Dept Rep 192, Decision No. 14,818; *Appeal of a Student Suspected of Having a Disability*, 41 *id.* 390, Decision No. 14,722; *Appeal of J.G.*, 39 *id.* 393, Decision No. 14,270; *Appeals of McMahon and Mosely, et al.*, 38 *id.* 22, Decision No. 13,976). For such a waiver to be valid, however, it must be "voluntary, knowing and intelligent." The district must provide the student and parents with a written document clearly and concisely stating all of the rights to be waived, as well as the *consequences* of waiving such rights (emphasis added) (*Appeal of a Student with a Disability*, *supra*; *Appeal of J.G.*, *supra*; *Appeals of McMahon and Mosely, et al.*, *supra*).

The stipulation in this case does not meet this standard. Although petitioners' counsel orally agreed to the stipulation at the hearing, the only written document in the record is the February 10, 2004, letter from the superintendent to S.S., setting forth the terms of the stipulation as articulated. There is no evidence that petitioners signed this document or otherwise consented in writing. Among other things, the stipulation provided that, if S.S. failed to graduate by the end of summer school, he would voluntarily withdraw from school and enroll in an alternative program, a consequence essentially equivalent to a permanent suspension or expulsion. Significantly, the stipulation fails to articulate this consequence or explain that petitioners were waiving S.S.'s right to attend school until such time as he either earned a high school diploma or turned 21 years of age (*see*, Education Law §3202(1)). The fact that petitioners seek their son's return to school suggests that they may not have fully understood the terms of the stipulation and its consequences.

In addition, a permanent suspension is an extreme penalty that is generally educationally unsound except under extraordinary circumstances, such as where the student exhibits "an alarming disregard for the safety of others" and where it is necessary to safeguard the well-being of other students (*Appeal of L.T.*, 44 Ed Dept Rep ___, Decision No. 15,107; *Appeal of Coleman*, 41 *id.* 101, Decision No. 14,628).

In the event petitioners pursue their administrative remedies, as is their right, by appealing directly to respondent, respondent should consider the issues outlined above. Any final determination by respondent can be appealed by petitioners to the Commissioner pursuant to Education Law §310.

THE APPEAL IS DISMISSED.

Decision No. 15,123

Appeal of M.P., on behalf of her son J.P., from action of the Board of Education of the Albion Central School District regarding student discipline.

(October 7, 2004)

APPEARANCES OF COUNSEL

Shirley A. Gorman, Esq., attorney for petitioner

David W. Lippitt, Esq., attorney for respondent

DECISION OF THE COMMISSIONER

MILLS, Commissioner.—Petitioner appeals the decision of the Board of Education of the Albion Central School District ("respondent") to affirm her son's suspension from school for the remainder of the 2003-2004 school year. The appeal must be dismissed.

Petitioner's son, J.P., is enrolled in the Charles D'Amico High School ("high school") in respondent's district. On January 14, 2004, J.P. allegedly offered to sell oxycontin, a controlled substance, to another student for $5.00. By letter of the same date, the high school principal notified petitioner that he was suspending J.P. for five days commencing January 14 as a result of this incident. Additionally, by letter dated January 15, 2004, respondent's superintendent notified petitioner that she would conduct a superintendent's hearing on January 22, 2004, to consider whether a further suspension was warranted. The notice charged J.P. with possession of a controlled substance with intent to sell on school property based on the allegation that "[o]n Wednesday, January 14th, during 2nd block, [J.P.] offered oxycontin to another student for $5.00. James took $4.00 from the student and told him to meet him in the lobby after school."

At the superintendent's hearing, the district called J.P. as its first witness. He testified that the substance confiscated by school officials was "crushed up" hydro-codeine, which had been prescribed for him more than a year earlier when he broke his leg. The district also called S.W., a student, who testified that during 2nd block on January 14, 2004, J.P. offered to sell her some oxycontin and that after she declined, she overheard J.P. making arrangements to sell some to D.M., another student. Immediately after class, S.W. reported the incident to the high school's resource officer ("officer"). S.W.'s testimony was corroborated by D.M., who testified that J.P. showed him a white envelope containing a white powdery substance that he identified as oxycontin, which he offered to sell to D.M. for five dollars. D.M. gave J.P. four dollars and the two agreed to meet after school to complete the transaction.

The officer testified that after speaking with S.W., he reported the incident to the high school vice-principal. The two then escorted J.P. from class and after searching his locker and belongings, recovered an envelope containing a white powdery substance. The officer also testified that oxycontin is a controlled substance and that it is "pretty much the same thing" as hydro-codeine.

In addition, D.M. testified that J.P. telephoned him on January 14, 2004, and threatened him about his testimony. The officer also testified that D.M. had reported this threat to him.

At the conclusion of the hearing, the superintendent found J.P. guilty of the charge and after considering his anecdotal record, recommended a suspension for the remainder of the school year. Petitioner appealed the superintendent's determination to respondent. By letter dated March 2, 2004, the district clerk advised petitioner that respondent had sustained the superintendent's determination. This appeal ensued.

Petitioner contends that J.P. was denied due process because the disciplinary notice did not charge J.P. with making a threat and because the superintendent allowed the district to call J.P. as a witness and did not offer petitioner the opportunity to call witnesses. Petitioner also claims that respondent improperly permitted the superintendent to be present during executive session while respondent considered petitioner's appeal. Petitioner requests that I annul J.P.'s suspension, direct expungement of his records and permit him to return to school. Respondent generally denies that it violated J.P.'s due process rights and maintains the petition should be dismissed in its entirety.

Because J.P. was suspended for the remainder of the 2003-2004 school year, which has ended, the appeal is moot except to the extent that petitioner seeks expungement of J.P.'s records (*Appeal of a Student with a Disability*, 43 Ed Dept Rep ___, Decision No. 15,021; *Appeal of M.K.*, 42 *id.* 405, Decision No. 14,894; *Appeal of Mace*, 40 *id.* 110, Decision No. 14,433).

A decision to suspend a student from school pursuant to Education Law §3214 must be based on competent and substantial evidence that the student participated in the objectionable conduct (*Bd. of Educ. of Monticello CSD v. Commissioner of Education, et al.*, 91 NY2d 133; *Bd. of Educ. of City School Dist. of City of New York v. Mills*, 293 AD2d 37; *Appeal of J.C. and P.C.*, 41 Ed Dept Rep 395, Decision No. 14,723; *Appeal of Harlan*, 40 *id.* 309, Decision No. 14,488). A hearing officer may draw reasonable inferences if the record supports the inference (*Bd. of Educ. of Monticello CSD v. Commissioner of Education, supra*; *Appeal of J.C., supra*; *Appeal of Harlan, supra*). In cases of student discipline, the sanction imposed must be proportionate to the severity of the offense involved (*Appeal of J.C. and P.C., supra*; *Appeal of Harlan, supra*). The test to be applied in reviewing a penalty is whether it is so excessive as to warrant substitution of the Commissioner's judgment for that of the board (*Appeal of J.C., supra*; *Appeal of Harlan, supra*).

The Court of Appeals has stated that the charges in a student disciplinary proceeding need only be "sufficiently specific to advise the student and his counsel of the activities or incidents which have given rise to the proceeding and which will form the basis for the hearing." (*Bd. of Educ. of Monticello CSD v. Commissioner of Education, et al., supra*). "As long as students are given a fair opportunity to tell their side of the story and rebut the evidence against them, due process is served." (*Id.*) Reasonable notice must provide the student with enough information to prepare an effective defense but need not particularize every single charge against a student (*Bd. of Educ. of Monticello CSD v. Commissioner of Education, supra*; *Appeal of a Student with a Disability*, 39 Ed Dept Rep 427, Decision No. 14,278).

The hearing notice charged J.P. solely with possession of a controlled substance with intent to sell on school property. Accordingly, I find the notice did not provide J.P. with sufficient information to prepare a defense to the charge that he had threatened D.M. The superintendent, therefore, erred by permitting this testimony. However, because the hearing testimony on the charge that J.P. offered to sell a controlled substance to a classmate is sufficient to support both the hearing officer's finding of guilt and the penalty recommendation, I find the error harmless.

I also find no merit to petitioner's claim that her son was denied the opportunity to call witnesses. The notice of discipline advised petitioner that she had the right to call witnesses at the superintendent's hearing. Additionally, at the beginning of the hearing, the superintendent advised petitioner and her son, among other things, that they had the right to call witnesses and would be given that opportunity after the district finished presenting its witnesses. Petitioner did not indicate at any point during the hearing that she, in fact, wished to call witnesses. Moreover, aside from her claim that J.P. did not have an opportunity to respond to testimony concerning his alleged threat, petitioner does not identify in this appeal any witnesses she was allegedly prevented from calling, or specify the substance of their testimony. Under these circumstances, I find that petitioner has failed to establish that she was deprived of her right to call witnesses.

Nor has petitioner established that respondent acted improperly by permitting the superintendent to be present during the executive session when respondent considered petitioner's appeal. Respondent's attorney explains that although both he and the superintendent were present during the executive session neither commented on the merits of appeal. Under these circumstances, I find no violation of petitioner's procedural rights.

I have considered petitioner's remaining contentions and find them without merit.

THE APPEAL IS DISMISSED.

Decision No. 15,124

Appeal of a STUDENT WITH A DISABILITY, by his parent, from action of the Board of Education of the Hyde Park Central School District regarding student discipline.

(October 7, 2004)

APPEARANCES OF COUNSEL

Donoghue, Thomas, Auslander and Drohan, attorneys for respondent, *Daniel Petigrow, Esq.*, of counsel

DECISION OF THE COMMISSIONER

MILLS, Commissioner.—Petitioner appeals a determination by the Board of Education of the Hyde Park Central School District ("respondent") suspending her son from school. The appeal must be sustained in part.

On October 21, 2003, petitioner's son allegedly threatened his bus driver while riding the school bus home. After the bus driver reported the incident to district officials, the high school principal ("principal") decided to suspend petitioner's son for five days, commencing October 23, 2003. The following morning, petitioner's son was escorted from the bus by the assistant principal, who telephoned petitioner to advise her that her son was being suspended from school for threatening the bus driver and that she should pick him up immediately. Petitioner was also notified by the principal, by letter dated October 23, 2003, that her son was being suspended for "5 days, commencing 10/23/03 and concluding 10/29/03." The letter, which apparently was sent by regular mail, further advised petitioner that she and her son had the right to an immediate informal conference with the principal and to ask questions of the complaining witnesses.

By letter dated October 24, 2003, respondent's superintendent ("superintendent") advised petitioner that a superintendent's hearing would be held on October 29, 2003, based on the allegation that on October 21, 2003, her son threatened the bus driver by stating "I am going to [expletive] blow up your house and I hope your [expletive] kids and [expletive] pet is in there." The hearing commenced on October 29, 2003, and reconvened on November 6, 2003, at petitioner's request, to allow her to call additional witnesses.

At the hearing, the bus driver testified to the threat allegedly made by petitioner's son. Petitioner's son admitted cursing at the bus driver, but denied threatening her. Petitioner also called two students who testified that they were on the bus and did not hear petitioner's son threaten the bus driver. A school resource officer testified that S.S., another student who was on the bus that day, admitted to him outside the vice principal's office that he, not petitioner's son, had threatened the bus driver.

On November 7, 2003, the hearing officer issued a report and recommendation finding substantial evidence to support the charge and referring the matter to the district's committee on special education ("CSE") for a manifestation hearing to determine whether there was any relationship between the student's disability and the behavior that was the subject of the disciplinary action. The district's CSE met on November 12, 2003, and determined that the student's conduct was not a manifestation of his handicapping condition and that his IEP is appropriate to meet his educational needs. That same day, the hearing officer issued a report recommending that the student be suspended from school until January 30, 2004, and from bus transportation for the balance of the school year. By letter dated November 13, 2003, the superintendent advised petitioner that he accepted the hearing officer's findings and recommendations. By letter dated December 12, 2003, respondent's president advised petitioner that respondent had adopted the superintendent's determination. This appeal ensued.

Petitioner contends, among other things, that she was not advised of her right to an informal conference with the principal and did not receive timely written notice of her son's short-term suspension. Additionally, petitioner claims that the hearing officer was not objective and that the punishment imposed was excessive. Finally, petitioner claims that alternative education provided to her son was inadequate. Petitioner requests that I order her son's suspension annulled and his records expunged.

Respondent contends that the hearing officer's findings and penalty recommendation are supported by substantial evidence and that the principal properly notified petitioner of her right to an informal conference. Respondent also contends that the appeal is moot because the suspension period has ended.

At the outset, I note that respondent objects to petitioner's reply. The purpose of a reply is to respond to new material or affirmative defenses set forth in an answer (8 NYCRR §§275.3 and 275.14). A reply is not meant to buttress allegations in the petition or to belatedly add assertions that should have been in the petition (*Appeal of General*, 43 Ed Dept Rep ___, Decision No. 14,948; *Appeal of Crosier*, 42 *id*. 232, Decision No. 14,835). Therefore, while I have reviewed petitioner's reply, I have not considered those portions containing new allegations or exhibits that are not responsive to new material or affirmative defenses set forth in the answer.

Preliminarily, I find that because the student has served the suspension, the appeal is moot except to the extent that petitioner seeks expungement of his records (*Appeal of a Student with a Disability*, 43 Ed Dept Rep ___, Decision No. 15,021; *Appeal of M.K.*, 42 *id*. 405, Decision No. 14,894).

I now turn to petitioner's complaints about the initial short-term suspension of her son. Education Law §3214(3)(b)(1) provides:

> The board of education, board of trustees, or sole trustee, superintendent of schools, district superintendent of schools and the principal of the school where the pupil attends shall have the power to suspend a pupil for a period not to exceed five school days. In the case of such a suspension, the suspending authority shall provide the pupil with notice of the charged misconduct. If the pupil denies the misconduct, the suspending authority shall provide an explanation of the basis for the suspension. The pupil and the person in parental relation to the pupil shall, on request, be given an opportunity for an informal conference with the principal at which the pupil and/or person in parental relation shall be authorized to present the pupil's version of the event and to ask questions of the complaining witnesses. The aforesaid notice and opportunity for an informal conference shall take place prior to suspension of the pupil unless the pupil's presence in the school poses a continuing danger to persons or property or an ongoing threat of disruption to the academic process, in which case the pupil's notice and opportunity for an informal conference shall take place as soon after the suspension as is reasonably practicable.

Section 100.2(l)(4) of the Commissioner's regulations provides:

> Parental notice concerning student suspensions. When suspension of a student from attendance for a period of five days or less pursuant to section 3214(3) of the Education Law is proposed, school district officials shall

> immediately notify the parents or the persons in parental relation in writing that the student may be suspended from school. *Written notice shall be provided by personal delivery, express mail delivery, or equivalent means reasonably calculated to assure receipt of such notice within 24 hours of the decision to propose suspension* at the last known address or addresses of the parents or persons in parental relation. Where possible, notification shall also be provided by telephone if the school has been provided with a telephone number(s) for the purpose of contacting parents or persons in parental relation. Such notice shall provide a description of the incident(s) for which suspension is proposed and shall inform the parents or persons in parental relation of their right to request an immediate informal conference with the principal in accordance with the provisions of Education Law, section 3214(3)(b). Such notice and informal conference shall be in the dominant language or mode of communication used by the parents or persons in parental relation to the pupil. *Such notice and opportunity for an informal conference shall take place prior to the suspension of the student unless the student's presence in the school poses a continuing danger to persons or property or an ongoing threat of disruption to the academic process, in which case the notice and opportunity for an informal conference shall take place as soon after the suspension as is reasonably practicable.* (Emphasis added)

Respondent did not comply with these mandates in several respects. The record reflects that the principal notified petitioner of her son's suspension by telephone on October 22, 2003, and by letter dated October 23, 2003, which was apparently sent by regular mail. The Commissioner has repeatedly held that written notification by regular mail does not meet the required standard (*Appeal of R.F.*, 43 Ed Dept Rep ___, Decision No. 14,972; *Appeal of a Student Suspected of Having a Disability*, 41 *id.* 390, Decision No. 14,722; *Appeal of Lloyd*, 39 *id.* 537, Decision No. 14,303). Nor is oral communication with parents regarding a suspension a substitute for the required written notification (*Appeal of a Student Suspected of Having a Disability*, *supra*; *Appeal of J.G.*, *supra*). Further, because respondent does not allege that the student's presence in school posed a continuing danger or threat, the principal was obligated to conduct an informal conference before suspending the student (Education Law §3214(3)(b)(1)). He did not. The student's suspension from October 23 to October 29, 2003, must therefore be annulled and expunged from his record (*Appeal of B.C. and A.C.*, 42 Ed Dept Rep 395, Decision No. 14,891).

I also find that the short-term suspension exceeded the five-day limit set forth in §3214(3)(b). Although the principal's October 23, 2003, letter states that the student would be suspended for five days from October 23, 2003, through October 29, 2003, the record reflects that the student was not permitted to attend school for six days, beginning on October 22, 2003. I remind respondent of the need to abide by the statutory five-day limit in the future.

With respect to the student's long-term suspension, I find no basis to disturb respondent's determination of guilt. Education Law §3214(3)(a) authorizes a school district to suspend a "pupil who is insubordinate or disorderly or violent or disruptive, or whose conduct otherwise endangers the safety, morals, health or welfare of others." The decision to suspend a student from school must be based on competent and substantial evidence that the student participated in the objectionable conduct (*Bd. of Educ. of Monticello CSD v. Commissioner of Educ.*, 91 NY2d 133, 140-41; *Bd. of Educ. of City School Dist. of City of New York v. Mills*, 293 AD2d 37; *Appeal of B.C. and A.C., supra*). A hearing officer may draw a reasonable inference if the record supports the inference (*Appeal of B.C. and A.C., supra*; *Appeal of J.C. and P.C.*, 41 Ed Dept Rep 395, Decision No. 14,723). With respect to findings of fact in matters involving the credibility of witnesses, I will not substitute my judgment for that of a hearing officer unless there is clear and convincing evidence that the determination of credibility is inconsistent with the facts (*Appeal of T.R. and M.D.*, 43 Ed Dept Rep ___, Decision No. 15,036; *Appeal of K.M.*, 41 *id.* 318, Decision No. 14,699).

Although petitioner's witnesses supported her son's assertion that he did not threaten the bus driver, the hearing officer credited the bus driver's testimony and found the student witnesses incredible. Under these circumstances, I will not substitute my judgment for that of the hearing officer and find substantial evidence to support the hearing officer's determination.

I have examined petitioner's remaining claims regarding her son's long-term suspension and find them to be without merit.

THE APPEAL IS SUSTAINED IN PART.

IT IS ORDERED that respondent remove any reference to the student's short-term suspension from his records.

Decision No. 15,125

Appeal of NANCY STANTON from action of the Board of Education of the Deposit Central School District regarding an election.

(October 7, 2004)

APPEARANCES OF COUNSEL

Hogan, Sarzynski, Lynch, Surowka & DeWind, LLP, attorneys for respondent, *Wendy K. DeWind, Esq.*, of counsel

DECISION OF THE COMMISSIONER

MILLS, Commissioner.—Petitioner challenges actions of the Board of Education of the Deposit Central School District ("respondent") regarding its May 18, 2004, school board election. The appeal must be dismissed.

On May 18, 2004, respondent conducted an annual meeting to vote on the proposed school district budget and to elect members to the board of education. Two incumbents, David Bergstrom and Mark Clark, and one new candidate, Thomas Keefe, ran for two seats on the board. Candidates Bergstrom, Clark and Keefe received 228, 191 and 65 votes, respectively. This appeal ensued.

Petitioner alleges that respondent failed to provide notice to district residents regarding the school board election and that the placement of the candidates on the voting machine was confusing. Petitioner further alleges that after the election, respondent held an unannounced school board meeting regarding the election, and failed to invite the reporter for the official newspaper for the district and candidate Keefe. Petitioner also alleges that the respondent's attorney made incorrect statements at the meeting about how to appeal the election results. Petitioner requests that I invalidate the school board election and order a new election.

Respondent denies petitioner's allegations and contends that petitioner has failed to state a cause of action. Respondent also contends that the appeal must be dismissed for petitioner's failure to join the school board candidates as necessary parties to this appeal.

The appeal must be dismissed for failure to join necessary parties. A party whose rights would be adversely affected by a determination of an appeal in favor of petitioner is a necessary party and must be joined as such (*Appeal of Milazzo*, 43 Ed Dept Rep ___, Decision No. 14,999; *Appeal of Stolbach*, 43 *id.* ___, Decision No. 14,977; *Appeal of Gilmore and Jordon-Thompson*, 42 *id.* 334, Decision No. 14,874). The rights of the successful candidates would be affected if the school board election were declared void and a new election ordered. Section 275.8(d) of the Commissioner's regulations provides in pertinent part: "If an appeal involves the validity of a school district meeting or election, . . . a copy of the petition must be served upon the trustee or board of trustees or board of education as the case may be, *and upon each person whose right to hold office is disputed and such person must be joined as a respondent*" (emphasis added). Joinder requires that an individual be clearly named as a respondent in the caption of the petition and served with a copy of the notice of petition and petition to inform the individual that he or she should respond to the petition and enter a defense (*Appeal of Milazzo, supra*; *Appeal of Stolbach, supra*; *Appeal of Gilmore and Jordon-Thompson, supra*).

Although it appears that petitioner attempted to personally serve a petition on David Bergstrom on June 2, 2004, it failed to name Mr. Bergstrom in the caption and, in any event, was rejected as defective by my Office of Counsel on June 15, 2004. While petitioner subsequently served a corrected petition, she failed to name or serve either Mr. Bergstrom or Mark Clark. The appeal must, therefore, be dismissed for failure to join them as necessary parties.

Since the appeal is dismissed on procedural grounds, I need not address the parties' remaining contentions.

THE APPEAL IS DISMISSED.

Decision No. 15,126

Appeal of L.S. from action of the Board of Education of the Commack Union Free School District regarding censure.

(October 7, 2004)

APPEARANCES OF COUNSEL

Smith Mazure Director Wilkins Young & Yagerman, P.C., attorneys for petitioner, *Joel M. Simon, Esq.,* of counsel

Bond, Schoeneck & King, PLLC, attorneys for respondent, *Howard M. Miller, Esq.*, of counsel

DECISION OF THE COMMISSIONER

MILLS, Commissioner.—Petitioner challenges a resolution adopted by the Board of Education of the Commack Union Free School District ("respondent") concerning petitioner's behavior. The appeal must be sustained.

Petitioner is a member of respondent board. On September 18, 2003, respondent adopted a resolution regarding several actions taken by petitioner:

> WHEREAS, the Board has long had serious concerns about whether [petitioner] has engaged in conduct that violates District policy and is otherwise inappropriate and unbecoming of a member of the Board of Education; and
>
> WHEREAS, the Board retained special outside counsel to investigate and advise the Board as to whether [petitioner's] conduct warrants his removal from the Board; and
>
> WHEREAS, [petitioner] has stated that he has not been given clear direction as to the rules and protocol governing the conduct of a member of the Board of Education, nor has he been given clear notice as to when, if at all, he has violated those rules.
>
> NOW, THEREFORE, IT IS HEREBY RESOLVED THAT:
>
> a) upon the recommendation of the District's special counsel, the action of [petitioner] on April 8, 2002, in which he sent staff members who report to the Superintendent information regarding his private lawsuit with the Superintendent, is deemed improper and representative of poor judgment and [petitioner] is hereby notified of same;
>
> b) upon the recommendation of the District's special counsel, the action of [petitioner] in April 2003, in which without the authorization of the Board of Education, he contacted the New York State Council of School Superintendents, identifying himself as a member of the Board of Education, for the purposes of furthering his own private interests, is deemed improper and

representative of poor judgment and [petitioner] is hereby notified of same;

c) upon the recommendation of the District's special counsel, the following additional conduct of [petitioner] is deemed improper and representative of poor judgment, and [petitioner] is hereby notified of same:

1) using profanity towards employees of the District;

2) threatening legal action against employees of the District;

3) soliciting proposals for professional services on behalf of the Board without Board approval;

4) participating in locker searches at the high school or any other school within the District without authorization;

5) using hostile language in written correspondences to other board members;

6) contacting staff members on matters unrelated to his own children without authorization from the Superintendent or Board.

BE IT FURTHER RESOLVED that it is expected that [petitioner] will, in the future, exhibit appropriate conduct and judgment warranted in all matters relating to School District or Board of Education affairs, including conduct of a nature specifically mentioned herein or reasonably related thereto; and be it further

RESOLVED, that if [petitioner] so requests, the District's general and/or special counsel shall meet with [petitioner] and any representative(s) of his choice, to provide to him with any additional detail regarding the incidents described above to ensure that [petitioner] is on clear notice of what is expected of him; the substance of such meeting shall be confirmed in writing; and be it further

RESOLVED, that if [petitioner] is unclear as to the circumstances under which he may have contact with District employees on matters that do not directly pertain to his own children, he is directed to obtain clarification from the Superintendent or Board President; and be it further

> RESOLVED, that the Board will request the District Superintendent of Western Suffolk BOCES to arrange a seminar on school district governance and [petitioner] is directed to include himself with the rest of the Board in attending this seminar.

This appeal ensued.

Petitioner claims that the resolution constitutes a censure, in violation of Education Law §§306 and 1709. Petitioner also asserts that the actions set forth in the resolution are unsubstantiated. He maintains the resolution infringes on his First Amendment rights.

Respondent contends that the resolution was not a censure or reprimand but merely a criticism of petitioner's poor judgment. Respondent also asserts that, other than conclusory allegations, petitioner submits no proof that the actions, as described in the resolution, are unsubstantiated. Thus, respondent maintains that the resolution is, in all respects, proper.

Before considering the merits, I must address a procedural matter. Petitioner's memorandum of law contains a new exhibit that was not a part of his original pleadings. A memorandum of law may not be used to belatedly add exhibits that are not part of the record (*Appeal of Smolen*, 43 Ed Dept Rep ___, Decision No. 15,000; *Appeal of George*, 40 *id.* 509, Decision No. 14,540). Accordingly, I have not considered the new exhibit appended to petitioner's memorandum of law.

Petitioner contends that the resolution constitutes an unlawful censure of him as a member of the board of education. While the Commissioner of Education is authorized to remove a board member from office pursuant to Education Law §306, the Education Law does not authorize the censure or reprimand of a board member by the Commissioner (*Matter of Legatos*, 23 Ed Dept Rep 10, Decision No. 11,113; *Matter of Graham*, 11 *id.* 220, Decision No. 8,426). Similarly, while a board of education is authorized to remove one of its members for misconduct pursuant to Education Law §1709(18), the Education Law does not authorize the censure or reprimand of a board member by a board of education (*Appeal of Silano*, 33 Ed Dept Rep 20, Decision No. 12,961).

A board of education, however, is authorized to criticize the actions of a board member for exhibiting poor judgment (*Appeal of Silano*, *supra*). In an appeal to the Commissioner of Education, the petitioner bears the burden of establishing the facts upon which he or she seeks relief and the burden of demonstrating a clear legal right to the relief requested (8 NYCRR §275.10; *Appeal of D.R.*, 43 Ed Dept Rep ___, Decision No. 15,035; *Appeal of Kirschenbaum*, 43 *id.* ___, Decision No. 15,020).

Black's Law Dictionary (8th Ed. 2004) defines "censure" as "an official reprimand or condemnation" or a "harsh criticism." The current Merriam-Webster Online Dictionary defines "reprimand" as "a severe or formal reproof." Respondent maintains that the resolution does not amount to a censure or reprimand, but instead merely criticizes petitioner's judgment on several occasions and instructs him as to future behavior. Although the resolution avoids the use of the words "censure" or "reprimand," the circumstances surrounding its adoption, as well as its tone, undercut respondent's position.

The incidents of petitioner's alleged poor judgment and inappropriate behavior, that are cited in the resolution, spanned a period of approximately 17 months. The fact that respondent waited almost one and one-half years before adopting the resolution belies respondent's contention that the resolution was intended merely to criticize such actions, caution and instruct (*cf. Silano, supra*).

Petitioner maintains that the resolution constitutes a thinly veiled threat of discipline. Although respondent denies that assertion, the resolution is prefaced by a "whereas" clause indicating that the purpose of investigating the underlying incidents that gave rise to the resolution was to determine "whether [petitioner's] conduct warrants removal." Indeed, the language of the resolution is akin to that used in formal disciplinary charges. Such language elevates the tone of the resolution to more than mere criticism. Moreover, unlike the resolution in *Silano*, no specific corrective action is directed toward petitioner with respect to the conduct that formed that basis of the resolution. Thus, I agree that the September 18, 2003, resolution constitutes an impermissible censure or reprimand. This result, however, should not be read as support or endorsement of petitioner's actions.

Petitioner also maintains that respondent's action violates the U.S. Constitution in that it has a chilling effect on his First Amendment rights. An appeal to the Commissioner of Education is not the proper forum to adjudicate novel issues of constitutional law (*Appeal of Murray*, 43 Ed Dept Rep ___, Decision No. 15,031; *Appeals of American Quality Beverages*, 42 *id.* 144, Decision No. 14,804). Therefore, I decline to address petitioner's constitutional claim.

In view of the above disposition, I need not address petitioner's remaining claims.

THE APPEAL IS SUSTAINED.

IT IS ORDERED that the September 18, 2003, resolution is annulled.

Decision No. 15,127

Appeal of MARK E. EWART from action of the Board of Education of the Starpoint Central School District regarding an election.

(October 16,2004)

APPEARANCES OF COUNSEL

Norton / Radin / Hoover / Freedman, attorneys for respondent, *Andrew J. Freedman, Esq*., of counsel

DECISION OF THE COMMISSIONER

MILLS, Commissioner.—Petitioner, an unsuccessful candidate for election to the Board of Education of the Starpoint Central School District ("respondent"), challenges the conduct of the school district election held on May 18, 2004. The appeal must be dismissed.

Petitioner contends that the successful candidate, Gary Braun, improperly electioneered within 100 feet of the polling place by talking to voters and soliciting votes in violation of Education Law §2031-a. Petitioner also asserts that respondent failed to name and provide the mandatory number of election officials required by Education Law §2025(3)(b). Petitioner requests that Mr. Braun resign from his position, and that I reprimand respondent and order it to review its election policies.

Respondent denies any wrongdoing and asserts that the appeal must be dismissed for failure to join a necessary party. Respondent contends that petitioner has failed to demonstrate that any irregularities occurred in the conduct of the election or that any electioneering took place.

To the extent that petitioner seeks Mr. Braun's resignation or removal, the petition must be dismissed for failure to join him as a necessary party. A party whose rights would be adversely affected by a determination of an appeal in favor of petitioner is a necessary party and must be named as such and served with a notice of petition and petition (*Appeal of Milazzo*, 43 Ed Dept Rep ___, Decision No.

14,999; *Appeal of Stolbach*, 43 *id.* ___, Decision No. 14,977; *Appeal of Gilmore and Jordon-Thompson*, 42 *id.* 334, Decision No. 14,874). Mr. Braun would be adversely affected by a determination that he resign or be removed. In this case, petitioner did not name or personally serve Mr. Braun. Therefore, his failure to do so requires dismissal of petitioner's claims and demands for Mr. Braun's resignation or removal.

To the extent that petitioner seeks a reprimand of respondent, there is no provision in the Education Law to authorize the reprimand of board members by the Commissioner of Education (*See Appeal of Mead*, 42 Ed Dept Rep 359, Decision No. 14,881; *Appeal of Kozak*, 39 *id.* 278, Decision No. 14,237; *Appeal of Kane*, 34 *id.* 116, Decision No. 13,251).

Petitioner's remaining claims and demands must be dismissed for lack of proof. In an appeal to the Commissioner, petitioner has the burden of establishing the facts upon which he seeks relief (8 NYCRR §275.10; *Appeal of Brown, et al.*, 43 Ed Dept Rep ___, Decision No. 14,980) and the burden of demonstrating a clear legal right to the relief requested (*Appeal of Goldin*, 43 Ed Dept Rep ___, Decision No. 15,048).

Petitioner has not established that Mr. Braun engaged in electioneering in violation of Education Law §2031-a. An activity does not constitute electioneering absent proof that the activity was used to influence voters to vote a particular way (*Appeal of Collins*, 39 Ed Dept Rep 226, Decision No. 14,223; *Appeal of Gang*, 32 *id.* 337, Decision No. 12,847; *Appeal of Fitzpatrick*, 30 *id.* 124, Decision No. 12,408). A portion of petitioner's evidence consists of newspaper articles. It is well settled that newspaper articles do not constitute evidence of the truth of the statements contained therein (*Appeal of Mead, supra*; *Appeal of Decastro*, 41 Ed Dept Rep 415, Decision No. 14,730; *Appeal of Wilson*, 41 *id.* 196, Decision No. 14,663). The remainder of petitioner's alleged proof, consisting of two notarized letters (one from his mother), establishes only that Mr. Braun talked to voters within the 100-foot markers. He presents no evidence that these conversations constituted electioneering or that the alleged electioneering affected the outcome of the election. Accordingly, petitioner has failed to meet his burden of proof on this claim.

Petitioner also fails to establish that respondent lacked the requisite number of election inspectors. Education Law §2025(3)(b) requires the appointment of at least two election inspectors for each ballot box or voting machine. In her affidavit, the district clerk avers that 11 inspectors were appointed prior the May 18, 2004, election for the four voting machines used in the election, and petitioner offers no proof to the contrary. (*See also Appeal of Uciechowski*, 32 Ed Dept Rep 511, Decision No. 12,903).

THE APPEAL IS DISMISSED.

Decision No. 15,128

Appeal of ROBERT A. and PAMELA R. ROMEO, on behalf of their daughters ARIELLA and MARISA, from action of the Board of Education of the Westhill Central School District regarding residency.

(November 5, 2004)

APPEARANCES OF COUNSEL

Romeo and Romeo, P.C., attorneys for petitioner, *Robert A. Romeo, Esq.*, of counsel

Bond, Schoeneck & King, PLLC, attorneys for respondent, *Henry H. Melchor, Esq.*, of counsel

DECISION OF THE COMMISSIONER

MILLS, Commissioner.—Petitioners appeal the determination of the Board of Education of the Westhill Central School District ("respondent") that their daughters, Ariella and Marisa, are not district residents. The appeal must be dismissed.

In August 2003, petitioners purchased their present residence located in the Broadview Heights subdivision. It appears from the record that their southern property line is very close to, if not coincident with, the boundary line dividing the City of Syracuse and the Town of Onondaga, which is also the boundary line between the City School District of the City of Syracuse ("Syracuse") and the Westhill Central School District ("Westhill"). Upon purchase, they were provided with a survey of the property, which did not include a metes-and-bounds description, but merely described petitioners' two-lot parcel by lot and block number.

Because of uncertainty over the location of their property's southern boundary line, petitioners engaged a professional surveyor to provide a metes-and-bounds description of the exact property line. The survey indicated that, although the majority of petitioners' property is within Syracuse, their property's southern boundary line extends a small distance into Westhill. Petitioners also had their southern neighbors' property surveyed.

On January 23, 2004, petitioners and their southern neighbors executed a boundary line agreement, which they filed with the Onondaga County Clerk's Office. Pursuant to the agreement, the neighbors conveyed all of their property lying north of the survey's southern boundary line to petitioners and petitioners conveyed all of their property lying south of the boundary line to the neighbors. The Onondaga County tax mapping authority established a taxable parcel of petitioner's property within Westhill, and the Town Assessor issued a tentative assessment for the parcel.

Petitioners sent a letter dated April 19, 2004, to Westhill designating that district, pursuant to Education Law §3203, as the district their children would attend beginning with the 2004-2005 school year. At its meeting on June 21, 2004, respondent determined that petitioners' daughters were not district residents and were not eligible for enrollment. The record indicates that respondent based its determination on a May 12, 2004, letter from the Town of Onondaga Codes Enforcement Office to petitioners' southern neighbors, stating that, because the parties had failed to obtain the approval of the Town Planning Board, the boundary line agreement with petitioners violated the Town of Onondaga's subdivision regulations.

This appeal ensued. Petitioners' request for interim relief to allow their children to attend school in respondent's district was denied in August 2004.

Petitioners allege that their residence is located on property intersected by the boundary line between respondent's district and Syracuse and that their daughters are entitled to attend respondent's schools pursuant to petitioners' designation under Education Law §3203. They contend that the boundary line agreement did not transfer property, but merely clarified the existing boundary line.

Respondent denies petitioners' allegations and contends that petitioners' designation of respondent's district under Education Law §3203 is invalid because it is based upon the boundary line agreement which on its face, transferred property. Such transfer allegedly created a resubdivision in violation of the subdivision approval requirements of local and State law.

Education Law §3203(1) provides:

> The owner of taxable property that is so located that the boundary line between two school districts intersects (a) the dwelling on said property or (b), in the case of an owner-occupied single family dwelling unit, the property on which the dwelling unit is located may designate the school in either of such districts to which the children lawfully residing in said dwelling on said property shall attend by filing with the district clerk of each of such districts a notice of such designation on or before August first in any year and thereafter . . . and, until a subsequent designation shall be made and filed, such children shall be deemed to be resident children of the district designated and shall be entitled to the school privileges of such district as resident pupils without the payment of tuition.

To effect a valid designation under Education Law §3203(1), petitioners must establish that "the boundary line between two school districts intersects" their property. The size of the parcel is not determinative (*Crowe, et al. v. MacFarland, et al.*, 138 AD2d 788; *Appeal of Bd. of Educ. of the Harborfields Cent. School Dist.*, 41 Ed Dept Rep 15, Decision No. 14,597; *Appeal of Bd. Educ. of the Syosset Cent. School Dist.*, 38 *id.* 791, Decision No. 14,144). Petitioners have submitted the results of a survey by a professional surveying firm that places the southern boundary of their property "several inches," as described in the surveyor's affidavit, within respondent's district.

Nevertheless, according to the May 12, 2004, letter from the Town of Onondaga Codes Enforcement Office, petitioners' boundary line agreement with their southern neighbors, which incorporates petitioners' survey, constitutes a property transfer that seeks to alter the filed subdivision map for Broadview Heights Section 6, thereby disputing the southern boundary line established by petitioners' survey. The record also indicates that the Onondaga Town Assessor rescinded the prior assessed valuation of petitioners' property allegedly lying within the Town, on the ground that the assessment was based upon an "Error in Essential Fact" because the "transfer concerns a strip of land which altered the filed Subdivision map for Broadview Heights Section 6, without first obtaining Subdivision approval as required by the Town Subdivision regulations (Parcel Deleted)." Thus, the Town of Onondaga maintains that petitioners' property boundary lines are as set forth in the filed subdivision map and, unless and until the map is properly altered, no part of petitioners' parcel lies within the Town.

Petitioners contend that a subdivision map may differ from the proven exact property line since subdivision lines are "guesstimates" or "estimates" of boundary lines between properties that are used for convenience and not for certainty in title. However, petitioners have failed to establish that the filed subdivision map for Broadview Heights Section 6 is based upon "guesstimates" or "estimates", or otherwise does not reflect the actual property boundary lines.

In an appeal to the Commissioner, petitioners have the burden of demonstrating a clear legal right to the relief requested and the burden of establishing the facts upon which they seek relief (*Appeal of Pope*, 40 Ed Dept Rep 473, Decision No. 14,530; *Appeal of Logan*, 38 *id.* 694, Decision No. 14,120; *Appeal of Catherine B.*, 37 *id.* 34, Decision No. 13,797). On the record before me, I am unable to conclude that petitioners' parcel is intersected by the boundary line between Syracuse and Westhill. Accordingly, I find that petitioners have failed to carry their burden of proof to establish their entitlement to designate respondent's district pursuant to Education Law §3203.

THE APPEAL IS DISMISSED.

Decision No. 15,129

Appeal of W.T.B. and M.B., on behalf of their son M.B., from action of the Assistant Superintendent for Pupil Personnel Services and the Board of Education of the Arlington Central School District regarding nursing services.

(November 5, 2004)

APPEARANCES OF COUNSEL

Raymond G. Kuntz, P.C., attorney for respondents

DECISION OF THE COMMISSIONER

MILLS, Commissioner.—Petitioners challenge the decision of the Assistant Superintendent for Pupil Personnel Services ("assistant superintendent") on behalf of the Board of Education of the Arlington Central School District ("the board") to deny a request for nursing services. The appeal must be dismissed.

Petitioners' son has type 1 diabetes and attends the St. Martin de Porres School ("St. Martin"), a nonpublic school located within the Arlington Central School District. The board provides St. Martin with a health aide from 9:30 a.m. to 11:15 a.m. and a registered nurse from 12:00 p.m. to 3:15 p.m.

By letter dated May 6, 2003, to the assistant superintendent, the principal of St. Martin requested that the district provide St. Martin with a full-time nurse, citing the health needs of three diabetic children. By letter dated May 22, 2003, the assistant superintendent denied the request. This appeal ensued.

Petitioners contend that respondents have failed to provide their son with nursing services that are equivalent to the services they provide in district schools, as required by Education Law §912. Among other things, petitioners note that respondents provide at least one full-time nurse to every public school in the district and argue that respondents are required to provide a full-time nurse at St. Martin. Petitioners also claim that respondents have failed to arrange for "appropriate" health care coverage for St. Martin students at "off site school activit[ies]," as they do for public school students.

Petitioners also contend that respondents' refusal to provide a full-time nurse is unlawful because it forces the health aide, who is not a registered professional nurse, to provide services that are required to be performed by a nurse under the Nurse Practice Act (Education Law §6900 *et seq.*). Petitioners request that I order respondents to provide "equitable access to health services" and monitor respondents' performance for three years. Petitioners also request that I subpoena St. Martin's student health records to substantiate their claim that the health aide improperly delivers health care without supervision.

Respondents contend that the services provided at St. Martin are equivalent to those provided at district schools because they are based on the same nurse-to-student ratio.

Preliminarily, I must deny petitioners' request to subpoena respondents' student health records because an appeal to the Commissioner under Education Law §310 is appellate in nature and does not provide for discovery or investigations (*Appeal of Krantz*, 38 Ed Dept Rep 485, Decision No. 14,077; *Appeal of Schonfeld*, 38 *id.* 306, Decision No. 14,040).

Education Law §902(2)(b) provides that any board of education "may employ one or more" nurses.[1] In addition, Education Law §912 provides, in pertinent part:

> The voters and/or trustees or board of education of every school district shall, upon request of the authorities of a school other than public, provide resident children who attend such school with any or all of the health and welfare services and facilities which are made available by such voters and/or trustees or board of education to or for children attending the public schools of the district.

This section obligates a school district to provide its resident children who attend nonpublic schools with certain services, including those of a nurse, equivalent to those provided to resident children who attend public school (*see*, *Cornelia v. Bd. of Educ. of Cent. School Dist. No. 1, Town of Greece*, 36 AD2d 576, aff'd 29 NY2d 586; *Appeal of Burke*, 34 Ed Dept Rep 3, Decision No. 13,213).

In an appeal to the Commissioner, petitioners bear the burden of establishing all of the facts upon which they seek relief (8 NYCRR §275.10; *Appeal of Laurie*, 42 Ed Dept Rep 313, Decision No. 14,867; *Appeal of Boiko*, 40 *id*. 409, Decision No. 14,513; *Appeal of Taylor*, 39 *id*. 368, Decision No. 14,261) and to demonstrate a clear legal right to the relief requested (*Appeal of Boiko*, *supra*; *Appeal of Taylor*, *supra*).

I find that petitioners have not established that respondents failed to comply with Education Law §912. Respondents explain that they determine the level of nursing staff assigned to each public school based on the number of students in a particular building and use the same criteria for nonpublic schools. To substantiate this contention, respondents submit a chart listing the student population and corresponding nursing staff levels at each public and nonpublic school in the district. This chart reflects that every public school in respondents' district is staffed with at least one full-time nurse, while three of the four private schools are staffed with half-time nurses. However, the chart further reflects that the three private schools have smaller student populations than the public schools. St. Martin,

---

[1] Effective September 1, 2004, this section was amended to require that any nurse so employed be a "registered professional nurse" (Ch. 477, L. 2004). It was also renumbered from §902(1)(b) to §902(2)(b).

the smallest of the nonpublic schools, has an enrollment of 275, compared to 395 at Travers Road Primary, the smallest public school. The remainder of the public schools staffed with full-time nurses are significantly larger than St. Martin, with populations ranging from 472 to 847.

There is no requirement that a school district staff each of its schools with a full-time nurse (Education Law §902(2)(b), *Appeal of Burke*, *supra*). Therefore, Education Law §912 cannot be read to require a board of education to staff every nonpublic school, regardless of size, with a full-time nurse. Accordingly, there is nothing that prohibits respondents from basing their nursing staff decisions on the size of the student population at each facility (*Appeal of Burke*, *supra*). Based on the relatively small student population at St. Martin, I find that respondents' provision of a half-time nurse supplemented by a part-time health aide is equivalent to the nursing services provided to public school students. To the extent that St. Martin wishes to provide its students with a higher level of service, it is free to hire additional nursing staff to supplement the services provided by respondents.

Similarly, with respect to off-site activities, petitioners have failed to establish a lack of comparability of available services. Although petitioners complain that respondents have not provided nursing staff to accompany their child on field trips, petitioners have failed to establish that respondents provide such services to its public school students. Nor have they established that they have made a specific request that was denied.

I also find no merit to petitioners' claim that respondents' refusal to provide a full-time nurse is unlawful because it forces the health aide to perform nursing services unsupervised, in violation of the Nurse Practice Act. First, petitioners have failed to establish that the health aide has acted improperly and, as set forth above, their allegations cannot be investigated in an appeal pursuant to Education Law §310. Contrary to petitioners' unsubstantiated allegations, respondents maintain that the health aide is supervised by a registered nurse. Moreover, to the extent that St. Martin feels that the health aide requires additional supervision, it is free to supplement the nursing services provided by respondents.

In sum, while I can understand petitioners' concern over their son's health, I do not find respondents' actions improper in any respect.

THE APPEAL IS DISMISSED.

Decision No. 15,130

Appeal of E.M., on behalf of his son P.M., from action of the Board of Education of the Penfield Central School District regarding an athletic suspension.

(November 5, 2004)

APPEARANCES OF COUNSEL

Joyce B. Berkowitz, Esq., attorney for petitioner

Harris Beach LLP, attorneys for respondent, *Alfred Streppa, Esq.*, of counsel

DECISION OF THE COMMISSIONER

MILLS, Commissioner.—Petitioner appeals the decision of the Board of Education of the Penfield Central School District ("respondent") suspending his son from interscholastic sports. The appeal must be dismissed.

Petitioner's son, P.M., was enrolled as a senior in respondent's high school during the 2003-2004 school year. At the high school homecoming dance on September 20, 2003, two deputy sheriffs detected the odor of alcohol on P.M. and referred him to the high school associate principal, who also detected the odor. As a result of this incident, P.M. received a three-day suspension. In addition, pursuant to the district's athletic code of conduct, P.M. was suspended for 20 days from extra-curricular activities and directed to attend three counseling sessions. After failing to attend the counseling sessions, P.M. was suspended from interscholastic athletics for the entire hockey season. Thereafter, P.M.'s mother attempted to appeal P.M.'s athletic suspension to respondent's superintendent. In an email response dated November 19, 2003, the superintendent informed P.M.'s mother that she supported the athletic director's decision to suspend her son from hockey. Petitioner commenced this appeal on December 30, 2003. Petitioner's request for interim relief was denied on January 13, 2004.

Petitioner contends that the district's athletic code of conduct is vague, that there was insufficient evidence that her son was under the influence of alcohol and that the district failed to advise him of his right to appeal the athletic suspension to the Commissioner of Education. Petitioner requests that P.M. be permitted to play hockey during the 2003-2004 season and that I require respondent to revise its athletic code of conduct.

Respondent contends, among other things, that P.M. was properly suspended from interscholastic sports pursuant to the district's athletic code of conduct, that the appeal is moot and untimely, and that it had no obligation to advise petitioner of his right to appeal his son's suspension.

The appeal must be dismissed as untimely. An appeal to the Commissioner of Education must be commenced within 30 days from the making of the decision or the performance of the act complained of, unless any delay is excused by the Commissioner for good cause shown (8 NYCRR §275.16). It is unclear when P.M. was notified of his suspension from hockey for the 2003-2004 season. However, P.M.'s mother attempted to appeal the suspension to the superintendent, who responded by email dated November 19, 2003, that she supported the athletic director's decision. Petitioner, however, did not commence his appeal until December 30, 2003, more than 30 days after the athletic director's decision and the superintendent's November 19, 2003, email. The only excuse for the delay offered by petitioner is that respondent did not inform P.M.'s parents of their right to appeal to the Commissioner. Except in unusual circumstances, ignorance of the appeal process does not excuse a delay in commencing an appeal (*Appeal of R.A. and D.A.*, 43 Ed Dept Rep ___, Decision No. 14,995; *Appeal of Biggins*, 35 *id*. 357, Decision No. 13,569; *Appeal of Pitney Bowes, Inc.*, 31 *id*. 290, Decision No. 12,646). In this case, I find no unusual circumstances to excuse the delay, and the appeal, therefore, must be dismissed as untimely (*Appeal of Biggins*, *supra*).

The appeal must also be dismissed as moot to the extent that petitioner seeks to have his son participate in the 2003-2004 hockey season. The Commissioner of Education will only consider matters in actual controversy and will not render a decision on a state of facts which no longer exist or which subsequent events have laid to rest (*Appeal of P.F. and M.F.*, 42 Ed Dept Rep 390, Decision No. 14,890; *Appeal of Lascala*, 38 *id*. 16, Decision No. 13,974). Petitioner's stay request was denied and the 2003-2004 hockey season has ended, leaving no possibility of any meaningful relief.

In light of this disposition, I need not address the parties' remaining contentions.

THE APPEAL IS DISMISSED.

Decision No. 15,131

Appeal of a STUDENT SUSPECTED OF A DISABILITY by his parent, from action of the Board of Education of the East Irondequoit Central School District regarding student discipline.

(November 5, 2004)

APPEARANCES OF COUNSEL

Joyce B. Berkowitz, Esq., attorney for petitioner

Ferrara, Fiorenza, Larrison, Barrett & Reitz, attorneys for respondent, *Norman H. Gross, Esq.*, of counsel

DECISION OF THE COMMISSIONER

MILLS, Commissioner.—Petitioner appeals a determination of the Board of Education of the East Irondequoit Central School District ("respondent") to suspend her son from school. The appeal must be dismissed.

During the 2003-2004 school year, petitioner's son was enrolled in the eighth grade in respondent's middle school. By letter dated October 9, 2003, the middle school principal advised petitioner and her husband that their son was being suspended for five days commencing October 9, 2003, for possessing marijuana. By letter dated October 10, 2003, respondent's superintendent advised petitioner and her husband that a superintendent's hearing would be held on October 16, 2003, to determine whether further discipline was warranted.

At the hearing, the student admitted possessing marijuana. By letter dated October 16, 2003, respondent's superintendent informed petitioner and her husband that, based on the hearing officer's findings, he found their son guilty of the possession charge and imposed a suspension through December 19, 2003.

By letter dated October 21, 2003, petitioner and her husband appealed the superintendent's determination to respondent. On November 7, 2003, petitioner apparently referred her son to the district's Committee on Special Education ("CSE") for evaluation. By letter dated November 25, 2003, the district clerk advised petitioner and her husband that, at its November 24, 2003, meeting, respondent affirmed the superintendent's determination, but expunged their son's short-term suspension. This appeal ensued. Petitioner's request for interim relief was denied on December 18, 2003.

Petitioner contends that respondent did not provide her with timely notice of the short-term suspension, that respondent should have presumed that her son is a student with a disability and that the penalty imposed is excessive. For relief, petitioner requests that respondent permit her son to return to school and expunge his records. Additionally, petitioner requests that respondent provide her son with additional tutoring "to assist him in his transition back to class."

Respondent contends that it had no basis to suspect that the student is disabled and points out that, the district's CSE later determined that the student did not, in fact, have a disability.

Petitioner's claim that she did not receive timely notice of the short-term suspension and her claim that respondent should have presumed her son to be a student with a disability must be dismissed as moot. The Commissioner will only decide matters in actual controversy and will not render a decision on a state of facts which no longer exists or which subsequent events have laid to rest (*Appeal of Cordisco*, 44 Ed Dept Rep ____, Decision No. 15,089; *Appeal of Kushner*, 43 *id.* _ ___, Decision No. 15,040; *Appeal of Reynolds*, 42 *id.* 231, Decision No. 14,834). Respondent has expunged the student's short-term suspension from his record. Further, following an expedited evaluation, the district's CSE determined that the student does not, in fact, have a disability. Because there is no meaningful relief that can be granted, these claims must be dismissed as moot.

Petitioner's claim that the penalty was excessive must also be dismissed. In cases of student discipline, the sanction imposed must be proportionate to the severity of the offense involved. The test to be applied in reviewing a penalty is whether it is so excessive as to warrant substitution of the Commissioner's judgment for that of the board (*Appeal of D.C.*, 43 Ed Dept Rep ___, Decision No. 14,976; *Appeal of J.C. and P.C.*, 41 *id.* 395, Decision No. 14,723; *Appeal of Harlan*, 40 *id.* 309, Decision No. 14,488). I find that the penalty imposed in this case is not irrational or unreasonable and is within respondent's discretion (*see*, *Appeal of Hyde*, 38 Ed Dept Rep 719, Decision No. 14,125). Accordingly, I will not substitute my discretion for that of respondent.

THE APPEAL IS DISMISSED.

Decision No. 15,132

Appeal of V.L., on behalf of her son J.L., from action of the Board of Education of the Huntington Union Free School District regarding student discipline.

(November 5, 2004)

APPEARANCES OF COUNSEL

William G. Ripp, Esq., attorney for petitioner

Guercio & Guercio, attorneys for respondent, *Barbara P. Aloe, Esq.*, of counsel

DECISION OF THE COMMISSIONER

MILLS, Commissioner.—Petitioner appeals the suspension of her son, J.L., by the Board of Education of the Huntington Union Free School District ("respondent"). The appeal must be dismissed.

During the 2003-2004 school year, J.L. was a junior in respondent's high school. By letter dated November 3, 2003, the high school principal notified petitioner's husband that J.L. was suspended for five days for possessing marijuana and "3 dangerous instruments, to wit, 3 syringes with needles." By letter also dated November 3, 2003, respondent's superintendent notified petitioner and her husband of a superintendent's hearing on charges that J.L. had endangered the safety, health and welfare of himself and/or others and was insubordinate for possessing marijuana and dangerous instruments while on school property on October 31, 2003, in violation of school rules and policies.

On November 7, 2003, petitioner, her husband and J.L. appeared without counsel for the scheduled hearing. Prior to the commencement of the hearing, they met with respondent's attorney, who advised them that in light of J.L.'s arrest for possession of marijuana and hypodermic needles, the district would agree to a settlement of the charges. According to respondent's attorney, J.L. and his parents agreed to waive their rights to a hearing and accept a five-month suspension from school from November 7, 2003, to April 16, 2004, to coincide with the end of the grading period. The attorney informed J.L. and his parents that the district would not provide home tutoring to J.L. during the suspension period because he was beyond compulsory school age.

Thereafter, the hearing officer commenced the hearing on the record. The two November 3 letters were introduced as evidence and the charges were read into the record. J.L. and his parents were informed of their rights concerning the hearing and appeal process. Respondent's attorney then informed the hearing officer that J.L. and his parents had "agreed and [had] elected to waive their rights to a hearing, and the rights that attach to a hearing, and [had] agreed and elected, in lieu of a hearing, to accept a suspension from attendance effective immediately and continuing up to and including April 16th, 2003 [sic]." All three responded "yes" when asked if they were entering into this agreement and disposition "voluntarily, knowingly, and without coercion."

By letter to respondent dated November 26, 2003, petitioner's attorney appealed the length of the suspension as excessive and requested a stay permitting J.L. to return to class. The attorney apparently wrote a second letter to respondent on December 9, 2003, but that letter is not in the record before me. By letter dated January 14, 2004, the superintendent informed petitioner's attorney that at its January 12, 2004, regular meeting, respondent upheld the disposition of the superintendent's hearing and that J.L.'s suspension would remain in effect through April 16, 2004. This appeal ensued. Petitioner's request for interim relief was denied on February 12, 2004.

Petitioner contends that syringes should not be classified as a weapon, and maintains that J.L. did not threaten anyone with the syringes and did not intend to use the syringes to harm anyone. She asserts that a five-month penalty is excessive for the offense committed, and requests that J.L. be permitted to return to school.

Respondent asserts that petitioner knowingly waived her rights and cannot appeal the suspension because she consented to it. Respondent asserts that petitioner admitted that J.L. possessed the syringes and what he believed was marijuana, and that the penalty is appropriate. Respondent also asserts that the petition fails to comply with §§275.8, 275.11 and 275.16 of the Commissioner's regulations. Finally, respondent contends that the appeal is moot because J.L. served the suspension and returned to school as of April 19, 2004.

The appeal must be dismissed as moot. The Commissioner of Education will only consider matters in actual controversy and will not render a decision on a state of facts that no longer exists or that subsequent events have laid to rest (*Appeal of P.F. and M.F.*, 42 Ed Dept Rep 390, Decision No. 14,890; *Appeal of Lascala*, 38 *id.* 16, Decision No. 13,974). Petitioner requests only that J.L. be permitted to return to Huntington High School and does not seek expungement of his records. Since the suspension ended on April 16, 2004, and J.L. has returned to school, no meaningful relief can be granted and the appeal must be dismissed as moot (*Appeal of D.W.*, 43 Ed Dept Rep ___, Decision No. 14,965; *Appeal of R.R. and K.R.*, 41 *id.* 405, Decision No. 14,726).

Although the appeal is dismissed on procedural grounds, I remind respondent that to effectuate a waiver of rights under Education Law §3214, the waiver must not only be voluntary, knowing and intelligent, but the district must also provide the student and parents with a written document clearly and concisely stating all of the rights to be waived, as well as the consequences of waiving such rights (*Appeal of a Student with a Disability*, 42 Ed Dept Rep 192, Decision No. 14,818; *Appeal of J.G.*, 39 *id.* 393, Decision No. 14,270; *Appeals of McMahon and Mosely, et al.*, 38 *id.* 22, Decision No. 13,976).

In light of this disposition, I need not address the parties' remaining contentions.

THE APPEAL IS DISMISSED.

Decision No. 15,133

Appeal of STEVE FRATELLO from action of the Board of Education of the Bay Shore Union Free School District regarding substitute teaching services.

(November 5, 2004)

APPEARANCES OF COUNSEL

Ingerman Smith, L.L.P., attorneys for respondent, *Anna M. Scricca, Esq.*, of counsel

DECISION OF THE COMMISSIONER

MILLS, Commissioner.—Petitioner challenges the decision of the Board of Education of the Bay Shore Union Free School District ("respondent") to remove him from the district's per diem substitute teaching roll. The appeal must be dismissed.

Petitioner served as a per diem substitute teacher for respondent from November 2002 until January 2003. On December 16, 2002, petitioner accepted a half-day work assignment and was compensated at half the daily rate in accordance with the applicable collective bargaining agreement. Petitioner believed that he was entitled to a whole day's pay for his services. He made his position known to district personnel in what he admits was a confrontational and unprofessional manner.

In February 2003, respondent's president informed petitioner that he had been removed from the approved per diem substitute roll because of his unprofessional behavior toward district staff members. By letter dated February 4, 2003, to the superintendent of schools, petitioner requested that he be reinstated to the district's per diem substitute teaching roll. By letter dated March 19, 2003, the superintendent declined petitioner's request. This appeal ensued.

Petitioner alleges that the district did not provide him with a copy of the applicable collective bargaining agreement. He contends that the only document which he received relating to pay was the substitute teacher handbook which did not contain information regarding half-day pay.

Petitioner requests that he be reinstated to respondent's per diem substitute teaching roll. He also requests that certain district employees be reprimanded for what he characterizes as unethical behavior. Finally, he asks that I investigate certain matters relating to the justification for payment of union dues.

Respondent asserts that petitioner's appeal is untimely and fails to state a claim upon which relief may be granted. It also alleges that petitioner failed to exhaust his administrative remedies both by not appealing the superintendent's decision to the board of education and by not invoking the grievance procedure under the applicable collective bargaining agreement. Finally, it argues that its actions were proper.

An appeal to the Commissioner must be commenced within 30 days from the making of the decision or the performance of the act complained of, unless excused by the Commissioner for good cause shown (8 NYCRR §275.16; *Appeals of Villien*, 44 Ed Dept Rep ___, Decision No. 15,101; *Appeal of O'Brien*, 44 *id.* ___, Decision No. 15,092). Petitioner was informed of his removal from the per diem substitute teaching roll in February 2003 and of the superintendent's denial of his reinstatement by letter dated March 19, 2003. The petition was served on May 4, 2004, more than one year later. The only reasons petitioner offers for his delay is ignorance of the appeal process and personal reasons. Under these circumstances, I find no basis to excuse petitioner's lengthy delay. Accordingly, the appeal must be dismissed as untimely.

Even if the appeal were not dismissed on procedural grounds, it would be dismissed on the merits. In an appeal to the Commissioner, petitioner has the burden of demonstrating a clear legal right to the relief requested (8 NYCRR § 275.10; *Appeal of Sloley-Raymond*, 44 Ed Dept Rep ___, Decision No. 15,085; *Appeal of Holder*, 44 *id.* ___, Decision No. 15,088). Petitioner has neither alleged nor established that respondent acted for a constitutionally impermissible reason or in violation of a statutory or contractual proscription. On the record before me petitioner, by his own admission, acted in a confrontational and unprofessional manner when interacting with district employees and that, in and of itself, is sufficient justification for respondent's action.

In light of this disposition, I need not address the parties' remaining contentions.

THE APPEAL IS DISMISSED.

Decision No. 15,134

Appeal of S.C., on behalf of her son B.C., from action of the Board of Education of the Half Hollow Hills Central School District regarding student discipline.

(November 10, 2004)

APPEARANCES OF COUNSEL

Ehrlich, Frazer & Feldman, attorneys for respondent, *Sanjay B. Malhotra, Esq.*, of counsel

DECISION OF THE COMMISSIONER

MILLS, Commissioner.—Petitioner appeals the suspension of her son, B.C., by the Board of Education of the Half Hollow Hills Central School District ("respondent"). The appeal must be dismissed.

When this appeal arose, B.C. was enrolled in the eighth grade in respondent's district. On October 3, 2003, B.C. refused to dress for gym class, and when confronted about his conduct by a member of respondent's administrative staff, he allegedly cursed and threw his books into the hallway. As a result of the incident, the middle school principal imposed a one day in-school suspension and a one day out-of-school suspension.

By letter dated October 3, 2003, the principal informed petitioner that B.C. would serve the in-school suspension on October 7, 2003, and the out-of-school suspension on October 8, 2003. The letter also informed petitioner that she would have the opportunity for an informal conference with the principal, at which she could question complaining witnesses.

On October 17, 2003, B.C. allegedly intimidated and physically threatened another student. The middle school principal imposed a one day in-school suspension and a one day out-of-school suspension. By letter dated October 17, 2003, the principal informed petitioner that B.C. would serve the in-school suspension for the remaining class periods of October 17, 2003, and the out-of-school suspension on October 20, 2003. The letter also informed petitioner that she would have the opportunity for an informal conference with the principal, at which she could question complaining witnesses.

Petitioner claims that respondent failed to provide her with timely written notice and denied her the opportunity for an informal conference with respect to each of her son's suspensions. Petitioner seeks a finding that the suspensions were improper and that they be expunged from her son's record.

Respondent asserts that petitioner fails to state a cause of action and failed to exhaust her administrative remedies. Respondent further contends that petitioner was afforded timely written notice and was afforded the opportunity for informal conferences. Respondent submits that the suspensions were in all respects proper.

Respondent's contention that the appeal must be dismissed because petitioner failed to exhaust her administrative remedies is without merit. Students who are suspended from school for five days or less may appeal their suspension directly to the Commissioner, unless a school district has adopted a policy that would require students to appeal short-term suspensions to the board of education before appealing to the Commissioner (*Appeal of Amara S.*, 39 Ed Dept Rep 90, Decision No. 14,182). The record does not demonstrate that respondent has such a policy. Therefore, I will not dismiss the appeal on that basis.

Because B.C. has already served the suspensions, the appeal is moot except to the extent that petitioner seeks expungement of his records (*Appeal of D.J.*, 42 Ed Dept Rep 382, Decision No. 14,888).

Education Law §3214(3)(b)(1) provides that in the case of a suspension up to five days in length:

> [T]he suspending authority shall provide the pupil with notice of the charged misconduct. . . . The pupil and the person in parental relation to the pupil shall, on request, be given an opportunity for an informal conference with the principal at which the pupil and/or person in

> parental relation shall be authorized to present the pupil's version of the event and to ask questions of the complaining witnesses. The aforesaid notice and opportunity for an informal conference shall take place prior to suspension of the pupil unless the pupil's presence in the school poses a continuing danger to persons or property or an ongoing threat of disruption to the academic process. . . .

Further, §100.2(l)(4) of the Commissioner's regulations provides in pertinent part:

> When suspension of a student from attendance for a period of five days or less pursuant to section 3214(3) of the Education Law is proposed, school district officials shall immediately notify the parents or the persons in parental relation in writing that the student may be suspended from school. Written notice shall be provided by personal delivery, express mail delivery, or equivalent means reasonably calculated to assure receipt of such notice within 24 hours of the decision to propose suspension. . . . Such notice shall provide a description of the incident(s) for which suspension is proposed and shall inform the parents. . . .of their right to request an immediate informal conference with the principal in accordance with the provisions of Education Law section 3214(3)(b). . . . Such notice and opportunity for an informal conference shall take place prior to the suspension of the student unless the student's presence in the school poses a continuing danger to persons or property or an ongoing threat of disruption to the academic process. . . .

The purpose of this provision is to make the parents of a student suspended for five days or less aware of the statutory right provided in Education Law §3214(3)(b) to question the complaining witnesses in front of the principal who imposed the suspension in the first instance, who also has the authority to terminate or reduce the suspension. This procedure affords the principal the opportunity to decide whether his original decision to suspend was correct or should be modified.

Petitioner claims that she did not receive the written notice regarding the October 7, 2003, incident until October 9, 2003, and that she did not receive any written notification from the district regarding the October 17, 2003, incident. Respondent has submitted an affidavit from a staff member who states that she personally delivered the notice of suspension letter dated October 3, 2003, to petitioner's residence on October 3, 2003. She further states that she personally delivered the notice of suspension letter dated October 17, 2003, to petitioner's residence on October 17, 2003. Both notices were also sent by regular mail.

Petitioner further claims that her availability for the informal conference scheduled for October 7, 2003, was not confirmed and that she left messages with several district officials regarding the same that went unanswered. Respondent submits an affidavit from its principal stating that petitioner did not call to inform district officials that she was unavailable or to ask that the informal conference be rescheduled. He further states that had she done so, he would have accommodated such request.

In an appeal to the Commissioner, petitioner has the burden of demonstrating a clear legal right to the relief requested and the burden of establishing the facts upon which she seeks relief (8 NYCRR §275.10; *Appeal of M.F. and J.F.*, 43 Ed Dept Rep ___, Decision No. 14,960; *Appeal of Kessler*, 43 *id.* ___, Decision No. 14,958). In this case, respondent submitted evidence in the form of affidavits to show that the district complied with the notice and informal conference requirements of the Education Law and Commissioner's regulations. Significantly, petitioner failed to submit a reply to respondents' answer and affidavits in support thereof. After careful review of the record before me, I find petitioner has not met her burden of proving the facts upon which her claim is based.

THE APPEAL IS DISMISSED.

Decision No. 15,135

Appeal of LAWRENCE LOMBARDO from action of the Board of Education of the Lynbrook Union Free School District regarding alleged conflicts of interest.

(November 10, 2004)

APPEARANCES OF COUNSEL

Ehrlich, Frazer & Feldman, attorneys for respondent, *James H. Pyun, Esq.*, of counsel

DECISION OF THE COMMISSIONER

MILLS, Commissioner.—Petitioner objects to the participation by certain members of the Board of Education of the Lynbrook Union

Free School District ("respondent") in matters involving the district's teacher contracts. The appeal must be dismissed.

Petitioner alleges that two unnamed board members have spouses who are district teachers and requests that I prohibit board members from negotiating or voting on future teacher contracts. Petitioner's request for interim relief was denied on July 12, 2004.

Respondent asserts that the petition does not raise a justiciable controversy because the district is not currently negotiating a contract with its teachers and has not done so since June 2002. Respondent also asserts that board members whose spouses are employed by the district are legally permitted to participate in contract negotiations and votes.

The appeal must be dismissed on procedural grounds. The Commissioner of Education will not render an advisory opinion on an issue before it becomes justiciable (*Appeal of Jacobson*, 37 Ed Dept Rep 75, Decision No. 13,808; *Appeal of Rhodes*, 21 *id.* 632, Decision No. 10,815). Because respondent is not currently negotiating a contract with district teachers, any ruling on this matter would be purely advisory. The Commissioner of Education does not issue advisory opinions in appeals brought pursuant to Education Law §310 (*Appeal of Coleman, et al.*, 42 Ed Dept Rep 256, Decision No. 14,845; *Appeal of Razzano*, 39 *id.* 303, Decision No. 14,244).

Even if the appeal were not dismissed on procedural grounds, it would be dismissed on the merits. In an appeal to the Commissioner of Education, the petitioner has the burden of demonstrating a clear legal right to the relief requested and the burden of establishing the facts upon which he seeks relief (8 NYCRR §275.10; *Appeal of B.H. and B.H.*, 43 Ed Dept Rep ___, Decision No. 14,919; *Appeal of J.T.*, 43 *id.* ___, Decision No. 14,917).

General Municipal Law §801 generally prohibits municipal officers and employees from having an interest in contracts with the municipality they serve. General Municipal Law §800(3) defines an "interest" as "a direct or indirect pecuniary or material benefit accruing to a municipal officer or employee as the result of a contract with the municipality which such officer or employee serves." That subdivision further provides that "a municipal officer or employee shall be deemed to have an interest in the contract of (a) his spouse, minor children and dependents, *except a contract of employment* with the municipality which such officer or employee serves . . ." (emphasis added). Thus, the General Municipal Law explicitly excludes a spouse's employment contract from coverage under the conflict of interest provision and therefore, does not bar a board member from negotiating or voting on the contract of a spouse (*see*, *Appeal of Grinnell*, 37 Ed Dept Rep 504, Decision No. 13,914). Nor does petitioner cite any other legal authority prohibiting board members from doing so. Under these circumstances, petitioner has failed to establish any basis for relief.

THE APPEAL IS DISMISSED.

Decision No. 15,136

Appeal of JAMES OCKIMEY from action of the Board of Education of the Uniondale Union Free School District regarding an election.

(November 17, 2004)

APPEARANCES OF COUNSEL

Ingerman Smith, LLP, attorneys for respondent, *Lawrence W. Reich, Esq*., of counsel

DECISION OF THE COMMISSIONER

MILLS, Commissioner.—Petitioner, an unsuccessful candidate for election to the Board of Education of the Uniondale Union Free School District ("respondent"), appeals the conduct of a school district election. The appeal must be dismissed.

On May 18, 2004, respondent conducted its annual meeting and election for the purpose of voting on a proposed school district budget and filling two seats on respondent board. Incumbent Raymond Rhoden defeated petitioner by a margin of 345 votes, incumbent Deborah Mabry defeated Elaine Portuondo-Smith by 484 votes, and the voters approved the annual budget by a margin of 215 votes.

Petitioner contends that respondent improperly permitted members of the Uniondale Teachers Association ("Union") to disseminate a flyer at polling places during school hours. He asserts that the flyer improperly urged voters to reelect the two incumbent board members and vote in favor of the budget. Petitioner contends that district facilities, employees and funds were used to disseminate the flyer. He further contends that "[t]he budget passed by about 320 votes which could not be verified with the Buff cards for the books." Petitioner maintains that these irregularities affected the outcome of the election. Petitioner seeks to overturn the election and requests that respondent be prohibited from spending any funds in excess of the amount it could have levied under a contingent budget. Petitioner's request for interim relief was denied on July 7, 2004.

Respondent asserts that the appeal is untimely and must be dismissed for failure to join necessary parties. Respondent alleges that the Union prepared and distributed the flyer, which was on Union letterhead, without any support, knowledge or funding from district sources. Respondent denies any wrongdoing in the conduct of the election and asserts that petitioner has failed to demonstrate that any alleged irregularities occurred or affected the outcome of the election.

I must first address petitioner's attempt to bring this appeal on his behalf and behalf of "all others similarly situated." An appeal may only be maintained on behalf of a class where the class is so numerous that joinder of all members is impracticable and where all questions of fact and law are common to all members of the class (8 NYCRR §275.2; *Appeal of Garmaeva*, 43 Ed Dept Rep ___, Decision No. 14,988; *Appeal of Colety, et al.*, 42 *id.* 162, Decision No. 14,806; *Appeal of Broardt, et al.*, 42 *id.* 126, Decision No. 14,796). A petitioner must set forth the number of individuals he or she seeks to represent and must show that all questions of law and fact would be common to all members of the class (*Appeal of Recore*, 42 Ed Dept Rep 283, Decision No. 14,856; *Appeal of Colety, et al., supra*). Petitioner makes no assertion that he represents any individuals other than those identified in the caption of the petition. Accordingly, class status is denied.

The appeal must be dismissed as untimely. An appeal to the Commissioner of Education must be commenced within 30 days of the making of the decision or the performance of the act complained of, unless any delay is excused by the Commissioner for good cause shown (8 NYCRR §275.16; *Appeal of Long*, 39 Ed Dept Rep 463, Decision No. 14,284). Petitioner did not commence this appeal until June 18, 2004, 31 days after the election, and offers no excuse for the delay.

The petition must also be dismissed for failure to join the successful board candidates as necessary parties. A party whose rights would be adversely affected by a determination of an appeal in favor of petitioner is a necessary party and must be named as such and served with a notice of petition and petition (*Appeal of Ewart*, 44 Ed Dept Rep ___, Decision No. 15,127; *Appeal of Milazzo*, 43 *id.* ___, Decision No. 14,999; *Appeal of Stolbach*, 43 *id.* ___, Decision No. 14,977). If an appeal involves the validity of a school district meeting or election, the petition must be served upon each successful candidate whose right to hold office is disputed and such person must be joined as a necessary party (8 NYCRR §275.8(d); *Appeal of VanAllen*, 38 Ed Dept Rep 701, Decision No. 14,122). In this case, a decision in petitioner's favor would clearly affect the rights of Mr. Rhoden and Ms. Mabry, and neither was named as a respondent or served with a copy of the notice of petition or petition. Accordingly, petitioner's failure to do so requires dismissal of the appeal.

In light of this disposition, I need not address the parties' remaining contentions.

THE APPEAL IS DISMISSED.

Decision No. 15,137

Appeal of ARMAND REO from action of the Board of Education of the Enlarged City School District of the City of Troy regarding an employment contract.

(November 24, 2004)

APPEARANCES OF COUNSEL

Whiteman Osterman & Hanna, LLP, attorneys for petitioner, *Melvin H. Osterman, Esq*., of counsel

Girvin & Ferlazzo, P.C., attorneys for respondent, *James A.P. McCarthy, Esq*., of counsel

DECISION OF THE COMMISSIONER

MILLS, Commissioner.—Petitioner alleges that the Board of Education of the Enlarged City School District of the City of Troy ("respondent") breached his employment contract. The appeal must be dismissed.

On January 31, 2001, respondent and petitioner executed an employment contract providing that petitioner's employment as Superintendent "shall commence on July 1, 2001, and expire on June 30, 2005." Under the heading, "Agreement Renewals," the contract states:

> 1. [Respondent] shall notify [petitioner], prior to January 1, 2004, whether it intends to offer him a new term commencing July 1, 2005. Such notification shall be in writing and delivered to [petitioner] by certified or registered mail, or by personal delivery.

At a meeting on December 8, 2003, respondent discussed petitioner's employment in executive session. During that meeting, the school district's attorney was directed to draft a letter to petitioner indicating that respondent did not intend to offer him a new term commencing July 1, 2005. Respondent did not vote concerning petitioner's employment.

On December 26, 2003, respondent's attorney sent petitioner a letter by certified mail stating, in relevant part:

> Please be advised that I have been directed by a majority of the Board of Education to advise you that pursuant to [the agreement renewals' section] of your employment agreement the Board hereby notifies you that the Board does not intend to offer you a new term of employment commencing July 1, 2005.

This appeal ensued.

Petitioner alleges that respondent breached the agreement renewals' provision of his employment contract which required respondent to notify him prior to January 1, 2004, whether it intended to offer him a new term. He asserts that the attorney's December 26, 2003, letter did not meet this contractual requirement because respondent's members never voted to notify petitioner that it was not renewing his contract nor voted to authorize respondent's attorney to do so. He asks that I direct respondent to extend the term of his agreement by one year.

Respondent argues that the appeal is untimely, that the claims are not ripe because respondent might still decide to extend the term of his employment, and that petitioner has failed to exhaust administrative remedies. Respondent also argues that the contract only required respondent to notify petitioner if it was going to renew his agreement, not if it declined to do so.

The appeal must be dismissed as untimely. An appeal to the Commissioner of Education pursuant to Education Law §310 must be commenced within 30 days of the action or decision complained of, unless any delay is excused by the Commissioner for good cause shown (8 NYCRR §275.16).

Petitioner alleges that his contract was breached because respondent failed to properly notify him before January 1, 2004, whether his contract would be renewed. Respondent argues that it did not have to notify petitioner by that date if it decided not to renew petitioner's contract. In either case, as of January 1, 2004, the issue of whether there had been a breach of contract became ripe for review. Therefore, petitioner needed to commence the appeal within 30 days of January 1, 2004. Petitioner commenced this appeal on March 25, 2004, more than 30 days later, and provides no excuse for his delay.

Further, I find no merit to petitioner's assertion that the alleged breach constitutes a continuing wrong that may be appealed at any time. The continuing wrong doctrine applies when the ongoing action is itself an unlawful action, such as unlawful appointments to a district's shared decision-making team (*Appeal of Sadue-Sokolow*, 39 Ed Dept Rep 6, Decision No. 14,155) or certain ongoing expenditures under an austerity budget that did not comply with the law (*Appeal of Aarseth*, 32 Ed Dept Rep 506, Decision No. 12,901). The doctrine does not apply where the specific action being challenged is a single action, inaction or decision and the resulting effects are not intrinsically unlawful (*see*, *Appeals of Simpson, et al.*, 40 Ed Dept Rep 5, Decision No. 14,402). Petitioner challenges respondent's alleged failure to notify him whether his contract was going to be renewed, which is not inherently unlawful, and therefore the continuing wrong doctrine does not apply (*see*, *Appeals of Pascasi*, 43 Ed Dept Rep ___, Decision No. 14,997; *Appeals of American Quality Beverages*, 42 *id.* 144, Decision No. 14,804). Accordingly, the appeal must be dismissed as untimely.

THE APPEAL IS DISMISSED

Decision No. 15,138

Appeal of LINDA RIZZO from action of the Board of Education of the Enlarged City School District of the City of Troy regarding an employment contract.

(November 24, 2004)

APPEARANCES OF COUNSEL

McCary & Huff, LLP, attorneys for petitioner, *Kathryn McCary, Esq.*, of counsel

Girvin & Ferlazzo, P.C., attorneys for respondent, *James A.P. McCarthy, Esq.*, of counsel

DECISION OF THE COMMISSIONER

MILLS, Commissioner.—Petitioner alleges that the Board of Education of the Enlarged City School District of the City of Troy ("respondent") breached her employment contract. The appeal must be dismissed.

On January 31, 2001, respondent and petitioner executed an employment contract providing that petitioner's employment as Associate Superintendent "shall commence on July 1, 2001, and expire on June 30, 2005." Under the heading, "Agreement Renewals," the contract states:

> 1. [Respondent] shall notify [petitioner], prior to January 1, 2004, whether it intends to offer her a new term commencing July 1, 2005. Such notification shall be in writing and delivered to [petitioner] by certified or registered mail, or by personal delivery.

At a meeting on December 8, 2003, respondent discussed petitioner's employment in executive session. During that session, the school district's attorney was directed to draft a letter to petitioner indicating that respondent did not intend to offer her a new term commencing July 1, 2005. Respondent's members did not vote concerning petitioner's employment.

On December 26, 2003, respondent's attorney sent petitioner a letter by certified mail stating, in relevant part:

> Please be advised that I have been directed by a majority of the Board of Education to advise you that pursuant to [the agreement renewals' section] of your employment agreement the Board hereby notifies you that the Board does not intend to offer you a new term of employment commencing July 1, 2005.

This appeal ensued.

Petitioner alleges that respondent breached the agreement renewals' provision of her employment contract which required respondent to notify her prior to January 1, 2004, whether it intended to offer her a new term. She asserts that the attorney's December 26, 2003, letter did not meet this contractual requirement because respondent's members never voted to notify petitioner that it was not renewing her contract nor voted to authorize respondent's attorney to do so. She asks that I direct respondent to extend the term of her agreement by one year.

Respondent argues that the appeal is untimely, that the claims are not ripe because respondent might still decide to extend the term of her employment, and that petitioner has failed to exhaust administrative remedies. Respondent also argues that the contract only required respondent to notify petitioner if it was going to renew her agreement, not if it decided not to renew her agreement.

The appeal must be dismissed as untimely. An appeal to the Commissioner of Education pursuant to Education Law §310 must be commenced within 30 days of the action or decision complained of, unless any delay is excused by the Commissioner for good cause shown (8 NYCRR §275.16).

Petitioner alleges that her contract was breached because respondent failed to properly notify her before January 1, 2004, whether her contract would be renewed. Respondent argues that it did not have to notify petitioner by that date if it had decided not to renew petitioner's contract, only if it was going to renew it. In either case, as of January 1, 2004, the issue of whether there had been a breach of contract on that date could have been decided, and no subsequent action by respondent would impact that determination. Therefore, petitioner needed to commence the appeal within 30 days of January 1, 2004. Petitioner commenced this appeal on March 29, 2004, more than 30 days later, and provides no excuse for his delay.

Petitioner relies on *Matter of Pine and Costello* (18 Ed Dept Rep 207, Decision No. 9807) and *Matter of Sammon* (20 Ed Dept Rep 335, Decision No. 10,429) which both held that where a determination becomes effective at a later date, the time within which an appeal may be brought begins to run on the effective date. These cases are not applicable in the present case. Petitioner does not complain about a decision that will take effect at a later date, but rather respondent's alleged failure to act prior to January 1, 2004, thus allegedly resulting in a breach of contract at that time.

Further, I find no merit to petitioner's assertion that this constitutes a continuing wrong that may be appealed at any time. The continuing wrong doctrine applies when the ongoing action is itself an unlawful action, such as unlawful appointments to a district's shared decision-making team (*Appeal of Sadue-Sokolow*, 39 Ed Dept Rep 6, Decision No. 14,155) or certain ongoing expenditures under an austerity budget that did not comply with the law (*Appeal of Aarseth*, 32 Ed Dept Rep 506, Decision No. 12,901). The doctrine does not apply where the specific action being challenged is a single action, inaction or decision and the resulting effects are not intrinsically unlawful (*see*, *Appeals of Simpson, et al.*, 40 Ed Dept Rep 5, Decision No. 14,402). Petitioner challenges respondent's failure to notify her whether her contract was going to be renewed, which is not inherently unlawful, and therefore the continuing wrong doctrine does not apply (*see*, *Appeals of Pascasi*, 43 Ed Dept Rep ___, Decision No. 14,997; *Appeals of American Quality Beverages*, 42 *id*. 144, Decision No. 14,804). Accordingly, the appeal must be dismissed as untimely.

THE APPEAL IS DISMISSED.

Decision No. 15,139

Appeal of JOSEPH E. SWEENEY from action of the Board of Cooperative Educational Services for the Second Supervisory District of Erie, Chautauqua and Cattaraugus Counties, District Superintendent Richard G. Timbs, and Kelly Services, Inc. regarding a contract for substitute teaching services.

(November 24, 2004)

APPEARANCES OF COUNSEL

James R. Sandner, Esq., attorney for petitioner, *Mary Scalise Perillo* and *James D. Bilik, Esqs.*, of counsel

Hodgson Russ LLP, attorneys for respondents, *David A. Farmelo, Esq.*, of counsel

DECISION OF THE COMMISSIONER

MILLS, Commissioner.—Petitioner, a resident taxpayer of the Fredonia Central School District, a component district of the Board of Cooperative Educational Services for the Second Supervisory District of Erie, Chautauqua and Cattaraugus Counties ("BOCES"), brings this appeal against BOCES, its District Superintendent Richard G. Timbs and Kelly Services, Inc. ("Kelly"), collectively "respondents," to annul a contract between BOCES and Kelly, and to annul the alleged delegation of substitute teaching instruction to Kelly. The appeal must be sustained.

On August 25, 2003, BOCES and Kelly entered into a contract for "per diem" substitute teaching services. The contract provides that Kelly will recruit, interview, select, hire and assign employees to render per diem substitute teaching services for BOCES. It further provides that Kelly will ensure that each per diem substitute meets any applicable teacher certification and criminal background check requirements, pay the per diem substitutes' wages and benefits, and maintain their personnel and pay records. The contract further provides that the substitute teachers shall remain Kelly's employees and shall not be employees of the BOCES.

In accordance with the terms of the contract, Kelly began providing per diem substitutes to BOCES at the beginning of the 2003-2004 school year. This appeal ensued. Petitioner's request for interim relief was denied on December 19, 2003.

Petitioner asserts that BOCES has no legal authority to contract with Kelly for the services of per diem substitutes. He also asserts that the contract is a violation of the respondent superintendent's obligation under §80-5.4 of the Commissioner's regulations to employ appropriately qualified substitute teachers.

Respondents contend that petitioner does not have standing to bring this appeal. Respondents further assert that BOCES does have authority to contract for the services of the per diem substitutes.

I decline to dismiss the appeal for lack of standing. An individual may not maintain an appeal pursuant to Education Law §310 unless aggrieved in the sense that he or she has suffered personal damage or injury to her or his civil, personal or property rights (*Appeal of Giardina and Carbone*, 43 Ed Dept Rep ___, Decision No. 15,030; *Appeal of Allard*, 43 Ed Dept Rep ___, Decision No. 14,957). Petitioner is a resident of a component district of BOCES. District residents have standing to challenge an allegedly illegal expenditure of district funds (*Appeals of Giardina and Carbone, supra*; *Appeal of Allard, supra*). Petitioner makes such a challenge in that he alleges that the BOCES has expended funds on the contract with Kelly without statutory authority and in violation of the Commissioner's regulations. Respondents argue that district residents should not have standing based on an alleged illegal expenditure of funds by a BOCES because district residents do not vote on the members of the BOCES board or the approval of a BOCES budget. However, the budgets of a BOCES are charged against the component districts (Education Law § 1951(1)). Thus, an unlawful expenditure of funds by a BOCES is, in effect, an unlawful expenditure of the funds of each component district. Accordingly, I find that petitioner does have standing to maintain this appeal.

I find that BOCES does not have the authority to contract with Kelly for instructional services. I have repeatedly held that a board of education lacks authority to provide instructional services through an independent contractor (*Appeal of McKenna*, 42 Ed Dept Rep 54, Decision No. 14,774; *Matter of Friedman*, 19 Ed Dept Rep 522, Decision No. 10,236).

Respondent argues that *Matter of Friedman*, *supra*, and *Appeal of McKenna*, *supra*, are factually distinguishable from the present case. In *Friedman*, I determined that the respondent board of education did not have authority to retain an independent contractor for psychological services as an alternative to the appointment of a school psychologist pursuant to Education Law § 3012(1). In *McKenna*, I determined that the respondent board of education did not have authority to enter into a contract with a private entity to provide alternative instruction to suspended students and dropouts.

Respondents observe that in *Friedman* the contracting of the services at issue allowed the board of education to avoid the requirement of Education Law § 2510(1) that when a board of education abolishes a position and creates a position with similar duties the person holding the abolished position must be appointed to the new position. Similarly, in *McKenna* the contracting of the services at issue allowed the board of education to avoid the requirement of Education Law § 3012(1)(a) that when a new instructional position is created it must be filled by making a probationary appointment. Thus, in both cases, respondents attempted to avoid their obligation to fill positions in accordance with the requirements of the Education Law. I agree that there are factual differences between these cases and the present case and that there is no evidence that the contracting arrangement in the present case is an attempt to avoid specific requirements of the Education Law related to teacher tenure.

Nevertheless, a BOCES is a creature of statute and has no inherent powers and possesses only those powers expressly delegated by statute. Education Law §1950(4) enumerates the powers and duties of a BOCES. Specifically, paragraph h provides the entities with which a BOCES may contract and the limited purposes of such contracts. The contract at issue here is not authorized by this statute. Therefore, I conclude that BOCES acted without legal authority when it contracted for substitute teaching services.

THE APPEAL IS SUSTAINED.

IT IS ORDERED that the contract between the Board of Cooperative Educational Services for the Second Supervisory District of Erie, Chautauqua and Cattaraugus Counties and Kelly Services, Inc. is hereby annulled.

Decision No. 15,140

Appeal of LARRY R. BONHAM from action of the Board of Education of the Voorheesville Central School District regarding the sale of plaques for installation on school district property.

(November 24, 2004)

APPEARANCES OF COUNSEL

Whiteman Osterman & Hanna, LLP, attorneys for respondent, *Robert T. Schofield, Esq*. of counsel

DECISION OF THE COMMISSIONER

MILLS, Commissioner—Petitioner appeals the decision of the Board of Education of the Voorheesville Central School District ("respondent") to permit the Voorheesville Friends of Music ("FOM") to raise funds by selling dedication plaques for the district's high school auditorium. The appeal must be dismissed.

FOM is a non-profit organization formed to support respondent's music education program. On June 11, 2001, respondent approved several of FOM's fundraising plans, including membership drives, community concerts and the "Best Seat in the House Campaign" ("campaign"). The money raised is used to purchase specialized equipment for the district, award scholarships and underwrite special musical presentations. Expenditures of money raised by FOM is subject to board approval.

The campaign raised money by selling, for $30-$50, a seat dedication in the district's new high school auditorium. A small (approximately one inch by three inch) plaque, engraved with text was affixed to each seat. In the case of corporate donors, one line of text identifying the corporation was permitted. Private individuals could select one of several dedication lines (*i.e.*, "In Memory of") and a second line with the donor or honoree's name. Donors were not able to pick specific seats, and no right to the seat was conveyed. FOM donated the money raised from this campaign, nearly $6,000, to respondent, and it was used as partial payment to purchase a concert grand piano for the auditorium.

Petitioner contends that this fundraising activity violates Article VIII, §1 of the New York State Constitution by allowing an outside organization to profit from the sale of the plaques. Petitioner asserts that respondent had no authority to permit ownership of district property by an outside organization. Petitioner asks that the plaques be removed, that no further plaques be allowed and that I "cite" respondent and its superintendent for their actions in this matter.

Petitioner also argues that respondent's answer was served late and should not be considered. Section 275.13 of the Commissioner's Regulations requires a respondent to answer a petition within 20 days from the time of service. Since the petition was served on November 19, 2003, respondent was required to serve its answer by December 9, 2003. Respondent, however, did not serve its answer until December 10, 2003, and offered no excuse for the delay. Accordingly, I find no basis to accept the late answer, and the factual allegations set forth in the petition are deemed to be true statements (8 NYCRR §275.11).

Additionally, petitioner submitted a reply that contains new allegations that should have been raised in the petition. The purpose of a reply is to respond to new material or affirmative defenses set forth in the answer (8 NYCRR §§275.3 and 275.14). A reply is not meant to buttress allegations in the petition or to belatedly add assertions that should have been in the petition (*Appeal of Goldin*, 43 Ed Dept Rep ___, Decision No. 14,904; *Appeal of Hollister*, 39 *id.* 109, Decision No. 14,188). Since no answer has been accepted, there is no reason to consider petitioner's reply.

Turning to the merits, in an appeal to the Commissioner, petitioner bears the burden of establishing all of the facts upon which he or she seeks relief (8 NYCRR §275.10; *Appeal of Apgar*, 43 Ed Dept Rep ___, Decision No. 15,015; *Appeal of Taylor*, 39 *id.* 368, Decision No. 14,261).

Article VIII, §1 of the New York State Constitution provides in pertinent part, "No. . .school district shall give or loan any money or property to or in aid of any individual, or private corporation or association, or private undertaking. . . ." This section generally prohibits the expenditure of school district moneys for the benefit of private parties unless it is in furtherance of a proper public purpose and is undertaken pursuant to a statutory obligation or properly authorized contract under which the municipality receives fair and adequate consideration (*see*, *Antonopoulou v. Beame*, 32 NY2d 126; 1989 Opn. State Compt. No. 89-50). However, where the expenditure primarily furthers a proper public purpose and only incidentally benefits an individual, the incidental private benefit will not invalidate the action (*Waldo's v. Village of Johnson City*, 74 NY2d 718; *Murphy v. Erie County*, 28 *id.* 80; Opn. State Compt. No. 92-5).

Petitioner has not established that FOM profited from the campaign or that affixing a small dedication plaque to a seat constitutes ownership of public property either by FOM or the donor. In fact, the campaign information flier specifically states that the campaign conveyed no rights or obligations to the donors of the seats. Here, any incidental benefit to donors or FOM was offset by the benefit respondent received in the form of a substantial cash gift applied toward the purchase of a piano for the school community.

Education Law §§1709(12) and 1804(1) authorize a central school district to accept gifts. In this case, the seat dedications were basically in the nature of gifts, notwithstanding the fact that donors were recognized with plaques (see, 33 Opn. State Compt. No. 77-229). In addition, the New York State Comptroller has opined that a county governing board could accept a corporate grant to provide day care services which was conditioned upon naming a day care room in a county building after the grantor or installing a plaque of nominal value identifying the grantor, so long as the condition was subject to the board's power to rename the room in its discretion in the future (Opn. State Compt. No. 90-6). Nothing in the record before me establishes that respondent has ceded its authority over the seats and its ability to remove the plaques in its discretion. Therefore, I cannot conclude that respondent has violated Article VIII, §1 of the State Constitution.

THE APPEAL IS DISMISSED.

Decision No. 15,141

Appeal of R.S. and R.S., on behalf of their daughter M.S., from action of the Board of Education of the Minisink Valley Central School District regarding student discipline.

(November 24, 2004)

APPEARANCES OF COUNSEL

Alan L. Joseph, Esq., attorney for petitioners

Shaw & Perelson, LLP, attorneys for respondent, *Margo L. May, Esq.*, of counsel

DECISION OF THE COMMISSIONER

MILLS, Commissioner—Petitioners challenge the suspension of their daughter, M.S., by the Board of Education of the Minisink Valley Central School District ("respondent"). The appeal must be dismissed.

During the evening of September 30, 2003, M.S., a ninth grade student at respondent's high school, used her home computer to electronically send threatening messages to several other district students. Using alternate screen names to hide her identity, the messages included the statements "I will not be shot you will. Watch your back after 5th period [expletive]" and "A rampage is gonna happen at the big MV and deaths will occur." Parents of students who received the messages contacted the police and respondent's superintendent. On October 1, 2003, police were present at respondent's high school to monitor the situation. According to respondent, as many as 400 to 500 students, or approximately one third of the high school student population, were absent from school because of the threats.

At some point that day, one of the petitioners contacted the superintendent and indicated that M.S. was responsible for the messages. After one postponement at petitioners' request, a superintendent's hearing was held on October 23, 2003. M.S., who was represented by an attorney at the hearing, admitted that she was responsible for the threats. By report dated October 24, 2003, the hearing officer recommended that M.S. be suspended for the remainder of the 2003-2004 school year. By letter dated October 28, 2003, the superintendent informed petitioners that she concurred with the hearing officer's recommendation. Petitioners appealed this decision to respondent and by decision dated November 25, 2003, respondent denied the appeal and upheld the suspension. This appeal ensued and petitioners' request for interim relief was denied on January 9, 2004.

Petitioners contend that the length of the suspension was unduly harsh and request that it be terminated. Petitioners also challenge the applicability of respondent's policy regarding off-campus misconduct. Respondent maintains that the suspension was warranted by the serious nature of the misconduct and the disruption it caused to the school community.

The appeal must be dismissed as moot. The Commissioner will only decide matters in actual controversy and will not render a decision on a state of facts which no longer exists or which subsequent events have laid to rest (*Appeal of A.F.*, 44 Ed Dept Rep ___, Decision No. 15,120; *Appeal of D.W.*, 43 *id.* ___, Decision No. 14,965; *Appeal of L.B.*, 43 *id.* ___, Decision No. 14,952). Petitioners do not request expungement of M.S.'s records. Since M.S. has served the suspension, no further meaningful relief can be granted and the appeal must be dismissed as moot (*Appeal of A.F.*, supra; *Appeal of R.R. and K.R.*, 41 Ed Dept Rep 405, Decision No. 14,726; *Appeal of D.H.*, 41 *id.* 142, Decision No. 14,640).

In light of this disposition, I need not address the parties remaining contentions.

THE APPEAL IS DISMISSED.

Decision No. 15,142

Appeal of GEORGE R. HUBBARD from action of the Board of Education of the Greece Central School District regarding the district's financial practices.

(November 24, 2004)

APPEARANCES OF COUNSEL

Harris Beach LLP, attorneys for respondent, *Alfred Streppa, Esq.*, of counsel

DECISION OF THE COMMISSIONER

MILLS, Commissioner.—Petitioner, a member of the Board of Education of the Greece Central School District ("respondent"), challenges a number of respondent's financial practices. The appeal must be sustained in part.

On August 12, 2003, respondent issued a tax warrant for $61.1 million and voted to apply $4.5 million of its surplus funds from the 2002-2003 school year toward the 2003-2004 budget. On September 9, 2003, respondent used $600,000 of the remaining $3.6 million 2002-2003 budget surplus to establish a tax certiorari reserve fund to bring the retained surplus within the two percent limit permitted by State law. This appeal ensued. Subsequently, respondent published its annual financial statement on or about October 9, 2003.

Petitioner alleges, among other things, that respondent improperly held unexpended surplus funds at the end of the 2002-2003 school year in violation of Real Property Tax Law ("RPTL") §1318(1), improperly created a tax certiorari reserve fund, and failed to timely publish its annual financial statement for 2002-2003. Additionally, petitioner claims that respondent's 2003-2004 tax warrant did not correctly identify the amount of surplus funds used to reduce the tax levy. Petitioner requests that I direct respondent to publish a financial statement for the 2002-2003 school year and in the future file timely financial statements, prepare an accurate fund balance at the time of adopting a proposed budget, and comply with legal requirements for preparing its tax warrant. He also asks that I direct respondent to rescind its tax certiorari reserve fund.

Respondent admits that it did not publish its annual financial statement until October, but explains that it was unable to do so by

July or August, as required by Education Law §1721, because year-end budget information was not yet available. Respondent also claims that it properly retained $600,000 in a tax certiorari reserve fund and therefore only retained approximately $3.0 million in surplus funds, within the two percent allowed under RPTL §1318(1). Finally, respondent denies that its 2003-2004 tax warrant failed to reflect the amount of surplus funds used to reduce the tax levy.

At the conclusion of each fiscal year, a board of education must apply any unexpended surplus funds to reduce its tax levy for the upcoming school year (RPTL §1318(1)). Surplus funds are defined as "any operating funds in excess of two percent of the current school year budget, and shall not include funds properly retained under other sections of law" (*Id.*). Accordingly, at the end of each school year, all unexpended operating funds in excess of two percent of the amount of the budget for the upcoming school year must be applied to reduce the tax levy (*Appeal of Gorman*, 43 Ed Dept Rep ___, Decision No. 14,906; *Appeal of Schadtle*, 40 *id.* 60, Decision No. 14,421; *Appeal of Siver*, 37 *id.* 498, Decision No. 13,912).

For the 2003-2004 school year, respondent is operating under a contingency budget of $154.6 million. Accordingly, respondent had authority to retain $3.1 million in unexpended surplus funds from the 2002-2003 school year. Petitioner alleges that respondent improperly retained $3.6 million. Respondent does not dispute that it had a $3.6 million unappropriated fund balance at the end of 2002-2003 school year, but claims that it properly retained $600,000 of this amount in a tax certiorari reserve fund, leaving a retained surplus of approximately $3 million, within the two percent permitted under RPTL §1318(1).

RPTL §1318(1) permits a board of education to retain additional unexpended operating funds when authorized to do so "under other sections of law." Thus, the authority to exceed the two-percent limit applies only to reserve funds specifically authorized by law (*Appeal of Gorman*, *supra*; *Appeal of Simons*, 39 *id.* 744, Decision No. 14,367; *Appeal of Mills*, 34 *id.* 92, Decision No. 13,243). If surplus money is to be used to establish a reserve fund, the fund should be established before the tax levy (*Appeal of Gorman*, *supra*; *Appeal of Simons*, *supra*). Education Law §3651(1-a) authorizes the establishment of a reserve fund for the payment of judgments and claims in tax certiorari proceedings without voter approval, provided that "the total of the monies held in such reserve fund shall not exceed the amount which might reasonably be deemed necessary to meet anticipated judgments and claims arising out of such tax certiorari proceedings."

Although this provision grants respondent the authority to establish a tax certiorari fund, respondent did not create the fund until after the tax warrant was issued. Accordingly, the $600,000 was not "properly retained under other sections of law" when the tax warrant was issued. Respondent had no authority to retain surplus funds in excess of the two percent limit for future funding of a tax certiorari reserve fund (*Appeal of Mills*, *supra*). With the inclusion of the $600,000, the record reflects that respondent retained approximately $3.6 million in unexpended surplus funds, and therefore exceeded the two percent limit set forth in RPTL §1318(1). I admonish respondent to comply fully with the requirements of RPTL §1318(1) in the future.

While I find that the $600,000 was improperly carried over and used to establish a tax certiorari reserve fund in 2003-2004, I find no need to direct respondent to rescind the fund. Pursuant to respondent's resolution, any amount not used or required for tax certiorari claims and judgments as of July 1, 2006 will be returned to the general fund. I further remind respondent that such funds may only be expended for judgments from claims arising from the tax roll in the year such monies are deposited (Education Law §3651(1-a)).

Petitioner also claims that respondent's 2003-2004 tax warrant failed to correctly identify the amount of surplus funds used to reduce the tax levy. As discussed above, although respondent improperly retained unexpended surplus funds in the 2003-2004 school year, the tax warrant correctly states the amount that respondent applied toward the 2003-2004 budget.

Petitioner further claims that respondent did not timely publish its annual financial statement. Pursuant to Education Law §1721, a board of education is required to publish a detailed statement of the district's finances in July or August. Respondent concedes that it did not issue an annual financial statement until October 9, 2003, explaining that it was unable to gather all the necessary fiscal information within the statutory time frame. While I am sympathetic to the constraints identified by the assistant superintendent, they do not excuse respondent's failure to issue the financial statement in a timely manner. Accordingly, respondent is directed to comply with Education Law §1721 in the future.

I have examined petitioner's remaining claims and find them to be without merit.

THE APPEAL IS SUSTAINED TO THE EXTENT INDICATED.

IT IS ORDERED that respondent henceforth fully comply with Education Law §§1721 and 3651 and Real Property Tax Law §1318.

Decision No. 15,143

Appeal of ELIZABETH G. QUATTRONE from action of the Board of Education of the Chautauqua Lake Central School District, the Board of Education of the City School District of the City of Dunkirk, Mary Anzalone and Donna Reiman regarding teacher employment.

(November 24, 2004)

APPEARANCES OF COUNSEL

Hodgson Russ, LLP, attorneys for respondents, *Karl W. Kristoff* and *David Farmelo, Esqs*., of counsel

DECISION OF THE COMMISSIONER

MILLS, Commissioner.—Petitioner appeals the refusal of the Board of Education of the Chautauqua Lake Central School District and the Board of Education of the City School District of the City of Dunkirk to appoint her to a full-time teaching position. Mary Anzalone ("Anzalone") is a teacher in the Chautauqua Lake Central School District ("Chautauqua Lake"), and Donna Reiman ("Reiman") is a teacher in the City School District of the City of Dunkirk ("Dunkirk"). The appeal must be dismissed.

Petitioner is a tenured elementary education teacher employed by Erie 2 — Chautauqua-Cattaraugus Board of Cooperative Educational Services ("BOCES"). Prior to the 2003-2004 school year, petitioner was assigned to provide a gifted and talented program for component school districts that had contracted for such services, including Chautauqua Lake and Dunkirk.

Before the 2003-2004 school year, Chautauqua Lake and Dunkirk apparently notified BOCES that they were discontinuing their participation in the BOCES gifted and talented program. By letter dated June 17, 2003, petitioner received notification from BOCES that her teaching position had been eliminated effective July 1, 2003. Petitioner was subsequently recalled by the BOCES for a .2 position to teach a gifted and talented program at another component district of the BOCES. Petitioner accepted the part-time position, but allegedly stated in her acceptance letter that she was not waiving any of her rights under Education Law §3014-b or any other law. This appeal ensued.

Petitioner contends that the actions of Chautauqua Lake and Dunkirk constituted a "takeover" within the meaning of Education Law §3014-b and that she is entitled to all of the rights and privileges provided therein. She seeks a determination that she is entitled to an appointment to a full-time teaching position in the elementary tenure area within Dunkirk.

Respondents contend that Chautauqua Lake and Dunkirk did not takeover the gifted and talented program formerly provided by the BOCES and, therefore, petitioner is not entitled to any rights under Education Law §3014-b. Respondents argue that petitioner failed to prove that a takeover occurred and, therefore, the petition must be dismissed in its entirety.

Initially I must address several procedural issues. Pursuant to §276.4 of the Commissioner's regulations, respondents were required to serve their memoranda of law within 30 days after service of their answers. Respondents served their answers on October 20, 2003, but did not submit their memoranda of law until December 1, 2003. While the Commissioner may permit the late filing of a memorandum of law where a party has established good cause for the delay and demonstrated the necessity of such memorandum to the determination of the appeal (8 NYCRR §276.4(a)), respondents have not shown either in this appeal. Therefore, I have not considered respondents' memoranda of law.

Petitioner's memorandum of law contains several new exhibits that were not part of her original pleadings. A memorandum of law may not be used to belatedly add exhibits that are not part of the record (*Appeal of Smolen*, 43 Ed Dept Rep ___, Decision No. 15,000; *Appeal of George*, 40 *id.* 509, Decision No. 14,540; *Appeal of Adriatico*, 39 *id.* 248, Decision No. 14,228). Therefore, I have not considered the new exhibits submitted with petitioner's memorandum of law.

Where a component school district withdraws its students from a BOCES program and establishes an equivalent program of its own, it has "taken over" the program as contemplated by Education Law §3014-b thereby conferring certain rights on the teachers of such programs. In order to determine whether such a takeover has occurred, certain relevant factors should be considered, including (1) the reason why the school district withdrew from the BOCES program, (2) the program offered by BOCES, (3) the new program offered by the school district, (4) whether the programs are equivalent, (5) the reasons why the school district may have hired new probationary teachers, and (6) the reasons why the BOCES teachers were excessed (*Cooper v. Bd. of Educ. of Shenendehowa Cent. School Dist.*, 206 AD2d 811; *Sklar v. Bd. of Coop. Educ. Services of Nassau County*, 104 AD2d 622). It was the intent of the statute that a school district taking over a program would no longer be free to hire probationary teachers to staff its newly established equivalent program (*Buenzow v. Lewiston-Porter Cent. School Dist.*, 101 AD2d 30, *aff'd*, 64 NY2d 676; *Acinapuro v. Bd. of Coop. Educ. Services of Nassau County*, 89 AD2d 329).

In an appeal to the Commissioner, petitioner has the burden of demonstrating a clear right to the relief requested and the burden of establishing the facts upon which she seeks relief (8 NYCRR §275.10; *Appeal of D.M.L.*, 43 Ed Dept Rep ___, Decision No. 14,990; *Appeal of M.F. and J.F.*, 43 *id.* ___, Decision No. 14,960). Upon examination of the factors in the present case, I find that petitioner has not established that a takeover by either Chautauqua Lake or Dunkirk has occurred.

Dunkirk avers that it discontinued the BOCES program because of the high cost of maintaining the program and decreased interest in the program. While cost may have been a factor, petitioner has provided evidence that the number of Dunkirk students enrolled in the BOCES program has been consistent and, therefore, I find the argument that there was decreased interest in the program unpersuasive. However, based on the record before me, it is clear that Dunkirk did not create a new gifted and talented program within the district, but rather its regular classroom teachers now include gifted and talented instruction within their general classroom instruction. Moreover, Dunkirk did not hire Reiman to fill a position that was created by a new gifted and talented program within the district, but rather hired her to teach in a program for students who experience behavioral problems in the classroom.

With respect to the issue as to why petitioner was excessed, petitioner's excess letter does not state a reason, but I find that it is reasonable to conclude that it was due, at least in part, to the fact that four component districts decided not to contract with the BOCES for such services. Accordingly, I find that petitioner failed to establish that a takeover occurred with respect to Dunkirk.

Chautauqua Lake avers that it discontinued the BOCES program because it no longer has as many gifted students and because it was dissatisfied with the BOCES program. While dissatisfaction may have been a factor, petitioner has provided evidence that the number of Chautauqua Lake students enrolled in the BOCES program has been consistent and, therefore, I find the argument that there was a decrease in the number of gifted students unpersuasive.

The record indicates that Chautauqua Lake established an "Enrichment Program" after it terminated its participation in the BOCES gifted and talented program. Petitioner contends that this new program is equivalent to the program she provided at BOCES. Respondent argues that the program is not equivalent because it was created to serve a greater number of students with a broader range of academic abilities in comparison to the students that participated in the BOCES program. Moreover, it includes field trips and has a "push-in" component where the enrichment teacher works in the general education classrooms with general education teachers. Significantly, Chautauqua Lake did not hire a new probationary teacher to fill the position created by the new Enrichment Program, but instead assigned Anzalone, who was already on staff (*Cooper v. Bd. of Educ. of Shenendehowa Cent. School Dist., supra*).

As stated above, with respect to the issue as to why petitioner was excessed, petitioner's excess letter does not state a reason, but I find that it is reasonable to conclude that it was due, at least in part, to the fact that four component districts decided not to contract with the BOCES for such services. After careful review of the record before me, I find petitioner has not met her burden of proving that a takeover occurred with respect to Chautauqua Lake.

THE APPEAL IS DISMISSED.

Decision No. 15,144

Appeal of ANTHONY STIFFLER from action of the New York City Department of Education regarding teacher excessing.

(November 24, 2004)

APPEARANCES OF COUNSEL

Michael A. Cardozo, Corporation Counsel, attorney for respondent, *Shivani Soni, Esq.*, of counsel

DECISION OF THE COMMISSIONER

MILLS, Commissioner.—Petitioner appeals a determination of the New York City Department of Education ("respondent") excessing him from a teaching position. The appeal must be dismissed.

Effective September 5, 2000, respondent appointed petitioner as a probationary teacher in physical education at P.S. 198. Because of declining enrollment, the principal of P.S. 198 decided to excess ten teachers in June 2003. By letter dated June 13, 2003, the principal informed petitioner that he was being excessed, effective June 26, 2003. (Petitioner also received a letter dated June 24, 2003, stating that he was being excessed as of June 27.) Petitioner grieved his excessing to the principal. The principal denied his grievance, stating that his excessing was conducted pursuant to the contract between respondent and United Federation of Teachers ("UFT"). This appeal ensued. Petitioner's request for interim relief was denied on August 12, 2003.

Petitioner contends that he was excessed in violation of his seniority rights, that respondent violated §135.4 of the Commissioner's regulations because P.S. 198 no longer has a licensed physical education teacher, and that P.S. 198 teachers no longer have union representation because he was the sole union chapter leader at that school. Petitioner seeks a determination that the excessing violated his seniority rights and demands reinstatement to his former position at P.S. 198.

Respondent argues that the Commissioner lacks subject matter jurisdiction over this appeal, that the appeal is moot, that petitioner lacks standing to assert the rights of other teachers in regard to union representation, and that P.S. 198 will not be without union representation. Respondent contends that petitioner was lawfully and properly excessed pursuant to the collective bargaining agreement and that petitioner has not exhausted his administrative remedies. Respondent contends that any alleged violation of the excessing rules should be grieved pursuant to the collective bargaining agreement, after which the proper forum for petitioner is an Article 78 proceeding in State Supreme Court, not an appeal to the Commissioner.

Petitioner's claim that he was excessed in violation of his seniority rights must be dismissed. A school employee who elects to submit an issue for resolution through a contractual grievance procedure may not elect to bring an appeal to the Commissioner of Education for review of the same matter (*Bd. of Educ., Commack UFSD v. Ambach*, 70 NY2d 501; *Appeal of Kassenbrock*, 31 Ed Dept. Rep 324, Decision No. 12,654; *Appeal of Almeter*, 30 *id.* 439, Decision No. 12,526; *Appeal of Perri*, 30 *id.* 277, Decision No. 12,464). Petitioner brought a Step 1 Grievance which was denied by the principal because teachers were "being excessed in accordance with UFT contractual rules of excessing." Evidently, petitioner did not complete Step 2 (District Level) or Step 3 (Chancellor) of the grievance process and, under the terms of the contract, he was deemed to have accepted the decision rendered at Step 1 (Article 22 B8). Petitioner thus elected to pursue his claim through the contractual grievance process and cannot appeal to the Commissioner for relief on the same issue.

Petitioner also claims that his excessing violates §135.4 of the Commissioner's regulations because P.S. 198 will not have a licensed physical education teacher. Respondent contends that it is in compliance with the regulations because a common branch teacher may teach physical education at the elementary level. Section 135.4(c)(4) of the Commissioner's regulations (addressing Physical Education) states that "[e]lementary classroom teachers may provide instruction under the direction and supervision of a certified physical education teacher." In an appeal to the Commissioner, petitioner has the burden of establishing the facts upon which he seeks relief (8 NYCRR §275.10; *Appeal of Brown, et al.*, 43 Ed Dept Rep ___, Decision No. 14,980) and the burden of demonstrating a clear legal right to the relief requested (*Appeal of Goldin*, 43 Ed Dept Rep ___, Decision No. 15,048). Here petitioner has failed to meet his burden of establishing that respondent's actions resulted in a violation of the Commissioner's regulations.

Finally, petitioner asserts that his excessing would leave P.S. 198 without union representation. Again, petitioner has failed to meet his burden of establishing that respondent's actions resulted in a lack of union representation at P.S. 198, or that such alleged lack of representation would entitle him to the relief requested.

THE APPEAL IS DISMISSED.

Decision No. 15,145

Appeal of R.J. and D.J., on behalf of their daughter A.J., from action of the Board of Education of the Jamesville-Dewitt Central School District regarding student discipline.

(November 24, 2004)

APPEARANCES OF COUNSEL

Martin, Martin & Woodard, LLC, attorneys for petitioners, *David P. Martin, Esq.*, of counsel

Bond, Schoeneck & King, PLLC, attorneys for respondent, *Dan Bordoni, Esq.*, of counsel

DECISION OF THE COMMISSIONER

MILLS, Commissioner.—Petitioners challenge the decision of the Board of Education of the Jamesville-Dewitt Central School District ("respondent") and its high school principal to suspend their daughter A.J. The appeal must be sustained.

On September 12, 2003, A.J. attended a school-sponsored dance at respondent's high school cafeteria. At some point, a chaperone noticed several students, including petitioners' daughter, lingering outside a doorway in a parking lot and instructed the students to come inside. The chaperone, along with an Onondaga County Deputy Sheriff who was on duty at the event, later went to the area where the students had gathered and discovered a water bottle, which contained alcohol (tequila). The chaperone reported this to an assistant principal, who then had the students sent to his office.

The assistant principal interviewed A.J. and she admitted that she took a drink from the bottle, initially indicating that it was one "sip" or "gulp." The parties disagree about whether A.J. made a written statement that evening or whether she made any admissions to another assistant principal. At some point respondent's high school principal arrived on the scene and spoke with R.J, the assistant principal and A.J. The principal informed R.J. that the incident would be reviewed Monday morning.

On Monday, September 15, 2004, the principal interviewed A.J. and she admitted that she had taken more than one sip from the bottle. Petitioners were notified by telephone that the principal intended to suspend A.J. Petitioners met with the principal and assistant principal at 11:45 a.m. that day. At the end of the meeting A.J. was suspended for five days. Petitioners requested an appeal to the superintendent and the principal arranged for them to meet with the superintendent later that day. At the end of that meeting the superintendent upheld the suspension. A letter dated September 15, 2003, notifying petitioners of the suspension and their right to an informal conference with the principal, was mailed via regular mail on September 16, 2003.

By letter dated September 22, 2003, petitioner D.J. asked the principal to arrange a conference "to ask questions of the complaining witness(s)." By letter dated September 25, 2003, the principal refused her request.

On November 3, 2003, respondent heard petitioners' appeal. By letter dated November 4, 2003, respondent notified petitioners that it was upholding the suspension. This appeal ensued.

Petitioners contend that they were denied an informal conference with the principal and the opportunity to question complaining witnesses before the suspension was imposed. Petitioners assert that the written suspension notice was insufficient, untimely, improperly mailed and in violation of law, regulation and district policy. Petitioners also assert that A.J. was unaware that there was alcohol in the bottle, and maintain that the punishment imposed was unduly harsh and did not comply with district policy. Petitioners object to the submission of affidavits by the superintendent, principal and two assistant principals because they allegedly contain information and allegations that were not part of the evidence considered by respondent in upholding the suspension. Petitioners ask that the suspension be expunged from the student's record.

Respondent contends that it substantially complied with applicable law and that petitioners did have an informal conference with the principal before the suspension. Respondent asserts that the student gave conflicting accounts of her actions and that the decision to suspend her was based on her own statements. Respondent argues that both the procedure and the penalty are proper.

Education Law §3214(3)(b)(1) provides that in the case of a suspension up to five days in length:

> [T]he suspending authority shall provide the pupil with notice of the charged misconduct. . . . The pupil and the person in parental relation to the pupil shall, on request, be given an opportunity for an informal conference with the principal at which the pupil and/or person in parental relation shall be authorized to present the pupil's version of the event and to ask questions of the complaining witnesses. The aforesaid notice and opportunity for an informal conference shall take place prior to suspension of the pupil unless the pupil's presence in the school poses a continuing danger to persons or property or an ongoing threat of disruption to the academic process. . . .

Section 100.2(l)(4) of the Commissioner's regulations provides:

> Parental notice concerning student suspensions. When suspension of a student from attendance for a period of five days or less pursuant to section 3214(3) of the

> Education Law is proposed, school district officials shall immediately notify the parents or the persons in parental relation in writing that the student may be suspended from school. *Written notice shall be provided by personal delivery, express mail delivery, or equivalent means reasonably calculated to assure receipt of such notice within 24 hours of the decision to propose suspension. . . .* Where possible, notification shall also be provided by telephone. . . . Such notice shall provide a description of the incident(s) for which suspension is proposed and shall inform the parents or persons in parental relation of their right to request an immediate informal conference with the principal in accordance with the provisions of Education Law, section 3214(3)(b). . . . *Such notice and opportunity for an informal conference shall take place prior to the suspension of the student unless the student's presence in the school poses a continuing danger to persons or property or an ongoing threat of disruption to the academic process, in which case the notice and opportunity for an informal conference shall take place as soon after the suspension as is reasonably practicable.* (Emphasis added.)

In this case, respondent did not comply with the written notice requirements of §100.2(l)(4) as mandated under these circumstances, *i.e.*, personal delivery, express mail delivery or equivalent means reasonably calculated to assure receipt of such notice within 24 hours of the decision to propose a suspension. I have repeatedly held that sending the written notice by regular mail does not satisfy the regulation (*Appeal of a Student with a Disability*, 43 Ed Dept Rep ___, Decision No. 15,021; *Appeal of a Student Suspected of Having a Disability*, 41 *id*. Dept Rep 390, Decision No. 14,722; *Appeal of J.G.*, 39 *id*. 393, Decision No. 14,270). Oral communication with parents regarding a suspension is not a substitute for the required written notification (*Appeal of a Student Suspected of Having a Disability*, *supra*; *Appeal of J.G.*, *supra*; *Appeal of a Student with a Disability*, 38 Ed Dept Rep 378, Decision No. 14,059).

Holding an informal conference with the principal does not excuse the requirement for written notification to students and their parents and/or guardians explaining their rights to the conference and the opportunity to question complaining witnesses. (*see*, *Appeal of a Student with a Disability*, 40 Ed Dept Rep 47, Decision No. 14,418; *Appeal of a Student with a Disability*, 38 *id*. 378, Decision No.

14,059). Accordingly, the five-day suspension must be annulled and expunged from the student's records.

In view of this disposition, I need not address petitioners' remaining contentions.

THE APPEAL IS SUSTAINED.

IT IS ORDERED that respondent's suspension of A.J. from September 15-19, 2003, be annulled and expunged from her record.

Decision No. 15,146

Appeal of B.K. and R.K., on behalf of their son D.K., from action of the Board of Education of the City School District of the City of Port Jervis regarding student discipline.

(December 1, 2004)

APPEARANCES OF COUNSEL

Cuddeback & Onofry, attorneys for respondent, *Robert A. Onofry, Esq.*, of counsel

DECISION OF THE COMMISSIONER

MILLS, Commissioner.—Petitioners challenge the decision of the Board of Education of the City School District of the City of Port Jervis ("respondent") to suspend their son, D.K., from school. The appeal must be dismissed.

D.K. was an 11th grade student at respondent's high school during the 2003-2004 school year. On September 25, 2003, a school monitor observed D.K. smoking what he thought was marijuana in a school stairway. The monitor called the Assistant Principal to come to the stairway and D.K. ran out a nearby exit door. D.K. returned and was escorted to the Assistant Principal's office. D.K. admitted that he smoked a cigarette and allowed the Assistant Principal to search his jacket, but refused numerous requests by the Assistant Principal to submit to a search of his person. The Assistant Principal called the police, and D.K. left the office. As D.K. left, he came into contact with the monitor, who was standing in front of the office door, causing him to lose his balance. A short time later D.K. returned and offered to be searched. The police arrived thereafter and harassment charges were filed against D.K.

By notice dated September 24, 2003, D.K. was charged with "Conduct which endangers the safety, morals, health or welfare of others. Supporting details: Alleged possession of marijuana" and was suspended for five days.

By notice dated October 1, 2003, petitioners were notified of a superintendent's hearing, which was held on October 7, 2003, before a hearing officer designated by the superintendent. The hearing officer, by decision dated October 10, 2003, found that on September 25, D.K. had been smoking a cigarette on school property during school hours, had left school twice without permission and had physical contact with the monitor. He therefore found D.K. guilty of "endangering the health, welfare, and morals of others on school property during a school day." After reviewing D.K.'s anecdotal record, the hearing officer recommended that D.K. be suspended for the remainder of the 2003-2004 school year and that he be placed in an alternative education setting. By letter dated October 21, 2003, respondent's superintendent accepted the hearing officer's recommendation. By letter dated November 5, 2003, respondent upheld the superintendent's decision and placed D.K. in the Alternative Education Program for the balance of the school year. This appeal ensued.

Petitioners allege that the hearing officer misstated the nature of the charges and that the report and recommendation do not accurately reflect the proceeding. Petitioners argue that the hearing officer's determination fails to reflect that the original charge of smoking marijuana was unfounded and that they were not given notice of the charge of smoking a cigarette or leaving school grounds without permission. Petitioners also argue that the penalty is excessive. They request an investigation into the alleged inequity of the penalty, reinstatement to school and additional tutoring to help D.K. catch up on schoolwork.

Respondent contends the appeal should be dismissed as untimely. Respondent also asserts that its decision to discipline D.K. was based on substantial evidence and that the penalty was appropriate.

An appeal to the Commissioner must be commenced within 30 days from the making of the decision or the performance of the act complained of, unless delay is excused by the Commissioner for good cause shown (8 NYCRR §275.16; *Appeal of O'Brien*, 44 Ed Dept Rep ___, Decision No. 15,092; *Appeal of Recore*, 42 *id.* 283, Decision No. 14,856). Petitioners were informed of respondent's determination by letter dated November 5, 2004. Petitioners initially served the petition on respondent on December 5, 2003, within the 30-day period. The petition was received in my Office of Counsel without the Notice required by §275.11 of the Commissioner's Regulations. By letter dated December 23, 2003, my Office of Counsel returned the petition to petitioners and allowed them two weeks from the date of that letter to correct their mistake and re-serve the petition. On January 6, 2004, the corrected petition was re-served on respondent. Accordingly, I find the petition timely.

The appeal must be dismissed as moot. The Commissioner will only decide matters in actual controversy and will not render a decision on a state of facts which no longer exist or which subsequent events have laid to rest (*Appeal of Cordisco*, 44 Ed Dept Rep ___, Decision No. 15,089; *Appeal of Kushner*, 43 *id.* ___, Decision No. 15,040; *Appeal of Reynolds*, 42 *id.* 231, Decision No. 14,834). D.K. was suspended for the remainder of the 2003-2004 school year. That school year has ended and D.K.'s penalty has been served.

I further find that petitioners were given adequate notice of all the charges against D.K. The superintendent's hearing notice pursuant to Education Law §3214(3) alleged that D.K. engaged in behavior "which endangers the safety, morals, health or welfare of others." Beneath this charge, under a sub-heading of "Supporting details", is a comprehensive account of D.K's actions on the date in question, including his attempts to flee and the allegation that he was smoking "something resembling a cigarette."

Education Law §3214(3)(a) authorizes a school district to suspend a "pupil who is insubordinate or disorderly or violent or disruptive, or whose conduct otherwise endangers the safety, morals, health or welfare of others." Respondent's code of conduct clearly states that students are subject to disciplinary action when they "[e]ngage in any conduct that endangers the safety, morals, health or welfare of others," including but not limited to smoking cigarettes. The decision to suspend a student from school pursuant to Education Law §3214 must be based on competent and substantial evidence that the student participated in the objectionable conduct (*Matter of Bd. of Educ., Monticello Cent. School Dist. v. Commissioner of Educ., et al.*, 91 NY2d 133; *Matter of Bd. of Educ., City School Dist. of the City of New York v. Mills, et al.*, 293 AD2d 37; *Appeal of D.G.*, 43 Ed Dept Rep ___, Decision No. 15,001).

In this case, D.K. had admitted to smoking cigarettes on school property during school hours and repeatedly refused the Assistant Principal's request to search him. The hearing officer also credited the testimony of the Assistant Principal and monitor regarding D.K.'s physical contact with the monitor, D.K.'s refusal to cooperate and attempts to leave school property without permission. With respect to findings of fact in matters involving the credibility of witnesses, I will not substitute my judgment for that of a hearing officer unless there is clear and convincing evidence that the determination of credibility is inconsistent with the facts (*Appeal of T.R. and M.D.*, 43 Ed Dept Rep ___, Decision No. 15,036; *Appeal of K.M.*, 41 *id.* 318, Decision No. 14,699). I find no basis to substitute my judgment in this case.

In cases of student discipline, the sanction imposed must be proportionate to the severity of the offenses involved (*Appeal of D.G.*, *supra*; *Appeal of Alexander*, 36 Ed Dept Rep 160, Decision No. 13,689). The test to be applied in reviewing a penalty is whether it is so excessive as to warrant substitution of the Commissioner's judgment for that of the board (*Appeal of Cynthia and Robert W.*, 37 Ed Dept Rep 437, Decision No. 13,899; *Appeal of Alexander*, *supra*; *Appeal of Forestiero*, 34 Ed Dept Rep 592, Decision No. 13,419). In support of the penalty imposed, respondent emphasizes D.K.'s conduct (i.e., smoking, flight from the building and physical altercation) and his anecdotal record. A review of the record indicates that most of D.K.'s offenses are tardiness. However, I must agree with respondent that D.K.'s conduct in school became more problematic during the 2002-2003 school year with incidents such as hitting other classmates with objects, forging passes and using inappropriate language toward teachers. Based therefore upon the totality of the record before me and the seriousness of D.K.'s conduct, I will not overturn the penalty imposed as excessive.

Finally, an appeal to the Commissioner is appellate in nature and does not provide for investigations (*Appeal of Laurie*, 42 Ed Dept Rep 313, Decision No. 14,867; *Appeal of Allen*, 39 Ed Dept Rep 528, Decision No. 14,300; *Appeal of Van Zile and Crowell*, 37 *id.* 213, Decision No. 13,846). Accordingly, petitioners' request for an investigation is denied.

THE APPEAL IS DISMISSED.

Decision No. 15,147

Appeal of MEE JO from action of Judith P. Staples, Superintendent of Schools for the City School District of the City of Corning, concerning parental complaints.

(December 6, 2004)

APPEARANCES OF COUNSEL

Harris Beach LLP, attorneys for respondent, *Alfred L. Streppa, Esq.*, of counsel

DECISION OF THE COMMISSIONER

MILLS, Commissioner.—Petitioner appeals the actions of Judith P. Staples ("respondent"), Superintendent of Schools for the City School District of the City of Corning ("the district"), in response to petitioner's complaints concerning her daughter's education. The appeal must be dismissed.

During the 2003-2004 school year, petitioner's daughter was a seventh grade student in the district. Between September 28, 2003, and February 9, 2004, petitioner sent 12 letters to various district employees expressing concern about her daughter's education. She raised a number of issues, but focused primarily on the teaching and grading methods used by her daughter's math teacher. During that time period, district administrators met with petitioner on several occasions to attempt to address her concerns. District administrators also sent petitioner five letters attempting to respond to her concerns.

On February 25, 2004, respondent sent petitioner a letter confirming that her daughter was being appropriately instructed. Respondent further indicated that the district would not schedule any more meetings or respond to petitioner's correspondence on the subject. The letter stated that future issues concerning petitioner's daughter would be restricted to the channels used by other parents in the district. This appeal ensued.

Petitioner questions whether various district practices are supported by the Education Law and whether her daughter's math teacher is certified. She asks that respondent's decision of February 25, 2004, be reversed and that she "recover" her right to correspond and meet with her daughter's teachers and district administrators. She also asks that I "reopen" the issue of the math teacher's instructional methods.

Respondent asserts that the appeal must be dismissed because petitioner requests an advisory opinion. Respondent also argues that, to the extent petitioner requests any relief regarding any issue involving her daughter's math teacher, the appeal must be dismissed for failure to join a necessary party. Respondent also contends that the appeal must be dismissed for failure to exhaust administrative remedies.

Respondent further asserts that the petition does not contain a clear and concise statement showing that petitioner is entitled to relief. Respondent argues that questions of academic freedom and teaching methods fall within the discretion of the district pursuant to Education Law §1709(33). Respondent also argues that she did not render any "decision" in her February 25, 2004, letter and that she did not deny petitioner any rights. She also submits documentation showing that the teacher in question is certified.

Initially, I must address petitioner's reply. The purpose of a reply is to respond to affirmative defenses or new material contained in an answer; it is not meant to buttress or add to the petition's allegations (8 NYCRR §§275.3 and 275.14; *Appeal of Hubbard*, 43 Ed Dept Rep ___, Decision No. 14,981). Portions of petitioner's reply buttress and add to petitioner's claims. Accordingly, although I have accepted petitioner's reply, I have considered only those portions responding to new material or affirmative defenses in respondent's answer.

In her reply, petitioner argues that the answer was untimely. Section 275.13 of the Commissioner's regulations requires a respondent to answer the petition within 20 days of the time it was served. However, when the period ends on a Saturday, Sunday or a public holiday, the answer may be served on the next succeeding business day (*see*, General Construction Law §25-a(1)). Here, petitioner served the district clerk on March 8, 2004. The 20-day period ended on March 28, 2004, a Sunday, and respondent served the answer on Monday, March 29, 2004. The answer is therefore timely.

Petitioner also argues that respondent's answer must be dismissed because her attorney failed to affirm that he does not have first-hand knowledge of the facts. Consistent with Commissioner's regulations, the answer is endorsed with the name, address and telephone number of respondent's attorney (8 NYCRR §275.4) and verified by respondent (8 NYCRR §275.5). Therefore, respondent's answer is proper.

To the extent petitioner requests an advisory opinion in response to her "questions presented," the appeal must be dismissed. It is well established that the Commissioner does not issue advisory opinions or declaratory rulings in appeals brought pursuant to Education Law §310 (*Appeal of Bach*, 43 Ed Dept Rep ___, Decision No. 14,962; *Appeals of Tesser and Kavitsky*, 42 *id.* 341, Decision No. 14,876; *Appeal of a Student with a Disability*, 42 *id.* 111, Decision No. 14,791).

In an appeal to the Commissioner of Education, the petitioner has the burden of establishing the facts upon which she seeks relief and of demonstrating a clear legal right to the relief requested (*Appeal of McBeth*, 43 Ed Dept Rep ___, Decision No. 14,913). Petitioner has neither alleged nor established that she has a legal right to the relief requested. Respondent's February 25, 2004, letter does not, as petitioner alleges, eliminate her opportunity to meet and correspond with her daughter's teachers and school administrators. Respondent simply notified petitioner that school administrators would not continue to respond to petitioner's correspondence and schedule meetings with her concerning the issues previously raised by petitioner.

It is not clear whether petitioner challenges the math teacher's instructional or grading methods in this appeal. She states that she seeks to "reopen" the issue of her daughter's math teacher's teaching methods, but her petition indicates, and her reply specifically states, that the petition is directed to respondent's February 25, 2004, letter. In any event, I find that petitioner has not demonstrated the right to any legal relief based on the teaching or grading methods of her daughter's math teacher. It is well settled that decisions regarding student grading rest initially with the classroom teacher and ultimately with the board of education (Education Law §1709(3)). Absent a finding that a grade determination was arbitrary, capricious or unreasonable, it will not be set aside (*Appeal of Conley*, 34 Ed Dept Rep 376, Decision No. 13,349). Moreover, a teacher must be given some latitude to determine how to teach a lesson (*Appeal of Conley*, *supra*). Petitioner has failed to meet her burden of proving that the grading or teaching methods of her daughter's math teacher were arbitrary and capricious.

THE APPEAL IS DISMISSED.

Decision No. 15,148

Appeal of ANNE SMITH, on behalf of her children JASON and MORGAN EDWARDS, from action of the Board of Education of the Saugerties Central School District regarding transportation.

(December 9,2004)

APPEARANCES OF COUNSEL

Shaw & Perelson, LLP, attorneys for petitioner, *Marc E. Sharff, Esq.*, of counsel

DECISION OF THE COMMISSIONER

MILLS, Commissioner.—Petitioner challenges the determination of the Board of Education of the Saugerties Central School District ("respondent") denying her children door-to-door transportation. The appeal must be dismissed.

Petitioner resides within respondent's district with her two elementary school-aged children, Jason and Morgan. In August 2003, petitioner inquired as to why her children were not picked up in front of their house. According to petitioner, respondent's transportation director advised her that, if students live within one-half mile of a bus stop, the district does not pick them up at their home. Petitioner then hired a professional surveyor who determined that the distance from petitioner's home to their bus stop exceeded one-half mile. Petitioner provided this information to district officials.

By letter dated December 22, 2003, respondent's acting superintendent advised petitioner that the district had surveyed the distance and found it to be less than one-half mile. Shortly thereafter, petitioner met with the acting superintendent who informed her that the district would move the bus stop closer to petitioner's home to eliminate any question that the stop was more than one-half mile from petitioner's home. According to petitioner, he further explained that the district would not provide bus service to petitioner's house because that would require a small bus, which was not available. This appeal ensued.

Petitioner alleges that respondent picks up other children in front of their homes and contends that its refusal to provide similar service to her children is arbitrary and capricious. Petitioner requests that I order respondent to provide her children with door-to-door transportation, or alternatively, to alter its transportation policy "to ensure equal treatment of all children who are similarly situated."

Respondent avers that it does not pick up students in front of their homes unless the district is unable to designate a safe bus stop within one-half mile of the home or the district is required by law to pick up the student. Respondent maintains that its decision regarding the bus stop location was properly based on safety concerns and was rational. Additionally, respondent contends that the appeal is moot.

To the extent that petitioner argues that the former bus stop location exceeds respondent's half-mile policy limit for elementary students, the appeal is moot. The record reflects that respondent moved the bus stop closer to petitioner's home, and petitioner does not dispute that the new stop is less than a half-mile from her home.

To the extent that petitioner claims that similarly situated children are not treated equally and that her children are entitled to door-to-door transportation, petitioner has failed to carry her burden of proof. In an appeal to the Commissioner, petitioner has the burden of establishing the facts upon which he or she seeks relief (8 NYCRR §275.10; *Appeal of Brown, et al.*, 43 Ed Dept Rep ___, Decision No. 14,980) and the burden of demonstrating a clear legal right to the relief requested (*Appeal of Goldin*, 43 Ed Dept Rep ___, Decision No. 15,048).

A board of education may exercise its discretion when designating pick-up and drop-off points, provided that the board uses reasonable care in exercising such discretion (*Appeal of Raymond*, 39 Ed Dept Rep 774, Decision No. 14,376; *Appeal of Hobbs*, 38 *id.* 203, Decision No. 14,015; *Appeal of Kaufman*, 36 *id.* 45, Decision No. 13,650). In establishing a pick-up point, a board of education must balance considerations of pupil safety and convenience, routing efficiency and costs (*Appeal of Hobbs*, *supra*; *Appeal of Marsh*, 36 Ed Dept Rep 134, Decision No. 13,680; *Appeal of Krauciunas*, 35 *id.* 107, Decision No. 13,480). The law does not require a school district to provide transportation for the pupil directly to and from home (*Ossant v. Millard*, 72 Misc 2d 384) and boards of education have discretion to require students to walk to pick-up points from which transportation will be provided (*Appeal of Marsh*, *supra*; *Appeal of Mechanick, et al.*, 33 *id.* 692, Decision No. 13,200). Where a student's home is on a dangerous road or at a remote location, the parents are not free from the obligation to assist the student in reaching the pick-up point (*Appeal of Warner*, 37 Ed Dept Rep 469, Decision No. 13,907; *Appeal of Rheaume-Wellenc*, 37 *id.* 83, Decision No. 13,811; *Appeal of Kaufman*, *supra*). It is the responsibility of the parent, not the district, to see that the child safely reaches the pick-up point (*Appeal of Warner*, *supra*; *Appeal of Rheaume-Wellenc*, *supra*).

Respondent asserts that generally, the district does not provide students with door-to-door transportation and petitioner offers no proof to the contrary. Accordingly, petitioner has failed to establish any right to such service. Moreover, based on the record before me, I cannot conclude that respondent's determination regarding the pick-up point was arbitrary, capricious or unreasonable. Accordingly, I will not substitute my judgment for that of respondent.

In light of this disposition, I need not address the parties' remaining contentions.

THE APPEAL IS DISMISSED.

Decision No. 15,149

Appeal of J.P., on behalf of his son M.P., from action of the Superintendent of the City School District of the City of Cohoes regarding a suspension from interscholastic athletics.

(December 9, 2004)

APPEARANCES OF COUNSEL

Girvin and Ferlazzo, P.C., attorneys for respondent, *Kristine Amodeo Lanchantin, Esq.*, of counsel

DECISION OF THE COMMISSIONER

MILLS, Commissioner.—Petitioner appeals the determination of the Superintendent ("respondent") of the City School District of the City of Cohoes ("district") to suspend his son, M.P., from interscholastic athletics for one year. The appeal must be dismissed.

While enrolled in the eleventh grade at the district's high school in November 2003, M.P. signed a pledge promising to obey all school rules and acknowledging that he read the district's co-curricular eligibility policy. M.P.'s mother cosigned the form.

The co-curricular policy provides in pertinent part:

> *SUBSTANCE ABUSE*: No smoking or drinking is allowed. Any violation of the rule will result in the following:
>
> 1st violation: Suspension from the team or co-curricular activity for the remainder of the season.
>
> 2nd violation: Suspension from all athletic teams or co-curricular activities for six months from the date of the infraction.
>
> Any possession, sale or use of drugs will lead to immediate dismissal from the team or co-curricular activity and suspension from all sports or co-curricular activities for one (1) year: *this includes during and after school, on or off school property.* Legal authorities will be notified.

On Friday night, December 19, 2003, a police officer came upon M.P. and three other students in a car off school property. Finding marijuana in the car, the police notified the students' parents, but did not pursue criminal charges.

On Monday, December 22, 2003, after several staff members told the assistant principal of the weekend incident, the assistant principal called the students individually to her office. The school resource officer, a police officer assigned by the Cohoes Police Department, came to the assistant principal's office as part of his morning routine and remained after the students arrived. When the assistant principal asked M.P. what occurred over the weekend, M.P. admitted that the police had found him and other students in a car with marijuana. The assistant principal conveyed the student's admission to the athletic coordinator, who determined that the student's conduct violated the district's co-curricular eligibility policy and imposed a one-year suspension from interscholastic athletics.

On January 5, 2004, petitioner appealed to a committee composed of the athletic coordinator, the high school principal and the junior varsity basketball coach. The committee upheld the penalty. On January 13, 2004, respondent met with the four students involved and their parents. By letter dated January 27, 2004, respondent sustained the committee's determination but offered an alternative resolution that would consider a reduction in the penalty if the students maintained good conduct. Petitioner did not accept the offer, and this appeal ensued. Petitioner's request for interim relief was denied on March 2, 2004.

Petitioner asserts that the district's co-curricular eligibility policy is arbitrary because the predetermined penalty for the possession, sale or use of drugs is much greater than the penalty related to tobacco products or alcohol. Petitioner argues that imposing different penalties is irrational because persons under 21 years of age cannot legally use any of these products; because alcohol use is as detrimental to a student's health as marijuana use; and because the school's interest in encouraging healthful habits and good citizenship is the same whether prohibiting alcohol or marijuana use. Petitioner also contends the student admitted to the assistant principal that marijuana was in the car because the police officer's presence intimidated him and because he was not advised of his rights under respondent's Code of Conduct. Petitioner seeks to invalidate the district's policy and M.P.'s suspension, and requests expungement of M.P.'s records.

Respondent asserts that the petition fails to state a claim, that the co-curricular policy establishes reasonable conduct standards, and that the procedure used was fair.

A board of education has broad authority to establish reasonable standards of conduct for participation in extracurricular activities, and unless it can be shown that the board has abused its discretion, its policy will be upheld (*Appeal of G.M.D.*, 43 Ed Dept Rep ___, Decision No. 14,998; *Appeal of Wright*, 38 *id.* 756, Decision No. 14,134; *Appeals of Cynthia and Robert W. and Melani and James H.*, 37 *id.* 437, Decision No. 13,899). Petitioner has not established that the district's current policy of imposing a greater penalty for drugs than for tobacco or alcohol is irrational or an abuse of discretion.

Petitioner contends that his son admitted to the assistant principal that marijuana was in the car because the police officer's presence intimidated him and because he was not advised of his rights under the district's Code of Conduct. The Code of Conduct provides that before police officials are permitted to question any student on school property, the principal (or designee) will try to notify the student's parent to give the parent an opportunity to be present. Also, the code provides that students must be informed of their legal rights, that the student may remain silent, and that the student may request the presence of an attorney. Respondent denies that the officer questioned M.P. and also argues that this does not apply to situations in which the district is investigating violations of its own rules and the police officer is involved in his capacity as the School Resource Officer.

In an appeal to the Commissioner of Education, petitioner has the burden of establishing the facts upon which relief is requested (8 NYCRR §275.10; *Appeal of V.P.*, 42 Ed Dept Rep 3, Decision No. 14,754) and the burden of demonstrating a clear legal right to the relief sought (*Appeal of D.T.*, 43 Ed Dept Rep ___, Decision No. 14,916). Petitioner alleges that the officer "actively participated in the interrogation." While the assistant principal acknowledges that M.P. engaged in "casual conversation" with the resource officer on December 22, she states the officer did not threaten or question the student. Petitioner was not present when his son was questioned and did not reply to the new material and affirmative defenses set forth in respondent's answer and accompanying affidavits. Therefore, since petitioner has failed to establish that the officer questioned M.P., I need not reach the question of whether respondent violated the district's Code of Conduct.

The procedures governing suspension of student privileges or the imposition of administrative discipline need only be fair and give students and parents an opportunity to discuss the conduct being reviewed with the person or body authorized to impose discipline (*Appeal of Michael J.A.*, 39 Ed Dept Rep 501, Decision No. 14,293; *Appeal of Forster*, 31 *id.* 443, Decision No. 12,693). Having read the co-curricular eligibility policy, petitioner's son was aware of the potential penalty when he engaged in the prohibited conduct. Petitioner's son admitted his misconduct. The district's administrators provided more than one opportunity for petitioner to informally discuss his son's admission and the penalty imposed. Under these circumstances, I find that petitioner's son was afforded sufficient due process, and I do not find respondent's imposition of the penalty to be improper.

THE APPEAL IS DISMISSED.

Decision No. 15,150

Appeal of C.C., on behalf of his son C.C., from action of the Superintendent of the City School District of the City of Cohoes regarding a suspension from interscholastic athletics.

(December 9, 2004)

APPEARANCES OF COUNSEL

Girvin and Ferlazzo, P.C., attorneys for respondent, *Kristine Amodeo Lanchantin, Esq.*, of counsel

DECISION OF THE COMMISSIONER

MILLS, Commissioner.—Petitioner appeals the determination of the Superintendent ("respondent") of the City School District of the City of Cohoes ("district") to suspend his son, C.C., from interscholastic athletics for one year. The appeal must be dismissed.

While enrolled in the eleventh grade at the district's high school in November 2003, petitioner's son, C.C., signed a pledge promising to obey all school rules and acknowledging that he read the district's co-curricular eligibility policy. Petitioner cosigned the form.

The co-curricular policy provides in pertinent part:

> *SUBSTANCE ABUSE*: No smoking or drinking is allowed. Any violation of the rule will result in the following:
>
> 1st violation: Suspension from the team or co-curricular activity for the remainder of the season.

2nd violation: Suspension from all athletic teams or co-curricular activities for six months from the date of the infraction.

Any possession, sale or use of drugs will lead to immediate dismissal from the team or co-curricular activity and suspension from all sports or co-curricular activities for one (1) year: *this includes during and after school, on or off school property.* Legal authorities will be notified.

On Friday night, December 19, 2003, a police officer came upon C.C. and three other students in a car off school property. Finding marijuana in the car, the police notified the students' parents, but did not pursue criminal charges.

On Monday, December 22, 2003, after several staff members told the assistant principal of the weekend incident, the assistant principal called the students individually to her office. The school resource officer, a police officer assigned by the Cohoes Police Department, came to the assistant principal's office as part of his morning routine and remained after the students arrived. When the assistant principal asked C.C what occurred over the weekend, C.C. admitted that the police had found him and other students in a car with marijuana. The assistant principal conveyed the student's admission to the athletic coordinator, who determined that the student's conduct violated the district's co-curricular eligibility policy and imposed a one-year suspension from interscholastic athletics.

On January 5, 2004, petitioner appealed to a committee composed of the athletic coordinator, the high school principal and the junior varsity basketball coach. The committee upheld the penalty. On January 13, 2004, respondent met with the four students involved and their parents. By letter dated January 27, 2004, respondent sustained the committee's determination but offered an alternative resolution that would consider a reduction in the penalty if the students maintained good conduct. Petitioner did not accept the offer, and this appeal ensued. Petitioner's request for interim relief was denied on March 2, 2004.

Petitioner asserts that the district's co-curricular eligibility policy is arbitrary because the predetermined penalty for the possession, sale or use of drugs is much greater than the penalty related to tobacco products or alcohol. Petitioner argues that imposing different penalties is irrational because persons under 21 years of age cannot legally use any of these products; because alcohol use is as detrimental to a student's health as marijuana use; and because the school's interest in encouraging healthful habits and good citizenship is the same whether prohibiting alcohol or marijuana use. Petitioner also contends the student admitted to the assistant principal that marijuana was in the car because the police officer's presence intimidated him and because he was not advised of his rights under respondent's Code of Conduct. Petitioner seeks to invalidate the district's policy and C.C.'s suspension, and requests expungement of C.C.'s record.

Respondent asserts that the petition fails to state a claim, that the co-curricular policy establishes reasonable conduct standards, and that the procedure used was fair.

A board of education has broad authority to establish reasonable standards of conduct for participation in extracurricular activities, and unless it can be shown that the board has abused its discretion, its policy will be upheld (*Appeal of G.M.D.*, 43 Ed Dept Rep ___, Decision No. 14,998; *Appeal of Wright*, 38 *id.* 756, Decision No. 14,134; *Appeals of Cynthia and Robert W. and Melani and James H.*, 37 *id.* 437, Decision No. 13,899. Petitioner has not established that the district's current policy of imposing a greater penalty for drugs than for tobacco or alcohol is irrational or an abuse of discretion.

Petitioner contends that his son admitted to the assistant principal that marijuana was in the car because the police officer's presence intimidated him and because he was not advised of his rights under the district's Code of Conduct. The Code of Conduct provides that before police officials are permitted to question any student on school property, the principal (or designee) will try to notify the student's parent to give the parent an opportunity to be present. Also, the code provides that students must be informed of their legal rights, that the student may remain silent, and that the student may request the presence of an attorney. Respondent denies that the officer questioned C.C. and also argues that this does not apply to situations in which the district is investigating violations of its own rules and the police officer is involved in his capacity as the School Resource Officer.

In an appeal to the Commissioner of Education, petitioner has the burden of establishing the facts upon which relief is requested (8 NYCRR §275.10; *Appeal of V.P.*, 42 Ed Dept Rep 3, Decision No. 14,754) and the burden of demonstrating a clear legal right to the relief sought (*Appeal of D.T.*, 43 Ed Dept Rep ___, Decision No. 14,916). Petitioner alleges that the officer "actively participated in the interrogation." While the assistant principal acknowledges that C.C. engaged in "casual conversation" with the resource officer on December 22, she states the officer did not threaten or question the student. Petitioner was not present when his son was questioned and did not reply to the new material and affirmative defenses set forth in respondent's answer and accompanying affidavits. Therefore, since petitioner has failed to establish that the officer questioned C.C., I need not reach the question of whether respondent violated the district's Code of Conduct.

The procedures governing suspension of student privileges or the imposition of administrative discipline need only be fair and give students and parents an opportunity to discuss the conduct being reviewed with the person or body authorized to impose discipline (*Appeal of Michael J.A.*, 39 Ed Dept Rep 501, Decision No. 14,293; *Appeal of Forster*, 31 *id.* 443, Decision No. 12,693). Having read the co-curricular eligibility policy, petitioner's son was aware of the potential penalty when he engaged in the prohibited conduct. Petitioner's son admitted his misconduct. The district's administrators provided more than one opportunity for petitioner to informally discuss his son's admission and the penalty imposed. Under these circumstances, I find that petitioner's son was afforded sufficient due process, and I do not find respondent's imposition of the penalty to be improper.

THE APPEAL IS DISMISSED.

Decision No. 15,151

Appeal of SHARLEEN RESHARD from action of the Board of Education of the Hempstead Union Free School District regarding personnel decisions.

(December 22, 2004)

APPEARANCES OF COUNSEL

Ingerman Smith, LLP, attorneys for respondents, *Neil M. Block, Esq.*, of counsel

DECISION OF THE COMMISSIONER

MILLS, Commissioner.—Petitioner challenges certain personnel decisions of the Board of Education of the Hempstead Union Free School District ("respondent") and seeks the removal of three board members, Regina L. Gordon, Betty Cross and Perre Smalls. The appeal must be dismissed.

On September 4, 2003, respondent passed a resolution to terminate the probationary appointment of the Assistant Superintendent for Personnel effective October 3, 2003. On March 9, 2004, respondent passed another resolution to rescind the September 4 action with board members Regina L. Gordon, Betty Cross and Perre Smalls (hereinafter referred to as Gordon, Cross and Smalls) voting in the majority. This appeal ensued. Petitioner's request for interim relief was denied on April 26, 2004.

Petitioner alleges that Gordon, Cross and Smalls intentionally and wrongfully violated Education Law §3012 by providing a new probationary appointment without the recommendation of the superintendent, thereby allegedly usurping the power of the superintendent, and seeks the removal of the three board members. Petitioner requests I hear this appeal as a class appeal.

Respondent alleges that the board acted lawfully when it rescinded the termination, and that the petition should be dismissed for lack of standing, failure to join necessary parties, and failure to meet the notice requirements required for the removal of board members under Education Law §306. In addition, respondent maintains that there is no basis for a class appeal.

An appeal may only be maintained on behalf of a class where the class is so numerous that joinder of all members is impracticable and where all questions of fact and law are common to all members of the class (8 NYCRR §275.2; *Appeal of Colety*, 42 Ed Dept Rep 162, Decision No. 14,806; *Appeal of Broardt*, 42 *id.* 126, Decision No. 14,796). A petitioner must set forth the number of individuals he or she seeks to represent and show that all questions of law and fact would be common to all members of the class (*Appeal of Colety*, *supra*; *Appeal of Broardt*, *supra*). In the instant appeal, petitioner, representing an unnamed class, has not set forth the number of prospective members. Petitioner broadly asserts that the members of this proposed class have a right to expect that elected officials abide by the law. However, petitioner does not demonstrate that all questions of law and fact would be common to all members. Therefore, class status is denied.

To the extent petitioner seeks the removal of Regina L. Gordon and Perre Smalls, the appeal must be dismissed as moot since neither is currently serving on respondent board.

The appeal must also be dismissed for failure to join necessary parties. A party whose rights would be adversely affected by a determination of an appeal in favor of petitioner is a necessary party and must be joined as such (*Appeal of K.S.*, 43 Ed Dept Rep 492, Decision No. 15,063; *Appeal of Lawson*, 38 *id.* 713, Decision No. 14,124; *Appeal of Heller*, 38 *id.* 335, Decision No. 14,048). Such individual must be clearly named as a respondent in the caption of the petition and served with a copy of the notice of petition and petition, to inform the person that he or she should respond to the petition and enter a defense (*Appeal of K.S.*, *supra*; *Appeal of Lawson*, *supra*; *Appeal of Heller*, *supra*).

The essence of petitioner's appeal, and relief sought, is for the removal of Gordon, Cross and Smalls. The board members were not named in the caption of the petition or in the notice of petition such that they would have been on notice that they were intended to be parties to the appeal and were required to submit an answer. The appeal, therefore, must be dismissed for failure to join necessary parties (*Appeal of Heller*, *supra*).

In light of this disposition, I need not address the parties remaining contentions.

THE APPEAL IS DISMISSED.

Decision No. 15,152

Appeal of STEVEN P. SCHILDHORN, on behalf of his son DANIEL, from action of the Board of Education of the Windham-Ashland-Jewett Central School District regarding a physical education requirement.

(December 22, 2004)

APPEARANCES OF COUNSEL

Ferrara, Fiorenza, Larrison, Barrett & Reitz, P.C., attorneys for respondent, *Donald E. Budmen, Esq.*, of counsel

DECISION OF THE COMMISSIONER

MILLS, Commissioner.—Petitioner appeals the decision of the Board of Education of the Windham-Ashland-Jewett Central School District ("respondent") to deny his son, Daniel, academic credit for participation in extracurricular sports programs. The appeal must be dismissed.

Daniel was an eleventh grade student at respondent's high school during the 2003-2004 school year. His class schedule did not include a study hall, and, at respondent's October 2003 meeting, petitioner requested that Daniel be excused from his physical education classes to attend study hall during those periods instead. Petitioner asked that Daniel be allowed to fulfill his physical education requirement by participating in several district extracurricular sports and a non-district sponsored year-round soccer league.

At its November 13, 2003, meeting, respondent denied petitioner's request. Petitioner then requested a written response, and respondent's interim superintendent, by letter dated November 17, 2003, stated that respondent had not approved the use of extracurricular activities for physical education credit. That letter also stated that respondent's administrators had rearranged Daniel's schedule to provide him with study halls by shifting Daniel's physical education class to the Board of Cooperative Education Services ("BOCES") facility and using part of the time allotted to his automotive technology class. This appeal ensued.

Petitioner asserts that the Commissioner's regulations mandate respondent to give Daniel physical education credit for participating in extracurricular athletics. Petitioner contends that respondent's decision to reduce Daniel's automotive technology class time in order to provide study halls may negatively affect his grades in that class. Petitioner requests that I interpret the regulation to require respondent to grant physical education credits for extracurricular athletics. Petitioner also asks that I approve Daniel's extracurricular activities as equivalent to a physical education program for providing credits toward his graduation requirements.

Respondent asserts that its decision to require students to fulfill their physical education requirements through participation in physical education classes is rational, educationally sound and within its discretion. Respondent contends that Daniel's revised schedule would provide him with physical education classes and study halls without compromising his ability to meet the automotive technology requirements. Respondent objects to petitioner's reply and argues that the appeal is moot because Daniel has stopped participating in the district's extracurricular sports programs.

The purpose of a reply is to respond to new material or affirmative defenses set forth in an answer (8 NYCRR §§275.3 and 275.14). A reply is not meant to buttress allegations in the petition or to belatedly add assertions that should have been in the petition (*Appeal of General*, 43 Ed Dept Rep 146, Decision No. 14,948; *Appeal of Crosier*, 42 *id*. 232, Decision No. 14,835). Therefore, while I have reviewed petitioner's reply, I have not considered those portions containing new allegations that are not responsive to new material or affirmative defenses set forth in the answer.

The appeal must be dismissed in part as moot. The Commissioner will only decide matters in actual controversy and will not render a decision on a state of facts which no longer exists or which subsequent events have laid to rest (*Appeal of A.F.*, 44 Ed Dept Rep ___, Decision No. 15,120; *Appeal of N.S.*, 42 *id.* 190, Decision No. 14,817). Petitioner admits that Daniel has withdrawn from the district's extracurricular sports programs for which he was seeking physical education credit. Therefore, the appeal is moot as to petitioner's request that Daniel be given academic credit for participation in those programs.

The appeal must be dismissed as to petitioner's request that respondent be required to grant academic credit for participation in extracurricular athletic programs. At issue is §135.4(c)(2)(ii) of the Commissioner's regulations which states, in pertinent part:

> Secondary instructional program—grades 7 through 12. All secondary pupils shall have the opportunity for regular physical education, but not less than three times per week in one semester and two times per week in the other semester, taught by a certified physical education teacher, and all such pupils shall participate in the physical education program either:
>
> (a) a minimum of three periods per calendar week during one semester of each school year and two periods during the other semester; or
>
> (b) a comparable time each semester if the school is organized in other patterns; or
>
> (c) for pupils in grades 10 through 12 only, a comparable time each semester in extraclass programs for those pupils who have demonstrated acceptable levels of physical fitness, physical skills, and knowledge of physical education activities; or
>
> (d) for pupils in grades 10 through 12 only, a comparable time each semester in out-of-school activities approved by the physical education staff and the school administration; or
>
> (e) as provided in an equivalent program approved by the Commissioner of Education.

Respondent states that it does not have standards to evaluate extracurricular programs and that it does not grant physical education credit for such activities. Respondent's policy is that regular physical education classes provide important educational components that a student would not be taught merely by participating on athletic teams. Petitioner, on the other hand, argues that respondent does not have the choice to deny credit for extracurricular activities. Rather, petitioner asserts that it is mandatory for boards of education to recognize each of the options listed in the regulation as satisfying a student's physical education requirement. I disagree.

To read such a requirement into the regulation would be at odds with Education Law §1709(3), which gives boards of education broad authority to prescribe courses of study. The decision as to what instructional programs are to be offered in schools within a district is within the discretion of the board of education (*Appeal of Reilly*, 20 Ed Dept Rep 191, Decision No. 10,373; *Appeal of Talbot and Suskind*, 10 *id*. 83, Decision No. 8,210). While the regulation permits certain alternative options, nothing in the regulation requires a board of education to recognize each of the options as meeting physical education requirements. Furthermore, the language of clauses (c) and (d) of §135.4(ii)(2)(ii), (which refer to "acceptable levels," and to approval by the school staff and administration) indicates that the district has discretion as to what extent it wishes to recognize such activities.

In this case, respondent elected not to permit the extracurricular option. Instead, it established a reasonable education policy that requires all students to earn physical education credits through respondent's physical education curriculum. I find that it was wholly within respondent's authority to do so.

Finally, petitioner contends that respondent's decision to rearrange Daniel's schedule so that he would have less class time in his automotive technology class would negatively impact Daniel's grades in that class. Respondent states that Daniel would be able to meet all of his Automotive Technology class requirements with the modified schedule. In an appeal to the Commissioner, petitioner has the burden of establishing the facts upon which he seeks relief (8 NYCRR §275.10; *Appeal of Ewart*, 44 Ed Dept Rep ___, Decision No. 15,127; *Appeal of Brown, et al.*, 43 *id*. 231, Decision No. 14,980). Petitioner has not supported his contention with any evidence that Daniel's academic performance would, in fact, be impacted. Petitioner has thus failed to meet his burden of proof on this issue.

THE APPEAL IS DISMISSED.

Decision No. 15,153

Appeal of N.L. from action of the Board of Education of the Lynbrook Union Free School District regarding student discipline.

(December 22, 2004)

APPEARANCES OF COUNSEL

Ehrlich, Frazer & Feldman, attorneys for respondent, *Jacob Feldman, Esq.*, of counsel

DECISION OF THE COMMISSIONER

MILLS, Commissioner—Petitioner challenges the action of the Board of Education of the Lynbrook Union Free School District ("respondent") regarding student discipline. The appeal must be dismissed.

During the 2003-2004 school year, petitioner's daughter was enrolled in the tenth grade in respondent's high school. Although the petition is unclear, it appears that petitioner primarily complains about a two-day suspension imposed on her daughter for a May 26, 2004, altercation with another student. Petitioner claims that her daughter was treated unfairly because the other student only received a one-day suspension and requests that I order respondent to suspend the other student for an additional day. Petitioner also complains, among other things, that in November 2003 and April 2004, school administrators failed to appropriately respond to her daughter's complaints of harassment by students at school.

Respondent asserts, among other things, that the petition is untimely and fails to establish any basis for relief. Respondent also claims that petitioner failed to join necessary parties.

Preliminarily, I must address a number of procedural matters. Respondent objects to petitioner's reply and memorandum of law. The purpose of a reply is to respond to new material or affirmative defenses set forth in the answer (8 NYCRR §§275.3 and 275.14). A reply is not meant to buttress allegations in the petition or to belatedly add assertions that should have been in the petition (*Appeal of Goldin*, 43 Ed Dept Rep 20, Decision No. 14,904; *Appeal of Hollister*, 39 *id.* 109, Decision No. 14,188). Petitioner's reply, in large measure, improperly reargues points made in the petition, and although I have reviewed it, I have not considered those portions containing new allegations that are not responsive to new material or affirmative defenses set forth in the answer.

A memorandum of law may not be used to belatedly add new assertions that are not part of the pleadings (*Appeal of Hager, et al.*, 43 Ed Dept Rep 363, Decision No. 15,019; *Appeal of Hubbard*, 39 *id.* 363, Decision No. 14,259). Therefore, I have not considered the new assertions regarding respondent's conduct raised in petitioner's memorandum. Petitioner also requests for the first time in her memorandum of law that I expunge her daughter's record. Petitioner was required to request such relief in her petition (8 NYCRR §275.10). Accordingly, I will not entertain this request.

On October 20, 2004, my Office of Counsel received a letter with attachments from petitioner raising new issues that were not included in her petition. Additional supporting papers may only be submitted with the prior permission of the Commissioner (8 NYCRR §276.5). While this provision permits the submission of additional evidence, it cannot be used to add new claims against a respondent for which notice has not been provided (*Appeal of Gehl, et al.*, 42 Ed Dept Rep 287, Decision No. 14,857; *Appeal of Johnson*, 38 *id.* 524, Decision No. 14,086). I have not accepted these materials because I find that they raise new issues that are not relevant to the claims originally raised in this appeal (*see*, *Appeal of Gehl, et al.*, *supra*; *Appeal of Johnson*, *supra*).

The appeal must be dismissed as untimely to the extent petitioner challenges the district's response to her daughter's complaints of harassment in November 2003 and April 2004. An appeal to the Commissioner must be commenced within 30 days from the making of the decision or the performance of the act complained of, unless any delay is excused by the Commissioner for good cause shown (8 NYCRR §275.16). Petitioner commenced her appeal on June 7, 2004, well beyond the 30-day period, and offers no excuse for the delay. Accordingly, these claims must be dismissed as untimely.

The appeal must also be dismissed to the extent that petitioner requests that I order respondent to impose an additional one-day suspension on another student. The rights of this individual would be adversely affected by a determination in petitioner's favor. Accordingly, he is a necessary party to this appeal and should have been named and served with a copy of the notice and petition (*see*, *Appeal of a Student with a Disability*, 38 Ed Dept Rep 378, Decision No. 14,059). Inasmuch as petitioner failed to join him as a party, those claims directed against him must be dismissed (*Appeal of Andela*, 38 Ed Dept Rep 249, Decision No. 14,026; *Appeal of Basil*, 37 *id.* 568, Decision No. 13,929). Moreover, although petitioner has standing to challenge the penalty imposed on her daughter, she lacks standing to compel respondent to impose an additional suspension on the student with whom her daughter had the altercation.

The appeal must also be dismissed on the merits. In an appeal to the Commissioner, petitioner has the burden of demonstrating a clear legal right to the relief requested and the burden of establishing the facts upon which she seeks relief (8 NYCRR §275.10; *Appeal of V.E.*, 43 Ed Dept Rep 244, Decision No. 14,985; *Appeal of Vazquez*, 42 *id.* 245, Decision No. 14,841). The record reflects that petitioner's daughter had an altercation, threw soda on another student and scratched him in the face after he threw a beverage on her. Respondent explains that both students were given a one-day suspension for inappropriate language and behavior on school grounds and that petitioner's daughter was given an additional one-day suspension for inappropriate physical contact. Under these circumstances, I do not find the penalty inappropriate and find no basis to interfere with respondent's determination.

I have reviewed petitioner's remaining contentions and find them without merit.

THE APPEAL IS DISMISSED.

Decision No. 15,154

Appeal of R.M. and L.M., on behalf of their daughter M.M., from action of the Board of Education of the Northern Adirondack Central School District regarding student discipline.

(December 22, 2004)

APPEARANCES OF COUNSEL

Harris Beach, LLP, attorneys for respondent, *Jacqueline M. Kelleher, Esq.*, of counsel

DECISION OF THE COMMISSIONER

MILLS, Commissioner.—Petitioners appeal the suspension of their daughter by the Board of Education of the Northern Adirondack Central School District ("respondent"). The appeal must be sustained in part.

During the 2002-2003 school year, petitioners' daughter was an eighth grade student in respondent's district. On the afternoon of April 29, 2003, a physical altercation occurred on the school bus between petitioners' daughter and another female student.

On April 30, 2003, the bus driver made a disciplinary referral and an investigation was conducted. The middle school principal met with the student and her mother on April 30, 2003. That same day, the high school principal spoke by telephone with the student's mother. Seven of the students on the bus were interviewed, including petitioners' daughter and the other girl involved in the fight. Upon completing her investigation, the middle school principal placed petitioners' daughter on in-school suspension for the remainder of the day on April 30, and suspended her from school through May 5, 2003. Written notice of the suspension, dated April 30, 2003, was sent to petitioners by regular mail. Respondent contends it put the notice in the mail no later than May 1, 2003. Petitioners contend that they received the notice on May 4.

After her daughter served the suspension, the student's mother identified to school personnel a provision in respondent's code of conduct which provides that any student who is found to have committed a violent act other than bringing a weapon onto school property and whose proposed penalty exceeds a one-day suspension, will be given the same notice and opportunity for a hearing given to all students subject to a long-term suspension.

On June 19, 2003, a hearing was held pursuant to this provision of the code of conduct. On June 26, 2003, the hearing officer issued his findings and recommendations. The superintendent notified petitioners on June 30, 2003, of his determination that their daughter was guilty of fighting on the school bus on April 29, 2003, and that the suspension imposed was justified. On July 28, 2003, petitioners were notified of respondent's decision to uphold the superintendent's decision. Petitioners then commenced this appeal. Petitioners' request for interim relief was denied on September 22, 2003.

Petitioners contend that they did not receive written notice of the suspension until May 4, 2003, and that they were not informed of the right to an informal conference. Petitioners also contend that their daughter was left unsupervised while serving in-school suspension and request an order requiring respondent to have a teacher present during future in-school suspensions. Petitioners request that the suspension be expunged from their daughter's record, that the bus driver be removed from his assigned route and given training, and that all buses have running videotapes reviewed daily. Petitioners further request that respondent transfer and transport her daughter to a school in another school district for the remainder of the 2003-2004 school year.

Respondent contends that the petition should be dismissed for failure to set forth a clear and concise statement of issues and failure to join the school bus driver as a necessary party. Respondent argues that the suspension was based upon competent and substantial evidence and is proportionate to the severity of the offense. Respondent contends that there is no basis to transfer or transport the student to a school in another school district.

Initially I will address the procedural matters. A party whose rights would be adversely affected by a determination of an appeal in favor of a petitioner is a necessary party and must be joined as such (*Appeal of M.C.*, 43 Ed Dept Rep 276, Decision No. 14,993; *Appeal of M.M.*, 42 *id.* 323, Decision No. 14,870; *Appeal of Loveland and Hazelton*, 42 *id.* 294, Decision No. 14,858). Here, petitioners seek sanctions against the school bus driver. Therefore, he should have been joined as a party and petitioners' failure to do so requires dismissal of the appeal as to him.

The Commissioner of Education will only decide matters in actual controversy and will not render a decision on a state of facts which no longer exist or which subsequent events have laid to rest (*Appeal of M.F. and J.F.*, 43 Ed Dept Rep 174, Decision No. 14,960; *Appeal of a Student Suspected of Having a Disability*, 41 *id.* 253, Decision No. 14,678). As the 2003-2004 school year has ended, petitioners' claim regarding transfer and transportation of their daughter to a different school for the remainder of the school year is moot and must be dismissed.

Turning to the merits, when a principal proposes to suspend a student from attendance for a period of five days or less, §100.2(l)(4) of the Commissioner's regulations requires that immediate written notice be provided to parents to advise them of the reason for the proposed suspension and their right to an immediate informal conference with the principal. The purpose of this regulation is to ensure that parents of a student suspended for five days or less are made aware of the statutory right provided in Education Law §3214(3)(b)(1) to question the complaining witnesses in the presence of the principal who imposed the suspension in the first instance, and who has authority to terminate or reduce the suspension. This procedure affords the principal the opportunity to decide whether his original decision to suspend was correct or should be modified (*Appeal of L.H.*, 43 Ed Dept Rep 315, Decision No. 15,005; *Appeal of M.F. and J.F.*, *supra*; *Appeal of a Student Suspected of Having a Disability*, 40 *id.* 542, Decision No. 14,552). Written notice must be provided by personal delivery, express mail delivery, or equivalent means reasonably calculated to assure receipt within 24 hours of the decision to propose suspension. Education Law §3214(3)(b)(1) provides that written notice and an opportunity for a conference must take place prior to the suspension unless the student presents a continuing danger or ongoing threat of disruption.

In this case, respondent failed to provide timely written notice of the suspension and petitioners' right to request an immediate informal conference, as required by the Commissioner's regulation. Accordingly, the suspension must be expunged from the student's record (*Appeal of L.H.*, *supra*; *Appeal of M.F. and J.F.*, *supra*; *Appeal of Coleman*, 41 Ed Dept Rep 101, Decision No. 14,628).

I have considered the parties' remaining contentions and find them to be without merit. In an appeal to the Commissioner, petitioner has the burden of demonstrating a clear legal right to the relief requested (*Appeal of Goldin*, 43 Ed Dept Rep 453, Decision No. 15,048). Here, petitioners have failed to meet that burden.

THE APPEAL IS SUSTAINED TO THE EXTENT INDICATED.

IT IS ORDERED that respondent remove all references to M.M.'s suspension during April 30 — May 5, 2003, from her records.

Decision No. 15,155

Appeal of SCOTT POLMANTEER, on behalf of his son NICHOLAS POLMANTEER, HAROLD and CYNTHIA TITUS MANSFIELD, on behalf of their children JACQUELINE and FRANK MANSFIELD, CATHERINE BOVEE, on behalf of her son BRIAN WEGMAN, and ROXANNE MILLER, on behalf of her children ETHAN and JULIA PRATT, from action of the Board of Education of the Cato-Meridian Central School District, Robert Vogel, president, Margaret Meccariello, Donald Thompson, Deborah Kolb, Katherine Bratt, Joanne Lloyd and Herbert Thomas, trustees, regarding a contingency budget.

(December 24, 2004)

APPEARANCES OF COUNSEL

Andrew S. Fusco, Esq., attorney for petitioners

Matthew R. Fletcher, Esq., attorney for respondents

DECISION OF THE COMMISSIONER

MILLS, Commissioner.—Petitioners challenge the 2004-2005 contingency budget adopted by the Board of Education of the Cato-Meridian Central School District ("respondent board"). The appeal must be dismissed.

On June 24, 2004, after district voters twice defeated a proposed budget, respondent board adopted a contingency budget as required by Education Law §§2022 and 2023. The contingency budget did not include appropriations for interschool athletics, extracurricular activities or field trips. On July 22, 2004, petitioners initiated this appeal on behalf of their children, and purportedly on behalf of a class of parents and students in the district, challenging the contingency budget. Thereafter, petitioners commenced a proceeding pursuant to Article 78 of the Civil Practice Law and Rules in New York State Supreme Court, Cayuga County, also challenging the contingency budget.

Petitioners object to the contingency budget on several grounds. They allege that respondents' failure to include appropriations for interschool athletics, extracurricular activities and field trips violates the requirements of Education Law §2023. Petitioners also allege that respondents exceeded the maximum cap on administrative expenditures imposed by Education Law §2023.

Petitioners further assert that, to avoid exceeding the cap, respondents improperly reallocated certain administrative expenditures to the program expenses portion of the budget. Petitioners also disagree with respondents' decision to allocate funds to reduce a pre-existing budget deficit. Finally, petitioners claim that respondents have employed unsound accounting methods and principles. Petitioners request an opportunity to present evidence at a hearing regarding their claims.

Respondents contend that petitioners lack standing to maintain the appeal, that class status must be denied and that petitioners failed to file a notice of claim. Respondents maintain that the contingency budget is in all respects proper.

Respondents claim that petitioners lack standing to maintain this appeal. Pursuant to Education Law §310, an individual may not maintain an appeal unless aggrieved in the sense that he or she has suffered personal damage or injury to his or her civil, personal or property rights. Only persons who are directly affected by the action being appealed have standing to bring an appeal (*Appeal of Murphy*, 39 Ed Dept Rep 562, Decision No. 14,311; *Appeal of Lucente*, 39 *id.*

244, Decision No. 14,227). A district resident has standing to challenge an allegedly illegal expenditure of district funds (*Appeal of Patton, et al.*, 42 Ed Dept Rep 226, Decision No. 14,832; *Appeal of Gargan*, 40 *id.* 465, Decision No. 14,528; *Appeal of Goldin*, 38 *id.* 322, Decision No. 14,044). Petitioners, as residents of the district, challenge certain expenditures included in the contingency budget adopted by respondents. Petitioners also challenge, on behalf of their children, respondents' determination to eliminate interscholastic sports, extracurricular activities and field trips in which the students had previously participated. I find, therefore, that petitioners have standing to maintain this appeal (*Appeal of Gargan*, *supra*; *Appeal of Murphy*, *supra*).

Class certification, however, is denied. Petitioners purport to represent "the present parents and students of the Cato-Meridian Central School District, who are likewise harmed by the adoption by respondents of the 2004-2005 Cato-Meridian Central School District 'contingency budget'." An appeal may only be maintained on behalf of a class where the class is so numerous that joinder of all members is impracticable and where all questions of fact and law are common to all members of the class (8 NYCRR §275.2; *Appeal of Cartagena*, 43 Ed Dept Rep 272, Decision No. 14,992; *Appeal of Colety*, 42 id. 162, Decision No. 14,806). A petitioner must set forth the number of individuals he or she seeks to represent and must show that all questions of law and fact would be common to all members of the class (*Appeal of Cartagena*, *supra*; *Appeal of Colety*, *supra*). Petitioners have failed to meet this requirement.

The Commissioner of Education will not entertain an appeal where it appears that the issue in controversy is simultaneously being litigated in another forum (*Appeal of the Bd. of Educ. of the Town of Webb U.F.S.D.*, 40 Ed Dept Rep 449, Decision No. 14,524; *Appeal of a Student with a Disability*, 36 *id.* 287, Decision No. 13,726). The record indicates that petitioners commenced an action against respondents in Cayuga County, Supreme Court, raising similar claims regarding the funding of interschool athletics, extracurricular activities and field trips, and seeking similar relief. On August 23, 2004, the court rendered an order and decision in favor of petitioners, directing respondent board to fund such activities in its contingency budget. Respondents appealed this decision to the Appellate Division, Fourth Department. Since petitioners' claims regarding the funding of interschool athletics, extracurricular activities and field trips are pending in the courts, this appeal must be dismissed as to those claims (*Appeal of the Bd. of Educ. of the Town of Webb U.F.S.D.*, *supra*; *Appeal of a Student with a Disability*, *supra*).

Petitioners' claims regarding the administrative expense cap, respondent board's allocation of expenses to the program component of the contingency budget and its reduction of the deficit must be dismissed on the merits. In their pleadings, petitioners set forth a number of conclusory allegations regarding the contingency budget adopted by respondents. In an appeal to the Commissioner of Education, the petitioner has the burden of demonstrating a clear legal right to the relief requested and establishing the facts upon which he seeks relief (8 NYCRR §275.10; *Appeal of Antoniadis*, 44 Ed Dept Rep ___, Decision No. 15,106; *Appeal of Coleman, et al.*, 42 *id.* 256, Decision No. 14,845; *Application of Wilson*, 41 *id.* 196, Decision No. 14,663). Petitioners fail to submit any affidavits, exhibits or other documentation in support of their claims. Instead, petitioners request an opportunity to present proof at an evidentiary hearing that the contingency budget violates Education Law §2023.

An appeal to the Commissioner under Education Law §310 is appellate in nature and does not provide for discovery or evidentiary hearings (*Lilley v. Mills*, 274 AD2d 644; *Akshar v. Mills*, 249 AD2d 786, *lv denied* 92 NY2d 962; *Appeal of Coleman*, *supra*). While oral argument may be granted at the discretion of the Commissioner, "[a]ll evidentiary material [must] be presented by affidavit or by exhibits. No testimony is taken and no transcript of oral argument [is] made" (8 NYCRR §276.2(d)). The burden is on petitioners to allege and prove facts upon which relief may be granted, not on respondents to rebut conclusory allegations set forth in the petition (*Application of Wilson*, *supra*).

On the record before me, petitioners fail to establish a basis for their factual claims on the administrative cap, allocation of expenses to the program component of the budget or the deficit reduction. Petitioners claim that respondents have exceeded the maximum cap on administrative expenses in a contingency budget imposed by Education Law §2023(3). A school district budget consists of an administrative component, a program component and a capital component (8 NYCRR §170.8). All parties agree that the administrative component of respondent board's contingency budget must not exceed 12.19% of the total budget, exclusive of the capital component. Petitioners assert in conclusory fashion that, in fact, the administrative component of the contingency budget approved by respondents constitutes 12.57% of the total budget, exclusive of the capital component. Petitioners present no documentary evidence to support their claim.

Respondents assert that, although the administrative component of the June 24, 2004, contingency budget initially exceeded the statutory cap, at a July 21, 2004, meeting, they recalculated the administrative component. Respondents assert that the administrative portion of the contingency budget currently does not exceed the 12.19% maximum cap imposed by Education Law §2023(3). Respondents submit the minutes of the July 21, 2004, meeting in support of their assertion, while petitioners submit no contravening evidence.

Petitioners allege that, when they revised the administrative component of the contingency budget, respondents improperly reallocated certain expenses from the administrative component to the program component. In support of their contention, petitioners cite only one example, alleging that respondents improperly reallocated $18,064 in legal expenses for a "BOCES negotiator" to the program component from the administrative component. Respondents deny the allegation and assert that the allocation of legal costs from the administrative component to the program component of the contingency budget is permissible. Respondents state that the allocation of legal expenses to the program component represents costs for negotiations with teachers and other employees within the program component, student discipline hearings and impartial hearings for students with disabilities. Respondents claim the allocation of those costs to the program component is consistent with Commissioner's regulations.

Section 170.8 of the Commissioner's regulations sets forth the types of expenses included in each component of a school district budget. Section 170.8(c) describes the expenses to be included in the program component and includes, "legal services relating directly to other accounts and functions in the program component." Inclusion in the program component of legal expenses related to student discipline hearings and impartial due process hearings for students with disabilities is permissible (New York State Education Department, School Business Management - Handbook Number 3, Revised February 1998). However, respondents may not include legal expenses associated with contract negotiations. Although petitioners contend that respondents included legal expenses for a "BOCES negotiator," they do not explain the nature of that position. Nor do they provide any evidence regarding the actual amount attributable to that position. Therefore, on the record before me, it is not possible to determine whether the expense has been improperly allocated or what effect, if any, the allocation would have on the statutory cap.

Finally, petitioners challenge respondents' determination to expend $250,000 to eliminate, over a three to five year period, an accumulated deficit of approximately $750,000. In challenging that expenditure, petitioners assert in a conclusory fashion that respondents' determination is unfair, inequitable and an unsound accounting practice. Petitioners argue that the funds more appropriately could have been used to pay for the eliminated activities they desire.

Respondents correctly maintain that boards of education are not permitted to engage in deficit spending and are required to adopt a balanced budget annually (Education Law §1718). Respondent board is required to eliminate its deficit as soon as possible. Petitioners incorrectly assert that the $250,000 could be included in the budget appropriations to support the eliminated programs. The $250,000 is not included in the annual budget appropriation on which respondents calculate the administrative and total spending caps imposed on contingency budgets pursuant to Education Law §2023(4). Even if respondents did not identify revenues to eliminate the accumulated deficit, they could not increase the annual budget appropriations to fund the eliminated activities petitioners desire without running afoul of the statutory annual budget appropriation spending caps. Petitioners' disagreement with respondents' plan to eliminate its deficit does not render respondents' action arbitrary or capricious or contrary to law.

In light of this disposition, I need not address the parties' remaining claims.

Although the appeal is dismissed for the above-stated reasons, I am compelled to comment on the funding of interschool athletics, extracurricular activities and field trips because of the statewide implications of this issue. For the reasons set forth below, I must respectfully disagree with the conclusion of the Supreme Court, Cayuga County.

Petitioners contend that Education Law §2023(1), as amended by Chapter 436 of the Laws of 1997, *requires* a board of education to include funding for these activities in a contingency budget. Historically, interscholastic athletics, field trips and extracurricular activities were non-contingent expenditures that could not be included in a contingency budget. If a board of education adopted a contingency budget, and wanted to offer such programs to students, it was required to submit a proposition and obtain voter approval to fund such programs or obtain donations in advance from an outside source (*Appeal of Gallagher*, 39 Ed Dept Rep 623, Decision No. 14,331; *Appeals of Scarrone and Tierney*, 35 *id.* 443, Decision No. 13,594; *Appeal of Farrell*, 30 *id.* 81, Decision No. 12,397).

In 1997, extensive changes were made to the Education Law by Chapter 436 of the Laws of 1997 relating to the impact of a budget defeat and the adoption of a contingency budget. One major change was that school boards were prohibited from submitting to district voters a school district budget or a proposition for the expenditure of money more than twice (Education Law §2022(4) and (5)). Adoption of a contingency budget became mandatory after a second budget defeat (*Id.*). Another major change was that expenses incurred for interscholastic athletics, field trips and other extracurricular activities were made ordinary contingent expenses (Education Law §2023(1)). As such, voter approval was no longer required for a school district on a contingency budget to offer such programs to students.

Education Law §2023(1), thus currently provides:

> If the qualified voters shall neglect or refuse to vote the sum estimated necessary for teachers' salaries, after applying thereto the public school moneys, and other moneys received or to be received for that purpose, or if they shall neglect or refuse to vote the sum estimated necessary for ordinary contingent expenses, including the purchase of library books and other instructional materials associated with a library and expenses incurred for interschool athletics, field trips and other extracurricular activities and the expenses for cafeteria or restaurant services, the sole trustee, board of trustees, or board of education shall adopt a contingency budget including such expenses and *shall levy* a tax for the same, in like manner as if the same had been voted by the qualified voters, subject to the limitations contained in subdivisions three and four of this section. (Emphasis added)

Petitioners point out that Chapter 436 of the Laws of 1997 added the phrase "shall levy" in place of "may levy" and contend that this amendment indicates the Legislature's intent to mandate the inclusion of the enumerated items of expenses and activities in a contingency budget. However, this amendment must be interpreted in the context of the sweeping changes made by Chapter 436 of the

Laws of 1997, including the addition of the phrase "shall adopt a contingency budget." When considered in this context, the change in language from "may levy" to "shall levy" is explicable as a consequence of making the adoption of a contingency budget mandatory after a second budget vote.

Moreover, Education Law §§1709 and 1804 confer specific powers and duties on the board of education of a central school district, including the power to prescribe the course of study by which the pupils of the schools shall be graded and classified, to prescribe the textbooks to be used in the schools, to make provision for the instruction of pupils in all subjects in which instruction is required to be given pursuant to Education Law and to have in all respects the superintendence, management and control of the schools. While Education Law §2023(1) requires a board of education to adopt a contingency budget, it does not abrogate the discretion of a board of education to determine whether to include or exclude specific items of expense or activities in the district's educational program. Boards of education have always had discretion to determine ordinary contingent expenses, including whether to purchase library books or instructional materials or to participate on interschool athletics or conduct field trips. (*See*, New York State Education Department, School Business Management — Handbook Number 3, Revised February 1998, Appendix F, page 58.)

Although the legislative history of Chapter 436 of the Laws of 1997 provides minimal guidance regarding the intent of the amendment to Education Law §2023(1), the sponsor's memorandum to a subsequent similar amendment is illustrative and does not support petitioners' contention. Chapter 682 of the Laws of 2002 also amended Education Law §2023(1) to include as ordinary contingency expenses, expenses for cafeteria or restaurant services. The sponsor's memorandum states that the purpose of the legislation is to "*allow* school districts the ability to continue to provide cafeteria services, as part of ordinary contingent expenses" (emphasis added). In the "Summary of Provisions" section of the memorandum, the sponsor states:

This legislation *allows* school districts, including Union Free and Common school districts, *the ability to* include expenses for cafeteria or restaurant services, as ordinary contingency expenses for which the sole trustee, board of trustees or board of education *may* levy a tax (emphasis added).

Thus, in the 2002 amendment to Education Law §2023(1), the Legislature clearly articulated an intent to continue to vest the board of education with discretion to include certain expenses as part of a contingency budget.

In sum, I find no indication in the language or legislative history of Education Law §2023(1) of an intent to compel boards of education to expend funds for programs or activities they have not approved. Accordingly, a board's decision not to fund interscholastic sports, extracurricular activities and field trips, would appear to be within its authority and discretion (*See*, *Appeal of Baisch*, 40 Ed Dept Rep 405, Decision No. 14,512.)

THE APPEAL IS DISMISSED.

Decision No. 15,156

Appeal of CHARLES WARE from action of the Board of Education of the Cato-Meridian Central School District and the Superintendent of Schools regarding a contingency budget.

(December 24, 2004)

APPEARANCES OF COUNSEL

Matthew R. Fletcher, Esq., attorney for respondents

DECISION OF THE COMMISSIONER

MILLS, Commissioner.—Petitioner challenges the action of the Board of Education of the Cato-Meridian Central School District ("respondent board") and its superintendent of schools in calculating the administrative component of a contingency budget. The appeal must be dismissed.

Petitioner was elected to respondent board at the district's annual election on May 18, 2004. On June 24, 2004, after district voters twice defeated a proposed budget, respondent board adopted a contingency budget as required by Education Law §§2022 and 2023. On July 13, 2004, after taking office, petitioner initiated this appeal challenging the calculation of the administrative expense component of the contingency budget.

Petitioner claims that the administrative component of the proposed contingency budget, published prior to the second vote on the district's proposed budget on June 18, 2004, exceeded the statutory limitation imposed by Education Law §2023(3). Petitioner also asserts that the contingency budget adopted by respondent board on June 24, 2004, continued to exceed the statutory cap on the administrative component. Petitioner asks that I direct respondents to properly calculate any contingency budget in the future.

Respondents contend that petitioner lacks standing to maintain this appeal, and that petitioner seeks an advisory opinion. Respondents assert that the contingency budget was revised on July 21, 2004, and the final contingency budget is in all respects proper.

Respondents claim that petitioner is not aggrieved and lacks standing to bring this appeal. A district resident has standing to challenge an alleged illegal expenditure of district funds (*Appeal of Gargan*, 40 Ed Dept Rep 465, Decision No. 14,528; *Appeal of Goldin*, 38 *id*. 322, Decision No. 14,044). Thus, I find petitioner has standing to maintain this appeal.

The Commissioner of Education does not issue advisory opinions or declaratory rulings in appeals brought pursuant to Education Law §310 (*Appeal of L.M.*, 43 Ed Dept Rep 279, Decision No. 14,994; *Appeal of Bach*, 43 *id*. 182, Decision No. 14,962). Although petitioner alleges that at the June 18, 2004, budget vote district voters were misinformed about the proposed contingency budget that respondent board would adopt if the proposed budget was defeated, he does not seek to have the results of that budget vote annulled. Nor does petitioner request annulment of the contingency budget adopted by respondent board on June 24, 2004, or the revised contingency budget approved on July 21, 2004. In his request for relief, petitioner merely asks for an order directed to respondents "stating when future budgets are developed, they must meet the requirements, intent, and spirit of Education Law §2023." Thus, while respondents are obligated to abide by all provisions of the Education Law, the relief sought constitutes an impermissible request for an advisory opinion.

THE APPEAL IS DISMISSED.

Decision No. 15,157

Appeal of D.B. from action of the Board of Education of the Huntington Union Free School District regarding parent participation in school activities.

(December 24, 2004)

APPEARANCES OF COUNSEL

Guercio & Guercio, attorneys for respondent, *Vanessa M. Sheehan* and *Barbara P. Aloe, Esqs*., of counsel

DECISION OF THE COMMISSIONER

MILLS, Commissioner.—Petitioner appeals the determination of the Board of Education of the Huntington Union Free School District ("respondent") that her ex-husband may participate in their daughter's school activities. The appeal must be dismissed.

During the 2003-2004 school year, petitioner's eight-year-old daughter attended respondent's Southdown Primary School. Petitioner and her husband were divorced in March 2001 and petitioner was awarded custody of the child with the father having weekend and evening visitation. The father has participated in his daughter's school programs and activities. Petitioner has made repeated written and verbal requests to the district that the father not be permitted access to their daughter at school without her permission.

By letter dated October 31, 2001, respondent's attorney first advised petitioner's attorney that it would not ban the father from school activities. Petitioner continued to object to the father's access to school activities involving her child. By letter dated October 17, 2003, the principal of Southdown Primary School advised petitioner that the school could not deny the father the right to participate in school-sponsored activities related to her daughter. Following a series of letters between petitioner's and respondent's attorneys, by letter dated February 5, 2004, respondent's attorney confirmed the district's position. This appeal ensued.

Petitioner contends that because she has sole custody of her child, respondent cannot allow the father access to her daughter during school hours without her permission.

Respondent maintains that its actions were lawful and had a rational basis. Further, respondent asserts that the Commissioner lacks jurisdiction over this matter, that the appeal is untimely, that petitioner has failed to prove that she has suffered injury and that petitioner failed to join the child's father as a necessary party. Finally, respondent objects to petitioner's reply.

Respondent objects to portions of petitioner's reply. A reply is not meant to buttress allegations in the petition or to belatedly add assertions that should have been included in the petition (8 NYCRR §§275.3 and 275.14; *Appeal of O'Herron*, 40 Ed Dept Rep 204, Decision No. 14,461; *Appeals of Simpson, et al.*, 40 *id.* 5, Decision No. 14,402). Therefore, while I have reviewed petitioner's reply, I have not considered the portion that contains new assertions that are not responsive to new material or affirmative defenses set forth in the answer.

Respondent also argues that I lack jurisdiction to hear this appeal. However, §310 of the Education Law provides for an appeal to the Commissioner by any person aggrieved by any official act or decision of any officer or school authority. Respondent's decision denying petitioner's request to restrict her ex-husband's access to her daughter while in school is such an act and is therefore properly before me (*Appeal of Sans*, 29 Ed Dept Rep 62, Decision No. 12,223). I likewise decline to dismiss the appeal for lack of standing.

An appeal to the Commissioner must be instituted within 30 days from the making of the decision or the performance of the act complained of, unless any delay is excused by the Commissioner for good cause shown (8 NYCRR §275.16). Respondent contends that the appeal is untimely because it was not commenced within 30 days from the October 31, 2001, letter sent to petitioner's attorney. I do not agree. The 2001 communication was an advisory letter informing petitioner's attorney that a more explicit court order would be needed before respondent would bar the father from school.

Two years later, petitioner requested that the school deny her ex-husband access to their daughter at school. She began with the principal of her child's school. An exchange of letters between petitioner's and respondent's attorneys ensued. Petitioner finally wrote to respondent on January 20, 2004, asking for a determination of the issue. She received a response from respondent's attorney by letter dated February 5, 2004, informing petitioner that the district, "will not prohibit a parent from participating in his or her child's everyday schooling and school activities unless the District is provided with a court order expressly setting forth this limitation." Therefore, I find this appeal which was commenced on March 5, 2004, to be timely (*see*, *Appeal of a Student with a Disability and his Sister*, 42 Ed Dept Rep 199, Decision No. 14,821).

The appeal, however, must be dismissed for failure to join the father as a necessary party. A party whose rights would be adversely affected by a determination of an appeal in favor of petitioner is a necessary party and must be joined as such (*Appeal of Hoffman*, 43 Ed Dept Rep 160, Decision No. 14,953; *Appeal of Monahan*, 42 *id.* 206, Decision No. 14,824; *Appeal of J.W. and C.W.*, 41 *id.* 106, Decision No. 14,629). Joinder requires that an individual be clearly named as a respondent in the caption of the petition and served with a copy of the notice of petition and petition to inform the individual that he or she should respond to the petition and enter a defense

(*Appeal of Hoffman, supra*; *Appeal of Monahan, supra*). If I were to decide the appeal in petitioner's favor, the rights of the child's father would be adversely affected, in that he could be barred from access to his daughter's activities and programs at her school. Accordingly, he is a necessary party to this appeal and should have been named and served with a copy of the notice and petition. Since petitioner failed to join the father as a party, the appeal must be dismissed.

Even if this appeal were not dismissed on joinder grounds, it would be dismissed on the merits. As respondent accurately notes, the divorce decree does not expressly limit the father's participation in school activities and programs during the school day. Absent such an express limitation, I cannot conclude that respondent's action was arbitrary or capricious (See *Appeal of Sans, supra*).

THE APPEAL IS DISMISSED.

Decision No. 15,158

Application of JULIANNE C. GABRYEL for the removal of James T. Crean as a member of the Board of Education of the Orchard Park Central School District.

(January 6, 2005)

APPEARANCES OF COUNSEL

Bouvier, O'Connor, LLP, attorneys for petitioner, *Charles D.J. Case*, Esq., of counsel

Harter Secrest & Emery LLP, attorneys for respondent, *Anthony D. Mancinelli, Esq*., of counsel

DECISION OF THE COMMISSIONER

MILLS, Commissioner.—Petitioner seeks the removal of James T. Crean ("respondent") from the Board of Education of the Orchard Park Central School District ("district"). The application must be denied.

Respondent served as president of the seven-member board of education of the Orchard Park district during the 2003-2004 school year. Petitioner alleges that respondent prohibited the district's superintendent from presenting the annual budget to the board of education at a public session, on February 10, 2004, in violation of Education Law §1711 and district policy. Petitioner also asserts that respondent improperly engaged in partisan political activity by advocating against the proposed budget before the budget vote, distributed misleading materials and made inappropriate public statements.

Petitioner further contends that respondent harassed another board member by forcing her to read aloud a letter she had written criticizing respondent at the board's May 11, 2004, public meeting and publicly threatened to sue the board member for libel and slander. Petitioner generally alleges that respondent treats board members, administrators, staff, students and community members disrespectfully and that he smoked a cigar on district property in violation of school rules. Petitioner's request for interim relief to prevent respondent from participating in the district's budget process was denied on June 18, 2004.

Respondent denies petitioner's allegations and argues that the appeal should be dismissed as untimely and for failure to join other board members as necessary parties. Respondent argues that the rest of the board should be joined because a majority voted at the February 10 meeting against allowing the superintendent to make an oral budget presentation at that meeting. Respondent also argues that petitioner's memorandum of law was untimely and contains new assertions and evidence that should have been included with the petition.

Respondent denies that the superintendent did not have an opportunity to present the budget proposal and contends that the superintendent made oral presentations at subsequent public meetings. Respondent asserts that he campaigned against the budget in his individual capacity as a private citizen and did not improperly use district resources to espouse his views. Respondent denies harassing others or engaging in any conduct warranting his removal from the board. Respondent further denies that he publicly threatened legal action against the board member although he did tell her in private that he was exploring his legal options.

Although respondent argues that petitioner's memorandum of law was untimely, I find it was timely submitted within a period of extension granted by my Office of Counsel. Petitioner, however, included new assertions and exhibits with her memorandum of law. A memorandum of law may not be used to belatedly add new materials and assertions that are not part of the pleadings (*Application of Lilly*, 43 Ed Dept Rep 459, Decision No. 15,050; *Appeal of T.M.*, 41 *id.* 443, Decision No. 14,740; *Appeal of D.C.*, 41 *id.* 190, Decision No. 14,661). I have therefore not considered the new exhibits or assertions.

Petitioner also submitted newspaper articles to support her position. It is well settled that newspaper articles do not constitute evidence of the truth of the statements contained therein (*Application of Lilly*, *supra*; *Appeal of Decastro*, 41 Ed Dept Rep 415, Decision No. 14,730; *Application of Wilson*, 41 *id.* 196, Decision No. 14,663). In addition, petitioner sent numerous newspapers and letters raising additional claims to my Office of Counsel without leave and, with few exceptions, without service on respondent as required by §276.5 of the Commissioner's regulations. Therefore, I have not considered any of these submissions.

The appeal, as it relates to respondent's conduct at the February 10, 2004, meeting, is dismissed as untimely. An appeal to the

Commissioner must be instituted within 30 days from the making of the decision or the performance of the act complained of, unless any delay is excused by the Commissioner for good cause shown (8 NYCRR §275.16). The 30-day limitation period also applies to removal applications made pursuant to Education Law §306 (8 NYCRR §277.1; *Application of Lilly, supra*; *Application of Bean*, 42 Ed Dept Rep 171, Decision No. 14,810; *Application of Downing*, 40 *id.* 396, Decision No. 14,509).

Petitioner did not commence this appeal until June 5, 2004, well beyond the 30-day period, and offers no excuse for her delay. Moreover, the case relied upon by petitioner (*Appeal of Maliha*, 41 Ed Dept Rep 367, Decision No. 14,716) is inapplicable since petitioner is not contesting the validity of the election or seeking to overturn the election results. Thus, petitioner's claims regarding those acts that occurred more than 30 days before the appeal was commenced are untimely and the appeal is dismissed as to them (*Appeal of Hubbard*, 43 Ed Dept Rep 3, Decision No. 14,898; *Appeals of Tesser and Kavitsky*, 42 *id.* 341, Decision No. 14,876; *Appeal of Carroll, et al.*, 42 *id.* 326, Decision No. 14,871).

The remainder of the appeal must be dismissed on the merits. A member of the board of education may be removed from office pursuant to Education Law §306 when it is proven to the satisfaction of the Commissioner that the board member has engaged in a willful violation or neglect of duty under the Education Law or has willfully disobeyed a decision, order, rule or regulation of the Board of Regents or the Commissioner of Education (*See also*, *Application of Kavitsky*, 41 Ed Dept Rep 231, Decision No. 14,672; *Application of Lilker*, 40 *id.* 704, Decision No. 14,588; *Application of Kozak and Hetey*, 40 *id.* 195, Decision No. 14,459). To be considered willful, respondent's actions must have been intentional and with a wrongful purpose. In an appeal or removal application to the Commissioner of Education, the petitioner has the burden of demonstrating a clear legal right to the relief requested and the burden of establishing the facts upon which she seeks relief (8 NYCRR §275.10; *Application of Lilly, supra*; *Appeal of a Student Suspected of Having a Disability*, 41 Ed Dept Rep

329, Decision No. 14,702; *Appeal of L.S.*, 41 *id.* 270, Decision No. 14,683).[1]

Petitioner argues that respondent improperly advocated against the proposed budget and submits budget election fliers which she claims respondent was responsible for distributing. While it is improper for a board of education, as a corporate body, to be involved in partisan activity, individual board members are entitled to express their personal views about issues concerning the district and engage in partisan activity, provided school district funds or resources are not used (*Appeal of Goldin*, 40 Ed Dept Rep 628, Decision No. 14,572; *Appeal of Allen*, 39 *id.* 528, Decision No. 14,300). Respondent admits that he campaigned against the proposed budget in his individual capacity and denies responsibility for the campaign fliers. Petitioner does not contend that respondent used district resources to publicly advocate against the proposed budget, nor does she offer any evidence connecting respondent to the fliers or to the private group(s) apparently responsible for distributing them.

Petitioner also submitted an affidavit from the board member who was allegedly harassed and two emails allegedly sent to that board member by respondent. The board member admits that she requested the opportunity to read her critical letter to the board in public session, but that respondent insisted that she finish reading the letter and claims he later threatened her with legal action. The board member, along with petitioner, objects to respondent's conduct, including his use of offensive language, his written reference to himself as "King James" and his written statement that he was going to use a "chainsaw" to cut the budget proposal. Petitioner has also submitted two petitions, from students and residents, in support of removing respondent from the board and requesting that he not speak at the district's high school graduation ceremonies in June 2004. Petitioner makes a number of conclusory allegations regarding respondent's behavior, including smoking on school property without any evidence in the record to support her allegations.

---

[1] A school board may also in the first instance remove any of its own members for official misconduct. Education Law §§1709(18) & 2503(1); *Appeal of Taber*, 42 Ed Dept Rep 251.

Removal may be warranted where a board member's improper conduct occurs during a board meeting and disrupts the meeting or interferes with the board's ability to function (*Application of Lilly*, *supra*; *Application of Kozak*, 34 Ed Dept Rep 501, Decision No. 13,396). Petitioner, however, has not established that respondent's conduct rises to this level. Although the record indicates that respondent used profanities in one email sent to another board member, and may have used profanities in executive sessions of the board, there is no evidence that those profanities were aimed at other board members, or that they were said to degrade or threaten other board members. Nor is there any evidence that this behavior interfered with the board's ability to function. Thus, on the record before me, I cannot conclude that those actions rise to a willful violation or neglect of duty under the law.

While respondent's conduct on this limited record may not warrant removal, I urge respondent to ensure that his personal opinions regarding budgetary or other election matters are clearly identified as such. I also strongly urge respondent to be mindful of his conduct and language as a school district official. A board member has a duty to proceed with constructive discussions aimed at achieving the best possible governance of the school district (*Application of Lilly*, *supra*; *Application of Kozak*, *supra*), and respondent's apparent approach to his responsibilities is not likely to result in creating the positive and respectful relationships necessary to an effective governing board.

In light of this determination, I need not address the parties' remaining contentions.

THE APPLICATION IS DENIED.

Decision No. 15,159

Appeal of ELIZABETH and DAVID PASSER, on behalf of their children RACHEL and SAMUEL, from action of the Board of Education of the Mexico Central School District regarding the playing of the song "Where Were You When the World Stopped Turning?"

(January 6, 2005)

APPEARANCES OF COUNSEL

Ferrara, Fiorenza, Larrison, Barrett & Reitz, P.C., attorneys for respondent, *Donald E. Budmen, Esq.,* of counsel

DECISION OF THE COMMISSIONER

MILLS, Commissioner.—Petitioners appeal the action of the Board of Education of the Mexico Central School District ("respondent") permitting school personnel of the Mexico Middle School to play the song "Where Were You When the World Stopped Turning?" over the school's public address system. The appeal must be dismissed.

Petitioners' son Samuel and daughter Rachel attended the sixth and eighth grades at the Mexico Middle School during the 2002-2003 school year. On September 11, 2002, the school held a series of commemorative events including moments of silence coinciding with the times that the planes hit the World Trade Center and the times the towers collapsed. After each moment of silence, a song was played over the school's public address system including "Where Were You When the World Stopped Turning?", "Proud to Be an American" and the National Anthem. Petitioners assert that the school's administration requested that students sing along. Respondent's staff memo, however, indicates that students would receive a copy of the lyrics and "may follow along." At noon, the Pledge of Allegiance was recited and students presented representatives of the local fire departments with a banner thanking them for their work.

By letter dated September 16, 2002, petitioners complained to respondent that the school's use of the song "Where Were You When the World Stopped Turning?" violated the Establishment Clause of the United States Constitution. By letter dated September 24, 2002, respondent advised petitioners that their complaint would be discussed at the next board meeting. Respondent, however, did not discuss the complaint until its October 22, 2002, meeting. Respondent had not yet provided a response to the complaint when petitioners commenced this appeal on November 20, 2002. Petitioners' request for interim relief was denied.

Petitioners assert that respondent's use of the song "Where Were You When the World Stopped Turning?" advances Christianity and fosters an excessive government entanglement with religion in violation of the Establishment Clause of the United States Constitution. Petitioners further contend that various prior actions by respondent occurring from December 1997 through October 2001 also violated their constitutional rights.

Petitioners ask for the termination of the middle school principal, the removal of several board members, a public apology, a district multicultural sensitivity training program, and a requirement that 25 percent of the district faculty and administration be minorities. Petitioners also seek a prohibition against school events reciting prayerful verses or other entreaties to God and an assurance that there will be no further violation of the United States Constitution or the New York State Education Law. Petitioners further request that the New York State Education Department approve any future district plans to commemorate American tragedies, such as September 11, 2001, and that all holiday displays be culturally equal.

Respondent asserts that the appeal should be dismissed because the petition is unverified and untimely. It also contends that petitioners failed to join necessary parties and meet the requisite standard for the removal of board members. Respondent further contends that an appeal to the Commissioner is an inappropriate forum for novel questions of constitutional law. Finally, respondent asserts that the challenged song is not a "prayerful verse."

Respondent asserts that the petition is not verified as required by §275.5 of the Commissioner's regulations. However, the petition submitted to my Office of Counsel contained the requisite verification. Although petitioner should have included a copy of the verification with the papers served on respondent, I will excuse this omission because petitioners are not represented by counsel and my Office of Counsel received a verified petition (*Appeal of McSween*, 42 Ed Dept Rep 59, Decision No. 14,775; *Appeals of Campbell and Coleman, et al.*, 41 *id.* 207, Decision No. 14,665).

An appeal to the Commissioner must be commenced within 30 days from the making of the decision or the performance of the act complained of, unless any delay is excused by the Commissioner for good cause shown (8 NYCRR §275.16; *Appeal of Recore*, 42 Ed Dept Rep 283, Decision No. 14,856; *Appeal of Phillips*, 40 *id.* 241, Decision No. 14,471). The petition includes allegations regarding acts occurring from December 1997 through October 2001. Since petitioners offer no excuse or reason for their delay in challenging those acts, the allegations are dismissed as untimely.

Petitioners' appeal, however, concerning the September 11, 2002, events is timely. Petitioners promptly sought respondent's review of their complaints, but respondent did not reply. In fact, respondent asserts that the superintendent was still drafting a response to petitioners' complaint when the petition was served.

A party whose rights would be adversely affected by a determination of an appeal in favor of a petitioner is a necessary party and must be joined as such (*Appeal of Lawson*, 42 Ed Dept Rep 210, Decision No. 14,826; *Appeal of Olsen*, 42 *id.* 20, Decision No. 14,761; *Appeal of Reed, et al.*, 33 *id.* 216, Decision No. 13,029). Petitioners seek to remove the middle school principal and several board members. Clearly, a determination in petitioners' favor would adversely affect these individuals. Accordingly, petitioners' failure to join them as parties requires dismissal of petitioners' claims for removal.

Although an appeal to the Commissioner is not the proper forum for litigating novel issues of constitutional law, this case does not present a novel issue. Applying established principles, I previously determined that a school assembly held on September 14, 2001, in which students were encouraged to sing "God Bless America," did not violate the United States Constitution (*Appeal of Cayot*, 42 Ed Dept Rep 97, Decision No. 14,786; judgment granted dismissing petition to review, Sup. Ct., Albany Co., Lamont J., February 19, 2004, n.o.r.).

The Establishment Clause of the First Amendment which provides that "Congress shall make no law respecting an establishment of religion" applies to the states and school districts through the Fourteenth Amendment. At a minimum, the Establishment Clause guarantees that government may not coerce anyone to support or participate in a religious exercise (see, *Lee v. Weisman*, 505 U.S. 577). However, the song "Where Were You When the World Stopped Turning?" is neither an invocation nor a benediction, and petitioners have not established here that the song's inclusion in a commemorative event constitutes a religious exercise.

In *Lemon v. Kurtzman*, 403 U.S. 602, the United States Supreme Court set out a three-pronged test to determine whether a governmental practice is consistent with the Establishment Clause: (1) does it have a secular purpose; (2) does it have a principal or primary effect that neither advances nor inhibits religion; and (3) does it foster an excessive government entanglement with religion.

With regard to the first prong, the record in this case indicates that the Governor requested that all schools in New York State observe moments of silence on the anniversary of the tragic events of September 11, 2001. Respondent's middle school administration decided that playing songs on the public address system following the moments of silence would further this secular purpose by aiding students' reflection. On the record before me, petitioners have not demonstrated that respondent's actual purpose was to endorse or disapprove of religion or to advance religious views (see, *Edwards v. Aguillard*, 482 U.S. 578, 585).

In regard to the second prong of the test, petitioners have not established objectively that a reasonable observer would find that playing of the song "Where Were You When the World Stopped Turning?" had the effect of endorsing religion (see, *County of Allegheny v. ACLU*, 492 U.S. 573). As the title suggests, the song questions the individual experience of its audience on September 11, 2001. While the songwriter, Alan Jackson, may seem to profess his own religious belief, the lyrics do not suggest that such belief was or should be a universal response:

> *Where Were You When the World Stopped Turning?*
>
> Where were you when the world stop turning that September day
> Were you in the yard with your wife and children
> Or working on some stage in L.A.
> Did you stand there in shock at the sight of that black smoke
> Rising against that blue sky
> Did you shout out in anger, in fear for your neighbor
> Or did you just sit down and cry
>
> Did you weep for the children who lost their dear loved ones
> And pray for the ones who don't know
> Did you rejoice for the people who walked from the rubble
> And sob for the ones left below
> Did you burst out in pride for the red, white and blue
> And the heroes who died just doin' what they do
> Did you look up to heaven for some kind of answer
> And look at yourself and what really matters?
>
> I'm just a singer of simple songs
> I'm not a real political man. I watch CNN but I'm not sure I could
> Tell you the difference in Iraq and Iran
> But I know Jesus and I talk to God
> And I remember this from when I was young
> Faith, hope and love are some good things He gave us
> And the greatest is love

Where were you when the world stopped turning on that September day
Teaching a class full of innocent children
Or driving down some cold interstate
Did you feel guilty 'cause you're a survivor
In a crowded room did you feel alone
Did you call up your mother and tell her you loved her
Did you dust off that Bible at home

Did you open your eyes, hope it never happened
And you close your eyes and not go to sleep
Did you notice the sunset the first time in ages
Or speak to some stranger on the street
Did you lay down at night and think of tomorrow
Go out and buy you a gun
Did you turn off that violent old movie you're watchin'
And turn on "I Love Lucy" reruns

Did you go to a church and hold hands with some strangers
Stand in line and give your own blood
Did you just stay home and cling tight to your family
Thank God you had somebody to love

©2001 EMI Music/Tri-Angels Music (ASCAP)[2]

These lyrics present a diverse list of possible responses to the events of that day rather than supporting any particular one. For example, the song's reference to buying a gun does not endorse gun-buying, merely because such a reference appears. Instead, the songwriter invites the listener to recall his or her individual response. I find that an objective observer would view this song as an expression of the wide range of emotions experienced on September 11, 2001, rather than having a "principal or primary" effect of advancing religion.

Concerning the third prong of the test, petitioners make only the conclusory allegation that the song fosters an entanglement with religion. However, there is no evidence that the middle school

---

[2] The lyrics are printed here as they appeared on the songsheet distributed to students and vary in minor and insignificant ways from the copyrighted version.

administration had any contact with church authorities concerning the commemorative event, and there is no assertion of any other type of entanglement.

In an appeal to the Commissioner of Education, petitioner has the burden of demonstrating a clear right to the relief requested (8 NYCRR §275.10) and the burden of establishing the facts upon which he seeks relief (*Application of Bean*, 42 Ed Dept Rep 171, Decision No. 14,810; *Application of Lilker*, 40 *id.* 704, Decision No. 14,588). Although the challenged song may reasonably be interpreted to reference the lyricist's own religious belief, the song was used for a secular purpose and is not a prayer or a religious exercise. On the record before me, I find that petitioners have failed to meet their burden of proof.

In light of this disposition, I need not reach the parties' remaining contentions.

THE APPEAL IS DISMISSED.

Decision No. 15,160

Appeal of ELIZABETH PASSER from action of the Board of Education of the Mexico Central School District regarding a budget vote.

(January 6, 2005)

APPEARANCES OF COUNSEL

Ferrara, Fiorenza, Larrison, Barrett & Reitz, P.C., attorneys for respondent, *Donald E. Budmen, Esq.*, of counsel

DECISION OF THE COMMISSIONER

MILLS, Commissioner.—Petitioner challenges actions of the Board of Education of the Mexico Central School District ("respondent") relating to an annual budget vote. The appeal must be dismissed.

Petitioner requested that respondent produce budget documents prior to the May 18, 2004, vote on the 2004-2005 school budget. Petitioner commenced this appeal on May 17, 2004, requesting that the vote be stayed and that the budget documents be found improper. Petitioner's request for interim relief was denied on May 28, 2004.

The appeal must now be dismissed as moot. The Commissioner of Education will only consider matters in actual controversy and will not render a decision on a state of facts which no longer exist or which subsequent events have laid to rest (*Appeal of Colety, et al.*, 42 Ed Dept Rep 162, Decision No. 14,806; *Appeal of Bazemore*, 41 *id.* 449, Decision No. 14,742). The May 18, 2004, budget vote was held, and the district voters rejected the proposed budget. Respondent revised the budget, prepared new budget documents for distribution, and resubmitted the budget for a vote, which took place on June 22, 2004. Therefore, the sole relief requested by petitioner cannot be granted and the appeal is moot.

THE APPEAL IS DISMISSED.

Decision No. 15,161

Appeal of the BOARD OF EDUCATION OF THE WHITEHALL CENTRAL SCHOOL DISTRICT from actions taken at a special meeting of the district.

(January 25, 2005)

APPEARANCES OF COUNSEL

Judge & Duffy, attorneys for petitioner, *Monica A. Duffy, Esq.*, of counsel

DECISION OF THE COMMISSIONER

MILLS, Commissioner.—Petitioner, the Board of Education of the Whitehall Central School District, seeks an order pursuant to Education Law §2037 annulling the results of a special meeting conducted by petitioner. The appeal is sustained.

On November 17, 2004, petitioner conducted a special meeting to obtain voter approval to renovate the kitchen in the Junior-Senior High School building. The vote was held from 12:00 p.m. until 8:00 p.m. and sixty four voters appeared and cast their ballots on a voting machine. After the polls were closed and the voting machine was secured and opened, the district clerk and the election inspectors discovered that the voting machine had malfunctioned in that only one of the sixty four votes cast had registered on the machine. Consequently, the district clerk was unable to certify the results of the election.

Petitioner requests an order setting aside the results of the November 17, 2004, special meeting and authorizing petitioner to call a special district meeting to revote the proposition presented to the voters on November 17, 2004.

The Commissioner of Education will set aside the results of a school district election on the basis of alleged irregularities only when it is probable from the evidence that the irregularities affected the outcome of the election (*Boyes, et al. v. Allen, et al.*, 32 AD2d 990, aff'd 26 NY2d 709; *Appeal of Holliday*, 42 Ed Dept Rep 242, Decision No. 14,840; *Appeal of Huber, et al.*, 41 *id.* 240, Decision No. 14,676), were so pervasive that they vitiated the electoral process (*Appeal of Meyer, et al.*, 40 Ed Dept Rep 34, Decision No. 14,413; *Appeal of Roberts*, 33 *id.* 601, Decision No. 13,162), or demonstrate a clear and convincing picture of informality to the point of laxity in adherence to the Education Law (*Matter of Levine*, 24 Ed Dept Rep 172, Decision No. 11,356, aff'd sub nom *Capobianco v. Ambach and Bd. of Educ., Glen Cove City School Dist*, 112 AD2d 640).

The record before me clearly shows that the voting machine used in the November 17, 2004, vote had malfunctioned by registering only one of the 64 votes cast. Therefore, I find that the voting machine malfunction vitiated the electoral process and that a new vote is necessary (*Appeal of Bd. of Educ. of the Fonda-Fultonville Central School Dist.*, 33 Ed Dept Rep 682, Decision No. 13,195).

THE APPEAL IS SUSTAINED.

IT IS ORDERED that the results of the special meeting conducted by petitioner on November 17, 2004, are hereby annulled; and

IT IS FURTHER ORDERED that petitioner is hereby authorized to call a special meeting of the district for the purpose of revoting on the proposition presented to the voters on November 17, 2004.

Decision No. 15,162

Appeal of ANDRÉ and JENNIFER CIOTTI, on behalf of their daughters STEPHANIE and CHELSEA, from action of the Board of Education of the Whitesboro Central School District regarding a required summer reading program.

(January 25, 2005)

APPEARANCES OF COUNSEL

Ferrara, Fiorenza, Larrison, Barrett & Reitz, P.C., attorneys for respondent, *David W. Larrison, Esq.*, of counsel

DECISION OF THE COMMISSIONER

MILLS, Commissioner.—Petitioners appeal the implementation by the Board of Education of the Whitesboro Central School District ("respondent") of a required summer reading program. The appeal must be sustained in part.

Petitioners' daughters, Jennifer and Chelsea, attend respondent's schools and were required to participate in respondent's 2004 summer reading program. In a letter dated June 1, 2004, but sent some time later in June, respondent's English Department chairperson ("chairperson") advised parents that all students in grades six through twelve would be required to read one book over the summer, and that students should purchase the books so they could write in them. The chairperson also advised parents that a limited number of books would be available to borrow from the district for students with financial hardship. At the end of the school year, students brought home a packet that informed students of the title of the book that they would have to read and provided related assignments.

In June 2004, petitioners advised the chairperson and respondent's superintendent of their objections to the program. On July 6, 2004, petitioner André Ciotti addressed respondent board, stated his objections and requested that the summer reading program be rescinded. On July 13, 2004, the superintendent responded to petitioner on behalf of respondent, indicating that the summer reading program would continue. This appeal ensued. Petitioners' request for interim relief was denied on August 20, 2004.

Respondent modified its summer reading program after this proceeding commenced. In a letter to parents dated August 1, 2004, the chairperson advised parents that teacher support would be available to students during the summer. Respondent established an e-mail address and telephone numbers to be used by students who wished to address questions to teachers, and teachers were made available on four days in August to work with students at school facilities. In addition, students were advised that they would be given additional time with teacher support to work on their assignments without penalty at the beginning of the new school year, if needed. The letter also stated that the "entire project" would count as one test grade for the quarter.

Petitioners claim that respondent's summer reading program is impermissible because it requires parents to purchase books, does not provide teacher support to students during the summer when assignments must be completed, and intrudes on the authority of parents to determine how their children spend the summer. Petitioners request the discontinuation of the summer reading program.

Respondent claims that petitioners have not established grounds in fact or in law upon which to conclude that the summer reading program is impermissible. Respondent also claims that the petition should be dismissed as untimely.

An appeal to the Commissioner must be commenced within 30 days from the making of the decision or the performance of the act complained of, unless the Commissioner excuses any delay for good cause shown (8 NYCRR §275.16). In a letter dated July 13, 2004, to petitioners, the superintendent responded on behalf of respondent to petitioners' request to the board that the summer reading program be rescinded, indicating that the program would continue. The petition was served on July 26, 2004, within 30 days of this determination. Therefore, the petition is timely.

A board of education has broad authority to prescribe the course of study in the schools of the district (Education Law §§1709(3), 1804(1); *Appeal of Lahm*, 41 Ed Dept Rep 193, Decision No. 14,662; *Appeal of Lease*, 39 *id.* 215, Decision No. 14,219; *Appeal of Smith*, 34 *id.* 346, Decision No. 13,335). The Supreme Court has confirmed that school authorities enjoy broad discretion in regulating matters of curriculum (*Bd. of Educ., Island Trees U.F.S.D. No. 26 v. Pico*, 457 US 853, 869). I will not substitute my judgment for that of a board of education on curriculum issues absent evidence that the board has acted in an arbitrary, capricious or unreasonable manner (*Appeal of Lahm, supra*; *Appeal of Lease, supra*; *Appeal of Smith, supra*).

I have in the past reviewed summer reading programs and found them to be permissible when properly structured and administered (*see, Appeal of Lahm, supra*). However, a summer reading program is unreasonable and impermissible when it requires students to perform mandatory written assignments for a grade without the benefit of a teacher's direction and supervision and does not ensure that books that are being used as part of a mandatory assignment are reasonably available to all students (*Appeal of Lease, supra*).

I find that respondent's summer reading program, as modified, provided students with adequate teacher direction and supervision, while students were performing mandatory written assignments for a grade. During the summer, students were permitted to address questions to teachers through telephone calls and e-mails, and four in-person sessions were scheduled for students who needed assistance. In addition, students were permitted to complete the written assignments without penalty upon returning to school in September, while under the direction and supervision of the teacher.

However, I find that respondent did not ensure that books in the summer reading program were reasonably available in all grades. The required texts in a summer reading program must be reasonably available to students (*Appeal of Lease*, *supra*). To accomplish this, a district may, for example, provide the books to the students or establish a large enough list of titles to reasonably ensure that books on the list are available at a public library for all students (*Appeal of Lahm*, *supra*). A district may not require the purchase of books for a summer reading program (*see*, *Appeal of Lease*, *supra*).

In this case, the district's June 1, 2004, letter to parents said "Students should purchase the books so they can write in them." It also stated that only a limited number of books were available to students in financial need. Grades seven through ten students were required to read one book, specified for each grade by the district. Grade twelve students were required to choose one book from among ten titles specified by the district. Petitioners state that there are approximately three hundred students in each grade, a fact respondent does not dispute. Given these numbers, it is unlikely that a sufficient number of books were available at local libraries or available for loan at the district for grades seven through ten and grade twelve. Therefore, I find the summer reading program for grades seven, eight, nine, ten, and twelve to be unreasonable due to respondent's failure to ensure the availability of an adequate number of books to all students.

The summer reading program for grades six and eleven is a different matter. Respondent's directions for grade six students indicate that respondent provided the assigned book to each student. It is not clear from the record whether respondent provided the assigned book to grade eleven students. In an appeal to the Commissioner, petitioners have the burden of demonstrating a clear legal right to the relief requested and the burden of establishing the facts upon which they seek relief (*Appeal of Pope*, 40 Ed Dept Rep 473, Decision No. 14,530; *Appeal of Logan*, 38 *id.* 694, Decision No. 14,120; *Appeal of Catherine B.*, 37 *id.* 34, Decision No. 13,797). Petitioners have failed to establish that respondent did not provide the required reading material to grade six and eleven students. Therefore, I cannot conclude that respondent failed to ensure an adequate supply of books for grades six and eleven.

Although I find respondent's summer reading program to be unreasonable in part, I find no basis to invalidate student grades earned on the summer reading assignments. At this point in the school year, students have read the books, completed the assignments and received grades. It would not serve any educational purpose to invalidate the grades that have already been earned, especially where petitioners have failed to show that any student was unable to complete the assignment because he or she lacked a book.

However, respondent's summer reading program is ongoing. Therefore, respondent must modify its program to ensure that in the future required texts are reasonably available to students.

Notwithstanding the above, a summer reading program, properly implemented helps sharpen the reading, language and writing skills that often deteriorate over the long summer vacation. The State Education Department recommends that students read at least 25 books each year. Requiring reading over the summer is a positive step toward this goal.

THE APPEAL IS SUSTAINED TO THE EXTENT INDICATED.

IT IS ORDERED that respondent modify its summer reading program consistent with this decision.

Decision No. 15,163

Appeal of VINCENT VUOTO from action of the Eastern Suffolk Board of Cooperative Educational Services regarding tenure.

(January 31, 2005)

APPEARANCES OF COUNSEL

Minerva and D'Agostino, P.C., attorneys for petitioner, *Albert A. D'Agostino, Esq.*, of counsel

Grotta, Glassman & Hoffman, P.A., attorneys for respondent, *David M. Wirtz, Esq.*, of counsel

DECISION OF THE COMMISSIONER

MILLS, Commissioner.—Petitioner challenges actions of the Eastern Suffolk Board of Cooperative Educational Services ("respondent") concerning his tenure area designation. The appeal must be dismissed.

Petitioner is employed by respondent as lead Teacher Coordinator of Diversified Cooperative Work Experience in the Occupational Education Program. Petitioner initially received a probationary appointment in October 1990 and was granted tenure, effective October 8, 1992, as a "Teacher of Diversified Cooperative Work Study in the Occupational Education Program" by the Board of Cooperative Educational Services First Supervisory District, Suffolk County ("BOCES 1"). During the 1993-1994 school year, BOCES 1 merged with the BOCES Second Supervisory District to form respondent, which has continuously employed petitioner since then.

In the summer of 2003, respondent issued seniority lists designating district teachers by their respective tenure areas and listed petitioner under the tenure area of Agriculture/Plant Science/Horticulture. By letter dated January 21, 2004, petitioner's counsel asserted that this designation was incorrect and requested that respondent place petitioner instead on the Occupational Business Education and Distributive Occupation Subjects tenure list. In a responsive letter dated February 12, 2004, respondent's counsel advised that petitioner's tenure area was correctly designated. This appeal ensued.

Petitioner claims that respondent unlawfully changed his tenure area without his consent and requests that I order respondent to designate his tenure area as Occupational Business Education and Distributive Occupational Subjects.

Respondent raises a number of procedural objections, including that the appeal is untimely and petitioner has failed to join necessary parties. Respondent also maintains that it properly designated petitioner's tenure area.

The appeal must be dismissed on procedural grounds. The record reflects that petitioner has served continuously as a Teacher Coordinator of Diversified Cooperative Work Experience in the Occupational Education Program since October 1990. Although petitioner claims that respondent changed his tenure area without his consent, petitioner does not allege that respondent has altered his duties in any way, or even threatened to do so (*see, e.g.*, *Matter of Bell v. Bd. of Educ. Vestal CSD*, 61 NY2d 149; *Appeal of Daly*, 23 Ed Dept Rep 226, Decision No. 11,196). Nor does he allege that his salary has been reduced, that he has been excessed from his position, or that he has otherwise suffered economic harm from respondent's actions. Rather, petitioner simply challenges respondent's designation of his tenure area as Agriculture/Plant Science/Horticulture rather than Occupational Business Education and Distributive Occupational Subjects.

Seniority rights, however, do not exist in the abstract. There must be an impact upon the individual to cause him to be aggrieved, and a party may not maintain an appeal solely to obtain a declaration of his tenure rights or relative seniority (*Matter of Greco v. Bd. of Educ. Patchogue-Medford UFSD, et al.*, 98 AD2d 721; *Appeal of Eaton*, 24 Ed Dept Rep 88, Decision No. 11,326; *Appeal of Murphy*, 21 *id.* 419, Decision No. 10,738). In essence, petitioner seeks an advisory opinion concerning his seniority status, relief that is unavailable in an Education Law §310 appeal (*Appeal of Murphy*, *supra*). Therefore, the appeal must be dismissed. Such dismissal, however, is without prejudice to any future application for similar relief should petitioner hereafter become actually aggrieved within the purview of Education Law §310.

In light of this disposition, I need not address the parties' remaining contentions.

THE APPEAL IS DISMISSED.

Decision No. 15,164

Appeal of ELIZABETH and DAVID PASSER, on behalf of their children RACHEL, SAMUEL, EMILY and DAYNA, from action of the Board of Education of the Mexico Central School District regarding a seasonal display.

(January 31, 2005)

APPEARANCES OF COUNSEL

Ferrara, Fiorenza, Larrison, Barrett & Reitz, P.C., attorneys for respondent, *Donald E. Budmen, Esq.*, of counsel

DECISION OF THE COMMISSIONER

MILLS, Commissioner.—Petitioners appeal the action of the Board of Education of the Mexico Central School District ("respondent") permitting the seasonal display of single candles in the windows of its high school. The appeal must be dismissed.

The Dollars for Scholars Foundation is a national network of community volunteers that raises money to award scholarships for postsecondary education. The local chapter of Dollars for Scholars in respondent's district awards scholarships to selected seniors of respondent's high school who plan to enroll in a college, university, vocational or business school. Since the Fall of 2000, the local chapter has raised funds by displaying single electric candles in the windows of respondent's high school in exchange for monetary donations to the scholarship fund from donors who sponsor a candle in memory of a family member, student, teacher or other loved one.

In 2001, petitioners donated to the fund for a "memory light" in honor of a Jewish immigrant from Russia. However, on September 30, 2003, petitioners complained to respondent that the display was exclusionary promoting Christianity and its cultural customs. Respondent did not respond to petitioners' complaint and permitted the Dollars for Scholars Foundation to proceed with its seasonal candle lighting from October 30, 2003, until February 2, 2004. Petitioners commenced this appeal on November 19, 2003. Petitioners' request for interim relief was denied.

Petitioners assert that a single candle placed in a window is an advent candle. They contend that respondent violated the First and Fourteenth Amendments of the United States Constitution when it permitted the Dollars for Scholars Foundation to display an alleged Christian symbol in its high school. Respondent asserts *inter alia* that petitioners failed to join necessary parties and that a single candle in a window is neither an exclusively religious symbol nor was it used as a religious symbol in this context. Respondent also maintains that the appeal should be dismissed on procedural grounds.

At the outset, I note that respondent objects to petitioners' reply. The purpose of a reply is to respond to new material or affirmative defenses set forth in an answer (8 NYCRR §§275.3 and 275.14). A reply is not meant to buttress allegations in the petition or to belatedly add assertions that should have been in the petition (*Appeal of General*, 43 Ed Dept Rep 146, Decision No. 14,948; *Appeal of*

Crosier, 42 *id*. 232, Decision No. 14,835). Therefore, while I have reviewed petitioners' reply, I have not considered those portions containing new allegations or exhibits that are not responsive to new material or affirmative defenses set forth in the answer.

A party whose rights would be adversely affected by a determination of an appeal in favor of a petitioner is a necessary party and must be joined as such (*Appeal of Simmons*, 43 Ed Dept Rep 7, Decision No. 14,899; *Appeal of Recore*, 42 *id*. 283, Decision No. 14,856; *Appeal of Dickinson*, 39 *id*. 41, Decision No. 14,168). Petitioners seek to prevent the local chapter of the Dollars for Scholars Foundation from conducting a fundraising activity. Clearly, a determination in petitioners' favor would adversely affect this organization. Accordingly, petitioners' failure to join the foundation as a party requires dismissal of the appeal.

The petition must also be dismissed on the merits. In an appeal to the Commissioner of Education, petitioner has the burden of demonstrating a clear right to the relief requested (8 NYCRR §275.10) and the burden of establishing the facts upon which he seeks relief (*Application of Bean*, 42 Ed Dept Rep 171, Decision No. 14,810; *Application of Lilker*, 40 *id*. 704, Decision No. 14,588). Petitioners' request for relief requires that they first establish that single candles displayed in the windows of respondent's high school are religious symbols. However, they have offered no evidence beyond their conjecture that the display was religious. To the contrary, the evidence submitted by petitioners and respondent establishes that the display of single candles in the windows of respondent's high school was nonreligious. On the record before me, I find that petitioners have failed to meet their burden of proof.

In light of this disposition, I need not address the parties' remaining contentions.

THE APPEAL IS DISMISSED.

Decision No. 15,165

Appeal of FRANK BARNEY, PATRICIA GODREAU, ROBERT LAVOIE and SUZANNE MCLEAN from action of the Board of Education of the St. Regis Falls Central School District and Superintendent Patricia A. Dovi, regarding shared decision-making.

(January 31, 2005)

APPEARANCES OF COUNSEL

James R. Sandner, Esq., attorney for petitioners, *Mary Scalise Perillo, Esq.*, of counsel

Silver and Silver, attorneys for respondents, *Andrew W. Silver, Esq.,* of counsel

DECISION OF THE COMMISSIONER

MILLS, Commissioner.—Petitioners, employees of the St. Regis Falls Central School District ("district") and members of the district's Shared Decision-Making Committee ("SDM Committee"), contend that the district's superintendent and board of education ("respondents") violated the district's shared decision-making plan ("plan") and failed to comply with the Commissioner's regulations by not including the SDM Committee in staffing decisions. The appeal must be dismissed.

Section 100.11 of the Commissioner's regulations requires school districts to develop and adopt a district plan for the participation by teachers and parents with administrators and school board members in school-based planning and shared decision-making. Under the district's plan, adopted on December 13, 1993, the list of educational issues subject to shared decision-making may include, but is not limited to, staffing needs, along with a dozen other issues.

Petitioners contend that from the plan's adoption until July 2003, the SDM Committee participated by giving input in the hiring of school personnel. Respondents admit that, on occasion, the SDM Committee has participated in hiring to a limited extent. Petitioners assert that since July 2003, the SDM Committee has not been allowed to participate in the interview and selection process for numerous staff positions filled by respondents.

On December 1, 2003, petitioners Barney and Godreau met with the superintendent regarding the exclusion of the SDM Committee from staffing interviews. According to petitioners, the superintendent indicated that individual SDM Committee members would need training to participate in interviews.

Petitioners assert that respondents' exclusion of the SDM Committee from the interview and selection process for new staff is a continuing wrong, is arbitrary and capricious, violates the district's plan, and fails to comply with §100.11. Petitioners request that I order respondents to comply with the regulation and plan.

Respondents contend that the appeal is untimely and that petitioners have failed to demonstrate a clear legal right to the relief sought. Respondents assert that the board of education has sole authority for personnel decisions. They contend that neither §100.11 nor the plan requires participation by the SDM Committee in the hiring process. They also state that they are contemplating amending the plan to allow the SDM Committee members to participate, to some extent, in the hiring process and to require training of Committee members.

An appeal to the Commissioner of Education must be instituted within 30 days from the making of the decision or performance of the act complained of, unless any delay is excused by the Commissioner for good cause shown (8 NYCRR §275.16). Respondents argue that the appeal is untimely because it was not commenced until March 1, 2004, more than seven months after July 2003 when the SDM Committee alleges it was denied participation in the selection and hiring process. Respondents argue that even if the operative date is the December 1, 2003, meeting with the superintendent, the appeal is still untimely because it was not commenced until three months after that meeting.

Although petitioners did not commence the appeal within the 30-day period, respondents' alleged failure to permit the SDM Committee to participate in staffing needs in accordance with its shared decision-making plan, if unlawful, is a continuing wrong (*Appeal of Sadue-Sokolow*, 39 Ed Dept Rep 6, Decision No. 14,155; *Appeal of Fitch*, 34 *id.* 486, Decision No. 13,391). Therefore, I decline to dismiss the appeal as untimely.

Petitioners acknowledge that pursuant to Education Law §1709, hiring of employees is within the purview of the board of education and is not a delegable responsibility (*Appeal of Lawrence Teachers' Assoc.*, 39 Ed Dept Rep 119, Decision No. 14,190). Petitioners argue, however, that in the plan, "staffing needs" is an educational issue subject to shared decision-making and nothing in the Education Law precludes respondents from allowing the SDM Committee to provide input in the hiring process, including the interviewing and selection of candidates.

Although respondents previously permitted the SDM Committee to participate in the hiring process by giving input in the interview and selection process for personnel, nothing in the plan or §100.11 mandates that respondents continue to afford petitioners that level of participation. Notably, the plan is silent on how the SDM Committee should participate in addressing the undefined issue of "staffing needs." I find, therefore, that petitioners have failed to establish a violation of the plan for failing to include the SDM Committee in interviews and selection of candidates.

Respondents indicate that they are contemplating amending the plan to allow the participation of the SDM Committee in the hiring process and to mandate training. Given the vagueness of the current plan, and the disagreement of the parties, I encourage them to work together to resolve these issues in any subsequent plan, which may be amended in accordance with §100.11.

THE APPEAL IS DISMISSED.

Decision No. 15,166

Appeal of the TOWN OF NEW WINDSOR from action of Robert J. Hanna, District Superintendent of Schools for the Sole Supervisory District of Orange-Ulster Counties, and the Board of Education of the Enlarged City School District of the City of Newburgh regarding formation of a new school district.

(January 31, 2005)

APPEARANCES OF COUNSEL

Duggan, Crotty & Dunn, P.C., attorneys for petitioner, *Philip A. Crotty, Esq.,* of counsel

Donoghue, Thomas, Auslander & Drohan, attorneys for respondent *Robert J. Hanna, Daniel Petigrow, Esq.,* of counsel

Shaw & Perelson, LLP, attorneys for respondent Enlarged City School District of the City of Newburgh, *David S. Shaw* and *Margo L. May, Esqs.,* of counsel

DECISION OF THE COMMISSIONER

MILLS, Commissioner.—Petitioner appeals the decision by Dr. Robert J. Hanna, District Superintendent of Schools for the Sole Supervisory District of Orange-Ulster Counties ("Hanna"), to deny petitioner's request to form a new school district. The appeal must be dismissed.

Petitioner, the Town of New Windsor, is divided among four school districts. Part of the town lies within the Enlarged City School District of the City of Newburgh ("Newburgh ECSD"), and the remainder of the town lies in three other school districts, Valley Central School District, Cornwall Central School District, and Washingtonville Central School District.

On November 7, 2002, petitioner's attorney sent a letter to respondent Hanna, asking him to consider forming a new school district for the town. Respondent denied petitioner's request, and petitioner commenced an appeal pursuant to Education Law §310 (*Appeal of the Town of New Windsor*, 43 Ed Dept Rep 56, Decision No. 14,915), which was dismissed on August 1, 2003. The appeal was dismissed because petitioner failed to name and serve the Newburgh ECSD, a necessary party to the appeal. My decision did not suggest any further course of action to be followed by petitioner, nor did I issue any order requiring that the Newburgh ECSD be named as a respondent in any "next proceeding" or appeal, as petitioner now claims.

In December 2003, petitioner's attorney prepared another letter addressed to both respondent Hanna and the district clerk of the Newburgh ECSD. The letter, dated December 10, 2003, contained this heading: "Re: Petition to form New Windsor School District out of Newburgh Enlarged City School District NYS Education Law, Section 1504.1." This letter again requested that respondent Hanna form a new school district by removing from the Newburgh ECSD that portion of its territory which lies within the Town of New Windsor, and creating a new school district to be known as the New Windsor Central School District or Union Free School District. Petitioner states that this letter was "served" on January 7 and 8, 2004.

By letter dated January 13, 2004, respondent Hanna again denied petitioner's request. He cited petitioner's ineligibility to act as a municipality as defined in Education Law §2218, and his own lack of authority under Education Law §1504(1) to "de-consolidate" an enlarged city school district that had been formed by order of the Commissioner of Education pursuant to Education Law §1526. (Respondent Newburgh ECSD did not respond to this letter, which did not make any request of it.)

This appeal was commenced by service of a notice of petition and petition on respondent Hanna on May 4, 2004, and on the district clerk of respondent Newburgh ECSD on May 10, 2004. The contentions of petitioner and respondent Hanna are essentially the same as those recited in Decision No. 14,915, but respondent Hanna also contends that this appeal is untimely. Petitioner again requests an order directing respondent Hanna to form a new school district pursuant to Education Law §1504(1).

The appeal must be dismissed as untimely. This appeal challenges a determination by respondent Hanna made on January 13, 2004, but was not commenced until almost four months later, in clear of violation of §275.16 of the Commissioner's regulations. That provision allows me to excuse the failure to commence an appeal in a timely fashion, where good cause is shown, and the reasons for such failure are set forth in the petition. Here, no such reason is shown. Petitioner apparently believes, mistakenly, that by sending the December 10, 2003, letter to both respondents, it is somehow excused from the clear requirements of §275.16 that an appeal must be commenced within 30 days after the determination it challenges. To be timely, this appeal should have been commenced by service of the notice of petition and petition upon both respondent Hanna and necessary party respondent Newburgh ECSD no later than February 18, 2004, (allowing five days for mailing and receipt, assuming the January 13, 2004, decision was mailed to petitioner).

In view of this disposition, it is unnecessary to address any of petitioner's remaining contentions, which I find without merit.

THE APPEAL IS DISMISSED.

Decision No. 15,167

Appeal of ANONYMOUS from action of the Board of Education of the City School District of the City of Plattsburgh and Superintendent Michelle Kavanaugh regarding denial of access to school functions.

(January 31, 2005)

APPEARANCES OF COUNSEL

Lori A. Cantwell, Esq., attorney for petitioner

Harris, Beach, LLP, attorneys for respondents, *Dennis Curtin* and *Jacqueline M. Kelleher, Esqs.*, of counsel

DECISION OF THE COMMISSIONER

MILLS, Commissioner.—Petitioner challenges certain directives of the Board of Education of the City School District of the City of Plattsburgh ("board") and its superintendent, Michelle Kavanaugh ("superintendent"), which have limited her access to certain school functions. The appeal must be dismissed.

At the time the appeal was commenced, petitioner was a tenured physical education teacher in the school district, and formerly coached the district's various track programs. On August 28, 2003, petitioner was placed on paid administrative leave pending the filing of charges pursuant to Education Law §3020-a. Such charges were voted by the board on November 6, 2003, and additional charges were voted on January 8, 2004. At the time the appeal was commenced, petitioner was also the parent of a child attending school in the district.

On August 29, 2003, the superintendent informed petitioner by letter that she was to have no contact with district staff or students, and would be allowed on school property only "with respect to your role as a parent in addressing your child's educational issues." Petitioner was required to seek permission to enter school grounds in advance. By letter dated November 14, 2003, the superintendent further defined the restrictions placed on petitioner. The November 14 letter indicated that petitioner could not attend any "home" athletic events that took place off district property, nor could she attend any district function that took place off district property. On May 20, 2004, the superintendent sent petitioner another letter which directed her not to attend any home or away track meets, including qualifiers, sectionals, or state events, where district students were participating. On June 8, 2004, respondent's attorney sent a letter to petitioner denying her permission to attend an academic awards ceremony on June 9, 2004, in which petitioner's daughter was to receive an academic award. (It appears that the June 8 letter was the only instance when petitioner was denied permission, as a parent, to attend an event held on school property in which her daughter was a participant.)

Petitioner argues that respondents have no legal authority to restrict her access to track meets off school property, as stated in the May 20, 2004, letter, and argues that, with respect to events on school property (the June 8, 2004, letter), respondents must adhere to a consistent policy regarding her attendance as a parent, and avoid making decisions which are arbitrary and capricious.

Respondents argue that they have the authority to restrict the activities of petitioner, a paid district employee on suspension, with respect to events both on and off school property. They also argue that they have allowed petitioner to attend all but one event she has asked to attend as a parent, and that they have not been arbitrary or capricious. Respondents also assert a number of affirmative defenses, including mootness and untimeliness.

After commencement of the appeal, my Office of Counsel received a letter from respondents' attorney and an affidavit of the superintendent indicating that petitioner's daughter was no longer a student in the district, but had transferred to the Chazy Central School District prior to the commencement of the 2004-2005 school year. Petitioner has not contradicted that information.

Petitioner did not bring an appeal with respect to the restrictions on her activities imposed by the letters dated August 29, 2003, and November 14, 2003. Those letters directed her to have no contact with staff or students (with no territorial limits expressed), banned her from school grounds (except as a parent regarding her child's educational issues), and banned her from home athletic contests and all functions sponsored by the school district to be held off school property. To the extent that the petition purports to challenge respondents' actions of November 14, 2003, and earlier, it is dismissed as untimely (8 NYCRR §275.16). This appeal was not commenced until June 2004, some seven months after the November 14, 2003, letter, and petitioner offers no excuse in the petition for her delay with respect to that letter (8 NYCRR §275.16; *Appeal of Parker*, 34 Ed Dept Rep 379, Decision No. 13,351).

Petitioner's challenge to the June 8, 2004, denial of her request to attend a ceremony on June 9 in which petitioner's daughter was to receive an academic award is moot, both because the award ceremony has already taken place, and because petitioner's daughter is no longer a student in the district. It is well settled that the Commissioner of Education will only consider matters in actual controversy and will not render a decision on a state of facts which no longer exists or which subsequent events have laid to rest (*Appeal of J.F.*, 42 Ed Dept Rep 136, Decision No. 14,800, [where the student had left the school district]; *Appeal of Denise W.*, 40 *id.* 503, Decision 14,538, [where the teacher had left the district]; *Appeal of a Student with a Disability*, 39 *id*. 223, Decision No. 14,221, [where the student had left the district]).

Petitioner also challenges the restrictions contained in the letter dated May 20, 2004. That letter directs that, in addition to the restrictions in the previous letter, petitioner was not to attend "any home or away outdoor track meets, including qualifiers, sectional and state events, where Plattsburgh City School District students are participating." This letter expands the restriction on petitioner from only home athletic activities off district property to all outdoor track meets, whether home or away.

Neither side has submitted relevant citations with respect to this portion of the appeal. The ability of an employer to restrict activities of a paid employee outside working hours is not unlimited (*cf.*, Labor Law §201-d). However, as respondents point out, many of the §3020-a charges pending against petitioner involve an allegedly improper relationship between petitioner and a student who was a member of the track team. Other charges against petitioner involve allegedly improper conduct by petitioner in her capacity as track coach in conspiring with other coaches to "fix" the outcome of various track events. Respondents also point out that some members of the track team may be called as witnesses in the §3020-a proceeding.

Accordingly, I find that petitioner has not met her burden of demonstrating a clear legal right to the relief requested and of establishing the facts upon which relief is sought (8 NYCRR §275.10; *Appeal of Washington*, 42 Ed Dept Rep 197, Decision No. 14,820; *Appeal of Siwula*, 41 *id*. 375, Decision No. 14,718; *Appeal of L.S.*, 41 *id*. 270, Decision No. 14,683). I find respondents' directive of May 20, 2004, to be reasonably and narrowly limited in scope, since it extends only to track meets, with the single purpose of restricting petitioner from contacting student athletes with whom she had previously been closely associated. I do not find such a restriction under these circumstances to be arbitrary or capricious.

THE APPEAL IS DISMISSED.

Decision No. 15,168

Appeal of D.V., on behalf of her son C.V., from action of the Board of Education of the Eldred Central School District regarding student discipline.

263 EDUC 01-31-2005

(January 31, 2005)

APPEARANCES OF COUNSEL

Robert N. Isseks, Esq., attorney for petitioner

Shawn Law Offices, attorneys for respondent, *Thomas H. Cragan, Esq.*, of counsel

DECISION OF THE COMMISSIONER

MILLS, Commissioner.—Petitioner appeals a determination by the Board of Education of the Eldred Central School District ("board") suspending her son, C.V., from school for alleged misconduct. The appeal must be dismissed.

During the week of March 8, 2004, C.V. used a home computer to access the website of a female teacher at the Eldred Junior-Senior High School. The website had been created as part of a continuing education program for teachers. C.V. altered the website by adding sexually explicit comments concerning both the teacher and the teacher's spouse. These alterations were discovered by a student during a computer lab in the school, reported to a teaching assistant, and ultimately reported to school authorities. It appears that C.V. was suspended from school on March 17, 2004.

A superintendent's hearing was held on March 22. C.V. was charged with violating the school's code of conduct, by engaging in conduct that endangered the safety, morals, health or welfare of others, specifically by defamation and by using vulgar or abusive language in altering the website. After a discussion between the superintendent and petitioner as to the rationale for charging C.V. with conduct which actually occurred outside the school, C.V. pled guilty to the charge. As a result of his guilty plea, he was suspended from the date of the hearing, March 22 to April 22, 2004.

The next day, petitioner made a written request to appear before the board on April 1 to appeal "the additional 15 day out of school suspension of my son . . ." By letter dated April 2, 2004, the board president advised petitioner that the board had upheld the superintendent's determination, and that her son's suspension would continue until April 22. This appeal was commenced on April 29, after the suspension had been served.

Petitioner claims that all of the activity charged against C.V. occurred outside the school, off school premises, and did not violate any provisions of the code of conduct. She further argues that the superintendent had no jurisdiction to adjudicate this matter, because the comments made by C.V. on the website were protected speech under both the Federal and State constitutions.

Respondent agrees that the conduct occurred off school premises, but points out that the conduct had a very real disruptive effect within the school, where numerous students attempted to access the website. Respondent further points out that C.V. pled guilty at the superintendent's hearing, and that the appeal taken by petitioner to the board was limited only to a consideration of the length of the suspension, and did not seek to overturn the guilty plea.

To the extent petitioner raises the issue of guilt, the appeal must be dismissed. Petitioner's appeal letter dated March 23, 2004, to the board was limited to contesting the length of her son's suspension. As respondent points out, petitioner's previous counsel argued the matter before the board on April 1, 2004, only with respect to the length of the suspension. Petitioner has not challenged that statement by serving a reply. Because the issue of guilt was not raised before, and considered by, the board, and, indeed, was a plea rather than a determination, it may not be raised in an appeal before the Commissioner under Education Law §310 (*Appeal of Ravick*, 40 Ed Dept Rep 262, Decision No. 14,477). Petitioner's appeal must therefore be limited to the length of the suspension.

Because the suspension has already been served, and in fact was served before the appeal was commenced, the matter of the penalty is moot, since no meaningful relief can be afforded (*Appeal of N.S.* 42 Ed Dept Rep 190, Decision No. 14,817; *Appeal of Deborah F.*, 42 *id.* 178, Decision No. 14,813; *Appeal of a Student with a Disability*, 40 *id.* 42, Decision No. 14,416).

Even if I were not dismissing for mootness, I would dismiss the challenge to the penalty on the merits. Where a suspension is imposed, it must be proportionate to the severity of the offense (*Appeal of Alexander*, 36 Ed Dept Rep 160, Decision No. 13,689; *Appeal of Durkee*, 20 *id.* 94, Decision No. 10,329). The test to be applied in reviewing a penalty is whether it is so excessive as to warrant substitution of the Commissioner's judgment for that of the board of education (*Appeal of B.B.*, 38 *id.* 666, Decision No. 14,113; *Appeal of Forestiero*, 34 *id.* 592, Decision No. 13,419). Upon the record before me, I find no basis for determining that respondent acting arbitrarily, unfairly, or excessively in imposing a suspension from March 22 to April 22, 2004, (*cf.*, *Appeal of David and Cynthia L.*, 40 *id.* 297, Decision No. 14,484; *Appeal of Leahy*, 39 *id.* 375, Decision No. 14,264; *Appeal of B.B.*, *supra*).

In light of this disposition, I need not address the parties' remaining contentions.

THE APPEAL IS DISMISSED.

Decision No. 15,169

Appeal of the BOARD OF EDUCATION OF THE EAST HAMPTON UNION FREE SCHOOL DISTRICT from action of the Board of Education of the Springs Union Free School District, and the Parent of a Student with a Disability regarding an impartial hearing.

(January 31, 2005)

APPEARANCES OF COUNSEL

Cooper, Sapir & Cohen, P.C., attorneys for petitioner, *Robert E. Sapir, Esq.*, of counsel

Mark A. Cuthbertson, Esq., attorney for respondent Board of Education of the Springs Union Free School District

Phyllis K. Saxe, Esq., attorney for respondent Parent of a Student with a Disability

DECISION OF THE COMMISSIONER

MILLS, Commissioner.—Petitioner challenges the jurisdiction of an impartial hearing officer ("IHO") to consolidate into one impartial hearing claims by a parent of a student with a disability ("respondent parent") against petitioner and respondent Board of Education of the Springs Union Free School District ("Springs"). The appeal must be dismissed.

Respondent parent resides in Springs' district with her son, a student with a disability, who attended eighth grade in the Springs Elementary School during the 2002-2003 school year. Prior to the conclusion of the 2002-2003 school year, respondent parent withdrew her son and placed him in a residential school in Texas, where he remained until October 2003, the beginning of ninth grade. In September 2003, respondent parent requested an impartial hearing from Springs seeking reimbursement for tuition for 2002-2003.

Springs contracts with petitioner to educate all of its resident students in grades 9 through 12. In November 2003, respondent parent enrolled her son at East Hampton High School in petitioner's district. Petitioner's Committee on Special Education ("CSE") scheduled a meeting regarding the student to be held on November 20, 2003. By letter dated November 7, 2003, respondent parent requested an impartial hearing from petitioner because no individualized education program ("IEP") had been developed for her son. On December 3, 2003, respondent parent notified the chairperson of petitioner's CSE that she had withdrawn her son and placed him in a residential school in upstate New York.

In January 2004, petitioner and respondents agreed to consolidate the two hearing requests into one impartial hearing before a single IHO. The consolidated hearing was scheduled to begin March 4, 2004. The hearing was postponed when petitioner commenced this appeal. Petitioner's request for interim relief was denied on March 15, 2004.

Petitioner contends that it is not a proper party to the impartial hearing because Springs is the student's school district of residence and, therefore, is responsible for providing him with a free appropriate public education ("FAPE"). Petitioner concedes that its CSE is responsible for the student but contends that it must provide Springs with the student's test results and evaluations and must approve the recommendations of petitioner's CSE. Petitioner argues that its contractual obligations are limited and do not extend to providing the student with a FAPE. Petitioner contends that the Commissioner, and not the IHO, has authority to determine the proper parties to an impartial hearing.

Springs contends that the appeal is untimely because it was not commenced within 30 days of receipt of the November 7, 2003, hearing request, the act of which petitioner complains. Springs further contends that the appeal should be dismissed because the Commissioner does not have jurisdiction over an appeal from an interim ruling of an IHO. Springs argues that its contract with petitioner is broadly worded to require petitioner to provide like and equal instruction to that imparted to the children of like ages, grades and departments and accords Springs students with the same rights and privileges enjoyed by petitioner's resident children. Springs thus contends that petitioner is a proper party to the impartial hearing because it must assume all CSE responsibilities for the student and provide him with a FAPE.

Section 275.16 of the Commissioner's regulations requires that an appeal be initiated with 30 days of the making of the decision or the performance of the act complained of. The Commissioner, in his sole discretion, may excuse the failure to commence an appeal within the time specified for good cause shown in the petition (8 NYCRR §275.16).

The appeal must be dismissed for lack of jurisdiction pursuant to §276.10(b) of the Commissioner's regulations, which provides, in relevant part:

> Appeals from an impartial hearing officer's ruling, decision or refusal to decide an issue prior to or during a hearing shall not be permitted. . .

Petitioner may object to the IHO's jurisdiction at the impartial hearing and in an appeal of the IHO's final determination to the State Review Officer, at the conclusion of the impartial hearing.

In light of this disposition, I need not address the parties remaining contentions.

THE APPEAL IS DISMISSED.

Decision No. 15,170

Appeal of S.G. and J.G., on behalf of their daughter L.G., from action of the Board of Education of the City School District of the City of Elmira regarding student discipline.

(February 10, 2005)

APPEARANCES OF COUNSEL

Roe & Hamm, LLP, attorneys for petitioners, *Denice A. Hamm, Esq.*, of counsel

Sayles & Evans, attorneys for respondent, *James F. Young, Esq.*, of counsel

DECISION OF THE COMMISSIONER

MILLS, Commissioner.—Petitioners appeal the decision of the Board of Education of the City School District of the City of Elmira ("respondent") suspending their daughter, L.G., from school. The appeal must be dismissed.

L.G. attends high school in respondent's district. On March 16, 2004, L.G. was involved in a fight with two other female students that resulted in injury to a teacher and teaching assistant, both of whom intervened to break up the fight. L.G. was initially suspended for five days, and by letter dated March 17, 2004, petitioners were notified that L.G. was being charged with "conduct that was disorderly, insubordinate, violent and endangering to the safety, health, morals and welfare of others."

A superintendent's hearing was held on March 22, 2004, to consider whether an additional suspension was warranted, and the hearing officer found L.G. guilty of the charge and recommended, among other things, that she be suspended until February 1, 2005. By decision dated March 29, 2004, respondent's superintendent adopted both the hearing officer's finding of guilt and penalty recommendation. By letter dated June 16, 2004, petitioners were notified that respondent had affirmed the superintendent's determination. This appeal ensued. Petitioners' request for interim relief was denied on August 4, 2004.

Petitioners contend that the hearing evidence was insufficient to support the superintendent's determination, that the penalty imposed is excessive, and that the hearing officer erred by failing to review the videotape of the incident from the school's security cameras. For relief, petitioners request that I reverse the suspension and allow L.G. to return to school at the beginning of the 2004-2005 school year or, in the alternative, find the punishment excessive and unduly harsh.

Respondent contends that the hearing evidence was sufficient to sustain the charges and that the penalty imposed was appropriate. Additionally, respondent contends that pursuant to petitioners' request, the hearing officer and superintendent viewed the security videotape, which was forwarded to respondent as part of the record.

To the extent petitioners seek L.G.'s reinstatement, the appeal must be dismissed as moot. The Commissioner of Education will only decide matters in actual controversy and will not render a decision on a state of facts which no longer exist or which subsequent events have laid to rest (*Appeal of D.C.*, 43 Ed Dept Rep 217, Decision No. 14,976; *Appeal of D.H.*, 41 *id.* 142, Decision No. 14,640). By letter dated December 10, 2004, respondent's attorney advised my Office of Counsel that the superintendent modified L.G.'s suspension by permitting her to return to school on January 3, 2005. Accordingly, because L.G. has served the suspension, and petitioners did not request expungement of L.G.'s records, the appeal is moot (*Appeal of D.H., supra*; *Appeal of Camille S.*, 39 *id*. 574, Decision No. 14,316).

Even if the appeal were not dismissed on procedural grounds, it would be dismissed on the merits. A decision to suspend a student from school pursuant to Education Law §3214 must be based on competent and substantial evidence that the student participated in the objectionable conduct (*Bd. of Educ. of Monticello Cent. School Dist. v. Commissioner of Educ., et al.*, 91 NY2d 133; *Bd. of Educ. of City of New York v. Mills*, 293 AD2d 37). The record reflects that L.G. was involved in an altercation with a number of other girls that required the intervention of several members of respondent's staff to restore order. When a teacher attempted to subdue L.G., she continued to struggle, and upon breaking free, flailed her arms, striking the teacher in the head and injuring her. Additionally, when a second staff member attempted to restrain L.G., she punched and kicked the staff member, causing her to sustain a number of bruises. In sum, L.G. was involved in a dangerous and violent altercation that resulted in injury to two members of respondent's staff. I find substantial evidence in the record to support the superintendent's finding of guilt.

Furthermore, the sanction imposed must be proportionate to the severity of the offense involved (*Appeal of D.C.*, 43 Ed Dept Rep 217, Decision No. 14,976; *Appeal of Alexander*, 36 *id*. 160, Decision No. 13,689). The test to be applied in reviewing a penalty is whether it is so excessive as to warrant substitution of the Commissioner's judgment for that of the board of education (*Appeal of D.C., supra*; *Appeal of J.C. and P.C.*, 41 *id*. 395, Decision No. 14,723). In light of the seriousness of L.G.'s conduct, I do not conclude that a suspension of approximately seven and a half months was unreasonable (*see*, *Appeal of Mace*, 40 Ed Dept Rep 110, Decision No. 14,433; *Appeal of Simon*, 33 *id*. 582, Decision No. 13,157). Under the circumstances I find no basis to disturb respondent's finding of guilt or penalty determination.

Nor do I find any merit to petitioners' contention that the videotape was not included in the record. In an appeal to the Commissioner, petitioners have the burden of demonstrating a clear legal right to the relief requested and the burden of establishing the facts upon which they seek relief (8 NYCRR §275.10; *Appeal of M.F. and J.F.*, 43 Ed Dept Rep 174, Decision No. 14,960; *Appeal of Kessler*, 43 *id*. 170, Decision No. 14,958). The record reflects that at the superintendent's hearing, petitioner S.G. requested that the superintendent and hearing officer review the security videotape from the high school's security system and that, in fact, on April 27, 2004, the hearing officer and superintendent, along with petitioners and their attorney, reviewed the videotape, which was forwarded to respondent as part of the record available for respondent's review.

THE APPEAL IS DISMISSED.

Decision No. 15,171

Appeal of V.G., on behalf of her son D.G., from action of the Board of Education of the Odessa-Montour Central School District and Superintendent Carol Boyce regarding student discipline.

(February 10, 2005)

APPEARANCES OF COUNSEL

Sayles & Evans, attorneys for respondents, *Conrad R. Wolan, Esq.*, of counsel

DECISION OF THE COMMISSIONER

MILLS, Commissioner.—Petitioner appeals the suspension of her son, D.G., by the Board of Education of the Odessa-Montour Central School District ("respondent board"). The appeal must be dismissed.

On March 18, 2004, D.G.'s idle play with the protective cage covering a building fire alarm at Crossroads, an alternative high school program of the Schuyler-Chemung-Tioga BOCES, caused the alarm to activate. The building was evacuated, and its occupants were required to remain outside for approximately 30 minutes. Based on information provided by another student, the principal called D.G. to her office, and he admitted to playing with the alarm's protective cage. After discussing the incident with petitioner, the principal suspended D.G. for five days. By letter dated March 19, 2004, the superintendent scheduled a hearing for March 26, 2004. The hearing was adjourned and held on March 29, 2004, to enable D.G. to attend.

At the hearing, D.G. testified that he was opening and closing the metal cage covering the fire alarm when it activated, but he asserted that he did not intend to set off the alarm. In his March 30, 2004, decision and recommendation, the hearing officer stated that a 19-year-old such as D.G. was capable of recognizing that a fire alarm is not a toy and found that D.G. endangered the safety and welfare of other students. By letter dated April 2, 2004, the superintendent suspended D.G. through April 7, 2004, for a total of 13 days. Petitioner appealed to respondent board, which issued a determination on April 22, 2004, upholding the superintendent's decision. This appeal ensued. Petitioner's request for interim relief was denied on May 20, 2004.

Petitioner asserts that the decision to suspend her son was arbitrary and intended to form the basis for further disciplinary action. She requests an investigation into the district's suspension practices and seeks to prevent the superintendent from suspending her son in the future.

Respondents assert that the appeal process does not provide for investigations and that the superintendent must ensure the safety of all students. Respondents further contend that petitioner's request for a stay of the superintendent's suspension authority is premature because the student is not threatened by any action at this time.

The appeal must be dismissed as moot. The Commissioner will only decide matters in actual controversy and will not render a decision on a state of facts which no longer exists or which subsequent events have laid to rest (*Appeal of D.W.*, 43 Ed Dept Rep 188, Decision No. 14,965; *Appeal of L.B.*, 43 *id.* 159, Decision No. 14,952; *Appeal of N.S.*, 42 *id.* 190, Decision No. 14,817). Petitioner does not request expungement of her son's records. Since her son has served the suspension, no further meaningful relief can be granted, and the appeal of respondent board's determination must be dismissed as moot (*Appeal of R.R. and K.R.*, 41 Ed Dept Rep 405, Decision No. 14,726; *Appeal of D.H.*, 41 *id.* 142, Decision No. 14,640; *Appeal of N.B.*, 40 *id.* 515, Decision No. 14,542).

While I am constrained to dismiss this appeal, I must comment on the district's failure to comply with the student's due process rights related to the initial five-day suspension. Education Law §3214(3)(b)(1) provides that in the case of a suspension by a principal, not to exceed five days, the student be provided with notice of the charged misconduct and the student and his parents "shall, on request, be given an opportunity for an informal conference with the principal at which the pupil and/or person in parental relation shall be authorized to present the pupil's version of the event and to ask questions of the complaining witnesses." That section further provides:

The aforesaid notice and opportunity for an informal conference shall take place prior to suspension of the pupil unless the pupil's presence in the school poses a continuing danger to persons or property or an ongoing threat of disruption to the academic process, in which case the pupil's notice and opportunity for an informal conference shall take place as soon after the suspension as is reasonably practicable.

The parental notice shall be in writing and "shall be provided by personal delivery, express mail delivery, or equivalent means reasonably calculated to assure receipt of such notice within 24 hours of the decision to propose suspension" (8 NYCRR §100.2(l)(4)). The written notice must "inform the parents or persons in parental relation of their right to request an immediate informal conference with the principal in accordance with the provisions of Education Law, section 3214(3)(b)" (*id.*).

Although the principal had a telephone conversation with petitioner regarding the incident and her intention to suspend D.G., her written notice to petitioner did not comply with §100.2(l)(4) of the Commissioner's regulations. Oral communication with parents regarding a suspension is not a substitute for the required written notification (*Appeal of R.F.*, *supra*; *Appeal of a Student Suspected of Having a Disability*, 41 Ed Dept Rep 390, Decision No. 14,722). Further, because respondents do not allege that the student's presence in school posed a continuing danger or threat, the principal was obligated to conduct an informal conference before suspending the student (Education Law §3214(3)(b)(1)). I remind respondents of the obligation to comply with Education Law §3214 and §100.2(l)(4) of the Commissioner's regulations.

With respect to petitioner's request for an investigation, an appeal to the Commissioner is appellate in nature and does not provide for investigations (*Appeal of Coleman, et al.*, 42 Ed Dept Rep 256, Decision No. 14,845; *Application of Wilson*, 41 *id.* 196, Decision No. 14,663).

Finally, petitioner's request that I stay the superintendent's authority to suspend her son must be dismissed as premature. While the superintendent's letter includes a general reminder that a student may be subject to further disciplinary action if he or she violates the school's code of conduct, petitioner does not establish that her son is currently threatened with any further suspension. It is well established that the Commissioner will not render advisory opinions or decide issues that have not yet become justiciable (*Appeal of L.M.*, 43 Ed Dept Rep 279, Decision No. 14,994; *Appeal of Sheppard*, 41 *id.* 150, Decision No. 14,643).

THE APPEAL IS DISMISSED.

Decision No. 15,172

Appeal of LYNDA ALEXANDER from action of the Board of Education of the South Orangetown Central School District and Joseph Zambito, Superintendent, regarding tenure.

(February 16, 2005)

APPEARANCES OF COUNSEL

James R. Sandner, Esq., attorney for petitioner, *Neil J. Dudich, Esq.*, of counsel

Kuntz, Spagnuolo, Scapoli & Schiro, PC, attorneys for respondents, *Mario L. Spagnuolo, Esq.*, of counsel

DECISION OF THE COMMISSIONER

MILLS, Commissioner.—Petitioner appeals the determination of the Board of Education of the South Orangetown Central School District ("respondent board") and its superintendent to terminate her services. The appeal must be sustained.

Prior to 1993, petitioner held a teaching certificate issued by the State Education Department in elementary education. In 1993, petitioner became employed by the Ramapo Central School District ("Ramapo") not as a teacher, but as a teaching assistant, although she held a teaching certificate. She was granted tenure as a teaching assistant in Ramapo effective October 24, 1996, and continued to work in Ramapo until the spring of 2000, when she acquired an additional teaching certificate in general special education.

Petitioner became employed by respondent board in 2001, when she was given a three year probationary appointment as a teacher of special education effective September 1, 2001. At the time petitioner was appointed, respondent board was aware that she had previously received tenure in Ramapo as a teaching assistant, but it also appears that petitioner did not request a shorter probationary term than the three year term to which she was appointed. Petitioner taught continuously in the South Orangetown Central School District ("Orangetown") from September 1, 2001, until February 14, 2003, when she took maternity leave for the balance of that school year. She returned to full time teaching in September 2003, and continued as an Orangetown employee until her services were terminated on June 30, 2004, in accordance with the procedures governing dismissal of probationary employees. This appeal was commenced on July 27, 2004, and interim relief was denied on August 16, 2004.

Petitioner claims that her rights under Education Law §3012 were violated. Education Law §3012(1)(a) provides in pertinent part:

> Teachers and all other members of the teaching staff . . . shall be appointed . . . for a probationary period of three years . . . provided, however, that in the case of a teacher who has been appointed on tenure in another school district within the state, the school district where currently employed, or a board of cooperative educational services, and who was not dismissed from such district or board as a result of charges brought pursuant to subdivision one of section three thousand twenty-a of this chapter, the probationary period shall not exceed two years.

Petitioner claims that her prior grant of tenure in Ramapo legally reduced her probationary period to two years in Orangetown, and that her two-year probationary period, after subtracting the maternity leave of Spring 2003, was completed near or at the end of the Fall 2003 term. Petitioner claims that respondents failed to take the action required by law to grant or deny tenure, and permitted her to teach beyond the expiration of her probationary term. Thus, petitioner argues that when she completed her two-year probationary period, she acquired tenure by estoppel, had a protected property right in her position, and could not be legally discharged except for cause in accordance with Education Law §3020-a.

Respondents argue that acquiring prior tenure as a teaching assistant does not reduce the probationary term for a teacher pursuant to Education Law §3012(1)(a). Respondents further contend that, because petitioner failed to request or demand a reduced probationary term in September 2001, she cannot now seek equitable relief of tenure by estoppel.

No party to this appeal has cited any case in which a New York educator has first received tenure as a teaching assistant, then claimed a shortened probationary period when later appointed as a teacher. Petitioner's position is that Education Law §3012(1)(a) must be read literally, *i.e.*, that petitioner was appointed as a teacher effective September 1, 2001, that she had been previously "appointed on tenure in another school district within the state," and, as a result, her probationary appointment may not exceed two years. Respondents argue that the statute should be read to require that the prior tenure appointment must have been as a teacher, because a teacher's required qualifications and duties differ substantially from those of a teaching assistant, and a person holding prior tenure as a teaching assistant has never been previously evaluated as a teacher. Respondents argue that a shortened probationary period only makes sense where the teacher has previously "endured the rigors of the teacher tenure process in another district" and "has performed well enough to be awarded tenure as a teacher."

I find respondents' arguments persuasive, but I am constrained to sustain the appeal because of the holding in *Matter of Gould v. Board of Educ.* (81 NY2d 446), which I believe is controlling. In *Gould*, petitioner was granted tenure as an elementary school teacher in New York City in 1965. Twenty-one years later, she applied for and obtained a position in the Sewanhaka Central High School District as a special education teacher. Her application indicated that she had previously obtained tenure in New York City, but on September 1, 1986, she was given a three-year probationary appointment.

On February 24, 1989, after serving more than two years, she was advised that she would not be recommended for tenure and would be terminated on June 23, 1989. Petitioner then elected to resign her position after being assured that the negative tenure recommendation would not be placed in her personnel file. Thereafter, petitioner sought to rescind her resignation claiming that she had obtained tenure by estoppel before she resigned because she should have been given only a two-year probationary appointment.

Supreme Court granted petitioner's Article 78 petition, but the Appellate Division, Second Department, unanimously reversed (184 AD2d 640). The Court of Appeals then unanimously reversed the Appellate Division (81 NY2d 446). In a sweeping decision by Judge Hancock, the Court of Appeals held, at pp. 450-451:

Education Law §3012(1)(a) states:

> "Teachers * * * shall be appointed * * * for a probationary period of three years; provided, however, that in the case

> of a teacher who has been appointed on *tenure in another school district within the state,* * * * and who was not dismissed from such district or board * * * *the probationary period shall not exceed two years*" (emphasis added).

The language of the section is plain and the meaning unambiguous. Because of petitioner's previous tenure in New York City, the acquired term of her probationary service had been reduced from three years to two years. The statute itself is self-executing. It makes no difference that her tenured status was in a different tenure area in another school district or that she had left her tenured position more than 20 years before. Thus, after September 1, 1988, she was eligible to acquire tenure.

Tenure by estoppel "results when a school board fails to take the action required by law to grant or deny tenure and, with full knowledge and consent, permits a teacher to continue to teach beyond the expiration of [the] probationary term" (*Matter of Lindsey v Board of Educ.*, 72 AD2d 185, 186). Here, petitioner's required probationary period had unquestionably been reduced from three years to two years. Although the Superintendent and the Board had constructive knowledge of the facts pertaining to petitioner's 1965 tenure from the information contained in her application, they were presumably not cognizant of the legal implications of continuing to employ petitioner beyond September 1, 1988, when her two years of probation ended. Respondents were, however, concededly aware of the operative facts—petitioner's continuing service as a teacher in the District's employ. It is of no legal significance that respondents did not know that petitioner's continued employment would enable her to acquire tenure by estoppel (see, *Lindsey, supra; Matter of Dwyer v Board of Educ.,* 61 AD2d 859).

As in *Gould*, there is no question here that petitioner received prior tenure (although here as a teaching assistant rather than as a teacher) in a different tenure area in another school district. Respondent does not deny that it knew of the prior award of tenure at the time of petitioner's probationary appointment. And petitioner served more than two years as a probationary teacher, even allowing a deduction for maternity leave (*see*, *Matter of Mulholland*, 70 Misc 2d 852, aff'd 41 AD2d 704, and cases cited therein, suggesting that time spent on maternity leave does not count toward fulfilling the probationary period), before her dismissal on June 30, 2004.

The only significant difference between *Gould* and this case is that here petitioner received prior tenure as a teaching assistant, not as a teacher, and the parties differ as to the meaning of the word "tenure" in these circumstances. McKinney's Consolidated Laws of New York, Book 1, Statutes §76, provides:

> Some statutes are framed in language so plain that an attempt to construe them is superfluous. The function of the courts is to enforce statutes, not to usurp the power of legislation, and to interpret a statute where there is no need for interpretation, to conjecture about or to add to or to subtract from words having a definite meaning, or to engraft exceptions where none exist are trespasses by a court upon the legislative domain.

While the word "teacher" has a somewhat fluid meaning in the Education Law (*see, e.g., Matter of Madison-Oneida BOCES v. Mills*, 2 AD3rd 1240; aff'd ____ NY3d ___, December 21, 2004), the word "tenure" does not. If the Legislature intended to exclude prior tenure as a teaching assistant for purposes of a shortened probationary period, it could simply have done so. To carve out an exception to the clear phrase "in the case of a teacher who has been appointed on tenure" with respect to prior tenure as a teaching assistant would be an incursion on the province of the Legislature, and I decline to do so.

THE APPEAL IS SUSTAINED.

IT IS ORDERED that petitioner acquired tenure by estoppel prior to her termination; and

IT IS FURTHER ORDERED that petitioner be restored to a tenured position in the general special education tenure area; and

IT IS FURTHER ORDERED that respondent board pay to petitioner back pay and benefits retroactive to June 30, 2004, less any compensation she may have otherwise earned.

Decision No. 15,173

Appeal of DANIEL M. DEVINE, SUE LANE, MAUREEN ESPOSITO, DAVID EHRHARDT, and ADRIAN GONZALEZ, from action of the Board of Education of the Central Islip Union Free School District regarding a proposition.

(February 16, 2005)

APPEARANCES OF COUNSEL

James R. Sandner, Esq., attorneys for petitioners, *Catherine V. Battle* and *Maria Elena Gonzalez, Esqs.*, of counsel

Kevin A. Seaman, Esq., attorney for respondent

DECISION OF THE COMMISSIONER

MILLS, Commissioner.—Petitioners, residents of the Central Islip Union Free School District, challenge the refusal by the Board of Education ("respondent") to place a proposition before the voters at the annual meeting. The appeal must be dismissed.

On February 18, 2004, respondent's District Clerk received a petition to place a proposition on the May 18, 2004, ballot to increase the number of seats on the board from seven to nine ("first petition"). The petition contained a legally sufficient number of signatures and was filed pursuant to Education Law §1703.

On March 1, 2004, the District Clerk received a second petition ("second petition"), prepared and circulated by petitioners to decrease the number of board seats from seven to five. The second petition also contained a legally sufficient number of signatures, and was filed pursuant to Education Law §1703.

On March 8, 2004, at a regular meeting of the board, respondent discussed the propositions before it. After discussion in executive session, the board returned to public session and voted, by a margin of 5-2, to accept the first petition filed, and to approve the notice of annual meeting with the inclusion of notice as to the first proposition. The board then voted, by a margin of 5-2, to reject the second petition. It also voted to reject a proposal made by a board member to place both propositions on the ballot and to add a third proposition which would have allowed voters to vote affirmatively to keep the number of board seats at seven.

Pursuant to the vote of the board, the District Clerk submitted the notice of annual meeting, including the first proposition, to two newspapers of general circulation for publication. This appeal ensued. Petitioners' request for interim relief was denied on March 31, 2004, and petitioners' request for reconsideration was denied on April 30, 2005.

Petitioners argue that Education Law §1703(2) requires that a board of education place before the voters a proposition either to increase or decrease the number of seats on the board, as long as the petition is signed by at least 25 voters or 5% of the number of voters who voted in the previous annual election of the members of the board, whichever is greater. (Both petitions filed with the District Clerk met this requirement.) The petition seeks an order staying the annual meeting, declaring that the board's actions were unlawful, directing the board to accept the second petition and place it on the May 2004 ballot whenever conducted, and giving notice to the voters in such manner as the Commissioner directs concerning the second proposition.

Respondent acknowledges that Education Law §1703 appears to require the acceptance of any legally sufficient petition to increase or decrease the number of board seats, but cites prior Commissioners' decisions which state that a board of education may refuse a proposition or propositions where contradictory propositions appearing on the ballot may result in ambiguity, unfeasibility, or difficulty in interpreting election results. Respondent argues that Education Law §1703 requires the vote of a majority, not merely a plurality, of qualified voters to either increase or decrease the number of seats on a board, and argues that placing propositions both to increase and to decrease board membership on the same ballot would have led to confusing results, particularly where voters were not offered a clear option to vote to keep the number of seats at seven.

The appeal must be dismissed as moot. The Commissioner will only decide matters in actual controversy and will not render a decision on a state of facts which no longer exists or which subsequent events have laid to rest (*Appeal of Loveland and Hazelton*, 42 Ed Dept Rep 294, Decision 14,858; *Appeal of Colety*, 42 *id.* 162, Decision 14,806). The annual meeting was conducted as scheduled on May 18, 2004, at which time the first proposition to increase the number of seats on the board was defeated by a vote of 1,572 to 361. All the relief sought in the petition was based upon my staying the annual meeting and requiring a vote on the second proposition. Since the annual meeting was not stayed and the vote was conducted, no meaningful relief is now available.

Although the appeal is dismissed on procedural grounds, I will comment on the merits for the benefit of the parties, particularly since a similar situation could arise in the future. In *Appeal of Krause* (27 Ed Dept Rep 57, Decision No. 11,870), the Commissioner articulated the duties and responsibilities of a board of education with respect to propositions:

> The role of the board in allowing propositions to come before the voters under Education Law §3035(2) [sic] has never been merely ministerial. In *Matter of Kaufman and Levine*, 2 Ed Dept Rep 315, the rejection by the board of education of a proposition relating to transportation which appropriated a sum of money wholly inadequate for its purpose was upheld, although the proposition was proper in form and timely submitted under the board's bylaws. *Matter of Prout, et al.*, 10 Ed Dept Rep 67, and *Matter of Gang, et al.*, 23 Ed Dept Rep 118, further illustrate the authority of a board in this context. In *Prout*, it was specifically held that a board of education has the power to alter the language of propositions submitted by voters to conform to law. In *Gang*, it was held that the right of voters to submit propositions does not include the right to require the deletion of corresponding items from the budget submitted to the voters by the board of education.
>
> These decisions make clear that a board may not be compelled to place before the voters at an annual meeting all propositions submitted in conformity with §2035 and its bylaws, regardless of ambiguity, feasibility, or difficulty in interpreting election results when conflicting matters are voted on simultaneously. A board must exercise its independent judgment within the law to be certain that the will of the voters can be ascertained.

In *Appeal of Martin* (32 Ed Dept Rep 567, Decision 12,915), the Commissioner wrote:

> . . . [P]etitioner's claim that respondent board was required to place his proposition as submitted to the electorate is without merit. Pursuant to Education Law §1716, it is a board of education's duty to present the voters with an annual budget. A board of education may not be compelled to place before the voters at an annual meeting all propositions submitted in conformity with §2035 and its bylaws, regardless of ambiguity, feasibility, or difficulty in interpreting election results when conflicting matters are voted on simultaneously (*Matter*

> *of Prout, et al.*, 10 Ed Dept Rep 67; *Matter of Gang, et al.*, 23 *id.* 118; *Appeal of Krause*, 27 *id.* 57). A board must exercise its independent judgment to ensure that the will of the voters can be ascertained. Placing two propositions before the electorate covering the exact same matter with two different appropriations, such as the propositions offered by petitioner and respondent board, would be confusing. Respondent board did not abuse its discretion and authority by declining to put petitioner's proposition before the voters.

In this appeal, petitioners do not contest the acceptance of the first petition by respondent, although they suggest that the second petition, which had more signatures, should have been given preference. They also do not contend that the board was required to put up a proposition of its own to allow for an affirmative vote to keep the number of board seats at seven. The appeal is instead limited to the propriety of rejecting the second petition. To succeed, petitioners must establish that the board acted arbitrarily, and they have the burden of demonstrating a clear legal right to the relief sought.

The parties agree that if the second petition seeking a decrease in the number of board seats had been the only proposition submitted to the board pursuant to Education Law §1703, the board would have been obligated to place the proposition on the ballot (*Appeal of Martin*, 29 Ed Dept Rep 148, Decision 12,248). However, where two competing propositions in conflict with each other are presented to the board, petitioners argue that the board's role becomes purely ministerial, and that conflicting propositions must be presented to voters regardless of ambiguity, feasibility, or difficulty in interpreting election results. I disagree.

There can be no question that the propositions at issue are contradictory. A voter confronted with two diametrically opposite proposals, and no affirmative opportunity to keep the number of board seats at seven, would necessarily be confused. There certainly existed the possibility that a confused electorate could have approved both propositions by a majority, leaving the proper number of board seats in debate. Where boards have allowed contradictory propositions, appeals have followed (*see e.g.*, *Appeal of Board of Trustees of the George F. Johnson Memorial Library*, 40 *id.* 331, Decision No. 14,490; *Appeal of Kohilakis*, 33 Ed Dept Rep 513, Decision No. 13,133). It would seem that the wiser course is to try to eliminate confusion prior to a vote (*Appeal of Huber, et al.*, 41 Ed

Dept Rep 240, Decision 14,676). As in *Huber*, I do not find that respondent acted arbitrarily in declining to place petitioners alternative proposition on the ballot.

The courts have been reluctant to interfere or substitute their judgment where administrative bodies have had to choose between or among apparently equal persons or options. For example, in *Matter of Bennett v. City School Dist. of New Rochelle* (114 AD2d 58), the Second Department approved the use of a random lottery to select 27 participants from a pool of 109 students for a gifted education program, all of whom met the criteria for participation, but could not all be accommodated.

In *Matter of Schoenfeld v. BOCES of Nassau County* (98 AD2d 723), the Second Department scrutinized a multi-level system for establishing relative seniority of teachers. The court found the system to be rational, and said:

> In *Matter of Sommers* [19 Ed Dept Rep 99] the Commissioner of Education held that a board of education may determine a means by which to establish the relative seniority of teachers. If the system used by the board is reasonable, the seniority determination will not be set aside. Clearly, the method of determining seniority promulgated by BOCES was reasonable. The criteria used and priorities set among those criteria constituted a rational process sufficient to eliminate subjective determinations.

In *Eisbruck v. New York State Educ. Dept.* (137 Misc 2d 241), Supreme Court considered the tie-breaking process used by the State Education Department with respect to the awarding of Empire State Scholarships of Excellence. The court dismissed the petition and said, "The applicable standard in reviewing a determination of the Commissioner of Education is whether it is arbitrary or capricious (*Matter of Chauvel v. Nyguist*, 43 NY2d 48). The role of the judiciary is thus drastically limited." The same standard is applicable in my review of respondent's actions in this appeal.

Respondent has complied with prior Commissioner's Decisions, and its decision to accept the petition filed first and reject the second is not arbitrary. I have considered the parties' other arguments and find that they lack merit.

THE APPEAL IS DISMISSED.

Decision No. 15,174

Appeal of N.M., individually and on behalf of her daughter N.C., from action of the Board of Education of the City School District of the City of New York, the Chancellor, and Kathleen M. Cashin, Superintendent of Region 5, regarding provision of school related information.

(February 16, 2005)

APPEARANCES OF COUNSEL

Anusuya Chatterjee, Esq., attorney for petitioner

Michael A. Cardozo, Corporation Counsel, attorney for respondents, *Theresa Crotty* and *Joshua Chao, Esqs.*, of counsel

DECISION OF THE COMMISSIONER

MILLS, Commissioner.—Petitioner appeals the alleged failure of the Board of Education of the City School District of the City of New York, the Chancellor, and Superintendent Cashin (hereinafter "respondents") to provide her with school related information in a language that she understands. The appeal must be sustained in part.

Petitioner's daughter, N.C., is a student who attends ninth grade at Richmond Hill High School in Region 5. Petitioner's primary language is Spanish. According to her petition, she does not speak or understand English proficiently.

Petitioner alleges that respondents failed to provide her with required translation or interpretation services. Petitioner claims that she is forced to rely on N.C. to translate school related information, including information about parents' associations or school leadership teams, and has not received translations of her daughter's report card or standardized assessments. Petitioner also alleges that she has requested interpreters for parent-teacher conferences and has been told that there are no interpreters available. Petitioner further claims that she did not receive translated information in connection with N.C.'s suspension from school from March 16 through March 22, 2004.

Petitioner contends, therefore, that respondents have violated her rights under federal law, including Title I of the Elementary and Secondary Education Act , Title III of the Elementary and Secondary Education Act , Title VI of the Civil Rights Act of 1964, and the Equal Educational Opportunities Act of 1974. Petitioner further claims that respondents have violated her rights under New York State Education Law §3201, Part 154 of the Commissioner's regulations and the related New York State Education Department guidelines, Chancellor's Regulations pertaining to disciplinary proceedings and Parent Association meetings and a New York City Board of Education Resolution on the "Establishment of Policy on Provision of Translation and Interpretation Services for Limited-English Speaking Parents." She seeks an order directing respondents to comply with these provisions. On June 28, 2004, petitioner's request for interim relief was denied.

Respondents seek dismissal of petitioner's federal claims on procedural grounds. Respondents also contend, among other things, that the appeal is untimely and that they provide school related information to petitioner in Spanish and, therefore, are in compliance with applicable law.

An appeal to the Commissioner pursuant to Education Law §310 is not an appropriate forum to adjudicate claims under Title VI of the Civil Rights Act of 1964 (*Appeal of Cartagena*, 43 Ed Dept Rep 267, Decision No. 14,991; *Appeal of Finkel*, 41 *id.* 74, Decision No. 14,619) or the Equal Educational Opportunities Act (*Appeal of Rits*, 43 Ed Dept Rep 257, Decision No. 14,989; *Appeal of Seligman, et al.*, 31 *id.* 131, Decision No. 12,594) or to obtain relief under the No Child Left Behind Act (*See*, 20 USC §7844(a)(3)(C) ; *Appeal of Garmaeva*, 43 Ed Dept Rep 253, Decision No. 14,988). Therefore, these claims are dismissed.

An appeal to the Commissioner must also be commenced within 30 days from the making of the decision or the performance of the act

---

Effective January 8, 2002, Title I of the Elementary and Secondary Education Act was repealed and re-enacted as Title I of the No Child Left Behind Act. Also, effective January 8, 2002, former Title VII of the Elementary and Secondary Education Act was omitted and re-enacted as Title III of the No Child Left Behind Act.

Accordingly, I have referred petitioner's complaints alleging violations of the No Child Left Behind Act to the appropriate Department staff for resolution.

complained of, unless any delay is excused by the Commissioner for good cause shown (8 NYCRR §275.16). The appeal is timely with respect to N.C.'s suspension from school from March 16 through March 22, 2004. Petitioner was notified of the suspension on March 16, 2004, and commenced this appeal on April 1, 2004, well within the 30-day period.

The appeal is also timely with regard to petitioner's claim that respondents failed to provide her with required translation or interpretation services, which if determined to be unlawful, would constitute a continuing wrong subject to complaint at any time (*Appeal of Upstate Home for Children, Inc.*, 43 Ed Dept Rep 505, Decision No. 15,067; *Appeal of Nettles*, 31 *id.* 437, Decision No. 12,691). Therefore, her claims under State law, regulation and policy are timely.

In an appeal to the Commissioner, petitioner has the burden of demonstrating a clear legal right to the relief requested and the burden of establishing the facts upon which she seeks relief (8 NYCRR §275.10; *Appeal of Cartagena*, *supra*; *Appeal of Kessler*, 43 Ed Dept Rep 170, Decision No. 14,958). Education Law §3201 prohibits discrimination in student admission or assignment to public schools based on race, creed, color or national origin. The petition is devoid of any allegation that petitioner's daughter has been denied admission to the district schools or assigned to a school on a prohibited ground. Consequently, I find no basis for petitioner's §3201 claim (*Appeal of Cartagena*, *supra*).

Part 154 of the Commissioner's regulations requires each board of education to "distribute to parents, or other persons in parental relation to pupils with limited English proficiency, school related information in English or when necessary, the language they understand" (8 NYCRR §§154.3(c) and 154.4(a)). Petitioner claims that she does not know whether respondent assessed her daughter to determine if she qualifies as a limited English proficient student. Respondents have provided undisputed evidence that N.C. took the Language Assessment Battery in 1994 and, based on her score, was not identified as a limited English proficient student. Since petitioner has failed to establish that her daughter is a pupil with limited English proficiency, Part 154 does not apply. Consequently, I find no basis for petitioner's Part 154 claim.

Moreover, petitioner has failed to submit the regulation and resolution that she contends were violated as part of her petition and has failed to establish that respondents violated any specific provision of the regulation or resolution. Accordingly, petitioner has not sustained her burden on claims that respondents violated either the resolution or regulation (*Appeal of Ravick*, 40 Ed Dept Rep 262, Decision No. 14,477).

To maintain an appeal pursuant to Education Law §310, a party must be aggrieved in the sense of having suffered personal injury to his or her civil, personal or property rights (*Appeal of J.L.*, 41 Ed Dept Rep 62, Decision No. 14,615). As the parent of a student who has been suspended from school, I find that petitioner has standing to challenge respondents' failure to provide her with appropriate written and oral information in conjunction with her daughter's suspension.

With respect to N.C.'s short-term suspension, Education Law §3214(3)(b)(1) authorizes a board of education or trustees, superintendent of schools, district superintendent or a school principal to suspend a student for a period of five days or less. Requirements related to a suspension of five days or less are also set forth in §100.2(l)(4) of the Commissioner's regulations. That section states, in pertinent part, "Such notice and informal conference shall be in the dominant language or mode of communication used by the parents or persons in parental relation to the pupil."

In the present appeal, the notice of the superintendent's suspension was not translated into Spanish, which is petitioner's dominant language. The informal conference between petitioner and the school official was also in English and translated by N.C. in the presence of a school aide fluent in Spanish. Accordingly, I find that respondents failed to comply with the requirements of §100.2(l)(4) of the Commissioner's regulations and I admonish respondents to comply with such requirements in future disciplinary proceedings.

In light of this disposition, I need not address the parties' remaining contentions.

THE APPEAL IS SUSTAINED TO THE EXTENT INDICATED.

IT IS ORDERED that respondents henceforth fully comply with the written notice and informal conference requirements in §100.2(l)(4) of the Commissioner's regulations.

Decision No. 15,175

Appeal of I.S., individually and on behalf of her daughter G.V., from action of the Board of Education of the City School District of the City of New York, the Chancellor, and Reyes Irizarry, Superintendent of Region 4, regarding provision of school related information.

(February 16, 2005)

APPEARANCES OF COUNSEL

Anusuya Chatterjee, Esq., attorney for petitioner

Michael A. Cardozo, Corporation Counsel, attorney for respondents, *Theresa Crotty* and *Joshua Chao, Esqs.*, of counsel

DECISION OF THE COMMISSIONER

MILLS, Commissioner.—Petitioner appeals the alleged failure of the Board of Education of the City School District of the City of New York, the Chancellor, and Superintendent Irizarry (hereinafter "respondents") to provide her with school related information in a language that she understands. The appeal must be dismissed.

Petitioner's daughter, G.V., is a limited English proficient student who attended kindergarten at P.S. 145 in Region 4 during the 2003-2004 school year. Petitioner's primary language is Spanish. According to her petition, she does not speak or understand English proficiently.

Petitioner alleges that respondents failed to provide her with required translation or interpretation services, that respondents failed to provide her with translated information regarding the district's bilingual program, that fifty percent of the information sent from G.V.'s school is translated into Spanish and fifty percent is in English, that she has requested interpretation services at school and has had to wait for over two hours for the same, that parent association information and meetings are not translated and that she has not received translations of her daughter's report card or standardized assessments. Petitioner also alleges that the school nurse does not speak Spanish and that her daughter has asthma and has not been able to take her medicine at school.

Petitioner contends, therefore, that respondents have violated her rights under federal law, including Title I of the Elementary and Secondary Education Act , Title III of the Elementary and Secondary Education Act , Title VI of the Civil Rights Act of 1964, and the Equal Educational Opportunities Act of 1974. Petitioner further claims that respondents have violated her rights under New York State Education Law §3201, Part 154 of the Commissioner's regulations and related New York State Education Department guidelines, a New York City Board of Education Resolution on the "Establishment of Policy on Provision of Translation and Interpretation Services for Limited-English Speaking Parents," and a Chancellor's regulation pertaining to Parent Association meetings. She seeks an order directing respondents to comply with these provisions. On June 28, 2004, petitioner's request for interim relief was denied.

Respondents seek dismissal of petitioner's federal claims on procedural grounds. Respondents also contend, among other things, that the appeal is untimely and that they provide school related information to petitioner in Spanish and, therefore, are in compliance with applicable law.

An appeal to the Commissioner pursuant to Education Law §310 is not an appropriate forum to adjudicate claims under Title VI of the Civil Rights Act of 1964 (*Appeal of Cartagena*, 43 Ed Dept Rep 267, Decision No. 14,991; *Appeal of Finkel*, 41 *id.* 74, Decision No. 14,619) or the Equal Educational Opportunities Act (*Appeal of Rits*, 43 Ed Dept Rep 257, Decision No. 14,989; *Appeal of Seligman, et al.*, 31 *id.* 131, Decision No. 12,594) or to obtain relief under the No Child Left Behind Act (*See*, 20 USC §7844(a)(3)(C)) ; *Appeal of Garmaeva*, 43 Ed Dept Rep 253, Decision No. 14,988). Therefore, these claims are dismissed.

Respondents contend that the appeal is untimely. An appeal to the Commissioner must also be commenced within 30 days from the making of a decision or the performance of the act complained of,

---

Effective January 8, 2002, Title I of the Elementary and Secondary Education Act was repealed and re-enacted as Title I of the No Child Left Behind Act. Also, effective January 8, 2002, former Title VII of the Elementary and Secondary Education Act was omitted and re-enacted as Title III of the No Child Left Behind Act.

Accordingly, I have referred petitioner's complaints alleging violations of the No Child Left Behind Act to the appropriate Department staff for resolution.

unless any delay is excused by the Commissioner for good cause shown (8 NYCRR §275.16). Petitioner's claim that respondents failed to provide her with required translation or interpretation services, which if determined to be unlawful, would constitute a continuing wrong subject to complaint at any time (*Appeal of Upstate Home for Children, Inc.*, 43 Ed Dept Rep 505, Decision No. 15,067; *Appeal of Nettles*, 31 *id.* 437, Decision No. 12,691). Therefore, her claims under State law, regulation and policy are timely.

In an appeal to the Commissioner, petitioner has the burden of demonstrating a clear right to the relief requested and the burden of establishing the facts upon which she seeks relief (8 NYCRR §275.10; *Appeal of Cartagena*, *supra*, *Appeal of Kessler*, 43 Ed Dept Rep 170, Decision No. 14,958). Education Law §3201 prohibits discrimination in student admission or assignment to public schools based on race, creed, color or national origin. The petition is devoid of any allegation that petitioner's daughter has been denied admission to the district schools or assigned to a school on a prohibited ground. Consequently, I find no basis for petitioner's §3201 claim.

Moreover, petitioner has failed to submit the regulation and resolution she contends were violated as part of her petition and has failed to establish that respondent violated any specific provision of the regulation or resolution. Accordingly, petitioner has not sustained her burden on claims that respondents violated either the resolution or regulation (*Appeal of Ravick*, 40 Ed Dept Rep 262, Decision No. 14,477).

Part 154 of the Commissioner's regulations requires each board of education to "distribute to parents, or other persons in parental relation to pupils with limited English proficiency, school related information in English or when necessary the language they understand" (8 NYCRR §§154.3(c) and 154.4(a)). Petitioner asserts that she speaks Spanish and that respondents have not provided all school related information in Spanish.

As part of their answer, respondents submit unrefuted affidavits from I.S.'s bilingual education teacher and the principal of P.S. 145, both of whom are fluent in Spanish.

I.S.'s teacher avers that in September 2003 she held an introductory presentation conducted in Spanish regarding her bilingual kindergarten class and that petitioner was present and received translated materials regarding the topics and subjects that would be covered in class. The teacher avers that in November 2003 petitioner met with her at the school's "Open School Afternoon" where parents were invited in to discuss their child's progress with their teacher. She states that she and petitioner discussed I.S.'s academic progress in Spanish and that she gave petitioner I.S.'s translated report card. The teacher attached copies of translated materials she provided to petitioner during the school year, including I.S.'s translated report card with petitioner's signature evidencing receipt thereof.

The principal of P.S. 145 avers that eighty-one of the one hundred thirty eight staff members at the school are fluent in Spanish. She avers that there are staff members always available to translate written and oral information for parents who do not understand English upon request. The principal states that Parent Teacher Association meetings are conducted in Spanish and English. She also avers that documents are routinely sent home to parents in Spanish and English and has attached examples of such translated documents including a notice of Parent Teacher Association meeting, school calendars, and a pamphlet describing the dual language program at the school. The principal further avers that petitioner enrolled I.S. in a bilingual class and attaches a copy of petitioner's translated Home Language Survey and Parent Survey and Program Selection forms. The principal further states that petitioner attended a parent workshop in November 2003 entitled "Aims and Objectives of Bilingual Programs" presented by a representative from Region 4 and the bilingual coordinator from P.S. 145, who is fluent in Spanish. Finally, the principal states that while the school nurse does not speak Spanish, the school's health aide in the medical room is present throughout the day and is available for translation.

The principal further states that petitioner submitted forms for her daughter's medication and that both the bilingual coordinator and the parent coordinator contacted petitioner several times and spoke to her in Spanish regarding her need to bring her daughter's medication to school. Petitioner subsequently brought the medication to school in April 2003.

As noted above, in an appeal to the Commissioner, petitioner has the burden of establishing the facts entitling her to relief. After careful review of the record before me, I find petitioner has not met her burden of proving that respondents have violated Part 154 of the Commissioner's regulations.

THE APPEAL IS DISMISSED.

Decision No. 15,176

Appeal of A STUDENT SUSPECTED OF HAVING A DISABILITY, by his parent, from action of the Board of Education of the City School District of the City of New York, the Chancellor, and Marcia Lyles, Superintendent of Region 8, regarding provision of school related information.

(February 16, 2005)

APPEARANCES OF COUNSEL

Anusuya Chatterjee, Esq., attorney for petitioner

Michael A. Cardozo, Corporation Counsel, attorney for respondents, *Theresa Crotty* and *Joshua Chao, Esqs.*, of counsel

DECISION OF THE COMMISSIONER

MILLS, Commissioner.—Petitioner appeals the alleged failure of the Board of Education of the City School District of the City of New York, the Chancellor, and Superintendent Lyles (hereinafter "respondents") to provide her with school related information in a language that she understands. The appeal must be dismissed.

Petitioner's son is a student who attended third grade at P.S. 18 in Region 8 during the 2003-2004 school year. Petitioner's son is not a limited English proficient student. Petitioner's primary language is Spanish. According to her petition, she does not speak or understand English proficiently.

Petitioner alleges that respondents failed to provide her with required translation and interpretation services. Petitioner contends, therefore, that respondents have violated her rights under federal law, including Title I of the Elementary and Secondary Education Act , Title III of the Elementary and Secondary Education Act , Title VI of the Civil Rights Act of 1964, and the Equal Educational

---

Effective January 8, 2002, Title I of the Elementary and Secondary Education Act was repealed and re-enacted as Title I of the No Child Left Behind Act. Also, effective January 8, 2002, former Title VII of the Elementary and Secondary Education Act was omitted and re-enacted as Title III of the No Child Left Behind Act.

Opportunities Act of 1974. Petitioner further claims that respondents have violated her rights under New York State Education Law §3201, Part 200 of the Commissioner's regulations, a New York City Board of Education Resolution on the "Establishment of Policy on Provision of Translation and Interpretation Services for Limited-English Speaking Parents," and Chancellor's Regulations pertaining to Parent Association meetings and student promotions. She seeks an order directing respondents to comply with these provisions. On June 28, 2004, petitioner's request for interim relief was denied.

Respondents seek dismissal of petitioner's federal claims on procedural grounds. Respondents also contend, among other things, that the appeal is untimely and that they provide school related information to petitioner in Spanish and, therefore, are in compliance with applicable law.

An appeal to the Commissioner pursuant to Education Law §310 is not an appropriate forum to adjudicate claims under Title VI of the Civil Rights Act of 1964 (*Appeal of Cartagena*, 43 Ed Dept Rep 267, Decision No. 14,991; *Appeal of Finkel*, 41 *id.* 74, Decision No. 14,619) or the Equal Educational Opportunities Act (*Appeal of Rits*, 43 Ed Dept Rep 257, Decision No. 14,989; *Appeal of Seligman, et al.*, 31 *id.* 131, Decision No. 12,594) or to obtain relief under the No Child Left Behind Act (*See*, 20 USC §7844(a)(3)(C) ; *Appeal of Garmaeva*, 43 Ed Dept Rep 253, Decision No. 14,988). Therefore, these claims are dismissed.

An appeal to the Commissioner must also be commenced within 30 days from the making of the decision or the performance of the act complained of, unless any delay is excused by the Commissioner for good cause shown (8 NYCRR §275.16). Petitioner's claim that respondents failed to provide her with required translation or interpretation services, which if determined to be unlawful, would constitute a continuing wrong subject to complaint at any time (*Appeal of Upstate Home for Children, Inc.*, 43 Ed Dept Rep 505, Decision No. 15,067; *Appeal of Nettles*, 31 *id.* 437, Decision No. 12,691). Therefore, her claims under State law, regulation and policy are timely.

** Accordingly, I have referred petitioner's complaints alleging violations of the No Child Left Behind Act to the appropriate Department staff for resolution.

In an appeal to the Commissioner, petitioner has the burden of demonstrating a clear legal right to the relief requested and the burden of establishing the facts upon which she seeks relief (8 NYCRR §275.10; *Appeal of Cartagena, supra*; *Appeal of Kessler*, 43 Ed Dept Rep 170, Decision No. 14,958). Education Law §3201 prohibits discrimination in student admission or assignment to public schools based on race, creed, color or national origin. The petition is devoid of any allegation that petitioner's son has been denied admission to the district schools or assigned to a school on a prohibited ground. Consequently, I find no basis for petitioner's §3201 claim (*Appeal of Cartagena, supra*).

Moreover, petitioner has failed to submit the regulations or resolution she contends were violated as part of her petition and has failed to establish that respondent violated any specific provision of the regulations or resolution. Accordingly, petitioner has not sustained her burden on claims that respondents violated either the regulations or resolution (*Appeal of Ravick*, 40 Ed Dept Rep 262, Decision No. 14,477).

Finally, to maintain an appeal pursuant to Education Law §310, a party must be aggrieved in the sense of having suffered personal injury to his or her civil, personal or property rights (*Appeal of J.L.*, 41 Ed Dept Rep 62, Decision No. 14,615). The record in this appeal is devoid of any evidence that petitioner's son has been identified as a student with a disability as defined under Education Law §4401(1) and §200.1(zz) of the Regulations of the Commissioner. Consequently, I find petitioner has no standing for her Part 200 claim (*Appeal of Finkel, supra*).

THE APPEAL IS DISMISSED.

Decision No. 15,177

Appeal of M.L., individually and on behalf of her daughter J.L., from action of the Board of Education of the City School District of the City of New York, the Chancellor, and Reyes Irizarry, Superintendent of Region 4, regarding provision of school related information.

(February 17, 2005)

APPEARANCES OF COUNSEL

Anusuya Chatterjee, Esq., attorney for petitioner

Michael A. Cardozo, Corporation Counsel, attorney for respondents, *Theresa Crotty, Esq.*, of counsel

DECISION OF THE COMMISSIONER

MILLS, Commissioner.—Petitioner appeals the alleged failure of the Board of Education of the City School District of the City of New York, the Chancellor, and Superintendent Irizarry (hereinafter "respondents") to provide her with school related information in a language that she understands. The appeal must be dismissed.

Petitioner's daughter, M.L., is a student who attended sixth grade at I.S. 291-Roland Hayes in Region 4 during the 2003-2004 school year. M.L. is not a limited English proficient student. Petitioner's primary language is Spanish. According to her petition, she does not speak or understand English proficiently.

Petitioner alleges that respondents failed to provide her with required translation or interpretation services. Petitioner contends, therefore, that respondents have violated her rights under federal law, including Title I of the Elementary and Secondary Education Act , Title III of the Elementary and Secondary Education Act , Title VI of the Civil Rights Act of 1964, and the Equal Educational Opportunities Act of 1974. Petitioner further claims that respondents have violated her rights under New York State

Education Law §3201, Part 154 of the Commissioner's regulations and related New York State Education Department guidelines, and a Chancellor's Regulation pertaining to Parent Association meetings. She seeks an order directing respondents to comply with these provisions. On June 28, 2004, petitioner's request for interim relief was denied.

Respondents seek dismissal of petitioner's federal claims on procedural grounds. Respondents also contend, among other things,

---

Effective January 8, 2002, Title I of the Elementary and Secondary Education Act was repealed and re-enacted as Title I of the No Child Left Behind Act. Also, effective January 8, 2002, Title VII of the Elementary and Secondary Education Act was omitted and re-enacted as Title III of the No Child Left Behind Act.

that the appeal is untimely and that they provide school related information to petitioner in Spanish and, therefore, are in compliance with applicable law.

An appeal to the Commissioner pursuant to Education Law §310 is not an appropriate forum to adjudicate claims under Title VI of the Civil Rights Act of 1964 (*Appeal of Cartagena*, 43 Ed Dept Rep 267, Decision No. 14,991; *Appeal of Finkel*, 41 *id.* 74, Decision No. 14,619) or the Equal Educational Opportunities Act (*Appeal of Rits*, 43 Ed Dept Rep 257, Decision No. 14,989; *Appeal of Seligman, et al.*, 31 *id.* 131, Decision No. 12,594) or to obtain relief under the No Child Left Behind Act (*See*, 20 USC §7844(a)(3)(C) ; *Appeal of Garmaeva*, 43 Ed Dept Rep 253, Decision No. 14,988). Therefore, these claims are dismissed.

An appeal to the Commissioner must also be commenced within 30 days from the making of the decision or the performance of the act complained of, unless any delay is excused by the Commissioner for good cause shown (8 NYCRR §275.16). Petitioner's claim that respondents failed to provide her with required translation or interpretation services, which if determined to be unlawful, would constitute a continuing wrong subject to complaint at any time (*Appeal of Upstate Home for Children, Inc.*, 43 Ed Dept Rep 505, Decision No. 15,067; *Appeal of Nettles*, 31 *id.* 437, Decision No. 12,691). Therefore, her claims under State law, regulation and policy are timely.

In an appeal to the Commissioner, petitioner has the burden of demonstrating a clear legal right to the relief requested and the burden of establishing the facts upon which she seeks relief (8 NYCRR §275.10; *Appeal of Cartagena, supra*; *Appeal of Kessler*, 43 Ed Dept Rep 170, Decision No. 14,958). Education Law §3201 prohibits discrimination in student admission or assignment to public schools based on race, creed, color or national origin. The petition is devoid of any allegation that petitioner's daughter has been denied admission to the district schools or assigned to a school on a prohibited ground. Consequently, I find no basis for petitioner's §3201 claim (*Appeal of Cartagena, supra*).

** Accordingly, I have referred petitioner's complaints alleging violations of the No Child Left Behind Act to the appropriate Department staff for resolution.

Part 154 of the Commissioner's regulations requires each board of education to "distribute to parents, or other persons in parental relation to pupils with limited English proficiency, school related information in English or when necessary, the language they understand" (8 NYCRR §§154.3(c) and 154.4(a)). Petitioner concedes that her daughter is not a limited English proficient student. Consequently, I find no basis for petitioner's Part 154 claim.

Moreover, petitioner has failed to submit the regulation she contends was violated as part of her petition and has failed to establish that respondents violated any specific provision of the regulation. Accordingly, petitioner has not sustained her burden on her claim that respondents violated the regulation (*Appeal of Ravick*, 40 Ed Dept Rep 262, Decision No. 14,477).

THE APPEAL IS DISMISSED.

Decision No. 15,178

Appeal of CATALINA MARTINEZ, individually and on behalf of her son ROGER, from action of the Board of Education of the City School District of the City of New York, the Chancellor, and Reyes Irizarry, Superintendent of Region 4, regarding provision of school related information.

(February 17, 2005)

APPEARANCES OF COUNSEL

Anusuya Chatterjee, Esq., attorney for petitioner

Michael A. Cardozo, Corporation Counsel, attorney for respondents, *Theresa Crotty* and *Joshua Chao, Esqs.*, of counsel

DECISION OF THE COMMISSIONER

MILLS, Commissioner.—Petitioner appeals the alleged failure of the Board of Education of the City School District of the City of New York, the Chancellor, and Superintendent Irizarry (hereinafter "respondents") to provide her with school related information in a language that she understands. The appeal must be dismissed.

Petitioner's son is a student who attended fifth grade at P.S. 81Q in Region 5 during the 2003-2004 school year. Roger is not a limited English proficient student. Petitioner's primary language is Spanish.

According to her petition, she does not speak or understand English proficiently.

Petitioner alleges that respondents failed to provide her with required translation and interpretation services. Petitioner contends, therefore, that respondents have violated her rights under federal law, including Title I of the Elementary and Secondary Education Act , Title III of the Elementary and Secondary Education Act , Title VI of the Civil Rights Act of 1964, and the Equal Educational Opportunities Act of 1974. Petitioner further claims that respondents have violated her rights under New York State Education Law §3201 and a Chancellor's Regulation pertaining to Parent Association meetings. She seeks an order directing respondents to comply with these provisions. On June 28, 2004, petitioner's request for interim relief was denied.

Respondents seek dismissal of petitioner's federal claims on procedural grounds. Respondents also contend, among other things, that the appeal is untimely and that they provide school related information to petitioner in Spanish and, therefore, are in compliance with applicable law.

An appeal to the Commissioner pursuant to Education Law §310 is not an appropriate forum to adjudicate claims under Title VI of the Civil Rights Act of 1964 (*Appeal of Cartagena*, 43 Ed Dept Rep 267, Decision No. 14,991; *Appeal of Finkel*, 41 *id.* 74, Decision No. 14,619) or the Equal Educational Opportunities Act (*Appeal of Rits*, 43 Ed Dept Rep 257, Decision No. 14,989; *Appeal of Seligman, et al.*, 31 *id.* 131, Decision No. 12,594) or to obtain relief under the No Child Left Behind Act (*See*, 20 USC §7844(a)(3)(C)[**]; *Appeal of Garmaeva*, 43 Ed Dept Rep 253, Decision No. 14,988). Therefore, these claims are dismissed.

An appeal to the Commissioner must also be commenced within 30 days from the making of the decision or the performance of the act

---

Effective January 8, 2002, Title I of the Elementary and Secondary Education Act was repealed and re-enacted as Title I of the No Child Left Behind Act. Also, effective January 8, 2002, former Title VII of the Elementary and Secondary Education Act was omitted and re-enacted as Title III of the No Child Left Behind Act.

[**] Accordingly, I have referred petitioner's complaints alleging violations of the No Child Left Behind Act to the appropriate Department staff for resolution.

complained of, unless any delay is excused by the Commissioner for good cause shown (8 NYCRR §275.16). Petitioner's claim that respondents failed to provide her with required translation or interpretation services, which if determined to be unlawful, would constitute a continuing wrong subject to complaint at any time (*Appeal of Upstate Home for Children, Inc.*, 43 Ed Dept Rep 505, Decision No. 15,067; *Appeal of Nettles*, 31 *id.* 437, Decision No. 12,691). Therefore, her claims under State law, regulation and policy are timely.

In an appeal to the Commissioner, petitioner has the burden of demonstrating a clear legal right to the relief requested and the burden of establishing the facts upon which she seeks relief (8 NYCRR §275.10; *Appeal of Cartagena*, *supra*; *Appeal of Kessler*, 43 Ed Dept Rep 170, Decision No. 14,958). Education Law §3201 prohibits discrimination in student admission or assignment to public schools based on race, creed, color or national origin. The petition is devoid of any allegation that petitioner's son has been denied admission to the district schools or assigned to a school on a prohibited ground. Consequently, I find no basis for petitioner's §3201 claim (*Appeal of Cartagena*, *supra*).

Moreover, petitioner has failed to submit the regulation she contends was violated as part of her petition and has failed to establish that respondent violated any specific provision of the regulation. Accordingly, petitioner has not sustained her burden on her claim that respondents violated the regulation (*Appeal of Ravick*, 40 Ed Dept Rep 262, Decision No. 14,477).

THE APPEAL IS DISMISSED.

Decision No. 15,179

Appeal of INOCENCIA NOLASCO, individually and on behalf of her daughter BRENDA BATISTA, from action of the Board of Education of the City School District of the City of New York, the Chancellor, and Reyes Irizarry, Superintendent of Region 4, regarding provision of school related information.

(February 24, 2005)

APPEARANCES OF COUNSEL

Anusuya Chatterjee, Esq., attorney for petitioner

Michael A. Cardozo, Corporation Counsel, attorney for respondents, *Theresa Crotty* and *Joshua Chao, Esqs*., of counsel

DECISION OF THE COMMISSIONER

MILLS, Commissioner.—Petitioner appeals the alleged failure of the Board of Education of the City School District of the City of New York, the Chancellor, and Superintendent Irizarry (hereinafter "respondents") to provide her with school related information in a language that she understands. The appeal must be dismissed.

Petitioner's daughter, Brenda, attended twelfth grade at EBC High School for Public Service during the 2003-2004 school year. Brenda is not a limited English proficient student. Petitioner's primary language is Spanish. According to her petition, she does not speak or understand English proficiently.

Petitioner alleges that respondents failed to provide her with required translation and interpretation services. Petitioner contends, therefore, that respondents have violated her rights under federal law, including Title I of the Elementary and Secondary Education Act , Title III of the Elementary and Secondary Education Act , Title VI of the Civil Rights Act of 1964, and the Equal Educational Opportunities Act of 1974. Petitioner further claims that respondents have violated her rights under New York State Education Law §3201 and a New York City Board of Education Resolution on the "Establishment of Policy on Provision of Translation and Interpretation Services for Limited-English Speaking Parents." She seeks an order directing respondents to comply with the above provisions. On June 28, 2004, petitioner's request for interim relief was denied.

Respondents seek dismissal of petitioner's federal claims on procedural grounds. Respondents also contend, among other things, that the appeal is untimely and that they provide school related information to petitioner in Spanish and, therefore, are in compliance with applicable law.

Effective January 8, 2002, Title I of the Elementary and Secondary Education Act was repealed and re-enacted as Title I of the No Child Left Behind Act. Also, effective January 8, 2002, former Title VII of the Elementary and Secondary Education Act was omitted and re-enacted as Title III of the No Child Left Behind Act.

The Commissioner will only consider matters in actual controversy and will not render a decision on a state of facts which no longer exists or which subsequent events have laid to rest (*Appeal of T.D.*, 43 Ed Dept Rep 83, Decision No. 14,927; *Appeal of Baronti*, 42 *id.* 140, Decision No. 14,802; *Appeal of Schrader*, 42 *id.* 47, Decision No. 14,771). In response to a request from my Office of Counsel, respondents report that Brenda has graduated from high school and petitioner has not refuted this information. Accordingly, petitioner's appeal is moot (*Appeal of T.D.*, *supra*; *Appeal of Berkman*, 43 Ed Dept Rep 71, Decision No. 14,921).

THE APPEAL IS DISMISSED.

Decision No. 15,180

Appeal of a STUDENT WITH A DISABILITY from action of the Board of Education of the Enlarged City School District of the City of Newburgh regarding student discipline.

(February 25, 2005)

APPEARANCES OF COUNSEL

Benjamin Ostrer & Associates, P.C., attorneys for petitioner, *Michael Meth, Esq.*, of counsel

Shaw & Perelson, LLP, attorneys for respondent, *David S. Shaw* and *Jillian E. Cass, Esqs.*, of counsel

DECISION OF THE COMMISSIONER

MILLS, Commissioner.—Petitioner appeals a determination by the Board of Education of the Enlarged City School District of the City of Newburgh ("respondent") to suspend petitioner for the remainder of the 2003-2004 school year. The appeal must be dismissed.

Petitioner was involved in a fight that took place on April 20, 2004, at respondent's high school. A disciplinary hearing and a manifestation determination ensued. Respondent's committee on special education ("CSE") found that petitioner had the ability to control his behavior and that his conduct was not a manifestation of his disability. The disciplinary hearing officer found petitioner guilty on one count and recommended that petitioner be suspended for the remainder of the 2003-2004 school year. This recommendation was upheld on appeal to respondent by decision dated May 12, 2004. This appeal ensued. Petitioner alleges that the penalty was excessive and seeks to have his record expunged.

Petitioner also filed a complaint against the district, the high school principal and respondent in New York State Supreme Court on April 30, 2004. The matter was subsequently moved to Federal District Court and on June 3, 2004, the Second Circuit affirmed the granting of a preliminary injunction returning petitioner to school.

On June 24, 2004, petitioner graduated from the district and on June 28, 2004, respondent passed a resolution to expunge the April 20, 2004, incident from petitioner's disciplinary record.

The appeal must be dismissed as moot. The Commissioner of Education will only decide matters in actual controversy and will not render a decision on a state of facts which no longer exists or which subsequent events have laid to rest (*Appeal of M.F. and J.F.*, 43 Ed Dept Rep 174, Decision No. 14,960; *Appeal of a Student With a Disability*, 42 *id.* 111, Decision No. 14,791). Since petitioner has graduated and his record has been expunged, no further meaningful relief can be granted.

In light of the foregoing disposition, I need not address the parties' remaining contentions.

THE APPEAL IS DISMISSED.

Decision No. 15,181

Appeal of JERICHO EDUCATIONAL ADMINISTRATORS ASSOCIATION and JOHN CATUOGNO from action of the Board of Education of the Jericho Union Free School District regarding a retirement incentive.

(February 25, 2005)

APPEARANCES OF COUNSEL

Robert Saperstein, Esq., attorney for petitioners

Ingerman Smith LLP, attorneys for respondent, *Susan Fine, Esq.*, of counsel

DECISION OF THE COMMISSIONER

MILLS, Commissioner.—Petitioners challenge the refusal of the Board of Education of the Jericho Union Free School District ("respondent") to provide petitioner Catuogno ("Catuogno") with a retirement incentive. The appeal must be dismissed.

Catuogno was employed as an assistant principal at Jericho High School until his retirement, effective June 30, 2003. In March 2003, respondent voted to offer certain eligible teachers a $25,000 incentive to retire effective June 30, 2003, or June 30, 2004. The incentive was announced by respondent's superintendent of schools in a March 14, 2003, letter that was apparently sent to district staff.

Shortly thereafter, petitioners consulted with district officials to determine whether Catuogno, whose employment was governed by an agreement between respondent and the Jericho Educational Administrators Association ("the Agreement"), would be eligible for the incentive pursuant to Part Two, Article V(A) ("Article V(A)") thereof, which provides, in part, that "[a]ll . . . fringe benefits provided for teachers shall also be provided for administrators . . . ." After being advised that Catuogno was not eligible for the incentive, petitioners filed a contract grievance. By memorandum dated October 10, 2003, respondent's superintendent notified the Association's president that the grievance had been denied. Petitioners then commenced this appeal, which constitutes the final step of the grievance process under the Agreement.

Petitioners contend that the retirement incentive offered to respondent's teachers is a "fringe benefit" to which petitioner Catuogno is entitled under Article V(A). Petitioners claim that respondent has previously interpreted this provision to include retirement incentives, but refused to do so here in retaliation for the Association's public endorsement and support of certain candidates for the board of education at the district's 2003 annual election. Petitioners request that I find that the district violated the Agreement and direct respondent to pay Catuogno the $25,000 retirement incentive, with interest.

Respondent denies that it previously paid administrators a retirement incentive pursuant to the parity provision (in Article V[A]) and asserts that historically, the provision has generally been limited to the benefits explicitly delineated therein, namely, health, disability, dental and life insurance.

The appeal must be dismissed. In an appeal to the Commissioner, petitioners have the burden of demonstrating a clear legal right to the relief requested and the burden of establishing the facts upon which they seek relief (8 NYCRR §275.10; *Appeal of M.F. and J.F.*, 43 Ed

Dept Rep 174, Decision No. 14,960; *Appeal of Kessler*, 43 *id.* 170, Decision No. 14,958). When construing contractual provisions, the appropriate standard is not whether a particular clause is susceptible of a different interpretation, but whether the school board's interpretation is unreasonable or otherwise arbitrary or capricious (*Appeal of Caruana*, 41 Ed Dept Rep 227, Decision No. 14,671; *Appeal of Lilly*, 39 *id.* 601, Decision No. 14,324; *Appeals of Bodnar, et al.*, 29 *id.* 516, Decision No. 12,369). I find that petitioners have failed to establish that the administrators' parity provision entitles Catuogno to the retirement incentive offered to district teachers.

The contract provisions at issue provide, in pertinent part:

ARTICLE V — FRINGE BENEFITS

> A. All (except the provision listed in Section B below) of the fringe benefits provided for teachers shall also be provided for administrators. This shall include such items as health; disability; dental and life insurances. The Jericho Educational Administrators Association shall be an equal party with the other staff organizations to all activities relative to the implementation of all fringe benefits.
>
> B. The list of benefits does not include released time for Association officers. In addition, the per employee amount previously granted as an equivalent for the teacher welfare trust is excluded.

Petitioners argue that a retirement incentive constitutes a "fringe benefit" because Article V includes a provision addressing administrators' entitlement to a lump sum payment upon retirement. Petitioners further argue that because retirement incentives are not specifically excluded under section B, they constitute a fringe benefit to which administrators are entitled under section A. In further support of this interpretation, petitioners assert that respondent applied this parity provision to teacher retirement incentives offered during the 1992-1993 and 1998-1999 school years.

Respondent's assistant superintendent for educational operations and human resources ("assistant superintendent") denies that the parity provision has ever been applied to an extra-contractual retirement incentive. He explains that although respondent previously provided certain administrators with a retirement incentive, on each occasion, the incentive was separately negotiated.

To support this contention, respondent submits two agreements dated June 25, 1992, and February 11, 1999, each amending the Agreement in effect between the parties to include a retirement incentive for eligible administrators retiring at the end of the 1992-1993 and 1998-1999 school years, respectively. The assistant superintendent further explains that in this case, respondent did not want to offer administrators a retirement incentive because the district recently had difficulty filling vacant administrator positions.

On the record before me, I find that petitioners have failed to establish that the teacher's retirement incentive is a "fringe benefit" covered by Article V(A) of the Agreement or that respondent's interpretation was unreasonable. Preliminarily, I reject petitioners' contention that the retirement incentive is covered by Article V(A) simply because is it not specifically excluded under Article V(B). There is nothing in the Agreement that suggests that only those benefits that are specifically listed under Article V(B) may be excluded. Further, although Article V(A) refers to "[a]ll" fringe benefits, the provision also provides examples of the types of benefits covered: health, disability, dental and life insurances. Under the rule of *ejusdem generis*, the meaning of "[a]ll . . . fringe benefits" in this context is understood to cover only the type or kind of fringe benefits specifically enumerated (*see*, 22 N.Y. Jur.2d, Contracts, §255). While I need not decide the precise scope of benefits covered by Article V(A), I find that the lump sum payment offered to induce teachers to retire does not fall within the class of benefits intended for coverage under this provision. Thus, I cannot conclude that respondent's interpretation was unreasonable.

I further find that petitioners have failed to establish that respondent has previously applied the parity provision to a teacher retirement incentive. Neither the June 25, 1992, nor the February 11, 1999, agreements amending the parties' existing Agreement references the teachers' retirement incentive or the administrators' parity provision. In addition, the 1992 administrators' retirement incentive exceeded the incentive initially offered that year to the district's teachers. Moreover, as respondent correctly points out, if in fact, administrators were entitled to the 1992 and 1999 teacher retirement incentives by virtue of the Agreement's parity provision, the parties would not have needed to amend the Agreement to explicitly provide for such. Accordingly, petitioners have failed to demonstrate that the earlier administrator incentives were provided pursuant to the parity provision at issue here. Thus, I cannot conclude that respondent was arbitrary or capricious.

In light of this disposition, I need not address the parties' remaining contentions.

THE APPEAL IS DISMISSED.

Decision No. 15,182

Appeal of MARY McCOLLUM from action of the Board of Education of the Sidney Central School District, Stephanie Fredenburg, and Cathryn Barnes, regarding a reduction of services.

(March 7, 2005)

APPEARANCES OF COUNSEL

James R. Sandner, Esq., attorney for petitioner, *Kevin H. Harren,* Esq., of counsel

Ferrara, Fiorenza, Larrison, Barrett & Reitz, PC, attorneys for respondent Board of Education of the Sidney Central School District, *Marc H. Reitz* and *Norman H. Gross, Esqs.*, of counsel

DECISION OF THE COMMISSIONER

MILLS, Commissioner.—Petitioner seeks to annul a determination of the Board of Education of the Sidney Central School District ("respondent") reducing her services from a full-time position to a .5 part-time position at the end of the 2002-2003 school year. The appeal must be sustained.

Petitioner is a certified teaching assistant who was employed full-time by respondent during the 2002-2003 school year. On June 26, 2003, respondent terminated two of its five full-time teaching assistants, and reduced petitioner from full-time to a .5 part-time position effective September 1, 2003. Petitioner claims, and respondent admits, that the two teaching assistants who were terminated had less seniority as teaching assistants than petitioner, and were terminated properly.

Petitioner claims that she was improperly reduced from full-time to .5 part-time in violation of Education Law §§2510 and 3013, and Part 30 of the Commissioner's regulations, because she was not the least senior person in the tenure area of teaching assistant. Petitioner has named two individual respondents, who were not terminated, and petitioner claims, and respondent admits, that these named respondents also had less seniority than petitioner, but were retained in full-time status. (Respondents Fredenburgh and Barnes were personally served with copies of the notice of petition and petition, but have not appeared in this appeal.)

This appeal arose because of respondent's practice of classifying teaching assistants by specific subject assignments. As a result, respondent purportedly created three "layoff units" within the tenure area of teaching assistant, which it characterizes as teaching assistants with special skills, teaching assistants in the special education program, and teaching assistants in the general instructional program. In making its determination, respondent made reductions only in the "special education layoff unit" that included petitioner and the two persons terminated, and did not make its decision based on seniority among all of its teaching assistants.

Respondent maintains that such "layoff units are permissible" and that the provisions of Education Law §3013 regarding seniority and layoffs are not applicable to teaching assistants.

These same arguments were advanced in *Appeal of Krason, et al.* (41 Ed Dept Rep 305, Decision No. 14,695), and were rejected. While that determination was originally annulled (*sub nom., Matter of Madison-Oneida BOCES v. Mills*, Sup. Ct., Albany County, Kavanagh, J., December 20, 2002), Supreme Court's determination was reversed by the Appellate Division, Third Department (2 AD3d 1240), and the determination of the Appellate Division was recently affirmed by the Court of Appeals (_____ NY3d ______, December 21, 2004). The Court of Appeals held:

> The legislative history of §3013(2) supports the conclusion that persons hired by a board of education or a BOCES should be laid off according to seniority. Thus, for lay-off purposes, TAs fall within the ambit of §3013[2]) (*Sic.*, uncorrected slip op., p.7.) Teaching assistants, which is a separate tenure area from teachers, should not have their abolition rights judged by whether or not they meet the qualifications and credentials of teachers . . . Their separate credentials

have been accorded tenure, and the TAs should have due process rights within that system.

As a result, the three-part system of "layoff units" that respondent has fashioned is invalid, and has been from its inception. Respondent was, and is, obligated to abolish any position within the tenure area of teaching assistant in accordance with Education Law §3013(2).

Consistent with the determination of the Court of Appeals, the appeal must be sustained.

THE APPEAL IS SUSTAINED.

IT IS ORDERED that the determination of respondent Board of Education of the Sidney Central School District reducing petitioner's services as of September 1, 2003, be, and the same hereby is annulled; and

IT IS FURTHER ORDERED that respondent reinstate petitioner to a position as a full-time teaching assistant as of September 1, 2003, with back salary and benefits from that date, less any compensation she may have otherwise earned in excess of her salary as a .5 part-time teaching assistant.

Decision No. 15,183

Appeal of MARYANNE DENOVA, KATHY EATON, JANET EZMAN, PATRICIA HIGGINS, JANET LENHART, ROSE LOMANACO, JULIE MOOLENSCHOT, MICHELE STEVENS, and LAURA WICKMAN from action of the Madison-Oneida Board of Cooperative Educational Services, Amy Galway, Mark Russell, Kelly Ingalls, Tammy Foster, Richard Dando, Deborah Flagler, Michael Schwartz, Christine McCurdy, and John Rork regarding termination of services.

(March 7, 2005)

APPEARANCES OF COUNSEL

James R. Sandner, Esq., attorney for petitioners, *Kevin H. Harren, Esq.*, of counsel

Ferrara, Fiorenza, Larrison, Barrett & Reitz, PC, attorneys for respondent Madison-Oneida Board of Cooperative Educational Services, *Henry F. Sabota* and *Craig M. Atlas, Esqs.*, of counsel

DECISION OF THE COMMISSIONER

MILLS, Commissioner.—Petitioners seek to annul a determination of the Madison-Oneida Board of Cooperative Educational Services ("BOCES") terminating their services at the end of the 2001-2002 school year. The appeal must be dismissed.

Petitioners are nine certified teaching assistants, who were employed by BOCES during the 2001-2002 school year. On June 1, 2002, BOCES terminated 11 of the approximately 65 teaching assistants it then employed, including petitioners, effective June 30, 2002. Petitioners claim that one of the 11 teaching assistants was terminated properly, and that another was recalled to service prior to the commencement of this appeal on July 19, 2002.

Petitioners claim that they were improperly terminated pursuant to Education Law §§2510 and 3013, and Part 30 of the Commissioner's regulations, because they were not the least senior persons in the tenure area of teaching assistant. Petitioners have named nine individual respondents, all of whom are teaching assistants whose services were not terminated. Petitioners claim that the individual respondents are among the nine least senior teaching assistants, and that all have less seniority than petitioners. (Although all nine individual respondents were personally served with copies of the notice of petition and petition, none has entered an appearance in this matter.)

This appeal arose because of BOCES' maintenance, since at least 1979, of a policy of classifying tenure areas by both position and specific subject assignment. In applying this policy to teaching assistants BOCES created approximately 30 different specific tenure areas (*e.g.*, "teaching assistant-heavy equipment" and "teaching assistant-science"), and teaching assistants received probationary appointments to these specific subject-related areas (*see Appeal of Krason, et al.*, 41 Ed Dept Rep 305, Decision No. 14,695).

I issued an interim order in this appeal on August 26, 2002, directing BOCES to reinstate petitioners as teaching assistants.

Thereafter, BOCES' director of personnel submitted an affidavit indicating that prior to the issuance of my interim order, petitioners

Eaton, Higgins, Lenhart, and Lomanaco had already been recalled by BOCES to positions as full-time teaching assistants. (Petitioners Eaton, Higgins, and Lenhart accepted these offers of employment, while petitioner Lomanaco declined.) As a result, the appeal must be dismissed for lack of standing as to petitioners Eaton, Higgins, and Lenhart, since they have been reemployed and thus are no longer aggrieved.

The record also indicates that, on August 29, 2002, after receiving my order, BOCES offered teaching assistant positions to petitioners DeNova, Ezman, Moolenschot, Stevens, and Wickman. Petitioners Ezman, Moolenschot, and Stevens accepted the positions offered and presumably continued to work through the 2002-2003 school year. Petitioner DeNova declined the offer. Petitioner Wickman also declined the offer, because she had been offered and accepted a position as a full-time case manager on August 1, 2002. As a result, the appeal must be dismissed for lack of standing as to petitioners Ezman, Moolenschot, Stevens, and Wickman, since they have been reemployed and thus are no longer aggrieved.

Petitioners Lomanaco and DeNova also lack standing to pursue this appeal. The record indicates that petitioner Lomanaco was offered reinstatement to a full-time teaching position on August 19, 2002, and declined on August 27. She was again offered a full-time teaching assistant position on August 29, 2002, and declined the position in writing on August 29. Petitioner DeNova was offered a full-time teaching assistant position on August 29, 2002, and declined in writing on August 31. Neither written declination contains any indication that the petitioner wished to be reemployed but for some reason was unable to accept respondent's offer, nor do they state any other significant circumstances. Petitioners Lomanaco and DeNova did not indicate any temporary impediment to being reemployed, and they expressed no interest in the positions (*cf.*, *Matter of Lewis v. Cleveland Hill UFSD*, 119 AD2d 263; *Matter of Sopher v. Board of Educ., East Ramapo CSD*, 97 AD2d 768). Based upon the record before me, I must conclude that these petitioners have no interest in the positions offered, and can no longer be considered aggrieved.

Although the appeal is dismissed on procedural grounds, I note that the "layoff units" at issue here have been found impermissible (*Appeal of Krason*, *supra*). On review of *Krason*, the courts have also determined that Education Law §3013(2) does apply to teaching assistants (*Matter of Madison-Oneida BOCES v. Mills*, 2 AD3d 1240; aff'd ____NY3d ____, December 21, 2004).

THE APPEAL IS DISMISSED.

Decision No. 15,184

Appeal of A STUDENT SUSPECTED OF HAVING A DISABILITY, by his parents, from action of the Board of Education of the Lakeland Central School District regarding student discipline.

(March 7, 2005)

APPEARANCES OF COUNSEL

Peter D. Hoffman, Esq., attorney for petitioners

Shaw & Perelson, LLP, attorneys for respondent, *David S. Shaw, Esq.*, of counsel

DECISION OF THE COMMISSIONER

MILLS, Commissioner.—Petitioners appeal a determination by the Board of Education of the Lakeland Central School District ("respondent") to suspend their son from school. The appeal must be dismissed.

On December 10, 2003, petitioners' son was involved in an incident at respondent's high school and was accused of physically attacking another student. A superintendent's hearing was held on January 6 and 14, 2004. Prior to the conclusion of the hearing, petitioners requested that the school district conduct a manifestation determination to ascertain whether their son's misconduct was related to a disability. Petitioners' request was denied and their son was found guilty of the charges against him. The hearing officer recommended that petitioners' son be suspended for the remainder of the 2003-2004 school year.

By letter dated January 23, 2004, respondent's superintendent affirmed the hearing officer's findings on guilt and penalty. Petitioners appealed to respondent. Respondent affirmed on March 4, 2004. Respondent's decision was mailed to petitioners on March 9, 2004, and received on March 10, 2004. This appeal ensued.

Petitioners contend that the decision to suspend their son was inappropriate and the penalty excessive. Petitioners contend that their son should have been afforded protection under the Individuals with Disabilities Education Act ("IDEA") and that the hearing officer erred by refusing to permit a manifestation determination prior to imposing the penalty. Petitioners further allege that the decision to suspend their son was not based on substantial evidence and that the hearing officer failed to adequately consider the testimony of their psychologist. Petitioners also allege a number of procedural and evidentiary defects and maintain that the hearing officer was biased and incompetent. Petitioners request that their son's suspension be vacated or reduced, or that their son be placed in an alternative school setting.

Respondent asserts that the appeal is untimely and there was no notice of petition included with the pleadings. Respondent further asserts that petitioners' son was not entitled to a manifestation review prior to the conclusion of the superintendent's hearing. Respondent contends that the finding of guilt and penalty were proper.

A memorandum of law may not be used to add belated assertions or exhibits that are not part of the pleadings (*Appeal of Smolen*, 43 Ed Dept Rep 296, Decision No. 15,000; *Appeal of T.M.*, 41 *id.* 443, Decision No. 14,740; *Appeal of George*, 40 *id.* 509, Decision No. 14,540). Petitioners offer new allegations and exhibits in their memorandum of law. Therefore, I have not considered the new exhibits or those portions of petitioners' memorandum of law that raise new arguments.

The appeal must be dismissed because petitioners failed to serve a notice of petition on respondent. The notice of petition secures jurisdiction over the intended respondent and alerts a party that he or she is required to appear in the appeal and answer (8 NYCRR §275.11(a); *Appeal of Hauk*, 44 Ed Dept Rep 36, Decision No. 15,090; *Appeal of Khalid*, 40 *id.* 621, Decision No. 14,570; *Appeal of Heller*, 38 *id.* 335, Decision No. 14,048). A petition that does not contain the language required by §275.11 is fatally defective, and does not secure jurisdiction over the intended respondent (*Appeal of Hauk*, *supra*).

The appeal must also be dismissed as untimely. An appeal to the Commissioner must be commenced within 30 days from the making of the decision or the performance of the act complained of, unless any delay is excused by the Commissioner for good cause shown (8 NYCRR §275.16; *Appeal of C.D.*, 41 Ed Dept Rep 147, Decision No. 14,642; *Appeal of Miller*, 35 *id.* 451, Decision No. 13,598). Petitioners received respondent's determination on March 10, 2004. The 30-day period in which to file an appeal therefore expired no later than April

9, 2004. Although petitioners attempted to effectuate service on April 8, 12 and 19, none of the methods of service complied with the requirements of §275.8 of the Commissioner's regulations. Petitioners have the burden of proving service in compliance with the Commissioner's regulations (*Appeal of Cauley*, 33 Ed Dept Rep 359, Decision No. 13,077). Since proper service was not effectuated until April 21, 2004, and there being no good cause shown for petitioners' delay, the appeal must be dismissed as untimely.

The appeal must also be dismissed as moot. The Commissioner of Education will only consider matters in actual controversy and will not render a decision on a state of facts that no longer exists or that subsequent events have laid to rest (*Appeal of P.F. and M.F.*, 42 Ed Dept Rep 390, Decision No. 14,890; *Appeal of Lascala*, 38 *id.* 16, Decision No. 13,974). Petitioners requested that their son's suspension be "vacated," but did not seek expungement of his records. Since the suspension has been served and petitioners' son has returned to school, no meaningful relief can be granted, and the appeal is moot (*Appeal of V.L.*, 44 Ed Dept Rep ___, Decision No. 15,132; *Appeal of D.W.*, 43 *id.* 188, Decision No. 14,965; *Appeal of R.R. and K.R.*, 41 *id.* 405, Decision No. 14,726).

Nor do I find merit to petitioners' contention that their son was a student with a disability at the time of the incident. There is no evidence that a referral was ever made to respondent's Committee on Special Education ("CSE") pursuant to §200.4 of the Commissioner's regulations, or that the standard was met to deem the school district to have had knowledge that he was a student with a disability before the behavior that precipitated disciplinary action. Section 201.5(b)(1)-(4) of the Commissioner's regulations sets forth that a school district shall be deemed to have knowledge that a student had a disability if prior to the time the behavior occurred: (1) the parent of such student has expressed concern to school personnel in writing that the student is in need of special education; (2) the behavior or performance of the student demonstrates the need for special education; (3) the parent of the student has requested that an individual evaluation of the student be conducted; or (4) a teacher of the student, or other personnel of the school district, has expressed concern about the behavior or performance of the student to the director of special education or to other school district personnel. To the extent petitioners suspected after the incident that their son had a disability, they were entitled to make a referral to respondent's CSE. The record indicates that the student was referred to the CSE following the disciplinary hearing and the CSE determined that the student was not a student with a disability.

In light of this disposition, I need not address the parties' remaining contentions.

THE APPEAL IS DISMISSED.

Decision No. 15,185

Appeal of DENNIS CENTOFRANCHI from action of the Board of Education of the Salem Central School District, Thomas Steele, Board President, and Richard Wheeler, Superintendent, regarding the distribution of textbooks.

(March 7, 2005)

APPEARANCES OF COUNSEL

Bartlett, Pontiff, Stewart & Rhodes, P.C., attorneys for respondents, *J. Lawrence Paltrowitz, Esq.*, of counsel

DECISION OF THE COMMISSIONER

MILLS, Commissioner.—Petitioner challenges the policy of the Board of Education of the Salem Central School District ("respondent board" or "board") and the actions of its president and superintendent (collectively referred to with the board as "respondents") pertaining to the loan of textbooks to nonpublic school students. The appeal must be dismissed.

Petitioner and his two sons reside in the Salem Central School District ("district"). Petitioner's children attend The Albany Academy, a nonpublic school. By letter dated June 30, 2004, petitioner notified the superintendent that he believed the district's proposed policy concerning distribution of textbooks was unlawful. On July 7, 2004, respondent board adopted the policy despite petitioner's objection. By letter dated July 7, 2004, petitioner requested a listing of all textbooks, by subject and grade, that the district would be providing to his sons and to similar public school students. By letter dated July 12, 2004, the superintendent replied that the district was in the process of comparing textbook requests with the supply available in the district's inventory, and that the petitioner would be notified as to what textbooks would be provided to his sons once the review was complete. This appeal ensued. Petitioner's request for interim relief was denied on August 17, 2004.

Petitioner alleges that the board's textbook loan policy violates Education Law §701 and Part 21 of the Rules of the Board of Regents. Petitioner also contends that respondents failed to provide him with a list of textbooks that will be supplied to his sons and to public school students in the same classes as his sons. Petitioner requests that I declare the textbook loan policy illegal and direct respondent board to adopt a new policy in accordance with the Education Law. Petitioner also demands that all textbook loan requests from The Albany Academy and other nonpublic schools be filled in a timely manner. Finally, petitioner requests that I withhold public monies from the district for willfully violating the Education Law.

Respondents contend that the textbook policy does not violate the Education Law or the Rules of the Board Regents. Respondents also contend that petitioner fails to state a cause of action, lacks standing and has failed to join necessary parties.

Subsequent to the filing of this appeal respondents filed a supplemental affidavit and exhibit pursuant to §276.5 of the Commissioner's regulations which I have accepted for consideration herein. The affidavit indicates that on September 1, 2004, respondent board adopted a revised textbook loan policy regarding the provision of textbooks and/or workbooks to resident pupils attending nonpublic schools.

The Commissioner of Education only decides matters in actual controversy and will not render a decision on a state of facts which no longer exist or which subsequent events have laid to rest (*Appeal of Cordisco*, 44 Ed Dept Rep 35, Decision No. 15,089; *Appeal of Kushner*, 43 *id.* 423, Decision No. 15,040). Because respondent board has adopted a revised textbook loan policy, this appeal must be dismissed as moot.

In light of this disposition, I need not address the parties' remaining contentions.

THE APPEAL IS DISMISSED.

Decision No. 15,186

Appeal of T.C., on behalf of her son J.M., from action of the Board of Education of the LaFayette Central School District regarding student discipline.

(March 7, 2005)

APPEARANCES OF COUNSEL

Ferrara, Fiorenza, Larrison, Barrett, Reitz, P.C., attorneys for respondent, *Craig M. Atlas, Esq.*, of counsel

DECISION OF THE COMMISSIONER

MILLS, Commissioner.—Petitioner appeals the decision of the Board of Education of the LaFayette Central School District ("respondent") to permanently suspend her son, J.M. from the LaFayette Junior-Senior High School ("high school"). The appeal must be sustained in part.

During the 2003-2004 school year, J.M. attended the 11th grade at the high school. On January 21, 2004, the high school principal notified petitioner that J.M. was being suspended for five days for use of an illegal substance (marijuana) on school property, endangering the safety of himself and others, and possession of a lighter.

A superintendent's hearing was held on January 26, 2004, to consider the charges against J.M. and to determine whether additional discipline should be imposed. By letter dated January 27, 2004, the superintendent informed petitioner that he found J.M. guilty of marijuana usage and endangering the welfare of others and advised that J.M. would be permanently suspended from the high school. The letter also advised petitioner that J.M. was eligible to receive tutoring for the remainder of the 2003-2004 school year and that he would be allowed to attend a BOCES alternative education high school ("BOCES program") in September 2004 on the condition that he receive counseling. Petitioner appealed this determination to respondent.

Petitioner was notified by letter dated February 26, 2004, that a portion of "phase two" of the hearing (penalty phase) had to be reconvened since the tape recorder malfunctioned at the superintendent's hearing. On March 1, 2004, the superintendent reheard evidence about J.M.'s anecdotal record. The superintendent did not modify the initial penalty determination.

By letter dated March 26, 2004, respondent affirmed the superintendent's findings of guilt and the penalty with the modification that counseling could not be a condition to J.M.'s entry into the BOCES program. This appeal ensued.

Petitioner contends that J.M. was not guilty of smoking marijuana and that he was found guilty before she was given the opportunity to question a relevant witness. She alleges that her son was denied his civil and due process rights. Petitioner requests that J.M. be permitted to attend the BOCES program at the district's cost and expense. She also requests that I reverse the superintendent's decision and expunge the charges from J.M.'s school record. Finally, she requests that respondent and the superintendent be reprimanded for the "improper handling of this matter."

Respondent contends that the appeal is moot. Respondent also contends that its decision is supported by the evidence and that petitioner fails to state a claim upon which relief may be granted. Respondent alleges that petitioner was given the opportunity to question her witness prior to a final determination of guilt and maintains that the constitutional rights of petitioner and her son were not violated. Respondent also asserts that the district and petitioner have agreed that J.M. will attend the BOCES program beginning September 2004. Finally, respondent alleges that there is no basis for a reprimand.

I will first address a preliminary issue. Respondent submitted an affidavit in response to petitioner's reply, and petitioner submitted a reply to that affidavit. These submissions address whether an application had been made to enroll petitioner's son in the BOCES program. Neither party has objected to the others submission. Therefore, pursuant to §276.5 of the Commissioner's regulations I will accept them for consideration.

Respondent argues that the appeal should be dismissed as moot. The Commissioner of Education only decides matters in actual controversy and will not render a decision on a state of facts which no longer exist or in which subsequent events have laid to rest. (*Appeal of L.H.*, 43 Ed Dept Rep 315, Decision No. 15,005; *Appeal of D.T. and M.M.*, 43 *id.* 58, Decision No. 14,916). In this appeal, petitioner requests that the student's records be expunged. I find, therefore, that a current controversy remains and the appeal will not be dismissed as moot.

Education Law §3214(3)(c) provides that no pupil may be suspended in excess of five days unless the pupil and person in parental relation are given an opportunity for a fair hearing, upon reasonable notice, at which the pupil should have the right to representation by counsel, with the right to question witnesses against the pupil and to present witnesses and other evidence on the pupil's behalf. Petitioner has failed to supply any evidence that due process violations occurred in connection with the disciplinary hearing. Petitioner's claim that she was denied the opportunity to question her witness prior to a final determination of guilt is without merit. The hearing transcript reveals that there was some initial confusion as to whether petitioner's witness would testify during phase one or phase two of the hearing. As a result, the superintendent initially found J.M. guilty prior to the testimony of petitioner's witness. However, once it was determined that the witness's testimony was relevant to phase one of the hearing, the superintendent immediately allowed petitioner to question the witness fully.

Petitioner also claims, in a conclusory fashion, that respondent has violated her son's civil rights. Petitioner presents no facts or details with respect to this claim, nor does she allege the basis upon she believes her son may have been discriminated against by respondent. In an appeal to the Commissioner, the petitioner has the burden of establishing the facts upon which he seeks relief and the burden of demonstrating a clear legal right to the relief sought (8 NYCRR §275.10; *Appeal of L.T.*, 44 Ed Dept Rep 89, Decision No. 15,107; *Appeal of D.T. and M.M., supra*). Petitioner has failed to meet this burden.

Petitioner further appeals the determination of guilt. A decision to suspend a student from school pursuant to Education Law §3214 must be based on competent and substantial evidence that the student participated in the objectionable conduct (*Bd. of Educ. of Monticello Central School Dist. v. Commissioner of Educ., et al.*, 91 NY2d 133, 140-141; *Bd. of Educ. of City School Dist. of City of New York v. Mills*, 293 AD2d 37). In this case, the teacher witness provided direct testimony that he entered the boy's bathroom on three separate occasions, one right after another. On the first occasion, he did not see or smell smoke, but looked under the stall and observed J.M.'s sneakers. On the second occasion, he heard a marijuana pipe known as a "bubbler." On the third occasion, he smelled marijuana and saw smoke. After exiting the bathroom for the third time, he waited in the hall a short distance from the bathroom door. Shortly thereafter he observed J.M. exit. At no time did he observe anyone other than J.M. in or near the bathroom. J.M. admitted that he was in the bathroom and did not see or hear anyone else in the vicinity at that time of the incident. Petitioner produced no witnesses and introduced no evidence to refute this testimony. The Commissioner will not substitute his judgment on witness credibility unless findings are not supported by the facts or the record (*Appeal of T.R. and M.D.*, 43 Ed Dept Rep 411, Decision No. 15,036; *Appeal of S.C.*, 43 *id.* 222, Decision No. 14,978). On the record before me, I find that respondent based its decision on competent and substantial evidence.

In cases of student discipline, the sanction imposed must be proportionate to the severity of the offense involved (*Appeal of K.S.*, 43 Ed Dept Rep 492, Decision No. 15,063; *Appeal of Student with a Disability*, 43 *id.* 213, Decision No. 14,975; *Appeal of M.F. and J.F.*, 43 *id.* 174, Decision No. 14,960). The test to be applied in reviewing a penalty is whether it is so excessive as to warrant substitution of the Commissioner's judgment for that of the board (*Appeal of M.F. and J.F.*, *supra*; *Appeal of K.S.*, *supra*). A permanent suspension is an extreme penalty that is generally educationally unsound except under extraordinarily circumstances, such as where the student exhibits "an alarming disregard for the safety of others" and where it is necessary to safeguard the well being of other students (*Appeal of L.T.*, *supra*; *Appeal of Y.M.*, 43 *id.* 193, Decision No. 14,968; *Appeal of Coleman*, 41 *id.* 101, Decision No. 14,628). The circumstances in this case do not meet those criteria.

Although respondent's decision referred to a permanent suspension, what respondent actually imposed amounted to a suspension until the end of the 2003-2004 school year followed by an involuntary transfer to the BOCES program. In light of the seriousness of J.M.'s conduct, I cannot conclude that the five-month suspension actually imposed was inappropriate.

With respect to the transfer, such a transfer imposes a disciplinary penalty that is not authorized by Education Law §3214 and is therefore invalid (*Appeal of K.B.*, 41 Ed Dept Rep 431, Decision No. 14,737; *Appeal of a Student Suspected of Having a Disability*, 40 *id.* 212, Decision No. 14,464, judgment granted dismissing petition to review, January 18, 2001, Sup. Ct., Albany Co., (Keegan J.), n.o.r.; aff'd 293 AD2d 37). Petitioner, however, has since agreed to the reassignment of her son to the BOCES program, and her pleadings actually demand it. Nevertheless, respondent is reminded of the need to fully comply with all laws and regulations governing student discipline in the future.

Finally, I decline to grant petitioner's request for a reprimand. I do not have the authority to censure or reprimand a board of education or district staff (*Appeal of Angrisani and Hamilton*, 41 Ed Dept Rep 6, Decision No. 14,593; *Appeal of D. H.*, 41 *id.* 142, Decision No. 14,640).

THE APPEAL IS SUSTAINED IN PART.

IT IS ORDERED that respondent expunge any reference to a permanent suspension from J.M.'s disciplinary record and adjust such record in accordance with the terms of this decision.

Decision No. 15,187

Appeal of FATHER CONSTANTINE L. SITARAS and SAINT BASIL ACADEMY from actions of the Board of Education of the Garrison Union Free School District and Stan Freilich, Anthony Haskell, Marilyn Palefsky, Anita Prentice, Frances DiSarro and Rebecca Malone regarding denial of admission.

(March 11, 2005)

APPEARANCES OF COUNSEL

White & Case LLP, attorneys for petitioners, *Dana E. Foster* and *Glenn M. Kurtz, Esqs.*, of counsel

Donoghue, Thomas, Auslander & Drohan, attorneys for respondents, *Daniel Petigrow, Esq.*, of counsel

DECISION OF THE COMMISSIONER

MILLS, Commissioner.—Petitioner Sitaras is the Executive Director of Saint Basil Academy ("St. Basil"), which is affiliated with the Greek Orthodox Church and operates a residential facility for children whose parents are unable to care for them. St. Basil and Sitaras (collectively referred to as "petitioners") challenge, among other things, the alleged failure of the Board of Education of the Garrison Union Free School District ("respondent board" or "board") and individual board members (collectively referred to as "respondents"), to comply with my April 6, 2004, consolidated decision sustaining, in part, petitioners' challenge to the board's determinations that 26 children then residing at St. Basil were not district residents of the Garrison Union Free School District ("Garrison" or "district"). The appeal must be sustained in part.

The facts underlying petitioners' previous appeals are set forth in the original decision (*Appeals of Sitaras, et al.*, 43 Ed Dept Rep 434, Decision No. 15,044) and briefly summarized here. St. Basil is located within Garrison. Garrison operates a school for grades K-8 and pays tuition to send its residents to high school in neighboring school districts. Prior to the 2002-2003 school year, St. Basil paid nonresident tuition for the children in its care ("St. Basil children") to attend school in neighboring districts, primarily the Highland Falls Central School District ("Highland Falls").

At the beginning of the 2002-2003 school year, petitioners sought to enroll 26 St. Basil children in Garrison's schools as district residents. Shortly thereafter, respondent board conducted residency hearings pursuant to §100.2(y) of the Commissioner's regulations to determine the children's residency. In separate decisions, the board found that none were district residents. Petitioner then commenced three separate appeals challenging the board's determinations, and in August 2003, I granted interim relief directing the board to admit the children to Garrison's schools and treat them as district residents pending a determination on the merits.

In a decision dated April 6, 2004, I found, among other things, that although petitioners failed to establish that any of the children were district residents, under Education Law §3202(6) those children with a parent or guardian residing in New York State are entitled to attend Garrison's schools on a tuition basis at the expense of each child's school district of residence or responsible social services district.[1] Consequently, I directed petitioners to provide respondent board, within 30 days of the decision, with any and all information concerning each child's district of residence or social services district responsible for their maintenance and support, and further ordered that "upon receipt of such information, respondent [board] contact

---

[1] In my April 6, 2004, decision, I noted that St. Basil's application for licensure was pending before the Office of Children and Family Services ("OCFS"). My Office of Counsel has been informed by OCFS's Office of Counsel that the application is still pending.

each such school district of residence or local social services district and make arrangements for the payment of tuition and continuing education for the children in question." None of the parties sought judicial review of my decision. Respondent board's application to reopen the decision was denied on September 1, 2004, (*Application to reopen Appeals of Sitaras, et al.*, 44 Ed Dept Rep ___, Decision No. 15,112).

By letter dated April 16, 2004, petitioners supplied respondent board with residency information, including parent or guardian name, address and corresponding school district, for ten St. Basil children who were presumably New York State residents. Shortly thereafter, Garrison's superintendent sent letters and invoices to the respective school districts for eight St. Basil children requesting payment for educational expenses for the 2003-2004 school year. The superintendent sent another series of letters with invoices in June 2004 to school districts for ten children, again requesting payment for educational expenses for 2003-2004. Although both series of letters reference my April 6, 2004, decision, none of the letters mention the 2004-2005 school year or request that the districts make tuition arrangements for the children's future education.

Thereafter, the parties exchanged a series of letters concerning the implementation and interpretation of my decision. By letter dated June 30, 2004, the superintendent advised petitioners that Garrison intended to hold St. Basil responsible for tuition for the 2003-2004 school year because it had been unable to identify and determine a responsible school district for the ten students. The superintendent further advised that, pursuant to district policy, Garrison would admit St. Basil children only if St. Basil reimbursed Garrison for "expenses incurred during the 2003-04 school year" and paid all educational expenses for the 2004-2005 school year 15 days before the start of the school year. By letter dated July 8, 2004, St. Basil's attorney disputed St. Basil's liability for tuition for the 2003-2004 school year and requested that Garrison document both its tuition figures and efforts to make tuition arrangements for the St. Basil children for the upcoming school year.

In a response dated July 20, 2004, the board's attorney advised that it had no obligation to educate St. Basil children unless and until a responsible school district or social services district had been identified and determined. Further, by letter dated July 28, 2004, respondent board's attorney provided St. Basil's attorney with a copy of the board's "Compliance Policy Education Law 3202(6)" as well as supporting documentation for its 2003-2004 tuition bills and requested that St. Basil provide the names of those children it planned to send to Garrison's K-8 school for the 2004-2005 school year, as well as certain custody and residency information it needed to comply with my decision.

By letter dated August 5, 2004, St. Basil's attorney again disputed St. Basil's liability for tuition for the 2003-2004 school year, accused respondent board of violating my decision by, among other things, conditioning the children's admission on the payment of tuition for the 2003-2004 school year and by failing to make sufficient effort to arrange for tuition for the 2004-2005 school year. By letter dated August 18, 2004, St. Basil's attorney requested that Garrison enroll the St. Basil children in the district's schools. This appeal ensued. Petitioners' request for interim relief was denied on September 1, 2004, and petitioners' request for reconsideration was denied on September 10, 2004.

Petitioners contend that respondents violated my April 6, 2004, decision by failing to make tuition arrangements with the appropriate school districts and social services districts and by refusing to admit the children unless St. Basil reimbursed Garrison for their educational expenses from the 2003-2004 school year and paid tuition in advance for the 2004-2005 school year. Petitioners also complain that Garrison's tuition bills for the 2003-2004 school year lack detail and are "suspiciously high." For relief, petitioners request that I direct respondents to: admit the St. Basil children to Garrison's schools; arrange and pay for the St. Basil children to attend Highland Falls' schools; collect tuition for the appropriate responsible school districts and social services districts; and require payment only at the conclusion of the school year. Petitioners also request that I remove each of the individually named board members for willfully violating my decision.

Respondents contend that St. Basil lacks standing and has failed to join necessary parties. Respondents further claim that I lack subject matter jurisdiction to compel Garrison to collect tuition from school districts and social services districts for nonresident children or make arrangements for the children to attend Highland Falls, or to compel Garrison to accept payment of tuition only at the conclusion of the school year. Respondents also allege that Garrison is not obligated to receive any of the St. Basil children because St. Basil has a charter to operate a private boarding school. Finally, respondents assert that none of the board members have committed any willful violation of the law or disobeyed any decision or order of the Commissioner.

In addition, respondent board seeks permission pursuant to Education Law §3202(6) to deny admission to the St. Basil children on the grounds that it has established valid and sufficient reasons to do so.

In reply, petitioners assert, among other things, that respondents are precluded from challenging my authority to order respondent board to make arrangements for tuition because respondent board did not seek judicial review of my prior decision.

As a threshold matter, I find that petitioners have standing to maintain this appeal. An individual may not maintain an appeal pursuant to Education Law §310 unless aggrieved in the sense that he or she has suffered personal damage or injury to her or his civil, personal or property rights (*Appeal of Sweeney*, 44 Ed Dept Rep ___, Decision No. 15,139; *Appeal of Bermudez*, 41 *id.* 355, Decision No. 14,712). In large measure, petitioners' claims relate to respondents' alleged failure to comply with my decision in their earlier appeals. As parties to those appeals, petitioners clearly have standing to maintain such a challenge. Further, because Education Law §306 authorizes the removal of a board member for willful failure to obey a decision or order of the Commissioner, I find that petitioners have standing to seek such relief.

I decline, however, to address petitioners' challenge to Garrison's tuition bills. The Commissioner of Education lacks authority to award money damages (*Appeals of Sitaras, et al.*, 43 Ed Dept Rep 434, Decision No. 15,044; *Appeal of Moore*, 41 *id.* 436, Decision No. 14,738; *Appeal of a Student with a Disability*, 41 *id.* 52, Decision No. 14,613). Accordingly, in the context of a residency appeal, the Commissioner of Education has declined to award a school district tuition for educating a nonresident student or to order a district to reimburse a petitioner for tuition paid on behalf of a resident student who was entitled to attend district schools (*see*, *Appeal of Baronti*, 42 Ed Dept Rep 140, Decision No. 14,802; *Appeal of a Student with a Disability*, *supra*; *Appeal of Zavesky*, 40 *id.* 517, Decision No. 14,543). Any dispute regarding petitioners' liability for tuition should thus be resolved in the New York State Supreme Court or other court of competent jurisdiction.

As discussed more fully below, I also find that Garrison may not require St. Basil to pay the children's tuition from the 2003-2004 school year as a condition to their admission on a tuition basis for the 2004-2005 school year.

A party whose rights would be adversely affected by a determination of an appeal in favor of petitioner is a necessary party and must be joined as such (*Appeal of American Quality Beverages, LLC*, 43 Ed Dept Rep 402, Decision No. 15,032; *Appeal of Lynch*, 42 *id*. 398, Decision No. 14,892; *Appeal of Roff*, 41 *id*. 346, Decision No. 14,708). Respondents claim that those school districts that have been identified and determined to be responsible for tuition are necessary parties to this appeal. I disagree. Petitioners essentially challenge respondents' alleged failure to comply with my order directing respondent board to contact and make arrangements for the payment of tuition with the resident school districts and social services districts identified by petitioners. I do not find that the rights of any school district would be adversely affected by a determination of the merits of this appeal, and therefore, do not find that petitioners have failed to join any necessary parties.

Before turning to petitioners' claim that respondents did not comply with my decision, I will briefly address respondents' claim that I lack subject matter jurisdiction to order respondents to "collect tuition" for the St. Basil children from resident school districts and social services districts. Although respondents do not explicitly phrase their claim as such, respondents essentially challenge my authority to order the relief granted in *Appeals of Sitaras, et al.* (*supra*). However, the record reflects that respondent board never sought judicial review of that decision and as a result, it is now final and binding on respondent board (*see*, *Bd. of Educ. Oneonta City School Dist. v. Manning*, 119 AD2d 971).

I further find this claim without merit. Pursuant to Education Law §310, I have jurisdiction to examine and decide any petition made in consequence of, among other things, any "official act or decision of any officer, school authorities, or meetings." Petitioners' challenge to respondent board's residency determinations clearly fall within that scope of authority under Education Law §310.

Education Law §311 also vests the Commissioner with the authority to "make all orders . . . which may, in his judgment, be proper or necessary to give effect to his decision." As I noted in *Appeals of Sitaras, et al.* (*supra*), because the parties apparently did not contemplate that the St. Basil children's educational rights were governed by Education Law §3202(6), it appeared that none of the respective resident school districts or social services districts had been contacted about arranging for the children's education. Because the relief ordered was designed to give effect to my finding that the children were entitled to attend Garrison's schools on a tuition basis, I find it within my authority under Education Law §311.

Based on the record before me, I find that respondent board did not fully comply with that portion of my decision and order that directed respondent board to contact social services districts and school districts identified by petitioners to make tuition arrangements. Although respondent board billed various school districts for the children's tuition for the 2003-2004 school year, there is no evidence in the record that respondent board's administrative staff made diligent efforts to contact such school districts to make tuition arrangements for the children's education for the 2004-2005 school year. As noted above, none of the letters accompanying the tuition bills requested that the school districts contact Garrison to make tuition arrangements for the 2004-2005 school year. Further, although it appears that many of the school districts did not respond to Garrison's letters, there is no evidence that Garrison's administration attempted to contact the districts by telephone to pursue the matter further.

Although respondent board's lack of diligence contributed to the fact that tuition arrangements are not in place, I nevertheless find that respondent board had no obligation to make arrangements with Highland Falls for the education of any St. Basil children because Education Law §3202(6) does not impose an obligation on respondent board to "receive" children unless it is requested to do so on a tuition basis.

While I find that respondent board did not fully comply with my decision, I do not find that petitioners have established any legal basis to remove any individual board members. The Commissioner of Education has authority to remove a board member or school official when it is proven to the Commissioner's satisfaction that the board member or school official has engaged in a willful violation or neglect of duty under the Education Law or other law pertaining to the public schools or has willfully disobeyed a decision, order, rule or regulation of the Board of Regents or the Commissioner of Education (Education Law §306; *Appeal of Simmons*, 43 Ed Dept Rep 7, Decision No. 14,899; *Application of Lilker*, 40 *id.* 704, Decision No. 14,588; *Appeal of Gaul, et al.*, 40 *id.* 105, Decision No. 14,432). To be considered willful, respondents' actions must have been intentional and with a wrongful purpose (*id.*). In an appeal to the Commissioner, the petitioner has the burden of establishing the facts upon which he or she seeks relief and the burden of demonstrating a clear legal right to the relief requested (8 NYCRR §275.10; *Application of Lilker, supra*; *Appeal of Gaul, et al., supra*). There is no evidence on the record that any board members engaged in conduct that could be construed as willful disobedience of my decision.

I agree with petitioners, however, that respondent board's "Compliance with Education Law 3202(6)" policy contravenes Education Law §3202(6) and my prior decision. Respondent board's obligation to admit the St. Basil children on a tuition basis is absolute and unconditional, absent a showing that the board has "valid and sufficient reasons" for refusing to do so. Accordingly, respondent board may not condition its receipt of the children on St. Basil's payment of tuition from the prior school year (2003-2004), especially since, as discussed above, there has been no determination that St. Basil is legally responsible for that tuition.

I further find that the board's policy contravenes Education Law §3202(6) to the extent that it requires payment of tuition-in-full 15 days before the start of the school year. The Commissioner has repeatedly held that tuition payments between school districts for nonresident students are due at the completion of the school year in which they are incurred (*Appeal of the Bd. of Educ. of the East Quogue Union Free School Dist.*, 43 Ed Dept Rep 385, Decision No. 15,026; *Appeal of the Bd. of Educ. of the Port Jefferson Union Free School Dist.*, 26 *id.* 525, Decision No. 11,841). In *Matter of Appeal from the action of the Bd. of Educ. of Union Free School Dist. No. 1 of the Town of Mentz* (34 St. Dept. 237, Decision No. 1072), the Commissioner found that because there was no statutory provision establishing the conditions for tuition collection, respondent could exercise reasonable discretion in fixing the terms of payment. However, in that appeal, the Commissioner found that it was unreasonable for respondent to require the district of residence to provide tuition-in-full in advance of the school year.

Similarly, although respondent board has the right to require a written, unconditional commitment for the payment of tuition prior to accepting any of the St. Basil children, and to impose other reasonable requirements, I find that respondent board's requirement of full payment of tuition by a school district of residence in advance of the school year contravenes the statute. There is no language in Education Law §3202(6) that would authorize Garrison to refuse a request from a school district of residence for instruction on a tuition basis that is received either before or after the start of the school year. Therefore, I find that it is an abuse of discretion to impose such a requirement.

In addition, respondent board's application to establish valid and sufficient reasons for denying admission to the St. Basil children must be denied. Education Law §3202(6) requires the local school district where the institution is located to receive the institution's children on a tuition basis, unless it can "establish to the satisfaction of the commissioner of education that there are valid and sufficient reasons for refusal to receive such children" (Education Law §3202(6)).

Respondent board's argument that it will suffer a financial hardship if it is forced to educate the St. Basil children without receiving tuition payments is without merit because it has no obligation to educate those St. Basil children for whom no tuition arrangements are in place. Accordingly, I find that respondent board has not established any financial hardship.

The fact that Garrison only operates a K-8 school does not relieve respondent board of its obligation to "receive" St. Basil's high-school-aged children. Just as respondent board makes arrangements for its resident children to attend high school in neighboring district schools, so too, can respondent board make such arrangements for the St. Basil children. Moreover, there are important public policy reasons for rejecting the board's argument. By requiring the local school district to receive the children cared for in an Education Law §3202(6) institution on a tuition basis, the statute ensures that such children are able to receive a public education while under the institution's care. If I were to relieve respondent board of this responsibility, the children would not be guaranteed the opportunity to attend public school at the expense of their respective resident school districts because the statute does not impose an obligation on any other school district to receive such children.

Finally, although I am again ordering respondent board to contact the children's respective school and social services districts concerning the arrangement of tuition for the current school year, there is nothing that prohibits petitioners from engaging in similar efforts to facilitate such tuition arrangements, and I encourage them to do so.

I have examined the parties' remaining contentions and find them without merit.

THE APPEAL IS SUSTAINED TO THE EXTENT INDICATED.

IT IS ORDERED that respondent board's "Compliance Policy Education Law 3202(6)" is hereby annulled to the extent it is inconsistent with this decision; and

IT IS FURTHER ORDERED that within 30 days of this decision respondent board contact, both in writing and by telephone, each of the school districts and social services districts identified by petitioners pursuant to my earlier order to make tuition arrangements for the education of the children in question for the current school year; and

IT IS FURTHER ORDERED that respondent board advise petitioners of the results of its efforts on an ongoing basis; and

IT IS FURTHER ORDERED that respondent board immediately receive each of the St. Basil children when tuition arrangements are in place in accordance with this decision.

Decision No. 15,188

Appeal of B.S., on behalf of his daughter J.S., from action of the Board of Education of the Sachem Central School District regarding attendance zones.

(March 11, 2005)

APPEARANCES OF COUNSEL

The Law Office of Kenneth M. Mollins, P.C., attorneys for petitioner, *Kenneth M. Mollins, Esq.*, of counsel

Ingerman Smith, LLP, attorneys for respondent, *Neil M. Block, Esq.*, of counsel

DECISION OF THE COMMISSIONER

MILLS, Commissioner.—Petitioner appeals the determination of the Board of Education of the Sachem Central School District ("respondent") that his daughter may not attend school outside the attendance zone in which she resides. The appeal must be dismissed.

Prior to September 2004, respondent maintained a high school campus for grades 9-10 named Sachem High School South ("Sachem South") and a separate campus for grades 11-12 named Sachem High

School North ("Sachem North"). Effective September 2004, Sachem South was transformed into the Samoset Middle School. Sachem North was expanded to accommodate grades 9-12 and a new, separate high school campus also for grades 9-12 was formed and named Sachem High School East ("Sachem East"). The determination as to whether a student would attend Sachem North or Sachem East was based on residence.

J.S. attended Sachem South during the 2003-2004 school year. At the beginning of the school year, her registration records reflected that she resided at an address on Van Horn Avenue, Holbrook, which is within the Sachem North attendance zone. However, sometime during the 2003-2004 school year petitioner relocated to a residence on Inverness Drive, Holbrook, which is in the Sachem East attendance zone.

In anticipation of students attending either Sachem North or Sachem East in the 2004-2005 school year, two cheerleading squads were established at Sachem South. Cheerleaders were assigned to the respective squads based on their residence. During the 2003-2004 school year, based on residency information provided by petitioner and/or his daughter, J.S. was designated as a Sachem North student and allowed to participate on the Sachem North cheerleading squad. A rivalry developed between that squad and the Sachem East squad. Because of J.S.'s "high profile" on the Sachem North squad, she was allegedly singled out and physically and psychologically abused by the girls on the Sachem East squad.

By letter dated August 27, 2004, petitioner was notified that because J.S.'s legal domicile was on Inverness Drive, she was required to attend Sachem East. By letter dated September 1, 2004, petitioner requested that respondent transfer her to Sachem North. By letter dated September 9, 2004, respondent's superintendent notified petitioner that his request for a transfer was denied, that Sachem East was a safe environment for J.S. and that petitioner had not presented a compelling reason for J.S. to attend school out of her attendance zone. This appeal ensued. Petitioner's request for interim relief was denied on September 28, 2004.

Petitioner alleges that during J.S.'s sophomore year, she resided in the Sachem North attendance zone and therefore should be permitted to attend school in that zone. Petitioner also alleges that his daughter should be permitted to attend Sachem North because she has been verbally and physically abused by students attending Sachem East, and that her placement at that school poses a serious threat to her health and safety. Finally, petitioner alleges that respondent's decision to place J.S. in Sachem East was arbitrary and capricious.

Respondent alleges that J.S. currently resides in the Sachem East attendance zone and is therefore required to attend school in that zone. Respondent further alleges that petitioner has failed to demonstrate that Sachem East is an unsafe environment for J.S. or that her placement there was arbitrary, capricious or contrary to sound education policy.

Petitioner submitted letters dated September 10 and 23, 2004, from J.S.'s psychiatrist and an affidavit from J.S.'s sister to support arguments made in his petition. Respondent did not object to these submissions. Pursuant to §276.5 of the Commissioner's regulations, I will accept these documents for consideration.

Pursuant to Education Law §1709(3) and (33), a board of education has the authority and responsibility to manage and administer the affairs of the school district, including the assignment of pupils to schools therein (*Matter of Older, et al. v. Board of Educ.*, 27 NY2d 333; *Appeal of P.S.*, 39 Ed Dept Rep 806, Decision No. 14,387; *Appeal of Ibrahim*, 39 *id.* 155, Decision No. 14,200). In the assignment of pupils to schools, a board of education has broad discretion (*Matter of Addabbo v. Donovan*, 22 AD2d 383; aff'd 16 NY2d 619, cert den 382 US 905; *Appeal of the Lancaster Parent Alliance*, 38 Ed Dept Rep 356, Decision No. 14,053). Accordingly, a board's decision regarding school assignments will only be overturned when found to be arbitrary, capricious or contrary to sound educational policy (*Matter of Older, supra*). Moreover, petitioner bears the burden of demonstrating that respondent's action is arbitrary, capricious or contrary to sound educational policy (*Appeals of Johnson, et al.*, 37 Ed Dept Rep 465, Decision No. 13,906; *Appeal of Sherwood, et al.*, 33 *id.* 410, Decision No. 13,096; *Appeal of McNerney, et al.*, 28 *id.* 250, Decision No. 12,097).

Petitioner provides no evidence, other than the unsubstantiated allegations in the petition, that J.S. was harassed, that her personal property was destroyed, or that her safety will be jeopardized by her placement in Sachem East. In an affidavit submitted in opposition to the petition, however, the principal of Sachem East avers that J.S. never complained to any school official that she was threatened or bullied, nor did she notify school officials that her personal property had been destroyed. Furthermore, the record reflects that there are "bullying boxes" in the school building where students can place anonymous complaints and, there is no evidence that J.S. ever used a box to lodge a complaint.

Petitioner contends that forcing J.S. to attend Sachem East will adversely affect her psychological and emotional well-being and, therefore, she should be permitted to attend Sachem North. In support of this contention, petitioner submits a letter dated August 30, 2004, from J.S.'s physician who states that "[J.S.] needs a stable, familiar environment for her mental health [and that] [s]he has been advised not to make sudden, big changes in her life." Petitioner also submits two letters from a psychiatrist that indicate J.S. should be permitted to attend Sachem North due to feelings of insecurity, anxiety, panic and depression resulting from being bullied. Finally, petitioner submits an ambulance report which indicates that J.S. was found upset, sobbing and hyperventilating reportedly because she was anxious about entering a different high school.

The fact that J.S. may have some difficulty adjusting to a new school, while certainly regrettable, is not a basis for overturning respondent's decision (*Appeal of Giovanniello*, 44 Ed Dept Rep 17, Decision No. 15,081; *Appeal of Sponcy*, 33 *id.* 126, Decision No. 12,998; *Appeal of Cullen*, 32 *id.* 179, Decision No. 12,798). While I am sympathetic to petitioner's assertion that his daughter has experienced anxiety about attending a different high school, there is no legal basis to reverse the local district's decision unless it is proven to be arbitrary, capricious or contrary to sound educational policy (*Appeal of Giovanniello*, *supra*; *Appeal of Kershaw*, 37 Ed Dept Rep 186, Decision No. 13,837).

On the record before me, I cannot conclude that respondent's decision meets that standard, and therefore, I will not disturb it.

THE APPEAL IS DISMISSED.

Decision No. 15,189

Appeal of K.G.B., on behalf of her daughter K.W., from action of the Board of Education of the City School District of the City of Elmira regarding student discipline.

Appeal of K.G.B., on behalf of her daughter C.W., from action of the Board of Education of the City School District of the City of Elmira regarding student discipline.

(March 11, 2005)

APPEARANCES OF COUNSEL

Sayles & Evans, attorneys for respondent, *James F. Young, Esq.*, of counsel

DECISION OF THE COMMISSIONER

MILLS, Commissioner.—Petitioner appeals the decision of the Board of Education of the City School District of the City of Elmira ("respondent") to suspend her daughters from school. Because the appeals involve common issues of law and fact, they are consolidated for decision. The appeals must be dismissed.

On March 15, 2004, C.W. was involved in an altercation with another student as they were exiting the school bus after school. The next day, C.W. and K.W. were both involved in an altercation on school property with that same student and several others. C.W. and K.W. were suspended and superintendent's hearings were held before a hearing officer on March 22, 2004. The hearing officer recommended that C.W. be suspended for the remainder of the school year, summer school and the first half of the 2004-2005 school year. The hearing officer recommended that K.W. be suspended for the remainder of the 2003-2004 school year. By decision dated March 29, 2004, the superintendent accepted the hearing officer's recommendations. By decision dated May 18, 2004, respondent upheld the superintendent's decision. These appeals ensued and petitioner's requests for interim relief were denied on July 14, 2004. K.W.'s suspension ended on June 24, 2004, and C.W. was allowed to return to school as of January 3, 2005.

Petitioner argues that the suspensions are excessive and requests a determination that C.W. was the victim of the attack and that she be allowed to return to school no later than February 2005. Petitioner further requests a determination that K.W. was only assisting her sister and that she be allowed to return to school no later than September 2004.

The appeals must be dismissed as moot. The Commissioner of Education will only decide matters in actual controversy and will not render a decision on a state of facts which no longer exist or which subsequent events have laid to rest (*Appeal of R.M. and L.M.*, 44 Ed Dept Rep ___, Decision No. 15,154; *Appeal of M.F. and J.F.*, 43 *id.* 174, Decision No. 14,960). Petitioner did not request expungement of her daughters' records. Since the suspensions have been served, no further meaningful relief can be granted and the appeals must be dismissed as moot (*Appeal of R.S. and R.S.*, 44 Ed Dept Rep ___, Decision No. 15,141; *Appeal of R.R. and K.R.*, 41 *id.* 405, Decision No. 14,726; *Appeal of D.H.*, 41 *id.* 142, Decision No. 14,640).

In light of this disposition, I need not address the parties' remaining contentions.

THE APPEALS ARE DISMISSED.

Decision No. 15,190

Appeal of JO ANNE ALVES, on behalf of her daughter JULIANNA, from action of the Board of Education of the Port Chester-Rye Union Free School District regarding attendance zones.

(March 18, 2005)

APPEARANCES OF COUNSEL

Sisca and Sisca, P.C., attorneys for respondent, *Francis J. Sisca*, Esq., of counsel

DECISION OF THE COMMISSIONER

MILLS, Commissioner.—Petitioner appeals a decision by the Board of Education of the Port Chester-Rye Union Free School District ("respondent") to transfer her daughter from the district's King Street Elementary School ("King Street") to the John F. Kennedy Elementary School ("Kennedy"). The appeal must be dismissed.

Petitioner has three daughters residing in respondent's district. Respondent's district is divided into attendance zones for its elementary schools. In the 1996–1997 school year, petitioner resided in the King Street attendance zone and petitioner's oldest daughter, Adrianna, attended King Street. On December 2, 1996, petitioner moved out of the King Street attendance zone and into the Kennedy attendance zone. Although petitioner moved out of the attendance zone, Adrianna was allowed to continue attending King Street and, because of a sibling exception to the attendance zones, in 1998 petitioner's second daughter, Emily, was allowed to attend King Street. In September 2003, Emily started fifth grade at King Street and under the sibling exception to the attendance zones, petitioner's third daughter, Julianna, was able to attend kindergarten at King Street.

By letter dated July 1, 2004, respondent's Residency Committee notified petitioner that it had determined that, for the 2004-2005 school year, Julianna would be required to attend first grade at Kennedy. The letter stated that this decision was based on the fact that Julianna was not a resident of the King Street attendance zone and would no longer have any siblings attending King Street. This appeal ensued. Petitioner's request for interim relief was denied on August 12, 2004. Beginning September 2004, Julianna was enrolled in a local parochial school.

Petitioner argues that Julianna should never have been admitted to King Street for kindergarten if she would not be allowed to complete elementary school there. Additionally, petitioner asserts that Kennedy does not meet the standards of King Street. Finally, petitioner asserts that transferring Julianna to Kennedy would be an "injustice" that could affect Julianna's entire outlook on schooling.

Respondent asserts that its policy requires students to attend the elementary school in their attendance zone. Respondent further asserts that over the past three years it has made a concerted effort to return students to their neighborhood schools. As part of this effort, respondent established a residency committee to review students' residency within the district and within the district's attendance zones. Petitioner was permitted to appear before the residency committee and express her concerns with regard to Julianna's placement.

The appeal must be dismissed as moot. The Commissioner of Education only decides matters in actual controversy and will not render a decision on a state of facts which no longer exists or which subsequent events have laid to rest (*Appeal of Welch*, 44 Ed Dept Rep 57, Decision No. 15,097; *Appeal of Patel*, 43 *id.* 518, Decision No. 15,071). Julianna has been enrolled at a local parochial school beginning with the 2004-2005 school year. Therefore, Julianna's elementary school assignment is no longer at issue.

Even if the appeal were not dismissed on procedural grounds, it would be dismissed on the merits. Pursuant to Education Law §1709(3) and (33), a board of education has the authority and responsibility to manage and administer the affairs of the school district, including the assignment of pupils to schools therein (*Matter of Older, et al. v Board of Ed.*, 27 NY2d 333; *Appeal of Giovanniello*,

44 Ed Dept Rep 17, Decision No. 15,081; *Appeal of DePaolo*, 38 *id.* 4, Decision No. 13,970). A board of education has broad discretion regarding the assignment of students to schools (*Matter of Addabbo v Donovan*, 22 AD2d 383; *aff'd* 16 NY2d 619, *cert den* 382 US 905; *Appeal of Teel*, 33 Ed Dept Rep 309, Decision No. 13,058). Therefore, a board's decision regarding school assignments will only be overturned when found to be arbitrary, capricious or contrary to sound educational policy (*Matter of Older*, *supra*; *Appeal of DePaolo*, *supra*; *Appeal of Cullen*, 32 Ed Dept Rep 179, Decision No. 12,798). Moreover, petitioner bears the burden of demonstrating that respondent's action is arbitrary, capricious or contrary to sound educational policy (*Appeal of Giovanniello*, *supra*).

Petitioner does not dispute that she and Julianna live in the Kennedy attendance zone. Nor does she establish that Julianna falls within an exception to respondent's attendance zone policy. Because petitioner has failed to show that respondent's determination was arbitrary, capricious or contrary to sound educational policy, the appeal must be dismissed.

THE APPEAL IS DISMISSED.

Decision No. 15,191

Appeal of LISA McLOUGHLIN, on behalf of BONNIE McLOUGHLIN, and CATHY CARUSI, on behalf of KELLY CARUSI, from action of the Locust Valley Central School District regarding a budget proposition.

(March 29, 2005)

APPEARANCES OF COUNSEL

Ehrlich, Frazer & Feldman, attorneys for respondent, *Kevin G. McMorrow, Esq.*, of counsel

DECISION OF THE COMMISSIONER

MILLS, Commissioner.—Petitioners challenge the refusal of the Board of Education of the Locust Valley Central School District ("respondent") to place a budget proposition before the voters at the district's annual meeting on May 17, 2005. The appeal must be dismissed.

In February 2004, the International Baccalaureate Organization ("IBO") in Geneva, Switzerland, approved respondent's high school to offer the curriculum of the International Baccalaureate ("IB") Diploma Programme, a pre-university course of study. The high school began to offer the program in September 2004 for students in the 11th and 12th grades.

Petitioners allege that respondent violated their civil, personal and property rights by refusing to place before the voters a proposition on whether respondent should be authorized to conduct and levy taxes to fund the IB program. Petitioners maintain that the IB program is a discretionary program similar to driver education, which was submitted to the voters for approval. They argue, therefore, that respondent has set a precedent for placing propositions on discretionary programs before the voters.

Petitioners also claim that respondent violated their rights by using public funds to enter into a contract with the IBO that grants exclusive jurisdiction over disputes to courts in Switzerland. They also allege that respondent is violating the New York State Student Record Privacy Act ("Privacy Act") by allowing personal student data to be transmitted through the IBO Online Curriculum Center to non-secure countries. Petitioners ask that a proposition to fund the IB program be allowed on the ballot at the May 17, 2005, election. They also seek determinations regarding respondent's legal authority to allocate public monies to the IBO and whether the privacy of student records is being violated.

Respondent contends that the petition is untimely and fails to state a claim for which relief can be granted. Respondent further alleges that petitioners lack standing. With regard to the merits, respondent asserts that it was not required to present a proposition on the IB program to the voters because it is a matter of curriculum, which is within the board's discretion. Respondent also asserts that the previous proposition concerning driver education is irrelevant and does not establish any precedent. Respondent contends that the jurisdictional waiver clause in the IBO contract relates only to the application process and since its application has been approved, petitioners' claims are moot. Finally, respondent denies that there is a State Privacy Act. To the extent petitioners intended to refer to the federal Family Education Rights and Privacy Act ("FERPA"), the respondent avers that the Commissioner lacks jurisdiction.

I must first address several procedural issues. The purpose of a reply is to respond to procedural defenses or new material contained in an answer (8 NYCRR §§275.3 and 275.14). A reply is not meant to buttress allegations in the petition or to belatedly add assertions or exhibits that should have been in the petition (*Appeal of O'Brien, et al.*, 42 Ed Dept Rep 317, Decision No. 14,868; *Application of Bean*, 42 *id.* 171, Decision No. 14,810). Accordingly, while I have reviewed petitioners' reply, I have not considered those portions containing new allegations that are not responsive to new material or affirmative defenses in respondent's answer.

An appeal to the Commissioner of Education must be commenced within 30 days of the making of the decision or the performance of the act complained of, unless any delay is excused by the Commissioner for good cause shown (8 NYCRR §275.16). Respondent contends that the appeal is untimely because the budget authorizing the district's funding of the IB program was approved on June 19, 2004, and the program commenced on September 1, 2004, but petitioners did not initiate this appeal until November 30, 2004. Petitioners counter that respondent denied their request for a proposition by letter dated November 8, 2004, and they served their petition within 30 days of the denial, on November 30, 2004. Under these circumstances, I decline to dismiss the appeal as untimely.

Pursuant to Education Law §310, an individual may not maintain an appeal unless aggrieved in the sense that she has suffered personal damage or injury to her civil, personal or property rights. Only persons who are directly affected by the action being appealed have standing to bring an appeal (*Appeals of Giardina and Carbone*, 43 Ed Dept Rep 395, Decision No. 15,030; *Appeal of Murphy, et al.*, 39 *id.* 562, Decision No. 14,311; *Appeal of Goldin*, 38 *id.* 322, Decision No. 14,044). However, district residents have standing to challenge an alleged illegal expenditure of district funds (*Appeals of Giardina and Carbone, supra*). Therefore, to the extent that petitioners are district residents who challenge whether the IB program is an appropriate use of district funds and whether district residents have a right to place a budget proposition before the voters, petitioners have standing (*Appeals of Giardina and Carbone, supra*; *Appeal of Goldin, supra*). However, since their children do not currently participate in the program, I agree with respondent that petitioners lack standing regarding the IBO's rules governing waivers, use of its web sites and use of student information. Accordingly, those portions of the appeal must be dismissed for lack of standing.

Boards of education have broad authority to prescribe the course of study in the schools of the district (Education Law §1709(3); *Appeal of Murphy, et al.*, *supra*; *Appeal of Graham*, 39 Ed Dept Rep 498, Decision No. 14,292; *Appeal of Smith*, 34 *id.* 346, Decision No. 13,335). Curriculum decisions are not to be made by district voters. Indeed, because the Legislature has given boards of education the authority to prescribe the curriculum in their schools, it is inappropriate to put a proposition before the voters that would override or limit the board's authority, as petitioners sought to do here (*Appeal of Lombardo*, 38 Ed Dept Rep 676, Decision No. 14,115).

The United States Supreme Court has confirmed that school authorities enjoy broad discretion in regulating matters of curriculum (*Bd. of Educ., Island Trees U.F.S.D. No. 26 v. Pico*, 457 US 853, 869). I will not substitute my judgment for that of a board on curriculum issues absent evidence that the board has acted in an arbitrary, capricious or unreasonable manner (*Appeal of Smith*, *supra*). I can make no such finding on the record before me.

In light of this disposition, I need not address the parties' remaining contentions.

THE APPEAL IS DISMISSED.

Decision No. 15,192

Appeal of WILLIAM SCOTT from action of the Board of Education of the City School District of the City of Utica regarding tenure.

(March 29, 2005)

APPEARANCES OF COUNSEL

David B. Savlov, Esq., attorney for petitioner

Donald R. Gerace, Esq., attorney for respondent

DECISION OF THE COMMISSIONER

MILLS, Commissioner.—Petitioner challenges the decision of the Board of Education of the City School District of the City of Utica ("respondent") to deny tenure and dismiss him, effective September 3, 2004, from the administrative position of Director of Staff Development, Planning and Technology. The appeal must be dismissed.

Prior to April 1998, petitioner was a tenured teacher in the City School District of the City of Syracuse ("Syracuse"). In February 1998, respondent posted and advertised a teaching position entitled "Staff Development Trainer/Facilitator (Teacher on Special Assignment — Full-time Position)." Respondent appointed petitioner to that position on March 24, 1998, and he began work on or about April 1, 1998. Respondent and Syracuse arranged for petitioner to remain on the Syracuse payroll, with respondent reimbursing Syracuse.

On August 18, 1998, respondent continued petitioner's appointment to the position of Staff Development Trainer/Facilitator, as an employee of respondent's district, at an annual salary of $59,000. Petitioner continued to be employed in that position through a series of one-year appointments and extensions through July 2001.

On July 24, 2001, respondent voted to establish the position of Director of Staff Development, Planning and Technology, effective September 1, 2001. Unlike the position petitioner then held, which required teaching certification, this new position required certification as a school district administrator, and was subject to the collective bargaining agreement between the district and the Utica Administrators Association. Petitioner applied for this new position and was appointed by respondent on August 28, 2001, effective September 4, 2001, at a salary of $79,153 per year.

Petitioner continued to serve in the Director position until Spring 2004, when the superintendent recommended him for tenure. At its meeting on April 27, 2004, respondent voted 5-2 to deny tenure. By letter dated April 30, 2004, respondent's clerk advised petitioner of the negative action, and further advised that a final vote would be taken on June 22, 2004.

On May 7, 2004, petitioner wrote to the clerk and requested that he be given in writing the reasons for denial of his tenure. Respondent met on May 11, 2004, in executive session to discuss a response to petitioner's request. By letter dated May 13, 2004, respondent's clerk enumerated six reasons for the denial of tenure. Thereafter, petitioner sent a letter dated May 17, 2004, to the clerk responding in detail to the reasons that had been provided.

After several months of discussion and negotiation, on August 24, 2004, respondent voted again by a 5-2 margin to deny tenure. That determination was sent to petitioner by the clerk in a letter dated August 26, 2004, which also advised him that his final date of employment would be September 3, 2004. It appears that petitioner was paid through September 24, 2004.

Petitioner claims that his dismissal was wrongful in several respects. He argues that from 1998 to 2004 he served in the same basic job description and performed the same or similar duties, both before and after respondent's actions of July 24 and August 28, 2001, and that he could not be denied tenure, which he had acquired by estoppel. He claims further that respondent did not comply with Education Law §3031(b) because the reasons he was given for denial of tenure were not the "board's reasons," in that they were not properly formulated, or were vague, ambiguous, and inadequate, and were communicated to him by the clerk rather than by respondent itself. He alleges that his termination was in violation of his constitutional right of free speech, and was also in violation of the collective bargaining agreement between the district and the Utica Administrator's Association. Petitioner asks that I annul respondent's August 24, 2004, action and order that he be reinstated to his position from September 3, 2004, with full pay and benefits as a tenured employee.

Respondent denies that it acted contrary to law, and asks that the petition be dismissed in its entirety.

I cannot accept petitioner's argument that he acquired tenure by estoppel because he performed the same or similar job duties during his entire time with the district. The vacancy announcement for the original job he held, Staff Development Trainer/Facilitator at Proctor High School, required experience in school-based staff development and the ability to train staff in block scheduling, cooperative learning, diversity, technology, behavior management and learning styles. The position required a teaching certificate, and was a school-year position which also included 25 days of work in the summer. The position reported to the principal of Proctor High School, paid $59,000 per year, and was subject to the collective bargaining agreement with the Utica Teacher's Association.

The position created in 2001, Director of Staff Development, Planning and Technology, was substantially different. The position encompassed substantial supervisory responsibilities and a district-wide role:

> Encompasses the overall district leadership in the on-going process of district-wide and site planning, staff development, and implementation and evaluation of the

> District Technology Plan, and development, implementation and evaluation of the District Professional Development Plan (PDP) and the Comprehensive District Education Plan (CDEP). Performs any other duties assigned by the Superintendent.

The new position required certification as a school district administrator, was a twelve-month position, and reported directly to the superintendent. Petitioner was hired at a salary of $79,153, more than $18,000 per year above his salary of $61,000 in his previous position and was subject to the collective bargaining agreement with the Utica Administrator's Association.

While there was a considerable carryover of duties, it is clear that petitioner was appointed to a newly-created position on August 28, 2001, and that both employer and employee were well aware of that fact. It is true that the Board's action was characterized as a "change of assignment," and that there is no specific mention of a probationary appointment beginning September 4, 2001. However, on the record before me, petitioner's claim that he essentially did the same job the entire time he was employed by the district exalts form over substance. Based upon the affidavit of the district's Director of Personnel and the extensive documentation attached thereto, I find that petitioner did not acquire tenure by estoppel, but that he entered upon a new administrative position as a probationary appointee effective September 4, 2001.

Generally, a board of education has the unfettered right to terminate a probationary employee's employment for any reason unless the employee establishes that he was terminated for a constitutionally impermissible reason or in violation of a statutory proscription (*James v. Bd. of Educ.*, 37 NY2d 891; *Matter of Strax v. Rockland County Bd. of Coop. Educ. Services*, 257 AD2d 578; *Appeal of Jackolski*, 43 Ed Dept Rep 418, Decision No. 15,038). Here petitioner claims that respondent violated Education Law §3031(b) because the reasons for the board's action stated in the clerk's letter of May 13, 2004, are legally insufficient. Education Law §3031(b) provides that when a candidate for tenure has been rejected by a board of education, the candidate may "request in writing that he be furnished with a written statement giving the board's reasons for such intended action and within seven days thereafter such written statement should be furnished."

In this case, after petitioner's May 7, 2004, request, respondent met on May 11, 2004, to discuss a response. Prior to the meeting, on

May 10, the then-president of respondent sent an e-mail to the superintendent, clerk, and board members outlining five reasons why tenure should be denied. Several affidavits give conflicting versions of the discussion at the ensuring May 11 meeting. It appears that at least some of the other board members who had earlier voted to deny tenure presented additional reasons. It does not appear that any formal vote was taken during this meeting. However, the then-president, counsel, and current president of respondent indicate that a "head count" was taken by the then-president, and that a majority of board members was in agreement at least as to the reasons stated in his e-mail. The then-president thereafter directed the clerk to respond to petitioner's demand, apparently directing that all reasons brought forth in the meeting be included in such letter.

The clerk's letter of May 13 stated six reasons for the denial of tenure, is similar in many respects to the e-mail sent by the then-board president, and, according to affidavits in the record, does not present all of the board's reasons for denying tenure. Based upon these conflicting affidavits, petitioner claims that he is entitled to tenure.

Where a superintendent has failed to provide reasons for a negative recommendation pursuant to Education Law §3031(a), the proper remedy is not to grant tenure, but to direct the formulation of appropriate specific reasons, and to give the aggrieved petitioner the opportunity to respond (*Appeal of Ruff*, 33 Ed Dept Rep 648, Decision No. 13,181). Similarly, where reasons given pursuant to §3031(a) were deemed insufficiently specific, the proper remedy is also to require new reasons, but not to reinstate petitioner (*Matter of Rathbone v. Bd. of Educ.*, 47 AD2d 172; aff'd, 41 NY2d 825). Neither party has cited any case where the reasons supplied pursuant to §3031(b) are allegedly incomplete. It would seem that where, as here, not all reasons discussed by the board were included in its response to petitioner, respondent must be limited to the reasons actually given, and precluded from now attempting to add additional reasons. For that reason, I will limit my analysis to the reasons given in the clerk's letter of May 13, 2004. Although disputed by the superintendent's affidavit, I conclude that the reasons given in the letter were supported by a majority of board members, and are the "board's reasons" for denying tenure.

The first five reasons given in the May 13, 2004, letter pertain to petitioner's failure to articulate certain district policies at a public meeting, failure to submit certain language to the Utica Teachers

Association with regard to its contract, failure to respond to telephone calls by the Utica Teachers Association president, acting in an unprofessional manner at board meetings, and failure to provide certain information after requests were made by the board of education. These are essentially the reasons given by the then-board president in his May 10 e-mail. The sixth reason charges petitioner's failure to supervise his secretarial staff properly.

In response, on May 17, 2004, petitioner submitted a four-page, single-spaced response, ably addressing the reasons given. In only one response did petitioner indicate any uncertainty as to the reason given, and there is no indication in the record that petitioner ever sought clarification of the reasons given to him prior to the due date of his response. In *Matter of Rathbone*, *supra*, the Appellate Division said that §3031 requires only that "the district superintendent would advise the teacher of the reasons for his recommendation so that in turn the teacher might be able to make a reasonable and logical reply" (47 AD2d at p. 175). The court further stated: "While the reasons ascribed for petitioner's termination could have been more explicit, it clearly expressed dissatisfaction . . . this being so, the board had the absolute right to end her employment regardless of specifics" (concurring opinion at p. 177). The specificity of a bill of particulars is not required (*Matter of Stevens*, 13 Ed Dept Rep 64, Decision No. 8,712). The same standard applies under both §3031(a) and (b) (*Appeal of Dituri and Blake*, 42 Ed Dept Rep 363, Decision No. 14,882). Based on this standard, I am satisfied that the reasons given in the clerk's letter of May 13, 2004, are sufficiently specific.

It would have been better practice had respondent formally voted upon the exact reasons for its intended action, but I find that the reasons ultimately posed were supported by a majority of board members. The fact that the reasons were transmitted by the clerk rather than by some member of the board is of no consequence, especially since it appears that this respondent routinely directed the clerk to make responses on its behalf.

Petitioner further claims that his determination was in violation of his constitutional right of free speech, apparently based on one of the reasons given in the clerk's letter objecting to his "non-professional and non-business-like manner when addressing the Board of Education publicly at meetings." In support of his claim, petitioner cites a single occasion when he addressed the board as a member of the public, rather than in his administrative capacity, on March 18, 2003. The board minutes for that meeting indicate that petitioner addressed the board because he "felt compelled to address Board Members and pledged that he would fight the battle of the students of the District to defeat those forces that were using the problems of the District for political gains." However, affidavits submitted by several board members indicate their dissatisfaction with petitioner's ability to articulate policy and explain various district actions at board meetings in his administrative capacity. There is no mention anywhere in respondent's papers regarding the incident to which petitioner refers. Petitioner fails to establish that respondent terminated him for a constitutionally impermissible purpose. Petitioner has the burden of proof to make an "evidentiary showing" of a statutory violation or a constitutionally impermissible purpose, not mere accusations or speculation (*Matter of Sachs*, 71 AD2d 898, aff'd 50 NY2d 830; *Appeal of Mahoney*, 43 Ed Dept Rep 483, Decision No. 15,060). I find that petitioner has failed to make the required showing of proof as to this claim.

Finally, I have examined the collective bargaining agreement between the Utica Administrators Association and the district covering the relevant period, and I do not find that there has been any violation. Further, I note that petitioner has not filed a grievance with respect to such contract.

Based upon the record before me, I cannot find that respondent's action in denying tenure to petitioner was arbitrary or capricious, in violation of lawful procedure, or for a constitutionally impermissible purpose.

THE APPEAL IS DISMISSED.

Decision No. 15,193

Appeal of KENNETH RUSSELL, on behalf of his daughter TYISHA KING-RUSSELL, from action of the Board of Education of the South Country Central School District, and Dr. Michael LaFever, Superintendent, regarding involuntary transfer.

(March 29, 2005)

APPEARANCES OF COUNSEL

Guercio & Guercio, attorneys for respondents, *Gary L. Steffanetta, Esq.*, of counsel

DECISION OF THE COMMISSIONER

MILLS, Commissioner.—Petitioner appeals actions of the Board of Education of the South Country Central School District and Superintendent Michael LaFever ("respondents") regarding an alleged involuntary transfer of his daughter Tyisha. The appeal must be dismissed.

Tyisha is a student at respondents' Bellport High School ("Bellport"). By letter dated July 30, 2004, district administrators informed petitioner that Tyisha had been selected as a candidate for the district's South Haven High School Academy ("South Haven") program to begin in September 2004. At a meeting on September 9, 2004, petitioner told the superintendent that he did not want Tyisha to attend South Haven. The superintendent told petitioner that Tyisha could continue to attend Bellport pending due process procedures for an involuntary transfer. On September 9, 2004, petitioner withdrew Tyisha from Bellport and, thereafter, commenced this appeal. Petitioner re-enrolled Tyisha in Bellport on September 14, 2004.

Petitioner contends that Tyisha was involuntarily transferred to South Haven in violation of Education Law §3214(5) and that she was denied due process. He further alleges that the facilities at South Haven are inferior to those at Bellport, and that his daughter's assignment to South Haven was unconstitutionally based upon her race. He requests that Tyisha be allowed to remain at Bellport and asks that the decision to implement the South Haven program be reversed.

The Commissioner will only decide matters in actual controversy and will not render a decision on a state of facts which no longer exists or which subsequent events have laid to rest (*Appeal of K.M.*, 41 Ed Dept Rep 318, Decision No. 14,699; *Appeal of N.B.*, 40 *id*. 515, Decision No. 14,542; *Appeal of N.C.*, 40 *id*. 445, Decision No. 14,522). Here, petitioner's daughter was readmitted to Bellport before this appeal was filed. The record also reflects that respondents do not plan to require petitioner's daughter to attend South Haven; she may continue to attend Bellport. Therefore, this appeal is moot (*Appeal of K.M., supra*; *Appeal of D.C.*, 41 Ed Dept Rep 277, Decision No. 14,684; *Appeal of Camille S.*, 39 *id*. 574, Decision No. 14,316).

In light of this disposition, I need not address the parties' remaining contentions.

THE APPEAL IS DISMISSED.

346 EDUC 03-31-2005

Decision No. 15,194

Appeal of APRIL JONES-WHITE from action of the Board of Education of the Hempstead Union Free School District and Regina Lattimore-Gordon, President, regarding her removal as a trustee.

(March 29, 2005)

APPEARANCES OF COUNSEL

C. Robinson, Thompson & Assoc., LLP, attorneys for petitioner, *Princess M. Tate, Esq*., of counsel

Meyer, Suozzi, English & Klein, P.C., attorneys for respondents, *A. Thomas Levin* and *Robert N. Zausmer, Esqs*., of counsel

DECISION OF THE COMMISSIONER

MILLS, Commissioner.—Petitioner appeals the decision of the Board of Education of the Hempstead Union Free School District ("respondent board") and its past president, Regina Lattimore-Gordon ("respondent Lattimore–Gordon"), to remove her as a trustee. The appeal must be dismissed.

Petitioner was initially elected as one of five trustees of respondent board in May 1998 and reelected to a second three-year term in May 2001. In October 2001, respondent board retained a special counsel to investigate six allegations against petitioner, including two allegations that between 1998 and 2001 she improperly charged to the district over $8,000 in personal expenses. In December 2001, the special counsel issued his confidential report. Although petitioner demonstrated the propriety of certain expenses totaling $3,053.43, she could not provide documentation for many other expenditures. Accordingly, after several discussions between petitioner and respondent board, the parties signed an agreement on March 1, 2002, that petitioner would repay the district $3,398.14 for disallowed expenses according to a specific payment schedule. The parties also agreed to meet within 60 days of the signing of the agreement to attempt to resolve an additional $2,242.08 remaining in dispute. According to respondents, although petitioner eventually repaid the full $3,398.14 pursuant to the March 2002 agreement, she failed to comply with the payment schedule and never arranged to resolve the disputed $2,242.08.

Respondents assert that in the Spring of 2003, petitioner abused her trustee position by involving herself in a district investigation of a family member and by preventing respondent board from conducting official business, among other things. On July 1, 2003, respondents were presented with a petition signed by 537 citizens calling for petitioner's resignation or for respondent board to remove petitioner from office.

At respondent board's meeting on July 17, 2003, a majority of the board voted to proceed with formal charges seeking petitioner's removal pursuant to Education Law §1709(18). Petitioner was served with notice of seven formal charges of official misconduct and notice of a hearing scheduled for August 7, 2003. She was also notified of the charges and hearing date by certified letter dated July 18, 2003.

Petitioner was charged with seven counts of official misconduct by abusing her position as a trustee for her personal benefit. Charge number one alleged that between August 1998 and August 2001, petitioner charged various personal expenses on a district credit card and obtained reimbursement from the district for various other personal expenses not related to her official duties, and refused to account for or reimburse those expenses (including the $2,242.08 in contested funds enumerated in the March 2002 agreement). The remaining six charges involved allegations that she interfered with a district investigation concerning her brother and improperly exerted her influence as a trustee in several instances. Charges one and seven had previously been considered as part of the special counsel's 2001 investigation.

At the hearing on August 7, 2003, respondent board convened in executive session to hear the charges against petitioner, then reconvened in public session to deliberate further and issue its determination in the early morning hours of August 8, 2003. Respondent board sustained five of the seven charges of official misconduct against petitioner (charges 1 through 3, 5 and 6) and resolved to remove her from office pursuant to Education Law §1709(18). This appeal ensued. Petitioner's request for interim relief was denied on September 30, 2003.

Petitioner asserts that her removal from respondent board was motivated by the political animus of the other trustees, especially in light of the fact that in February 2003, the board had already considered and found no official misconduct for her failure to meet the terms of the March 2002 financial agreement. She claims, therefore, that reconsideration of the financial charges is barred by the doctrine of *res judicata*. Petitioner also contends that the removal proceeding was not in accordance with Education Law, the Commissioner's regulations or §2410 of the official Hempstead policy manual. She contends further that the acts complained of do not constitute official misconduct and do not justify her removal from respondent board. She also maintains that the notice of charges and the August 7 hearing were insufficient; she was not afforded due process; and she was denied access to documents necessary for the filing of her petition. In addition, petitioner claims that respondent board should not have proceeded under Education Law §1709, but that the Commissioner should have exercised his jurisdiction under Education Law §306. Petitioner seeks reinstatement to her position as a trustee.

Respondents assert that the appeal is untimely. They also contend that the five sustained charges of official misconduct are supported by credible evidence. Respondents maintain that petitioner was afforded due process and had a full and fair opportunity to defend herself.

I will first address several procedural issues. The Commissioner of Education will only consider matters in actual controversy and will not render a decision on a state of facts which no longer exist or which subsequent events have laid to rest (*Appeal of Passer*, 44 Ed Dept Rep ___, Decision No. 15,160; *Appeal of Colety, et al.*, 42 *id*. 162, Decision No. 14,806). For relief, petitioner requests an interim order (which was denied) and reinstatement to the board. The parties agree that petitioner's term of office expired. Therefore, since reinstatement is no longer possible, the appeal must be dismissed as moot.

Even if the appeal were not dismissed on procedural grounds, it would be dismissed on the merits. Petitioner alleges that respondent board should have deferred to the Commissioner and sought to have her removed pursuant to Education Law §306. While Education Law §306 authorizes the Commissioner of Education to remove a member of a board of education in certain circumstances (see, e.g., *Appeal and Application of Davis*, 43 Ed Dept Rep 323, Decision No. 15,007; *Application of Kavitsky*, 41 *id*. 231, Decision No. 14,672; *Application of Lilker*, 40 *id*. 704, Decision No. 14,588), the board of education of a union free school district has the power, among other things, "[t]o remove any member of their board for official misconduct" (Education Law §1709(18)). Therefore, I find no merit to this claim.

I also find no merit to petitioner's due process claims. Section 1709(18) requires that a written copy of the charges must be served at least ten days before the hearing and the trustee must be "allowed a full and fair opportunity to refute such charges before removal." On the record before me, I find that petitioner was afforded sufficient due process to satisfy this standard. The record reflects that on July 17, 2003, respondents' attorney hand-delivered to petitioner a copy of the charges and notice of the hearing, and sent the same by certified letter dated July 18, 2003, and the hearing was held on August 7, 2003, more than ten days later.

Further, I find that the charges were sufficiently detailed to apprise petitioner of the conduct that would be at issue at the hearing. I also find that petitioner was not deprived of any due process by respondent board's alleged failure to respond to her discovery requests. Petitioner cites no statutory or constitutional right to formal discovery in a removal proceeding conducted pursuant to Education Law §1709(18). As long as petitioner receives adequate notice of the charges, due process is served (*Appeals of Gill and Burnett*, 42 Ed Dept Rep 89, Decision No. 14,785; *Gill v. Mills and St. Ed. Dept.*, Supreme Court, Albany County, Bradley, J.; Judgment granted dismissing petition to review; October 6, 2003, n.o.r.).

Petitioner also cites no statutory or constitutional right to counsel in a removal proceeding conducted pursuant to Education Law §1709(18). The hearing record reflects that petitioner was afforded a full and fair opportunity to refute the charges and that she was permitted the opportunity to cross-examine the hearing witnesses, examine respondent board's documentary evidence, and introduce her own witnesses and evidence. Petitioner was served notice of the hearing on July 17, 2003, and had ample time to prepare for the hearing, especially since she had previously participated in the investigation of the most serious charge regarding the financial improprieties.

To constitute grounds for removal pursuant to Education Law §1709(18), the "official misconduct" must clearly relate to a board member's official duties, either because of the allegedly unauthorized exercise of the member's powers or the intentional failure to exercise those powers to the detriment of the school district (*Appeals of Gill and Burnett*, *supra*; *Appeal of Balen*, 40 Ed Dept Rep 479, Decision No. 14,532; *Appeal of Cox*, 27 *id.* 353, Decision No. 11,973).

Based on my review of the record, including the hearing transcript, I find sufficient proof to establish grounds for petitioner's removal based on charge one alone regarding the financial improprieties. The record contains the special counsel's December 2001 report of the investigation of over $8,000 of questioned expenses, including district credit card statements, board expense reports, and interviews with the district's assistant business manager, district clerk, board president and petitioner. The $3,398.14 in disallowed expenses included over $1,200 of undocumented cash advances and credit card charges for auto care, Ritz Camera, Walgreen's, Wal-Mart, Walbaums, and 16 months of AOL, among other personal items. The $2,242.08 in unresolved expenditures included credit card charges for People Magazine, rental cars, auto care and airline tickets, among other things. Not only were these items fully investigated in the fall of 2001, but petitioner also signed an agreement in March of 2002 to repay $3,398.14 for disallowed expenditures and executed a confession of judgment for the same amount to be held in escrow by the district's attorneys in the event she defaulted. Since petitioner did not adhere to the payment schedule specified in the agreement, respondent board could have filed the confession of judgment in court at any time. In addition, although petitioner agreed in 2002 to meet to resolve the $2,242.08 of questioned expenses, she had not taken any steps to do so by the time charges were preferred on July 17, 2003. Indeed, petitioner has yet to present any documentation demonstrating the legitimacy of these expenses.

For petitioner to assert that respondents erred in not requesting timely reimbursement from her or that her only error was solely a lack of documentation caused by various moves and relocations is disingenuous and not persuasive. The record indicates that petitioner was not only fully cognizant of respondent board's policies and rules regarding expenses, credit cards and reimbursements, but had been a member of respondent board and had voted to enact some of those policies. There is clear documentary evidence dating back more than five years that petitioner made improper charges and failed to reimburse the district for those charges. There can be no question that petitioner is guilty of official misconduct for improperly using district funds for her personal benefit and/or failing to provide documentation to justify the propriety of those expenditures.

Nor do I find relevant to the issue of petitioner's removal any alleged improper expenditures by other board members. Moreover, petitioner misstates the nature of respondent board's motion in February 2003. At that time, the board merely failed to pass a resolution to request that the Commissioner remove petitioner from the board; it did not make an affirmative finding that petitioner had not engaged in any misconduct. The mere fact that an earlier motion to request petitioner's removal failed to pass is irrelevant to the clear and rational finding of misconduct by respondent board at the hearing on August 7, 2003. Respondent board's finding of guilt on charge one is supported by substantial evidence and provides more than sufficient grounds for petitioner's removal under Education Law §1709(18).

Finally, petitioner seeks a certificate of good faith pursuant to Education Law §3811 so that the district can reimburse her reasonable and necessary legal costs. Education Law §3811 provides for the reimbursement of legal expenses incurred by a member of a board of education arising out of the exercise of his or her powers or the performance of his or her duties, except where they are incurred to defend either "a criminal prosecution or an action or proceeding brought against [her] by a school district." School board members are not entitled to recover costs incurred in defending themselves in removal proceedings (*In re Singer*, 153 Misc. 755). Accordingly, petitioner is not entitled to indemnification for her legal expenses, and her request for a certificate of good faith is denied.

In light of this disposition, I need not address the merits of the remaining charges against petitioner or the parties' remaining contentions.

THE APPEAL IS DISMISSED.

Decision No. 15,195

Appeal of ALAN H. and BARBARA T. AUSTIN, on behalf of their daughter ANNE, from action of the Board of Education of the Albion Central School District regarding dual enrollment.

(March 29, 2005)

APPEARANCES OF COUNSEL

David W. Lippitt, Esq., attorney for respondent

DECISION OF THE COMMISSIONER

MILLS, Commissioner.—Petitioners challenge the refusal of the Board of Education of the Albion Central School District ("respondent") to enroll their daughter, Anne, in a program run jointly through Genesee Community College ("GCC") and Genesee Valley Board of Cooperative Educational Services ("BOCES").

Anne attends a nonpublic school. On March 23, 2004, she applied to the College Tech Prep Legal Careers Academy ("Academy") run by GCC and BOCES for the 2004-2005 school year. She was accepted on June 10, 2004, and on July 28, 2004, received a second letter inviting her to an orientation session on August 18, 2004. Mrs. Austin states that on August 31, 2004, a BOCES representative verbally informed her that Anne could not attend the Academy because respondent's superintendent would not allow her participation in the program. According to petitioners, that was the first time they heard of the requirement to submit a request for dual enrollment to the home school district by June 1.

Petitioners contend that they were unaware of the June 1 filing deadline and were never advised by any school official to submit a request for dual enrollment. Moreover, Anne was not accepted into the program until June 10, after the deadline had passed. They claim that other school districts permit students from Anne's school to attend the Academy and may "waive" the deadline. They also imply that respondent should have posted a notice regarding the June 1 requirement. Petitioners request a waiver of the June 1 deadline, a determination that Anne is entitled to attend the Academy, and a determination that respondent is required to pay tuition for Anne to attend the Academy.

Respondent contends that petitioners failed to comply with the statutory deadline, which is also incorporated in its Board Policy 8600. Respondent further contends that petitioners have provided no authority to excuse their delay or to permit a waiver.

Education Law §3602-c permits a nonpublic school pupil to enroll in a public school program in career education. However, the student's parent, guardian or legal custodian must file a written request to enroll the student in such program no later than the first day of June preceding the school year for which the request is made (Education Law §3602-c(2)). Here, petitioners admit that they did not submit a written request for Anne's enrollment in the Academy.

In an appeal to the Commissioner of Education, petitioners have the burden of establishing the facts upon which relief is requested and the burden of demonstrating a clear legal right to the relief sought (8 NYCRR §275.10; *Appeal of Ritters*, 44 Ed Dept Rep 117, Decision No. 15,117; *Appeal of Beauman*, 43 *id.* 212; Decision No. 14,974). Petitioners cite no authority for waiver of the statutory deadline for enrollment applications. Their allegation that they were unaware of the deadline does not provide a legal basis for the requested relief, nor does the fact that Anne's acceptance occurred after the deadline. In addition, §3602-c(2) does not require respondent to post a notice of the deadline.

THE APPEAL IS DISMISSED.

Decision No. 15,196

Appeal of DONNA M. BATES, on behalf of her daughter BARBARA J. REID, from action of the Board of Education of the Bainbridge-Guilford Central School District regarding residency.

(March 29, 2005)

APPEARANCES OF COUNSEL

Hogan, Sarzynski, Lynch, Surowka, & DeWind, LLP, attorneys for respondent, *Wendy K. DeWind, Esq*., of counsel

DECISION OF THE COMMISSIONER

MILLS, Commissioner.—Petitioner appeals the determination of the Board of Education of the Bainbridge-Guilford Central School District ("respondent") that her daughter, Barbara, is not entitled to attend respondent's schools for the 2004-2005 school year. The appeal must be dismissed.

Petitioner resides at an address on State Highway No. 7 in Bainbridge. The parties agree that petitioner's property intersects the boundary line between respondent's district and the Afton Central School District ("Afton"). During the 2003-2004 school year, petitioner elected to send Barbara to Afton.

On August 27, 2004, petitioner requested that respondent admit Barbara to respondent's schools for eighth grade. According to petitioner, respondent denied her request on September 1, 2004. By letter dated September 13, 2004, the superintendent advised petitioner that her request was denied because she had failed to notify both districts in writing prior to August 1 that she desired a change in enrollment. This appeal ensued. Petitioner's request for interim relief was denied on September 28, 2004.

Petitioner asserts that she pays taxes in both school districts and seeks a determination that her daughter is entitled to attend school in respondent's district without the payment of tuition. Petitioner also asserts that she contacted the superintendent in July about enrolling Barbara, and he did not inform her of the need to make a written request prior to August 1. She states that had she been so informed, she would have done so. Petitioner also states that she orally informed personnel at Afton that she was withdrawing Barbara, and they also did not inform her that she needed to give notice in writing prior to August 1.

Respondent denies that Barbara is entitled to attend school in the district for the 2004-2005 school year. Respondent asserts that its district clerk never received a notice of designation from petitioner on or before August 1. Respondent also avers that the superintendent first spoke with petitioner regarding Barbara's enrollment in respondent's district at the end of August 2004 when petitioner attempted to enroll her.

The appeal must be dismissed. Education Law §3203 (1) provides, in pertinent part:

> The owner of taxable property that is so located that the boundary line between two school districts intersects (a) the dwelling on said property or (b), in the case of an owner-occupied single family dwelling unit, the property on which the dwelling unit is located may designate the school in either of such districts to which the children lawfully residing in said dwelling on said property shall attend *by filing with the district clerk of each of such districts a notice of such designation on or before August first* in any year and thereafter ... and, until a subsequent designation shall be made and filed, such children shall be deemed to be resident children of the district designated and shall be entitled to the school privileges of such district as resident pupils without the payment of tuition. (Emphasis added)

The designation requirement in Education Law §3203(1) is clear and unambiguous. Thus, petitioner was required to notify each district by filing a notice of designation on or before August 1, which she failed to do.

Even if petitioner had relied on the alleged conversation with the superintendent in July, which respondent denies occurred, she would not be entitled to the requested relief. Equitable estoppel does not apply against a government subdivision except in limited circumstances not applicable here (*Parkview Assoc. v. City of New York*, 71 NY2d 274; *Appeal of Perez*, 42 Ed Dept Rep 71, Decision No. 14,779; *Appeal of Holzer, et al.*, 37 *id.* 549, Decision No. 13,924).

THE APPEAL IS DISMISSED.

Decision No. 15,197

Appeal of S.H., on behalf of her son S.H., from action of the Board of Education of the Patchogue-Medford Union Free School District regarding student discipline.

(March 30, 2005)

APPEARANCES OF COUNSEL

Tarsha C. Smith, Esq., attorney for petitioner

Ingerman Smith, L.L.P., attorneys for respondent, *Susan E. Fine, Esq.*, of counsel

DECISION OF THE COMMISSIONER

MILLS, Commissioner.—Petitioner appeals the suspension of her son, S.H., by the Board of Education of the Patchogue-Medford Union Free School District ("respondent"). The appeal must be sustained in part.

S.H.'s suspension arose from an incident at respondent's high school cafeteria on Thursday, November 6, 2003. S.H. allegedly struck two security guards as they tried to remove him from the cafeteria, and he continued to kick and punch at the guards as they attempted to restrain him. S.H. finally accompanied the guards and principal into an adjacent classroom, but continued to curse and yell, overturn desks, throw chairs and spit on the floor. The principal suspended S.H. for insubordination for five days, commencing Friday, November 7, 2003.

The principal avers that petitioner was telephoned as soon as S.H. was removed from the cafeteria and that S.H.'s father called the school about 40 minutes after the incident and spoke with the dean of students. The principal also avers that she spoke by telephone with petitioner on the morning of November 7. The suspension notice, dated November 6, 2003, was mailed by certified mail on Monday, November 10, 2003.

By letter dated November 7, 2003, the superintendent notified petitioner and her husband of a superintendent's hearing scheduled for November 13, 2003. In the afternoon of November 12, 2003, petitioner's attorney requested an adjournment. The hearing was rescheduled for November 17, 2003, at which time petitioner appeared and requested a second adjournment because her attorney was unavailable. The hearing was rescheduled for December 10, 2003, at which time petitioner requested a third adjournment, to a date between December 29 and January 15, 2004, and thereafter commenced this appeal. Petitioner's request for interim relief was denied on December 29, 2003.

The hearing scheduled for January 15, 2004, was canceled due to a snowstorm and rescheduled for February 5, 2004. At that time, petitioner's attorney requested another adjournment until such time as criminal charges against S.H. arising from the same incident were resolved.

Petitioner contends that respondent violated Education Law §3214 and her son's constitutional right to due process. She contends that she was not afforded proper notice of S.H.'s initial five-day suspension. She also claims that she did not receive adequate notice of the November 17, 2003, superintendent's hearing. She further asserts that S.H. was inadequately supervised and protected on the day of the incident, and was provoked, humiliated, taunted, assaulted and battered by district personnel. Petitioner contends that her son was subject to an illegal transfer, that the home instruction provided to him was inadequate, and that her requests for S.H's readmission to school were denied. Petitioner seeks to have S.H. readmitted to school, requests that the five-day suspension be annulled and expunged from S.H.'s record, and seeks a determination precluding respondent from taking further disciplinary action against him.

Respondent contends that the petition fails to state a claim upon which relief may be granted, and maintains that the suspension and notice were proper. Respondent further asserts that petitioner lacks standing with respect to her claims under Education Law §3214(3)(c)(1), and contends that petitioner failed to exhaust administrative remedies. Respondent further alleges that petitioner is responsible for S.H.'s extended time out of school because she requested repeated adjournments of the superintendent's hearing and argues that the principal was not obligated to inform petitioner of the five-day suspension in advance because of the danger S.H. presented.

In addition, respondent states that petitioner requested an adjournment of the superintendent's hearing and agreed to keep S.H. on home instruction until pending criminal charges against him were resolved. Respondent also asserts that although it was not required to provide alternative instruction for S.H. because he is over 16 years of age, it nevertheless provided such instruction.

With regard to S.H.'s initial five-day suspension, respondent's contention that the appeal must be dismissed because petitioner failed to exhaust her administrative remedies is without merit. Education Law §3214 does not require a petitioner to appeal a suspension of five days or less to the board of education unless a school district has adopted a policy requiring appeals of short-term suspensions to the board of education before appealing to the Commissioner (*Appeal of S.C.*, 44 Ed Dept Rep 164, Decision No. 15,134; *Appeal of Amara S.*, 39 *id.* 90, Decision No. 14,182). The record does not demonstrate that respondent has such a policy. Therefore, I will not dismiss petitioner's claims regarding the short-term suspension for failure to exhaust.

In the case of a suspension of five days or less, the suspending authority must provide the pupil with notice of the charged misconduct. The pupil and the person in parental relation to the pupil must be given an opportunity for an informal conference with the principal. The notice and opportunity for an informal conference must take place prior to the suspension of the pupil, unless the pupil's presence in the school poses a continuing danger or threat, in which case the notice and opportunity for an informal conference must take place as soon after the suspension as is reasonably practicable. (Education Law §3214(3)(b)(1), 8 NYCRR §100.2(l)(4)).

The record indicates that S.H.'s actions "pose[d] a continuing danger to persons or property or an ongoing threat of disruption to the academic process" (*Id.*). Accordingly, the principal was authorized to suspend S.H. without prior notice. However, the statute and regulation require that notice and opportunity for an informal conference "take place as soon after the suspension as is reasonably practicable." In this case, S.H. was suspended commencing Friday, November 7, the principal mailed the notice, by certified mail, on Monday, November 10, and petitioner did not receive the notice until November 15. Thus, S.H. served the entire five-day suspension before petitioner received the written notice. Although petitioner was informed of the suspension by telephone, oral communication with a parent regarding a suspension is not a substitute for the required written notification (*Appeal of J.G.*, 39 Ed Dept Rep 393, Decision No. 14,270). Accordingly, the five-day suspension must be expunged from petitioner's son's records (*see*, *Appeal of A Student with a Disability*, 40 Ed Dept Rep 47, Decision No. 14,418; *Appeal of J.G., supra*).

Petitioner also claims that the notice of the Monday, November 17, 2003, superintendent's hearing was unreasonable because petitioner received the notice on Saturday, November 15, and her attorney did not receive the notice until November 17. However, even if the notice were found unreasonable, petitioner requested and received an adjournment and has failed to demonstrate how she was aggrieved by any delay.

Because this appeal was commenced prior to any superintendent's hearing or disposition, there is no indication in the record whether any further penalty was imposed on S.H. Accordingly, I need not address the parties' remaining arguments concerning the merits of the suspension.

THE APPEAL IS SUSTAINED IS PART.

IT IS ORDERED that respondent's suspension of petitioner's son from November 7, 2003, through November 14, 2003, be annulled and expunged from his record.

Decision No. 15,198

Appeal of MINDY WARSHAW from action of the Board of Education of the City School District of the City of Long Beach regarding the conduct of an annual budget vote.

(April 1, 2005)

APPEARANCES OF COUNSEL

Ingerman Smith L.L.P., attorneys for respondent, *Neil M. Block, Esq.*, of counsel

DECISION OF THE COMMISSIONER

MILLS, Commissioner—Petitioner challenges certain actions of the Board of Education of the City School District of the City of Long Beach ("respondent") with respect to the annual budget vote held on May 18, 2004. The appeal must be dismissed.

On May 18, 2004, respondent conducted its annual district meeting to vote on the district's budget. At that meeting, the budget was approved by a margin of 175 votes. This appeal ensued.

Petitioner asserts that respondent improperly used district resources to advocate a "yes" vote on the budget by permitting the district's parent-teacher association ("PTA") to distribute pro-budget flyers using teacher mailboxes and sending such flyers home with students. Petitioner claims that respondent's action violates a stipulation of settlement of two prior appeals challenging similar action by the board. Petitioner also claims that respondent's high school principal made an announcement during the school day urging students and parents to vote "yes" on the budget. Petitioner seeks annulment of the May 18, 2004, budget vote and an order directing a re-vote on the budget. She also seeks removal of Lynn Gergen as president of the district's PTA and an order barring the PTA from distributing literature to students at school. As part of her appeal, petitioner requested a stay of any expenditures authorized by the May 18, 2004, budget. Petitioner's request for a stay was denied on June 29, 2004.

Respondent denies that it engaged in any improper electioneering. Respondent also asserts that, even if improper electioneering occurred, petitioner failed to demonstrate that it affected the outcome of the budget vote. Finally, respondent asserts that petitioner may not maintain the appeal on behalf of a class of individuals.

Class certification is denied to the extent that petitioner attempts to bring this appeal on behalf of a class of "all others similarly situated." An appeal may only be maintained on behalf of a class where the class is so numerous that joinder of all members is impracticable and where all questions of fact and law are common to all members of the class (8 NYCRR §275.2; *Appeal of Cartagena*, 43 Ed Dept Rep 272, Decision No. 14,992; *Appeal of Recore*, 42 *id.* 283, Decision No. 14,856). Petitioner's pleadings are entirely devoid of any allegations addressing those criteria. Class status, therefore, is denied.

To the extent that petitioner seeks removal of Lynn Gergen as president of the district's PTA, the appeal must be dismissed for failure to join her as a necessary party. A party whose rights would be adversely affected by a determination of an appeal in favor of petitioner is a necessary party and must be joined as such (*Appeal of* Merandy, 44 Ed Dept Rep 122, Decision No. 15,119; *Appeal of Stolbach*, 43 *id.* 218, Decision No. 14,977; *Appeals of Tesser and Kavitsky*, 42 *id.* 341, Decision No. 14,876). Section 275.8 of the Commissioner's regulations requires that a copy of the petition be personally served upon each named respondent. An individual must also be clearly named as a respondent in the caption of the petition and served with a copy of the notice of petition and petition, to inform the person that he or she should respond to the petition and enter a defense (*Appeal of Stolbach, supra*; *Appeals of Tesser and Kavitsky, supra*). It is the notice of petition which alerts a party to the fact that he or she is required to appear in the appeal and to answer the allegations contained in the petition (8 NYCRR §§275.11, 275.13; *Appeals of Tesser and Kavitsky, supra*; *Appeal of Monahan*, 42 Ed Dept Rep 206, Decision No. 14,824). Petitioner failed to name Ms. Gergen as a respondent in the caption of the petition and failed to personally serve her with the notice of petition and petition. Therefore, those portions of the appeal seeking relief as against Ms. Gergen are dismissed.

The petition must also be dismissed on the merits. While a board of education may distribute factual information to educate and inform voters regarding a vote or election, the use of district resources to distribute materials designed "to exhort the electorate to cast their ballots in support of a particular position advocated by the board" violates the constitutional prohibition against using public funds to promote a partisan position (*Phillips v. Maurer*, 67 NY2d 672; *Appeal of Hager and Scheuerman*, 43 Ed Dept Rep 363, Decision No. 15,019;

Appeal of Stolbach, supra). Statements that do not specifically urge a "yes" vote may nevertheless violate the holding in *Phillips v. Maurer*, if such statements otherwise seek to persuade or convey support for a particular position (*Appeal of Hager and Scheuerman, supra*; *Appeal of Stolbach, supra*). Moreover, it is improper for a board of education, as a corporate body, to be involved in partisan activity in the conduct of a school district election (*Appeal of Hager and Scheuerman, supra*; *Appeal of Eckert*, 40 Ed Dept Rep 433, Decision No. 14,520). Even indirect support, such as a school board giving a PTA access to its established channels of communication to parents to espouse a partisan position that the board itself was prohibited from doing directly, has been deemed improper (*Appeal of Hager and Scheuerman, supra*; *Appeals of Tesser and Kavitsky, supra*).

In an appeal to the Commissioner, petitioner has the burden of establishing a clear legal right to the relief sought and to establish facts upon which petitioner seeks relief (8 NYCRR §275.10; *Appeal of Brown*, 43 Ed Dept Rep 231, Decision No. 14,980; *Appeal of Stolbach, supra*; *Appeals of Tesser and Kavitsky, supra*). Petitioner asserts that, although the PTA flyer does not include any specific statement to vote "yes" on the budget, the information included "threatened massive cuts" if the budget was defeated and was meant to impose fear as a means of obtaining a "yes" vote. I have reviewed the flyer and find that it does not urge residents to vote in any particular manner. It presents information regarding the rate of the budget increase, the rate of the proposed tax levy, comparative tax rate information, student test score and college attendance information, and contingency budget information should the proposed budget be defeated. I conclude that the challenged flyer is primarily factual and informational in nature and cannot be fairly construed as advocating a "yes" vote.

Petitioner also asserts that the principal of respondent's high school made an announcement during school hours urging eligible students to vote in favor of the proposed budget and asking all students to tell their parents to vote for the budget. Respondent submits the principal's affidavit denying that allegation and petitioner did not submit a reply. Petitioner, thus, has not demonstrated that respondent engaged in improper electioneering in connection with the May 18, 2004, budget vote.

Moreover, to invalidate the results of a school district election, petitioner must establish not only that irregularities occurred, but also that the irregularities actually affected the outcome of the election (*Matter of Boyes v. Allen, et al.*, 32 AD2d 990, aff'd 26 NY2d 709; *Appeal of Brown, supra*; *Appeal of Stolbach, supra*) were so pervasive that they vitiated the electoral process (*Appeal of Brown, supra*; *Appeal of Stolbach, supra*; *Appeal of Laurie*, 42 Ed Dept Rep 313, Decision No. 14,867) or demonstrate a clear and convincing picture of informality to the point of laxity in adherence to the Education Law (*Appeal of Brown, supra*; *Appeal of Stolbach, supra*; *Matter of Levine*, 24 Ed Dept Rep 172, Decision No. 11,356, aff'd sub nom, *Capobianco v. Ambach and Bd. of Ed., Glen Cove City School Dist.*, 112 AD2d 640). Implicit in these decisions is a recognition that it is a rare case where errors in the conduct of a school election become so pervasive that they vitiate the fundamental fairness of the election (*Appeal of Brown, supra*; *Appeal of Stolbach, supra*; *Appeal of Laurie, supra*).

At the May 18, 2004, annual meeting, the budget was approved by a margin of 175 votes. Petitioner submits only two affidavits from district voters. In each affidavit, the voter challenges the content of the flyer and its distribution via teacher mailboxes and to students. However, neither voter indicates that the flyer influenced her vote. Moreover, given the margin of approval, petitioner has failed to establish that the alleged irregularity affected the outcome of the vote.

In sum, I find that petitioner has failed to establish that any alleged irregularity actually affected the outcome, demonstrated laxity in adherence to the Education Law or vitiated the fundamental fairness of the vote. In view of this determination, I need not address the parties' remaining contentions.

THE APPEAL IS DISMISSED.

Decision No. 15,199

Appeal of EDWARD H. CIFFONE from action of the Board of Education of the Yorktown Central School District, Dr. Gordon Bruno, Superintendent, and Regina M. Pitruzzello, District Clerk, regarding a bond vote.

Appeal of EDWARD H. CIFFONE, on behalf of school district voters, from action of the Board of Education of the Yorktown Central School District, Dr. Gordon Bruno, Superintendent, and Regina M. Pitruzzello, District Clerk, regarding a bond vote.

Appeal of GILBERT KAUFMANN, from action of the Board of Education of the Yorktown Central School District, Dr. Gordon Bruno, Superintendent, and Regina M. Pitruzzello, District Clerk, regarding a bond vote.

Appeal of GILBERT KAUFMANN, on behalf of school district voters, from action of the Board of Education of the Yorktown Central School District, Dr. Gordon Bruno, Superintendent, and Regina M. Pitruzzello, District Clerk, regarding a bond vote.

(April 6, 2005)

APPEARANCES OF COUNSEL

Shaw & Perelson, LLP, attorneys for respondents, *Margo L. May* and *Jillian E. Cass, Esqs.*, of counsel

DECISION OF THE COMMISSIONER

MILLS, Commissioner—Petitioners Ciffone and Kaufmann each filed two appeals, individually and on behalf of district voters, seeking an order setting aside the results of a special district meeting held by the Board of Education of the Yorktown Central School District ("respondent board or board") on October 13, 2004. Because the appeals raise common issues of law and fact, they are consolidated for decision. The appeals must be dismissed.

At the special district meeting, district voters approved funding for an addition to Yorktown High School, and renovation of the High School library for use as administrative offices, by a vote of 651 to 337. These appeals ensued. Petitioners allege that the published notice of the meeting was defective, and that the vote must therefore be set aside. Petitioners' requests for interim relief were denied on October 27, 2004.

Respondents contend that the petitions fail to demonstrate a clear legal right to the relief requested. Respondents deny that the notice is defective and assert that even if there was an error in the notice, it was *de minimus* and did not affect the legality of the notice or the outcome of the vote.

I must first address several procedural issues, starting with petitioners' replies. The purpose of a reply is to respond to new material or affirmative defenses set forth in an answer (8 NYCRR §§275.3 and 275.14). A reply is not meant to buttress allegations in the petition or to belatedly add assertions that should have been in the petition (*Appeal of Schildhorn*, 44 Ed Dept Rep 212, Decision No.

15,152; *Appeal of General*, 43 *id.* 146, Decision No. 14,948). Therefore, while I have reviewed petitioners' replies, I have not considered those portions containing new allegations that are not responsive to new material or affirmative defenses set forth in the answers.

In their respective replies, petitioners ask to join as a respondent the district's bond counsel who prepared the notice. A party whose rights would be adversely affected by a determination of an appeal in favor of a petitioner is a necessary party and must be joined as such (*Appeal of M.C.*, 43 Ed Dept Rep 276, Decision No. 14,993). I do not find that bond counsel's rights would be adversely affected by my determination and I therefore decline to join bond counsel as a party to these appeals.

In two of the four appeals, petitioners attempt to appeal on behalf of "school district voters." An appeal may only be maintained on behalf of a class where the class is so numerous that joinder of all members is impracticable and where all questions of fact and law are common to all members of the class (8 NYCRR §275.2; *Appeal of Ockimey*, 44 Ed Dept Rep 169, Decision No. 15,136; *Appeal of Garmaeva*, 43 *id.* 253, Decision No. 14,988; *Appeal of Colety, et al.*, 42 *id.* 162, Decision No. 14,806). Petitioners must set forth the number of individuals they seek to represent and must show that all questions of law and fact would be common to all members of the class (*Appeal of Recore*, 42 Ed Dept Rep 283, Decision No. 14,856; *Appeal of Colety, et al., supra*). Here, petitioners have not set forth the number of prospective members of the class, but merely assert that "some 8000 individuals are registered to vote" in the district. Nor have they demonstrated that all the potential class members have the same interests or claims. In any event, a determination as to the individual petitioners will resolve the issue concerning the vote. Thus, there is no need for class certification (*Appeal of Bluemke, et al.*, 39 Ed Dept Rep 447, Decision No. 14,281). Accordingly, class certification is denied.

Turning to the merits, notice of the special district meeting was published four times within the seven weeks prior to the vote on October 13, 2004. The notice appeared, in pertinent part:

> **NOTICE OF SPECIAL DISTRICT MEETING**
> **YORKTOWN CENTRAL SCHOOL DISTRICT,**
> **IN THE COUNTY OF WESTCHESTER, NEW YORK**
>
> NOTICE IS HEREBY GIVEN that pursuant to a resolution of the Board of Education of the Yorktown Central School District, in the County of Westchester, New York, adopted on August 12, 2004, a Special District Meeting of the qualified voters of said School District will be held on
>
> **Wednesday, October 13, 2004**
>
> from 7:00 o'clock A.M. to 9:00 o'clock P.M. (Prevailing Time) in the Mohansic Elementary School, 704 Locksley Road, Yorktown Heights, New York for the purpose of voting upon the following Bond Proposition: . . .

The substantive part of the notice contained five separately spaced paragraphs, (a)–(e), describing the bond proposition, followed by one longer paragraph containing the exact language that would appear on the ballot labels to be inserted in the voting machines.

Petitioners object to this sentence preceding the ballot language:

> Such Bond Proposition shall appear on the ballot labels to be inserted in the voting machines used for voting at *said Annual District Meeting and Election* in substantially the following form: (emphasis added).

They assert that the words "said Annual District Meeting and Election" are a critical part of the legal notice and clearly state that the bond proposition would occur at an annual district meeting. They argue, therefore, that the legal notice referred to the next annual meeting in May 2005, not the special meeting on October 13, 2004. Petitioners contend that the entire bond proposition must be declared null and void because it was erroneously placed before the voters at the special district meeting on October 13, 2004, instead of at an annual district meeting and election, as announced in the published legal notice. They also argue that many voters were misled and confused and presumably did not vote on October 13, 2004.

Respondents admit that the highlighted language appeared in the notice but assert that the language may be construed in two ways: that the bond proposition would appear on the ballot labels in the voting machines that had been used for the annual district meeting and election on May 18, 2004; or, that the use of the phrase "said Annual District Meeting and Election" was in error and should have read "Special District Meeting." Respondents contend that, to the extent the language was in error, the error was *de minimus* because it had no impact on the meaning of the notice. Respondents also assert that they received no questions or complaints concerning the wording or the date of the bond vote, that literature distributed to district residents contained the correct date, and that the total number of voters was substantially the same as the number who voted at the previous special district meeting in March 2004 at which the bond proposition was defeated. Respondents state that petitioners fail to allege that any voters were actually confused or misled by the notice.

Petitioners have failed to meet the burden of establishing the facts upon which they seek relief (8 NYCRR §275.10; *Appeal of Wierzchowski*, 39 Ed Dept Rep 682, Decision No. 14,348). The date of October 13, 2004, is clearly highlighted in bold letters near the center top of the notice and "October 2004" appears five more times in the body of the notice. I find that the date of the Special Meeting, October 13, 2004, is obvious when read in the context of the notice as a whole.

To the extent that the language at issue was erroneous, it is neither critical nor significant and does not warrant setting aside the election (*see* Education Law §2010; *Matter of Qualified Electors of CSD No. 6, Towns of Worcester, Westford, Decatur and Maryland, Otsego Cty*, 72 St. Dept. 13, Decision No. 5,561).

THE APPEALS ARE DISMISSED.

Decision No. 15,200

Appeal of LAWRENCE LOMBARDO from action of the Board of Education of the Lynbrook Union Free School District regarding training.

(April 6, 2005)

APPEARANCES OF COUNSEL

Ehrlich, Frazer & Feldman, attorneys for respondent, *Michael Perna, Esq.*, of counsel

DECISION OF THE COMMISSIONER

MILLS, Commissioner—Petitioner, a district resident, appeals the determination of the Board of Education of the Lynbrook Union Free School District ("respondent") to exclude him from training sessions for members of the district's Compact Team. The appeal must be dismissed.

Petitioner requested to participate in the district's training for Compact Team members. The superintendent and another district official denied his requests. He contends that since the training is being held in a district building, attendance at the training cannot be restricted. Petitioner's request for interim relief to participate in the district's training session on November 30, 2004, was denied on November 30, 2004.

The appeal must be dismissed as moot. The Commissioner of Education will only consider matters in actual controversy and will not render a decision on a state of facts which no longer exist or which subsequent events have laid to rest (*Appeal of E.M.*, 44 Ed Dept Rep 156, Decision No. 15,130). Because petitioner's stay request was denied and the training has already taken place, no further meaningful relief can be granted.

In light of this disposition, I need not address the parties' remaining contentions.

THE APPEAL IS DISMISSED.

Decision No. 15,201

Appeal of KEN UY and ARTHUR NORDEN from action of the Board of Education of the Sullivan West Central School District regarding the retention of surplus funds.

(April 6, 2005)

APPEARANCES OF COUNSEL

Shaw & Perelson, LLP, attorneys for respondent, *David Shaw, Esq.*, of counsel

DECISION OF THE COMMISSIONER

MILLS, Commissioner—Petitioners appeal the action of the Board of Education of the Sullivan West Central School District ("respondent") in retaining unexpended, unreserved surplus funds in excess of 2% of its 2003-2004 operating budget. The appeal must be sustained in part.

The district's budget for the 2003-2004 school year was $26,829,103. The district's balance sheet for June 30, 2003, reflected an unreserved, undesignated fund balance of $3,357,452. Respondent's tax warrant dated September 1, 2003, indicated the "amount of fund balance withheld for use in 2003-04" to be $1,088,588. Petitioners commenced this appeal on December 31, 2003, alleging that respondent improperly retained surplus funds from the 2002-2003 school year in violation of Real Property Tax Law ("RPTL") §1318(1). Petitioners also contend that respondent's tax warrant does not comply with RPTL §1318(1). Petitioners request, among other things, that I order respondent to comply with RPTL §1318.

Respondent acknowledges that it retained unexpended, unreserved funds in excess of the 2% limit permitted under RPTL §1318(1) but alleges that the petition is untimely.

Initially, I will address petitioners' reply. The purpose of a reply is to respond to new material or affirmative defenses set forth in an answer (8 NYCRR §§275.3 and 275.14). A reply is not meant to buttress allegations in the petition or to belatedly add assertions that should have been in the petition (*Appeal of General*, 43 Ed Dept Rep 146, Decision No. 14,948; *Appeal of Crosier*, 42 *id.* 232, Decision No. 14,835). Therefore, while I have reviewed petitioners' reply, I have not considered those portions containing new allegations or exhibits that are not responsive to new material or affirmative defenses set forth in the answer.

An appeal under RPTL §1318(1) is timely if it is brought within the fiscal year during which unexpended surplus funds are improperly retained (*Appeal of Gorman*, 43 Ed Dept Rep 32, Decision No. 14,906; *Appeal of Schadtle*, 40 *id.* 60, Decision No. 14,421; *Appeal of Siver*, 37 *id.* 498, Decision No. 13,912). This appeal was commenced on December 31, 2003, during the 2003-2004 school year, and therefore is timely with respect to allegations that respondent improperly retained surplus funds in the 2003-2004 school year.

Under RPTL §1318(1), at the conclusion of each fiscal year, a board of education must apply any unexpended surplus funds to reduce its tax levy for the upcoming school year. Surplus funds are defined as "any operating funds in excess of two percent of the current school year budget, and shall not include funds properly retained under other sections of law" (RPTL §1318(1)). Accordingly, at the end of each school year, all unexpended operating funds in excess of 2% of the amount of the budget for the upcoming school year must be applied to reduce the tax levy (*Appeal of Gorman, supra*; *Appeal of Schadtle, supra*; *Appeal of Siver, supra*).

Based on the foregoing, respondent was authorized to retain $536,582.06 of its unexpended operating funds from the 2002-2003 school year (2% of $26,829,103). Respondent acknowledges that it exceeded the 2% limit under RPTL §1318(1) by some $2,820,870, but implies that it was not fully aware of the problem until it consulted with its attorney and an accountant after the tax warrant was issued. Respondent's explanation, however, does not excuse its failure to comply with the law.

Additionally, respondent's tax warrant does not comply with RPTL §1318(1), which provides that "[t]he warrant of the collecting officer . . . shall state the amount of unexpended surplus funds in the custody of the board and shall further state that except as authorized or required by law, such unexpended surplus funds have been applied in determining the amount of the school tax levy." Respondent's tax warrant does not include this statutory language. In addition, the fund balance figure noted on the warrant is inaccurate and exceeds the 2% limit authorized by RPTL §1318(1).

The record indicates that this is not the first time that respondent has improperly retained excess surplus funds. By letter dated October 6, 2003, the State Education Department's Office of Audit Services advised respondent that it had improperly retained excess surplus funds in the 2002-2003, 2001-2002 and 2000-2001 school years. I admonish respondent to be scrupulous in its future budgetary practices and remind respondent of the need to comply fully with the requirements of RPTL §1318. I further remind respondent that willful violation of law is grounds for removal of school officers under Education Law §306.

THE APPEAL IS SUSTAINED TO THE EXTENT INDICATED.

IT IS ORDERED that respondent henceforth fully comply with Real Property Tax Law §1318 and approve tax warrants in strict compliance with the statutory requirements.

Decision No. 15,202

Appeal of C.L., on behalf of N.H., from action of the Board of Education of the Enlarged City School District of the City of Newburgh regarding student discipline.

Appeal of J.W., SR., on behalf of J.W., JR., from action of the Board of Education of the Enlarged City School District of the City of Newburgh regarding student discipline.

Appeal of J.W., SR., on behalf of J.W., from action of the Board of Education of the Enlarged City School District of the City of Newburgh regarding student discipline.

Appeal of W.S., on behalf of S.S., from action of the Board of Education of the Enlarged City School District of the City of Newburgh regarding student discipline.

Appeal of D.H., on behalf of L.P., from action of the Board of Education of the Enlarged City School District of the City of Newburgh regarding student discipline.

(April 6, 2005)

APPEARANCES OF COUNSEL

Shaw & Perelson, LLP, attorneys for respondent, *David S. Shaw* and *Jillian E. Cass, Esqs.*, of counsel

DECISION OF THE COMMISSIONER

MILLS, Commissioner—In separate appeals, petitioners challenge decisions of the Board of Education of the Enlarged City School District of the City of Newburgh ("respondent") suspending their children from school. Because the appeals present similar issues of fact and law, they are consolidated for decision. The appeals must be dismissed.

Petitioners' children were involved in an April 20, 2004, melee at respondent's high school. As a result, each child was suspended for five days by the high school principal. Additionally, petitioners were notified that a superintendent's hearing would be held to determine whether a further suspension was warranted. With the exception of student J.W., on the scheduled hearing date, each of the petitioners and their respective children executed a "Waiver of Long-Term Suspension Hearing Rights and Acceptance of Disciplinary Action" form admitting the student's involvement in the April 20, 2004, incident, waiving his or her right to a hearing and any appeal, and agreeing to the penalty specified in the waiver document.

The waiver agreements for J.W., Jr. and S.S. provide for a suspension "through and including graduation." Apparently both students were enrolled as seniors during the 2003-2004 school year. The waiver agreements for L.P. and N.H. provide for a suspension "through and until the student graduates," but further provide that "the suspension will be held in abeyance at the [end] of the [2003-2004] school year." The agreements for L.P. and N.H. further permitted the students to attend summer school and return to school during the 2004-2005 school year provided that they abide by a "probation contract," which specifies, among other things, that if the student fails to abide by the student code of conduct, the principal may refer the matter to the superintendent for a hearing pursuant to Education Law §3214 for further disciplinary action.

With respect to J.W., the superintendent's designee conducted a hearing on April 29, 2004. At the conclusion of the hearing, the hearing officer found J.W. guilty of the charges and recommended a suspension for the remainder of the school year. He further recommended that J.W. be permitted to attend summer school and return to school for the 2004-2005 school year on "probationary status," requiring that he abide by school district rules or be subject to a superintendent's hearing for possible additional punishment. By letter dated June 2, 2004, respondent's acting superintendent advised petitioner J.W., Sr., that she was adopting the hearing officer's penalty recommendation. Petitioner J.W., Sr., did not appeal the acting superintendent's determination to respondent.

These appeals ensued. Petitioners' requests for interim relief were denied on June 21, 2004.

Petitioners contend that the principal lacks the authority to impose a suspension, that the suspensions were imposed "without regard to the circumstances giving rise to the offense," and that suspension from graduation ceremonies is improper. Petitioners request that I find the suspensions improper, but do not seek expungement of their children's records.

Respondent claims, among other things, that the appeals are moot and that the appeals are not ripe for review because petitioners failed to appeal to respondent.

The appeals must be dismissed as moot with regard to the suspensions served. In all five appeals, the penalty imposed was essentially a suspension for the remainder of the 2003-2004 school year. Since the school year has ended and the students have served the suspensions, the appeals must be dismissed as moot (*Appeal of D.W.*, 43 Ed Dept Rep 188, Decision No. 14,965; *Appeal of R.R. and K.R.*, 41 *id.* 405, Decision No. 14,726; *Appeal of D.H.*, 41 *id.* 142, Decision No. 14,640). Moreover, it appears that respondent permitted those students who had met graduation requirements to attend graduation ceremonies.

To the extent that L.P. and N.H. were required to sign a probationary contract in order to return to school, their appeals are not moot. However, the requirement that these students enter into a probationary contract was a provision of the waivers into which L.P. and N.H. and their parents entered. To effectuate a waiver of rights under Education Law §3214, the waiver must not only be voluntary, knowing and intelligent, but the district must also provide the student and parents with a written document clearly and concisely stating all of the rights to be waived, as well as the consequences of waiving such rights (*Appeal of V.L.*, 44 Ed Dept Rep 160, Decision No. 15,132; *Appeal of a Student with a Disability*, 42 *id.* 192, Decision No. 14,818; *Appeal of J.G.*, 39 *id.* 393, Decision No. 14,270). In this case, there are no allegations that the waivers did not meet these criteria. Therefore, I find no basis on which to find the probationary contracts improper. Moreover, the contracts merely state that the student agrees to work diligently and to abide by the district's rules and regulations, and that in the event the student violates these terms, the building principal may refer the matter to the superintendent for a hearing pursuant to Education Law §3214 and seek additional discipline commensurate with the seriousness of the infraction. Therefore, none of the conditions of the contract imposed any special rules or regulations on the students that were not similarly imposed on their fellow students (*see*, *Appeal of a Student with a Disability*, *supra*).

To the extent that J.W. was allowed to return to school on "probationary status," his appeal is also not moot. However, Education Law §3214(3)(c)(1) provides that "[a]n appeal will lie from the decision of the superintendent to the board of education . . ." Accordingly, the decision of a superintendent following a hearing must be appealed to the board of education prior to initiating an appeal to the Commissioner of Education (*Application of a Student With a Disability*, 43 Ed Dept Rep 161, Decision No. 14,954; *Appeal of D.C.*, 41 *id.* 190, Decision No. 14,661; *Appeal of P.R. and C.R.*, 41 *id.* 48, Decision No. 14,611). J.W.'s parents did not appeal to respondent.

Therefore, this claim must be dismissed for failure to exhaust administrative remedies.

In light of the foregoing, I need not address the parties' remaining contentions.

THE APPEALS ARE DISMISSED.

Decision No. 15,203

Appeal of ANTHONY GAZZOLA, JR., on behalf of his son ANTHONY GAZZOLA III, from action of the Board of Education of the South Country Central School District, and Dr. Michael LaFever, Superintendent, regarding involuntary transfer.

(April 6, 2005)

APPEARANCES OF COUNSEL

Guercio & Guercio, attorneys for respondent, *Gary L. Steffanetta, Esq.*, of counsel

DECISION OF THE COMMISSIONER

MILLS, Commissioner—Petitioner appeals actions of the Board of Education of the South Country Central School District and Superintendent Michael LaFever ("respondents") regarding an alleged involuntary transfer of his son, Anthony. The appeal must be dismissed.

Petitioner's son is a student at respondent's Bellport High School ("Bellport"). By letter dated July 30, 2004, district administrators informed petitioner that Anthony had been selected as a candidate for the South Haven High School Academy ("South Haven") program to begin in September 2004. At a meeting on August 20, 2004, petitioner told the superintendent that he wanted Anthony to remain at Bellport.

On August 31, 2004, the superintendent conducted a hearing with petitioner and his advocate. He determined that South Haven was the most appropriate educational setting for Anthony and informed petitioner of this decision by letter dated September 2, 2004.

By letter dated September 7, 2004, respondent informed petitioner that Anthony could attend Bellport starting September 8 (the first day of school). Though petitioner requested interim relief allowing his son to stay at Bellport, I did not act on this request because respondent informed me shortly after this appeal was commenced that it allowed Anthony to remain at Bellport.

Petitioner contends that his son was involuntarily transferred to South Haven in violation of Education Law §3214(5). The Commissioner will only decide matters in actual controversy and will not render a decision on a state of facts which no longer exists or which subsequent events have laid to rest (*Appeal of K.M.*, 41 Ed Dept Rep 318, Decision No. 14,699; *Appeal of N.B.*, 40 *id.* 515, Decision No. 14,542; *Appeal of N.C.*, 40 *id.* 445, Decision No. 14,522). Here, petitioner's son was allowed to remain at Bellport. The record also reflects that respondents do not plan to require petitioner's son to attend South Haven; he may continue to attend Bellport. Therefore, this appeal is moot (*Appeal of K.M.*, *supra*; *Appeal of D.C.*, 41 Ed Dept Rep 277, Decision No. 14,684; *Appeal of Camille S.*, 39 *id.* 574, Decision No. 14,316).

In light of this disposition, I need not address the parties' remaining contentions.

THE APPEAL IS DISMISSED.

Decision No. 15,204

Appeal of GEORGE R. HUBBARD from action of the Board of Education of the Greece Central School District regarding financial practices.

(April 6, 2005)

APPEARANCES OF COUNSEL

Harris Beach, LLP, attorneys for respondent, *James A. Spitz, Jr.* and *Laura M. Purcell, Esqs.*, of counsel

DECISION OF THE COMMISSIONER

MILLS, Commissioner—Petitioner challenges certain actions of the Board of Education of the Greece Central School District ("respondent") with respect to the adoption and filing of the 2004-2005 real property tax report card and the liquidation of certain capital reserve funds. The appeal must be dismissed.

On April 6, 2004, respondent adopted its 2004-2005 budget resolution (the "budget resolution"). The budget resolution authorized the liquidation of three capital reserve funds (equipment, buses and repairs) (collectively "reserve funds") and the application of the proceeds to the bond indebtedness related to the original purpose of each fund. The budget resolution did not contain a provision whereby the board adopted the district's real property tax report card ("report card"). The district submitted its report card to the New York State Education Department ("SED") on April 7, 2004. This appeal ensued.

Subsequently, on May 11, 2004, respondent passed a resolution specifically adopting the report card. On May 18, 2004, voters approved the district's 2004-2005 budget and the liquidation of the reserve funds.

Petitioner alleges, *inter alia*, that respondent did not adopt its 2004-2005 report card and that the report card filed with SED was therefore improper. Petitioner further alleges that the report card publicly distributed with respondent's budget document did not show the date it was filed with SED as required by law and is therefore not an "authentic copy."

Petitioner also alleges that respondent has taken steps to liquidate the reserve funds which are "improper and deny voters clear choices." Specifically, he alleges that respondent has not established that the funds will be applied in a manner consistent with the budget proposition and as permitted by the Education Law. Petitioner contends respondent is improperly applying the proceeds of the reserve funds to the General Fund which will become part of the fund balance used to reduce the 2004-2005 tax levy. Petitioner also alleges that respondent is liquidating the reserve funds prior to ascertaining whether the voters have determined that they are "no longer desirable" as required by Education Law §3651(5). Finally, petitioner contends that respondent improperly used a single proposition to authorize the 2004-2005 budget and the liquidation of the reserve funds.

Petitioner requests that I direct respondent to properly adopt its 2004-2005 report card and properly adopt and file real property tax report cards in the future. Petitioner further requests that I nullify the voters' authorization to liquidate the reserve funds and that I instruct respondent to liquidate any capital reserve funds only after the voters have determined that the original purpose of the funds is "no longer desirable." Finally, petitioner requests that I instruct respondent to cease using single propositions to authorize unrelated purposes.

Respondent argues that it adopted a property tax report card on April 6, 2004, "through the adoption of the proposed budget" and that its subsequent resolution renders plaintiff's allegations related to the adoption and filing of the report card moot. Respondent denies that the report card omitted any required information. Respondent claims that petitioner's allegations regarding the budget proposition must be dismissed as untimely. Respondent further contends that petitioner's allegations related to the liquidation of the reserve funds must be dismissed as premature. Finally, respondent claims that petitioner's allegations regarding the ambiguity of the budget resolution and the inability of respondent to ascertain the voters' intent fail to state a claim upon which relief may be granted.

I must first address a procedural matter. Petitioner submitted proposed minutes of respondent's June 8, 2004, board meeting to support arguments made in his timely reply. Respondent has not objected to this submission. Pursuant to §276.5 of the Commissioner's regulations, I will accept this document for consideration.

An appeal to the Commissioner of Education must be commenced within 30 days of the making of the decision or the performance of the act complained of unless any delay is excused by the Commissioner for good cause shown (8 NYCRR §275.16; *Appeal of J.J.*, 44 Ed Dept Rep 113, Decision No. 15,115). Respondent contends that petitioner's claims regarding the budget proposition must be dismissed as untimely because it was adopted on April 6, 2004, and this appeal was commenced on May 7, 2004. I disagree. The budget proposition was not voted on until May 18, 2004, and, to the extent that petitioner's claims arise out of the proposition authorized by the voters on that date, petitioner's challenge is timely.

I find petitioner's claim that respondent did not adopt a property tax report card to be moot. The Commissioner of Education will only consider matters in actual controversy and will not render a decision on a state of facts which no longer exist or which subsequent events have laid to rest (*Appeal of Johnson*, 41 Ed Dept Rep 407, Decision No. 14,727; *Appeal of Martin*, 31 *id.* 441, Decision No. 12,692). The record reflects that on May 11, 2004, respondent passed a resolution specifically approving the report card. Because respondent has already taken the action requested by petitioner, this aspect of petitioner's appeal is moot. Nevertheless, I note that Education Law

§1716(7)(b) requires board approval of a real property tax report card prior to it being forwarded to SED. Accordingly, respondent is reminded of the need to fully comply with all aspects of §1716 in the future.

Education Law §1716 and §170.11(8)(c) of the Commissioner's regulations govern the content of the property tax report card. The school property tax report card must include a report of:

1) total spending;

2) percentage increase or decrease in total spending;

3) total estimated school tax levy;

4) percentage increase or decrease in total school tax levy;

5) projected enrollment growth;

6) percentage change in enrollment; and

7) percentage increase in the consumer price index.

(Education Law §1716(7)(a), 8 NYCRR §170.11(8)(c))

To the extent that petitioner alleges that the copy of the report card that was distributed with the budget was improper and not an "authentic copy" because it did not state the date on which it was submitted to SED, petitioner fails to carry his burden of proof. In an appeal to the Commissioner, the petitioner has the burden of demonstrating a clear right to the relief requested and the burden of establishing the facts upon which it seeks relief (8 NYCRR §275.10; *Appeal of Sloley-Raymond*, 44 Ed Dept Rep 27, Decision No. 15,085; *Appeal of Nelson*, 44 *id.* 20, Decision No. 15,082). I find that respondent's report card contains all required information and complies with the requirements of the Education Law and Commissioner's regulations.

Petitioner's claims regarding the liquidation of the reserve funds must be dismissed as premature. It is well settled that the Commissioner will not render advisory opinions or decide issues that have not yet become justiciable (*Appeal of L.M.*, 43 Ed Dept Rep 279, Decision No. 14,994). The record reveals that the reserve funds have not yet been liquidated and, therefore, it is premature and speculative to conclude that they will not be liquidated in accordance with the Education Law or budget proposition.

Moreover, in an appeal to the Commissioner, the petitioner has the burden of demonstrating a clear right to the relief requested and the burden of establishing the facts upon which it seeks relief (8 NYCRR §275.10; *Appeal of Sloley-Raymond, supra*; *Appeal of Nelson, supra*). Petitioner repeatedly asserts that respondent has failed to show that it has acted properly with respect to the liquidation of the reserve funds. However, it is petitioner's burden to establish that respondent acted in contravention of the law or the budget proposition. Petitioner has failed to meet his burden. Petitioner argues that respondent's proposed budget does not identify bond debt relating to the original purposes of each reserve fund and, therefore, voters have no assurance that the proceeds of the liquidated reserve funds will be applied in a manner consistent with the Education Law or the budget proposition. However, according to respondent's Assistant Superintendent for Finance and Support Services, outstanding bond indebtedness for capital building improvements and repairs as well as purchases of new instructional equipment exceeds the amounts remaining in the reserve funds for repairs and equipment. In addition, in March 2004 voters approved a bond proposition for the purchase of buses, the amount of which far exceeds the amount remaining in the bus reserve fund. Finally, respondent has indicated that it will apply the liquidated proceeds to actual outstanding bonded indebtedness associated with repairs, equipment and buses.

Petitioner also alleges that the "Determination of 2004-2005 Estimated Tax Levy And Rate" contained in respondent's proposed budget shows that the fund balance used for the 2004-2005 tax levy includes proceeds of $1.2 million from the liquidation of the reserve funds. In response, the Assistant Superintendent avers that for bookkeeping purposes, the reserve funds are first liquidated into the fund balance and then transferred to debt service to be applied to the district's outstanding bond indebtedness. The corresponding expenditure is included in the "Debt Service Fund" line item of respondent's proposed budget. Respondent believes that this is the best presentation of the relevant information and has agreed to maintain detailed records of the transaction evidencing the liquidation of the reserve funds. Accordingly, petitioner has failed to put forth facts sufficient to support his allegation that respondent has improperly taken steps to liquidate the reserve funds.

Petitioner's allegation, that respondent is liquidating the reserve funds prior to ascertaining whether the voters have determined that they are "no longer desirable" as required by §3651(5) of the Education Law, is also without merit.

Education Law §3651(5) provides, in pertinent part:

> Whenever the voters shall determine that the original purpose for which a reserve fund has been established is no longer desirable, the school authorities may liquidate the fund by first applying its proceeds to any outstanding bonded indebtedness and applying the balance, if any, to the annual tax levy . . .

Petitioner argues it is implausible that voters determined that the reserve funds were "no longer desirable" because the proposed budget contains appropriations for building repairs and the purchase of equipment and there could be appropriations for similar purposes in the future. Respondent argues that, taken to its logical conclusion, petitioner's analysis would mean that a reserve fund can never be liquidated. Respondent argues that voters made an informed decision based upon information presented in meetings and materials and that they manifested their purpose by voting for the proposition. Petitioner offers no proof that such a determination was not made. Therefore, despite the fact that the budget proposition did not contain specific language that the reserve funds were "no longer desirable," I find that such a determination was implicit in the voters approval of the proposition.

Petitioner's contention that the budget proposition was improper because it did not state separately the proposed budget and liquidation of the reserve funds is without merit. A board of education has broad discretion in determining the form of its propositions and the power rests with the voters to reject propositions not satisfactory to the majority (*Corbett v. Union Free School Dist. No. 21, Town of Hempstead*, (199 Misc. 930, *aff'd* 278 AD 960; *Appeal of Friedman, et al.*, 36 Ed Dept Rep 431, Decision No. 13,769).

In light of this disposition, I need not address the parties' remaining contentions.

THE APPEAL IS DISMISSED.

Decision No. 15,205

Appeal of VERNON DANIEL TILLMAN from action of the Board of Education of the City School District of the City of Long Beach regarding a substitute teaching position.

(April 13, 2005)

APPEARANCES OF COUNSEL

Ingerman Smith, L.L.P., attorneys for respondent, *Christopher Venator, Esq.*, of counsel

DECISION OF THE COMMISSIONER

MILLS, Commissioner—Petitioner attempts to appeal his suspension and termination from a substitute teaching position by the Board of Education of the City School District of the City of Long Beach ("respondent"). The appeal must be dismissed.

In May 2003, petitioner was appointed as a regular substitute English teacher in the district, effective September 2003. Petitioner was suspended with pay in May 2004 and terminated June 30, 2004.

By letter dated February 12, 2005, petitioner wrote to the Commissioner of Education requesting a redress of grievances previously considered by respondent. However, since this request did not comply with the regulations for appeals pursuant to Education Law §310, by letter dated February 18, 2005, my Office of Counsel returned petitioner's papers along with a copy of the regulations.

By letter dated March 4, 2005, petitioner submitted a Notice of Petition, Affidavit of Verification, Affidavit of Personal Service, and essentially the same letter of grievances previously presented to respondent, albeit with numbered paragraphs and a new date. Pursuant to §275.10 of the Commissioner's regulations, the petitioner must set forth a clear and concise statement of petitioner's claim showing that the petitioner is entitled to relief. Petitioner's letter of grievances does neither and does not constitute a petition. Petitioner's filing is still defective despite his being given an opportunity to correct such filing. Therefore, I am dismissing this matter pursuant to my authority under §276.9 of the Commissioner's regulations.

Petitioner's letter "appeal" is also untimely. An appeal to the Commissioner must be instituted within 30 days from the making of the decision or the performance of the act complained of, unless any delay is excused by the Commissioner for good cause shown (8

NYCRR §275.16). Petitioner was suspended in May 2004 and terminated June 30, 2004. However, he did not attempt to commence an appeal until February 2005. Accordingly, even if I were to construe his letter as constituting a petition, the appeal would be dismissed as untimely (*Appeals of St. Villien*, 44 Ed Dept Rep 69, Decision No. 15,101; *Appeal of Eveillard*, 42 *id.* 78, Decision No. 14,782; *Appeal of Perez*, 42 *id.* 71, Decision No. 14,779).

In light of this disposition, I need not address any other issues or petitioner's late submission dated March 28, 2005.

THE APPEAL IS DISMISSED.

Decision No. 15,206

Appeal of GLEN W. JOHNSON from action of the Board of Education of the Yorktown Central School District regarding the rejection of a voter petition.

(April 13, 2005)

APPEARANCES OF COUNSEL

Shaw & Perelson, LLP, attorneys for respondent, *Margo L. May, Esq.*, of counsel

DECISION OF THE COMMISSIONER

MILLS, Commissioner—Petitioner appeals the decision of the Board of Education of the Yorktown Central School District ("respondent") rejecting a petition to place a proposition on the ballot at the district's May 2004 annual election. The appeal must be dismissed.

In March 2000, district voters approved a proposition authorizing construction of additions to and renovations of the district's school buildings at a cost not to exceed $33,695,225. The text of the original proposition provided, in pertinent part:

> (a) That [respondent] is hereby authorized to undertake a school building improvement project (the "Project") . . . consisting of the construction of additions and/or improvements and renovations at all District school buildings and sites thereof to accommodate existing programs and to provide for projected enrollment

> increase, including (as and where required) construction of building additions to provide new classrooms, library, computer, art, special education, science, cafeteria and circulation space; . . . interior reconstruction and space reconfiguration; . . . and to expend therefor, . . . an amount not to exceed the estimated aggregate maximum cost of $33,695,225; *provided that the detailed costs of the components of the Project as set forth in the Report may be reallocated among such components if the Board of Education shall determine that such reallocation is in the best interests of the District* provided, however, that the aggregate amount to be expended shall not exceed the $33,695,225 estimated maximum cost of the Project and that no material change shall be made in the scope of the project . . . (emphasis added)

In June 2003, voters approved a proposition authorizing an additional amount not to exceed $5,205,000 to cover unanticipated cost increases. Although not explicitly referenced in the March 2000 proposition, respondent's initial plans included renovating space in the district's high school library to house its administrative offices. However, due to cost overruns, respondent was forced to prioritize various portions of the project. After considering the recommendations of the district's facilities committee, respondent chose not to renovate the library space for the district's administrative offices, and instead, leased space in a non-district owned facility for that purpose. This decision was apparently prompted, in part, by respondent's assessment that additional classroom space in the high school was a greater priority.

In early March 2004, the district clerk was served with a petition with the requisite number of signatures requesting that respondent place a proposition on the ballot at the district's May 18, 2004, annual election. The proposition sought to direct respondent to move the district's administrative offices from the leased location to the high school library, as envisioned under the original capital bond referendum authorized in 2000.

At respondent's March 29, 2004, meeting, a motion to place the proposition on the ballot failed by a vote of 1 to 3. This appeal ensued. Petitioner's request for interim relief was denied on May 7, 2004.

Petitioner contends that respondent improperly rejected the petition to place the proposition on the ballot and failed to timely act on the petition. Petitioner requests, among other things, that I order respondent to conduct a special district meeting to consider the proposition.

Respondent contends that it properly rejected the petition because the decision where to house district administrative offices is a matter within respondent's discretion.

Pursuant to §276.4 of the Commissioner's regulations, respondent was required to serve its memorandum of law within 30 days after service of its answer. Respondent served its answer on May 24, 2004, but did not submit its memorandum until July 2, 2004. While the Commissioner may permit the late filing of a memorandum of law where a party has established good cause for the delay and demonstrated the necessity of such memorandum to the determination of the appeal (8 NYCRR §276.4(a)), respondent has shown neither in this appeal. Therefore, I have not considered respondent's memorandum of law.

The purpose of a reply is to respond to new material or affirmative defenses set forth in the answer (8 NYCRR §§275.3 and 275.14). A reply is not meant to buttress allegations in the petition or to belatedly add assertions that should have been in the petition (*Appeal of Goldin*, 43 Ed Dept Rep 20, Decision No. 14,904; *Appeal of Hollister*, 39 *id.* 109, Decision No. 14,188). Petitioner submitted a lengthy reply that mainly reargues the points made in the petition. While I have reviewed petitioner's reply, I have not considered those portions containing new allegations or exhibits that are not responsive to new material or affirmative defenses set forth in the answer.

The appeal must be dismissed as moot. The Commissioner of Education will only consider matters in actual controversy and will not render a decision on a state of facts which no longer exist or which subsequent events have laid to rest (*Appeal of E.M.*, 44 Ed Dept Rep 156, Decision No. 15,130). At a special district meeting held on October 13, 2004, district voters approved, by a vote of 651 to 337, a proposition funding an addition to the district's high school and renovation of the high school library for use as administrative offices (see, *Appeals of Ciffone and Kauffman*, 44 Ed Dept Rep ___, Decision No. 15,199, dated April 6, 2005). The approval of this most recent proposition accomplishes the exact purpose underlying the petition rejected by respondent in March 2004. Accordingly, there is no further relief I can afford petitioner.

Even if the appeal were not dismissed as moot, it would be dismissed on the merits. A board need not present all propositions submitted to it (*Appeal of Osten*, 35 Ed Dept Rep 160, Decision No. 13,500) and may refuse to place a proposition before the voters where the matter is not within the voters' discretion (Education Law §2035; *Appeal of Lawson*, 36 Ed Dept Rep 450, Decision No. 13,774; *Appeals of Cappa*, 36 *id.* 278, Decision No. 13,724). Decisions concerning the use of school facilities are within the discretion of the board of education (Education Law §1709(7), (9) and (33); *Appeal of Rosenberg*, 31 Ed Dept Rep 398, Decision No. 12,680).

Furthermore, the March 2000 proposition explicitly vested respondent with the discretion to reallocate costs among various components of the project, provided that the total cost did not exceed the amount authorized by district voters. Accordingly, respondent's decision to forego renovations to the library space at that time, and instead, to lease space for its administrative offices, was within its discretion. Respondent therefore did not act arbitrarily or capriciously by rejecting the petition on the grounds that the proposition addressed a matter not within the power of the voters.

Moreover, contrary to petitioner's assertion, respondent properly considered and rejected the petition at its March 29, 2004, meeting. To conduct business, respondent must have a quorum, a simple majority of the total number of board members. To take any official action, it must have the vote of a majority of the total number of board members (General Construction Law §41; Opinion of Counsel No. 70, 1 Ed Dept Rep 770). The record reflects that four of the district's seven board members, a quorum, were present when the motion to place the proposition on the ballot was presented, but, in order for the motion to have passed, all four members would have had to have voted in favor of the motion. In this case, however, the motion was defeated by a vote of 1 to 3. Thus, because a majority of the board did not approve placing the proposition on the ballot, respondent properly declined to do so.

In light of this disposition, I need not address the parties' remaining arguments.

THE APPEAL IS DISMISSED.

Decision No. 15,207

Appeal of ELSY MECKLEMBOURG GUIBERT from action of the Board of Education of the Elmont Union Free School District regarding an election.

(April 13, 2005)

APPEARANCES OF COUNSEL

Colum P. Nugent, Esq., attorney for respondent

DECISION OF THE COMMISSIONER

MILLS, Commissioner—Petitioner, an unsuccessful candidate for election to the Board of Education of the Elmont Union Free School District ("respondent"), appeals the conduct of a school district election. The appeal must be dismissed.

On May 18, 2004, respondent conducted its annual meeting and school board election. Petitioner ran for the school board seat held by incumbent Lorraine Ferrigno. Ms. Ferrigno defeated petitioner by a one-vote margin, 976 to 975.

Petitioner alleges that several irregularities occurred in the conduct of the election. She alleges that poll workers failed to properly monitor and account for votes because at two of the seven voting venues there was a one-vote discrepancy between the voting machine total and the poll list. Petitioner also alleges that two registered voters were denied the opportunity to vote, and that several non-residents improperly voted in the election. Petitioner asserts that these irregularities are substantial and in light of the one-vote margin of victory, require that the Commissioner order a revote of the contest between her and Ms. Ferrigno. Petitioner's request for interim relief staying the installation of Ms. Ferrigno as a board member was denied on June 24, 2004.

Respondent provides a detailed explanation of the election process as evidence that it conducted the election properly in accordance with the Commissioner's regulations and New York State laws.

To the extent that petitioner seeks to prevent Ms. Ferrigno from being sworn in as a duly elected member of respondent, that portion of the appeal must be dismissed as moot. The Commissioner of Education will only consider matters in actual controversy and will not render a decision on a state of facts which no longer exist or which subsequent events have laid to rest (*Appeal of Passer*, 44 Ed Dept Rep ___, Decision No. 15,160; *Appeal of Colety, et al.*, 42 *id.* 162, Decision No. 14,806). The installation of elected board members was scheduled at respondent's reorganization meeting on July 6, 2004, after petitioner's request to stay the installation was denied. There is no evidence in the record indicating that the installation did not occur as scheduled.

The appeal must be dismissed for failure to join a necessary party. A party whose rights would be adversely affected by a determination of an appeal in favor of petitioner is a necessary party and must be named as such and served with a notice of petition and petition (*Appeal of Ewart*, 44 Ed Dept Rep 147, Decision No. 15,127; *Appeal of Milazzo*, 43 *id.* 294, Decision No. 14,999; *Appeal of Stolbach*, 43 *id.* 218, Decision No. 14,977). If an appeal involves the validity of a school district meeting or election, the petition must be served upon each successful candidate whose right to hold office is disputed and such person must be joined as a respondent (8 NYCRR §275.8(d); *Appeal of Milazzo, supra*). Here, petitioner named the board only in the caption of the appeal and served the district clerk, on behalf of the board. Ms. Ferrigno was neither named as a respondent nor personally served with a copy of the notice of petition or petition. Since a decision in petitioner's favor would clearly affect the rights of Ms. Ferrigno as the winning candidate, petitioner's failure to name and serve her requires dismissal of the appeal. Accordingly, I need not consider Ms. Ferrigno's request to intervene or appear as an *amicus*.

The appeal must also be dismissed on the merits. To invalidate the results of a school district election, petitioner must establish not only that irregularities occurred but also that any irregularities actually affected the outcome of the election (*Matter of Boyes v. Allen, et al.*, 32 AD2d 990, *affd* 26 NY2d 709; *Appeal of Roberts*, 33 Ed Dept Rep 601, Decision No. 13,162), were so pervasive that they vitiated the electoral process (*Appeal of Brannon*, 42 Ed Dept Rep 220, Decision No. 14,830; *Appeals of Laskas-Gillespie and Warshaw*, 40 *id.* 568, Decision No. 14,559; *Appeal of Roberts, supra*), or demonstrate a clear and convincing picture of informality to the point of laxity in adherence to the Education Law (*Appeal of Christe*, 40 Ed Dept Rep 412, Decision No. 14,514; *Matter of Levine*, 24 *id.* 172, Decision No. 11,356, *affd sub nom. Capobianco v. Ambach and Bd. of Educ., Glen Cove City School District*, 112 AD2d 640). Implicit in these decisions is a recognition that it is a rare case where errors in the conduct of an election become so pervasive that they vitiate the fundamental fairness of the election (*Appeal of Collins*, 39 Ed Dept Rep 226, Decision No. 14,223; *Appeal of Roberts, supra*; *Appeal of Como, et al.*,

28 Ed Dept Rep 483, Decision No. 12,177). Petitioner has the burden of establishing all the facts upon which she seeks relief (8 NYCRR §275.10; *Appeal of Wierzchowski*, 39 Ed Dept Rep 682, Decision No. 14,348). To warrant setting aside an election, petitioner must establish that the improprieties are substantial and not merely technical in nature (*Appeal of Morris, et al.*, 37 Ed Dept Rep 590, Decision No. 13,936; *Appeal of Taylor*, 31 *id.* 46, Decision No. 12,564). Petitioner has failed to meet that burden.

Respondent describes the voting procedure as follows. The Nassau County Board of Elections provides voter registration books containing buff cards, or signature cards, for all voters registered to vote in school elections, that are sent to each polling place the day prior to the election. The district clerk maintains a duplicate set of books at the administration building. There were seven polling places at which a chairperson, co-chairperson and election workers were present. When an individual presents himself or herself to vote, an election worker checks the election register for the buff card. Each individual signs the poll list, and then votes on a voting machine. The poll list total is matched with the number of votes on the voting machine periodically and at the end of the day.

If the buff card cannot be found in the election register, the potential voter is referred to the chair or co-chairperson who consults the registration books. If the individual's name cannot be found in the books, the chair or co-chair telephones the district clerk or her designee, who searches for the name again in the books or on disk. If the name still cannot be found, the chair or co-chair provides the potential voter with a paper ballot and form affidavit that is printed on an envelope. The individual completes the ballot and affidavit, a so-called "challenge vote," which are sent to the district clerk's office at the end of the day.

At the end of election night, the machine totals showed Ms. Ferrigno defeating petitioner 973 to 972. The district clerk received nine challenge votes. According to respondent, three days later the clerk sent the names and addresses of those nine individuals to the Nassau County Board of Elections, which responded that five of the nine individuals were registered to vote in the county. The clerk then opened these five envelopes in the presence of respondent's president, counsel, and superintendent, and petitioner, Ms. Ferrigno and her husband. Two votes were for petitioner, giving her 974 votes, and three were for Ms. Ferrigno, giving her a total of 976 votes.

According to respondent, one of the four other "challenge" voters had neglected to include his address. Subsequently, when his address was found, the buff card was located in the registration book. Accordingly, his envelope was accepted and opened by the clerk in the presence of petitioner and respondent's counsel. The vote was cast in favor of petitioner, bringing her total to 975, still one short of Ms. Ferrigno.

Petitioner contends that two individuals were turned away without being offered the opportunity to vote by affidavit. One is Mr. Frantz Baron, the challenge voter who neglected to include his address, as discussed above. Thus, contrary to petitioner's allegation, Mr. Baron did fill out an affidavit, and his challenge vote was accepted, opened and included in petitioner's vote total. According to petitioner, the other individual is James Vandezande. By letter dated May 28, 2004, Mr. Vandezande sent petitioner a copy of his letter to the district recounting his experience on election day. Mr. Vandezande states he was prevented from voting but was not offered the opportunity to submit a paper "challenge" ballot. However, there is nothing in his letter indicating for whom he would have voted had he been given the opportunity to do so.

In her reply, petitioner includes an affidavit from Mr. Vandezande stating that had he been able to vote, he would have voted for petitioner. However, the purpose of a reply is to respond to new material or affirmative defenses set forth in an answer (8 NYCRR §§275.3 and 275.14). A reply is not meant to buttress allegations in the petition or to belatedly add assertions that should have been in the petition (*Appeal of Schildhorn*, 44 Ed Dept Rep 212, Decision No. 15,152; *Appeal of General*, 43 *id.* 146, Decision No. 14,948). Petitioner failed to include Mr. Vandezande's affidavit with her petition even though she was aware of his earlier letter. Therefore, while I have reviewed petitioner's reply, I have not considered those portions, including the affidavit, containing new allegations that are not responsive to new material or affirmative defenses set forth in the answer.

Petitioner asserts that election workers failed to properly monitor and account for votes because the poll lists at two of the seven polling venues did not match the machine counts. She contends that at the Clara H. Carlson School ("Carlson"), the machine total was one greater than the poll list, and at the Gotham Avenue School ("Gotham"), the machine total was one less than the poll list.

In its answer, respondent states that three days after the election, the Carlson chairperson and a clerk checked each buff card signed by a voter on election day. They found that two buff cards with the same voter last name had been given the same poll list number. Respondent posits that this explains why the machine total was one greater that the poll list.

Although respondent also reviewed all the buff cards at Gotham, respondent admits that it could not find the cause of the discrepancy there. Respondent speculates that a potential voter signed a buff card, had his or her name placed on the poll list, received a number, and simply left without voting. In any event, it is not unusual for discrepancies to exist between the machine count and the poll list at the conclusion of an election (*see, e.g., Appeals of Laskas-Gillespie and Warshaw, supra*; *Appeal of Diamond*, 39 Ed Dept Rep 541, Decision No. 14,304), and petitioner has failed to meet her burden of proving that any alleged irregularity regarding the poll list actually occurred, much less that it affected the outcome of the election.

Finally, petitioner contends that several nonresidents were allowed to vote. She claims that three adult children of another member of respondent board, Deanna Doreson, who allegedly supported Ms. Ferrigno, used Ms. Doreson's address on the poll list in order to vote in the election even though they purportedly reside outside the district. Petitioner also claims that three other individuals who purportedly reside outside the district improperly voted in the election.

I decline to address with specificity the allegations regarding each individual because there is no indication that petitioner made any timely challenges with respect to the qualifications of any voters. A qualified voter may challenge, either prior to or at the district election, the qualifications of any other voter (Education Law §§2015(3) and 2019). Challenges to the qualifications of a voter must be made no later than the time the voter appears at the polls to vote (*Appeal of Brannon, supra*; *Appeal of Crowley, et al.*, 39 Ed Dept Rep 665, Decision No. 14,345; *Appeal of Fraser-McBride, et al.*, 36 *id.* 488, Decision No. 13,783). A person who has the right to challenge a voter and permits him to vote without such challenge is not allowed to object to such voter's participation (*Appeal of Crowley, et al., supra*; *Appeal of Fraser-McBride, supra*). Accordingly, petitioner's failure to timely object to the qualifications of any voters in a timely manner requires dismissal of these claims.

THE APPEAL IS DISMISSED.

Decision No. 15,208

Appeal of S.M., on behalf of her son M.M., from action of the Board of Education of the Lakeland Central School District regarding transportation.

(April 19, 2005)

APPEARANCES OF COUNSEL

Levy, Santoro & Santoro, Esqs., attorneys for petitioner, *Stephen M. Santoro, Sr., Esq.*, of counsel

Shaw & Perelson, LLP, attorneys for respondent, *Garrett L. Silveira, Esq.*, of counsel

DECISION OF THE COMMISSIONER

MILLS, Commissioner—Petitioner appeals the refusal of the Board of Education of the Lakeland Central School District ("respondent") to transport her son to a nonpublic school. The appeal must be dismissed.

In May 2004, petitioner's son was suspended from attending respondent's schools through June 30, 2005. Pursuant to a hearing waiver agreement, petitioner's son ". . .is prohibited from being on school property during the period of the suspension and is prohibited from attending any school related programs or activities during this period." Subsequently, petitioner enrolled her son in a nonpublic school for the 2004-2005 school year.

In August 2004, petitioner requested transportation for her son to the nonpublic school during the 2004-2005 school year. By letter dated September 2, 2004, respondent's superintendent denied petitioner's request on the grounds that school district buses are "school property" within the meaning of the hearing waiver agreement and, pursuant to such agreement, petitioner is prohibited from such property through June 30, 2005. In a letter dated September 23, 2004, petitioner's attorney disputed respondent's reliance on the waiver agreement to deny transportation and requested that respondent reconsider its determination. Petitioner commenced this appeal on October 4, 2004.

Petitioner contends that respondent is required to provide transportation to her son pursuant to Education Law §§1709 and 3635. Petitioner states that she did not request that respondent use its own buses to transport her son and alleges that respondent has alternative means to provide the requested transportation. Petitioner requests that I find respondent in violation of Education Law §§1709 and 3635 and direct respondent to provide transportation for her son during the 2004-2005 school year and to compensate petitioner for the cost of transportation not provided to date. Petitioner also requests that I hold a hearing.

Respondent denies that it is required to transport petitioner's son and alleges that its determination to deny transportation based upon the hearing waiver agreement was proper. Respondent also contends that the appeal must be dismissed because petitioner failed to submit a timely request for transportation pursuant to Education Law §3635(2).

With respect to petitioner's request for a hearing, the jurisdiction of the Commissioner in an appeal brought pursuant to Education Law §310 is appellate in nature and does not provide for evidentiary hearings or investigations (*Appeal of Schuler*, 37 Ed Dept Rep 512, Decision No. 13,915). Accordingly, I decline to grant petitioner's request.

Education Law §3635(2) requires that an application for transportation to a nonpublic school must be submitted no later than the first day of April preceding the school year for which transportation is requested. The purpose of the deadline is to enable school districts to budget funds and make necessary arrangements to provide transportation reasonably and economically (*Appeal of J.D.*, 42 Ed Dept Rep 373, Decision No. 14,884; *Appeal of Joanne M.*, 40 *id.* 686, Decision No. 14,584; *Appeal of Attubato*, 38 *id.* 511, Decision No. 14,082). However, a district may not reject a late request for transportation if there is a reasonable explanation for the delay (Education Law §3635(2); *Appeal of J.D., supra*; *Appeal of Joanne M., supra*; *Appeal of Attubato, supra*). A belated decision to enroll a student in a private school is not a reasonable explanation for a late submission of a transportation request (*Appeal of J.D., supra*; *Appeal of Attubato, supra*; *Appeal of Matero*, 36 Ed Dept Rep 242, Decision No. 13,713).

The record indicates that petitioner failed to submit a timely request for transportation pursuant to Education Law §3635(2) as a result of petitioner's belated decision to enroll her son in the nonpublic school after his suspension. Accordingly, petitioner has failed to provide a reasonable explanation for the delay in submitting her request (*Appeal of J.D., supra*).

However, even absent a reasonable explanation for the delay, a late transportation request must be granted if the requested transportation can be provided under existing transportation arrangements at no additional cost to the district (*Appeal of R.O.*, 40 Ed Dept Rep 137, Decision No. 14,441; *Appeal of Tarricone*, 38 *id.* 623, Decision No. 14,105; *Appeal of Shevlin*, 38 *id.* 365, Decision No. 14,056). It appears from the record that respondent provides transportation to students attending nonpublic schools from designated centralized pick-up points located at respondent's two high schools. Respondent contends that since the waiver agreement prohibits petitioner's son from being on school property, he cannot be transported from any of the high school pick-up points. Consequently, should petitioner's transportation request be granted, respondent would incur additional costs to arrange for alternative transportation of petitioner's son. The Commissioner has consistently sustained denials of untimely applications for transportation where the transportation requested would impose additional costs upon the school district (*Appeal of J.D., supra*; *Appeal of Joanne M., supra*; *Appeal of Matero, supra*).

In an appeal to the Commissioner pursuant to Education Law §310, the petitioner has the burden of demonstrating a clear right to the relief requested and the burden of establishing the facts upon which she seeks relief (8 NYCRR §275.10; *Appeal of Ritters*, 44 Ed Dept Rep 117, Decision No. 15,117; *Appeal of Nelson*, 44 *id.* 20, Decision No. 15,082; *Appeal of Green*, 40 *id.* 278, Decision No. 14,479).

On the record before me, I do not find respondent's interpretation of the waiver agreement to be unreasonable, and petitioner has otherwise failed to rebut respondent's contention that it would incur additional costs to arrange alternative transportation should petitioner's transportation request be granted.

THE APPEAL IS DISMISSED.

Decision No. 15,209

Appeal of ALEX SCHREIBER from action of the New York City Department of Education regarding an unsatisfactory rating.

(April 19, 2005)

APPEARANCES OF COUNSEL

Michael A. Cardozo, Corporation Counsel, attorney for respondent, *Shivani Soni, Esq*., of counsel

DECISION OF THE COMMISSIONER

MILLS, Commissioner—Petitioner challenges an unsatisfactory rating for his teaching performance during the 2001-2002 school year. The appeal must be dismissed.

During the 2001-2002 school year, petitioner was a tenured mathematics teacher at W.C. Bryant High School, a public school now operated by the New York City Department of Education ("respondent"). On or about January 24, 2002, one of petitioner's students made a formal complaint to the principal concerning certain sarcastic, demeaning, and embarrassing remarks allegedly made by petitioner about her and other students during classroom time. Following receipt of the complaint, the principal investigated and interviewed approximately 15 other students. The principal met with petitioner on February 14, 2002, and confronted him with the complaint and written statements of the other students. Following the conference, the principal issued a letter dated February 15, 2002. The conclusion of the letter stated:

> Based on the investigation of student statements as well as your admission to me . . . that you have used sarcasm in your classes and that you indeed made unprofessional and inappropriate comments about [the complaining student] when she was not in the room, I conclude that the allegations are true.
>
> . . .
>
> Finally, I advised you that this misconduct which violates the Chancellor's Regulations may lead to further disciplinary action, including an adverse rating for this school year.

Pursuant to the collective bargaining agreement, petitioner initiated a grievance to have the letter removed from his file. At Step II, the superintendent's representative issued a decision dated April

30, 2002, finding that "the Grievant did use inappropriate comments in the classroom regarding one student in particular and when referring to the class as a whole. The Principal was justified in her remarks and the Grievant presented no new information that would show the letter to be inaccurate or unfair." At Step III of the process, the Chancellor's representative again denied the grievance in a decision dated October 17, 2002. The Chancellor's representative found:

> The February 15, 2002, letter accurately and fairly describes the incident. The comments made by the grievant were shown to have embarrassed the student thereby causing harm to the student. Accordingly, the principal's finding that there was a violation of Chancellor's Regulation A-420 is not arbitrary or capricious . . .

Thereafter, petitioner's union did not pursue the matter further and did not go to arbitration under the collective bargaining agreement.

Between the Step II and Step III determinations, at the end of the 2001-2002 school year, petitioner was given an unsatisfactory rating by the principal. The rating sheet indicates more satisfactory areas of practice than unsatisfactory, but in the section entitled "Additional Remarks" the principal noted: "Substantiation of Corporal Punishment Charges [sic] (Violation of A420, Chancellor's Regulations.)" (Chancellor's Regulation A-420, regarding corporal punishment, contains this statement: "Language that belittles or subjects students to ridicule or is abusive or threatening verbal communication is a violation of this Regulation.")

In February 2004, a Chancellor's Review Committee convened to consider petitioner's appeal of his unsatisfactory rating. Petitioner, his principal, and a union representative were present, and presented testimony, oral argument, and documentary materials. With respect to the incident noted in the unsatisfactory rating, petitioner's union representative argued, among other things, that if the allegations were as serious as stated, the principal should have taken action against petitioner pursuant to Education Law §3020-a.

The Review Committee found, in its decision dated February 13, 2004:

> The written documentation gave little evidence of a consistent pattern of ineffective teaching and

> unsatisfactory performance. The verbal testimony of the Principal did not provide sufficient evidence to substantiate the fact that the Appellant rendered a level of service as a teacher of mathematics that was other than satisfactory during the rating period. The documents do not substantiate the weaknesses noted on the rating sheet and the overall evaluation of "U" in performance. There was only one incident used to justify an "Unsatisfactory" rating; the investigation that was conducted by the Principal seemed to focus on statements that could have an ambiguous interpretation. The Appellant's satisfactory teaching skills were attested to by the Principal. There were no other incidents alleged either prior to or subsequent to the incident cited in Document 3.
>
> It is, therefore, recommended that the appeal be sustained and the rating of "Unsatisfactory" be reversed.

(Petitioner states in his reply that he had never seen this decision until it was served on him as an attachment to respondent's answer on October 8, 2004.)

Thereafter, on August 2, 2004, the Chancellor's designee, Carmen Farina, Deputy Chancellor (Acting), Teaching and Learning, issued the final determination on petitioner's appeal: "Please be advised that the appeal of Mr. Alex Schreiber from the rating of 'Unsatisfactory' for the period ending June 30, 2002, has been denied and the said rating is sustained as a consequence of a substantiated charge of corporal punishment." Petitioner states that he received this determination on August 10, 2004, by regular mail; he commenced this appeal on August 27, 2004.

Petitioner asks for a confirmation that his rights were violated by the February 15, 2002, determination that he had engaged in unprofessional and inappropriate verbal conduct, and asks that I annul the unsatisfactory rating for the 2001-2002 school year.

Respondent denies any wrongdoing on its part, and argues that the Chancellor's final determination with respect to the unsatisfactory rating was proper in all respects. Respondent further claims that I lack jurisdiction with respect to the placement of the February 15, 2002, letter in petitioner's file, and that any challenge to the retention of the letter is untimely. Respondent further argues that the petition fails to state a claim to the extent that petitioner challenges the

February 15, 2002, letter as a disciplinary matter in violation of Education Law §3020-a.

With respect to the February 15, 2002, letter, petitioner, in his reply, states clearly that he is not challenging the placement of the letter in his file. Indeed, he cannot do so in this appeal, because it is clear that he elected to file a grievance pursuant to the collective bargaining agreement, and proceeded to Step III, but no further. I make no determination as to whether the letter was proper or improper (*see Holt v. Board of Educ., Webutuck CSD*, 52 NY2d 625; *cf.*, *Appeal of Fusco*, 39 Ed Dept Rep 836, Decision No. 14,396; *Appeal of Irving*, 39 *id.* 761, Decision No. 14,373). Because the grievance process has resulted in a final determination that the letter must remain in petitioner's file, I must accept it as an official school document, as did the Review Committee, and the factual statements contained in it.

With respect to the unsatisfactory rating, petitioner claims that the unsatisfactory rating was the result of the February 15, 2002, letter. He alleges: "There was no other documentation of any kind to support the unsatisfactory ratings [sic]." Respondent's answer denies that allegation, but "affirmatively states that petitioner's unsatisfactory rating is based on a substantiated charge of corporal punishment," clearly referring to the February 15, 2002, letter. Petitioner's rating sheet, dated June 21, 2002, shows 16 satisfactory ratings, and 4 unsatisfactory ratings: professional attitude and professional growth, effect on character and personality growth of pupils, maintenance of wholesome classroom atmosphere, and attention to pupil health, safety and general welfare. In the area of pupil guidance and instruction, petitioner was rated satisfactory in 7 of 10 categories.

The standard of proof required to overturn a teacher rating is very high. In *Appeal of Gordon* (36 Ed Dept Rep 343, Decision No. 13,743), which also concerned a teacher rating, I wrote:

> With respect to appeals challenging unsatisfactory ratings, in the absence of a showing of malice, prejudice, bad faith or gross error, the Commissioner will not substitute his judgment for that of the Chancellor (*Appeal of Bristol*, 33 Ed Dept Rep 202; *Matter of Taylor*, 23 *id.* 482). Petitioner has the burden of establishing the facts upon which he or she seeks relief (*Appeal of Marek*, 35 Ed Dept Rep 314; *Appeal of Nash*, 35 *id.* 203; *Appeal*

of Goldman, 35 *id*. 126) and the burden of demonstrating a clear legal right to the relief requested (*Appeal of Marek*, *supra*; *Appeal of Nash*, *supra*; *Appeal of DiMicelli*, 28 Ed Dept Rep 327).

Petitioner has established that the unsatisfactory rating he received was based on the incident described in the February 15, 2002, letter, and, indeed, the final decision by the Chancellor's designee concedes as much. However, petitioner has neither alleged nor proven that the rating was a result of malice, prejudice, bad faith, or gross error. Petitioner has also not alleged or proven that he was given an unsatisfactory rating based on a single incident, while other teachers similarly situated were not so rated. He has not claimed or shown that the Chancellor lacks the authority to base a rating on a finding of unprofessional and inappropriate comments. As a result, I have no basis for substituting my judgment for that of the Chancellor.

THE APPEAL IS DISMISSED.

Decision No. 15,210

Appeal of GREGORY M. MUENCH from action of the Board of Education of the Central Square Central School District regarding a tax levy.

(April 19, 2005)

APPEARANCES OF COUNSEL

Ferrara, Fiorenza, Larrison, Barrett & Reitz, P.C., attorneys for respondent, *Craig M. Atlas, Esq*., of counsel

DECISION OF THE COMMISSIONER

MILLS, Commissioner—Petitioner appeals the adoption of the tax levy for the 2004-2005 school year by the Board of Education of the Central Square Central School District ("respondent"). The appeal must be sustained in part.

At a special meeting on August 23, 2004, respondent voted to adopt a proposed tax levy and executed tax warrants for the 2004-2005 school year. This appeal ensued. Petitioner's request for interim relief was denied on September 10, 2004.

Petitioner contends that respondent failed to modify the tax levy to reflect an increase in the district's 2004-2005 State aid as provided for in the State budget for the 2004-2005 State fiscal year (Chapter 53, Laws of 2004) in violation of *Appeal of Muench*, 43 Ed Dept Rep 419, Decision No. 15,039 ("*Muench I*") and the Real Property Tax Law. The estimate of State aid used by respondent for development of the district's 2004-2005 budget was $29,526,386. However, the State budget enacted on August 20, 2004, provided for $31,497,661 in State aid to the district. Petitioner contends that the $1,971,275 in additional State aid should have been applied to reduce the tax levy, and requests that I order respondent to recalculate and re-issue the tax levy accordingly.

Respondent contends that its decision not to use the additional State aid solely for the purpose of reducing the tax levy had a rational basis, did not violate any laws, and was not arbitrary or capricious. Respondent also raises several procedural objections.

Respondent contends that the appeal is untimely. An appeal to the Commissioner of Education must be commenced within 30 days of the making of the decision or the performance of the act complained of unless any delay is excused for good cause shown (8 NYCRR §275.16). Respondent concedes that the appeal is timely with respect to its actions on August 23, 2004, when the board established the tax rates and adopted the tax warrants for the 2004-2005 school year. However, respondent contends the appeal is untimely as to any actions that occurred more than 30 days prior to August 25, 2004, the date petitioner commenced this appeal. I agree that to the extent petitioner raises similar allegations with respect to the 2003-2004 or earlier school years, such allegations are untimely (*Appeal of Molineaux*, 38 Ed Dept Rep 672, Decision No. 14,114; *Appeal of Aarseth*, 35 *id.* 211, Decision No. 13,519; *Appeal of Davis*, 33 *id.* 675, Decision No. 13,192).

Respondent further contends that the appeal is moot. The Commissioner of Education will only decide matters in actual controversy and will not render a decision on a state of facts which no longer exists or which subsequent events have laid to rest (*Appeal of L.D. and M.D.*, 43 Ed Dept Rep 144, Decision No. 14,947; *Appeal of Deborah F.*, 42 *id.* 178, Decision No. 14,813; *Appeal of Johnson*, 41 *id.* 407, Decision No. 14,727). Here, the 2004-2005 taxes were due by the time the parties had submitted all the necessary papers in this appeal. However, "[I]t is settled doctrine that an appeal will, nevertheless, be entertained where, as here, the controversy is of a character which is likely to recur not only with respect to the [same] parties . . . but with respect to others as well" (*East Meadow Community Concerts Ass'n v. Bd. of Educ., Union Free School Dist. No. 3, County of Nassau*, 18 NY2d 129, 135; *Appeal of Muench*, *supra*; *Appeal of Student Suspected of Having a Disability*, 38 Ed Dept Rep 796, Decision No. 14,145). Therefore, I decline to dismiss this appeal as moot because it raises important legal issues concerning the proper use of State aid estimates in preparation of tax warrants that affect all districts and taxpayers statewide. Moreover, it is the same issue which petitioner raised and I sustained in *Muench I*.

I also must address petitioner's reply. The purpose of a reply is to respond to new material or affirmative defenses set forth in the answer (8 NYCRR §§275.3 and 275.14). A reply may not be used to belatedly add new assertions that are not part of the pleadings (*Appeal of Kirschenbaum*, 43 Ed Dept Rep 366, Decision No. 15,020; *Appeal of Hollister*, 39 *id.* 109, Decision No. 14,188). The rationale for this procedural rule is to ensure an orderly framing of the issues (*Matter of a Handicapped Child*, 24 Ed Dept Rep 41, Decision No. 11,308). Therefore, while I have reviewed petitioner's submissions, I have not considered those portions containing new allegations that are not responsive to new material or affirmative defenses set forth in the answer.

In determining the tax levy, respondent should use the best estimate of State aid that is reasonably available at the time the tax warrant is issued (*Appeal of Muench*, *supra*). Relying on *Muench I*, petitioner contends that respondent must recalculate the tax levy using the State aid projection in the enacted State budget. Respondent alleges that when it met on August 23, 2004, to determine the tax warrants, the board did consider the district's updated State aid and discussed using it to lower the tax levy, but decided to levy taxes in the amount approved by the voters on May 18, 2004, which amount was based on the earlier State aid estimate.

Respondent contends that the State aid projection in the enacted State budget is still only an estimate, and that based upon the district's experience, it was prudent to treat it as an estimate and not a definitive prediction of the exact amount of State aid that the district would ultimately receive. Respondent submits an affidavit from the district's business manager in which she states, as an example, that for the 2002-2003 school year (the year involved in *Muench I*) the actual amount of State aid the district received ($29,182,394) was closer to their original estimate ($29,125,887), and if the district had used the higher estimate in the enacted State budget for 2002-2003 ($30,627,699), the district would have overestimated the amount of State aid it actually received.

The business manager further states that certain types of aid, such as BOCES, building, and transportation aid, are different from more general types of aid and the amount of State aid ultimately received by the district depends on the expenses actually incurred by the district for these purposes and such factors as changes in enrollment, utilization levels, and the actual amount of construction and financing. She states that most of the increase in State aid in the enacted State budget is due to these special types of aid which, being dedicated for particular purposes, are not available to the board to reduce the property tax levy.

I do not find that respondent's reasons provide sufficient justification for its failure to use the most recent State aid projection as set forth in the enacted State education budget. Other than an anecdotal example regarding the 2002-2003 school year, respondent has failed to provide any other evidence that establishes the State aid projections set forth in the State budget, including those for certain types of State aid such as BOCES, building, and transportation aid, are consistently overstated, or that the projections set forth in the 2004-2005 State budget are based upon outdated information or are otherwise unreliable. Accordingly, respondent should have used the State aid projections in the enacted State budget in determining the tax levy to be assessed for the 2004-2005 school year.

Although I sustain the appeal in this regard, there is no need to adjust the 2004-2005 tax levy at this time because the use of the lower estimate of State aid should lead to an excess of revenues over expenditures at the end of the 2004-2005 school year, which the district would then be obligated to apply to reducing the 2005-2006 tax levy (*Appeal of Muench*, *supra*). Furthermore, there is no mechanism for returning a pro rata share of funds to the taxpayers once the tax levy has been made (*Appeal of Liberatore*, 42 Ed Dept Rep 321, Decision No. 14,869).

THE APPEAL IS SUSTAINED TO THE EXTENT INDICATED.

IT IS ORDERED that respondent henceforth utilize the best estimate of State aid that is reasonably available to respondent at the time it calculates the tax levy and issues tax warrants, consistent with the terms of this decision.

Decision No. 15,211

Appeal of KEN UY from action of the Board of Education of the Sullivan West Central School District regarding a budget appropriation and expenditure.

(April 26, 2005)

APPEARANCES OF COUNSEL

Shaw & Perelson, LLP, attorneys for respondent, *David S. Shaw, Esq.*, of counsel

DECISION OF THE COMMISSIONER

MILLS, Commissioner—Petitioner challenges a transfer of funds by the Board of Education of the Sullivan West Central School District ("respondent") from the unappropriated fund balance during the 2003-2004 school year to an account for the payment of debt service on a capital project and an expenditure from that account. The appeal must be dismissed.

On June 22, 2000, district voters approved a proposition in the amount of $49,938,453 for a capital project to acquire property and construct a building, and authorized respondent to issue obligations to fund the project. In May 2001, respondent adopted a resolution authorizing the issuance of bonds and notes to fund the project. In June 2002, respondent issued bond anticipation notes in anticipation of the issuance of serial bonds for the capital project. These notes came due in June 2003 and June 2004. It is unclear whether and to what extent respondent issued serial bonds to fund the project.

During the 2002-2003 school year, respondent apparently submitted claims for State aid, pursuant to Education Law §§3602 and 3641, on capital project expenditures (capital outlay) made during the 2001-2002 school year. On June 26, 2003, the State Education Department's Office for State Aided Programs notified respondent that the 2001-2002 capital outlay expenditures would generate State aid, but that respondent was required to amend certain financial data submitted in support of its State aid claim. Although the record is unclear, it appears that respondent subsequently received the State aid and included it in the unappropriated fund balance of the previously approved 2003-2004 budget.

On April 15, 2004, respondent decided to transfer money from the unappropriated fund balance to pay for debt service on the capital project. On June 17, 2004, respondent adopted this resolution transferring money from the 2003-2004 unappropriated fund balance to enable such payment:

> BE IT RESOLVED, that the Board of Education hereby directs the Superintendent to increase the budgetary item Transfer Debt Service — SW Project A9901.96.0.000 in the amount of $1,500,000 with such funds to be used for the purpose of reducing principle [sic]; and
>
> BE IT FURTHER RESOLVED, that the appropriated fund balance is hereby increased by the amount of $1,500,000 as a result of the reduction in principle [sic].

On June 18, 2004, the district treasurer made the payment.

Petitioner claims that, by increasing the debt service appropriation, the transfer of money from the unappropriated fund balance to the debt service account improperly increased the total 2003-2004 budget appropriation above that approved by the voters. Petitioner contends that respondent's action violates Education Law §1718. Petitioner also contends that the intrafund transfer does not comply with the uniform system of accounts prescribed by the State Comptroller pursuant to General Municipal Law §36.

Petitioner seeks an order nullifying all expenditures that cause respondent to exceed the total 2003-2004 budget appropriation authorized by voters. Petitioner also asks, "[i]n the event that Respondent has made a payment under a debt service agreement. . . which causes Respondent to exceed authorized expenditures, relief in the form of nullifying said payment and causing Respondent to be in default of said debt service agreement."

As part of his appeal, petitioner sought a stay of the appropriation and expenditure, so that the money could be used to reduce the 2004-2005 tax levy. On June 28, 2004, petitioner's request was denied.

Respondent denies petitioner's allegations and asserts that it has properly complied with applicable provisions of the Education Law in managing the 2003-2004 budget and preparing the 2004-2005 budget. Respondent also argues that the appeal is moot because the contested expenditure was made on June 18, 2004, and that all 2003-2004 budget events have occurred. Respondent also objects to petitioner's verified reply, maintaining that it does not comply with the Commissioner's regulations.

The purpose of a reply is to respond to new material or affirmative defenses set forth in an answer (8 NYCRR §§275.3 and 275.14). A reply is not meant to buttress allegations in the petition or to belatedly add assertions that should have been in the petition (*Appeal of Schildhorn*, 44 Ed Dept Rep 212, Decision No. 15,152). Therefore, while I have reviewed petitioner's reply, I have not considered those portions containing new allegations that are not responsive to new material or affirmative defenses set forth in the answer.

The appeal must be dismissed for failure to join necessary parties. A party whose rights will be adversely affected by a determination in an appeal in favor of petitioner is a necessary party and must be joined as such (*Appeal of Reshard*, 44 Ed Dept Rep 210, Decision No. 15,151; *Appeal of K.S.*, 43 *id.* 492, Decision No. 15,063). Petitioner specifically seeks to void the June 18, 2004, expenditure to reduce the outstanding principal on the capital project indebtedness. To the extent that such expenditure paid off existing bond anticipation notes or serial bonds, the holders of such obligations to whom payments were made are necessary parties to the appeal. Petitioner's failure to join them requires dismissal.

The appeal is also moot. The Commissioner of Education will only consider matters in actual controversy and will not render a decision on a state of facts which no longer exists or which subsequent events have laid to rest (*Appeal of E.M.*, 44 Ed Dept Rep 156, Decision No. 15,130; *Appeal of S.Y.*, 44 *id.* 120, Decision No. 15,118). This appeal was initiated on June 18, 2004, — the day respondent's treasurer made the disputed expenditure — and was not received in my Office of Counsel until June 21, 2004. Petitioner's request for a stay of the disputed appropriation and expenditure, so as to permit an offset of the 2004-2005 tax levy, was denied on June 28, 2004. Respondent was required to issue its 2004-2005 tax warrant on or before September 1, 2004 (Real Property Tax Law §1306). Because the disputed appropriation and expenditure has already occurred and cannot be voided, as noted above, and the 2004-2005 warrant for the tax levy has also been issued, petitioner cannot obtain the relief sought. The appeal, therefore, is moot.

Even if the appeal were not dismissed on procedural grounds, I would dismiss it on the merits. In an appeal to the Commissioner, the petitioner has the burden of demonstrating the facts upon which relief is sought and a clear right to the relief requested (8 NYCRR §275.10; *Appeal of Smith*, 44 Ed Dept Rep 201, Decision No. 15,148; *Appeal of Goldin*, 43 *id.* 453, Decision No. 15,048). Petitioner asserts that respondent's transfer of $1,500,000 from the unappropriated fund balance to the debt service account improperly increased the appropriation in that account and, thus, improperly increased the total 2003-2004 budget appropriation authorized by district voters, in contravention of Education Law §1718(1). That section provides:

> No board of education shall incur a district liability in excess of the amount appropriated by a district meeting unless such board is specially authorized by law to incur such liability.

Respondent maintains that the $1,500,000 transfer to debt service and subsequent expenditure is permissible under Education Law §1718(1). Respondent asserts that the appropriation and expenditure were authorized by law because the expenditure was applied to debt service previously authorized by the voters.

The petition consists entirely of conclusory allegations. The only documentary evidence submitted by petitioner are copies of respondent's June 17, 2004, resolution and copies of pages setting forth accounting principles and account code numbers from the Uniform System of Accounts for School Districts. Petitioner submits no further evidence to support his conclusory statements.

Respondent's description of the appropriation and expenditure does not provide a clear explanation of exactly what was paid with the money. It is unclear whether respondent used the money to pay off any of the bond anticipation notes due in June 2004 or other "bonded indebtedness." It is also unclear to what degree respondent used the money transferred from the unappropriated fund balance to pay for debt service already included as a line item in the approved 2003-2004 budget. As noted above, petitioner has the burden of proof. On this record, I am unable to determine the appropriateness of respondent's action. Thus, petitioner has failed to meet his burden, and the appeal must be dismissed.

THE APPEAL IS DISMISSED.

Decision No. 15,212

Appeal of MICHAEL J. CIMINO from action of the Board of Education of the Plainedge Union Free School District regarding certain expenditures.

(April 26, 2005)

APPEARANCES OF COUNSEL

Ingerman Smith, LLP, attorneys for respondent, *Carrie E. Flynn, Esq.*, of counsel

DECISION OF THE COMMISSIONER

MILLS, Commissioner—Petitioner challenges the action of the Board of Education of Plainedge Union Free School District ("respondent") in adding certain expenditures to the budget approved by the voters for the 2004-2005 school year. The appeal must be dismissed.

On May 18, 2004, the original budget submitted by respondent to the voters was defeated. Respondent then prepared a second budget, reduced by $521,830 from the amount of the first budget, which was approved by the voters on June 29, 2004. Among the expenditures that were eliminated between the original budget and the second budget were the costs associated with the position of director of guidance, an athletic trainer position, and seventh grade winter and spring sports.

On August 10, 2004, respondent voted to restore the director of guidance position, the athletic trainer position, the seventh grade winter and spring sports, and in addition voted to hire an outside auditor and to approve a forensic audit. The net increase in expenditures of these additional items was approximately $130,000. The board minutes indicate that the additional expenditures would be paid with additional State aid for the 2004-2005 school year in the amount of $260,000.

The petition merely states the board's actions. It does not claim that the board violated any law or regulation, and it does not demand any form of relief.

Respondent admits the allegations of the petition, and argues that the appeal is untimely, fails to state a claim, fails to request any relief, and fails to make any allegation that the board has acted arbitrarily, capriciously, or without a rational basis.

The appeal must be dismissed as untimely. The board action complained of occurred on August 10, 2004, but the appeal was not commenced until October 22, 2004, well beyond the thirty days allowed by §275.16 of the Commissioner's regulations. While the Commissioner may excuse a failure to commence an appeal within the time specified for good cause shown and set forth in the petition, here there is no such ground for excuse.

The petition must also be dismissed pursuant to §275.10 of the regulations, which requires that a petition contain a clear and concise statement of petitioner's claim showing an entitlement to relief, and a demand for relief. The petition fails in both respects.

THE APPEAL IS DISMISSED.

Decision No. 15,213

Appeal of FREDERICK J. GORMAN from action of the Board of Education of the Sachem Central School District regarding financial practices.

(April 26, 2005)

APPEARANCES OF COUNSEL

Ingerman Smith, L.L.P., attorneys for respondent, *Neil M. Block, Esq*., of counsel

DECISION OF THE COMMISSIONER

MILLS, Commissioner—Petitioner challenges the financial practices of the Board of Education of the Sachem Central School District ("respondent"). The appeal must be dismissed.

Petitioner contends that respondent violated Real Property Tax Law ("RPTL") §1318 by improperly creating an unauthorized reserve fund in the amount of $4,636,176 for retirees' health insurance premiums for the 2003-2004 school year. Petitioner also contends that respondent failed to seek approval from district voters or an opinion from the New York State Education Department before creating the alleged reserve fund.

Petitioner requests that I order respondent to liquidate the alleged reserve fund and to reduce taxes or transfer the fund to a reserve account permitted by law. Petitioner also requests that I censure respondent and caution it against establishing reserves not authorized by law in the future.

Respondent asserts that petitioner's appeal is untimely and fails to state a claim upon which relief may be granted. Respondent also asserts that it did not create a reserve fund for retirees' health insurance premiums. Rather, it maintains that the amount petitioner characterizes as a reserve fund is actually an accrued liability.

Pursuant to §275.16 of the Commissioner's regulations, an appeal to the Commissioner must be commenced within 30 days from the making of the decision or the performance of the act complained of unless any delay is excused by the Commissioner for good cause shown. Under RPTL §1318(1), an appeal is timely if it is brought within the fiscal year during which unexpended surplus funds are improperly retained (*Appeal of Schadtle*, 40 Ed Dept Rep 60, Decision No. 14,421; *Appeal of Siver*, 37 *id*. 498, Decision No. 13,912). This appeal was commenced on March 29, 2004, during the 2003-2004 school year and, therefore, is timely to the extent that petitioner alleges that respondent created an unauthorized reserve fund for that school year.

In an appeal to the Commissioner, the petitioner has the burden of demonstrating a clear legal right to the relief requested and the burden of establishing the facts upon which he seeks relief (8 NYCRR §275.10; *Appeal of Sloley-Raymond*, 44 Ed Dept Rep 27, Decision No. 15,085; *Appeal of Nelson*, 44 *id*. 20, Decision No. 15,082). Petitioner has failed to prove that respondent created an unauthorized reserve fund.

Petitioner bases his claim, in part, on a document entitled "Sachem Central School District Analysis of Reserves" ("the Reserve Analysis"). This document includes a line for "Retirees Health Insurance" and reflects a balance of $4,636,176 as of June 30, 2003. Petitioner also submits a "General Fund Balance Sheet" that reflects accrued liabilities in the same amount. In addition he submits eight "General Ledger Transaction Analysis" sheets that appear to show the accumulation of the $4,636,176 from 2000 to 2003. None of these documents, however, indicate the existence of a reserve fund for retirees' health insurance; neither do the 2004-2005 budget documents that petitioner submits with his reply.

According to respondent's assistant superintendent for business, the district does not maintain a reserve fund for retirees' health insurance. The assistant superintendent avers that, although the Reserve Analysis includes reserve funds established by the district, it also sets forth liabilities for retirees' health insurance and teachers' and employees' retirement systems for which reserves have not been created. To avoid any future confusion respondent states that it will remove these liabilities from the Reserve Analysis in financial statements prospectively.

Thus, on the record before me, petitioner has failed to establish that respondent created an unauthorized reserve account. Accordingly, his allegations with respect thereto must be dismissed.

In light of this disposition, I need not address the parties' remaining contentions.

THE APPEAL IS DISMISSED.

Decision No. 15,214

Appeal of BENEDICT VIGLIETTA from action of the Board of Education of the Enlarged City School District of the City of Auburn, John Ferrara, Johnathan Roberts, Brian Piscotti, Janine Pellegrino, Jeannette Oliver, Jeffrey Evener, Elizabeth Case, Mark Angier, Jeffrey Alberici and Matthew Moskov regarding seniority.

(April 26, 2005)

APPEARANCES OF COUNSEL

James R. Sandner, Esq., attorney for petitioner, *Marilyn S. Dymond, Esq.*, of counsel

Randy J. Ray, Esq., attorney for respondent Board of Education of the Enlarged City School District of the City of Auburn

DECISION OF THE COMMISSIONER

MILLS, Commissioner—Petitioner appeals a determination by the Board of Education of the Enlarged City School District of the City of Auburn ("respondent board") to abolish his teaching position and its failure to appoint him to a social studies position in the district. The appeal must be dismissed.

In October 1998, respondent board hired petitioner to teach in the district's Air Force Junior ROTC ("AFJROTC") program and granted him a probationary appointment in the "technical subjects — AFJROTC" tenure area. In October 2001, respondent board awarded petitioner tenure in that same tenure area. On July 6, 2004, respondent board abolished the AFJROTC program and petitioner's position. On July 27, 2004, respondent board appointed Matt Dillon to a probationary appointment in the social studies tenure area.

Petitioner claims that respondent board appointed him to an unauthorized tenure area and that his duties most resemble those of a social studies teacher. Petitioner further asserts that he should be deemed to have served in the social studies tenure area and to have acquired tenure by estoppel in that tenure area. Petitioner contends that there are a number of other individual teachers with less seniority in the social studies tenure area, including Mr. Dillon. Petitioner seeks an order directing respondent board to appoint him to a social studies position with full pay and benefits, including back pay.

Respondent board contends, among other things, that petitioner did not accrue any seniority in the social studies tenure area and the appeal must be dismissed because petitioner failed to join Matt Dillon as a necessary party.

The appeal must be dismissed for failure to join a necessary party. A party whose rights would be adversely affected by a determination of an appeal in favor of petitioner is a necessary party and must be joined as such (*Appeal of Stanton*, 44 Ed Dept Rep 141, Decision No. 15,125; *Appeal of Milazzo*, 43 *id.* 294, Decision No. 14,999; *Appeal of Stolbach*, 43 *id.* 218, Decision No. 14,977). Mr. Dillon, as the undisputed least senior teacher, would be affected if petitioner prevails in this appeal. Respondent board raised this argument as an affirmative defense in its answer. On August 26, 2004, my Office of Counsel granted petitioner's request to join Mr. Dillon as a respondent and directed that the caption of the appeal be amended to include Mr. Dillon as a named respondent. Joinder requires that an individual be clearly named as a respondent in the caption of the notice of petition and petition to inform the individual that he or she should respond to the petition and enter a defense (*Appeal of Stanton*, *supra*; *Appeal of Milazzo*, *supra*; *Appeal of Stolbach*, *supra*).

There is no evidence in the record that petitioner amended the caption of the notice of petition and petition to include Mr. Dillon as a respondent. An amended notice of petition and petition were not filed with my Office of Counsel as required by §275.9 of the Commissioner's regulations.

In addition, according to the affidavit of service that was filed, petitioner did not serve Mr. Dillon with an amended notice of petition and petition naming him as a party. Instead, it appears he was only served with the original pleadings. Therefore, I am constrained to dismiss the appeal for failure to join Mr. Dillon as a necessary party.

Since the appeal is dismissed on procedural grounds, I need not address the parties' remaining contentions.

THE APPEAL IS DISMISSED.

Decision No. 15,215

Appeal of A.C., on behalf of her daughter A.C., from action of the Board of Education of the West Islip Union Free School District regarding a bullying complaint.

(April 26, 2005)

APPEARANCES OF COUNSEL

Guercio & Guercio, attorneys for respondent, *Thomas Voltz, Esq.*, of counsel

DECISION OF THE COMMISSIONER

MILLS, Commissioner—Petitioner appeals the actions of the Board of Education of the West Islip Union Free School District ("respondent") in response to her bullying complaint. The appeal must be dismissed.

Petitioner alleges that on June 2, 2004, at the West Islip High School, a student chased her daughter through the halls into the guidance office screaming threats and obscenities. The high school principal conducted an investigation and determined that there was insufficient evidence to take disciplinary action against the student.

Petitioner and her daughter then went to the district administrative offices and requested a meeting with the superintendent. Because the superintendent was not available, they were advised that petitioner's daughter could present her concerns in writing. On or about June 16, 2004, the superintendent's office received a letter from petitioner's daughter describing the June 2, 2004, incident and surrounding events, and setting forth her complaints regarding the district's response to the incident. Petitioner alleges that neither the superintendent nor respondent answered her letter.

At its August 12, 2004, meeting, respondent permitted petitioner's daughter to speak before the board and she expressed her dissatisfaction with respondent's handling of the incident and its alleged failure to respond to her June 16 letter.

On September 8, 2004, petitioner commenced this appeal on behalf of her daughter. Petitioner requests that the superintendent and board members formally respond to their complaint "with full resolution of the situation of 6/2 and 8/12/04"; that respondent and the superintendent explain why "they chose to ignore" her daughter and to publicly apologize for doing so; and for her daughter to be invited to speak with others on solutions to bullying.

Respondent denies petitioner's allegations and contends that it properly acted within its scope of authority in determining that no discipline would be imposed for the June 2, 2004, incident. Respondent also maintains that the appeal is untimely, that petitioner has failed to meet her burden of proof, that the petition fails to state a claim upon which relief may be granted, that petitioner has failed to join necessary parties, and that petitioner lacks standing.

Before proceeding to the merits, I will address several procedural issues. Respondent contends that petitioner's reply and reply affidavits fail to comply with §§275.3 and 275.14 of the Commissioner's regulations. The purpose of a reply is to respond to new material or affirmative defenses set forth in the answer (8 NYCRR §§275.3 and 275.14). A reply may not be used to belatedly add new assertions that are not part of the pleadings (*Appeal of Kirschenbaum*, 43 Ed Dept Rep 366, Decision No. 15,020; *Appeal of Hollister*, 39 *id.* 109, Decision No. 14,188; *Appeal of Muench*, 38 *id.* 649, Decision No. 14,110). The rationale for this rule is to ensure an orderly framing of the issues (*Matter of a Handicapped Child*, 24 Ed Dept Rep 41, Decision No. 11,308). Therefore, while I have reviewed petitioner's submissions, I have not considered those portions containing new allegations that are not responsive to new material or affirmative defenses set forth in the answer.

Pursuant to §275.16 of the Commissioner's regulations, an appeal to the Commissioner of Education must be initiated within 30 days of the action or decision complained of, unless any delay is excused for good cause shown. Respondent contends that the 30 days must be measured from the June 16, 2004, delivery to the superintendent of the complaint letter from petitioner's daughter. However, petitioner has framed her complaint in terms of respondent's alleged failure to respond to the letter. It appears from the record that petitioner was permitted to present her grievances regarding respondent's alleged lack of response at respondent's August 12, 2004, board meeting. Therefore, on the record before me, I find that the 30 days should be measured from the August 12, 2004, meeting. Since petitioner properly served a petition on the board's clerk on September 8, 2004, I find that the appeal is timely.

A party whose rights would be adversely affected by a determination of an appeal in favor of petitioner is a necessary party and must be joined as such (*Appeal of Roff*, 41 Ed Dept Rep 346, Decision No. 14,708; *Appeal of Gargan*, 40 *id.* 465, Decision No. 14,528; *Appeal of World Network International Services, Inc.*, 39 *id.* 30, Decision No. 14,164). Petitioner has named and served only respondent board of education in this appeal. However, petitioner requests certain relief against the superintendent, including a public apology for allegedly ignoring and failing to respond to petitioner's complaint. Since the superintendent's rights would be adversely affected by any determination that he acted improperly, the superintendent is a necessary party to this proceeding (*Appeal of Basil*, 37 Ed Dept Rep 568, Decision No. 13,929). Petitioner was therefore required to personally serve him with the notice of petition and petition (8 NYCRR §275.8; *Appeal of Wheeler*, 40 Ed Dept Rep 678, Decision No. 14,581; *Appeal of Heller*, 38 *id.* 335, Decision No. 14,048), and her failure to do so warrants the dismissal of this appeal with respect to petitioner's claims against the superintendent.

Moreover, with respect to petitioner's request for an apology, I lack the authority to order such relief (*Application of McDougall and Dacey*, 42 Ed Dept Rep 195, Decision No. 14,819; *Appeal of Basil*, *supra*).

Respondent also contends that petitioner failed to join the student who allegedly chased and threatened petitioner's daughter. However, in a letter submitted pursuant to §276.5 of the Commissioner's regulations, petitioner clarifies that she does not seek discipline of the student. Accordingly, since petitioner seeks no relief against the student, I do not find her to be a necessary party to this appeal. Furthermore, since petitioner does not seek to have respondent discipline the student, I need not consider respondent's contention that she lacks standing to do so.

It appears that the essence of petitioner's grievance is that respondent failed to directly communicate with her daughter concerning its investigation of the June 2, 2004, incident or respond in writing to her June 16, 2004, complaint letter.

In an appeal to the Commissioner, the petitioner bears the burden of establishing the facts upon which she seeks relief and demonstrating a clear legal right to the relief requested (8 NYCRR §275.10; *Appeal of L.M.*, 43 Ed Dept Rep 279, Decision No. 14,994; *Appeal of Brannon*, 42 *id.* 220, Decision No. 14,830). Petitioner's allegations consist of general, subjective expressions of her dissatisfaction with the district's response to the June 2, 2004, incident and her complaint. Her allegations are refuted by the affidavits of respondent's principal and superintendent, which establish that the assistant superintendent conducted two reviews of the principal's determination, one of which was conducted specifically in response to the June 16, 2004, complaint letter from petitioner's daughter. The district also took other measures such as assigning an escort to petitioner's daughter, allowing her to leave class early, and rearranging her fall schedule to ensure certain students would not be in her classes or lunch periods.

Although petitioner believes that respondent should have directly communicated with her and her daughter concerning its investigation and responded in writing to her June 16, 2004, complaint letter, there is no requirement in law that respondent do so. Furthermore, confidentiality requirements regarding student discipline and student records may constrain respondent's disclosure of certain information.

While a better effort on the part of both parties to communicate more effectively may have removed the necessity for an appeal, on the record before me, I do not find respondent's actions to be arbitrary, capricious or contrary to law.

THE APPEAL IS DISMISSED.

Decision No. 15,216

Appeal of KEELY DUNSHEE from action of the Board of Education of the Malone Central School District, Wayne C. Walbridge, Superintendent of Schools, and John Scheidegger, regarding an administrative appointment.

(April 26, 2005)

APPEARANCES OF COUNSEL

Louis J. Patack, Esq., attorney for petitioner

Ferrara, Fiorenza, Larrison, Barrett & Reitz, P.C., attorneys for respondents, *David W. Larrison, Esq.*, of counsel

DECISION OF THE COMMISSIONER

MILLS, Commissioner—Petitioner challenges her appointment by the Board of Education of the Malone Central School District ("respondent board" or "board") to the position of co-principal of Franklin Academy High School. The appeal must be dismissed.

Petitioner was first employed by respondent board on January 21, 1998 as interim principal of Malone Middle School, and was subsequently appointed principal of the middle school on July 1, 1998. In the Malone Central School District, only two tenure areas have been historically identified for secondary building administrators — "secondary principal" and "secondary assistant principal." Petitioner received tenure in the secondary principal tenure area, effective January 19, 2001.

At its May 25, 2004, meeting, respondent board appointed petitioner as "co-principal" of Franklin Academy High School, effective July 1, 2004. Respondent board also appointed respondent Scheidegger as interim principal of Malone Middle School, effective July 1, 2004. Prior to the effective date of his appointment as interim principal, respondent Scheidegger was assistant principal of the high school.

On June 8, 2004, petitioner received a letter, dated June 1, 2004, from respondent superintendent of schools advising of her appointment as co-principal. The letter further stated that she would maintain tenure in the secondary principal tenure area, that the current principal of the high school would be the "principal in-charge," and that it was expected that petitioner would fulfill those duties previously carried out by respondent Scheidegger.

Petitioner commenced this appeal on June 21, 2004. She contends that her appointment as a co-principal to allegedly perform assistant principal duties constitutes, in effect, an involuntary transfer from her secondary principal tenure area to a secondary assistant principal tenure area. Petitioner requests that her appointment be rescinded and that she be returned to her tenured position of middle school principal.

Respondents deny petitioner's allegations and contend that no involuntary transfer has occurred because petitioner's appointment to co-principal is within the secondary principal tenure area and petitioner will be performing the duties of co-principal within such tenure area. Respondents further contend that the appeal is premature, and object to petitioner's reply memorandum of law.

I will first address the procedural issues. Respondents contend that petitioner's reply memorandum of law fails to comply with §276.4(a) of the Commissioner's regulations. Under that provision, reply memoranda of law may be accepted only with the prior approval of the Commissioner (*Appeal of Schadtle*, 40 Ed Dept Rep 60, Decision No. 14,421). By cover letter dated October 19, 2004, petitioner requested that I accept and consider the reply memorandum as it addresses arguments advanced by respondents in their memorandum of law. However, I find that the reply memorandum also raises new allegations and issues not included in the petition. A reply memorandum of law may not be used to belatedly add new assertions that are not part of the pleadings (*Appeal of Kirschenbaum*, 43 Ed Dept Rep 366, Decision No. 15,020; *Appeal of T.M.*, 41 *id.* 443, Decision No. 14,470; *Appeal of Muench*, 38 *id.* 649, Decision No. 14,110). Therefore, while I have reviewed petitioner's submissions, I have not considered those portions containing new allegations.

Respondents contend that the appeal is premature since a determination of the actual duties to be performed by petitioner as co-principal will not be made until on or after the opening of the 2004-2005 school year. However, the gravamen of petitioner's appeal is her appointment to the position of co-principal. An appeal to the Commissioner must be instituted within 30 days from the making of the decision or the performance of the act complained of (8 NYCRR §275.16). Since petitioner commenced her appeal within 30 days of respondent board's appointment action on May 25, 2004, I do not find the appeal to be premature.

In an appeal to the Commissioner of Education, petitioner has the burden of establishing the facts upon which relief is requested (8 NYCRR §275.10; *Appeal of Beauman*, 43 Ed Dept Rep 212, Decision No. 14,974; *Appeal of McNamara*, 41 *id.* 134, Decision No. 14,638, judgment granted dismissing petition to review, *McNamara v. Mills, et al.*, Sup. Ct., Albany Co., Special Term (Kane, J.), January 10, 2002, n.o.r.) and the burden of demonstrating a clear legal right to the relief sought (*Appeals of T.M., Sr.*, 42 Ed Dept Rep 281, Decision No. 14,855). Section 30.9(b) of the Commissioner's regulations states:

> No professional educator, whether on tenure or in probationary status, may be assigned to devote a substantial portion of his time in a tenure area other than that in which he has acquired tenure or is in probationary status, without his prior written consent.

Petitioner alleges that she will be performing the duties of an assistant principal. However, according to the affidavit of respondent superintendent, the actual duties to be performed by petitioner during the 2004-2005 school year will be developed during the school year based upon some division of responsibilities between the co-principals, as need requires.

A board of education has broad discretion in assigning members of its professional staff, so long as the employee's tenure rights are not infringed upon (*Matter of Van Heusen v. Bd. of Ed., City School District of the City of Schenectady, et al.*, 26 AD2d 721; *Appeal of Dillon*, 43 Ed Dept Rep 333, Decision No. 15,010; *Appeal of Garry*, 19 *id.* 359, Decision No. 10,166). Although petitioner disputes respondents' assertions regarding the duties to be assigned to her as co-principal, it is clear that petitioner will maintain tenure in the secondary principal tenure area as a co-principal. Petitioner has otherwise failed to demonstrate that she has been involuntarily transferred to a position outside her tenure area or that her tenure rights have been otherwise infringed by her appointment as co-principal.

Nor do I find on the record before me that petitioner's appointment as co-principal was merely a thinly disguised attempt at disciplinary action (compare *Appeal of Irving*, 39 Ed Dept Rep 761, Decision No. 14,373). In *Irving*, the district cited incidents of alleged misconduct that immediately preceded the administrator's transfer and were the subject of a counseling letter given to her on the day before the transfer. In contrast, petitioner here has framed her complaint as an involuntary transfer outside of her tenure area and has failed to establish that the transfer was used as a subterfuge to discipline her for alleged misconduct (*see Appeal of Dillon*, *supra*).

THE APPEAL IS DISMISSED.

Decision No. 15,217

Appeal of S.M. and A.N., on behalf of their daughter S.N., from action of the Board of Education of the Bayport-Blue Point Union Free School District regarding exclusion from school due to lack of immunization.

(April 26, 2005)

APPEARANCES OF COUNSEL

Patricia A. Finn, Esq., attorney for petitioners

Cooper, Sapir & Cohen, P.C., attorneys for respondent, *David M. Cohen, Esq.*, of counsel

DECISION OF THE COMMISSIONER

MILLS, Commissioner—Petitioners appeal the determination of the Board of Education of the Bayport-Blue Point Union Free School District ("respondent") that their daughter is not entitled to an exemption from the immunization requirement under Public Health Law ("PHL") §2164. The appeal must be dismissed.

By letter dated February 17, 2004, petitioners requested that their daughter be permitted to attend respondent's schools without the immunizations required by PHL §2164 because "vaccination is contrary to our religious beliefs." The letter did not describe their beliefs. By letter dated March 6, 2004, petitioners provided additional information in support of their request for a religious exemption citing case law and legal authority, but again did not explain how their specific religious beliefs are contrary to the immunization requirements.

On March 26, 2004, the assistant superintendent for curriculum, instruction and general administration and respondent's attorney met with petitioners to ascertain the basis for their request. After hearing petitioners' arguments for a religious exemption and reviewing the information provided by petitioners in support of their request, respondent denied an exemption by letter dated July 14, 2004. Petitioners' request for interim relief was denied on September 3, 2004.

Petitioners contend that their objections to immunizations are based on sincerely held religious beliefs and seek an order reversing respondent's decision to exclude their daughter from school. They further seek attorneys' fees and costs.

Respondent maintains that petitioners' objections to immunizations are not based on sincerely held religious beliefs and that its determination should be upheld. Respondent further submits that the Commissioner lacks jurisdiction to award attorneys' fees and costs.

PHL §2164(9) provides:

> This section shall not apply to children whose parent, parents, or guardian hold genuine and sincere religious beliefs which are contrary to the practices herein required, and no certificate shall be required as a prerequisite to such children being admitted or received into school or attending school.

The issue in this appeal is whether petitioners' opposition to immunization stems from sincerely held religious beliefs. The exemption from immunization does not extend to persons whose views are founded upon medical or purely moral considerations, scientific or secular theories, or philosophical and personal beliefs (*Farina v. Bd. of Ed. of the City of New York*, 116 F Supp 2d 503). However, it is not necessary for persons to be members of a recognized religious organization whose teachings oppose inoculation (*Sherr v. Northport-East Northport Union Free School Dist.*, 672 F Supp 81). Whether a religious belief is sincerely held can be a difficult factual determination that must be made, in the first instance, by school district officials (*Appeal of D.L.*, 44 Ed Dept Rep 104, Decision No. 15,111; *Appeal of D.K.*, 44 *id.* 47, Decision No. 15,094; *Appeal of Quigley*, 41 *id.* 399, Decision No. 14,724). In making this determination, school officials must make a good faith effort to assess the credibility of petitioners' statements and sincerity and may consider petitioners' demeanor and forthrightness (*Appeal of D.K.*, *supra*; *Appeal of Quigley*, *supra*). While school officials are not required to simply accept a statement of religious belief without some explanation, they similarly should not simply reject a statement without further examination (*Appeal of D.K.*, *supra*).

In an appeal to the Commissioner, petitioners have the burden of demonstrating a clear legal right to the relief requested and the burden of establishing the facts upon which they seek relief (8 NYCRR §275.10; *Appeal of Garmaeva*, 43 Ed Dept Rep 253, Decision No. 14,988; *Appeal of Goldin*, 43 *id.* 20, Decision No. 14,904). In this appeal, the assistant superintendent and respondent's attorney gave petitioners an opportunity to explain their position. The parties disagree over what transpired at the meeting. Petitioners claim that they provided a clear explanation of their religious beliefs that are contrary to the immunization requirements. Respondent contends that petitioners did not clearly state their religious beliefs that are contrary to immunization. Respondent further asserts that petitioners stated that they thought immunizations were harmful to an individual's health. According to respondent, the only references to religious passages made in support of an exemption, were made by petitioners' attorney in a letter received subsequent to the meeting. Respondent contends that petitioners' opposition to immunization is based upon their medical, personal or philosophical beliefs. Petitioners failed to submit a reply to respondent's answer.

After affording petitioners an opportunity to explain their beliefs, and after assessing their credibility, respondent determined that they failed to articulate the religious basis or origins of their beliefs. Based on the record before me, I cannot find that petitioners have demonstrated that respondent's determination was arbitrary or capricious.

In light of this disposition, I need not address petitioners' remaining contentions.

THE APPEAL IS DISMISSED.

Decision No. 15,218

Appeal of J.V., on behalf of her children, from action of the Board of Education of the Greece Central School District regarding residency.

(May 2, 2005)

APPEARANCES OF COUNSEL

Harris Beach LLP, attorneys for respondent, *Alfred Streppa, Esq.*, of counsel

DECISION OF THE COMMISSIONER

MILLS, Commissioner.—Petitioner appeals the determination of the Board of Education of the Greece Central School District ("respondent") that her two children are not district residents. The appeal must be dismissed.

Respondent began an investigation into petitioner's residency in November 2003. Respondent's investigator conducted surveillance of a residence located outside of the district between November 3 and 18, 2003. On five mornings during this period, the investigator observed petitioner drive her children from the out-of-district residence to respondent's school. On two other mornings, the investigator observed petitioner's children being driven to school from the out-of-district residence but did not identify the driver.

Respondent's investigator resumed the surveillance of the out-of-district residence between June 15 and 17, 2004. On two mornings, petitioner drove her children from the out-of-district residence to a school bus stop from which her children were transported to respondent's school, and on the third morning, another individual drove the children from the out-of-district residence to the same school bus stop. On review of the district's records, respondent's designee for residency matters ("respondent's designee") found that the home telephone number provided by petitioner on student data forms in August 2003 belonged to the out-of-district residence.

In July 2004, respondent's investigator interviewed two neighbors who live near the address that petitioner claims to be her district residence. According to the investigator, one neighbor said that he knew petitioner and that she had not lived at that residence for at least one and one-half years, and the other neighbor said that no school-age children lived at the address.

By letter dated July 21, 2004, respondent's designee advised petitioner of the results of the investigation and the determination that petitioner and her children were not district residents, and provided petitioner with an opportunity to respond. In a letter dated July 27, 2004, respondent's designee made a final determination in the matter, finding that petitioner and her children were not district residents. He reiterated the findings of the investigation and added that when the July 21, 2004, letter was hand-delivered to petitioner at the out-of-district residence, her name was on the mailbox at that address. This appeal ensued.

Petitioner claims that she owns a house in the district and that this house is her permanent residence. She claims that she is temporarily residing outside of the district because she is afraid of her former husband but plans to return to the district residence by August 2005. Respondent claims that petitioner and her children reside outside of the district and consequently petitioner's children do not have the right to attend the district's schools free of charge.

Education Law §3202(1) provides, in pertinent part:

> A person over five and under twenty-one years of age who has not received a high school diploma is entitled to attend the public schools maintained in the district in which such person resides without the payment of tuition.

The purpose of this statute is to limit the obligation of school districts to provide tuition-free education to students whose parents or legal guardians reside within the district (*Appeal of Marshall*, 43 Ed Dept Rep 47, Decision No. 14,911; *Appeal of B.O. and D.O.*, 42 *id.* 42, Decision No. 14,769; *Appeal of Metze*, 42 *id.* 40, Decision No. 14,768). Residence for purposes of Education Law §3202 is established by one's physical presence as an inhabitant within the district and an intent to reside in the district (*Longwood Cent. School Dist. v. Springs Union Free School Dist.*, 1 NY3d 385; *Appeal of Marshall*, *supra*; *Appeal of B.O. and D.O.*, *supra*). Mere ownership of property in a school district does not confer residency status (*see Appeal of Rosen*, 43 Ed Dept Rep 87, Decision No. 14,929; *Appeal of O'Herron*, 41 *id.* 1, Decision No. 14,591).

A person's temporary absence from the school district of residence does not necessarily constitute either the establishment of a residence in the district where one is temporarily located, or the abandonment of one's permanent residence (*Appeal of Weisberg*, 39 Ed Dept Rep

737, Decision No. 14,365, judgment granted dismissing petition to review, *Weisberg v. Mills, et al.*, Sup. Ct., Albany Co., Special Term (Malone, J.), November 27, 2000, n.o.r.; *Appeal of Schwartzburt*, 37 *id.* 139, Decision No. 13,825; *Appeal of Kenneth R.*, 30 *id.* 297, Decision No. 12,471). To determine one's intent as to whether a living arrangement is indeed temporary, the Commissioner must consider evidence regarding the family's continuing ties to the community and their efforts to return (*Appeal of Collins*, 44 Ed Dept Rep 74, Decision No. 15,103; *Appeal of Weisberg, supra*; *Appeal of Schwartzburt, supra*).

A residency determination will not be overturned unless it is arbitrary and capricious (*Appeal of St. Villien*, 44 Ed Dept Rep 69, Decision No. 15,101; *Appeal of Holder*, 44 *id.* 32, Decision No. 15,088). In an appeal to the Commissioner, petitioner has the burden of establishing a clear legal right to the relief requested and the burden of establishing the facts upon which petitioner seeks relief (8 NYCRR §275.10; *Appeal of Smith, supra*; *Appeal of Holder, supra*).

The parties do not dispute the fact that petitioner owns a house in the district. Petitioner admits that she is allowing other individuals to live in that house. She states that she is residing outside of the district with her two children on a temporary basis because she is afraid of her former husband and wants to protect her children by living at a location unknown to him. Petitioner submits an order of protection, which prohibits her former husband from having any contact with her and requires a third party to arrange for her former husband's visitation with the children.

The issue in this appeal is whether or not petitioner's absence from the district is temporary. Petitioner submits a number of documents in support of her claim that her permanent residence is within the district, including a driver's license, a tax bill, water bills, utility bills, refuse removal bills, cable bills, and credit card bills, among others. Many of these documents have little probative value because they date to a period prior to November 2003, when respondent began its investigation. Others support the fact that petitioner owns a house in the district, but ownership of property in a district alone does not confer residency status. I do not find that these documents adequately establish continuing ties to the community demonstrating that petitioner's absence from the district is temporary.

While petitioner expresses an intent to return to the district by August 2005, she provides no explanation of the change in circumstance that would enable her to do so. Petitioner's claimed intent to return to the district is insufficient to establish residency, absent evidence of substantial progress toward meeting that objective or at the very least, a concrete and realistic plan to do so (*see Appeal of Collins*, *supra*). Petitioner has failed to supply sufficient evidence demonstrating substantial progress or a concrete and realistic plan. Thus, on the record before me, I cannot conclude that respondent's determination was arbitrary or capricious.

THE APPEAL IS DISMISSED.

Decision No. 15,219

Appeal of KEN UY and ARTHUR NORDEN from action of the Board of Education of the Sullivan West Central School District regarding a capital reserve fund.

(May 12, 2005)

APPEARANCES OF COUNSEL

Shaw & Perelson, LLP, attorneys for respondent, *David Shaw, Esq.*, of counsel

DECISION OF THE COMMISSIONER

MILLS, Commissioner.—Petitioners challenge certain actions of the Board of Education of the Sullivan West Central School District ("respondent") relating to a capital reserve fund. The appeal must be sustained in part.

Although the record is somewhat unclear, it appears that at respondent's May 16, 2000, annual election, district voters authorized respondent to establish a capital reserve fund with an ultimate amount of $3,000,000 "for the purpose of paying part of the costs of the new High School construction and reconstruction of other District buildings." In addition, at a June 22, 2000, special district meeting, district voters approved the following proposition:

> RESOLVED, that the Board of Education of Sullivan West Central School District at Callicoon-Jeffersonville-Youngsville-Narrowsburg, Sullivan and Delaware Counties, New York, is hereby authorized to purchase real property at a maximum estimated cost of $40,000 and construct and reconstruct school buildings, including

> site improvement, original furnishings, equipment, machinery, apparatus and other improvements and costs incidental thereto, at a maximum estimated cost of $49,898,453; and for such construction and reconstruction to expend up to $3,000,000 (plus accrued interest) from the "District-wide Construction and Reconstruction Reserve Fund"; and that the sum of $49,938,453, being the aggregate of the aforesaid costs, or so much thereof as may be necessary after taking into account the expenditure of Reserve Fund moneys, shall be raised by the levy of a tax upon the taxable property of said School District and collected in annual installments as provided by Section 416 of the Education Law; and, in anticipation of such tax, obligations of said School District shall be issued.

Respondent apparently expended the funds in its capital reserve fund during the 2001-2002 school year. This appeal ensued.

Petitioners essentially claim that respondent improperly expended monies from its capital reserve fund without voter authorization. Petitioners also maintain that at its December 4, 2003, meeting, respondent improperly accepted an inaccurate revised financial statement for the year ending June 30, 2002. Petitioners request, among other things, that I order respondent to rescind its acceptance of the revised financial statement, restore the capital reserve fund and comply with Education Law §3651 in the future.

Respondent objects to petitioners' reply and alleges that petitioners have failed to name as necessary parties certain unnamed State Education Department ("Department") officials who advised respondent on certain capital expenditures, reporting and State Aid issues. Respondent admits that it expended $1,037,477.28 from the Capital Reserve fund during the 2001-2002 school year, thereby depleting it, and asserts that district voters authorized this action by their approval of the June 22, 2000, proposition. Further, respondent explains that it properly accepted the revised financial statement to correct an earlier accounting error concerning the capital reserve expenditure.

Initially, I will address respondent's procedural objections. The purpose of a reply is to respond to new material or affirmative defenses set forth in an answer (8 NYCRR §§275.3 and 275.14). A reply is not meant to buttress allegations in the petition or to belatedly add assertions that should have been in the petition (*Appeal of General*, 43 Ed Dept Rep 146, Decision No. 14,948). Therefore, while I have reviewed petitioners' reply, I have not considered those portions containing new allegations or exhibits that are not responsive to new material or affirmative defenses set forth in the answer.

A party whose rights would be adversely affected by a determination of an appeal in favor of petitioners is a necessary party and must be joined as such (*Appeal of Hoffman*, 43 Ed Dept Rep 160, Decision No. 14,953; *Appeals of Branch, et al.*, 41 *id.* 334, Decision No. 14,704). Although respondent received advice from Department staff concerning the reserve fund, it is respondent's actions that petitioners challenge. Moreover, respondent fails to demonstrate how these unnamed State officials would be adversely affected by a determination in petitioners favor. Additionally, Education Law §310 does not authorize an appeal to the Commissioner from actions taken by staff of the State Education Department (*Appeal of Karpen*, 40 Ed Dept Rep 199, Decision No. 14,460; *Appeal of Molloy College*, 33 *id.* 361, Decision No. 13,078; *Matter of the Bd. of Educ. of the City School Dist. of the City of Rome*, 23 *id.* 382, Decision No. 11,253, *affd sub nom. Bd. of Educ. of the City School Dist. of the City of Rome v. Ambach*, 118 AD2d 932). Under these circumstances, I find no merit to respondent's claim that petitioners have failed to name necessary parties.

The purpose of a §3651 reserve fund is to permit a school district to set aside a sum of money for a future expenditure, rather than fund the expenditure through the current year's budget or through issuing bonds at the time of the expenditure. The reserve fund must be created for specific purpose(s), which must be disclosed to the voters at the time they approve the establishment of the fund. As I stated in *Appeal of Kackmeister* (40 Ed Dept Rep 577, Decision No. 14,560):

> [T]he expenditures from reserve funds should be for the specific purpose(s) for which the fund was established, and the proposition to approve the expenditure should explicitly state the purpose of the proposed expenditure (Education Law §3651(3)). Although the stated purpose(s) of a reserve fund may be somewhat broad, the spending authorization should be specific and give the voters adequate notice of the particular intended use of the funds. A proposition authorizing the funding of a reserve fund or an expenditure from a reserve fund is

limited to the fiscal year for which the voters approved the proposition, and may not contain language purporting to continue such authorization indefinitely into future fiscal years (*accord*, Opn. State Comptr. 83-223 [it is improper to use a single proposition to authorize a series of annual expenditures of a certain amount from a reserve fund]). As the Comptroller noted in Opinion 83-223, the statutory requirement of "specific purpose" mandates that each and every expenditure must be authorized separately by the voters, so that the voters can evaluate the expenditure in light of circumstances existing at the time each expenditure is to be made.

Based on the foregoing, I find that the June 23, 2000, referendum was insufficient to authorize respondent's expenditure from its capital reserve fund. First, the proposition fails to specifically identify the purpose for which the funds are sought (*see Appeal of Kackmeister, supra*). Further, the proposition improperly requests authorization to spend "up to" the ultimate amount of the reserve fund, rather than specifying a dollar figure. Such an open-ended request is improper. Respondent's failure to specify the amount and proposed use of the funds deprived the voters of their ability to properly evaluate respondent's request.

In addition, because voter authorization must be obtained during the same school year in which the board proposes to expend the funds, the June 22, 2000, proposition was insufficient to authorize the expenditure of reserve funds during the 2001-2002 school year (*Appeal of Kackmeister*, *supra*). Moreover, the record reflects that respondent did not have $3 million in reserve on June 22, 2000. Accordingly, respondent improperly sought approval to spend more than was actually available in the reserve fund.

I find no merit, however, to petitioners' claim that the revised financial statement is inaccurate. In an appeal to the Commissioner, petitioner has the burden of demonstrating a clear legal right to the relief requested and the burden of establishing the facts upon which she seeks relief (8 NYCRR §275.10; *Appeal of M.F. and J.F.*, 43 Ed Dept Rep 174, Decision No. 14,960; *Appeal of Kessler*, 43 *id.* 170, Decision No. 14,958). I find that petitioners have failed to meet this burden.

Finally, I remind respondent that a reserve fund is intended as a mechanism to reserve and accumulate funds over time for a future project, not as a vehicle to finance a current project or current needs. There is no sense whatsoever in depositing money received from current tax levies into a reserve fund, and then conveying the money via an interfund transfer to the district's capital fund to expend the money during the same fiscal year. If there is money from current tax levies available for such current needs, the money should simply be deposited directly into the capital fund for expenditure (*Appeal of Kackmeister, supra*).

THE APPEAL IS SUSTAINED TO THE EXTENT INDICATED.

IT IS ORDERED that respondent henceforth fully comply with the reserve fund requirements of Education Law §3651.

Decision No. 15,220

Appeal of LINDA TOWLER from action of the Board of Education of the Mount Sinai Union Free School District regarding an annual budget vote.

(May 12, 2005)

APPEARANCES OF COUNSEL

Kevin A. Seaman, Esq., attorney for respondent

DECISION OF THE COMMISSIONER

MILLS, Commissioner.—Petitioner challenges the actions of the Board of Education of the Mount Sinai Union Free School District ("respondent") in conducting its 2004-2005 budget vote. The appeal must be dismissed.

On May 18, 2004, district voters rejected respondent's proposed 2004-2005 budget. Respondent amended its proposed budget and, on June 22, 2004, presented three propositions to the voters. Proposition I sought voter approval of the amended budget in the amount of $39,337,817. Proposition II authorized up to $183,000 additional funds "to help maintain the current level of athletic teams (middle and high schools), co-curricular activities (elementary, middle and high schools) and field trips (elementary, middle and high schools)." Proposition III authorized up to $95,000 additional funds "for building security guard services."

Prior to both the May 18 and June 22, 2004, budget votes, respondent distributed material relating to the proposed budget informing voters of the consequences of a rejected budget, including information regarding the contingency budget respondent would adopt. On June 22, 2004, voters approved the proposed budget (Proposition I) and Proposition II, but rejected Proposition III. This appeal ensued. As part of her appeal, petitioner requested a stay of the appropriation of money for the budget (Proposition I) and Proposition II. Petitioner's request for a stay was denied on July 22, 2004.

Petitioner challenges respondent's conduct in relation to both budget votes. She contends that respondent was not authorized to submit separate propositions for the items set forth in Propositions II and III, but was required to include such items as part of the proposed budget in Proposition I. Petitioner alleges that respondent incorrectly calculated the contingency budget that might result should voters defeat the proposed budget, and that this alleged erroneous information was distributed to district residents prior to both votes. Petitioner also challenges the accuracy of the tax rate information that respondent provided prior to the votes and claims that respondent failed to append to the budget the school district report card and other required documents. Petitioner further asserts that a brochure respondent distributed prior to the votes contained erroneous information regarding the programmatic impact of a contingency budget and also described the propositions using different language than that which appeared on the sample ballot. Petitioner asks that I nullify the June 22, 2004, vote. She also requests an independent audit of respondent's internal controls and procedures. Finally, petitioner seeks an award of costs related to her appeal.

Respondent asserts that the appeal is untimely and that the equitable doctrine of laches also requires dismissal. Respondent maintains that it fully complied with all requirements of the Education Law with respect to both budget votes and that there is no basis for overturning the results of the June 22, 2004, vote.

As a procedural matter, petitioner's reply contains material that buttresses allegations in the petition. The purpose of a reply is to respond to new material or affirmative defenses set forth in the answer (8 NYCRR §§275.3 and 275.14). A reply is not meant to support allegations in the petition or to belatedly add assertions that should have been in the petition (*Appeal of Schildhorn*, 44 Ed Dept

Rep 212, Decision No. 15,152; *Application of Lilly*, 43 *id.* 459, Decision No. 15,050). Therefore, while I have reviewed petitioner's reply, I have not considered those portions containing new allegations that are not responsive to new material or affirmative defenses set forth in the answer.

The appeal is untimely to the extent that petitioner challenges the May 18, 2004, budget vote and respondent's conduct in relation to that vote. An appeal to the Commissioner must be commenced within 30 days of the making of the decision or the performance of the act complained of unless excused by the Commissioner for good cause shown (8 NYCRR §275.16). Petitioner initiated this appeal by service of a petition on June 30, 2004 — more than 30 days after the May 18, 2004, budget vote. Petitioner offers no excuse for the delay except to correctly note that her appeal from the subsequent June 22, 2004, budget vote is timely and is based on similar alleged irregularities. Because petitioner did not appeal the May 18, 2004, budget vote within the required time period, her challenge to respondent's conduct in relation to that vote is dismissed.

Respondent contends that the entire appeal should be dismissed under the doctrine of laches because petitioner waited until after the June 22, 2004, re-vote to commence it, asserting violations that allegedly occurred and were known to petitioner prior to the May 18, 2004, budget vote.

Laches may bar "the enforcement of a right where there has been an unreasonable and inexcusable delay that results in prejudice to a party" (*Skrodelis v. Norbergs*, 272 AD2d 316; *Appeal of Y.M.*, 43 Ed Dept Rep 193, Decision No. 14,968). Petitioner asserts that respondent repeated its alleged improper conduct in connection with the June vote. As noted above, petitioner initiated this appeal on June 30, 2004 — within 30 days of the challenged June 22, 2004, budget re-vote. Therefore, petitioner's claims regarding that vote and respondent's conduct in relation to it are clearly timely (*see* 8 NYCRR §275.16). Moreover, had petitioner commenced an appeal contesting actions taken by respondent prior to the scheduled June 22, 2004, re-vote, some or all of such claims could have been considered premature. Because the appeal from the June 22, 2004, vote is timely and petitioner's claims relate to respondent's conduct repeated again in connection with that vote, the doctrine of laches does not apply.

Petitioner's appeal from the June 22, 2004, budget vote must be dismissed on the merits. To invalidate the results of a school district election, petitioner must establish not only that irregularities occurred, but also that the irregularities actually affected the outcome of the election (*Matter of Boyes, et al. v. Allen, et al.*, 32 AD2d 990, *aff'd* 26 NY2d 709; *Appeal of Brown*, 43 Ed Dept Rep 231, Decision No. 14,980; *Appeal of Stolbach*, 43 *id.* 218, Decision No. 14,977) were so pervasive that they vitiated the electoral process (*Appeal of Brown, supra*; *Appeal of Stolbach, supra*; *Appeal of Laurie*, 42 Ed Dept Rep 313, Decision No. 14,867) or demonstrate a clear and convincing picture of informality to the point of laxity in adherence to the Education Law (*Appeal of Brown, supra*; *Appeal of Stolbach, supra*; *Matter of Levine*, 24 Ed Dept Rep 172, Decision No. 11,356, *affd sub nom, Capobianco v. Ambach and Bd. of Ed., Glen Cove City School Dist.*, 112 AD2d 640). Implicit in these decisions is a recognition that it is a rare case where errors in the conduct of a school election become so pervasive that they vitiate the fundamental fairness of the election (*Appeal of Brown, supra*; *Appeal of Stolbach, supra*; *Appeal of Laurie, supra*).

Although petitioner sets forth a number of alleged irregularities in relation to the June 22, 2004, budget vote, she does not provide a single affidavit from any individual stating that he or she would have voted differently but for the alleged irregularities. Indeed, the petition does not even contain an allegation that any vote was affected. Without proof that an irregularity occurred *and* affected the outcome of the vote, there is no basis on which to overturn the result.

Petitioner also alleges that respondent's budget process "was informal to the point of laxity." In an appeal to the Commissioner, the petitioner has the burden of demonstrating a clear legal right to the relief requested and establishing the facts upon which he seeks relief (8 NYCRR §275.10; *Appeal of Polmanteer, et al.*, 44 Ed Dept Rep 221, Decision No. 15,155; *Appeal of Antoniadis*, 44 *id.* 84, Decision No. 15,106). Specifically, petitioner alleges that respondent failed to append to the budget the school district report card or a detailed statement of compensation for the superintendent and other administrators, as required by Education Law §1716. The petition contains no affidavit or exhibit in support of this allegation. Respondent denies the allegation and submits an affirmation of the school attorney and an affidavit of the superintendent attesting to respondent's compliance with these requirements. Petitioner's conclusory allegations are insufficient to carry her burden.

Petitioner also claims that a budget brochure distributed to district residents prior to the June 22, 2004, vote included only the calculated tax rate that would result from approval of the proposed budget set forth in Proposition I and did not inform voters of the total tax rate impact should they approve Propositions II and/or III. However, by affidavit of its superintendent, respondent submits a postcard also mailed to district residents separately setting forth the tax rate implications of each proposition.

In addition, petitioner asserts that respondent distributed information to the voters incorrectly inferring that certain programs or activities would be curtailed or eliminated if it was required to adopt a contingency budget. Petitioner contends that respondent was required to inform voters that, where a donation is received covering the full cost of a program or activity, respondent would be permitted to offer such program or activity. Petitioner cites no legal basis, and indeed there is none, for her claim.

Finally, petitioner claims that, in a budget brochure mailed to district residents, respondent described the content of Propositions II and III using "different language" than that used in the sample ballot. However, petitioner neither claims nor offers evidence that any voter was confused or misled by the language used. Petitioner has failed to prove any of the allegations set forth in support of her claim of informality with respect to the June 22, 2004, vote.

In sum, petitioner has failed to demonstrate that any irregularities actually affected the outcome, were so pervasive that they vitiated the electoral process or demonstrate a clear and convincing picture of informality to the point of laxity in adherence to the Education Law.

Petitioner requests that I order an independent audit of respondent's internal controls and procedures. To the extent that petitioner requests an investigation of respondent's fiscal procedures to establish her claims, I note that an appeal to the Commissioner is appellate in nature and does not provide for investigations (*Appeal of Laurie, supra*; *Appeal of Julian, et al.*, 42 Ed Dept Rep 300, Decision No. 14,861).

In view of this disposition, I need not address petitioner's other claims.

THE APPEAL IS DISMISSED.

Decision No. 15,221

432 EDUC 05-31-2005

Appeal of DAN FARCASIU from action of the Board of Education of the Roslyn Union Free School District regarding a transportation referendum.

(May 12, 2005)

APPEARANCES OF COUNSEL

Ingerman Smith, LLP, attorneys for respondent, *Carrie E. Flynn, Esq.*, of counsel

DECISION OF THE COMMISSIONER

MILLS, Commissioner.—Petitioner appeals the actions of the Board of Education of the Roslyn Union Free School District ("respondent") regarding a transportation budget referendum. The appeal must be dismissed.

On May 18, 2004, respondent's proposed budget and a transportation proposition were defeated. The transportation proposition would have continued reduced distance eligibility for student transportation. On June 23, 2004, respondent decided to hold another budget vote and transportation referendum on July 13, 2004. The proposed transportation proposition stated that the budgetary impact of the continuation was $80,000. At respondent's meeting of July 6, petitioner questioned the method used to arrive at that amount and requested that respondent delay the referendum until an analysis of the cost was completed. Respondent moved forward with the referendum and this appeal ensued. Petitioner's request for interim relief was denied on July 12, 2004.

Petitioner contends that the actual cost of the transportation proposition is significantly higher than $80,000. He argues that information presented by respondent at its May 26, 2004, meeting indicated a reduction of $335,000 in equipment costs if there were no transportation referendum. Petitioner requests that respondent be required to recalculate the costs of the referendum, that all data and procedures used to arrive at that figure be made public and that the referendum vote be delayed until that information is released.

Respondent asserts that they have already fully examined the costs of providing the continued transportation and that those costs were accurately reflected in the transportation referendum. Respondent states that the $335,000 figure was initially listed as a potential savings to reflect the possibility of delaying the replacement of buses if there were no transportation referendum. Respondent also states that the $335,000 figure was properly included in the proposed budget presented to the voters on July 13, 2004. Respondent contends that the $80,000 figure reflects the costs of operating the two additional buses needed to provide the additional transportation. Respondent further alleges that State Education Department staff were consulted when the referendum was drafted, that respondent has acted in good faith, and that the voters were provided with complete and accurate information. Respondent also argues that the appeal should be dismissed as moot.

Initially, I must address the contents of petitioner's reply. The purpose of a reply is to respond to new material or affirmative defenses set forth in an answer (8 NYCRR §§275.3 and 275.14). A reply is not meant to buttress allegations in the petition or to belatedly add assertions that should have been in the petition (*Appeal of Passer*, 44 Ed Dept Rep __, Decision No. 15,164; *Appeal of General*, 43 *id.* 146, Decision No. 14,948). Petitioner's reply contains numerous calculations, graphs and arguments that should have been included with the petition. Therefore, while I have reviewed petitioner's reply, I have not considered those portions containing new allegations or exhibits that are not responsive to new material or affirmative defenses set forth in the answer.

The appeal must be dismissed as moot to the extent that petitioner requested a delay of the transportation referendum. The Commissioner will only decide matters in actual controversy and will not render a decision on a state of facts which no longer exists or which subsequent events have laid to rest (*Appeal of Passer*, 44 Ed Dept Rep __, Decision No. 15,160; *Appeal of Loveland and Hazelton*, 42 *id.* 294, Decision 14,858; *Appeal of Colety, et al.*, 42 *id.* 162, Decision 14,806). The vote was held on July 13, 2004, and the transportation proposition was passed.

The appeal must be dismissed on the merits. In an appeal to the Commissioner of Education, petitioner has the burden of demonstrating a clear right to the relief requested (8 NYCRR §275.10) and the burden of establishing the facts upon which he seeks relief (*Application of Bean*, 42 Ed Dept Rep 171, Decision No. 14,810; *Application of Lilker*, 40 *id.* 704, Decision No. 14,588). Petitioner has not provided any evidence establishing that respondent miscalculated the additional transportation costs associated with the reduced distance eligibility. Nor has petitioner cited any legal authority that would dictate that respondent place equipment costs in the transportation referendum.

In light of this disposition, I need not address the parties' remaining contentions.

THE APPEAL IS DISMISSED.

Decision No. 15,222

Appeal of FREDERICK J. GORMAN from action of the Board of Education of the Sachem Central School District regarding election irregularities.

(May 12, 2005)

APPEARANCES OF COUNSEL

Ingerman Smith, L.L.P., attorneys for respondent, *Neil M. Block, Esq.*, of counsel

DECISION OF THE COMMISSIONER

MILLS, Commissioner.—Petitioner challenges actions of the Board of Education of the Sachem Central School District ("respondent") relating to the district's June 17, 2004, budget vote. The appeal must be dismissed.

On May 18, 2004, respondent's proposed budget of $244,798,915 was defeated by a vote of 5,891 to 5,223. On June 17, 2004, voters passed respondent's revised budget of $242,798,915 by a vote of 5,533 to 5,021 (the "budget"). This appeal ensued. Petitioner's request for interim relief was denied on August 9, 2004.

Petitioner contends that respondent misrepresented the budget by overstating available funds, overstating the contingency budget, and overestimating State aid. Petitioner further asserts that respondent failed to inform voters that the tax levy associated with the budget was arrived at by applying reserve funds and a fund balance, thereby minimizing the difference between the budget and the contingency budget. Petitioner also alleges that the budget was not available until June 10, that respondent reduced the number of its budget mailings to two, and that respondent did not inform voters of their polling places. Petitioner claims that respondent also engaged in impermissible targeting, exhorting the public to vote in favor of the budget, and permitted others to dispense literature that it could not distribute itself.

Petitioner asks that I nullify the budget vote and order respondent not to misrepresent available funds. Petitioner requests that I order respondent to prepare its contingency budget in accordance with State regulations using the same growth estimate in both its proposed and contingency budgets. Finally, petitioner requests that I order respondent not to promote its budgets, impermissibly target voters or permit others to conduct such activities.

Respondent argues that petitioner has failed to establish that the alleged irregularities affected the outcome of the election, were so pervasive that they vitiated the electoral process or demonstrate a clear and convincing picture of informality to the point of laxity in adherence to the Education Law. Respondent also alleges that petitioner has not proven that the district improperly exhorted the passage of the budget in violation of *Phillips v. Maurer* (67 NY2d 672).

Initially, I must address a procedural matter. The purpose of a reply is to respond to new material or affirmative defenses set forth in an answer (8 NYCRR §§275.3 and 275.14). A reply is not meant to buttress allegations in the petition or belatedly add assertions that should have been in the petition (*Appeal of Cowley*, 44 Ed Dept Rep 125, Decision No. 15,121; *Appeal of General*, 43 *id.* 146, Decision No. 14,948). Although I have reviewed petitioner's reply, I have considered only those portions that respond to new material or affirmative defenses set forth in respondent's answer.

To invalidate the results of an election, petitioner must establish not only that irregularities occurred but also that any irregularities actually affected the outcome of the election (*Matter of Boyes, et al. v. Allen, et al.*, 32 AD2d 990, *affd* 26 NY2d 709; *Appeal of Shafer*, 43 Ed Dept Rep 9, Decision No. 14,900; *Appeal of Grant*, 42 *id.* 184, Decision No. 14,816), were so pervasive that they vitiated the electoral process (*Appeal of Meyer and Mittelstaedt*, 40 Ed Dept Rep 34, Decision No. 14,413; *Appeal of Roberts*, 33 *id.* 601, Decision No. 13,162) or demonstrate a clear and convincing picture of informality to the point of laxity in adherence to the Education Law (*Appeal of Shafer*, *supra*; *Appeal of Grant*, *supra*; *Appeal of Hubert*, *supra*). Implicit in these decisions is a recognition that it is a rare case where errors in the conduct of a school election become so pervasive that they vitiate the fundamental fairness of the election (*Appeal of Mead*, 42 Ed Dept Rep 359, Decision No. 14,881). Furthermore, in an appeal to the Commissioner, petitioner has the burden of demonstrating a clear legal right to the relief requested and the burden of establishing the facts upon which he seeks relief (8 NYCRR §275.10; *Appeal of General*, *supra*; *Appeal of Vazquez*, 42 Ed Dept Rep 245, Decision No. 14,841).

Respondent's budget passed by a margin of 512 votes. Even assuming petitioner's allegations to be true, the appeal must be dismissed because petitioner presents no evidence that any actions by respondent affected the outcome of the vote or that the alleged irregularities were so pervasive that they vitiated the electoral process or demonstrate a clear and convincing picture of informality to the point of laxity. Petitioner does not provide any affidavits from voters who allege that they would have voted differently but for the alleged misrepresentations, irregularities or exhortation. Petitioner provided just one affidavit from someone who failed to vote because he went to the incorrect polling place. Mere speculation as to the effect of alleged irregularities is insufficient to annul election results.

In light of this disposition, I will not address the parties' remaining contentions.

THE APPEAL IS DISMISSED.

Decision No. 15,223

Appeal of P.M., on behalf of J.M., from action of the Board of Education of the City School District of the City of North Tonawanda regarding student discipline.

(May 12, 2005)

APPEARANCES OF COUNSEL

Tisdale, Coykendall & Weber, Esqs., attorneys for petitioner, *W. Maxwell Coykendall, Esq.*, of counsel

Norton/Radin/Hoover/Freedman, Esqs., attorneys for respondent, *Bernard B. Freedman, Esq.*, of counsel

DECISION OF THE COMMISSIONER

MILLS, Commissioner.—Petitioner appeals the decision of the Board of Education of the City School District of the City of North Tonawanda ("respondent") to suspend her son, J.M., from school. The appeal must be dismissed.

During the 2003-2004 school year, J.M. attended respondent's high school. On May 4, 2004, J.M. was involved in a fight with another student. During the fight, J.M. punched the student in the face, breaking the student's nose. The high school principal suspended J.M. for five days and recommended to the superintendent that a longer suspension be imposed.

On May 10, 2004, a hearing officer, designated by the superintendent, conducted a disciplinary hearing pursuant to Education Law §3214. On May 14, 2004, the hearing officer issued a report and recommendation finding J.M. guilty of fighting on school grounds. The hearing officer recommended an additional five-day suspension, citing J.M.'s remorse and plea for leniency, with the proviso that a further long-term suspension would be warranted if J.M. violated school rules again prior to the end of the school year. On May 17, 2004, after considering the hearing officer's recommendation and reviewing the entire record, including J.M.'s prior disciplinary history, the superintendent issued his decision, finding J.M. guilty of fighting and suspending him until June 30, 2005.

Petitioner appealed to respondent. By letter dated June 10, 2004, respondent upheld the superintendent's determination. This appeal ensued.

Petitioner contends that her son acted in self-defense. She claims that he previously had been threatened and assaulted by the other student and had no choice but to fight. Petitioner also asserts that respondent failed to provide her with a copy of the transcript and exhibits from the disciplinary hearing. Petitioner further claims that respondent has not complied with Education Law §2801-a, which requires all school districts to develop a school safety plan and prescribes its required components.

Respondent contends that the appeal is untimely. Respondent maintains that J.M.'s suspension through June 30, 2005, is warranted based on the severe and dangerous nature of his conduct and on his anecdotal record. Respondent asserts that it is in compliance with Education Law §2801-a.

An appeal to the Commissioner must be commenced within 30 days from the making of the decision or performance of the act complained of, unless any delay is excused for good cause shown (8 NYCRR §275.16). Where a school district is named as a respondent, service must be effected upon the district clerk, a member of the board, the superintendent of schools or a person in the superintendent's office who has been designated by the board of education to accept service (8 NYCRR §275.8(a)). Petitioner attempted to commence this appeal on July 8, 2004, by serving a petition on the superintendent's secretary. Petitioner's affidavit of service did not indicate that the secretary was authorized to accept service, and, on July 14, 2004, my Office of Counsel returned the petition for improper service. Petitioner re-submitted her appeal with a new affidavit of service indicating that, on July 20, 2004, she served the petition on the district clerk — beyond the 30-day period. Petitioner offered no explanation in her petition to excuse the late filing nor did she submit a reply to respondent's timeliness argument. The appeal, therefore, is dismissed as untimely.

Even if the appeal were not untimely, I would dismiss it on the merits. In an appeal to the Commissioner, the petitioner has the burden of demonstrating the facts upon which relief is sought and a clear right to the relief requested (8 NYCRR §275.10; *Appeal of Smith*, 44 Ed Dept Rep 201, Decision No. 15,148; *Appeal of Goldin*, 43 *id*. 453, Decision No. 15,048).

As a procedural matter, petitioner claims that she was not provided a copy of the transcript of the disciplinary hearing or copies of exhibits introduced at the hearing. Respondent asserts that petitioner was informed of her right to such documents upon request, but that she never made such a request. Petitioner did not submit a reply to controvert respondent's assertion. Petitioner's allegation, therefore, is unsubstantiated.

The decision to suspend a student from school pursuant to Education Law §3214 must be based on competent and substantial evidence that the student participated in the objectionable conduct (*Bd. of Educ. of Monticello CSD v. Commissioner of Education, et al.*, 91 NY2d 133; *Bd. of Educ. of City of New York v. Mills*, 293 AD2d 37). In cases of student discipline, the sanction imposed must be proportionate to the severity of the offense involved (*Appeals of J.J.*, 44 Ed Dept Rep 113, Decision No. 15,115; *Appeal of M.F. and J.F.*, 43 *id*. 174, Decision No. 14,960). The test to be applied in reviewing a penalty is whether it is so excessive as to warrant substitution of the Commissioner's judgment for that of the board (*Appeals of J.J.*, *supra*; *Appeal of M.F. and J.F.*, *supra*).

Petitioner admits that J.M. engaged in a fight on school grounds, punched another student several times and broke the student's nose. Nevertheless, petitioner asserts that J.M. should not have been disciplined because he acted in self-defense. At the hearing J.M. stated that, because of prior off-campus altercations with the other student, in which J.M. was injured, J.M. felt threatened by him. J.M. also testified that during the altercation he felt threatened by the fact that 15 other students were present. He stated that he had no choice except to fight. However, the record indicates that J.M. is larger and stronger than the other student. J.M. and witnesses testified that, in response to being pushed and verbally harassed by the student, J.M. did not walk away. Instead, J.M. reacted by punching the student in the face, breaking the other student's nose. J.M. punched the other student twice more before staff members broke up the fight. Both the hearing officer and superintendent found that, despite J.M.'s claim of self-defense, he was guilty of the charge of fighting. After reviewing the record, I find no basis to overturn respondent's finding of guilt.

I also find a 13-month suspension is appropriate. As noted, J.M. admitted he was guilty of fighting, causing severe injury. He also admitted that the appropriate response in such situations is to walk away. Despite that admission, in this instance J.M. chose to fight. I note that respondent considered all the circumstances leading up to the fight. Respondent also considered the severity of J.M.'s conduct — that J.M.'s response to a push and verbal harassment was to punch the student in the face, breaking the student's nose. The record also indicates that the significant amounts of blood that resulted from the injury to the other student presented a danger to students and staff in the area.

Moreover, J.M.'s anecdotal record indicated that he had three prior disciplinary infractions, including one long-term suspension that had been reduced in response to J.M.'s plea for leniency at that time. I note that, in recommending an unusually short suspension as a penalty for the current charge, the hearing officer stated that he was throwing J.M. "the biggest bone that I have ever thrown a student." Respondent, however, determined not to grant J.M. leniency again.

In view of the severity of J.M.'s conduct, the serious injury he caused, the danger presented to others, and his prior disciplinary record, I will not substitute my judgment for that of respondent and its superintendent on penalty.

Finally, petitioner asserts, in conclusory fashion, that respondent has not complied with the requirements of Education Law §2801-a. That section requires all boards of education to adopt a school safety plan and sets forth the process to be followed in developing the plan, as well as required components of the plan. Petitioner requests that I commence an investigation to determine "the extent to which [respondent] is or is not in compliance" with Education Law §2801-a. As noted above, petitioner has the burden of proof. To the extent that she requests an investigation to establish her claim, I note that an appeal to the Commissioner is appellate in nature and does not provide for investigations (*Appeal of Laurie*, 42 Ed Dept Rep 313, Decision No. 14,867; *Appeal of Julian, et al.*, 42 *id.* 300, Decision No. 14,861).

THE APPEAL IS DISMISSED.

Decision No. 15,224

Appeal of G.S., on behalf of K.S., from action of the Board of Education of the Seaford Union Free School District regarding student discipline.

(May 12, 2005)

APPEARANCES OF COUNSEL

Alesia & Limmer, LLP, attorneys for petitioner, *Scott J. Limmer, Esq.*, of counsel

Ingerman Smith, L.L.P., attorneys for respondent, *Christopher Venator, Esq.*, of counsel

DECISION OF THE COMMISSIONER

MILLS, Commissioner.—Petitioner appeals the suspension of her son, K.S., by the Board of Education of the Seaford Union Free School District ("respondent"). The appeal must be dismissed.

During the 2003-2004 school year, K.S. was an eleventh grade student attending Seaford High School. On June 14, 2004, K.S. and several classmates allegedly engaged in a hazing ritual known as "Freshman Friday" that included paddling eighth grade middle school boys on the grounds of a nearby private school.

A superintendent's hearing was held on June 22, 2004, and the hearing officer found K.S. guilty of participating in behavior that resulted in intimidation and physical assault on Seaford eighth grade middle school students. The superintendent informed petitioner by letter dated July 12, 2004, that K.S. would be suspended from school through January 28, 2005, and from participation in extracurricular activities and/or interscholastic athletics through June 30, 2005.

Petitioner appealed the suspension to respondent. Respondent sustained the superintendent's findings, but modified the penalty to limit the suspension from extracurricular activities and/or interscholastic athletics to the same timeframe as the suspension from school, *i.e.* through January 28, 2005. This appeal ensued. On September 22, 2004, petitioner's request for interim relief was denied.

Petitioner seeks an order reversing respondent's penalty determination and expunging the suspension from the student's record, or, in the alternative, imposing a punishment of two to four weeks' suspension. Petitioner does not dispute the determination of guilt that her son participated in the paddling incident, but challenges the penalty as excessive. Petitioner argues that her son along with others at most caused an injury that caused one victim to miss school on the morning after the incident so he could see his doctor. Petitioner argues that due to recently publicized incidents in another school district in Nassau County, her son was treated harsher than he would have been previously.

Respondent contends that the penalty is not excessive, considering the gravity of the misconduct and the student's prior disciplinary record.

To the extent petitioner seeks a reduction in the suspension period, the appeal must be dismissed as moot. The Commissioner will only decide matters in actual controversy and will not render a decision on a state of facts which no longer exists or which subsequent events have laid to rest (*Appeal of B.K. and R.K.*, 44 Ed Dept Rep 195, Decision No. 15,146; *Appeal of A.F.*, 44 *id.* 124, Decision No. 15,120; *Appeal of D.W.*, 43 *id.* 188, Decision No. 14,965). Since K.S. has served the suspension, the request to shorten the suspension period is not meaningful relief that may be granted, and must be dismissed as moot (*Appeal of B.K. and R.K.*, *supra*; *Appeal of A.F.*, *supra*; *Appeal of D.W.*, *supra*).

In cases of student discipline, the sanction imposed must be proportionate to the severity of the offense involved (*Appeal of B.K. and R.K.*, *supra*; *Appeals of J.J.*, 44 Ed Dept Rep 113, Decision No. 15,115; *Appeal of D.C.*, 43 *id.* 217, Decision No. 14,976). The test to be applied in reviewing a penalty is whether it is so excessive as to warrant substitution of the Commissioner's judgment for that of the board (*Appeal of B.K. and R.K.*, *supra*; *Appeals of J.J.*, *supra*; *Appeal of D.C.*, *supra*).

In support of its penalty, respondent points to the seriousness of the hazing incident that resulted in injuries to eighth grade students as part of an initiation rite into Seaford High School. The middle school principal testified that he observed "a very large bruise with deep discoloration" on the upper right thigh of one of the eighth grade boys the following day. A photograph of the bruise was entered as an exhibit. The injured student testified that K.S. and three other juniors pulled up in a car as he was walking home with other students around 3:30 p.m. He got in the car after he was told to "just get it over with or it would be worse." He testified that he was taken alone to a nearby private school, told to face a wall, and was hit four times with a wooden paddle that broke as the juniors each took a turn. The middle school principal also testified that he met with the mother of another eighth grader who complained about the incident, and he observed that her son's buttocks "were severely bruised and very, very discolored." A third eighth grade student testified that K.S. was one of a group of eleventh graders who took turns hitting him with a wooden paddle described as "about 18 inches long, 3 inches wide, maybe an inch and a half thick." Respondent also considered K.S.'s prior disciplinary record that included detentions and in-school suspensions for loitering, disrupting class and using obscenities.

The nature of this incident in which intimidation and physical violence was used by high school juniors to "initiate" middle school eighth graders is a threat to both the safety and security of school children. School district officials must take any type of hazing seriously and act to eliminate the practice, as they properly did in this case. Under these circumstances, I find that the penalty is not irrational or unreasonable, and is within respondent's discretion.

THE APPEAL IS DISMISSED.

Decision No. 15,225

Appeal of J.W., on behalf of B.W., from action of the Board of Education of the Seaford Union Free School District regarding student discipline.

(May 12, 2005)

APPEARANCES OF COUNSEL

Alesia & Limmer, LLP, attorneys for petitioner, *Scott J. Limmer, Esq.*, of counsel

Ingerman Smith, L.L.P., attorneys for respondent, *Christopher Venator, Esq.*, of counsel

DECISION OF THE COMMISSIONER

MILLS, Commissioner.—Petitioner appeals the suspension of her son, B.W., by the Board of Education of the Seaford Union Free School District ("respondent"). The appeal must be dismissed.

During the 2003-2004 school year, B.W. was an eleventh grade student attending Seaford High School. On June 14, 2004, B.W. and several classmates allegedly engaged in a hazing ritual known as "Freshman Friday" that included paddling eighth grade middle school boys on the grounds of a nearby private school.

A superintendent's hearing was held on June 22, 2004, and the hearing officer found B.W. guilty of participating in behavior that resulted in intimidation and physical assault on Seaford eighth grade middle school students. The superintendent adopted the hearing officer's recommendation and suspended B.W. from school through January 28, 2005, and from participation in extracurricular activities and/or interscholastic athletics through June 30, 2005.

Petitioner appealed the suspension. Respondent sustained the superintendent's findings, but modified the penalty to limit the suspension from extracurricular activities and/or interscholastic athletics to the same timeframe as the suspension from school, *i.e.* through January 28, 2005. This appeal ensued. On September 22, 2004, petitioner's request for interim relief was denied.

Petitioner does not appeal respondent's determination of guilt, but seeks a determination that the penalty is excessive. Petitioner contends that the penalty is disproportionate to the offense and that a punishment of two to four weeks' suspension should be imposed. Alternatively, petitioner seeks a reversal of respondent's determination and expungement of B.W.'s record. Petitioner argues that B.W., along with others, at most injured one victim, causing him to miss school on the morning after the incident so he could see his doctor.

Respondent contends that the penalty is not excessive in light of the seriousness of the incident, in which several students were struck with wooden objects used as paddles. Respondent contends that an eighth grade student suffered severely bruised buttocks as a result of this hazing incident and identified B.W. as one of his attackers. Respondent contends that the penalty of a five-month suspension is not disproportionate to the offense, considering B.W.'s prior disciplinary record.

To the extent petitioner seeks a reduction in the suspension period, the appeal must be dismissed as moot. The Commissioner will only decide matters in actual controversy and will not render a decision on a state of facts which no longer exists or which subsequent events have laid to rest (*Appeal of B.K. and R.K.*, 44 Ed Dept Rep 195, Decision No. 15,146; *Appeal of A.F.*, 44 *id.* 124, Decision No. 15,120; *Appeal of D.W.*, 43 *id.* 188, Decision No. 14,965). Since B.W. has served the suspension, the request to shorten the suspension period is not meaningful relief that may be granted, and must be dismissed as moot (*Appeal of B.K. and R.K., supra*; *Appeal of A.F., supra*; *Appeal of D.W., supra*).

In cases of student discipline, the sanction imposed must be proportionate to the severity of the offense involved (*Appeal of B.K. and R.K., supra*; *Appeals of J.J.*, 44 Ed Dept Rep 113, Decision No. 15,115; *Appeal of D.C.*, 43 *id.* 217, Decision No. 14,976). The test to be applied in reviewing a penalty is whether it is so excessive as to warrant substitution of the Commissioner's judgment for that of the board (*Appeal of B.K. and R.K., supra*; *Appeals of J.J., supra*; *Appeal of D.C., supra*).

In support of its penalty, respondent points to the seriousness of the hazing incident that resulted in injuries to eighth grade students as part of an initiation rite into Seaford High School. The middle school principal testified that he observed bruises on two different eighth grade students the morning of June 15, 2004. He reported meeting with the mother of one of the injured boys and interviewing five eighth graders who were paddled in the "Freshmen Friday" incident. One of the eighth grade students testified that B.W. and seven other juniors were present when he and another student were hit from behind four times with a paddle. He testified that when a third boy started to cry and his face was turning red, he was not hit more than twice. Petitioner testified that this initiation has been going on for at least 15 years and that students told her four or five years ago that the paddles were made in the Seaford wood shop during school.

The high school principal testified that when he heard a rumor on Friday, June 11, 2004, that "Freshman Friday" was going to occur at the middle school, he notified police and drove to the middle school. He reported seeing B.W. and four other juniors run across the baseball field. He testified that B.W. was verbally abusive, belligerent and disobeyed a request to leave the grounds. Respondent also considered B.W.'s prior disciplinary record of suspensions and more than a hundred detentions for, *inter alia*, using profanities, disrupting classes, threatening a teacher and leaving school grounds.

The nature of this incident, in which intimidation and physical violence was used by high school juniors to "initiate" middle school eighth graders, is a threat to both the safety and security of school children. School officials must take any type of hazing seriously and act to eliminate the practice. Under these circumstances, I find that the penalty is not irrational or unreasonable and is within respondent's discretion.

I note that the school administration in this case appropriately considered these hazing activities serious offenses that cannot be tolerated. The high school principal is to be commended for intervening when he learned what was about to take place. Hazing is a growing problem and adults must make clear to students through words and actions that there is no place for such behavior.

THE APPEAL IS DISMISSED.

Decision No. 15,226

Appeal of S.W., on behalf of K.W., from action of the Board of Education of the Seaford Union Free School District regarding student discipline.

(May 12, 2005)

APPEARANCES OF COUNSEL

Thomas C. Monaghan, Esq., attorney for petitioner

Ingerman Smith, L.L.P., attorneys for respondent, *Christopher Venator, Esq.*, of counsel

DECISION OF THE COMMISSIONER

MILLS, Commissioner.—Petitioner appeals the suspension of his son, K.W., by the Board of Education of the Seaford Union Free School District ("respondent"). The appeal must be dismissed.

During the 2003-2004 school year, K.W. was an eleventh grade student attending Seaford High School. On June 14, 2004, K.W. and several classmates allegedly engaged in a hazing ritual known as "Freshman Friday" that included paddling eighth grade middle school boys on the grounds of a nearby private school.

A superintendent's hearing was held on June 22, 2004, and the hearing officer found K.W. guilty of participating in behavior that resulted in intimidation and physical assault on Seaford eighth grade middle school students. The superintendent informed petitioner by letter dated July 12, 2004, that K.W. would be suspended from school through September 24, 2005, and from participation in extracurricular activities and/or interscholastic athletics through September 24, 2005.

Petitioner appealed the suspension. Respondent sustained the superintendent's findings at its meeting on August 12, 2004. Petitioner received notice of this determination by a letter from the superintendent dated August 13, 2004. This appeal ensued. On September 22, 2004, petitioner's request for interim relief was denied.

Petitioner seeks an order reversing respondent's determination of guilt and penalty. Petitioner contends that respondent had no jurisdiction over the hazing incident because it occurred after school hours and off school grounds. Petitioner contends that the hearing process was flawed, arguing, *inter alia*, that only hearsay evidence was presented to sustain the charge that K.W. participated in the intimidation and physical assault on eighth grade Seaford students. Petitioner also argues that the hearing officer failed to set forth findings of fact supporting his determination. Petitioner admits that his son was present at the incident but contends that he remained at the top of the stairwell and did not paddle or injure any Seaford students. Petitioner contends that the penalty is disproportionate to the offense.

Respondent contends that its jurisdiction over the incident stems from a clear nexus between the paddling and the long-standing school-related "initiation" known as "Freshman Friday," targeting eighth grade Seaford students. Respondent contends that the fact that the paddling occurred after the school day and on private property does not overcome the connection with the school district.

Respondent further contends that there was substantial evidence to support the determination, including testimony from an eighth grade student who was paddled during the incident. Respondent contends that even though K.W. did not paddle students, he is responsible for his involvement in the hazing ritual by lying in wait with the other upper classmen. Respondent contends that the penalty of an additional two weeks suspension is not excessive considering the severity of the misconduct.

Because K.W. was suspended until September 24, 2004, which has passed, the appeal is moot except to the extent that petitioner seeks expungement of K.W.'s records (*Appeal of M.P.*, 44 Ed Dept Rep 132, Decision No. 15,123; *Appeal of a Student with a Disability*, 43 *id.* 372, Decision No. 15,021; *Appeal of M.K.*, 42 *id.* 405, Decision No. 14,894).

I will first consider petitioner's contention that respondent had no jurisdiction over the incident. Prior Commissioner's decisions have upheld the suspension of students for off-campus conduct (*see* e.g. *Appeal of K.S.*, 43 Ed Dept Rep 492, Decision No. 15,063; *Appeal of Ravick*, 40 *id.* 262, Decision No. 14,477; *Appeal of Rodriguez*, 8 *id.* 214, Decision No. 8015). Case law has also recognized that students may be disciplined for conduct that occurred outside of the school that may endanger the health or safety of pupils within the educational system, or adversely affect the education process (*Matter of Coghlan v. Board of Education*, 262 AD2d 949, *citing Pollnow v. Glennon*, 594 F.Supp. 220, 224, *affd*, 757 F2d 496). The incident for which petitioner's son was suspended involved an initiation rite perpetrated by and upon Seaford students. There is evidence in the record that there were communications among Seaford students about "Freshman Friday" prior to the incident and that eighth grade students feared going through the summer because they were told the paddling would be more severe closer to September and the beginning of their ninth grade school year. Because of the school-related nature of this incident, respondent was authorized to impose disciplinary sanctions and adjudicate this matter.

Education Law §3214(3)(a) authorizes a board of education to suspend a "pupil who is insubordinate or disorderly or violent or disruptive, or whose conduct otherwise endangers the safety, morals, health or welfare of others." A decision to suspend a student from school pursuant to Education Law §3214 must be based on competent and substantial evidence that the student participated in the objectionable conduct (*Matter of Bd. of Educ. of Monticello CSD v. Commissioner of Education, et al.*, 91 NY2d 133; *Matter of Bd. of*

Educ., City School Dist. of the City of New York v. Mills, et al., 293 AD2d 37; *Appeal of B.K. and R.K.*, 44 Ed Dept Rep 195, Decision No. 15,146). A hearing officer may draw reasonable inferences if the record supports the inference (*Matter of Bd. of Educ. of Monticello CSD v. Commissioner of Education, et al., supra*; *Appeal of a Student with a Disability*, 44 Ed Dept Rep 136, Decision No. 15,124; *Appeal of B.C. and A.C.*, 42 *id.* 395, Decision No. 14,891).

At the hearing, one of the eighth grade students who was paddled testified that K.W. was present at the scene. The witness placed K.W. at the top of the stairwell while the younger students were told to go down the stairs, face the wall, and put their hands against the wall where the paddling occurred. The middle school principal testified that he met with the mother of one of the eighth grade students and observed the injuries sustained by her son, who had difficulty sitting down the following day. The hearing officer stated on the record at the conclusion of the guilt phase of the hearing that, based upon the testimony, he found K.W. guilty as a participant in the incident, although not a paddler, and proceeded to take evidence on K.W.'s disciplinary history. Based on the parties' submissions and my review of the hearing transcript, I find that the hearing officer's finding of guilt is supported by the record, and there is no basis to substitute my judgment for that of the board.

In cases of student discipline, the sanction imposed must be proportionate to the severity of the offense involved. The test to be applied in reviewing a penalty is whether it is so excessive as to warrant substitution of the Commissioner's judgment for that of the board (*Appeal of B.K. and R.K., supra*; *Appeal of a Student Suspected of Having a Disability*, 44 Ed Dept Rep 158, Decision No. 15,131).

In support of the penalty, respondent points to the seriousness of the hazing incident that resulted in injuries to eighth grade students as part of an initiation rite to Seaford High School. Respondent argues that there can be no question that K.W.'s mere presence at the school, along with the other upper classmen, lying in wait for the eighth graders to arrive to receive their beating contributed to the scheme to intimidate these students. The middle school principal testified that he observed severe bruises on two different eighth grade students the morning of June 15, 2004. He reported meeting with the mother of one of the injured boys and interviewing five of the eighth graders who were paddled in the "Freshman Friday" incident. One of the eighth grade students testified at the hearing that, "it stung for a second" when he was hit four times and that another student "started to cry." He testified that, "I heard if you run and don't accept it, you get it worse like more hitting and harder hits, so then we just went and got it over with." Respondent also considered K.W.'s prior disciplinary record of 41 detentions and an in-school suspension for, *inter alia*, cutting classes and leaving school grounds.

The nature of this incident, in which intimidation and physical violence was used by high school juniors to "initiate" middle school eighth graders is a threat to both the safety and security of school children. School officials must take any type of hazing seriously and act to eliminate the practice. District officials acted properly in doing so here. In light of the seriousness of this hazing incident and K.W.'s role in contributing to the intimidation of younger students, I cannot conclude that the imposition of a one-month suspension was inappropriate. As such, there is no basis to expunge K.W.'s record.

I have considered petitioner's remaining contentions and find them without merit.

THE APPEAL IS DISMISSED.

Decision No. 15,227

Appeal of K.M., on behalf of M.M., from action of the Board of Education of the Seaford Union Free School District regarding student discipline.

(May 12, 2005)

APPEARANCES OF COUNSEL

Ingerman Smith, L.L.P., attorneys for respondent, *Christopher Venator, Esq.*, of counsel

DECISION OF THE COMMISSIONER

MILLS, Commissioner.—Petitioner appeals the suspension of her son, M.M., by the Board of Education of the Seaford Union Free School District ("respondent"). The appeal must be dismissed.

During the 2003-2004 school year, M.M. was an eleventh grade student attending Seaford High School. On June 14, 2004, M.M. and several classmates allegedly engaged in a hazing ritual known as "Freshman Friday" that included paddling eighth grade middle school boys on the grounds of a nearby private school.

A superintendent's hearing was held on July 9, 2004, and the hearing officer found M.M. guilty of participating in behavior that resulted in intimidation and physical assault on Seaford eighth grade middle school students. The superintendent informed petitioner by letter dated July 22, 2004, that M.M. would be suspended from school through January 28, 2005, and from participation in extracurricular activities and/or interscholastic athletics through June 30, 2005.

Petitioner appealed the suspension to respondent. Respondent sustained the superintendent's findings but modified the penalty to limit the suspension from extracurricular activities and/or interscholastic athletics to the same timeframe as the suspension from school, *i.e.* through January 28, 2005. This appeal ensued. On September 28, 2004, petitioner's request for interim relief was denied.

Petitioner seeks an order reversing respondent's penalty determination and expunging the suspension from the student's record or, in the alternative, imposing a punishment of two to four weeks' suspension. Petitioner does not dispute the determination of guilt that her son participated in the paddling incident, but challenges the penalty as excessive. Petitioner argues that her son was present when others paddled one victim to the point of injury and, at worst, participated in paddling a second victim that caused some discomfort. Petitioner argues that due to recently publicized incidents in another school district in Nassau County, her son was treated harsher than he would have been previously.

Respondent contends that its disciplinary determination is rationally based. Respondent contends that there was substantial eyewitness and documentary evidence to support the determination of his complicity and direct involvement, including detailed testimony from an eighth grade student who was injured during the incident. Respondent contends that the penalty is not excessive considering the gravity of the misconduct and the student's long disciplinary history.

To the extent petitioner seeks a reduction in the suspension period, the appeal must be dismissed as moot. The Commissioner will only decide matters in actual controversy and will not render a decision on a state of facts which no longer exists or which subsequent events have laid to rest (*Appeal of B.K. and R.K.*, 44 Ed Dept Rep 195, Decision No. 15,146; *Appeal of A.F.*, 44 *id.* 124, Decision No. 15,120; *Appeal of D.W.*, 43 *id.* 188, Decision No. 14,965). Since M.M. has served the suspension, the request to shorten the suspension period is not meaningful relief that may be granted, and must be dismissed as moot (*Appeal of B.K. and R.K., supra*; *Appeal of A.F., supra*; *Appeal of D.W., supra*).

In cases of student discipline, the sanction imposed must be proportionate to the severity of the offense involved (*Appeal of B.K. and R.K., supra*; *Appeals of J.J.*, 44 Ed Dept Rep 113, Decision No. 15,115; *Appeal of D.C.*, 43 *id.* 217, Decision No. 14,976). The test to be applied in reviewing a penalty is whether it is so excessive as to warrant substitution of the Commissioner's judgment for that of the board (*Appeal of B.K. and R.K., supra*; *Appeals of J.J., supra*; *Appeal of D.C., supra*).

In support of its penalty, respondent points to the seriousness of the hazing incident that resulted in injuries to eighth grade students, as part of an initiation rite into Seaford High School. One of the eighth grade students who was injured testified that he learned in sixth grade that "Freshman Friday" meant that "eighth grade students going into ninth grade get beat up by the eleventh graders." He testified that he and three other eighth graders were told to go down a stairwell and put their hands against the wall. He reported being hit from behind with a foot-long belt holder, a racquetball racket and a broken 17-inch piece of wood. He identified M.M. as one of the juniors at the bottom of the stairs. He also testified that he was told, "don't tell your mom or dad." He further testified that he couldn't sit on the toilet for two to four days and a photograph of his bruised buttocks was entered as an exhibit at the hearing.

Another eighth grader testified that he was hit by M.M., and a photograph of his bruised thigh was entered as an exhibit at the hearing. Respondent also considered M.M.'s extensive disciplinary record, including suspensions and over a hundred detentions for, *inter alia*, smoking, cutting classes, leaving school grounds and using profanities.

The nature of this incident in which intimidation and physical violence was used by high school juniors to "initiate" middle school eighth graders is a threat to both the safety and security of school children. School officials must take any type of hazing seriously and act to eliminate the practice, as they properly did here. Under these circumstances, I find that the penalty is not irrational or unreasonable, and is within respondent's discretion.

THE APPEAL IS DISMISSED.

Decision No. 15,228

Appeal of GORDON A. BUSHWAY, on behalf of his daughter ERIKA, from action of the Board of Education of the Hoosick Falls Central School District regarding residency.

(May 12, 2005)

APPEARANCES OF COUNSEL

Gunter Dully, Esq., attorney for respondent

DECISION OF THE COMMISSIONER

MILLS, Commissioner.—Petitioner appeals the determination of the Board of Education of the Hoosick Falls Central School District ("respondent") that his daughter is not a district resident and is not eligible to attend its schools without payment of tuition. The appeal must be dismissed.

Petitioner resides within the Brunswick Central School District ("Brittonkill") with his daughter, who is a senior. Petitioner's daughter resided with her mother in respondent's district and attended the Hoosick Falls Central School from May 2000 until August 6, 2004.

On September 3, 2004, petitioner informed respondent's superintendent that his daughter moved into his residence in Brittonkill and was advised that respondent's Policy No. 7131 required payment of tuition for non-resident students. Respondent's Policy No. 7131 permits a resident student enrolled in the district who becomes a non-resident to complete that school year without payment of tuition upon consideration of the superintendent and approval of the board. In addition, there had been a period of time during previous years when respondent made another exception for non-resident seniors. However, at respondent's November 18, 2003, meeting, it resolved that the "non-resident senior" exception would cease, effective with the 2004-2005 school year.

By letter dated September 3, 2004, the superintendent informed petitioner that his daughter would be allowed to attend respondent's schools until the September 21, 2004, meeting of respondent board, at which the final decision on her status would be made. Petitioner spoke with the board president and other board members regarding his daughter's move out of the district, and her preference to finish high school in respondent's district.

On September 15, 2004, the superintendent informed petitioner that respondent was advised by legal counsel not to admit his daughter to Hoosick Falls Central School without payment of tuition.

At its September 21, 2004, meeting, respondent determined that petitioner's daughter was a non-resident, ineligible to attend under Policy No. 7131 without payment of tuition. Petitioner was informed of the board's determination by letter dated September 28, 2004. The letter advised petitioner that unless payment for the first semester tuition on $1,800.50 was made by the end of the instructional day on October 15, 2004, his daughter would be excluded from district schools. This appeal ensued. Petitioner's request for interim relief was denied on October 27, 2004.

Petitioner alleges that he enrolled his daughter in Brittonkill on October 4, 2004, but that she was not attending school because she was not offered the same courses as she was at respondent's schools. Petitioner further contends that respondent did not notify parents, students or staff of its November 18, 2003, decision to discontinue the exception for senior non-resident students, effective with the 2004-2005 school year.

Respondent contends that it has authority to prescribe terms for admission of non-residents and did so with its Policy No. 7131, which requires payment of tuition for admission of non-resident students with one exception for students who become non-resident during a school year. Respondent contends that petitioner's daughter does not qualify for the sole exception to Policy No. 7131.

Education Law §3202(1) provides, in pertinent part:

> A person over five and under twenty-one years of age who has not received a high school diploma is entitled to attend the public schools maintained in the district in which such person resides without the payment of tuition.

The purpose of this statute is to limit the obligation of school districts to provide tuition-free education to students whose parents or legal guardians reside within the district (*Appeal of L.H.*, 44 Ed Dept Rep 100, Decision No. 15,110; *Appeal of D.K and R.S., Jr.*, 44 *id.* 23, Decision No. 15,083; *Appeal of Tucker*, 44 *id.* 14, Decision No. 15,080). The right to attend a district's schools does not extend to non-residents without the consent of the board of education, as set forth in §3202(2):

> (2) Nonresidents of a district, if otherwise competent, may be admitted into the schools of a district or city, upon the consent of the trustees or the board of education, upon terms prescribed by such trustees or board.

In an appeal to the Commissioner of Education, petitioner bears the burden of establishing a clear legal right to relief requested and establishing the facts upon which relief is sought (8 NYCRR §275.10; *Appeal of a Student with a Disability*, 44 Ed Dept Rep 94, Decision No. 15,108). Petitioner has failed to meet that burden. Petitioner admits residing with his daughter outside respondent's district. Under Education Law §3202(2), a school district may decide to accept non-resident students on terms prescribed by the board of education. Additionally, Education Law §§1709(3) and (13) grant boards of education the power to regulate the admission of pupils, to admit non-resident students and to regulate and establish tuition fees for such non-resident students (*Appeal of Volk*, 43 Ed Dept Rep 186, Decision No. 14,964).

Respondent's Policy No. 7131, prescribing terms for admission of non-resident students, was adopted on July 21, 1998 and its decision to discontinue an exception for senior non-resident students, effective 2004-2005, was published in the minutes for respondent's November 18, 2003, meeting. The record reflects that petitioner's circumstances were considered by respondent and that its determination is consistent with its policy. Accordingly, I find that respondent's decision was not arbitrary, capricious or an abuse of discretion.

THE APPEAL IS DISMISSED.

Decision No. 15,229

Appeal of M.G., on behalf of R.G., from action of the Board of Education of the Seaford Union Free School District regarding student discipline.

(May 12, 2005)

APPEARANCES OF COUNSEL

Murray & McCann, attorneys for petitioner, *Joseph D. McCann, Esq.*, of counsel

Ingerman Smith, L.L.P., attorneys for respondent, *Christopher Venator, Esq.*, of counsel

DECISION OF THE COMMISSIONER

MILLS, Commissioner.—Petitioner appeals the suspension of her son, R.G., by the Board of Education of the Seaford Union Free School District ("respondent"). The appeal must be dismissed.

During the 2003-2004 school year, R.G. was an eleventh grade student attending Seaford High School. On June 14, 2004, R.G. and several classmates allegedly engaged in a hazing ritual known as "Freshman Friday" that included paddling eighth grade middle school boys on the grounds of a nearby private school.

A superintendent's hearing was held on July 28, 2004, and the hearing officer found R.G. guilty of participating in behavior that resulted in intimidation and physical assault on Seaford eighth grade middle school students. The superintendent informed petitioner by letter dated August 10, 2004, that R.G. would be suspended from school through January 28, 2005, and from participation in extracurricular activities and/or interscholastic athletics through June 30, 2005.

Petitioner appealed the suspension to respondent. Respondent sustained the superintendent's findings but modified the penalty to limit the suspension from extracurricular activities and/or interscholastic athletics to the same timeframe as the suspension from school, *i.e.* through January 28, 2005. This appeal ensued. On September 10, 2004, petitioner's request for interim relief was denied.

Petitioner seeks an order reversing respondent's determination of guilt and the penalty of suspension. Petitioner contends that respondent had no jurisdiction over the hazing incident because it occurred after school hours and off school grounds. Petitioner contends that the hearing process was flawed, arguing, *inter alia*, that only one witness testified that R.G. participated in the initiation and hit an eighth grade student. Petitioner argues that the hearing officer should have given more weight to affidavits she presented as contradictory evidence.

Respondent contends that its jurisdiction over the incident stems from a clear nexus between the paddling and the school-related initiation known as "Freshman Friday," targeting eighth grade Seaford students. Respondent contends that there was substantial evidence to support its determination, including detailed testimony from an eighth grade student who was injured during the incident. Respondent contends that the penalty is not excessive considering the gravity of the misconduct and the student's prior disciplinary record.

The appeal must be dismissed as moot. The Commissioner will only decide matters in actual controversy and will not render a decision on a state of facts which no longer exists or which subsequent events have laid to rest (*Appeal of A.F.*, 44 Ed Dept Rep 124, Decision No. 15,120; *Appeal of D.W.*, 43 *id.* 188, Decision No. 14,965; *Appeal of L.B.*, 43 *id.* 159, Decision No. 14,952). Petitioner does not request expungement of R.G.'s records. Since R.G. has served the suspension, no further meaningful relief can be granted and the appeal must be dismissed as moot (*Appeal of A.F.*, *supra*; *Appeal of D.W.*, *supra*; *Appeal of L.B.*, *supra*).

In light of this disposition, I need not address the parties' remaining contentions.

THE APPEAL IS DISMISSED.

Decision No. 15,230

Appeal of MERCIA DESROCHES, on behalf of CHRISTOPHER DUSSECK, from action of the Board of the Education of the Sewanhaka Central High School District regarding residency.

(May 12, 2005)

APPEARANCES OF COUNSEL

Douglas E. Libby, Esq., attorney for respondent, *Bernadette Gallagher-Gaffney, Esq.*, of counsel

DECISION OF THE COMMISSIONER

MILLS, Commissioner.—Petitioner challenges the determination of the Board of Education of the Sewanhaka Central High School District ("respondent") that her nephew, Christopher Dusseck, is not a district resident. The appeal must be dismissed.

On October 4, 2004, petitioner, a district resident, requested Christopher's admission to respondent's schools. Prior to that time, Christopher lived with his mother, petitioner's sister, in Florida and attended high school there. Christopher's mother obtained employment in Haiti, withdrew Christopher from his Florida school on

October 8, 2004, and sent him to live with petitioner beginning October 10, 2004. On October 13, 2004, the administrative assistant to the superintendent denied Christopher admission, and petitioner requested a hearing.

Respondent's administrative review officer conducted a hearing on October 14, 2004. Petitioner was present and offered additional information. The transcript of that hearing indicates that Christopher was expected to live with petitioner for one year, at which time his mother's employment would terminate and she would return to Florida. The transcript also indicates that Christopher's mother would continue financial support for him, in the amount of $600.00 per month. Based upon this information, the administrative review officer issued a final denial on October 25, 2004. This appeal ensued. Petitioner's application for interim relief was denied on November 15, 2004.

Petitioner argues that Christopher should be allowed to attend respondent's schools because his mother was unable to take him to Haiti with her, and she has not yet found a suitable place to live. She further argues that living in Haiti would be unsafe for Christopher.

Respondent maintains that Christopher is not entitled to attend its schools because the purported transfer of custody and control to petitioner is neither total nor permanent.

Education Law §3202(1) provides in pertinent part:

> A person over five and under twenty-one years of age who has not received a high school diploma is entitled to attend the public schools maintained in the district in which such person resides without the payment of tuition.

The purpose of this statute is to limit the obligation of school districts to provide tuition-free education to students whose parents or legal guardians reside within the district (*Appeal of Humphrey*, 43 Ed Dept Rep 117, Decision No. 14,940; *Appeal of Thomas*, 41 *id.* 84, Decision No. 14,622; *Appeal of Oliver*, 41 *id.* 30, Decision No. 14,603). A child's residence is presumed to be that of his or her parents or legal guardian (*Appeal of Humphrey, supra*; *Appeal of Thomas, supra*; *Appeal of Santana*, 40 Ed Dept Rep 57, Decision No. 14,420). This presumption may be rebutted upon a determination that there has been a total, and presumably permanent, transfer of custody and control to someone residing in the district (*Appeal of Maxwell*, 42 Ed

Dept Rep 134, Decision No. 14,799; *Appeal of Donohue*, 41 *id.* 26, Decision No. 14,601; *Appeal of Juarez*, 39 *id.* 184, Decision No. 14,208).

Moreover, where the sole reason the child is residing with someone other than the parent is for the convenience of the family or to take advantage of the schools of the district, the child has not established residence (*Appeal of Gratton*, 43 Ed Dept Rep 72, Decision No. 14,922; *Appeal of Pierre*, 40 *id.* 538, Decision No. 14,551; *Appeal of Mendoza*, 39 *id.* 74, Decision No. 14,178). A residency determination will not be set aside unless it is arbitrary and capricious (*Appeal of A.F.*, 41 Ed Dept Rep 115, Decision No. 14,633; *Appeal of Karmin*, 41 *id.* 72, Decision No. 14,618).

I agree that the purported transfer of Christopher's custody and control to petitioner was neither total nor permanent. It clearly was intended to continue only as long as Christopher's mother remains in Haiti, and during that time his mother will be providing substantial support for him. Since petitioner has not established a total and permanent transfer of custody, I do not find respondent's determination to be arbitrary, capricious or unreasonable.

THE APPEAL IS DISMISSED.

Decision No. 15,231

Appeal of LAMIAA ELKOULILY, on behalf of her daughter LAYLA, from action of the Board of Education of the Lynbrook Union Free School District regarding residency.

(May 12, 2005)

APPEARANCES OF COUNSEL

Ehrlich, Frazer & Feldman, attorneys for respondent, *Kevin G. McMorrow, Esq.*, of counsel

DECISION OF THE COMMISSIONER

MILLS, Commissioner.—Petitioner appeals the determination of the Board of Education of the Lynbrook Union Free School District ("respondent") that her daughter, Layla, is not a district resident. The appeal must be dismissed.

Petitioner's daughter began attending kindergarten in respondent's district in September 2004. By letter dated October 4, 2004, respondent's assistant superintendent for business informed petitioner that her daughter was not a district resident and would no longer be enrolled in the district's schools as of October 29, 2004. This appeal ensued. On November 1, 2004, petitioner's request for interim relief was granted.

By letter dated December 23, 2004, respondent's attorney requested that the appeal be dismissed as moot because the district had withdrawn its October 4, 2004, residency determination letter.

The Commissioner will only consider matters in actual controversy and will not render a decision on a state of facts which no longer exists or which subsequent events have laid to rest (*Appeal of Steinbrecher*, 43 Ed Dept Rep 329, Decision No. 15,008; *Appeal of Shaffer*, 43 *id*. 79, Decision No. 14,925; *Appeal of T.B. and N.B.*, 42 *id*. 142, Decision No. 14,803). Since respondent has withdrawn its residency determination and is permitting petitioner's daughter to attend respondent's school as a district resident, the appeal must be dismissed as moot (*Appeal of Steinbrecher*, *supra*; *Appeal of Shaffer*, *supra*; *Appeal of T.B. and N.B.*, *supra*).

THE APPEAL IS DISMISSED.

Decision No. 15,232

Appeal of DEBRA MARCHESANI from action of the Board of Education of the Harrison Central School District, David Brunner, David Singer, Christine Rinaldi, and Georgia Riedel, Members of the Board of Education, Gene George, District Clerk, Robert Salierno, Director of Business, and George Brunner regarding an election.

(May 23, 2005)

APPEARANCES OF COUNSEL

Mann & Mann, attorneys for petitioner, *Monroe Yale Mann, Esq.*, of counsel

Ingerman Smith, L.L.P., attorneys for respondents, *Neil M. Block, Esq.*, of counsel

DECISION OF THE COMMISSIONER

MILLS, Commissioner.—Petitioner, an unsuccessful candidate for election to the Board of Education of the Harrison Central School District ("respondent board"), appeals the conduct of a school district election. The appeal must be dismissed.

On May 18, 2004, respondent board held its annual meeting and election for the purpose of voting on its annual budget and filling two seats on respondent board. The voting took place at four polling sites. The budget was approved by 530 votes, Georgia Riedel defeated Christine Rinaldi by 263 votes, and incumbent David Brunner defeated petitioner, 1705 to 1522 — a difference of 183 votes. This appeal ensued.

Petitioner alleges that the conduct of the election was "fraught with illegalities" related to absentee ballots, affidavit ballots, redistricting of voting boundaries, electioneering, opening and closing of polls, the actions of an election inspector, and the improper elimination of over 190 people from the polling books and lists. Petitioner claims that these alleged violations affected the outcome of the election and requests that I order a new election. She also asserts that respondent board failed to comply with her requests for information under the Freedom of Information Law ("FOIL").

Respondents state that the election was conducted fairly and in compliance with Education Law. Respondents admit that there were slight discrepancies with the election district boundaries and a problem with the voting machines being locked initially at one polling site, but they maintain that these problems were resolved without any effect on the conduct of the election or the election results. Respondents assert that petitioner has not met her burden of proving that any substantial irregularities occurred or affected the outcome of the election. Respondents also assert that the Commissioner does not have jurisdiction over FOIL claims, and in any event, respondent board timely complied with all petitioner's FOIL requests.

The purpose of a reply is to respond to procedural defenses or new material contained in an answer (8 NYCRR §§275.3 and 275.14). A reply is not meant to buttress allegations in the petition or to belatedly add assertions or exhibits that should have been in the petition (*Appeal of O'Brien, et al.*, 42 Ed Dept Rep 317, Decision No. 14,868; *Application of Bean*, 42 *id.* 171, Decision No. 14,810). Similarly, a memorandum of law may not be used to add new assertions that are not part of the pleadings (*Appeal of Sbrocchi*, 42 Ed Dept Rep 380, Decision No. 14,887; Appeal *of Grinnell*, 37 *id.* 504,

Decision No. 13,914). Accordingly, while I have reviewed petitioner's reply and memorandum of law, I have not considered those portions containing new allegations that are not responsive to new material or affirmative defenses in respondents' answer.

To invalidate the results of a school district election, petitioner must establish not only that irregularities occurred, but also that any irregularities actually affected the outcome of the election (*Matter of Boyes v. Allen, et al.*, 32 AD2d 990, affd 26 NY2d 709; *Appeal of Roberts*, 33 Ed Dept Rep 601, Decision No. 13,162), were so pervasive that they vitiated the electoral process (*Appeal of Brannon*, 42 Ed Dept Rep 220, Decision No. 14,830; *Appeals of Laskas-Gillespie and Warshaw*, 40 *id.* 568, Decision No. 14,559; *Appeal of Roberts, supra*), or demonstrate a clear and convincing picture of informality to the point of laxity in adherence to the Education Law (*Appeal of Christe*, 40 Ed Dept Rep 412, Decision No. 14,514; *Matter of Levine*, 24 *id.* 172, Decision No. 11,356, *affd sub nom Capobianco v. Ambach*, 112 AD2d 640). Implicit in these decisions is a recognition that it is a rare case where errors in the conduct of an election become so pervasive that they vitiate the fundamental fairness of the election (*Appeal of Collins*, 39 Ed Dept Rep 226, Decision No. 14,223; *Appeal of Roberts, supra*; *Appeal of Como, et al.*, 28 Ed Dept Rep 483, Decision No. 12,177).

In addition, petitioner has the burden of establishing all the facts upon which she seeks relief (8 NYCRR §275.10; *Appeal of Wierzchowski*, 39 Ed Dept Rep 682, Decision No. 14,348). To warrant setting aside an election, petitioner must establish that the improprieties are substantial and not merely technical in nature (*Appeal of Morris, et al.*, 37 Ed Dept Rep 590, Decision No. 13,936; *Appeal of Taylor*, 31 *id.* 46, Decision No. 12,564).

I will address petitioner's allegations *in seriatim*. Petitioner first alleges that respondent board failed to conspicuously post a list of absentee voters at two of the four polling venues, in violation of Education Law §2018-a(6), making it impossible for her or any other qualified voter to challenge absentee voters before the close of the polls. Petitioner, however, misstates the law and its applicability to respondent board. Respondent board adopted a resolution during the 2003-2004 school year discontinuing personal registration of voters. Therefore, §2018-b, not §2018-a, applies.

Moreover, the requirement in both §§2018-a and 2018-b to post a list of absentee voters in a conspicuous place was repealed effective

January 1, 2001 (*see* L. 2000, c. 29, §3). Section 2018-b(7) only requires the district clerk to maintain a list of all persons to whom absentee ballots have been issued, and have the list available for inspection during regular office hours until the day of the election. The clerk avers that he not only complied with this requirement by maintaining a list in his office, but also distributed a copy to each polling site. Accordingly, petitioner's claim is without merit.

Petitioner also asserts that she was not permitted to observe the opening of the lock boxes containing the absentee ballots, and thus was unable to object to or challenge them. The clerk admits that after the close of the polls, he removed the absentee ballots from locked boxes in his office and brought the ballots into a conference room at the administration office, where the ballots were opened in petitioner's presence. The record, therefore, indicates that petitioner had sufficient opportunity to observe and challenge the ballots when they were opened, and she offers no proof that the absentee ballots were otherwise tampered with or miscounted.

Petitioner similarly alleges that she was not permitted to observe the opening of the affidavit lock boxes and that the absentee and affidavit ballots were mixed in the same box. The district clerk avers that the absentee ballots were kept separate from the affidavit ballots, which were placed in locked boxes at each polling site. He avers that the boxes containing 47 affidavit ballots were collected from the four polling sites and brought to the district offices, and that he removed the ballots from the boxes and brought them to the conference room where the candidates were present. He then instructed the candidates that the ballots would not be opened that night because the district needed to verify the voters' residences and there were not enough ballots to affect the outcome of the election. The clerk also avers that the following day, he located six additional affidavit ballots from one polling site, for a total of 53 affidavit ballots.

In her reply, petitioner alleges that the six additional affidavit ballots were actually included in the 91 absentee ballots. She cites this misrecording of the ballots as an example of respondent board's lack of accountability and lax conduct of the election. However, petitioner has not demonstrated that the ballots were improperly recorded, nor has she offered any proof that the affidavit ballots were tampered with or miscounted. Moreover, she was defeated by 183 votes, more than the combined sum of the 91 absentee and 53 affidavit ballots (144). In addition, according to the vote tally sheet, petitioner trailed the incumbent by 154 votes even before the absentee and affidavit votes were counted. Accordingly, petitioner has failed to show that any irregularity regarding the ballots occurred or affected the outcome of the election.

Petitioner further alleges that names were missing from the polling books and county registration lists. She submits 190 "new or reactivated voter" sheets filled out the day of the election by voters she claims were left off the lists. Respondents assert that the inclusion or exclusion of names on the registration lists is irrelevant to the conduct of the election because the district does not have a system of personal registration. The only relevance and convenience of the registration books was that those persons whose names appeared in the books did not have to submit identification in order to vote. All others had to submit proof of residency in accordance with Education Law §2018-c, and those voters filled out the "new or reactivated voter" sheet for record-keeping purposes.

Respondents admit that at one polling site, some election inspectors mistakenly required several eligible voters whose names were not on the list to vote by affidavit ballot. Respondents maintain, however, that since these voters were nonetheless permitted to vote, any alleged irregularity did not affect the outcome of the election. I agree. Petitioner does not allege, much less demonstrate, that any voters were disenfranchised because they were not on the registration list. Nor does she show that the fact that voters had to sign a "new or reactivated voter" sheet in any way impacted the outcome of election.

Petitioner asserts that at one polling site it took at least 45 minutes for the voting machines to be unlocked. She alleges that many people left without voting and were not immediately offered the opportunity to fill out paper ballots. Respondents admit that the machines were mistakenly locked, but assert that it took only about 15 to 20 minutes to correct the problem, that four voters who did not want to wait or return later in the day completed affidavit ballots, and therefore this incident did not affect the outcome of the election. Petitioner fails to submit any affidavits from voters who were allegedly prevented from voting, and thus has not met her burden of proof on this issue.

In addition, petitioner alleges that four election districts were "redistricted" without public notice. She asserts that although voters were instructed to vote at their neighborhood elementary school, the boundaries of the election districts were changed so that many voters appeared at the wrong voting site and were instructed to go to a new site. She claims that many voters refused to leave and instead filled out affidavit ballots, but others left and failed to vote. Petitioner alleges that respondent board member David Singer gave verbal permission to the computer company that prepared the polling books to change the boundary lines of each polling place.

Mr. Singer denies that he gave permission to anyone to change boundary lines. Respondents admit that there were slight discrepancies between the published boundaries in the Legal Notices section of the local newspaper, which were accurate, and the boundary list maintained in the clerk's office, which was roughly 98% accurate. The clerk avers that the computer company utilized his list, and the discrepancies were not realized until election day. Consequently, some voters appeared at the wrong polling site and were not allowed to vote there because their names did not appear on the list for that site. The clerk avers that those voters were sent to the correct site, or, if they wanted, they were allowed to vote by affidavit. There is no evidence of malfeasance or intent on respondents' part regarding the discrepancy in boundaries, and petitioner fails to demonstrate that any voters were actually prevented from voting because of the discrepancy.

Petitioner challenges the appointment of George Brunner, incumbent Brunner's father, as an election inspector. Education Law §2025, which authorizes the appointment of election inspectors, contains no restriction barring relatives of board members or candidates from those positions. Therefore, the mere service of an incumbent's relative, without more, is not a reason to overturn the election (*Appeal of Goldman*, 35 Ed Dept Rep 126, Decision No. 13,487).

Petitioner also alleges that George Brunner improperly assisted voters in the voting booth with the curtain closed and that Mr. Singer electioneered within 100 feet of one polling site in contravention of Education Law §2031-a. Mr. Brunner and Mr. Singer both submit affidavits denying the allegations against them, and petitioner has failed to submit any evidence or affidavits from other voters to the contrary. Therefore, I find her claims to be unsubstantiated.

I must also dismiss petitioner's allegations that respondent board violated FOIL. The Public Officers Law vests exclusive jurisdiction over complaints alleging FOIL violations in the Supreme Court of the State of New York and alleged violations thereof may not be adjudicated in an appeal to the Commissioner (Public Officers Law §89; *Appeals of Tesser and Kavitsky*, 42 Ed Dept Rep 341, Decision No. 14,876; *Appeal of Rowe*, 41 *id*. 189, Decision No. 14,660).

I have considered petitioner's remaining contentions and find them without merit. Mere speculation as to the possible existence of irregularities is an insufficient basis to annul election results (*Appeal of Laurie*, 42 Ed Dept Rep 313, Decision No. 14,867; *Appeal of Brannon, supra*). Petitioner has failed to establish that any irregularities affected the outcome of the election, were so pervasive as to vitiate the electoral process, or demonstrate a clear and convincing picture of informality to the point of laxity in adherence to the Education Law. In the absence of such proof, the election will not be set aside and the appeal must be dismissed (*Appeal of Brannon, supra*).

THE APPEAL IS DISMISSED.

Decision No. 15,233

Appeal of BRUCE and MARISA HOROWITZ, on behalf of their daughter MADELYN, from action of the Board of Education of the Croton-Harmon Union Free School District regarding residency.

(May 23, 2005)

APPEARANCES OF COUNSEL

Castro & Remer, P.C., attorneys for petitioners, *Daniel V. Remer, Esq*., of counsel

Keane & Beane, P.C., attorneys for respondent, *Stephanie M. Roebuck, Esq*., of counsel

DECISION OF THE COMMISSIONER

MILLS, Commissioner.—Petitioners appeal the determination of the Board of Education of the Croton-Harmon Union Free School District ("respondent") that their daughter, Madelyn, is not a district resident. The appeal must be dismissed.

By letter dated February 9, 2004, a representative of respondent's Staff and Pupil Personnel Services Office notified petitioners of the district's determination that they were not district residents, and that Madelyn would be removed from the school rolls. This appeal ensued.

By letter dated February 18, 2004, respondent's superintendent informed petitioners that, based upon the district's review of the documentation submitted with their petition, it would permit Madelyn to remain enrolled as a student in the district's schools.

The appeal must be dismissed as moot. The Commissioner of Education will only consider matters in actual controversy and will not render a decision on a state of facts which no longer exist or which subsequent events have laid to rest (*Appeal of Passer*, 44 Ed Dept Rep ___, Decision No. 15,160; *Appeal of Colety, et al.*, 42 *id*. 162, Decision No. 14,806). Respondent has agreed to permit Madelyn to remain enrolled as a student in the district's schools. Accordingly, there is no further relief I can accord petitioners.

THE APPEAL IS DISMISSED.

Decision No. 15,234

Appeal of M.F. and T.L., on behalf of N.F.-L., from action of the New York City Department of Education regarding class placement.

(May 23, 2005)

APPEARANCES OF COUNSEL

Michael A. Cardozo, Corporation Counsel for the City of New York, *Martin Bowe, Esq*., of counsel

DECISION OF THE COMMISSIONER

MILLS, Commissioner.—Petitioners challenge a decision of the New York City Department of Education ("respondent") to retain their daughter in fifth grade for the 2004-2005 school year. The appeal must be dismissed.

Petitioners' daughter attended the fifth grade at the Clara Cardwell School, P.S./I.S. 308, in Brooklyn during the 2003-2004 school year. On April 5, 2004, respondent revised its policy for student promotion from the fifth grade as follows:

> *Promotion from Grades 5, 6, and 7 for General Education and Special Education Students and English Language Learners Tested in English*

> Promotion from grades 5, 6, and 7 to the next grade will be based on a comprehensive assessment of whether students:
>
> 1) meet New York City Performance Standards in Language Arts and Mathematics as evidenced by student work, teacher observation and assessment/grades;
>
> 2) achieve at or above Proficiency Level 2 on the Citywide ELA assessment;
>
> 3) achieve at or above Proficiency Level 2 on the Citywide Mathematics assessment;
>
> 4) attain 90% attendance.
>
> [Chancellor's Regulation A-501(6)(J)]

Beginning in September 2003, based upon the student's poor performance in mathematics in the fourth grade, she was enrolled in a mathematics intervention class until April 2004 to prepare her for the Citywide Mathematics Assessment. In January 2004, petitioners were informed that their daughter was at risk of being retained based upon her receiving a grade of 55 in mathematics. Petitioners' daughter received a failing grade of 55 in mathematics for each of the four marking periods during the 2003-2004 school year and the lowest score of Proficiency Level 1 on the Citywide mathematics assessment administered in April 2004. The test results were forwarded to the school and petitioners in early June 2004.

By letter dated June 16, 2004, petitioners were informed that their daughter would not participate in the promotion ceremony on June 18, 2004, due to her Citywide and classroom assessments in mathematics. Petitioners met with the assistant principal on June 16, 2004, and the principal on June 17, 2004. On June 17, 2004, petitioners met with the regional superintendent, who upheld the decision not to promote the student from the fifth grade.

On July 6, 2004, petitioners enrolled their daughter in summer school classes for English and Math. At the conclusion of the summer session on August 9, 2004, the student again sat for the standardized mathematics exam and received another score of Proficiency Level 1.

On August 12, 2004, the student's mother met with the regional superintendent. By letter dated August 30, 2004, petitioners were informed that the community superintendent upheld the decision to retain their daughter in the fifth grade, based on her mathematics classroom course work, data from both spring and summer sessions and standardized tests. Petitioners commenced this appeal and, on September 14, 2004, petitioners' request for interim relief was denied.

Petitioners contend that it is unfair to retain their daughter in the fifth grade because of one mathematics examination and grade when she was passing her other subjects. Petitioners contend they should have received notice earlier than June 16, 2004, that their daughter would not participate in the June 18, 2004, graduation ceremony. Petitioners contend that other children with the same issues as their daughter were allowed to participate in the ceremony. Petitioners also question their daughter's grade in mathematics.

Respondent contends that the determination to retain petitioners' daughter in fifth grade had a rational basis because the student failed to meet the standards for promotion from the fifth grade as set forth in Chancellor's Regulation A-501(6)(J). Respondent contends that it is in the student's best interest to be retained in fifth grade so that she can acquire the necessary skills, since she failed to achieve the minimum required proficiency in the mathematics assessment after intervention services during the 2003-2004 school year and the 2004 summer school session.

Education Law §1709(3) authorizes a board of education "to prescribe the course of study by which pupils of the schools shall be graded and classified, and to regulate the admission of pupils and their transfer from one class or department to another, as their scholarship shall warrant." Consistent with that authority, boards have the power to place students in particular classes (*Appeal of a Student with a Disability*, 41 Ed Dept Rep 259, Decision No. 14,680; *Appeal of J.K. and M.B.*, 40 *id*. 368, Decision No. 14,500; *Appeal of Dawn H.*, 39 *id*. 635, Decision No. 14,336). The Commissioner will not substitute his judgment for that of a board of education with respect to student placement, absent evidence that the board has acted in an illegal, arbitrary or capricious manner (*Appeal of Hillhouse*, 41 Ed Dept Rep 385, Decision No. 14,720; *Appeal of a Student with a Disability*, *supra*; *Appeal of J.K. and M.B.*, *supra*). In New York City, the powers of the board of education in this regard are exercised by the Chancellor (Education Law §§2554(1) and 2590-h(17)).

In an appeal to the Commissioner, petitioners have the burden of demonstrating a clear legal right to the relief requested and establishing the facts upon which they seek relief (8 NYCRR §275.10;

Appeal of a Student with a Disability, supra; *Appeal of Dawn H., supra*). Petitioners have not met their burden of showing that respondent's decision to retain their daughter in fifth grade was illegal, arbitrary or capricious.

Based on the record before me, I find that respondent has not acted arbitrarily or capriciously. Rather, respondent's determination is rationally based upon its standard for promotion from grades 5, 6 and 7, as set forth in Chancellor's Regulation A-501(6)(J). That standard was promulgated to ensure that students advance in grade level only where they demonstrate the knowledge to succeed in the next grade.

I have considered petitioners' remaining arguments and find them to be without merit.

THE APPEAL IS DISMISSED.

Decision No. 15,235

Appeal of BRIAN P. CURRAN, on behalf of his son BRIAN, from action of the Board of Education of the Carle Place Union Free School District and Dr. Patricia Hansen, Superintendent of Schools, regarding summer assignments.

(June 9, 2005)

APPEARANCES OF COUNSEL

Jaspan Schlesinger Hoffman LLP, Esq., attorneys for respondent, *Carol A. Melnick, Esq.*, of counsel

DECISION OF THE COMMISSIONER

MILLS, Commissioner.—Petitioner appeals the actions of the Board of Education of the Carle Place Union Free School District ("respondent board" or "board") and its superintendent (collectively referred to with the board as "respondents") concerning required summer reading, math and social studies assignments. The appeal must be sustained.

Petitioner's son, Brian, attended seventh grade in respondents' middle school during the 2003-2004 school year. By letter dated June 11, 2004, petitioner was notified that "upcoming" seventh and eighth grade students would be required to participate in a summer assignment involving the presidential election of 2004 (the "Summer Social Studies Assignment" or the "Project").

In accordance with the "Carle Place Middle School/High School Student Handbook," petitioner sequentially contacted the department chairperson, the middle school assistant principal and principal, the assistant superintendent for instruction and personnel and the superintendent of schools to discuss his concerns and express his belief that the Project was unreasonable. Later in June, petitioner's son received two additional summer assignments — the "Summer Reading Assignment" and the "Summer Math Assignment."

In July 2004, petitioner met with the superintendent to discuss his objection to all three summer assignments. Petitioner suggested that the due date of the Summer Social Studies Assignment be extended until the middle or end of October 2004, and the superintendent agreed to extend the due date to September 20, 2004. Petitioner was under the impression that the extension applied to all eighth grade students. However, the September 20 due date only applied to students who requested an extension.

By letter dated September 7, 2004, petitioner wrote to the president of the board objecting to all three mandatory summer assignments and expressing his desire to discuss the matter at the next board meeting. At its September 13, 2004, meeting, respondent board listened to petitioner's concerns but declined to take any action. This appeal ensued. Petitioner's request for interim relief was denied on October 13, 2004.

Petitioner requests that I find the summer assignments, either individually or collectively, unreasonable and beyond respondents' authority. He asks that students' grades relating to the summer assignments be discounted. Petitioner also requests that I direct respondents to discontinue, modify or make optional the current and future use of summer assignments. Finally, petitioner asks that I censure respondents.

Respondents allege that petitioner fails to state a claim upon which relief may be granted, and maintain that the summer assignments are within respondents' authority and are not arbitrary, capricious and/or unreasonable.

Initially, I must address several procedural matters. The purpose of a reply is to respond to new material or affirmative defenses set forth in an answer (8 NYCRR §§275.3 and 275.14). A reply is not meant to buttress allegations in the petition or belatedly add assertions that should have been in the petition (*Appeal of a Student with a Disability*, 44 Ed Dept Rep 136, Decision No. 15,124; *Appeal of*

General, 43 *id.* 146, Decision No. 14,948). Although I have reviewed petitioner's reply and "verified reply to respondents' affidavit in application to application for stay," I have considered only those portions that respond to new material or affirmative defenses set forth in respondents' pleadings.

Pursuant to §276.4 of the Commissioner's regulations, respondents were required to serve their memorandum of law within 30 days after service of the answer. Respondents served their answer on October 18, 2004, and submitted their memorandum of law on November 18, 2004, 31 days later. While the Commissioner may permit the late filing of a memorandum of law where a party has established good cause for the delay and demonstrated the necessity of such memorandum to the determination of the appeal (8 NYCRR §276.4(a)), there has been no such showing here. Therefore, I have not considered respondents' memorandum of law. In light of this decision, I need not consider the issues raised in petitioner's letter and affidavit in opposition to respondents' memorandum of law.

Similarly, petitioner's memorandum of law was served one day late (i.e. November 12, 2004) and petitioner offered no good cause for the delay or demonstrated the necessity of his memorandum to the determination of the appeal (*see* 8 NYCRR §276.4(a)). Accordingly, I have not considered petitioner's untimely memorandum of law.

With respect to the merits, boards of education have broad authority to prescribe the course of study in the schools of the district (Education Law §1709(3); *Appeal of Ciotti*, 44 Ed Dept Rep ___, Decision No. 15,162; *Appeal of Lahm*, 41 *id.* 193, Decision No. 14,662; *Appeal of Lease*, 39 *id.* 215, Decision No. 14,219). The U.S. Supreme Court has confirmed that school authorities enjoy broad discretion in regulating matters of curriculum (*Bd. of Educ., Island Trees U.F.S.D. No. 26 v. Pico*, 457 US 853, 869). I will not substitute my judgment for that of a board of education on curriculum issues absent evidence that the board has acted in an arbitrary, capricious, or unreasonable manner (*Appeal of Ciotti, supra*; *Appeal of Lahm, supra*; *Appeal of Lease, supra*).

I have, in the past, reviewed summer reading programs and found them to be permissible when properly structured and administered (*see Appeal of Ciotti, supra*; *Appeal of Lahm, supra*). However, a summer reading program is unreasonable and impermissible when it does not ensure that books that are being used as part of a mandatory assignment are reasonably available to all students and when it requires students to perform mandatory written assignments for a grade without the benefit of a teacher's direction or supervision (*Appeal of Ciotti*, *supra*; *Appeal of Lease*, *supra*). While I have not previously addressed mandatory summer assignments in subjects such as math and social studies, I find that the principles articulated in the summer reading decisions apply equally to those subjects. Fundamentally, class grades should reflect work done under a teacher's direction and supervision (*Appeal of Lease*, *supra*; *Appeal of Lahm*, *supra*).

I will address each of respondents' mandatory summer assignments individually, starting with the eighth grade Summer Reading Assignment.

The list for respondents' eighth grade reading assignment contains six books. All non-honors students were required to select one book. All honors students were required to read *A Tree Grows in Brooklyn* and one other book. Petitioner states that there are 100 eighth grade students in respondents' school district, a fact respondents do not dispute. The record does not reflect how many of these students are honors students. Petitioner alleges difficulty in obtaining one of the required books from a local bookstore, and that after a search at one local library he found only eight copies of *A Tree Grows in Brooklyn*. However, it appears that petitioner made only a limited effort to locate books from the list, and as in the *Appeal of Lahm* (*supra*), petitioner did not provide any evidence that families were compelled to purchase books due to their unavailability at local libraries. Furthermore, respondents allege that books were available at the public library, the school library or any of the 42 participating libraries in the Nassau library system. In an appeal to the Commissioner, petitioner has the burden of establishing the facts upon which he seeks relief (*Appeal of Pope*, 40 Ed Dept Rep 473, Decision No. 14,530; *Appeal of Logan*, 38 *id*. 694, Decision No. 14,120). Petitioner has failed to establish, and therefore I cannot conclude, that respondents failed to ensure that an adequate supply of books was reasonably available.

However, I nevertheless find the Summer Reading Assignment to be unreasonable due to lack of adequate teacher guidance or instruction. The Summer Reading Assignment required students to complete an extensive written "guideline sheet" without the benefit of any instruction. The "guideline sheet" was not graded but was used as an aid for students in completing a graded "open book" reading assessment given on September 9 or 10, 2004. The guideline sheet and the assessment required students to understand and describe complex concepts such as the book's "protagonist." Students had only four or five days after the start of school to review the guideline sheet and prepare for the assessment under the guidance of their teacher. On this record, I find that there was insufficient opportunity for students to obtain teacher guidance and instruction prior to completing the graded written assessment.

I also find the Summer Math Assignment to be unreasonable due to lack of adequate teacher direction and supervision. The mandatory Summer Math Assignment consisted of 100 multiple choice questions in a math workbook. Answers to the questions were provided at the end of the workbook, which also contained a list of websites to consult if students needed assistance in answering the problems. However, there were no teachers available to assist students who did not have access to a computer or who required additional assistance. A test was given on the material on September 10, 2004, only five school days after the start of the school year. Although respondents assert that the material was discussed and reviewed in class prior to the test, there is no explanation in the record of how teachers were able to cover all the concepts addressed in the workbook in such a short time frame. Indeed, this seems improbable. Therefore, on this record, I must overturn respondents' Summer Math Assignment for lack of sufficient instructional support.

Likewise, I find respondents' Summer Social Studies Assignment to be unreasonable due to lack of sufficient teacher direction and supervision concerning the mandatory written assignment which was reflected in the students' grades. The Project accounted for 10 to 20% of each student's first quarter grade, depending upon the number of assignments in that quarter. The Project required all students to read newspapers, watch part of the Republican and Democratic national conventions and interview ten people of voting age. Students were also asked to answer some fundamental questions regarding the presidential candidates, their political parties and the electoral process. Students were required to write a paragraph of five to seven sentences predicting which candidate would win the election and create a portfolio of their work. The written assignments were due on September 10, 2004.

I find the instructional support for this Project to be lacking in several respects. First, only one teacher was accessible by phone until July 2, 2004, a date prior to the national conventions. Second, although two teachers were available to assist students through email all summer, there was no provision made for students who did not have access to e-mail. Third, the Project was due on September 10, 2004, just five days after the start of school and accounted for up to one-fifth of the student's quarterly grade. Given the extensive nature of the project and its relative weight towards students' grades, the amount of teacher direction and supervision was inadequate. On this record, I conclude that respondents' Social Studies Summer Assignment was unreasonable.

Although I find respondents' summer assignments to be unreasonable, I find no basis to invalidate student grades earned on assessments based upon the summer assignments. At this point in the school year, students have completed the assignments and received grades. It will not serve any educational purpose to invalidate the grades that have already been earned, especially where petitioner has failed to show that Brian's, or any other student's grades suffered for lack of instruction.

Finally, I decline to censure respondents as requested by petitioner. The Commissioner of Education has no authority to order disciplinary action against district employees or to censure or reprimand a board of education (*Appeal of D.H.*, 41 Ed Dept Rep 142, Decision No. 14,640; *Appeal of Angrisani and Hamilton*, 41 *id.* 6, Decision No. 14,593).

In light of this disposition, I need not address the parties' remaining contentions.

THE APPEAL IS SUSTAINED.

IT IS ORDERED that respondent board modify its summer assignments consistent with this decision.

Decision No. 15,236

Appeal of a STUDENT SUSPECTED OF HAVING A DISABILITY, by her parent, from action of the Board of Education of the Smithtown Central School District regarding student discipline.

(June 16, 2005)

APPEARANCES OF COUNSEL

Law Offices of Peter G. Albert, attorneys for respondent, *Peter G. Albert, Esq.*, of counsel

DECISION OF THE COMMISSIONER

MILLS, Commissioner.—Petitioner appeals the suspension of his daughter by the Board of Education of the Smithtown Central School District ("respondent"). The appeal must be sustained in part.

Petitioner's daughter attended tenth grade at Smithtown High School during the 2003-2004 school year. On May 17, 2004, she and a classmate allegedly poured an oral laxative into their teacher's drink without the teacher's knowledge or consent. When petitioner picked up his daughter from school on May 17, 2004, he was provided written notice from the principal that his daughter would be suspended for five days, from May 18 through May 24, 2004, and provided daily alternative instruction after school hours. The notice advised petitioner of his right to request an immediate informal conference with the principal and that the matter was being referred to the superintendent to determine whether further disciplinary action would be taken.

By letter dated May 18, 2004, the superintendent advised petitioner that a hearing would be held on May 24, 2004, to determine whether his daughter engaged in conduct that warranted a suspension for more than five days. Petitioner's daughter was represented by counsel at the hearing. After reading the charge, the hearing officer adjourned the hearing pending an expedited meeting of respondent's Committee on Special Education ("CSE") and stated that the student would be provided home instruction during the interim. The student returned to school on June 3, 2004, and was assigned to in-school suspension.

The CSE met on June 9, 2004, and concluded that petitioner's daughter did not have a disability and was not eligible for special education. On June 10, 2004, petitioner's attorney requested an impartial hearing to challenge the CSE's determination. On June 21, 2004, the impartial hearing officer advised the parties and their counsel in writing that the impartial hearing would be delayed for 30 days at the request of petitioner's attorney because petitioner was not ready to go forward at that time. This appeal ensued. Petitioner's request for interim relief was denied on June 18, 2004.

Petitioner contends that respondent had knowledge prior to the May 17, 2004, incident that his daughter was a student with a disability entitled to the rights and protections of the Individuals with Disabilities Education Act ("IDEA") and should have provided him with notice of procedural safeguards due to students presumed to have a disability for discipline purposes. Petitioner contends that respondent failed to conduct a manifestation determination before suspending his daughter for more than ten consecutive days. Petitioner alleges that respondent provided inadequate alternative instruction and deprived his daughter of after-school review opportunities available to other students to prepare for final and Regents examinations. He requests that the suspension be annulled and her record expunged.

Respondent contends that it provided petitioner and his daughter with the rights and procedures required by Education Law §3214. Respondent admits that it was advised on March 9, 2003, that the student showed signs and symptoms of attention deficit hyperactivity disorder ("ADHD"), but contends that petitioner cancelled a May 9, 2003, CSE meeting to consider her IDEA eligibility. Respondent contends that the petition should be dismissed for failure to exhaust administrative remedies under the IDEA and §504 of the Rehabilitation Act ("§504"). Respondent further contends that petitioner failed to appeal its determinations of May 21, 2003, and May 5, 2004, that his daughter does not have a disability as defined by §504. Respondent maintains that the Commissioner lacks jurisdiction to determine an appeal raising claims pursuant to the IDEA and §504.

Education Law §3214(3)(b)(l) provides that, in the case of a suspension by a principal not to exceed five days, the student and her parents "shall, on request, be given an opportunity for an informal conference with the principal at which the pupil and/or person in parental relation shall be authorized to present the pupil's version of the event and to ask questions of the complaining witnesses." Notice of the right to request an informal conference, as required under §100.2(l)(4) of the Commissioner's regulations, provides in pertinent part:

> When suspension of a student from attendance for a period of five days or less pursuant to section 3214(3) of the Education Law is proposed, school district officials shall immediately notify the parents . . . in writing that the student may be suspended from school. . . . Such notice shall provide a description of the incident(s) for which suspension is proposed and shall inform the parents . . . of their right to request an immediate infor-

mal conference with the principal in accordance with the provisions of Education Law, section 3214(3)(b). . . .

The purpose of §100.2(l)(4) is to require that parents of a student suspended for five days or less are made aware of the statutory right provided in Education Law §3214(3)(b) to question the complaining witnesses in the presence of the principal who imposed the suspension in the first instance, and who has the authority to terminate or reduce the suspension, thereby allowing the principal to decide whether the original decision to suspend was correct or should be modified (*Appeal of T.R. and M.D.*, 43 Ed Dept Rep 411, Decision No. 15,036; *Appeal of a Student with a Disability*, 43 *id.* 372, Decision No. 15,021).

In this case, although respondent's letter of May 17, 2004, advised petitioner of his right to request an immediate informal conference with the principal, it did not inform him of his right to question the complaining witnesses. The suspension must therefore be annulled and expunged from the student's record (*Appeal of R.J. and D.J.*, 44 Ed Dept Rep 191, Decision No. 15,145; *Appeal of a Student with a Disability*, 40 *id.* 47, Decision No. 14,418; *Appeal of a Student with a Disability*, 38 *id.* 378, Decision No. 14,059).

With respect to petitioner's allegation that his daughter is eligible for and entitled to special education services, the record indicates that an impartial hearing officer (IHO) was appointed to decide that issue. The IHO's determination is not reviewable in an appeal to the Commissioner (Education Law §4404 and 8 NYCRR Part 279).

In light of this disposition, I need not address the parties' remaining contentions.

THE APPEAL IS SUSTAINED TO THE EXTENT INDICATED.

IT IS ORDERED that respondent's five-day suspension of petitioner's daughter be annulled and expunged from her record.

Decision No. 15,237

Appeal of M.S., on behalf of her son Z.S., from action of the Board of Education of the City School District of the City of Tonawanda regarding student discipline.

(June 16, 2005)

APPEARANCES OF COUNSEL

Suzanne M. Burns, Esq., attorney for petitioner

Norton/Radin/Hoover/Freedman, attorneys for respondent, *Andrew J. Freedman, Esq.*, of counsel

DECISION OF THE COMMISSIONER

MILLS, Commissioner.—Petitioner appeals the actions of the Board of Education of the City School District of the City of Tonawanda regarding her son's suspension. The appeal must be sustained in part.

In 2004, petitioner's son, Z.S., was a member of respondent's varsity football team. On October 1, 2004, Z.S. allegedly attended a high school football game under the influence of alcohol. By letter dated October 5, 2004, respondent's high school principal notified petitioner that Z.S. would be suspended from October 5, 2004, through October 13, 2004, because of the incident. By letter dated October 6, 2004, the superintendent notified petitioner that a hearing had been scheduled for October 13, 2004.

At the hearing, respondent's guidance counselor and Dean of Students/Director of Athletics testified that Z.S. admitted to them that he was under the influence of alcohol while at the football game. The superintendent found Z.S. guilty and imposed a ten-week suspension. On November 10, 2004, respondent upheld the finding of guilt and the penalty. This appeal ensued.

Petitioner claims that respondent's short-term suspension notice was insufficient. Petitioner also contends that respondent violated Z.S.'s right to privacy, privilege against self-incrimination and due process. Petitioner further asserts that respondent's determination of guilt is not supported by competent and substantial evidence. Petitioner requests that I order her son's suspension annulled and his records expunged.

Respondent contends that its short-term suspension notice was legally sufficient. Respondent further argues that the suspension was based on competent and substantial evidence.

Preliminarily, I find that because the student has served the suspension, the appeal is moot except to the extent that petitioner seeks expungement of his records (*Appeal of a Student with a Disability*, 44 Ed Dept Rep 136, Decision No. 15,124; *Appeal of a Student with a Disability*, 43 *id*. 372, Decision No. 15,021).

Education Law §3214(3)(b)(1) provides that, in the case of a suspension for a period not to exceed five days, the student and his parents "shall, on request, be given an opportunity for an informal conference with the principal" at which they may present the student's version of the facts and ask questions of complaining witnesses. Notice of the right to request an informal conference is required by §100.2(l)(4) of the Commissioner's regulations, which provides, in pertinent part:

> Parental notice concerning student suspensions. When suspension of a student from attendance for a period of five days or less pursuant to section 3214(3) of the Education Law is proposed, school district officials shall immediately notify the parents or the persons in parental relation in writing that the student may be suspended from school. . . *Such notice shall provide a description of the incident(s) for which suspension is proposed and shall inform the parents or persons in parental relation of their right to request an immediate informal conference with the principal in accordance with the provisions of Education Law, section 3214(3)(b)*. . . (Emphasis added)

The purpose of §100.2(l)(4) is to make the parents of a student suspended for five days or less aware of the statutory right provided in Education Law §3214(3)(b) to question the complaining witnesses in the presence of the principal who proposed the suspension in the first instance, and who has authority to terminate or reduce the suspension.

In this case, the principal's October 5, 2004, letter to petitioner does not meet the requirements described above. The letter failed to inform petitioner that she could request an opportunity to question complaining witnesses (*Appeal of R.M. and L.M*, 44 Ed Dept Rep 218, Decision No. 15,154; *Appeal of R.J. and D.J.*, 44 *id.* 191, Decision No. 15,145; *Appeal of P.F. and M.F.*, 42 *id.* 390, Decision No. 14,890). Accordingly, the short-term suspension must be annulled and expunged from Z.S.'s record (*Appeal of B.C. and A.C.*, 42 Ed Dept Rep 395, Decision No. 14,891).

I also find that the short-term suspension exceeded the five-day limit set forth in §3214(3)(b). The principal's October 5, 2004, letter states that the student was suspended from October 5, 2004, through October 13, 2004. I remind respondent of the need to abide by the statutory five-day limit in the future.

With respect to the student's long-term suspension, I find no basis to disturb respondent's determination of guilt. Education Law §3214(3)(a) authorizes a school district to suspend a "pupil who is insubordinate or disorderly or violent or disruptive, or whose conduct otherwise endangers the safety, morals, health or welfare of others." The decision to suspend a student from school must be based on competent and substantial evidence that the student participated in the objectionable conduct (*Bd. of Educ. of Monticello CSD v. Commissioner of Educ.*, 91 NY2d 133, 140-41; *Bd. of Educ. of the City School Dist. of the City of New York v. Mills*, 293 AD2d 37).

In this case, Z.S. admitted to two school officials that he was under the influence of alcohol while at the football game. I reject petitioner's argument that those admissions are protected by privilege. No decision of the courts or the Commissioner of Education has yet granted privileged status to communications between a student and school personnel (*Appeal of the Board of Education of the City School District of the City of New York*, 31 Ed Dept Rep 378, Decision No. 12,673). Moreover, to the extent the testimony constituted hearsay evidence, it is admissible in administrative hearings and hearsay evidence alone may constitute competent and substantial evidence (*Appeal of S.C.*, 43 Ed Dept Rep 222, Decision No. 14,978; *Appeal of a Student Suspected of Having a Disability*, 41 *id.* 341, Decision No. 14,707).

I have considered petitioner's remaining contentions and find them to be without merit. In an appeal to the Commissioner, petitioner has the burden of demonstrating a clear legal right to the relief requested (*Appeal of R.M. and L.M., supra*). Here, petitioner failed to meet that burden.

THE APPEAL IS SUSTAINED TO THE EXTENT INDICATED.

IT IS ORDERED that respondent's suspension of petitioner's son from October 5-13, 2004, be annulled and expunged from his record.

Decision No. 15,238

Appeal of S.A.M., on behalf of her son, A.S.M., from action of the Board of Education of the City School District of the City of Ithaca regarding denial of admission.

(June 17, 2005)

APPEARANCES OF COUNSEL

Bond, Schoeneck & King, PLLC, attorneys for respondent, *Jonathan B. Fellows, Esq.*, of counsel

DECISION OF THE COMMISSIONER

MILLS, Commissioner.—Petitioner appeals actions of the Board of Education of the City School District of the City of Ithaca ("respondent") regarding the discipline of her son, A.S.M., and his admission to district schools. The appeal must be dismissed.

By letter dated December 30, 2004, respondent's superintendent suspended petitioner's son from the district's high school through the end of the 2004-2005 school year. On April 5, 2005, the Committee on Special Education ("CSE") held an initial referral meeting regarding A.S.M. This appeal ensued.

Petitioner alleges that the high school principal improperly attended the CSE meeting and improperly denied her son "re-admission" to the high school. Petitioner requests that her son be permitted to attend summer school in the district, that he be allowed to return to the district's high school in September 2005, and that the principal acknowledge his improper actions.

Respondent asserts that to the extent petitioner challenges the suspension, the appeal is untimely, and to the extent petitioner challenges her son's 2005-2006 placement, the appeal is premature. Respondent further maintains that the Commissioner lacks jurisdiction to review actions of the CSE. Respondent also denies that the principal refused A.S.M. readmission to the high school.

An appeal to the Commissioner must be commenced within 30 days from the making of the decision or the performance of the act complained of, unless any delay is excused by the Commissioner for good cause shown (8 NYCRR §275.16; *Appeal of O'Brien*, 44 Ed Dept Rep 43, Decision No. 15,092; *Appeal of Spina*, 43 *id.* 354, Decision No. 15,016). To the extent petitioner appeals the suspension which was the subject of the December 30, 2004, letter, the appeal, which was commenced approximately four months later, without any explanation, must be dismissed as untimely.

To the extent petitioner seeks to challenge any alleged recommendations of the CSE, the appeal must be dismissed for lack of jurisdiction because those issues are properly the subject of an impartial hearing brought pursuant to Education Law §4404(1) and

§200.5(c) of the Commissioner's regulations and not an appeal pursuant to Education Law §310. An impartial hearing officer ("IHO") must, in the first instance, determine those issues. A person who is dissatisfied with the decision of an IHO may then appeal such decision to the State Review Officer ("SRO") pursuant to Education Law §4404(2) (*see* Education Law §4404(1) and (2); 8 NYCRR §200.5; *Appeal of a Student with a Disability*, 40 Ed Dept Rep 170, Decision No. 14,451; *Appeal of a Student with a Disability*, 39 *id.* 354, Decision No. 14,257; *Appeal of a Student with a Disability*, 39 *id.* 1, Decision No. 14,154).

To the extent petitioner appeals her son's 2005-2006 placement, the appeal must also be dismissed as premature. The Commissioner will not render an advisory opinion on an issue before it becomes justiciable (*Appeal of Lombardo*, 44 Ed Dept Rep 167, Decision No. 15,135; *Appeal of American Quality Beverages, LLC, et al.*, 42 *id.* 153, Decision No. 14,805; *Appeal of Sheppard*, 41 *id.* 150, Decision No. 14,643). There is no evidence in the record that A.S.M. will be denied admission to the high school in 2005-2006. Therefore, this claim must be dismissed as premature.

Similarly, the appeal is premature to the extent petitioner requests that her son be permitted to attend summer school. Pursuant to the superintendent's letter of December 30, 2004, A.S.M. will complete his suspension at the end of the 2004-2005 school year, which is June 30, 2005. He would then be eligible to apply for summer school like any other district student. There is no evidence that he applied for or has been denied admission to summer school.

In light of this disposition, I need not address the parties' remaining claims.

THE APPEAL IS DISMISSED.

Table of Decisions

A

B

C

D

E

F

G

S

T

U

V

W

Y

SUBJECT INDEX

PROCEDURE—Jurisdiction—(*cont'd*)

—Mootness

PROCEDURE—Jurisdiction—(*cont'd*)

STATUTORY REFERENCE TABLE

---

§ 2022(5) — Dec No. 15,155

§ 2023 — Dec No. 15,155, 15,156

§ 2023(1) — Dec No. 15,155

§ 2023(3) — Dec No. 15,155, 15,156

§ 2023(4) — Dec No. 15,155

§ 2025 — Dec. No 15,232

§ 2025(3)(b) — Dec No. 15,127

§ 2031-a — Dec No. 15,127, 15,232

§ 2035 — Dec. No 15,206

§ 2037 — Dec No. 15,161

§ 2218 — Dec No. 15,166

§ 2503(1) — Dec No. 15,158

§ 2510 — Dec No. 15,182, 15,183

§ 2510(1) — Dec No. 15,139

§ 2554(1) — Dec. No 15,234

§ 2590-h(17) — Dec. No 15,234

§ 2801-a — Dec. No 15,223

§ 3012 — Dec No. 15,151, 15,172

§ 3012(1) — Dec No. 15,139

§ 3012(1)(a) — Dec No. 15,139, 15,172

§ 3013 — Dec No. 15,182, 15,183

§ 3013(2) — Dec No. 15,182, 15,183

§ 3014-b — Dec No. 15,143

§ 3020-a — Dec No. 15,167, 15,172, 15,209

§ 3031(a) — Dec No. 15,192

§ 3031(b) — Dec No. 15,192

§ 3035(2) — Dec No. 15,173

§ 3201 — Dec No. 15,174, 15,174, 15,175, 15,175, 15,176, 15,177, 15,177, 15,178, 15,178, 15,179

§ 3202 — Dec. No. 15,077, 15,078, 15,086, 15,088, 15,096, 15,098, 15,101, 15,103, 15,104, 15,109, 15,218

§ 3202(1) — Dec. No. 15,075, 15,077, 15,078, 15,080, 15,082, 15,083, 15,085, 15,086, 15,088, 15,090, 15,093, 15,095, 15,096, 15,098, 15,099, 15,100, 15,101, 15,103, 15,104, 15,105, 15,108, 15,109, 15,110, 15,113, 15,122, 15,218, 15,228, 15,230

§ 3202(2) — Dec. No 15,228

§ 3202(6) — Dec. No. 15,112, 15,187

§ 3203 — Dec No. 15,128

§ 3203(1) — Dec No. 15,128, 15,196

§ 3209 — Dec. No. 15,108

§ 3209(1)(a) — Dec. No. 15,108

§ 3209(2) — Dec. No. 15,108

§ 3209(2)(a) — Dec. No. 15,108

§ 3214 — Dec. No. 15,107, 15,122, 15,123, 15,132, 15,146, 15,170, 15,171, 15,186, 15,186, 15,197, 15,202, 15,223, 15,226, 15,236

§ 3214(3) — Dec No. 15,124, 15,134, 15,145, 15,146, 15,236, 15,237

§ 3214(3)(a) — Dec No. 15,124, 15,146, 15,226, 15,237

§ 3214(3)(b) — Dec No. 15,124, 15,134, 15,145, 15,171, 15,236, 15,237

§ 3214(3)(b)(1) — Dec No. 15,124, 15,134, 15,145, 15,154, 15,171, 15,174, 15,197, 15,237, 15,236

§ 3214(3)(c) — Dec No. 15,186

§ 3214(3)(c)(1) — Dec. No. 15,107, 15,122, 15,197, 15,202

§ 3214(5) — Dec No. 15,193, 15,203

§ 3602 — Dec. No 15,211

§ 3602-c — Dec No. 15,195

§ 3602-c(2) — Dec No. 15,195

§ 3635 — Dec. No. 15,121, 15,208

§ 3635(2) — Dec. No. 15,117, 15,208

§ 3635-b — Dec. No. 15,121, 15,106, 15,106

§ 3635-b(2) — Dec. No. 15,106

§ 3635-b(4) — Dec. No. 15,106

§ 3641 — Dec. No 15,211

§ 3651 — Dec No. 15,142, 15,219

§ 3651(1-a) — Dec No. 15,142

§ 3651(3) — Dec. No 15,219

§ 3651(5) — Dec. No 15,204

§ 3811 — Dec No. 15,194

§ 4401(1) — Dec No. 15,176

§ 4404 — Dec. No. 15,079, 15,236

§ 4404(1) — Dec. No. 15,079, 15,238

§ 4404(2) — Dec. No. 15,079, 15,238

§§ 6900 *et seq.* — Dec No. 15,129

General Construction Law
§ 25-a(1) — Dec No. 15,147

§ 41 — Dec. No 15,206

General Municipal Law
§ 36 — Dec. No 15,211

§ 800(3) — Dec No. 15,135

§ 801 — Dec No. 15,135

Labor Law
§ 201-d — Dec No. 15,167

Public Health Law
§ 2164 — Dec. No. 15,091, 15,094, 15,111, 15,217

§ 2164(7)(b) — Dec. No. 15,094

§ 2164(9) — Dec. No. 15,091, 15,094, 15,217

Public Officers Law
§ 89 — Dec. No 15,232

Real Property Tax Law
§ 1306 — Dec. No 15,211

§ 1318 — Dec No. 15,142, 15,201, 15,213

§ 1318(1) — Dec No. 15,142, 15,201, 15,213

Nurse Practice Act
— Dec No. 15,129

REGULATIONS OF THE DEPARTMENT OF TRANSPORTATION

§ 191.4 — Dec. No. 15,106

FEDERAL ACTS

Civil Rights Act of 1964
Title VI — Dec No. 15,174, 15,175, 15,176, 15,177, 15,178, 15,179

Elementary and Secondary Education Act
Title I — Dec No. 15,174, 15,175, 15,176, 15,177, 15,178, 15,179

Title III — Dec No. 15,179 15,174 15,175, 15,176 15,177, 15,178

Title VII — Dec No. 15,174, 15,175, 15,176, 15,177 , 15,179

Equal Educational Opportunities Act of 1974
— Dec No. 15,174, 15,175, 15,176, 15,177, 15,178, 15,179

Family Education Rights and Privacy Act ("FERPA")
— Dec No. 15,191

Freedom of Information Law ("FOIL")
— Dec. No 15,232

Individuals with Disabilities Education Act ("IDEA")
— Dec. No. 15,079, 15,184, 15,236

McKinney-Vento Homeless Assistance Act
— Dec. No. 15,108

No Child Left Behind Act
— Dec No. 15,174, 15,175, 15,176, 15,176, 15,177, 15,178

Title I — Dec No. 15,174, 15,175, 15,176, 15,177, 15,179

Title III — Dec No. 15,174, 15,175, 15,176, 15,177, 15,179

§ 504 of the Rehabilitation Act
— Dec. No 15,236

FEDERAL STATUTES

20 USC
§ 1415 — Dec. No. 15,079

§ 7844(a)(3)(C)—Dec No. 15,174, 15,175, 15,176, 15,177, 15,178

42 USC
§ 11302 — Dec. No. 15,108

§ 11432(g)(3)(A) — Dec. No. 15,108

UNITED STATES CONSTITUTION

First Amendment — Dec No. 15,126, 15,164

First Amendment, Establishment Clause — Dec No. 15,159

Fourteenth Amendment — Dec No. 15,159, 15,164

NEW YORK STATE CONSTITUTION

Article VIII, § 1 — Dec No. 15,140

TABLE OF JUDICIAL REVIEW

Decision Appealed	
11,856	*Jackson v Sobol et al.*; Supreme Court, Albany County, Special Term; Doran, J.; Judgment granted dismissing petition to review; April 5, 1988, n.o.r.; aff'd 170 AD2d 718 (3d Dept 1991).
11,869	*Albion CSD v Canteen Company, et al.*; Supreme Court, Albany County, Special Term; Williams, J.; Judgment granted annulling decision; November 13, 1987, n.o.r.
11,881	*Blake, et al. v Sobol. et al.*; Supreme Court, Albany County, Special Tern; Cobb, J.; Judgment granted dismissing petition to review; May 3, 1988, n.o.r.
11,887	*Swezey v Sobol, et al.*; US District Court, Eastern District; Wexler, J.; Order of discontinuance entered; December 13, 1988, n.o.r.
11,893	*Goodline v Bd. of Ed., Warwick Valley CSD and Sobol*; US District Court, Southern District; Goettel, J.; case settled, order entered; February 12, 1990, n.o.r.
11,909	*Cronin v Bd. of Ed., East Ramapo CSD and Sobol*; US District Court, Southern District; Ward, J.; motion for prelim. inj. granted; 689 F.Supp. 197 (SDNY, 1988); case settled, order entered; March 17, 1989, n.o.r.
11,910	*Kron v Sobol et al.*; Supreme Court, Albany County, Special Term; Connor, J.; Judgment granted dismissing petition to review; February 19, 1990, n.o.r.
11,920	*Pronin v Sobol*; Supreme Court, Albany County, Special Term; Connor, J.; Judgment granted dismissing petition to review; September 21, 1988, n.o.r.
11,923	*Engel v Sobol*; Supreme Court, Albany County, Special Term; Bradley, J.; Judgment granted annulling decision; November 21, 1988, n.o.r.; aff'd 161 AD2d 873 (3d Dept. 1990).
11,976	*Birden v Sobol, et al.*; US District Court, Eastern District; Sifton, J.; case settled, order entered; October 21, 1988, n.o.r.

11,979 *Williamsville CSD v Sobol and Albert*; Supreme Court, Albany County, Special Term; Prior, J.; Judgment granted dismissing petition to review; February 10, 1989, n.o.r.

11,980 *Cardo v Sobol, et al.*; Supreme Court, Albany County, Special Term; Connor, J.; Judgment granted dismissing petition to review; April 25, 1989, n.o.r.; motion for reargument denied; December 7, 1989, n.o.r.

11,983 *Matter of Section XI NYS Public H.S. Athletic Association, Inc. v Sobol, et al.*; Supreme Court, Albany County, Special Term; Hughes, J.; Judgment granted dismissing petition to review; August 24, 1988, n.o.r.

11,985 *Holmes v Sobol, et al.*; 690 FSupp. 154 (WDNY 1988); case settled, order entered; September 12, 1990.

11,987 *Schuylerville CSD v Commissioner of Education, et al.*; Supreme Court, Albany County, Special Term; Cheeseman, J.; Judgment granted dismissing petition to review; October 26, 1988, n o r.; affd 152 AD2d 241 (3d Dept. 1989).

11,995 *Kron v Sobol, et al.*; Supreme Court, Albany County, Special Term; Connor, J.; Judgment granted dismissing petition to review; May 10, 1989, n.o.r.

12,028 *Floryan v Bd. of Ed., New Paltz CSD, et al.*; US District Court, Northern District; McAvoy, J.; Order of discontinuance entered; April 20, 1992, n.o.r.

12,045 *Schwarz v Mt. Pleasant Cottage UFSD, et al.*; Supreme Court, Albany County, Special Term; Cheeseman, J.; Judgment granted dismissing petition to review, subnom.; Mt Pleasant Cottage UFSD v Sobol; May 2, 1989, n.o.r.; aff'd 163 AD2d 715; aff'd 78 NY2d 938 (1991).

12,066 *Kron v Sobol, et al.*; Supreme Court, Albany County, Special Term; Connor, J.; Judgment granted dismissing petition to review; December 30, 1989, n.o.r.

12,076 *Pine Plains Central School District v Sobol*; Supreme Court, Albany County, Special Term; Conway, J.; Judgment granted dismissing petition to review; June 7, 1989, n.o.r.

12,077 *Dionisio v Sobol*; Supreme Court, Albany County, Special Term; Prior, J.; Judgment granted dismissing petition to review; August 17, 1989, n.o.r.

12,119 *Fogelman v Sobol, et al.*; Supreme Court, Albany County, Special Term; McDermott, J.; Judgment granted dismissing petition to review; November 22, 1989, n.o.r.

12,124 *Stellato v Bd. of Ed., Ellenville CSD, et al.*; US District Court, Northern District; McAvoy, J.; case settled, dismissed as against Commissioner of Education; September 10, 1991, n.o.r.

12,146 *Tombler v Bd. of Ed., Brookhaven-Comsewogue UFSD, et al.*; Order of discontinuance entered; June 1990.

12,155 *Bd. of Ed. of Northeast Central School District v Sobol, et al.*; Supreme Court, Albany County, Special Term; Kahn, J.; Judgment granted dismissing petition to review; December 14, 1989, n.o.r.; mod in part 170 AD2d 80; mod and decision of Commissioner aff'd 70 NY3d 598 (1992).

12,172 *Bd. of Ed., Uniondale UFSD v Sobol*; Supreme Court, Albany County, Special Term; Bradley, J.; Judgment granted dismissing petition to review; March 5, 1991, n.o.r.

12,216 *Cargill v Sobol, et al.*; Supreme Court, Albany County, Special Term; Harris J.; Judgment granted annulling decision; order entered May 10, 1990; aff'd 165 AD2d 131; appeal denied 78 NY2d 854.

12,219 *O'Connor v Sobol, et al.*; Supreme Court, Albany County, Special Term; Cobb, J.; Judgment granted dismissing petition to review; July 20, 1990, n.o.r.; aff'd 173 AD2d 74; appeal dismissed 80 NY3d 897 (1992).

12,220 *Bd. of Ed., Ramapo CSD v Sobol*; Supreme Court, Rockland County; Silverman, J.; Order of discontinuance entered; August, 1990.

12,230 *Alexandra V.N. v Sobol, et al.*; Stipulation and order dismissing petition as against Commissioner; October 9, 1990.

12,299 *Frutiger v Hamilton CSD and Sobol*; case settled; order of discontinuance; August 12, 1991.

12,318 *Shenendehowa CSD v Bd. of Ed., Waterford-Halfmoon UFSD and Sobol*; Supreme Court, Albany County, Special Term; Harris, J.; Judgment granted dismissing petition to review; January 10, 1991; aff'd 182 AD2d 944 (1992).

12,320 *BOE, Malverne UFSD v Sobol, et al.*; Supreme Court, Albany County, Special Term; Cobb, J.; Judgment granted dismissing petition to review; May 5, 1991; n.o.r.; aff'd 181 AD2d 370 (1992).

12,395 *Hable v Sobol, et al.*; Appliction to review decision pending.

12,409 *Vecchio v Sobol and Bd. of Ed., East Islip UFSD*; Supreme Court, Albany County, Special Term; Cobb, J,; Judgment granted dismissing petition to review; August 27, 1991; aff'd 189 AD2d 961, mot. for leave to appeal den. 81 NY2d 709, May 4, 1993.

12,438 *BOE, Brentwood UFSD v Sobol*; Supreme Court, Albany County, Special Term; Conway, J.; Judgment granted dismissing petition to review; September 3, 1991, n.o.r.

12,484 *Save Our Students v Sobol, et al.*; Application to review decision pending.

12,497 *Davis, et al. v Comm. of Educ. and Bd.of Ed., Roxbury CSD*; Supreme Court, Albany County, Special Term; Kahn, J.; Judgment granted dismissing petition to review; February 4,1992, n.o.r.; aff'd 189 AD2d 1046 (3d Dept. 1993).

12,499 *Sewanhaka CHSD v Sobol*; Supreme Court, Albany County, Special Term; Cardona, J.; Judgment granted dismissing petition to review; April 14, 1992, n.o.r.

12,515 *Jacobs v Sobol and BOCES of Putnam / Northern Westchester*; Supreme Court, Albany County, Special Term; Torraca, J.; Judgment granted dismissing petition to review; January 16, 1992, n.o.r.

12,534 *Levofsky v Sobol*; Supreme Court, Albany County, Special Term; Travers, J.; Judgment granted dismissing petition to review; March 30, 1992, n.o.r.

12,584 *Watkins v Sobol*; Supreme Court, Albany County, Special Term; Cardona, J.; Judgment granted annulling decision and remitting matter for further proceedings; July 23,1992, n.o.r.; appeal withdrawn; December 16, 1993.

12,594 *Rosenberg v Half Hollow Hills CSD and Sobol*; Supreme Court, Albany County, Special Term; Hughes, J; Judgment granted dismissing petition to review, March 13, 1992, n.o.r.; Appeal pending, 12,594 *Seligman v Sobol and Half Hollow Hills CSD*; Supreme Court, Albany County, Special Term; Connor, J; Judgment granted dismissing petition to review; June 16, 1992, n o r.

12,601 *Malley v Sobol*; Supreme Court, Albany County, Special Term; Keegan, J.; Judgment granted dismissing petition to review; June 22, 1992, n.o.r.

12,616 *Lessen v Sobol*; Supreme Court, Albany County, Special Term; Hughes, J.; Judgment granted dismissing petition to review; June 23, 1992, n.o.r.

12,637 *Troy v Sobol, et al.*; Supreme Court, Albany County, Special Term; Khan, J.; Judgment granted dismissing petition to review; March 11, 1996, n.o r.

12,743 *Danin v Sobol*; Supreme Court, Albany County, Special Term; Keegan, J.; Judgment granted dismissing petition to review; March 18, 1993; n.o r.

12,745 *Impellizzeri, et al. v Sobol, et al.*; Supreme Court, Albany County, Special Term; Judgment granted dismissing petition to review; February 1995, n.o.r.

12,768 *Garnett v Sobol*; Supreme Court, Albany County, Special Term; Harris, J.; Judgment granted dismissing petition to review; July 13, 1994, n.o.r.; aff'd 222 AD2d 850, 634 NYS2d 882 (3d Dept 1995) (December 14, 1995); mot. for lv. to appeal denied, 87 NY2d 810, 642 NYS2d 859, 665 NE2d 661 (1996) (March 28, 1996); cert denied 519 U.S. 849, 117 S. Ct. 138, 136 L. Ed. 2d 86 (1996).

12,789 *Schachter v Sobol, et al.*; Supreme Court, Queens County, Special Term; Application to review decision pending.

12,796 *Schachter v Sobol*; Supreme Court, Queens County, Special Term; Application to review decision pending.

12,797 *BOE, Beacon City School District v Sobol, et al.*; Supreme Court, Albany County, Special Term; Spain, J.; Judgment granted dismissing petition to review; August 17, 1994, n.o.r.; aff'd 212 AD2d 76 (1995).

12,837 *BOE, City School District, City of Lackawanna v Sobol, et al.*; Application to review decision pending.

12,838 *Fehr v Sobol, et al.*; complaint filed USDC, Northern District; March 24, 1993; Matter stayed pending administrative proceeding; Reopening issued, 33 Ed Dept Rep 403.

12,858 *Boron v Sobol, et al.*; Supreme Court, Albany County, Special Term; Toracca, J.; Judgment granted dismissing petition to review; July 20, 1993. n.o.r.; aff'd 205 AD2d 28, 617 NYS2d 243 (3d Dept 1994); mot. for lv. to appeal den. 86 NY2d 711, 635 NYS2d 947, 659 NE2d 770 (1995).

12,866 *Lawrence v Sobol, et al.*; Supreme Court, Albany County, Special Term; Canfield, J.; Judgment granted dismissing petition to review; January 3, 1994.

12,883 *Board of Education of the City of New York v Sobol, et al.*; Supreme Court, Albany County, Special Term; Cobb, J.; Judgment granted dismissing petition to review; July 16, 1993, n..o.r.

12, 937 *Sewanhaka CHSD v Sobol, et al.*; Supreme Court, Albany County, Special Term; Toracca, J.; Judgment granted dismissing petition to review; March 4, 1994, n.o.r.; aff'd 210 AD2d 675 (3rd Dept 1994).

12,961 *Silano v Sobol, et al.*; Supreme Court, Albany County, Special Term; Hughes, J.; Judgment granted dismissing petition to review; January 10, 1994, n.o.r.

12,969 *Ulster County BOCES v Sobol*; Supreme Court, Albany County, Special Term; Judgment granted dismissing petition to review; February 17, 1994, n.o.r.

12,999 *Board of Education, Sewanhaka CHSD v Sobol, et al.*; Supreme Court, Albany County, Special Term; Keegan, J.; Judgment granted dismissing petition to review; May 25, 1994, nor.; aff'd 213 AD2d 844 (1995).

13,013 *Palyo v Sobol*; Supreme Court, Albany County, Special Term; Canfield, J.; Judgment granted dismissing petition to review; May 12, 1994, n.o.r.

13,020 *Vaughan v Sobol*; Supreme Court, Albany County, Special Term; Canfield J.; Judgment granted dismissing petition to review; March 1994, n.o.r.

13,032 *Martin v Sobol, et al.*; Supreme Court, Albany County, Special Term; Williams, J.; Judgment granted dismissing petition to review; April 7, 1994, n.o.r.; appeal pending.

13,040 *Gaffney v Sobol, et al.*; Supreme Court, Albany County, Special Term; Connor, J.; Judgment granted dismissing petition to review; March 3l, 1994, n.o.r.; aff'd 2I0 AD2d 810 (1995).

13,041 *Blumenblatt v Sobol, et al.*; Supreme Court, New York County; Lehner, J.; Judgment transferring to Albany County; November 4, 1994; Supreme Court, Albany County, Special Term; Canfield, J.; Judgment granted dismissing petition to review: June 18, 1997, n.o.r.; appeal dismissed for failure to perfect.

13,052 *Friedman v Sobol, et al.*; Supreme Court, Albany County, Special Term; Hughes, J.; Judgment granted dismissing petition to review; May 20, 1994, n.o.r.

13,057 *Merritt v Sobol, et al.*; Supreme Court, Albany County, Special Term; Hughes, J.; Judgment granted dismissing petition to review; May 31, 1994, n.o.r.

13,075 *Gutilla v Sobol*; Supreme Court, Albany County, Special Term; Canfield, J.; Judgment granted dismissing petition to review; January 1995; appeal pending.

13,087 *Cerilli v Sobol*; Supreme Court, Albany County, Special Term; Connor, J.; Judgment granted dismissing petition to review; October 14, 1994, n.o.r.

13,104 *McMahon v Sobol et al.*; Supreme Court, Albany County, Special Term; Torraca, J.; Judgment granted annulling decision and remitting matter for further proceedings; December 20, 1994, n.o.r.; aff'd 235 AD2d 635, 651 NYS2d 742 (3d Dept, January 9, 1997).

13,159 *Bradshaw v Sobol, et al.*; Supreme Court, Albany County, Special Term; Torraca, J.; Judgment granted dismissing petition to review; December 20, 1994, n.o.r.; appeal pending.

13,166 *Newman v Sobol*; Supreme Court, Albany County, Special Term; Torraca, J.; Judgment transferring to Appellate Division, Third Department; February 3, 1995, n.o.r.

13,176 *Yastion v Sobol, et al.*; Supreme Court, Albany County Special Term; Canfield, J.; Judgment granted dismissing petition to review; March 6, 1994, n.o.r.; aff'd 229 AD2d 775, 645 NYS2d 585 (3d Dept. 1996).

13,223 *Lisbon CSD v Sobol, et al.*; Supreme Court, Albany County, Special Term; Ceresia, J.; Judgment granted dismissing petition to review; January 27, 1995, n.o.r.; aff'd 226 NY2d 945, 641 NYS2d 168 (3d Dept. 1996).

13,275 *Thomas v Sobol*; Supreme Court, Albany County, Special Term; Hughes, J.; Judgment granted dismissing petition to review; May 9, 1995, n.o.r.

13,290 *Manning v Sobol*; Supreme Court, Albany County, Special Term; Judgment granted dismissing petition to review.

13,323 *Martin v Sobol, et al.*; Supreme Court, Albany County, Special Term; Williams, J.; Judgment granted dismiissing petition to review; April 7, 1994, n.o.r.

13,397 *Greenburgh v Sobol*; Supreme Court, Albany County, Special Term; Ceresia, J.; Judgment granted dismissing petition to review; December 20, 1995, n.o.r.; aff'd 237 AD2d 721, 654 NYS2d 458 (3d Dept. March 6, 1997).

13,430 *Fiore v Sobol, et al.*; Supreme Court, Albany County, Special Term; Kahn, J.; Judgment granted dismissing petition to review; March 6, 1995, n.o.r.

13,433 *Allen, et al. v Mills, et al,*; Supreme Court, Albany County, Special Term; Carpinello, J.; Judgment granted dismissing petition and remanding to Commissioner for consideration of additional issues; January 15, 1996, n.o.r.

13,446 *Delhi Central School District v Mills, et al.*; Supreme Court, Albany County, Special Term; Hughes, J.; Judgment granting petition, annulling decision of Commissioner and remanding to Commissioner for further consideration; February 21, 1996, n.o.r.

13,501 *Boyle v Mills, et al.*; Supreme Court, Albany County, Special Term; Hughes, J.; Judgment granted dismissing petition to review; June 10, 1996, n.o.r.

13,505 *Bd. of Ed., Monticello CSD v Commissioner of Education, et al.*; Judgment granted transferring to Appellate Division, Third Department. Judgment granted annulling decision of Commissioner, 235 AD2d 734 (3d Dept. 1997) aff'd 91 NY2d 133 (1997).

13,517 *Crawmer v Mills*; Supreme Court, Albany County, Special Term; Hughes, J.; Judgment granted dismissing petition to review; May 17, 1996, n.o.r.; aff'd 239 AD2d 844, May 22, 1997.

13,523 *Winchall v Mills, et al.*; Supreme Court, Albany County, Special Term; Harris, J.; Judgment granted dismissing petition to review; May 6, 1996, n.o.r.

13,549 *Nasca v Mills*; Judgment granted transferring to Appellate Division, Third Department.

13.563 *Mulder v Mills, et al.*; Supreme Court, Albany County, All Purpose Term; Ceresia, J.; Judgment granted dismissing petition to review; September 25, 1996, n.o.r.

13,567 *Peikon-Cotz v Mills*; Supreme Court, Albany County, Special Term; Cobb, J.; Judgment granted dismissing petition to review; September 30, 1996, n.o.r.

13,583 *Bradley Industrial Park, et al. v Mills*; Supreme Court, Albany County, Special Term; Ceresia, J.; Judgment granted dismissing petition to review; March 31, 1997, n.o.r.; appeal never perfected.

13,589 *Cadet v Mills, et al.*; Supreme Court, Albany County, Special Term; Bradley, J.; Judgment granted dismissing petition to review; April 9,1997; aff'd 250 AD2d 122, November 12, 1998; mot. for leave to appeal den. 93 NY2d 803, March 25, 1999.

13,590 *Akshar v Mills, et al.*; Supreme Court, Albany County Special Term; Cobb, J.; Judgment granted dismissing petition to review; November 21, 1996, n.o.r. aff'd 249 AD2d 786, April 23, 1998; mot. for leave to appeal den. 92 NY2d 962, November 18, 1998.

13,607 *Forte v Mills, et al.*; Supreme Court, Albany County, Special Term; Judgment granted dismissing petition to review; May 7, 1998; aff'd 250 AD2d 882, May 7, 1998.

13,660 *Bd. of Ed., Baldwin UFSD v Mills, et ano.*; Supreme Court, Albany County, Special Term; Keegan, J.; Judgment granted dismissing petition to review; October 9, 1997.

13,681 *Donlon v Mills, et ano.*; Judgment granted dismissing petition to review; April 29, 1999, 260 AD2d 971; mot. for leave to appeal den. 94 NY2d 752, October 21, 1999.

13,701 *Domadeo, et al. v Mills, et al.*; Supreme Court, Albany County, Special Term; Keegan, J.; Judgment granted dismissing petition to review; June 12, 1997, n.o.r.

13,730 *Allen, et al. v BOE, Middle Country CSD*; Supreme Court, Albany County, Special Term; Judgment granted dismissing petition to review; November 1997, n.o.r.

13,760 *Education Alternatives, Inc. v Mills and SED*; Supreme Court, Albany County, Special Term; Lamont, Acting J.S.C.; Judgment granted dismissing petition to review; December 18, 1997, n.o.r.

13,779 *Owego-Apalachin CSD v Mills*; Supreme Court, Albany County; Connor, J.; Judgment granted dismissing petition to review; March 30, 1998, n.o.r.; aff'd 257 AD2d 739, January 7, 1999.

13,807 *Bd. of Ed., Northeast CSD v Mills, et al.*; Supreme Court, Albany County, Special Term; Ceresia, J.; Judgment granted dismissing petition to review; November 22, 1999.

13,813 *Bd. of Ed., North Tonawanda City SD v Mills, et al.*; Supreme Court, Albany County, Special Term; Torraca, J.; Judgment granting petition and annulling decision of the Commissioner; May 1, 1998, n.o.r.; aff'd 263 AD2d 574, July 1, 1999; mot. for leave to appeal den. 94 NY2d 751; October 19, 1999.

13,820 *Bd. of Ed., Uniondale UFSD v Mills, et al.*; Supreme Court, Albany County, Special Term; Lamont, J.; Judgment granted dismissing petition to review; May 27, 1998.

13,876 *Bd. of Ed., Alexandria CSD v Mills and SED*; Supreme Court, Albany County, Special Term; Judgment granted dismissing petition for review; June 18, 1998.

13,881 *Hessney v Mills, et al.*; Supreme Court, Albany County, Special Term; Sheridan, J.; Judgment granted dismissing petition to review; March 4, 1999, n.o.r.

13,883 *Matter of Schulman, et al. v BOE, Monticello CSD*; Supreme Court, Albany County, Special Term; Malone, J.; Judgment granted dismissing petition to review; December 16, 1998; n.o.r.; appeal dismissed for failure to perfect; April 28, 1999.

13,896 *Morehouse v Mills, et al.*; Supreme Court, Albany County; Special Term; Bradley, J.; Judgment granted dismissing petition to review; November 5, 1998; n.o.r.; aff'd 268 AD2d 767, January 13, 2000; mot. for leave to appeal den. 95 NY2d 751; May 4, 2000.

13,910 *Jordan v Mills*; Supreme Court, Albany County, Special Term; Keegan, J.; Judgment granted dismissing petition to review; March 30, 1999; appeal dismissed for failure to perfect.

13,964 *Chernoff v Mills, et al.*; Supreme Court, Albany County, Special Term; Canfield, J.; Judgment granted dismissing petition to review; May 24, 1999; n.o.r.; appeal withdrawn.

13,994 *Matter of Ogbunugafor v NYSED*; Supreme Court, Albany County, Special Term; Connor, J.; Judgment granted dismissing petition to review; July 22, 1999; n.o.r.; aff'd 279 AD2d 738, January 11, 2001; mot. for leave to appeal den 96 NY2d 712; May 8, 2001.

13,999 *Lilley v Mills, et al.*; Supreme Court, Albany County, Special Term; Ceresia, J.; Judgment granted dismissing petition to review; August 23, 1999; n.o.r.; aff'd 274 AD2d 644; July 6, 2000.

14,143 *Bojarczuk v Mills, et ano*; Supreme Court, Albany County, Special Term; Connor, J.; Judgment granted dismissing petition to review; October 3, 2000; n.o.r.; aff'd 287 AD2d 82, December 13, 2001; mot. for leave to appeal granted; March 21, 2002; Reversed and remitted to Supreme Court for further proceedings 98 NY2d 663; June 11, 2002; Reversed, Appellate Division, Third Department; April 1, 2004.

14,144 *Bd. of Ed., Oyster Bay-East Norwich CSD v Mills*; Supreme Court, Albany County, Special Term; Sheridan, J.; Judgment granted dismissing petition to review; January 31, 2000, n.o.r.

14,200 *Ibrahim v Mills*; Application to review decision abandoned.

14,214 *Bd. of Ed., Sewanhaka CSD v Mills, et al.*; Supreme Court, Albany County, Special Term; Connor, J.; Judgment granted dismissing petition to review; June 7, 2000; n.o.r.; appeal dismissed for failure to perfect.

14,217 *Bd. of Ed., Fairport CSD v Mills, et al.*; Supreme Court, Albany County; Hughes, J.; Judgment granted dismissing petition in its entirety, June 1, 1999.

14,236 *Davis v Mills, et al.*; Supreme Court, Albany County, Special Term; Ferradino, J.; Judgment granted dismissing petition to review; July 3, 2000; n.o.r.; aff'd 285 AD2d 703, July 5, 2001; mot. for leave to appeal granted; November 15, 2001; aff'd 98 NY2d 120; June 6, 2002.

14,245 *Mennella v Mills*; Supreme Court, Albany County, Special Term; Ferradino, J.; Judgment granted dismissing petition to review; September 28, 2001; n.o.r.

14,250 *Gersen, et al. v Mills, et al.*; Supreme Court, Albany County, Special Term; Sheridan, J.; Judgment granting petition and annulling decision of the Commissioner; October 10, 2000; n.o.r.; rev'd 290 AD2d 839; January 24, 2002.

14,280 *Bd. of Ed., Port Washington UFSD v. Mills, et al.*; Supreme Court, Albany County; Stip. of discontinuance, July 5, 2000.

14,365 *Weisberg v Mills, et anno*; Supreme Court, Albany County, Special Term; Malone, J.; Judgment granted dismissing petition to review; November 27, 2000; n.o.r.

14,430 *Bd. of Ed., Berkshire UFSD v Cate, et al.*; Application to review decision filed; discontinued by stipulation; June 15, 2001.

14,450 *Farago v Mills*; Supreme Court, Albany County, Special Term; McNamara. J.; Judgment granted dismissing petition to review; May 1, 2001; n.o.r.

14,464 *Bd. of Ed., City School District, City of New York v Mills*; Supreme Court, Albany County, Special Term; Keegan, J.; Judgment granted dismissing petition to review; January 18, 2001; n.o.r.; mot to reargue den.; March 30, 2001; aff'd 293 AD2d 37; April 18, 2002.

14,485 *Bd. of Ed., City School Dist., City of New York v Mills, et al.*; Supreme Court, Albany County, Special Term; Connor, J.; Judgment granted dismissing petition to review; September 22, 2001; n.o.r.; decision withheld and matter remitted to Supreme Court for further proceedings 300 AD2d 981; December 26, 2002; Remitted to Commissioner by Supreme Ct on January 21, 2003; additional decision (14,878) issued May 30, 2003; amended petition to review filed June 26, 2003; remitted to Appellate Division, Third Department, October 30, 2003; aff'd June 17, 2004; Contempt determination appealed to Appellate Division, Third Department; March 15, 2005.

14,527 *Karpoff, et al. v Mills, et al.*; Supreme Court, Albany County, Special Term; Cobb, J.; Judgment granted dismissing petition to review; August 1, 2001; n.o.r.; aff'd 296 AD2d 691; July 11, 2002; mot. for leave to appeal den. 99 NY2d 501; November 14, 2002.

14,534 *Finch, Pruyn & Co., Inc. v Mills, et al.*; Supreme Court, Albany County, Special Term; Cobb, J.; Judgment granted dismissing petition to review; October 2, 2001; n.o.r.; aff'd 297 AD2d 406; August 1, 2002.

14,557 *MacDonald v Mills, et al.*; Supreme Court, Albany County, Special Term; Canfield, J.; Judgment granted dismissing petition to review; January 11, 2002; n.o.r.

14,638 *McNamara v Mills*; Supreme Court, Albany County, Special Term; Kane, J.; Judgment granted dismissing petition to review; January 10, 2002; n.o.r.

14,666 *Boni, et al. v Mills, et al.*; Supreme Court, Albany County; Special Term; Bradley, J.; Judgment granted dismissing petition to review; February 27, 2003.

14,676 *Huber, et al.; v Mills, et al.*; Supreme Court, Albany County, Special Term; Spargo, J.; Judgment granted dismissing petition to review; January 7, 2003.

14,677 *Donato v Mills, et al.*; Supreme Court, Albany County, Special Term; Stein, J.; Judgment granted dismissing petition to review; January 14, 2003; n.o.r.; aff'd April 22, 2004.

14,695 *Madison-Oneida BOCES v Mills, et al.*; Supreme Court, Albany County, Special Term; Kavanagh, J.; Judgment granting petition and annulling decision of Commissioner; December 20, 2002; rev'd 2 AD3d 1240 December 31, 2003; mot. for lv. to appeal granted December 31, 2003; aff'd ___ NY3d ___; December 21, 2004.

14,741 *Cohn v Mills, et al.*; Supreme Court, Albany County, Special Term; Lamont, J.; Judgment granting petition and annulling decision of Commissioner; April 17, 2003.

14,750 *Mendez, et al. v Mills*; Supreme Court, Albany County, Special Term; Cannizzaro, J.; Judgment granted dismissing petition to review; June 30, 2003.

14,785 *Gill v Mills*; Supreme Court, Albany County, Special Term; Bradley, J.; Judgment granted dismissing petition to review; October 6, 2003; n.o.r.; appeal never perfected.

14,786 *Cayot v Mills*; Supreme Court, Albany County, Special Term; Judgment granted dismissing petition to review, February 19, 2004.

14,805 *American Quality Beverages, et al. v Mills, et al.*; Supreme Court, Teresi, J.; Judgment denied granting respondent's motion to dismiss; April 11, 2003; Supreme Court, Connor J.; Judgment granted dismissing petition on the merits; October 7, 2004; appeal pending.

14,842 *Lewtschenko v Mills*; Supreme Court, Albany County, Special Term; Lamont, J.; Judgment granted dismissing petition to review; October 27, 2003; n.o.r.

14,878 See, 14,485

14,961 *City of Albany, et al. v Mills, et al.*; Supreme Court, Albany County, Special Term; Connor, J.; Judgment granted dismissing petition to review, July 19, 2004; Stipulation of discontinuance terminating appeal; October 25, 2004.

14,969 *Bd. of Ed., Morristown CSD v Mills, et al.*; Supreme Court, Albany County, Bradley, J.; Judgment granted dismissing petition to review; appealed to Appellate Division, Third Department, July 2, 2004; Notice of discontinuance, August 10, 2004.

TABLE OF JUDICIAL REVIEW

14,972	*Fitch, et al. v Mills*; Supreme Court, Albany County, Special Term; Connor, J.; Judgment granted dismissing petition; July 9, 2004.
15,003	*Klein v Mills, et al.*; Supreme Court, Albany County, Special Term; Ceresia, J.; Judgment dismissing petition; December 6, 2004.
15,056	*Bd. of Ed., Uniondale UFSD v Mills, et al.*; Supreme Court, Albany County, Special Term; Kavanagh, J.; Judgment granted dismissing petition and stay vacated; December 7, 2004.
15,060	*Mahoney v Mills, et al.;* Supreme Court., Albany County, Special Term; Canfield, J.; Judgment granted dismissing petition; February 18, 2005; Appealed to Appellate Division, Third Department.
15,128	*Romeo, et al. v SED, et al.*; Supreme Court, Albany County; Application to review petition pending. Judgment denied motion to dismiss; July 12, 2005.
15,139	*Kelly Services, Inc. v SED, et al.*; Supreme Court, Albany County; Application to review petition pending.
	Second Supv. Dist. of Erie, Chautauqua and Cattaraugus BOCES, et al. v SED, et al.; Supreme Court, Albany County; Application to review petition pending.
15,143	*Quattrone v SED, et al.*; Supreme Court, Albany County; Application to review petition pending.
15,147	*Jo v SED, et al.*; Supreme Court, Albany County, Special Term; Bradstreet, J.; Judgment dismissing petition; February 8, 2005; Appealed to Appellate Division, Fourth Department.
15,187	*Bd. of Educ., Garrison UFSD v Mills, et al.*; Supreme Court, Albany County; Application to review petition pending.
15,192	*Scott v Mills, et al.*; Supreme Court, Albany County; Application to review petition pending.
15,214	*Viglietta v Mills, et al.*; Supreme Court, Albany County; Application to review petition pending.